International Organizations
A Dictionary and Directory

Third Edition

International Organizations
A Dictionary and Directory

Third Edition

Giuseppe Schiavone

St. Martin's Press
NEW YORK

® The Macmillan Press Ltd, 1983, 1986, 1992

All rights reserved. For information, write:
Scholarly and Reference Division,
St. Martin's Press, Inc., 175 Fifth Avenue,
New York, NY 10010

First published in the United States of America in 1993

Printed in Great Britain

ISBN 0-312-09143-5

Library of Congress Cataloging-in-Publication Data
Schiavone, Giuseppe.
     International organizations : a dictionary & directory / Giuseppe
  Schiavone. — 3rd ed.
       p.   cm.
     Includes indexes.
     ISBN 0-312-09143-5
     1. International agencies—Dictionaries.   2. International
  agencies—Directories.   I. Title.
  JX1995.S325   1993
  341.2'025—dc20   92-38142
  CIP

Contents

Introduction

(**1**) The dramatic and unexpected events of the past few years have brought about a major change in the international situation with far-reaching repercussions on the goals and activities of international organizations, at the global level (notably the UN system) as well as on a regional scale (notably the process of European union).

The long-standing East-West confrontation has subsided now that the demise of communism is an accomplished fact in all but a few countries and the transition to multi-party democracy and a market-driven system is under way in Central and Eastern Europe and in the republics of the erstwhile Soviet Union. As the East-West conflict has disappeared, the North-South polarization has taken on new features characterized by a clear shift by the developing countries toward less interventionist government policies and an acceptance of the 'democratic model' prevailing in major industrial nations. It is important to stress that the developing world now embraces not only the countries of the South, according to conventional wisdom, but also the countries of the former 'East'.

The traditional scenarios of bloc-to-bloc confrontation throughout the world have been replaced by a number of conflicts no longer directly inspired or controlled by the major powers. The variety of approaches and interests, largely unconditioned by traditional ideological tenets, presents unprecedented challenges to international co-operation in all areas, from security to trade and financial issues to environmental protection and drug abuse control. This is especially true with regard to the theory and practice of development in all its dimensions. It is now a widely recognized fact that economic growth does not automatically translate into a human progress which should ultimately lead to enlarging people's choices and putting the human being, not the economic system, at the core of the development process.

The concern about the rapid deterioration of the environment has contributed to the emergence of the notion of 'sustainable development', that is, development that does not threaten the well-being and survival of humanity itself. Sustainable development involves, in fact, not only the protection of natural resources and the physical environment but the protection of future economic growth and future human development. Radical changes will be necessary in both policies and institutions if the needs and options of the unborn generation are to be taken into account.

The 1990s will provide a decisive test for the capacities of international organizations to meet the challenge of sustainable development by taking stock of past experience and opening up new avenues for implementing global solidarity. The new spirit of co-operation among the 'great powers' and the growing awareness of the interdependence among all countries, large and small, should induce the international community to avail itself more extensively than in the recent past of the opportunities provided by international institutions at all levels and in all fields of activity.

(2) The emergence and, particularly during the last decades, the enormous expansion in number, range of tasks and functions of international organizations may be viewed as a response to the objective need for integration of international society at both the global (universal) and regional level.

It is important to emphasize, however, that the many and varied efforts towards integration have neither altered substantially the structure and dynamics of international society nor brought mankind any further towards the establishment of a world government within a more or less centralized international system.

Active nationalistic competition, fierce pressures for protectionism, and the stubborn defence of vested interests on a national scale, remain a constant feature of relations, even between countries such as those of Western Europe, which have set up supranational institutions endowed with very wide competences and far-reaching powers of co-ordination.

The proliferation of independent sovereign countries and the resulting sharp increase in membership of intergovernmental organizations are inevitably leading to the fragmentation of decision-making centres. Contrary to the widespread expectation of a gradual concentration of power in a few highly-integrated units, more and more countries are performing a significant role in the international system.

Many important international bodies have become overly politicized, with adverse effects on the performance of their institutional roles. Over-confidence in the possibilities of international organizations or gross miscalculations by the parties involved have often led to the raising of issues not yet ripe for fruitful discussion or outwardly intractable at a given moment. Furthermore, a tendency has emerged to extend the competences of certain bodies far beyond their pre-established boundaries.

Despite the magnitude of the political, economic and social problems, in the present phase of international relations, intergovernmental organizations stand a significant chance of improving the overall climate and of tackling successfully at least some aspects of major world issues on a multilateral basis. The heterogeneity of international society, made up of countries characterized by vastly different cultural backgrounds and huge variations in living standards, should not prevent the rational exploitation by all its members of the potentiality for co-operation provided by existing organizations. As in the past, the success of these bodies, born of good intentions but not by themselves representing a practical shortcut to world peace and stability, will ultimately depend on the resolve of member countries not to abuse a collective instrument for the mere pursuit of national interests and ends.

(3) From a legal point of view, international intergovernmental organizations are the products of treaties; the purely voluntary character of the participation of sovereign countries in international organizations and international co-operation efforts need not be emphasized. The formation of permanent international groupings, although almost inevitably involving a limitation of individual state sovereignty, cannot by itself be regarded as a preliminary stage towards the establishment of co-operative federal structures and the eventual institutionalization of world society. In fact, the majority of countries continue to emphasize the paramount value of the state and obstacles to any larger role for international organizations are not diminishing.

The evolution of the international legal system invites comparison with the evolution of national legal systems; the present legal framework of world society then emerges as a relatively weak and primitive system bound to develop gradually into a strong and highly organized pattern of rules. Whatever the wisdom of such an assumption and its long-term implications, existing international organizations essentially represent a more sophisticated means of conducting inter-state relations when national interests are better served through multilateral action or international concert.

In the absence of a generally agreed system of classification of international organizations, several possible criteria for distinction may be put forward, each concentrating on a specific feature or set of features. From a historical perspective, it can be observed that administrative and technical unions of fairly limited scope preceded the creation of institutions with broad political, economic and social aims. However, any clear-cut classification of organizations according to main objects of activity – preservation of peace and security, economic development, financial aid, technical, cultural and scientific exchange, humanitarian or military assistance – would prove to be less than accurate and lead to glaring inconsistencies in a number of cases, due to the overlap of functions and responsibilities.

A broad distinction may be made between organizations endowed with a wide array of powers (legislative, administrative, judicial) and with comprehensive competence and organizations with limited competence. Another suggested distinction is based on the global, regional or sub-regional scope of an organization. In a few cases the boundaries of a region are defined according to political or ideological rather than strictly geographical considerations. A further possible distinction – between supranational and non-supranational organizations – rests on the degree of integration which characterizes the organizations themselves and regards the nature and extent of the decision-making powers granted to particular organs. Supranational organizations have the ability to take decisions which are directly binding upon member states, public and private enterprises as well as individuals within these states, whereas traditional organizations can act or execute decisions only by or through member states.

The basic purposes, functions and powers of international organizations are usually set out, in a general or specific way, in their constituent documents which bear titles such as constitution, charter, covenant, statute or articles of agreement. Besides the functions and powers which are expressly mentioned in the relevant clauses of the basic instrument, it is generally assumed that an organization may be endowed with implied powers, that is such powers as are essential to the adequate fulfilment of its appointed tasks.

As a rule, the constituent instruments of international organizations provide that the original signatories may become members upon ratification or acceptance of the instruments themselves, while other states may be admitted to membership by a special majority vote of the competent organs. Since legal rights and obligations are the same for both original and subsequent members the distinction between the two categories is essentially of historical value. Although only states are normally envisaged as members, the constitutions of a number of organizations refer to 'governments', 'countries', 'sovereign countries' or 'nations'; these different expressions are of no consequence on the legal plane. Entities such as politically dependent territories or even independent and sovereign countries which are not acceptable as full members may be admitted to limited (associate) membership, usually without voting rights or representation in institutional organs. On occasion organizations grant observer status to countries which may be admitted to membership at a later stage.

Loss of membership of international organizations may derive from a multiplicity of causes. The first step towards termination of participation may be represented by suspension of a member's rights and privileges, notably voting rights, as a sanction for the non-fulfilment of financial obligations or the serious breach of other membership obligations. Persistent violations of the fundamental principles of an organization may eventually lead to expulsion or compulsory withdrawal from membership. Voluntary withdrawal of dissident members is envisaged in the constitutions of several organizations, although special conditions may be prescribed. In many cases withdrawal does not take effect immediately but is subject to a period of notice ranging from a few months to one or more years.

(4) The institutional structure of international organizations is generally based on a division of labour among three different types of organs: (a) a policy-making body on which all members are represented; (b) an executive or governing body of limited composition; and (c) a largely technical-administrative body made up of international civil servants and headed by a Secretary or Director.

The plenary organ – known usually as the Assembly, Conference, or Congress and meeting at regular intervals ranging from one to several years – is the supreme body. It determines basic policies, adopts recommendations and decisions, draws up conventions and agreements, approves the budget and exercises any other power conferred upon it by the constituent instrument.

The smaller executive organ is usually elected by the plenary body from among its members according to varying criteria – such as the adequate representation of leading members or main geographical areas – and meets with relative frequency to ensure continuity of the work of the organization between sessions of the supreme organ. It carries out the directions of the plenary organ and is responsible to it, administers finances, and directs all activities relating to the fulfilment of the tasks of the organization.

The administrative organ, generally known as the Secretariat or Bureau, is in charge of the practical working of the organization. It performs various administrative, executive, technical and co-ordinatory functions, centralizes the handling of numerous questions, collects and disseminates information and statistical data. Members are enjoined to respect the international character of the functions performed by the staff, whereas the civil servants themselves undertake not to accept instructions from outside authorities. Besides the standard principal organs, most organizations possess other lesser (subsidiary) organs designed to meet specific requirements.

The systems of representation and voting have played a crucial role in the decision-making process of international organizations, especially during periods of acute East-West or North-South confrontation. The basic principle of sovereign equality of all members should naturally lead to the one country-one vote procedure which is actually enshrined in the constitutions of many organizations. However, in a number of cases special consideration needs to be given to the different political, economic or financial weight and interests of members in order to ensure some kind of proportional representation. Weighted voting, veto rights and specific majorities are among the modes of decision which may be adopted with a view to balancing general equality against particular powers and responsibilities.

The majority principle is generally now applied in the decision-making process of international organizations and unanimity is hardly ever prescribed, except in a handful of bodies of limited membership. In most organizations the basic voting rule is currently a simple majority of members, although a qualified majority – usually a two-thirds majority of those present and voting – may be required for important matters. Nonetheless, full reliance on the results of formal voting may occasionally prove unrealistic, especially when a massive numerical majority forces through a resolution whose actual implementation depends largely on the goodwill and participation of a dissenting minority which happens to comprise some of the most important and influential members. More recent practices tend to avoid voting whenever a recorded vote would dramatically divide an organization or aggravate discord among members. Resolutions are therefore adopted – without taking formal votes – by acclamation, without objection, or by consensus. As a rule – and with the exception of supranational organizations – resolutions, recommendations, declarations and decisions are not legally binding upon members. Decisions in the substantive meaning of the term usually may be taken only with regard to the internal affairs of an organization.

It is generally held that international organizations enjoy some measure of international personality and are endowed with such treaty-making power as is necessary for the full performance of their functions. A fairly wide power has been expressly conferred upon the policy-making organs of certain organizations. Besides treaties concluded with both member and non-member countries, relationship and co-ordination agreements with other international organizations (in order, *inter alia*, to avoid unsound competition and duplication of efforts) may assume special relevance.

With a view to enabling them to fulfil their purposes and to exercise their functions in an impartial, independent and efficient manner, international organizations are ordinarily granted various privileges and immunities such as inviolability of premises and archives, immunity from jurisdiction, freedom from direct taxes and customs duties, freedom of official communications, special privileges and immunities for representatives of member countries and officials of the organization. These matters are dealt with in detail by separate agreements which supplement the general provisions contained in basic constitutional texts. Because of their functional basis, privileges and immunities are subject to waiver whenever the interests of an organization are not prejudiced. Questions concerning the status of the headquarters or other offices of an organization are regulated by bilateral agreements with the host country. The location of the headquarters of an organization is normally fixed by the constitution, although on occasion the matter is left undecided for further consideration by members.

As regards budgetary questions, the estimates of future expenditure of an organization are generally prepared by the executive head of the secretariat and submitted for review and approval – either directly or through the executive organ – to the plenary policy-making body. The budget consists of the administrative costs of running the organization (salaries of staff and costs of the various services) plus the expenses incurred as a result of activities undertaken to implement decisions taken by the organization. As a rule, the total amount is apportioned among members on the basis of percentage quotas which are graduated according to specific criteria such as national income or population. Not all expenses are necessarily borne by members since international organizations may derive an income from sources such as sales or investments. It should also be noted that certain activities may be financed as extra-budgetary programmes supported by voluntary contributions made by members in addition to normal budgetary commitments.

The eventual dissolution of an international organization and the liquidation of its assets and affairs may be expressly regulated in the constituent instrument. This is generally the case for organizations of a transitional nature or created for a limited period, as well as for financial bodies. It is generally admitted that, even in the absence of any specific provision concerning dissolution, members of an organization are endowed with the implied power to dissolve it. Succession – which is not necessarily associated with dissolution – takes place when the functions, rights and duties of an organization are transferred wholly or partly to another existing or new organization. In a number of cases the personality of the predecessor continues in the successor.

(5) In the course of history, the inadequacy of the traditional techniques of bilateral diplomacy to solve major problems involving the interests of more than two countries became evident as a result of the steady development of a complex web of relations between different peoples and between their rulers. From this state of affairs originated the international conference, that is the gathering of representatives from several countries to discuss and negotiate the settlement of common problems, normally through the conclusion of a multilateral treaty creating legal obligations for the contracting parties. The great post-war settlements of modern history – from the Peace of Westphalia (1648) and the Final Act of the Congress of Vienna (June, 1815) to the Peace Treaties concluded after World War I at Versailles, St Germain, Neuilly (1919), and Trianon (1920) – emanated from international conferences.

After the Napoleonic Wars, the creation in 1815 of a new balance of power system between the five great powers ('pentarchy') – Austria, Britain, France, Prussia and Russia – represented a major effort to secure international peace and stability within a multilateral framework. Through the Holy Alliance, concluded in Paris in September 1815, the monarchs of Austria, Prussia, and Russia (subsequently joined by other European rulers), committed themselves to govern their subjects 'as fathers of families' according to Christian principles and to practice solidarity in foreign affairs, holding consultations and regular meetings ('congress system'), in order to safeguard the settlement of Vienna. Although regular congresses were convened only four times (between 1818 and 1822), and European solidarity was weakened by the formation of a 'liberal' bloc (Britain and France) opposed to a 'conservative' bloc (Austria, Prussia and Russia), the 'Concert of Europe' succeeded in surviving recurring tensions between its partners and remained in operation until the outbreak of World War I.

The change from *ad hoc* to standing international conferences constituted another landmark in the development of international organization. From the 1850s, administrative international institutions, at both intergovernmental and non-governmental level, began to grow at a remarkably rapid pace. Hundreds of private international associations or unions were formed during the last half of the 19th century and their spread to cover a wide variety of fields paved the way to the establishment of a number of intergovernmental organizations.

The European Commission for the Danube (1856) was endowed with important administrative and legislative functions far wider than those entrusted to similar bodies responsible for other European rivers, such as the Central Commission for the Navigation of the Rhine (1815). Several institutions were charged with co-ordination of the activities of national administrations and/or the performance of supplementary liaison, information and consultation tasks including: the Geodetic Union (1864); the International Telegraph Union (1865), later renamed International Telecommunication Union (ITU); the General Postal Union (1874), later renamed Universal Postal Union (UPU); the Metric Union (1875); the International Meteorological Organization (1873); the International Copyright Union (1886); the Central Office for International Railway Transport (1890); and the United International Bureau for the

Protection of Intellectual Property (1893). Besides culture, sciences, transport and communications, intergovernmental co-operation gradually extended to other vital areas at the very beginning of this century: suffice it to mention the International Office of Public Health, established in 1903, and the International Institute of Agriculture, founded in 1905, which may be viewed as the forerunners of the World Health Organization (WHO) and the Food and Agriculture Organization (FAO) respectively.

(6) The League of Nations was created in 1919 to promote international co-operation and to achieve world peace and security by ensuring the respect 'for all treaty obligations in the dealings of organized peoples with one another'. In principle, it presented a unique opportunity to co-ordinate on a multilateral scale the activities of specialized unions and associations under the supervision of the League itself.

The League Covenant expressly provided that 'there shall be placed under the direction of the League all international bureaux already established by general treaties if the parties to such treaties consent'. Moreover, 'all such international bureaux and all commissions for the regulation of matters of international interest hereafter constituted shall be placed under the direction of the League'. For a number of reasons, the international bodies that were actually placed under the League's direction were comparatively few – only six, in fact, including the International Commission for Air Navigation (ICAN) and the International Hydrographic Bureau. Close co-ordination links existed with the International Labour Organization (ILO), whose original constitution formed part of the Peace Treaties of 1919 and 1920 and whose connection with the League lasted until the mid-1940s.

The League never attained a truly universal character, its membership being confined mostly to Europe and gravely prejudiced by the non-participation of the USA, but its political failure should not lead to an underestimation of the importance of its undertakings in several non-political fields and its overall contribution to the development of international organization as one of the salient features of interstate relations in the 20th century. The steadily deteriorating political climate of the period after World War I, and the major crises in international economic and social affairs substantially reduced the opportunities and prospects for fruitful multilateral collaboration within institutionalized frameworks.

The gradual extension of government intervention to nearly all aspects of economic life and the need to protect and insulate national economies plagued by depression, especially in the late 1920s and early 1930s, led to extreme forms of economic nationalism and to the consolidation of major trends away from the basic principles of economic liberalism, such as the introduction of severe measures hampering the international circulation of goods, capital and manpower, the abandonment of the gold standard and the continued manipulation of exchange rates. The World Economic Conferences, held in 1927 and 1933 under the auspices of the League and with the participation of the USA, could not prevent the disintegration of the world economy by the outbreak of World War II. The foundation of the Bank for International Settlements (BIS) in 1930 – with a view to solving, *inter alia*, the German reparations problem – may be regarded as one of the few notable achievements of international organization in the inter-war period. Another significant event was the adoption in 1931 of the Statute of Westminster, which is the basic charter of the modern Commonwealth.

(7) The firm commitment of the Allies to reorganize the whole network of international relations in the post-war world on the basis of friendship, co-operation and equal opportunities for all nations was clearly expressed from the early 1940s, well before the end of World War II. The principles of the Atlantic Charter of August 1941 and the Joint Declaration of the United Nations at war (that is the Allies fighting against the Axis Powers) of January 1942 were subsequently confirmed and supplemented in solemn declarations and treaties of the parties concerned.

As early as November 1943, the representatives of the 44 United Nations at war signed the Agreement establishing the United Nations Relief and Rehabilitation Administration (UNRRA) for providing assistance to the areas liberated from German domination. Between May and June 1943, the United Nations Conference on Food and Agriculture, held at Hot Springs, Virginia, set up an Interim Commission charged with the responsibility of drawing up the constitution of the Food and Agriculture Organization (FAO). The creation of the International Monetary Fund (IMF) and the International Bank for Reconstruction and Development (IBRD) was the outcome of another major United Nations Conference, devoted to monetary and financial problems, summoned at Bretton Woods, New Hampshire, in July 1944. The International Civil Aviation Organization (ICAO) was established under a Convention on International Civil Aviation concluded in Chicago in December 1944.

During that period, the features of the global institution to succeed the League of Nations were discussed and subsequently worked out in detail at Dumbarton Oaks, Yalta, and San Francisco. At the San Francisco Conference between April and June 1945, representatives from 50 countries eventually decided on the structure and mechanisms of the United Nations (UN). The Security Council was entrusted with primary responsibility for the maintenance of international peace and security while the Economic and Social Council, acting under the authority of the General Assembly, was to promote, assist and co-ordinate co-operation in the economic and social fields. The basic goal of a truly comprehensive and lasting peace had to be pursued in all its dimensions – political, economic, social, cultural and humanitarian. With a view to decentralizing the economic and social activities of the UN and making them more responsive to specific needs emerging at regional level, the following UN regional commissions were created between 1947 and 1974 and are currently in operation: the Economic Commission for Europe (ECE); the Economic Commission for Latin America and the Caribbean (ECLAC); the Economic Commission for Africa

(ECA); the Economic and Social Commission for Asia and the Pacific (ESCAP); the Economic and Social Commission for Western Asia (ESCWA). The last two bodies replaced the Economic Commission for Asia and the Far East (ECAFE).

Functional international co-operation was to play a prominent role within the newly created institutional framework through the Economic and Social Council. Specialized organizations, established by intergovernmental agreements and having wide international responsibilities in economic, social, cultural, educational, health and related fields had to be brought into relationship with the UN which would recognize them as its 'specialized agencies'. In addition to FAO, IMF, IBRD and ICAO, other important specialized bodies were set up in the last half of the 1940s and entered into relationship agreements, following the same general pattern, with the UN: the UN Educational, Scientific and Cultural Organization (UNESCO); the World Health Organization (WHO); the World Meteorological Organization (WMO); the International Maritime Organization (IMO). Similar agreements were also concluded by the UN with older international institutions, such as the UPU and ILO. In order to supplement the lending operations of IBRD and to meet a wider range of needs, with special regard to the developing countries, two more agencies were set up: the International Finance Corporation (IFC), in 1956, and the International Development Association (IDA), in 1960. Together with the IBRD, these two institutions form the World Bank Group to which the Multilateral Investment Guarantee Agency (MIGA) has been added in the late 1980s. Another specialized institution with special status with the UN is the International Atomic Energy Agency (IAEA). It was established in 1956 as a result of an International Conference on the Peaceful Uses of Atomic Energy.

While the basic principles of post-war monetary and financial co-operation were eventually embodied in the Bretton Woods Agreements on the establishment of the IMF and IBRD, the UN-sponsored plans to set the broad outlines for dealing with international trade issues failed to materialize and the creation of an agency especially responsible for trade matters proved impossible. The Havana Charter of 1948 – intended to serve as the constitution of the abortive International Trade Organization (ITO) – was never ratified by the signatory countries and an interim convention, the General Agreement on Tariffs and Trade (GATT), was virtually assigned the heavy task of promoting the gradual abolition of tariff and non-tariff barriers and improving the practices and mechanisms of international commercial relations through multilateral negotiations.

The Allies' comprehensive attempt to deal effectively with the vast economic, financial and social problems of the post-war era was largely based on the ideals and principles of economic liberalism rooted in an international structure that had long since ceased to exist. Failure to recognize the full impact of the shift from 'market economies' to 'command economies', and of the underlying forces which were to bring about dramatic changes in the system of international relations and the corresponding rules of the game (such as the formation in Eastern Europe of a group of countries within the Soviet sphere of influence and the emergence of scores of assertive developing nations) prevented a more far-sighted approach to the problems of the post-1945 world.

(8) The overall commitment to universality and to an open international trade and monetary system was not seen as an obstacle to the conclusion of arrangements, or the constitution of co-operation and integration groupings, on a regional scale. The nations of the European continent appeared particularly well-suited to that end, once recovery from the devastation caused by World War II had been achieved. The launching in 1947 of the Marshall Plan, open to any country 'willing to assist in the task of recovery', followed by the establishment in 1948 of the Organization for European Economic Co-operation (OEEC), may be regarded as a turning point in the reconstruction process of the Western half of Europe. On the Eastern side, the creation in 1949 of the Council for Mutual Economic Assistance (CMEA; Comecon) represented, to a considerable extent, the Soviet riposte to the Marshall Plan.

On a broad political plane, the appeal of European unity stimulated the creation of the Council of Europe which, according to the Statute signed in 1949, was intended to safeguard the common heritage as well as to facilitate the economic and social progress of the member countries. In 1952 Scandinavian countries established the Nordic Council, an organ for consultation between national parliaments and governments.

The rapprochement of wartime enemies in continental Europe found a most significant expression in the signature, in 1951, of the Treaty setting up the earliest of the European Communities, the European Coal and Steel Community (ECSC), by the representatives of the 'Six', that is France, the Federal Republic of Germany, Italy, and the Benelux countries. The Treaties of Rome establishing the European Economic Community (EEC) and the European Atomic Energy Community (Euratom) completed in 1957 the institutional framework for economic co-operation between the 'Six'. Following British initiative, other European countries (the 'Seven') which were not prepared to accept the far-reaching political and economic objectives of the 'Six' founded, in 1960, the European Free Trade Association (EFTA), largely conceived as an interim counterpart to the European Communities.

In 1960, the OEEC, which had virtually fulfilled its basic task of assisting in the reconstruction of Western Europe, was succeeded by the Organization for Economic Co-operation and Development (OECD). The OECD had a larger membership than its predecessor, notably with the participation of Canada and the USA as full members, and broader aims, such as the achievement of the highest sustainable growth and the promotion of sound economic expansion in member as well as non-member countries in the process of economic development.

On the defence side, as a response to growing Cold War tensions, the North Atlantic Treaty, signed in 1949 by the representatives of Canada, the USA, and ten European nations, provided for mutual assistance should any one contracting party be attacked.

In fact, the North Atlantic Treaty Organization (NATO) appeared far more adequate from the standpoint of regional security than the Brussels Treaty Organization, established in 1948 by the Benelux countries, France, and the UK. In 1954, following the rejection by the French National Assembly of the 1952 Treaty on the European Defence Community (EDC), a number of protocols were signed in order to transform the Brussels Treaty Organization into the Western European Union (WEU), with the inclusion of the Federal Republic of Germany and Italy as full members.

The participation of the Federal Republic of Germany in the Western security system and the need to supplement bilateral military treaties prompted the USSR and its Eastern European allies to establish a joint military command under the Warsaw Pact of 1955 which obliged contracting parties to assist each other to meet any armed attack on one or more of them in Europe.

Exports of strategic goods and technology that would contribute significantly to the military potential of Warsaw Pact members and socialist countries of Asia were to be kept under close control by a Co-ordinating Committee (CoCom) established by the USA and its NATO partners since 1949.

International co-operation on a regional or subregional scale also materialized outside Europe. In this connection, the Western hemisphere offered several examples of varying kinds and levels of co-operation. The foundation of the Organization of American States (OAS) in 1948 represented a milestone in the gradual development of Pan-American policies involving all independent countries of the continent, with the exception of Canada. Three years later, a subregional agency, the Organization of Central American States (ODECA), was set up by five nations of the area.

The achievements of the European Communities induced Latin American countries to concentrate their co-operation efforts on trade and financial issues. As a result, the Central American Common Market (CACM) and the Latin American Free Trade Association (LAFTA) were formed in 1960 to establish, by stages, subregional or regional 'common markets'. Development financing problems were to be dealt with on a continental scale by the Inter-American Development Bank (IDB), set up in 1959 with the inclusion of the USA as full member, and on a subregional scale by the Central American Bank for Economic Integration (CABEI), established in 1960. Regarding the Caribbean specifically, an agreement establishing a subregional institution, the Caribbean Organization, was signed in 1960.

In 1945, representatives of independent Arab countries signed the Pact of the League of Arab States [Arab League], an important though institutionally loose association favouring political and economic unity among member countries and promoting the adoption of common policies *vis-a-vis* third countries, notably on Middle Eastern issues. Another body, the Central Treaty Organization (CENTO), developed in 1955 out of the 'Baghdad Pact' between Iraq and Turkey, and was subsequently enlarged to include Iran, Pakistan, and the UK. Co-operation on military and political questions was expressly envisaged, without involving any mandatory form of mutual assistance.

In the Asian and Pacific region, various intergovernmental organizations had come into being from the early 1950s, especially in the fields of collective self-defence, economic co-operation and development assistance. The Security Treaty concluded between Australia, New Zealand and the USA (ANZUS Pact) in 1951 was intended to ensure mutual assistance should any signatory country be the victim of 'an armed attack in the Pacific area'. A more far-reaching collective security pact was signed in 1954 with a view to defending non-member countries in Indo-China and providing for the establishment of the South East Asia Treaty Organization (SEATO).

A very loose association for broad consultation on economic and social matters, the South Pacific Commission (SPC), was founded in 1947 by six countries with dependent territories in the area. The Colombo Plan for Co-operative Economic Development in South and South East Asia was launched in 1951 in order to provide capital and technical training to Asian countries closely associated with the UK. Both the membership and scope of the Colombo Plan were subsequently enlarged to include donor and recipient countries outside the Commonwealth.

The decolonization of Africa reached its climax in 1960 but the association of the newly independent African countries with different and often rival political groups delayed the constitution of a truly pan-African institution – the Organization of African Unity (OAU) – until 1963. The new regional institution was endowed with wide competence, despite its relatively weak institutional mechanism.

The foundations for a far-reaching change in the international political setting were laid in April 1955 when the leaders of 29 nations from the African and Asian continents meeting in Bandung, Indonesia, condemned colonialism, racial discrimination and atomic weapons and refused to be politically or militarily associated with either the West or the Soviet bloc, thereby emerging as a third force in world affairs.

The formal adoption of a 'non-aligned' attitude towards the cold war confrontation between East and West was the outcome of the first Conference of the Non-Aligned Movement (NAM) held in September 1961 in Belgrade, notwithstanding differences between moderate and anti-Western states. The 25 countries (mostly Afro-Asian) participating in the Belgrade summit meeting were shortly to be joined by Latin American countries, an event of the highest significance for the future of North-South relations.

Another significant event at the level of intergovernmental co-operation took place in 1960 when a group of oil exporting countries set up a cartel to regulate production and pricing of oil in the world market – the Organization of the Petroleum Exporting Countries (OPEC), destined to play a leading role in the 1970s.

(9) The political and economic events from the early 1960s to the end of the decade emphasized the need for a fresh approach to some basic problems of international organization, either by adapting existing institutions or by estab-

lishing further bodies in order to respond effectively to new situations, especially in the developing world. The UN itself had to change greatly – not only because of the dramatic increase in membership – in order to meet many pressing needs through the improvement of 'special help' activities for children, refugees and disaster victims, and to respond to a variety of problems through initiatives ranging from promotion of a new international economic order to the encouragement of sound environmental practices, campaigns against the remnants of colonialism and apartheid, and the negotiation of treaties and other agreements on matters of global concern such as the seas and outer space. A new specialized agency, the World Intellectual Property Organization (WIPO), entered into relationship with the UN. The co-operative efforts of the UN and related agencies in the economic and social sphere were expanded and streamlined, priority being given to problems having a direct bearing on the conditions of the poorest segments of society within the framework of the UN Development Decades.

The special problems of trade in relation to development were entrusted to the UN Conference on Trade and Development (UNCTAD), established in 1964 as a permanent organ of the UN General Assembly. Growing emphasis on direct field activities led to the creation in 1965 of the UN Development Programme (UNDP) as the world's largest channel for multilateral technical and pre-investment co-operation. The UN Industrial Development Organization (UNIDO) was set up in 1966 to foster and accelerate the industrial development of developing countries. With respect to food problems, the World Food Programme (WFP) was founded in 1963, under the joint sponsorship of the UN and FAO, with a view to providing aid in the form of food. Financial resources for technical co-operation activities in the population field were provided through the UN Fund for Population Activities (UNFPA), created in 1967. For their part, the specialized agencies in relation with the UN were increasingly co-ordinating their efforts and focusing on the promotion of sustained growth over the long term, with special regard to the needs of the poorer countries.

On the other hand, expenditure on arms and armies continued to grow throughout the world, consuming huge material and human resources that might have been employed for development purposes. In 1969, in an effort to slow and reverse the arms race, the UN General Assembly proclaimed the 1970s as a Disarmament Decade but little or no progress was actually made, despite a number of international agreements for the limitation and regulation of armaments.

The growing solidarity between developing countries and the ensuing pursuit of a unified approach to North-South issues represented one of the most significant features of international relations to emerge in the 1960s.

The cohesion of developing nations acquired a concrete operational meaning through the consultation and co-ordination procedures carried out within the Movement of Non-Aligned Countries with regard to broad political issues and within the Group of 77 (which was founded at the time of the first session of UNCTAD in 1964 and took its name from the number of signatories to a declaration of common aims) with regard to economic issues and multilateral negotiations. In fact, owing to the relatively high degree of overlap in membership, it became possible for the two groups to establish an original form of 'division of labour' in advancing development goals.

One of the earliest successes for developing countries was the establishment of the Generalized System of Preferences (GSP). After negotiation on the principles of the GSP between 1968 and 1970 within the UNCTAD framework, national preference schemes were put into operation by virtually all developed countries in order to help developing countries to expand their exports of manufactured goods.

Co-operation at the regional and subregional level made significant progress in the 1960s in a relatively favourable international setting characterized by fairly high rates of growth of income in developed market-economy countries and of world trade coupled with a reduction in international tension gradually leading to East-West détente.

In Western Europe, the EEC experiment progressed swiftly, achieving, *inter alia*, a customs union and free movement of workers between the 'Six', and developing step by step the essentials of the highly controversial Common Agricultural Policy (CAP). Within the CMEA area, efforts to improve monetary and financial relations eventually materialized in the foundation of two institutions, the International Bank for Economic Co-operation (IBEC) in 1963, and the International Investment Bank (IIB) in 1970.

In Latin America, an important step was made in 1967 by the signing of the Treaty of Tlatelolco which prohibited nuclear weapons in the region and established an Agency responsible for ensuring compliance with the obligations arising from the Treaty itself (OPANAL). Besides creating the first nuclear-weapon-free zone in a densely populated area, the Treaty was the first arms control agreement whose implementation had to be verified by an international organization. On the plane of economic integration, LAFTA's failure to establish a common market on the European model induced Andean countries to form a subregional group of their own in 1969, the Andean Group based on the Cartagena Agreement. A limited but promising form of co-operation was inaugurated by the River Plate Basin Treaty, signed in 1969 and aiming to develop physical integration between countries drained by the River Plate and its tributaries.

After the dissolution of the Caribbean Organization in 1965, a Caribbean Free Trade Association (CARIFTA), following the patterns of LAFTA and EFTA, was set up in 1968. An autonomous financial body, the Caribbean Development Bank (CDB; Caribank), was established in the following year.

In Africa, widespread dissatisfaction with the course followed by OAU in handling highly sensitive issues such as the Congo crisis prompted a group of French-speaking African countries to form in 1965 the African and Malagasy Common Organization (OCAM) as an agency for promoting economic, social, technical and cultural development. Given the fact that small subregional groupings seemed to offer far more favourable prospects for co-operation in the economic and financial sphere, a number of intergovernmental organizations were founded, such as the Maghreb Permanent Consultative Committee, the Customs Union of West African States (UDEAO), the Customs and Economic Union of Central Africa (UDEAC) and the short-lived Economic Community of East Africa.

On a continental scale, the African Development Bank (AfDB) was established in 1963 and entrusted with the task of dealing with development financing problems. In 1965 the Asian Development Bank (AsDB) was created to serve as the region's development financing body.

In the Asian and Pacific region, a significant achievement was the establishment in 1967 of the Association of South East Asian Nations (ASEAN) to encourage subregional co-ordination and co-operation in economic, social and cultural matters and to ensure political stability.

(10) The monetary events of 1971 – the suspension of the convertibility of the dollar into gold and its subsequent devaluation – represented a turning point in the history of international monetary relations and radically altered the conditions under which the IMF had been operating since its foundation. A system of floating exchange rates gradually emerged, encouraging speculation, increasing economic uncertainty and instability, and seriously threatening the orderly development of world trade. The monetary turmoil was accompanied by rising prices for such essentials as food and fuel, notably oil under OPEC's pressure, and growing burdens of debt and trade imbalances.

The steady progression of the economic crisis had a substantial impact on the growth rates and development programmes of developing countries, with depressed prices for exports of primary commodities (other than oil), soaring prices for imports of manufactured goods, reduced flows of official development assistance (ODA) from industrial countries, high interest rates, limited access to international capital markets and sharp aggravation of the external debt problem. In the developed countries, renewed protectionist pressures gradually led to the adoption of narrow and generally short-sighted nationalistic policies. Therefore, it became virtually impossible to deal effectively, in an integral and co-ordinated manner, with the vital questions concerning international trade and the global relationship between developing and developed countries.

At the political level, rising international tension in an ambience of escalating super-power antagonism and regional conflicts prepared the crisis of détente. In 1976, the meagre achievements of the first Disarmament Decade prompted the UN General Assembly to convene a special session, devoted entirely to the question of disarmament, which was held in 1978.

By the mid-1970s the increased awareness of the structural character of the rigidities and maladjustments of world trade and financial systems led to a drastic reappraisal of development policies and priorities. In the aftermath of the 'oil shock' of 1973, widespread concern that the experience of OPEC might encourage the producers of other commodities to form cartels to improve their terms of trade with the industrialized world contributed to create a new responsiveness on the part of the developed consumer countries. In May 1974 the UN General Assembly held a special session on the problems of raw materials and development and called for the establishment of a 'New International Economic Order' involving a reshaping of the world's trade and financial relations. As a further step, in December of the same year, the General Assembly adopted the Charter of Economic Rights and Duties of States. The Declarations and Action Programmes adopted by members of the Group of 77 at their pre-UNCTAD Ministerial Meetings presented ideas and proposals with a view to addressing the more difficult and less tractable structural problems related to trade and development.

To face the food crisis situations that had developed in several parts of the world a major effort was launched within the UN framework. The World Food Conference, held in November 1974, led to the creation of the World Food Council (WFC), in December of the same year, to co-ordinate policies and activities affecting the world food situation, and of the International Fund for Agricultural Development (IFAD), in June 1976, to mobilize additional financial resources to help developing countries improve their food production and nutrition. The UN Centre for Human Settlements (HABITAT) was set up by the General Assembly in 1978 to serve as a focal point for reviewing and co-ordinating human settlements activities.

On the institutional plane, a co-ordinated response to the first big escalation in oil prices was launched by most of the West's oil-importing countries in 1974 through the creation of the International Energy Agency (IEA), aimed at promoting stability in world energy markets as well as security of supplies.

As regards West European co-operation, an event of paramount importance was the accession as full members to the European Communities of Denmark, Ireland and the UK in January 1973. In the eastern half of the European continent, in July 1971 the CMEA adopted a far-reaching 'Comprehensive Programme' to improve co-operation and develop integration.

The Latin American Economic System (SELA) was set up in 1975 to advance mutual trade and co-operation, while respecting and supporting pre-existing arrangements, and to co-ordinate members' policies vis-a-vis third countries and international organizations. At the subregional level, the Amazonian Co-operation Treaty [Amazon Pact], concluded in July 1978, provided a multilateral framework for promoting the harmonious socio-economic development of the respective Amazon territories of the member countries. Other forms of co-operation emerged in specific sectors, such as the Latin American Energy Organization (OLADE), created in 1973. In the Caribbean, a new body endowed with broader competences and having wider aims – the Caribbean Community (CARICOM) – replaced CARIFTA in 1973.

In Africa reorganization efforts resulted in the foundation in 1973 of the West African Economic Community (CEAO), replacing UDEAO, and in 1975 in the establishment of the Economic Community of West African States (ECOWAS). An Economic Community of the Great Lakes Countries (CEPGL) was formed in 1976. The first Southern African Development Co-ordination Conference

(SADCC) was held in 1979 and laid the foundations for closer co-operation among majority-ruled states in the subregion.

Arab oil-exporting countries decided to use part of their revenue to help developing nations to face the impact of oil price rises by channelling substantial resources for the implementation of infrastructural, industrial and agricultural projects through financial institutions and development agencies: the Arab Bank for Economic Development in Africa (BADEA), created in 1974, and the Arab Fund for Economic and Social Development (AFESD), which began operations in 1973, are among the most important bodies in the field.

A large body with general competence, the Organization of the Islamic Conference (OIC), embracing the overwhelming majority of Islamic countries, was set up in 1971 to encourage effective solidarity and mutual assistance in all vital fields.

The South Pacific Bureau for Economic Co-operation (SPEC) was formed in 1973 to promote regional co-operation for development, following a recommendation by the South Pacific Forum (SPF) created in 1971. On the regional defence side, in 1975 changed conditions prompted the remaining member countries to decide to phase out SEATO, which could no longer fulfil its collective security function in South East Asia.

(11) With the aggravation and deepening of the world economic crisis several unfavourable developments emerged in the late 1970s and early 1980s. A steadily deteriorating political environment and the commitment of massive resources to armaments of unparalleled destructive capability compounded the economic difficulties manifested in the sluggish growth of developed and developing countries alike, high unemployment, and the widespread resurgence of inflation. In the developed countries, increasing demands for government intervention to protect specific sectors from external competition and to subsidize ailing industries led to the introduction of new trade barriers and extensive use of quotas and 'voluntary' export restraints.

The dangerous weakening of the fabric of multilateralism and of the corresponding institutional system adversely affected negotiating processes in virtually every international forum.

The beginnings of an economic recovery from the international recession of the early 1980s first became noticeable in the USA. The accelerated pace of American economic activity in 1983, sustained by rapid expansion of domestic demand, laid a sound basis for stronger output growth and slower inflation rates in other Western countries. By the mid-1980s, although the overall rate of expansion had become less rapid, the recovery was spreading increasingly if unevenly to the developing countries with beneficial effects on both the external position and domestic economic growth. The predominant themes of international debate revolved around the arms race, world trade and financial flows, and the external debt of developing countries.

On the political side, in Geneva in late 1985, after half-a-dozen years, regular talks were resumed between the leaders of the two superpowers. Expectations were aroused that arrangements would be made to lessen East-West confrontation and to prevent it turning into conflict.

The fortieth anniversary of the UN in 1985 seemed to offer one more occasion to analyse the close and complex inter-relationships of key policy issues which, although viewed from different perspectives by various countries and groups of countries, were of universal concern. Grave questions were raised about the value of the UN system and the general effectiveness of multilateral co-operation – making all the more arduous the search for a co-ordinated response to the new generation of global problems, in relation to both world peace and the world economy. In 1983 the inter-relationship of trade, finance, payments and development, in an international context of sharpened interdependence, was once more emphasized both in the Message for Dialogue and Consensus adopted by the Group of 77 (including 127 members) in Buenos Aires and in the New Delhi Message and the Economic Declaration of the Heads of State and Government of Non-Aligned Countries (numbering 101).

On a global plane, noting the crucial importance of continuing efforts to achieve general and complete disarmament under effective international control, the UN General Assembly, meeting in 1980, declared the 1980s as the Second Disarmament Decade and decided to hold the Second Special Session on disarmament in 1982. However, it did not prove possible to reach agreement on any specific course of action designed to help to halt and reverse the arms race throughout the world.

In 1980 the General Assembly adopted the International Development Strategy for the Third Development Decade setting out general goals and objectives and a series of policy measures. Despite a general perception of the crucial links between commodities and the development process and the adoption in 1976 of the ambitious Integrated Programme for Commodities (IPC), primary commodity markets continued to be volatile, showing a marked increase in certain cases. The need to provide special help for the particularly disadvantaged developing countries (the least developed, land-locked and island countries) led to the convening in Paris in 1981 of the Conference on the Least Developed Countries. The Substantial New Programme of Action (SNPA) for the 1980s, calling for considerable expansion of financial and technical assistance, was approved.

In 1985 the launching of a new GATT round of multilateral trade negotiations appeared to open up prospects of curbing protectionist tendencies and strengthening the trading system.

On the financial side, increased flows of concessional assistance became of the utmost priority to low-income countries, particularly in sub-Saharan Africa. A broad consensus emerged on the need to expand the World Bank's lending programme, with a view to meeting more adequately the demands of borrowing member countries and providing further impulses for generating capital flows from other sources. Substantial financial assistance was provided by the IMF to countries undertaking adjustment programmes. The Fund had experienced an unprecedented net use of its resources but by the mid-1980s net drawings began to subside, partly due to an improvement in the payments positions of the developing countries. The IMF continued to encourage developed countries to enlarge their ODA contributions.

Within the UN system, a significant event took place in 1985 when UNIDO eventually became a specialized agency. The long-term trend towards an increase in membership of UN specialized agencies was confirmed in the first half of the 1980s by the admission of several countries. In this connection, mention should also be made of China's plan to rejoin GATT after an absence of more than 35 years. Unfortunate developments took place in other agencies, notably UNESCO, with the withdrawals of the USA, the UK and Singapore.

At regional and subregional level, a number of significant events took place. In western Europe, the enlargement process of the European Communities continued: Greece became the tenth member of the Communities in January 1981, followed by Portugal and Spain in January 1986. As regards CMEA, the basic goals of socialist economic integration were solemnly restressed at the summit meeting in June 1984.

In Latin America, plans originally aimed at reorganizing LAFTA's mechanism eventually resulted in the creation in 1980 of a new region-wide institution, the Latin American Integration Association (LAIA), based on a tariff preference and regional and partial scope agreements. In Central America, political and social conflicts complicated by the economic recession adversely affected attempts to revive the integration process. In the Caribbean, seven small island countries set up the Organization of Eastern Caribbean States (OECS) in 1981 to foster economic co-operation and to defend their territorial integrity and independence. The new body was to play a role in the American intervention in Grenada in October 1983.

In the face of growing threats to regional stability, in 1981 the Arab oil-producing countries on the western side of the Gulf created the Gulf Co-operation Council (GCC) to strengthen political and economic solidarity between member countries.

In Africa, two new bodies were formed in the early 1980s: the Economic Community of Central African States (CEEAC) aiming to foster economic and financial integration; and the Preferential Trade Area for Eastern and Southern Africa (PTA) with the prospect of establishing an Economic Community within the region. In West Africa, little of substance was achieved since the establishment of ECOWAS. In early 1985, the remaining members of OCAM decided the dissolution of the organization.

A new organization with wide political and economic objectives was founded by India, Pakistan and five other countries at the end of 1985: the South Asian Association for Regional Co-operation (SAARC), which should enhance mutual solidarity and stability.

In the Pacific, the ANZUS crisis, arising from the sharply diverging views of the USA and New Zealand, deeply affected the operation of the security pact.

(12) The almost abrupt return to the realities of a multipolar world initiated in

1989 has altered deep-rooted equilibria which had inspired the theory and practice of international organizations for several decades. In the post-Cold War era, the UN seems bound to assume for the first time in history the role for which it was originally conceived, fostering genuine co-operation in an increasingly interdependent world. The reorganization and streamlining of the UN Secretariat, undertaken in 1992 by the new Secretary-General, may be viewed as the first and encouraging sign of a wholly new period in the life of the world body.

A form of 'economic realignment' has rapidly spread from the former socialist countries of Europe to Africa, Asia and Latin America demanding appropriate policy responses from the whole UN system and especially from international financial institutions. The IMF and the World Bank have become, in an incredibly short period of time, the truly global institutions envisioned by their founders nearly five decades ago and face a daunting task calling into question their traditional role.

The protection of the environment is being accorded growing importance – also in the context of the UN Conference on Environment and Development (UNCED) of June 1992 – and the impact of development projects (especially in agriculture and energy) on the environment is assessed and monitored. Continuing support is provided to the programme of debt and debt-service reduction; both the World Bank and the IMF are actively involved in the negotiation of packages between debtors and commercial banks. One major problem will remain that of the heavy indebtedness of many developing countries whose situation has not substantially improved because of inadequate policies and/or insufficient financial support. Last but not least is the daunting task of helping the Central and Eastern European countries as well as the republics of the erstwhile USSR make the massive changes in their institutional and regulatory framework that are necessary to establish open market-based economies in a relatively short time.

The eighth round of multilateral trade negotiations conducted under the sponsorship of GATT, known as the Uruguay Round, had not yet been completed in early 1992. The growing difficulties surrounding multilateral trade negotiations contributed to a proliferation of regional arrangements for co-operation and integration.

In Western Europe, the completion of the single market of the EC has been scheduled for the end of 1992 while the Maastricht Treaty, whatever its eventual outcome, has solemnly restressed the goals of political as well as economic and monetary union. The power of attraction of the European Communities has grown stronger for both the EFTA countries (establishing with the EC countries the European Economic Area since 1993) and the former members of CMEA, officially dissolved in 1991 along with its military counterpart, the Warsaw Pact. Pan-European co-operation will require new patterns and new institutions, such as the European Bank for Reconstruction and Development (EBRD) set up in 1991, as well as restructuring of existing bodies from the Council of Europe to NATO. The participation of NATO members and of their former adversaries of the Warsaw Pact in the newly-created North Atlantic Co-operation Council (NACC) is just an example of the radical transformations going on in Europe.

In the Western Hemisphere, significant events are taking place in both North and Central and South America. In North America, negotiations have been concluded among the USA, Canada and Mexico for the establishment of a North American Free Trade Area (NAFTA) which might eventually embrace countries in Central and South America. In Central America, the members of CACM have restressed their willingness to set up a regional common market and adopted the relevant timetable. In South America, both LAIA and the Andean Group countries are in the process of revitalizing their co-operation and integration schemes setting new deadlines. New schedules for completion of tariff reductions and adoption of a common external tariff have also been established by Caribbean countries within the framework of CARICOM and OECS. Moreover, a new grouping has been created, under the name of MERCOSUR, by Argentina, Brazil, Paraguay and Uruguay in early 1991 with a view to establishing a common market by 1995.

In Africa, efforts are going on to strengthen existing bodies in the prospect of enhanced co-operation in the southern part of the continent with the participation of the Republic of South Africa. In 1989 the Union of Arab Maghreb (UMA) has been created in an effort to renew efforts at closer economic co-operation.

The Asia-Pacific region has seen the positive evolution of ASEAN towards the creation of a free trade area and the launching of the Asia-Pacific Economic Co-operation (APEC) process which represents the first attempt at institutionalized intergovernmental collaboration among Pacific Rim nations. Furthermore, a number of proposals have been advanced to further regional trade liberalization among selected countries.

A

AfDB. *See* **African Development Bank.**

AFESD. *See* **Arab Fund for Economic and Social Development.**

African Development Bank (AfDB). The aims of the Bank are to contribute to the economic and social progress of its member countries, individually and jointly, by financing development projects, promoting public and private investment and stimulating economic co-operation between African countries.

The origins of the Bank date back to the Conference of the Peoples of Africa, held in Tunis in 1960, which passed a resolution concerning the creation of an African investment financing institution. Under the aegis of the *UN Economic Commission for Africa (ECA), an agreement was drawn up between 1962 and 1963 by a Committee of Experts of nine African countries. It was formally adopted by the Conference of African Ministers of Finance in August 1963 in Khartoum. The agreement entered into effect in September 1964 and the Bank started operations at its headquarters at Abidjan in July 1966. Unlike other regional development institutions, membership of the Bank was originally limited to independent countries within the region, thereby excluding non-African countries from subscribing to the capital stock. In May 1979 a decision was taken to admit non-regional members in accordance with a set of principles aimed at preserving the African character of the Bank. In December 1982, the capital stock was officially opened to

non-African countries. The present membership comprises 51 African countries – including Madagascar and other island states that surround the continent with the exclusion of the Republic of South Africa – and 25 non-African countries, including several Western European nations, Brazil, Canada, India, Japan, the Republic of Korea, Kuwait, Saudi Arabia and the USA. The agreement makes explicit provision for the withdrawal or suspension of member countries.

The Bank's basic aims are: to provide loans directly or indirectly for financing national and multinational projects; to encourage public and private investment; to assist member countries to improve the utilization of their resources; to increase the complementarity of economic systems and to promote the balanced growth of foreign trade; to extend technical assistance with a view to studying, preparing and implementing development programmes and projects; to co-operate with national, regional and subregional economic institutions in Africa, as well as with any other outside agency that aims to support African development efforts.

The Bank Group of development financing institutions comprises, in addition to the Bank itself, the African Development Fund (ADF) and the Nigeria Trust Fund (NTF) both providing concessionary loans. Over the past two decades four associated institutions have also been set up to channel further public and private resources for the development of Africa.

The Bank uses a unit of account (UA) equivalent to $1 before the devaluation of 1971 and now expressed on the basis of the special drawing right (SDR). The size of the authorized capital stock, initially set at UA250 million, has grown substantially; in 1986 a special committee approved an increase in the Bank's authorized capital from UA5,400 million to UA16,200 million ($19,600 million). At the end of 1989 the subscribed capital amounted to $18,647.7 million (of which the paid-up portion was equivalent to $2,173.4 million). Payments of amounts subscribed to the paid up capital are made in gold or convertible currencies. Loans from ordinary resources are not tied to purchases in any specific country and are repayable over a period ranging from 12 to 20 years, including the grace period.

The African Development Fund was established, as the Bank's soft window, in July 1972 and began operations in August 1973. Subscriptions to the Fund were made by the Bank itself and by 22 capital-exporting countries outside Africa – thus ensuring the financial contribution of non-regional members to the development of the continent. Concessional loans granted by the Fund for development projects are repayable over very long periods (50 years including a 10-year grace period) and usually carry no interest as such but only an annual service charge around 0.75 per cent. Loans concerning feasibility studies are repayable over 10 years, after a 3-year grace period. The fifth replenishment of the Fund, agreed upon in 1987 by donor countries, amounted to $2700 million for 1988-90.

The Nigeria Trust Fund was established by an agreement signed by the Bank and the government of Nigeria in February 1976 and entered into effect the following April. The Fund, which is under the Bank's administration, finances national and multinational projects, mainly in the infrastructural sector, granting loans for long periods (up to 25 years, including the grace period) and charging interest. The Fund's initial resources amounted to 50 million naira and were subsequently replenished.

The four associated institutions are specifically intended to support the Bank's finance and development efforts. The oldest among these institutions is the

Société internationale financière pour les investissements et le développement en Afrique (SIFIDA), with headquarters in Switzerland (22 rue François-Perreard, BP 310, 1225 Chêne-Bourg). It was created in November 1970 as a holding company for promoting the establishment and growth of productive enterprises in Africa. Besides the Bank its shareholders include the *International Finance Corporation (IFC) and several financial, industrial and commercial institutions in Europe, the USA, Canada and Japan. The initially authorized capital stock amounted to $50 million, of which $18.2 million subscribed.

The Africa Reinsurance Corporation (AFRICA-RE), with headquarters in Nigeria (Reinsurance House, 46 Marina, PMB 12765, Lagos), was established by an agreement signed in February 1976 and entered into force in January 1977. The Corporation – whose authorized capital amounts to $15 million of which 10 per cent is held by the Bank – aims to stimulate the insurance and re-insurance activities as well as the growth of national and regional underwriting capacities.

The Association of African Development Finance Institutions (AADFI), established in 1975 and based in the Côte d'Ivoire (c/o ADB, 01 BP 1387, Abidjan), promotes co-operation among the development banks of the region with regard to project design and financing.

Shelter-Afrique (Société pour l'habitat et le logement territorial en Afrique), with headquarters in Kenya (Mamlaka Road, POB 41479, Nairobi), is another associated institution, set up in 1982, whose purpose is to finance housing in the Bank's member countries. Besides the Bank, several African countries, AFRICA-RE and the Commonwealth Development Corporation participate in its share capital.

The Bank is organized like other international financing institutions and is run by the President, the Board of Directors, and the Board of Governors. Each member country nominates one governor to the Board, usually its Minister of Finance, and one alternate governor. The Board meets at least once a year. As the highest policy-making body, it is vested with all the powers, many of which have been delegated to the Board of Directors. The Board of Governors usually takes its decisions by a majority of the votes cast. Each member is allotted a pre-determined number of votes, plus one additional vote for each share (equal to UA10,000) of stock held; voting rights are therefore related to the amount of each country's share. Amendments to the agreement, such as the admission of non-regional members, require the approval of two-thirds of members possessing at least 75 per cent of the total voting power.

The Board of Directors is responsible for the current operations of the Bank, and is composed of 18 members (of whom six are non-African) nominated by the Board of Governors for a three-year term; it meets twice a month.

The President of the Bank serves for a five-year period and acts as Chairman of the Board of Directors, by whom he is elected; the five Vice-Presidents are nominated by the Board of Directors for a three-year term on the President's recommendation.

The Bank's organization was restructured in 1986 in connection with the expected increase in the authorized capital. Separate sections were set up for Eastern, Western and Central Africa and a new department responsible for disbursements was created. Regional offices of the Bank operate in Cameroon, Ethiopia, Guinea, Kenya, Morocco, Nigeria and Zimbabwe.

The Bank has developed close links with several regional and extraregional political, financial and technical institutions: the *Food and Agriculture Organization of the UN (FAO); the *International Bank for Reconstruction and Development (IBRD); the *International Labour Organization (ILO); the *Organization of African Unity (OAU); the *UN Educational, Scientific and Cultural Organization (UNESCO); and the *World Health Organization (WHO).

Since the first loan was granted in 1967, the Bank has progressively developed its lending activities, supplemented by the non-commercial loans extended by the ADF. Together with its soft loan affiliates (ADF and NTF), by the end of 1989 the Bank had cumulatively disbursed a total $6.8 billion for the development of the African economies. Agricultural projects (especially those concerning food production) receive the largest proportion of loans followed by public utilities, transport, education and health, industry, and multi-sector activities. The Bank also provides technical assistance which is financed to a large extent by bilateral aid funds contributed by developed member countries. Assistance to the private sector in Africa by providing advisory services and finance as well as by encouraging private investment from both within and outside the region may represent a major new area of activity for the Bank over the coming years.

Despite its modest capital base and the magnitude of the development problems facing its members, the Bank has managed to play a significant role. However, even with the admission of industrial countries as non-borrowing members, and the consequent substantial increase in its resources and enhanced capacity to borrow in the international financial markets, it will be difficult for the Bank to have more than a minimal impact on Africa's very fast-growing capital needs.

President: B. N'Diaye

Headquarters: P.O. Box 1387, Abidjan, Côte d'Ivoire (telephone: 320711 – 325010; telex: 23717 – 23498 – 23263 AFDEV; fax: 227004)

Publications: *Annual Report*; ADB News (monthly); *Basic Information* (two a year); *Statistical Handbook* (annually)

Agency for the Prohibition of Nuclear Weapons in Latin America and the Caribbean [Organismo para la Proscripción de las Armas Nucleares en la América Latina y el Caribe] (OPANAL). The basic purpose of the Agency is to provide the institutional framework for the fulfilment of the obligations set forth in the Treaty for the Prohibition of Nuclear Weapons in Latin America (Tlatelolco Treaty) signed in February 1967 by 14 countries. The signature followed a number of preparatory meetings on the denuclearization of Latin America relevant to resolutions of the UN General Assembly. The original contracting parties were subsequently joined by several other Latin American and Caribbean nations. Full contracting parties now total 24; other countries have signed but not ratified the Treaty. The Tlatelolco Treaty remains open for signature by all other sovereign states situated in their entirety South of latitude 35° North in the Western Hemisphere. The Treaty contains two Additional Protocols: Protocol I, open to the signature of countries which, *de jure* or *de facto*, are internationally responsible for territories lying within the geographical zone defined in the Treaty, and Protocol II, open to the signature of countries possessing nuclear weapons. Protocol I has been signed by France and signed and ratified by the Netherlands, the UK and the USA; Protocol II has been signed and ratified by China, France, Russia, the UK, and the USA.

To attain the objectives of the Treaty, the Agency aims to ensure the absence of all nuclear weapons in the area under the jurisdiction of the contracting parties, without prejudice to peaceful uses of atomic energy; to prohibit all testing, use, production, deployment and any form of possession of nuclear weapons; and to provide protection against possible nuclear attacks.

The principal organs of the Agency are the General Conference, the Council, and the Secretariat. The General Conference, consisting of representatives of all member countries, meets in ordinary sessions every two years to lay down policy guidelines and to approve the budget; extraordinary sessions have been held to deal with urgent problems. The Council is the executive body and is composed of five members elected by the General Conference, taking into account the necessity to obtain an equitable geographic representation. The Secretariat is headed by a Secretary General.

The Agency keeps the *UN and the *Organization of American States (OAS) informed about the results of on-site inspections and eventual violations of the Tlatelolco Treaty. A co-operation agreement between OPANAL and the *International Atomic Energy Agency (IAEA) was concluded in September 1972.

The Agency has made an important con-

tribution by restraining the proliferation of nuclear weapons and by establishing Latin America as a denuclearized zone under the guarantee of the nuclear powers which signed and ratified Protocol II to the Tlatelolco Treaty. Besides furthering the objectives of the Treaty, the Agency has promoted the development of the peaceful uses of atomic energy through research and fellowship programmes.

Secretary-General: Dr Antonio Stempel Paris

Headquarters: Temístocles 78, Col. Polanco, CP 11560, Mexico, D.F., Mexico (telephone: 250 6222)

ALADI. Asociación Latinoamericana de Integración; *see* **Latin American Integration Association.**

Andean Group [Cartagena Agreement]. The Group was originally established within the legal framework of the Latin American Free Trade Association (LAFTA), which was succeeded in 1980 by the *Latin American Integration Association (LAIA). Its aims are to strengthen the smaller economies of the Andean subregion through trade liberalization, industrial specialization agreements, common policies for regulating foreign investment, a common external tariff and special measures to favour the least-developed members.

In response to LAFTA's failure to develop a common market on the European model, the representatives of Chile, Colombia, Ecuador, Peru and Venezuela met in Bogotá in August 1966 and solemnly declared their intention to expedite Andean economic integration within the larger structure of LAFTA; Bolivia joined in the Declaration of Bogotá a year later. A Joint Commission was set up to prepare drafts for future agreements at the subregional level. Within this institutional framework, Bolivia, Chile, Colombia, Ecuador, Peru and Venezuela signed an agreement in February 1968 creating the Andean Development Corporation (CAF), a development-financing institution which began operations in 1970; Chile withdrew from CAF in August 1977.

At the conclusion of its sixth session, held in Cartagena, Colombia, the Joint Commission approved the final text of the Agreement on Subregional Integration which was formally signed on 26 May 1969 in Bogotá by the representatives of Bolivia, Chile, Colombia, Ecuador and Peru. Although actually signed in Bogotá, the treaty establishing the Group is officially known as the Cartagena Agreement in honour of the city where the conclusive negotiations took place. The Agreement was approved in July 1969 by LAFTA's Permanent Executive Committee and entered into force in October when the minimum number of ratifications was reached. In spite of active involvement at the initial stage of the negotiations, Venezuela did not join the Group until February 1973. Chile withdrew in October 1976 after a dispute on the common rules governing foreign investment. The text of the Cartagena Agreement has been revised and supplemented on several occasions, notably by the Quito Protocol of 1987.

The basic goals of the Group are to promote the balanced and harmonious development of member countries and to facilitate participation in the process of Latin American integration, with a view to achieving constant improvement in the standard of living of the peoples of the Andean subregion. This should lead to 'an equitable distribution of the benefits of integration' among participant countries in order to reduce the existing disparities in the levels of economic development. In the text of the Cartagena Agreement the listing of the Group's objectives is followed by an indication of the basic ways and means to be adopted. Explicit provision is made for: the harmonization of economic and social policies; the intensification of subregional industrialization through sectoral programming; the acceleration of trade liberalization; the adoption of a common external tariff; the development of agriculture; the channelling of capital resources from within and outside the subregion towards investment financing; and the granting of preferential treatment to Bolivia and Ecuador.

The functions and powers of the Group are further illustrated in a large section of the Cartagena Agreement which defines the main guidelines of the Group's action and establishes a full set of deadlines for carrying out the various tasks. These deadlines have been extended because of continuing difficulties in complying with the original schedules.

The co-ordination of sectoral programmes and the ensuing distribution of key industries among member countries are viewed as a major step towards joint planning at the subregional level. At the same time, an Andean common market is to be established gradually through automatic tariff cuts and the erection of a common tariff against imports from third countries. As the relatively least-developed partners, Bolivia and Ecuador are granted additional, non-reciprocal opportunities and are also allowed longer terms for eliminating tariff barriers to Andean trade and conforming with the final external tariff. The joint programmes, which represent the backbone of the Group's industrialization policies, involve both the rationalization of existing industries and the creation of new ones. For the adoption of each programme a two-thirds majority and the participation of at least four member countries are required. Under the programmes, exclusive production and investment opportunities in basic sectors are allocated among participating countries. Thus, each country manufactures assigned items which enjoy full access to the Andean market. The Group's Programme of Liberalization is directed towards the gradual elimination of all tariff and non-tariff barriers on the importation of goods from any member country; particular rules apply to products related to sectoral specialization agreements and to items included in national reserve lists and temporarily withdrawn from liberalization. The common external tariff, to be erected through periodic adjustments in the existing national rates, is dealt with in detail. Despite the instalment of a common external minimum tariff, new extended timetables had to be fixed due to the failure of member countries to meet the original deadlines.

With regard to agriculture, the member

countries agree to harmonize their policies and to co-ordinate their plans with the aim of establishing a common agricultural policy and a subregional plan. These objectives are to be achieved through joint programmes for the development of individual products or groups of products, common marketing systems, arrangements among the various national organizations to ensure supplies, co-ordination agreements among state planning agencies, measures for promoting exports and joint projects in the spheres of applied research and technical and financial assistance.

The member countries are responsible for deciding on the necessary regulations to prohibit dumping, price manipulation, disruption of normal supplies of raw materials and other equivalent practices which may distort conditions of competition in the Andean market. Various escape clauses and waivers are provided to allow a member to face a grave economic emergency. The promotion of physical integration, especially regarding energy, transportation and communications, is another major task facing the parties to the Cartagena Agreement. Whenever possible, this objective is to be pursued through the establishment of multinational agencies or enterprises. The co-ordination of monetary and financial policies is to take place to the extent necessary to ensure the proper functioning of the Group's mechanisms. Measures are to be taken to channel subregional public and private capital towards investments in industry, agriculture and infrastructure; to finance export trade; to facilitate capital movements; to strengthen the existing system of multilateral compensation among Central Banks; to eliminate double taxation; and, finally, to establish a common reserve fund.

Membership in the Group may not be subject to reservations and is open to other contracting parties to the Treaty of Montevideo which established LAFTA. The least-developed countries joining the Group will be granted the sort of preferential treatment enjoyed by Bolivia and Ecuador. Each member may withdraw from the Group by giving notice to that effect; such notice shall come into force immediately, except for the benefits received and granted under the Programme of Liberalization which are to remain in existence for a five-year period.

According to the Cartagena Agreement, the principal organs through which the Group accomplishes its purposes are the Commission and the Junta (Board), assisted by lesser organs (Committees and Councils) of a subsidiary nature. A new principal organ, the Andean Judicial Tribunal, was added to the Group's institutional machinery in 1979. Further developments in the organizational mechanism resulted from the institutionalization of the Meeting of Ministers of Foreign Affairs (Andean Council) in November 1979 and from the treaty of October 1979 establishing an Assembly consisting of representatives of Andean peoples (Andean Parliament).

The process of adjustment of the Group's structure over the coming years might lead to a stronger institutional framework, more suited to the growing requirements of integration. In particular, the meetings of the Heads of State of the member countries, according to a decision taken in 1990, are to be held on a regular basis twice a year.

Under the present organizational structure the Commission, consisting of a plenipotentiary representative from each country, is the supreme decision-making and political authority. It is empowered: to establish major policies and adopt such measures as may be deemed necessary for the attainment of the Group's objectives; to set the essential rules for the co-ordination of development plans and the harmonization of economic policies; to appoint and dismiss members of the Junta and consider proposals put forward by the same Junta; to supervise the fulfilment by participating countries of obligations arising from the Cartagena Agreement; to approve the Junta's annual budget and determine the amount of the contribution to be paid by each country. In its deliberations the Commission is assisted by two Consultative Councils; each Council comprises four representatives from each member country, elected respectively by national employers' and workers' organizations.

Regular sessions of the Commission are

held three times a year, generally at the seat of the Junta, with the participation of at least two-thirds of the member countries; non-participation is equivalent to abstention. Extraordinary sessions are convened at the request of any country or the Junta. Each country in turn has the presidency of the Commission for one year. As a rule the Commission adopts its decisions by a two-thirds majority; unanimity is required only for appointing members of the Junta. Decisions on proposals concerning highly sensitive matters, such as the delegation of powers to the Junta and the approval of sectoral programmes, may be made by a two-thirds majority only if the remaining countries have abstained; if any negative vote has been cast, the proposal is brought back to the Junta for further consideration.

The Junta, whose seat is in Lima, is a technical body composed of three members, assisted by a permanent staff, and acting unanimously in the general interest of the Andean subregion. Each member, chosen among the nationals of any Latin American country, is appointed for a renewable three-year term. In the discharge of their duties, members of the Junta, who are responsible to the Commission, are required to refrain from any action incompatible with the character of their functions and may not seek or take instructions from any government or from any other national or international body. The tasks assigned to the Junta include supervising the implementation of the Cartagena Agreement and the Commission's decisions; formulating proposals and projects for the development and intensification of the integration process; and evaluating at yearly intervals the results of such process, taking into consideration the objective of an equitable distribution of the benefits of integration. Moreover, the Junta acts as a Permanent Secretariat to the Group and keeps its contacts with member countries through national bodies especially appointed to this effect.

In carrying out their functions, the Group's principal organs are aided by several subsidiary bodies meeting a broadening range of requirements. Among the most important subsidiary organs are the Consultative Committee and the Economic and Social Committee. The Consultative Committee, consisting of the representatives of all member countries, performs the delicate task of co-ordinating national interests and priorities with the initiatives and proposals of the Junta. It may be convened at the seat of the Junta at the request of any member country, by the Junta itself, or by the President of the Commission. The Economic and Social Committee consists of three representatives of the workers and three representatives of the employers for each member country and issues opinions on the relevant aspects of the integration process. A number of specialized Councils have been established by the Commission for promoting the harmonization of economic and social policies and ensuring effective co-ordination between national agencies and bodies on the one hand and the Group's principal organs on the other. The Councils are composed of high-rank representatives who, in their respective countries, are directly responsible for the economic and social sectors with which the individual Councils are concerned. The existing Councils include those dealing with planning, foreign trade, currency and exchange, finance, fiscal policy, physical integration, social affairs, health, tourism, agriculture and livestock, and statistics.

The Andean Judicial Tribunal was established as a principal organ in May 1979 when the Group's members signed an international treaty. The Tribunal, which began operating in January 1984, is located in Quito. It consists of five judges, one from each member country appointed for a renewable six-year term; the Presidency is assumed annually by each judge in turn by alphabetical order of country. The Tribunal is competent to deal with cases relating to the alleged illegality of actions taken by the Commission or the Junta and the infringement by a member country of its obligations under the Cartagena Agreement. It also has jurisdiction to give preliminary rulings concerning the interpretation of the Cartagena Agreement. Matters may be brought before the Tribunal by any member country, the Commission, the Junta and any natural or legal person in the Andean subregion.

The Group has been developing co-operative relations with other international economic organizations, at both the regional and the extraregional level, and with several third countries. Besides co-operating with UN organs, especially regarding trade, technology and finance, the Group is making an effort to expedite Latin American integration. An active role was played by the Group in the so-called re-negotiation of LAFTA's heritage for revising the concessions granted and the obligations assumed under the Montevideo Treaty of 1960 and framing a new instrument of integration represented by LAIA (established by the Montevideo Treaty of 1980). A promising area of co-operation is represented by the Group's growing ties with economic integration areas outside Latin America, such as the *European Economic Community (EEC) and the *Economic Community of West African States (ECOWAS). A five-year agreement was signed in December 1983 with the EEC to eliminate obstacles to trade and to foster co-operation programmes. With reference to third countries, mention is to be made of the co-operation agreement signed with the USA in December 1979 and of bilateral agreements with other Latin American and Western European countries.

The Group's activity throughout the 1970s achieved substantial results, despite the frequent clash of national and subregional economic priorities, marked ideological differences and a complex set of external pressures which led to the postponement of several deadlines and other significant changes in the original version of the Cartagena Agreement. The Group demonstrated its ability to survive and adjust to major and unforeseen change during the grave crisis which occurred in 1975–6 and resulted in the withdrawal of Chile. To give new impetus to economic and political co-operation, including subregional industrial development programmes, and to reaffirm their commitment to the basic goals of the Group, the Heads of State of the member countries adopted in May 1979 the 'Mandate of Cartagena'.

Serious political and economic problems hindered the operations of the Group throughout the 1980s. A 'Plan of Reorientation' was adopted by the Junta in early 1983 with a view to adjusting to the changed economic and political environment. In front of increasing tensions, the Presidents of the five member countries restressed their willingness to pursue the objective of regional integration in a solemn declaration signed in Caracas in July 1983.

A turning point was represented, in May 1987, by the adoption by the representatives of the member countries of the Quito Protocol which modified to a considerable extent the Cartagena Agreement. The Protocol has been in force since May 1988. Further attempts at 'revitalizing' the process of Andean integration were undertaken in May 1989 when the Presidents of four member countries and the Bolivian Minister of Foreign Affairs decided to withdraw measures hindering trade liberalization and to apply reductions in customs duties. The May 1990 meeting of the Heads of State decided to co-ordinate negotiations with creditors, to strengthen co-operation in industrial development and to implement a common policy concerning energy exports. Efforts are currently under way for the creation of a common market by 1994.

As regards Andean trade, based on exports of member countries to the subregion, gains in volume and a clear trend toward diversification are a salient feature. Trade liberalization within the Group has been achieved to a sizeable extent. Non-tariff barriers have disappeared while annual, automatic and irrevocable tariff cuts involve 80 per cent of the total products. New and extended schedules have been drawn up for tariff reductions on the remaining products; in May 1986 an agreement was reached in order to further limit the number of 'sensitive' products exempted from trade liberalization.

By 1980 tariffs among Colombia, Peru and Venezuela were down about 75 per cent from the 1971 starting point; the reduction was completed in 1983. The reduction on the part of Bolivia and Ecuador was to take place over a much lomger period. Their products have enjoyed free admission to other member countries since the end of 1973.

In joint industrial programming, negotiations over product assignments ran into severe difficulties and deadlines had to be extended as only a few of the projected sectoral agreements were actually signed. The first programme, dealing with the metalworking sector, was approved in August 1972 and revised in July 1979. The petrochemical programme was approved in August 1975 and renegotiated in July 1978. The agreement on the automotive programme, generally regarded as one of the most important, was signed in September 1977. However, persistent differences and conflicts of interest ultimately led to shelve the more ambitious joint industrial programmes.

With reference to agriculture, significant advances have been made for co-ordinating national plans, fostering mutual co-operation and adopting integration projects in selected areas. The Meeting of Ministers of Agriculture was institutionalized in December 1977. The 1982 'Plan of Reorientation' had placed increased emphasis on agricultural development. The first Meeting of Ministers of Transport was held in 1982 when a plan of action for the improvement of road and maritime transport was adopted. Plans to improve posts and telecommunications are under consideration.

The Group had agreed to common rules on the treatment of foreign capital as a response to the threat of an increasing dependence of the subregion on non-Andean investors and transnational corporations. According to the rules adopted in December 1970 (through the well-known Decision 24) and subsequently revised and improved, foreign investors were not allowed to own more than 49 per cent of a local company and were required to complete the transfer of their shares by 1988 in Colombia, Peru and Venezuela, and by 1993 in Bolivia and Ecuador, in order to qualify for the benefits granted under the trade liberalization programme. Moreover, foreign companies were not allowed to repatriate dividends of more than 20 per cent annually unless the Commission had expressly given its approval.

The strict rules embodied in Decision 24 ultimately deterred foreign investors and led to the adoption in the mid-1980s of more liberal national laws on foreign investment by individual member countries. The Quito Protocol of 1987 annulled Decision 24 and replaced it with Decision 220, leaving to national authorities the determination of the extent of foreign participation. The maximum period allowed for completion of transfer of majority shareholding from foreign to local investors was extended to 30 years (37 years in the case of Bolivia and Ecuador). Specific rules have been in effect since 1982 (through Decision 169) to foster the creation of 'Andean Multinational Enterprises' by regional investors. The establishment in November 1976 of an Andean Reserve Fund was intended as a major step towards the harmonization of the Group's exchange, monetary and financial policies. The Fund, located in Bogotá, is responsible for extending credits to help solve balance-of-payments problems of the member countries. The decision to open the Fund to other Latin American countries was taken in 1988 in view of the creation of a Latin American Reserve Fund. The Andean Intermunicipal Bank was established in 1988 for financing public works.

The Andean Development Corporation (CAF), with headquarters in Caracas and an authorized capital of $1,000 million, has been providing loans and technical assistance to the least-developed countries of the subregion since 1970. Finally, the Group has made progress towards integrating social and labour policies, especially with regard to health, social security and workers' migration.

The Group has played a prominent role in the Andean development process and, notwithstanding failures and delays, may still be regarded among the most wide-ranging efforts at regional integration in the developing world.

Headquarters: Paseo de la República 3895, Lima 27; P.O. Box 18–1177, Lima 18, Peru (telephone: 414212; telex: JUNAC 20104 PU; fax: 420911)

Publications: *Annual Report*; *Carta Informativa* (monthly); occasional brochures dealing with general and particular aspects of Andean integration

References: W. Avery and J. Cochrane: 'Innovation in Latin American Regionalism: the Andean Common Market', *International Organization*, 27 (1973), 181–223; F. Parkinson: 'International Economic Integration in Latin America and the Caribbean: A Survey', *Year Book of World Affairs*, 31 (1977), 236–56; E.S. Milenky: 'The Cartagena Agreement in Transition', *Year Book of World Affairs*, 33 (1979), 167–79; C. Angarita and P. Coffey: *Europe and the Andean Countries: A Comparison of Economic Policies and Institutions* (London, 1988)

ANZUS Pact [ANZUS Security Treaty]. The Pact, which is no longer in full operation, was devised to co-ordinate the defence of the contracting parties in order to preserve peace and security in the Pacific. The Security Treaty between Australia, New Zealand and the USA (usually known as the ANZUS Pact from the initials of its signatory countries) was signed in San Francisco in September 1951 and entered into force in April 1952. It was intended to be the first step towards the development of a comprehensive system of regional security in the Pacific, within the framework of the defensive alliance systems of the Western world. This system was further developed by the creation of the South-East Asia Treaty Organization (SEATO) under the Manila Treaty of September 1954 which aimed also to protect non-member countries belonging to the region such as South Vietnam.

The parties to the Pact uphold the principles set forth in the UN Charter and affirm their desire to live in peace with all peoples and all governments. The purposes of the parties are to strengthen the fabric of peace in the Pacific; to declare publicly and formally their sense of unity against any potential aggressor; to further their efforts for collective defence and to co-ordinate their policies. Threats to the territorial integrity, political independence or security of any of the parties in the Pacific give rise to the obligation to consult together. In case of aggression by means of armed attack, each party is bound to act according to its constitutional processes since attack against any party constitutes a danger to the peace and safety of the others. According to the Pact, an armed attack includes aggression on the metropolitan territory of any of the parties or on the island territories under its jurisdiction in the Pacific or on its forces, vessels or aircraft in the Pacific. The UN Security Council is to be informed immediately of any armed attack and of all measures adopted to resist it. Such measures are to be terminated when the Security Council has taken appropriate action to restore and maintain peace and security. On the whole, the functions and powers arising out of the Pact are dealt with in general terms, in accordance with the largely declaratory character of the document. The duration of the Pact is unlimited although any party may withdraw upon one year's notice.

Co-operation to be carried out under the Pact embraces the exchange of strategic intelligence, scientific and technical assistance in defence matters, supply of defence equipment, training programmes, combined ground, air and naval exercises and visits by military aircraft and naval vessels.

The main consultative organ of the Pact is the Council, which consists of Foreign Ministers or their deputies. Closed meetings were held annually, rotating between the capitals of the three contracting parties, until the mid-1980s. Decisions were taken unanimously. The Council meetings were also attended by military representatives giving advice on matters related to military co-operation; these representatives also met separately, between sessions of the Council. Officials involved in other forms of practical co-operation held meetings whenever the governments deemed it necessary. The Pact is not endowed with any permanent staff or secretariat; costs are borne by the government in whose territory the meeting takes place.

The Pact has no formal or informal relationship with the *North Atlantic Treaty Organization (NATO), although both are intended to provide for collective self-defence. The activities carried out under the Pact are limited, as its weak organizational structure suggests. Moreover, the obligation to assist the attacked party is subordinated to compliance with 'constitutional processes' and is therefore not automatic, as in NATO. The influence of the Pact decreased as SEATO developed its activities in South-East Asia and Australasia. After the dissolution of SEATO, the Pact regained importance. Major issues of common concern to contracting parties have been reviewed at the annual sessions of the Council, such as events in Afghanistan and Kampuchea and the spread of nuclear weapons on a world scale.

Following the election of a Labour Government in July 1984, New Zealand decided not to allow US warships enter its ports unless assurance was given that they were not carrying nuclear arms, an information that the USA does not disclose as a matter of policy. Because of the New Zealand ban on visits by nuclear warships, joint naval exercises planned for March and October 1985 were cancelled; in August 1986 the USA formally announced the suspension of its security commitment to New Zealand and therefore the Pact ceased to be in full operation. The prospects of the Pact were also affected by the treaty, signed in August 1985 within the framework of the *South Pacific Forum (SPF), providing for the establishment of a South Pacific Nuclear-Free Zone. Instead of the annual trilateral meetings of the Council, bilateral talks are held every year between Australia and the USA. The Pact still governs security relations between Australia and the USA as well as between Australia and New Zealand since the suspension of obligations affects only the relationship between New Zealand and the USA. Full trilateral co-operation is unlikely to be resumed unless there is a major change in New Zealand's policy concerning potentially nuclear-armed vessels.

Headquarters: c/o Department of Foreign Affairs and Trade, Parkes, ACT 2600, Australia (telephone: 619111; telex: 62007; fax: 733577)

References: J.G. Starke: *The ANZUS Treaty*

Alliance (London, 1965); J. Bercovitch (ed): *ANZUS in Crisis. Alliance Management in International Relations* (London, 1987)

ANZUS Security Treaty. *See* **ANZUS Pact.**

APEC. *See* **Asia-Pacific Economic Co-operation.**

Arab Bank for Economic Development in Africa [Banque arabe pour le développement économique en Afrique] (BADEA). The purpose of the Bank is to contribute to the economic development of Africa by financing infrastructural, industrial and agricultural projects and by providing technical assistance.

The decision to establish the Bank was taken in November 1973 in Algiers at the Sixth Summit Conference of the *Arab League and the founding agreement was signed in Cairo in February 1974. The Bank started operations in March 1975 with headquarters in Khartoum, Sudan. Its subscribers include all countries participating in the Arab League, with the exception of Djibouti, Somalia, and Yemen. Egypt's membership was suspended in April 1979 and subsequently restored in April 1988. Recipient countries may be all members of the *Organization of African Unity (OAU), except those African countries that belong to the Arab League. A total of 41 countries are eligible for the Bank's aid.

The Bank's basic aims are: to provide loans to national and regional institutions for financing national and multinational projects; to supply expertise and to promote technical co-operation; and, generally, to co-ordinate aid provided by Arab financial institutions to Africa.

Loans on concessional terms for development projects may not exceed $15 million or 50 per cent of the total cost of each project (80 per cent for loans of under $10 million). The Bank also provides technical assistance, mainly in the form of grants for project feasibility studies, and generally stimulates the contribution of Arab capital to African development.

The Bank carries on operations through its ordinary capital resources. These were integrated in November 1976 with the capital stock of the Special Arab Assistance Fund for Africa (SAAFA) which had been created in January 1972, under the name of Arab Loan Fund for Africa, by Arab oil ministers in order to provide urgent aid to African countries. The subscribed capital stock of the Bank amounted to $1,048 million at the end of 1988. Saudi Arabia was by far the largest subscriber, followed by Libya, Kuwait, Iraq, the United Arab Emirates, Qatar and Algeria.

The structure of the Bank is similar to that of other international financing institutions. The Board of Governors, composed of the finance ministers of the Arab League member countries, is the supreme authority and meets at least once a year to set the general guidelines. The Board of Directors, composed of 11 members and meeting four times a year, performs executive functions and supervises the implementation of decisions adopted by the Board of Governors. The seven countries which are major subscribers to the capital stock have a permanent seat on the Board; appointments to the remaining four seats are made by the Governors for a four-year term. The Chairman is elected by the Board of Directors for a two-year term.

The links of the Bank with other Arab and African financial institutions have a special relevance in order to ensure co-ordination in channelling public and private resources for Africa's economic development: particularly close relations exist with the *African Development Bank (AfDB), subregional banks in Central and West Africa and Arab development agencies.

The Bank has been playing an active albeit modest role in promoting Arab investment in Africa and co-ordinating Arab aid for development projects. Between 1975 and 1989, the Bank had approved loans and grants involving 142 projects, 49 grants for technical assistance and nine lines of credit and totalling $946.4 million (or $1,160.6 million if aid granted by SAAFA is taken into account); total disbursements amounted to about 60 per cent of total commitments. Among the recipients were nearly all non-Arab members of OAU. In regional terms, West African countries received the largest proportion of total aid. The five leading recipients of project aid have been Ghana, Senegal, Madagascar, Guinea and Rwanda which together accounted for about one fourth of total lending. The largest share of total lending went to infrastructural projects; agricultural, industrial and energy development projects accounted for the balance. Over the past five years emphasis on agriculture has remarkably grown, representing on average over 40 per cent of total commitments.

Chairman: Ahmad Abdallah al-Akeil
Headquarters: Sayed Abdar-Rahman el-Mahdi Avenue, P.O. Box 2640, Khartoum, Sudan (telephone: 73646 – 74709; telex: 22248 – 22739)
Publications: *Annual Report*; *Co-operation for Development* (quarterly)

Arab Fund for Economic and Social Development (AFESD). The purpose of the Fund is to contribute to the progress of the Arab countries by financing economic and social development projects, encouraging, directly or indirectly, public and private investment and providing technical assistance.

The Agreement establishing the Fund was signed in May 1968 by the representatives of 17 Arab countries but the Fund did not begin operations until April 1973. The founder members were subsequently joined by other Arab countries; the present membership includes 20 countries plus the Palestine Liberation Organization (PLO). In response to the signing of a bilateral peace treaty with Israel, Egypt's participation was suspended in April 1979 but funds granted for projects already under way were not discontinued; the full reintegration of Egypt into the Fund took place in April 1988.

The Fund participates in the financing of investment projects by: granting loans on concessional terms to governments and public and private institutions of member countries, giving special regard to projects that interest specifically Arab peoples and to joint Arab projects; stimulating the flow of public and private capital resources for the growth of the Arab economy; and supplying technical expertise and assistance.

The size of the authorized capital stock of the Fund, expressed in Kuwaiti dinars (KD), was initially set at KD100 million and increased in 1975 to KD400 million and in 1982 to KD800 million, comprising 80,000 shares, each of them equivalent to KD10,000. Kuwait and Saudi Arabia are by far the largest subscribers, followed by Algeria and Libya. At the end of 1990 subscribed capital amounted to about KD695 million and paid-up capital to KD663 million. The Fund may borrow twice the amount of its capital; additional borrowing must be authorized by the Board of Governors.

The structure of the Fund comprises: the Board of Governors, which is the supreme decision-making organ, consisting of one governor and one alternate governor appointed by each member country; the Board of Directors, composed of eight members nominated by the Board of Governors for a renewable two-year term, which is charged with the general operation of the Fund and exercises the powers delegated to it by the Board of Governors; and the Director-General who serves as Chairman of the Board of Executive Directors.

The Fund maintains close working relations with the *League of Arab States and Arab economic and financial institutions such as the *Arab Monetary Fund (AMF) and the *Organization of Arab Petroleum Exporting Countries (OAPEC); in 1974/75 the Fund was charged with administrating loans from the OAPEC Special Account established to allievate balance-of-payments difficulties of Arab oil importing countries. Moreover, the Fund acts as the secretariat of the Co-ordination Group of Arab National and Regional Development Institutions.

Between 1973 and 1990, the Fund had granted 251 loans totalling about KD1,326 million; actual disbursements amounted to roughly half that sum. During the same period, technical assistance grants had been about 300 for a total amount exceeding KD30 million. More than three quarters of the Fund's cumulative commitments have been on concessional terms; the geographic distribution is biased toward the least developed countries in the Arab

world. The invasion, in August 1990, of Kuwait where the Fund's headquarters are located, interrupted the activities of the organization which temporarily moved to Bahrain; many projects financed by the Fund were affected and a redefinition of lending policies is under way.

Director-General: Abd al-Latif Yousuf al-Hamad

Headquarters: P.O. Box 21923, Safat, 13080 Kuwait (telephone: 245 1580; telex: 22153; fax: 241 6758)

Temporary address in 1991: P.O. Box 10915, Manama, Bahrain (telephone: 536300; telex: 8491; fax: 536583)

Arab League. *See* **League of Arab States.**

Arab Monetary Fund (AMF). The Fund is intended to assist member countries in coping with balance of payments difficulties and more generally to promote Arab monetary co-operation and integration.

The agreement establishing the Fund was drawn up under the auspices of the Economic Council, operating within the framework of the *League of Arab States, which gave its approval during a meeting held in Rabat, Morocco, in April 1976; it entered into force in February 1977. The present membership includes 19 Arab countries together with the Palestine Liberation Organization (PLO). Egypt's membership was suspended in April 1979, in response to the signing of the bilateral peace treaty with Israel, and restored in April 1988.

The Fund's basic aims are: to correct disequilibria in the balance of payments of member countries; to promote stability of exchange rates among Arab currencies, the realization of their mutual convertibility and the elimination of restrictions on current payments; to encourage the use of the Arab dinar as a unit of account, thus paving the way for the creation of a unified Arab currency; to co-ordinate policies of member countries with regard to international monetary problems; and to provide a mechanism for the settlement of current payments between members with a view to promoting trade among them.

The Fund, which functions both as a bank and a fund, is empowered: to provide short- and medium-term loans to finance balance of payments deficits; to issue guarantees to members with a view to strengthening their borrowing capabilities; to act as intermediary in the issuance of loans in Arab and international markets for the account and under the guarantee of members; to manage funds placed under its charge by members; to consult periodically with members on the situation of their economies; and to extend technical assistance to banking and monetary institutions in member countries.

Operations are carried out by the Fund through its ordinary capital resources. The establishment of a general reserve fund and, if necessary, of special reserve funds is envisaged by the agreement. The Fund uses its own unit of account, that is the Arab Accounting Dinar (AAD), which is expressed on the basis of special drawing rights (SDRs); more precisely AAD1 = SDR3. The size of the authorized capital stock of the Fund was initially set at AAD263 million (SDR789 million), comprising 5260 shares, each of them equivalent to AAD50,000. Algeria, Iraq and Saudi Arabia subscribed the largest number of shares, immediately followed by Egypt and Kuwait. Each member paid 5 per cent of the value of its shares upon ratification of the agreement and another 20 per cent when the agreement entered into effect. Besides these payments, made in convertible currencies, each member had to pay 2 per cent of its quota in its national currency. A further 25 per cent of the capital was to be paid, in convertible currencies, by September 1979.

In July 1981, members were obliged to pay the balance of their subscribed capital. In April 1983, the authorized capital was increased to AAD600 million, comprising 12,000 shares, each having the value of AAD50,000; the increase was to be paid in five equal annual instalments. However, only a fraction of the first instalment was actually paid up and further payments appeared uncertain. At the end of 1990, total paid-up capital was AAD312 million.

A member is normally entitled to borrow up to 75 per cent of its paid-up capital, in convertible currencies, in order to finance an overall balance of payments deficit (automatic loans). Loans in excess of 75 per cent may be granted only on the condition that the member adopts, in accord with the Fund, a programme for reducing its deficit (ordinary and extended loans). In the event of an unexpected deficit arising from a sudden decline in exports of goods and services or a large increase in agricultural imports, a member is entitled to draw up to 100 per cent of its paid-up capital (compensatory loans). Loans to an individual member in any one year may not exceed twice the amount of the member's paid-up convertible currency subscription and a member's outstanding loans at any one time may not exceed four times such amount; in special cases the limit may be raised to five times. Automatic as well as compensatory loans are repayable within three years, ordinary loans within five years and extended loans within seven years. Interest rates vary according to the length of the lending period.

In 1981 the Fund introduced an Inter-Arab Trade Facility with a view to encouraging trade among member contries. Under this facility, which was discontinued in 1989, a member was allowed to borrow up to 100 per cent of its subscription, paid in convertible currencies, but the amount could not exceed the member's trade deficit with other members. To foster laberalization of trade in goods and services (excluding petroleum) between Arab countries and to increase the competitive edge of their exporters, Arab financial institutions decided, in March 1989, the creation of the Arab Trade Financing Program (ATFP) to be based in Abu Dhabi. The Program extends lines of credit to national agencies for exports and imports; the Fund was expected to supply 50 per cent of the Program's capital of $500 million.

The structure of the Fund comprises the Board of Governors, the Board of Executive Directors, and the Director-General. The Board of Governors, composed of one governor and one deputy appointed by each member country for a five-year term, is the supreme policy-making body and meets at least once a year; extraordinary meetings may be convened at the request of half the members or of members possessing at least 50 per cent of the total voting power. The Board of Governors, which has delegated many of its powers to the Board of Executive Directors, takes its decisions by simple majority, with certain exceptions where a larger majority is required. Each member country has a fixed number of votes plus one additional vote for each share of stock held. The Board of Executive Directors, responsible for the general operation of the Fund, consists of eight members, nominated for a renewable three-year term, plus the Director-General of the Fund who serves as Chairman. The Director-General serves for a renewable five-year term and is responsible for supervising Committees on loans and investments respectively.

The Fund maintains close working relations with other economic and financial groupings of Arab countries but appears still far from achieving its wider political objectives such as the promotion of Arab economic integration and the introduction of a unified Arab currency. The Fund sponsors annual meetings of the Board of Governors of Arab central banks and Arab monetary agencies with a view to co-ordinating the policies of member countries on current international financial and monetary questions.

It has now become the policy of the Fund to focus on specific projects which directly foster economic growth in the country concerned. Between 1978 and 1990, total approved loans amounted to AAD561.6 million, of which automatic loans represented over 40 per cent. The Fund prepares surveys on inter-Arab trade and extends technical assistance; an Economic Policy Institute was set up in 1988 to conduct research, provide training for economists and policymakers and organize seminars and meetings.

The future prospects of the Fund will be affected to a very large extent by the continued delay by some member countries in discharging their financial obligations; arrears on loan repayments, notably from Sudan, Mauritania and Somalia, represented about one fourth of the Fund's loanable resources. This might ultimately disrupt the revolving nature of the resources of the Fund making them unavailable to other members needing support for the correction of macroeconomic disequilibria.

Director-General: Osama J. Faquih
Headquarters: P.O. Box 2818, Abu Dhabi, United Arab Emirates (telephone: 215000; telex: 22989; fax: 326454)
Publications: *Annual Report*; *Joint Arab Economic Report* (annually); *Balance of Payments and Public Debt of Arab Countries* (annually)

AsDB. *See* **Asian Development Bank.**

ASEAN. *See* **Association of South East Asian Nations.**

Asian Development Bank (AsDB). The Bank is a development financing institution which aims to foster economic growth and co-operation in the Asian and Pacific region and to contribute to the progress of developing member countries, collectively and individually, by lending funds, promoting investment and providing technical assistance.

The agreement establishing the Bank was drawn up under the auspices of the Economic Commission for Asia and the Far East (ECAFE) – a regional body of the UN later succeeded by the *Economic and Social Commission for Asia and the Pacific (ESCAP). It was formally adopted at the Ministerial Conference on Economic Co-operation in Asia in December 1965 in Manila; the agreement entered into effect in August 1966 and the Bank started operations at its headquarters in Manila in December of the same year. Membership of the Bank includes about 40 countries within the ESCAP region, all developing except Australia, New Zealand and Japan, plus 15 developed countries outside the region such as Canada, France, Germany, Italy, the UK and the USA. Among the Bank's developing countries are also centrally-planned economies such as the

Socialist Republic of Viet Nam, which succeeded the former Republic of Viet Nam as a regional member in September 1976, Laos, and Cambodia (which had not sent delegations to meetings for several years and resumed participation in 1992). China joined the Bank in March 1986; Taiwan, one the Bank's founder members, maintained its membership. Among prospective members are Iran as well as the Asian republics of the former USSR.

The basic aims of the Bank are: to raise funds from both public and private sources for development purposes, taking into special consideration projects of regional and subregional scope and the needs of the lesser developed member countries; to assist members with regard to co-ordination of development, trade and general economic policies; to extend technical assistance, including the formulation of specific proposals and the preparation and implementation of projects; and to co-operate with the UN and its specialized agencies and with other international and national institutions concerned with investment of development funds in the ESCAP region.

The Bank operates with its ordinary capital resources (composed of subscribed capital, funds raised through borrowings and reserves) to carry out lending on commercial terms and with the resources of Special Funds to grant concessional (soft) loans. The size of the capital stock, initially authorized at $1100 million, has been growing substantially; at 31 December 1990 the authorized capital amounted to $23,938 million, of which $22,884 million had been subscribed. Japan and the USA are by far the largest shareholders, each of them holding 12.4 per cent of total voting power.

The Bank has been borrowing funds from world capital markets since 1969. Loans from the ordinary resources, that is hard loans made on commercial terms, are not tied to the purchase of goods and services in any specific country and are repayable over a period usually ranging from 15 to 25 years, including the grace period. The system of fixed lending rates was abolished in July 1986 and replaced by a system of periodically adjusted rates.

In the first half of the 1970s the existing Special Funds – the Multi-Purpose Special Fund (MPSF) and the Agricultural Special Fund (ASF) – were restructured and a new mechanism, the Asian Development Fund (ADF), was established in June 1974 for the administration of resources available for concessional loans. The resources of the ASF were consolidated with those of the MPSF and the latter transferred most of its resources to the ADF. The initial mobilization of ADF resources (known as ADF I), intended to finance concessional lending up to the end of 1975, was followed by a replenishment (ADF II) of $809 million for 1976–8; a second replenishment (ADF III) of $2150 million for 1979–82; a third replenishment (ADF IV) of $3214 million for 1983–6; a fourth replenishment (ADF V) of $3600 million for 1987–90; a fifth replenishment (ADF VI) of $4200 million for 1992–95.

The Technical Assistance Special Fund (TASF) extends technical assistance grants on the basis of direct voluntary contributions. The Japan Special Fund was set up in 1988 in order to provide financing for technical assistance and equity investment.

The Bank's structure, which is similar to that of other international financing institutions, consists of the Board of Governors, the Board of Directors, and the President. All the powers are vested in the Board of Governors which is composed of one governor and one alternate governor appointed by each member country and meets at least once a year. Many of its powers may be and actually are delegated to the Board of Directors, with important exceptions concerning the admission of new members, changes in the capital stock, amendments of the Charter and election of Directors and President. The Board of Governors normally adopts its decisions by a majority of the votes cast; the voting power of each country is related to the amount of its quota in the Bank's authorized capital stock. At present the Board of Directors, responsible for the general direction of the Bank's operations, is composed of twelve members, eight representing countries within the ESCAP region (with about 65 per cent of the voting power) and four representing the remaining countries. Each director serves for a two-year term and may be re-elected. The President of the Bank serves for a five-year period and acts as Chairman of the Board of Directors. The Vice-Presidents are nominated by the Board of Directors on the President's recommendation.

The Bank acts as executing agency for projects financed by the *UN Development Programme (UNDP) and maintains close working relations with regional and extra-regional bodies to co-ordinate technical and financial development assistance efforts within the ESCAP region.

Between 1968 and 1991, the Bank had approved loans from ordinary capital resources totalling $25 billion, while loans from the ADF amounted to over $12 billion. Indonesia, Pakistan, the Philippines, Bangladesh, India and the Republic of Korea were the largest borrowers. Priority was given to the agriculture and agro-industry sector which accounted for nearly one third of total lending. Energy, transport and communications, and social infrastructure also took a sizeable share of total loans. In the near future the Bank is expected to play a significant role in development in China as well as in the countries of Indochina.

The Bank has had a remarkable impact on the progress of its borrowing members but to meet the fast-growing capital demands of the 1990s and the new development priorities it needs a substantial increase in its ordinary capital resources and adequate and timely replenishments of its soft window, the ADF. The demands on the Bank's resources over the next few years will be enormous and only a small proportion of the external financing gap of its developing member countries will be satisfied. Although the Bank's loans were to be usually granted for specific projects, a decision was taken in 1987 to support programmes of sectoral adjustment. A clear trend has emerged to extend the Bank's activities beyond the traditional sectors. Therefore, the Bank is being increasingly involved in assisting the private sector, including direct financial assistance to private enterprises, in supporting financial institutions and capital markets and in promoting privatization of public sector enterprises. The Bank may be expected to play a more active catalyst role than in the recent past in mobilizing external resources through innovative modes of co-financing from both official and commercial sources.

President: Kimimasa Tarumizu

Headquarters: 6 ADB Avenue, 1501 Mandaluyong, Metro Manila, Philippines; P.O. Box 789, 1099 Manila, Philippines (telephone: 711 3851; telex: 63587; fax: 741 7961)

Publications: *Annual Report*; *ADB Quarterly Review*; *Asian Development Outlook* (annually); *Asian Development Review* (twice a year)

Reference: D. Wilson: *A Bank for Half the World. The Story of the Asian Development Bank 1966–1986* (Manila, 1987)

Asia-Pacific Economic Co-operation (APEC). APEC has rapidly evolved from an 'informal process' to the leading intergovernmental forum for economic co-operation in the Asia-Pacific region, currently including 15 nations as full members.

A notable part has been played by Australia in developing the concept of a regional economic consultative forum since the speech made by then Prime Minister Hawke in Seoul in January 1989 suggesting the formation of an Asian version of the *Organization for Economic Co-operation and Development (OECD). At the meeting held in Canberra, Australia, in November 1989 an Asia-Pacific Economic Co-operation forum set up with the participation of the five Pacific industrial powers (Australia, Canada, Japan, New Zealand and the USA), the members of the *Association of South-East Asian Nations (ASEAN), and South Korea.

The consultation process further developed at APEC II, held in Singapore, and made a qualitative step forward at the ministerial meeting (APEC III) held in Seoul in November 1991. The admission of the 'three Chinas' – that is China, Hong Kong, and Taiwan (under the name of Chinese Taipei) – and the adoption of the

'Seoul Declaration' setting out aims and methods of operation marked a new stage in intergovernmental co-operation in the Asia-Pacific region.

According to the 'Seoul Declaration', the objectives of APEC will be: (a) to sustain the growth and development of the region; (b) to enhance the positive gains resulting from increasing economic interdependence, including by encouraging the flow of goods, services, capital and technology; (c) to develop and strengthen an open multilateral trading system; and (d) to reduce barriers to trade in goods and services among participants according to the principles of the *General Agreement on Tariffs and Trade (GATT) and without detriment to other economies. APEC will focus on those economic areas where there is scope to advance common interests and achieve mutual benefits, including co-operation in specific sectors such as energy, environment, fisheries, tourism, transportation and telecommunications.

APEC operates through a process of consultation and exchange of views among high-level representatives of the member countries, drawing upon research, analysis and policy ideas contributed by participants as well as by other relevant organizations such as ASEAN, the *South Pacific Forum (SPF) and the *Pacific Economic Co-operation Council (PECC). The relationship with PECC will be of special importance because of PECC's less formal character and wider membership allowing for the discussion of specific issues and proposals without committing governments to specific actions. On the other hand, the maturing of APEC will stimulate PECC's work programmes. Substantial input for APEC will also come from private sector bodies, notably the *Pacific Basin Economic Council (PBEC).

The direction and nature of APEC activities, within the framework of the 'Seoul Declaration', will be determined by annual ministerial meetings of member countries; responsibility for developing the APEC process in accord with the decisions of the ministerial meetings will lie with a senior officials' meeting of represen-

tatives from each participating country. It is to be expected that a small permanent secretariat will be created to perform administrative functions.

Future APEC ministerial meetings are to be held in Thailand (1992), the USA (1993), and Indonesia (1994).

Asociación Latinoamericana de Integración (ALADI). *See* **Latin American Integration Association.**

Association of South East Asian Nations (ASEAN). The Association, although it does not embrace the whole region, is the major body organizing co-operation in South East Asia and plays a leading role in facilitating economic, social and cultural development, promoting active co-ordination and mutual assistance in matters of common interest and ensuring regional peace and stability.

The Association originated in August 1967 in Bangkok when a solemn document, known as the Bangkok Declaration, was signed by representatives of Indonesia, Malaysia, the Philippines, Singapore and Thailand. The Declaration set out the aims and features of the new organization, which was intended to replace the Association of South East Asia (ASA), formed by Malaysia, the Philippines and Thailand in the early 1960s to deal with political and economic matters. Brunei joined in January 1984 the five founder members of the Association. Papua New Guinea enjoys observer status.

The eventual extension of ASEAN membership to include the whole of South East Asia now appears a realistic prospect. Besides the interest demonstrated on occasion by Myanmar [formerly Burma] in gaining observer status, Viet Nam has openly expressed its aspiration to join the Association. Viet Nam's entry would be subordinated, inter alia, to the resolution of the Cambodian problem. In such context, the subsequent admission to ASEAN of a fully sovereign and neutral Cambodia – and even of Laos – would not seem unlikely. Papua New Guinea might also be a prospective member but its close affiliation to South Pacific bodies prevents a full-scale participation in ASEAN.

The basic goals of the Association are rather widely phrased in the founding Declaration. They include: acceleration of economic growth, social progress and cultural development through joint efforts in the spirit of equality and partnership; provision of mutual assistance in training and research facilities in the educational, professional, technical and administrative fields; promotion of political stability in South East Asia and the development of close links with other international and regional organizations with similar aims. Within the framework of economic co-operation and development, provision is made for greater utilization of the agriculture and industries of member countries, intensification of trade within the region and with the rest of the world including study of the problems of international commodity trade, improvement of transportation and communications, and adoption of joint research and technological programmes and projects.

The functions and powers of the Association, in conformity with its basic features, are rather limited in scope and subject to the principle of consensus with regard to decision-making. Recurring crises in the region have placed very severe strains on the internal cohesion of the Association whose powers have thus far been confined to the promotion of voluntary co-ordination of efforts.

The present institutional framework comprises a Ministerial Conference, a Standing Committee, several specialized Committees and a Secretariat; Summits of the Heads of Government of the member countries take place at irregular intervals. The Ministerial Conference is composed of the Foreign Ministers of member countries and meets annually in the capital of each member in turn. It is the supreme decision-making and political authority, with the exception of the ASEAN Summits, and is empowered to establish major policies and to set the guidelines for the development of regional co-ordination and co-operation in specific areas of common interest. The Economic Ministers meet about two times a year to discuss major issues of economic co-operation.

The Standing Committee meets for consultations whenever necessary between ministerial sessions in each member country in annual rotation. It is composed of the Foreign Minister of the host country and the ambassadors of the other countries.

There are ten Committees, basically reporting to the Standing Committee. The five economic Committees consider matters relating to: finance and banking; food, agriculture and forestry; industry, minerals and energy; transportation and communications; and trade and tourism. The five non-economic Committees are concerned with: science and technology; culture and information; social development; drug matters; and protection of the environment. A permanent central Secretariat was established in 1976 in Jakarta, Indonesia, to perform administrative functions and keep contact with member countries through specially appointed National Secretariats. The post of Secretary-General revolves among member countries in alphabetical order at three-year intervals (originally for two years only). The Association's principal organs are assisted and advised by subcommittees, expert groups, working parties and other subsidiary bodies meeting a broadening range of requirements.

The meetings held during the last half of the 1970s and in the late 1980s by the Heads of Government of member countries have substantially contributed to developing and re-establishing South East Asian co-operation; the Summit meeting has therefore emerged as an important component of the Association's institutional machinery.

The Association has developed relations with other international economic organizations at both regional and extraregional level, and with various third countries. Special committees, composed of heads of diplomatic missions of member countries, have been set up in Western capitals in order to promote the co-ordination of foreign policies. These ASEAN committees presently operate in Australia, Belgium, Canada, France, Germany, Japan, New

Zealand, Switzerland, the UK and the USA.

A promising area of co-operation is represented by the Association's ties with the *European Economic Community (EEC). A renewable five-year co-operation agreement, strengthening trade relations and increasing joint action in scientific and agricultural spheres, was signed between the Association and the EEC in March 1980 and entered into force the following October. A joint co-operation committee meets at yearly intervals. Several joint initiatives have been launched by the two organizations in order, *inter alia*, to encourage European investment in South East Asia, to identify joint industrial projects and to facilitate access to ASEAN markets. Despite repeated efforts, European investment in the ASEAN region continues to lag behind Japanese and American investment. The relationship with the EEC is further complicated, in ASEAN's eyes, by the prospects of completion of the single European market by the end of 1992 – with fears of raised barriers to imports from third countries and a widening imbalance in bargaining power – and the increasing flow of aid extended by the EEC to former socialist countries in Central and Eastern Europe to the detriment of other regions of the world.

Over the past decade, the Association has developed relations with major industrial countries, the so-called dialogue partners whose Foreign Ministers participate in ASEAN's post-ministerial meetings. These 'partners' currently include Australia, Canada, the EC, Japan, the Republic of Korea, New Zealand, the USA and the *United Nations Development Programme (UNDP); the last-mentioned partner is the only one not representing a country or group of countries. ASEAN holds regular talks with these countries and organizations to discuss matters of mutual concern in trade, investment, technology transfer and development assistance.

Even if ASEAN's achievements in the economic field are far from impressive, the Association as a whole may be regarded as a possible source of inspiration for other groupings of developing countries. Besides promoting political stability and fostering co-operation in basic economic and non-economic sectors, the Association has succeeded in forging an 'ASEAN identity' taking common stands on regional as well as global issues, notably Viet Nam's invasion of Cambodia and the Soviet occupation of Afghanistan. In fact, the ASEAN experience started with a legacy of tense and volatile relations among its founder members and in the early stages the peaceful resolution of intra-ASEAN conflicts as well as the resistance to a perceived communist threat were the overriding concerns. Only in the late 1970s did economic issues become a key aspect of ASEAN co-operation both among members and with regard to third countries and international organizations.

The Association adopted in 1971 the concept of the creation of a Zone of Peace, Freedom and Neutrality (ZOPFAN) in South East Asia. The Indochina crises, the question of relations with China, and the continuing flood of refugees are among the factors which caused major concern to the Association's member countries and seriously affected prospects for effective co-operation on economic, social and cultural issues.

ASEAN's first Summit meeting was held at Denpasar, Bali, Indonesia, in February 1976 and two important documents were signed. The Treaty of Amity and Co-operation established the principles of mutual respect for the independence and sovereignty of all nations; non-interference in the internal affairs; peaceful settlement of disputes and effective co-operation. The Treaty was amended in 1987 by a Protocol allowing the accession of other countries within and outside South East Asia. The Declaration of Concord – the other document signed at the Bali summit – set guidelines with regard to economic, social and cultural relations.

Another Summit meeting was held in Kuala Lumpur, Malaysia, in August 1977. The intention to develop peaceful relations with other countries of South East Asia was solemnly reaffirmed. In particular ASEAN supported the right of the people of Cambodia to self-determination after the withdrawal of all foreign troops.

A Basic Agreement on the Establishment of Preferential Trading Arrangements (PTA) concluded in January 1977 provided the framework for gradual tariff cuts and other concessions on a widening range of items. However, only a fraction of the value of intra-ASEAN trade was actually accounted for by preferentially-traded items. Another initiative, the implementation of the ASEAN Industrial Joint Ventures (AIJV) scheme in selected branches to be carried out under the Basic Agreement on Industrial Projects concluded in June 1978, did not succeed in involving the private sector. Regional industrial complementation schemes, intended to give exclusive production and marketing rights to accredited manufacturers in specified countries, experienced serious difficulties because of the reluctance of some member countries to participate and meaningful industrial integration remained a distant goal.

The need to enhance economic co-operation programmes was addressed by the third Summit of Heads of Government which took place in Manila in December 1987; a new set of priorities for national and regional development was articulated through the improvement of the AIJV scheme and the extension of the PTA. With regard to agricultural research and technology, joint programmes were drawn up to investigate problems of common concern. Progress had also been made in promoting educational and cultural exchanges and tourism. Co-operation was enhanced in the sectors of minerals and energy, transport and communications, and science and technology.

At the beginning of the 1990s, the end of the East-West confrontation and the eventual solution of the Cambodian crisis are offering ASEAN countries a major opportunity to move forward with economic co-operation programmes in an environment which is no longer characterized by imminent security threats. The accelerating pace of economic development within the six member countries seems to make intra-ASEAN co-operation both more feasible and more imperative, also in view of the possible impact on ASEAN trade and investment flows of the Single European Market of 1992 and of the North American Free Trade Area (NAFTA). The Association should also better define its role within the context of the efforts for furthering economic co-operation currently going on in the Asia-Pacific region, especially through the *Pacific Economic Co-operation Council (PECC) and the *Asia Pacific Economic Co-operation (APEC) process of consultations.

The fourth Summit was held in Singapore in January 1992; participants expressed the hope that Viet Nam would join the Association within a few years, decided to allow their foreign ministers to discuss security issues at their future meetings although without giving the Association competences in the military sphere, and agreed to create an ASEAN Free Trade Area (AFTA) within 15 years. A 'Framework Agreement on Enhancing ASEAN Economic Co-operation' was adopted with a view to promoting the conclusion of more detailed implementing arrangements. Under a Common Effective Preferential Tariff (CEPT), intra-ASEAN tariffs on manufactured goods will be standardized and reduced to a level of 0–5 per cent over a 15-year period beginning in January 1993. The decisions taken at the 1992 Summit might represent a major step toward the realization of the Association's long-standing goal of closer economic co-operation without resorting, on the other hand, to any EC-type 'supranational' integration.

Headquarters: Jalan Sisingamangaraja 70A, Kebayoran Baru, Jakarta Selatan, P.O. Box 2072, Jakarta, Indonesia (telephone: 716451 – 712955; telex: 47214 ASEAN JKT)

Publications: *Annual Report of the ASEAN Standing Committee*; *ASEAN Newsletter* (bi-monthly); *ASEAN Journal on Science and Technology for Development* (twice a year)

References: J. Wong: *ASEAN Economies in Perspective* (London, 1979); R.H. Fifield: *National and Regional Interests in ASEAN* (Singapore, 1979); M.T. Skully: *ASEAN Financial Cooperation* (London, 1984); M. Rajendran: *ASEAN's Foreign Relations. The Shift to Collective Action* (Kuala

Lumpur,1985); G. Schiavone (ed): *Western Europe and South-East Asia: Cooperation or Competition?* (London, 1989); H.C. Rieger: 'Regional Economic Cooperation in the Asia-Pacific Region', *Asia-Pacific Economic Literature*, 2 (1989), 5–33

B

BADEA. Banque arabe pour le développement économique en Afrique; *see* **Arab Bank for Economic Development in Africa.**

Banco Centroamericano de Integración Económica (BCIE). *See* **Central American Bank for Economic Integration.**

Bank for International Settlements (BIS). The Bank aims to promote co-operation among national central banks, to provide additional facilities for international financial operations and to act as trustee or agent in connection with international financial settlements entrusted to it.

Although the first proposals to institutionalize co-operation among central banks date back to the late 19th century, the creation of the Bank resulted from conferences held in The Hague, the Netherlands, in 1929 and 1930 to settle the question of German reparations. Negotiations over the revision of the Dawes Plan led to the signing of an international agreement on the Young Plan in January 1930 in The Hague. As a result, the burdens of reparations and war debts were considerably eased and a Bank for International Settlements was established and empowered, *inter alia*, to act as trustee. Another agreement was signed between the governments of Belgium, France, Germany, Italy, Japan and the UK and the government of Switzerland for the constitution of the Bank as a limited company with its seat at Basel, Switzerland. The Bank was granted immunities from taxation as well as guarantees against expropriation.

The Charter of the Bank was formally signed in February 1930, in Rome, by the governors of the central banks of the founding countries joined by the representatives of a group of American banks. The Bank started operations at its Basel headquarters the following May. The central banks of other European countries, such as Austria, Denmark, Hungary, the Netherlands, Sweden and Switzerland, joined the founder members shortly afterwards. The aggravation of the economic crisis in Europe prevented other prospective members from participating in the newly-created institution. The Bank's membership substantially increased after World War II. The central banks of nearly all European countries have become members. Japan, which had withdrawn in 1953, resumed participation in 1969. Canada, Australia and South Africa have also joined, thereby increasing the importance of non-European members.

In order to fulfil its basic aims, the Bank is empowered to: buy and sell gold coin or bullion for its own account or for central banks; hold gold for its own account under earmark in central banks, and accept the custody of gold for these banks; make advances to or borrow from central banks against gold and short-term obligations of prime liquidity or other approved securities; discount, rediscount, purchase or sell short-term obligations of prime liquidity, including Treasury bills and other government short-term securities; buy and sell exchange and negotiable securities other than shares; open current or deposit accounts with central banks and accept deposits from them as well as deposits in connection with trustee agreements; act as

45

trustee or agent with regard to international settlements; conclude special agreements with central banks to facilitate the settlement of international transactions.

The Bank is obliged to maintain its liquidity and therefore has to retain assets appropriate to the maturity and character of its liabilities. The Bank's short-term liquid assets may include bank notes, cheques payable on sight drawn on first class banks, claims in course of collection, deposits at sight or at short notice and prime bills of exchange. All operations undertaken by the Bank must conform to the monetary policy of the central banks of the countries concerned.

The Bank uses as unit of account the gold franc equivalent to 0.290322 gram of fine gold. The size of the authorized capital stock, initially set at 500 million gold francs, was raised in June 1969 to 1500 million gold francs, divided into 600,000 shares of 2500 gold francs each. As of 30 June 1990, shares in issue numbered 473,125, paid up as to 25 per cent of nominal value. The major shareholders are the central banks which enjoy the corresponding voting rights; private shareholders are not entitled to vote.

The organizational structure of the Bank includes the General Meeting, the Board of Directors, and the President. The General Meeting, attended by representatives of the central banks voting in proportion to the number of shares subscribed, normally takes place every year to approve the budget and the annual report, to decide the distribution of the net income and to set down the general guidelines for the Bank's activities.

Administration is carried out by the Board of Directors which at present consists of the governors of the central banks of Belgium, France, Germany, Italy and the UK, each of whom appoints another member of the same nationality. The USA does not occupy the two seats to which it is entitled. According to the Charter, the governors of not more than nine other central banks may be elected to the Board; the governors of the central banks of the Netherlands, Sweden and Switzerland are currently serving. The Chairman of the

Board may also act as President, as is currently the case. The President conducts the ordinary business of the Bank and is assisted by a General Manager, several executive officers and the necessary staff. The Bank has developed close co-operative links with economic and financial institutions within the UN system and with regional or national bodies.

Since its establishment, the Bank has performed a significant role in a variety of fields and has effectively managed to maintain its liquidity. At the very beginning of its operations, the Bank had to face the consequences of the Great Depression in almost all the countries of Europe, with the ensuing suspension, in July 1931, of the implementation of the Young Plan and of its activities as trustee. The Bank's role was further reduced when many countries modified or went off the gold standard in the first half of the 1930s. Its difficulties were aggravated by the outbreak of World War II. Nearly all the participating banks represented belligerent countries and the Bank decided to pursue a policy of strict neutrality and therefore to abstain from any operation amounting to a breach of such neutrality. The UN Monetary and Financial Conference held at Bretton Woods in 1944 recommended the liquidation of the Bank because of the alleged illegitimacy of its custody of gold for the account of the Reichsbank. Moreover, the functions of the Bank appeared to a very large extent to overlap those of the *International Monetary Fund (IMF) and the *International Bank for Reconstruction and Development (IBRD). However, the peculiar role performed by the Bank through the provision of a framework for co-operation of central banks was eventually recognized and operations were fully resumed. Since the 1950s the Bank has substantially developed its activities on international financial markets, acted as an important forum for consultation and collaboration among central banks and has provided a helpful and informative analysis of the major features of the world economy through its annual reports.

The Bank provides the secretariat for several committees and groups of experts, such as the Committee on Banking

Regulations and Supervisory Practices which was established in 1974 by the governors of the central banks of the Group of Ten and Switzerland and is responsible for co-ordinating banking supervisory regulations and surveillance systems at the international level.

The Bank acted as a clearing agency for the Organization for European Economic Co-operation (OEEC) in connection with the agreements on intra-European payments and compensation, and the European Payments Union (EPU), replaced by the European Monetary Agreement (EMA) in December 1958. The EMA system was retained in the *Organization for Economic Co-operation and Development (OECD) which succeeded the OEEC in 1960. At present the Bank acts as depositary under an Act of Pledge concluded with the *European Coal and Steel Community (ECSC), and as agent, since June 1973, for the European Monetary Co-operation Fund (EMCF), set up by the member countries of the *European Economic Community (EEC). In 1986 the Bank assumed the functions of agent in a private international clearing and settlement system for bank deposits denominated in European Currency Units (ECUs).

In the early 1980s, with a view to safeguarding the viability of the international financial system, the Bank granted large-scale loans to central banks of Latin American countries (Argentina, Brazil and Mexico) experiencing an increasingly critical debt situation and to the IMF facing a 'commitment gap' because of its policy of enlarged access. Similar loans were subsequently made but with decreasing frequency. In the late 1980s several bridging facilities were arranged for central banks mostly of Latin America.

President: Bengt Dennis

Headquarters: Centralbahnplatz 2, 4002 Basel, Switzerland (telephone 280 8080; telex 962487; fax: 280 9100)

Publication: *Annual Report*

Banque arabe pour le développement économique en Afrique (BADEA). *See* **Arab Bank for Economic Development in Africa.**

BCIE. Banco Centroamericano de Integración Económica; *see* **Central American Bank for Economic Integration.**

Benelux Economic Union. The Union entails the free movement of persons, goods, capital and services between Belgium, Luxembourg and the Netherlands and implies the co-ordination of economic, financial and social policies as well as the pursuit of a joint policy in econmic and financial relations with third countries.

The Treaty establishing the Union was signed in The Hague, the Netherlands, in February 1958 and entered into force in November 1960. It represented the result of several moves initiated in the early 1930s towards closer economic co-operation between the three Benelux countries. An economic union had been formed between Belgium and Luxembourg by the convention concluded in Brussels in July 1921 and entered into force the following year. Dissolved in August 1940, the union was re-established in May 1945. After an unsuccessful attempt through the Ouchy Agreement (1932), the governments in exile of the Benelux countries made a fresh effort to advance mutual economic co-operation by signing a Customs Convention in September 1944 in London. This Convention was further defined and interpreted in a Protocol for the establishment of a customs union; it was signed in The Hague in March 1947 and came into force in January 1948. The customs tariffs of the Belgium-Luxembourg Economic Union and of the Netherlands were thus superseded by the joint external tariff of the Benelux customs union. Further protocols (1947, 1950, 1953, 1954) gradually expanded the scope of economic co-operation between the Benelux countries.

In November 1955, a Convention for the establishment of a Benelux Interparliamentary Consultative Council, consisting of members of the three national parliaments, was signed in Brussels. In 1958, the Benelux countries decided to set up a full economic union (as envisaged by the Customs Convention of 1944 and the Protocol of 1947), and concluded the present Treaty. In the Preamble to the Treaty, the signatory countries expressly noted that the Rome Treaties of 1957 do not prevent particular member countries from creating an economic union *inter se*. In March 1965, in Brussels, the Benelux countries signed a Treaty creating a Court of Justice with both a contentious and advisory jurisdiction.

According to the basic provisions of the Treaty establishing the Union, the nationals of each member country may freely enter and leave the territory of any other member country and are entitled to the same treatment as nationals of that country as regards: freedom of movement, sojourn and settlement; freedom to carry on a trade or occupation; capital transactions; conditions of employment; social security benefits; taxes and charges of any kind; exercise of civil rights as well as legal and judicial protection of their person, individual rights and interests.

Importation or exportation of goods between the territories of the member countries, irrespective of origin or destination, are freed of import, excise and any other duties, charges or dues of any kind as well as of prohibitions or restrictions of an economic or financial nature, such as quotas or currency restrictions. A common tariff with identical rates applies to goods coming from or destined to third countries. Restrictions concerning transfers of capital between the member countries are abolished; the rendering of services is also freed of taxes and charges of any kind. The member countries are bound to pursue a co-ordinated policy in the economic, financial and social fields.

With respect to their relations with third countries, the member countries: (a) accept and pursue a joint policy in the field of foreign trade and of payments related thereto; (b) jointly conclude treaties and conventions regarding foreign trade and the customs tariff; (c) conclude, either jointly or concurrently, treaties and conventions relating to payments in connection with foreign trade.

The organizational structure of the Union is rather elaborate and consists of the following institutions: the Committee of Ministers; the Consultative Inter-parliamentary Council; the Council of the Economic Union; the Committees and the Special Committees; the Secretariat-General; Joint Services; the College of Arbitrators; the Court of Justice; and the Economic and Social Advisory Council.

The real executive power lies with the Committee of Ministers which meets at least once every three months in order to supervise the application of the Treaty and ensure the realization of its aims. Each member country appoints at least three government members (generally the Ministers of Foreign Affairs, Foreign Trade, Economic Affairs, Agriculture, Finance and Social Affairs). All decisions are taken unanimously, each country having one vote, but the abstention of one country does not prevent a decision being taken.

The Consultative Inter-parliamentary Council, created by the Convention of 1955, is entrusted with advisory functions. It consists of 49 members, 21 each from the Netherlands States-General and the Belgian Parliament and 7 from the Luxembourg Chamber of Deputies.

The Council of the Economic Union, consisting of one chairman from each member country and of the presidents of the Committees, is responsible for: (a) co-ordinating the activities of the Committees and Special Committees; (b) putting into effect the relevant decisions of the Committee of Ministers; and (c) submitting proposals to the Committee of Ministers.

The following Committees are currently in operation: foreign economic relations; monetary and financial; industry and trade; agriculture, food and fisheries; customs tariffs and taxes; transport; social; movement and establishment of persons. There are also Special Committees in charge of: co-ordination of statistics; comparison of government budgets; tenders; public health; retail trade and handicrafts; movement of persons (control at external frontiers); tourism; territorial planning; administrative and judicial co-operation; environment. The Committees and the Special Committees, each within the limits of its competence, implement the relevant decisions of the Committee of Ministers, submit proposals and monitor the execution by national administrations of resolutions adopted.

The Secretariat-General, located in Brussels, is headed by a Secretary-General of Dutch nationality assisted by two deputies, one from Belgium and one from Luxembourg; all three are appointed and dismissed by the Committee of Ministers.

Joint Services have executive powers and may be set up by the Committee of Ministers. At present there are two: the Benelux Office on Trademarks and Brands, and the Joint Service for the Registration of Medicaments.

The College of Arbitrators is entrusted with the task of settling any disputes that may arise between member countries from the working of the Union. The Court of Justice, added in 1965, is designed to ensure uniformity in the interpretation of the legal rules common to the three member countries which are specified either in conventions or decisions of the Committee of Ministers. The College of Arbitrators suspends its function in any case where a matter of interpretation of such rules arises, pending a decision of the Court of Justice.

The Economic and Social Advisory Council consists of 27 members and 27 deputy members from representative economic and social organizations, each country supplying one third of the number. It offers advice on its own initiative or upon specific request of the Committee of Ministers.

The provisions of the Treaty do not affect the existence and development of the economic union between Belgium and Luxembourg insofar as the objectives of such union are not attained by the application of the Treaty itself.

The Union has brought substantial benefits to the economies of the member countries without jeopardizing their full participation in the European Communities and their efforts at closer economic and political integration on a wider scale.

Secretary-General: B.M.J. Hennekam

Headquarters: 39 rue de la Régence, 1000 Brussels, Belgium (telephone: 519 3811; fax: 513 4206)

Publications: *Benelux Newsletter* (monthly); *Benelux Review* (quarterly); *Bulletin Benelux*

BIS. *See* **Bank for International Settlements.**

C

CABEI. *See* **Central American Bank for Economic Integration.**

CACM. *See* **Central American Common Market.**

Caribank. *See* **Caribbean Development Bank.**

Caribbean Community (CARICOM). The main areas of activity of the Community are: economic integration by means of the Caribbean Common Market which replaced the former Caribbean Free Trade Association (CARIFTA); functional co-operation in specific sectors and operation of certain common services; co-ordination of foreign policies.

The basic legal instrument of the Community is the Treaty signed in July 1973 at Chaguaramas, Trinidad, by the Prime Ministers of Barbados, Guyana, Jamaica and Trinidad and Tobago which entered into effect the following August; eight other Commonwealth Caribbean countries acceded to full membership during 1974. The Treaty was amended in 1976 to facilitate the prospective admission of the Bahamas as a member of the Community without participating in the Common Market; the formal admission of the Bahamas took place in July 1983. A number of Caribbean islands, Mexico, Suriname and Venezuela have observer status while other islands have applied to join as full members.

During the 1950s efforts were made to promote Commonwealth Caribbean regionalism, resulting in the establishment of the short-lived Federation of the West Indies (January 1958). Proposals for a customs union were also put forward. An agreement establishing a regional institution, the Caribbean Organization, was signed in June 1960 in Washington. During the 1960s self-government was introduced and/or gradually extended until many of the former British colonies acquired full independence within the Commonwealth. The West Indies Federation was dissolved in February 1962 after withdrawal of Jamaica and Trinidad and Tobago. This substantially weakened the Caribbean Organization and its founding agreement was formally ended in 1965. Under the West Indies Act 1967, new constitutional arrangements raised Antigua, Dominica, Grenada, Saint Kitts-Nevis-Anguilla, Saint Lucia and Saint Vincent to the rank of Associated States of the UK.

In the last half of the 1960s, new initiatives for freeing trade among Commonwealth Caribbean countries led to the signing in April 1968, at St John's, Antigua, of the agreement establishing CARIFTA, following the patterns of the *European Free Trade Association (EFTA) and the Latin American Free Trade Association (LAFTA). The four original signatories (Antigua, Barbados, Guyana and Trinidad and Tobago) were joined, between May and August 1968, by Jamaica, Grenada, Dominica, Saint Lucia, Saint Vincent, Saint Kitts-Nevis-Anguilla, Montserrat and in May 1971 by Belize. In June 1968, seven small lesser developed countries of the subregion, initially reluctant to join CARIFTA, had formed their own customs union, the East Caribbean

Common Market (ECCM). An autonomous financial institution, the *Caribbean Development Bank (CDB; Caribank), was set up in 1969 with the participation of both regional and non-regional members.

A generalized consensus over the need to deepen and improve the integration process and the ensuing negotiations made it possible to replace CARIFTA with the broader and more advanced CARICOM.

The basic aim of the Community is to foster unity among peoples of the Caribbean through common or co-ordinated regional actions in spheres ranging from foreign policy to health, education, labour matters, transport, and economic, financial and trade relations. However, no future merger into a single political unit is envisaged. Foreign policy co-ordination is dealt with by the Ministers of Foreign Affairs of independent member countries. Functional co-operation involves several sectors which are expressly mentioned, though the list may be expanded.

The Common Market was established by an Annex to the Chaguaramas Treaty with a view to achieving the Community's objectives in the field of economic integration. It is founded on: the erection of a common external tariff, a common protective policy and the gradual co-ordination of commercial policies; the harmonization of fiscal incentives to industry; the elimination of double taxation; the co-ordination of economic policies and development planning; and, last but not least, the setting up of a special regime for the less developed members. Adequate recognition has been given to differences in levels of economic development in the Commonwealth Caribbean context; Barbados, Guyana, Jamaica and Trinidad and Tobago have been designated as more developed countries (MDCs) and the remaining members as less developed countries (LDCs). Measures specifically intended to meet the needs of the LDCs are included in the Common Market Annex to the Chaguaramas Treaty to ensure an equitable distribution of benefits from integration. The steady development of the ECCM, composed of seven LDCs, had to take place within the wider framework of the Caribbean Common Market. The Community's functions and

decision-making powers bear no supranational features and are fairly limited by the unanimity principle which is applicable in any delicate case. As regards the Common Market, its aims are often widely phrased, leaving ample room for further negotiations on specific issues and areas of activity.

Membership in the Community does not necessarily imply membership in the Common Market; the Bahamas, which were included in the list of countries which might be admitted to the Community, are omitted from the similar list regarding the Common Market. Provisions for associate membership are contained in both the Chaguaramas Treaty and its Common Market Annex.

Decisions, recommendations and directives are generally adopted unanimously, each member having one vote; non-participation is equivalent to abstention. Decisions which may involve constitutional problems are to be submitted for consideration to member countries before they become legally binding.

Caribbean political and functional co-operation and economic integration take place within a rather complex institutional structure. The Conference of Heads of Government (whose meetings have been held annally since 1983) is the supreme organ responsible for the determination of basic policies, including relations with third countries and international organizations, and the establishment of financial arrangements to meet the Community's expenses. The Conference has delegated a number of functions to the Common Market Council, including matters related to Community's expenses. The Council, consisting of one state minister from each country, is the principal organ of the Common Market, responsible for its operation and the settlement of any problem arising out of the integration process. It undertakes annual reviews of the Common Market mechanisms, taking into consideration the special needs of the less developed members and submitting relevant reports to the Conference; the latter may issue directives to the Council to this effect. Joint consultative status has been granted by the Council to the major economic groups in the Caribbean. The Council convenes whenever necessary, in particular before meetings of the Conference.

The Secretariat (successor to the Commonwealth Caribbean Regional Secretariat) is located in Georgetown, Guyana. It performs technical and administrative functions concerning both the Community and the Common Market, takes appropriate action on decisions of the various organs, initiates and carries out studies on regional co-operation and integration and provides services requested by member countries in order to achieve the Community's objectives. It is organized into five divisions: trade and agriculture; economics and industry; functional co-operation; legal matters; and general services and administration. The Secretary-General is appointed by the Conference on the recommendation of the Council for a term not exceeding five years and may be re-appointed.

There are also specialized institutions in charge of the advancement of co-operation in specific sectors. These institutions include the Conference of Ministers responsible for Health and the Standing Committees of Ministers responsible (respectively) for Education; Labour; Foreign Affairs; Finance; Agriculture; Industry; Transport; Energy, Mines and Natural Resources; Science and Technology; Tourism; and Environment.

The Treaty recognizes as Associate Institutions of the Community a number of regional bodies having their own constitutive documents and enjoying legal autonomy. Among these bodies are: the Caribbean Development Bank (CDB); the Caribbean Examinations Council (CEC); the Council of Legal Education (CLE); the University of Guyana (UG); the University of the West Indies (UWI); the Caribbean Meteorological Organization (CMO); and the West Indies Shipping Corporation (WISCO).

As regards the co-ordination of foreign policy, the Standing Committee of Ministers responsible for Foreign Affairs aims at developing the Community's relations with third countries and international organizations and preparing joint diplomatic action on matters of particular relevance to the Caribbean. The Community has established close ties with UN bodies and regional agencies; trading relations with the USA and Canada are regulated, respectively, by the Caribbean Basin Initiative of 1983 and the 'Caribcan' agreement of 1986. The Community's member countries have a special relationship – as African, Caribbean and Pacific (ACP) states – with the *European Economic Community (EEC) under the Lomé Convention.

In spite of serious economic and financial constraints and strong nationalistic tendencies, the Community has played a significant role in promoting broader understanding and increased trade and economic relations in the Commonwealth Caribbean. As regards trade liberalization, the Community inherited from its predecessor CARIFTA a free trade pattern with numerous exceptions whose complete elimination has proved extremely difficult. The first step towards the erection of a common external tariff was taken in August 1973 by the four MDCs, while longer and more flexible schedules were envisaged for the LDCs. As well as through the acceleration of intra-area trade, integration is promoted through the harmonization of economic policies and the establishment and operation of regional industrial and agricultural projects. This implies, *inter alia*, some form of control over foreign investments in key sectors. The co-ordination of development planning is carried out through a project-by-project approach since no comprehensive long-term scheme has as yet been agreed upon. Agreements have been concluded to harmonize fiscal incentives to industry and to avoid double taxation among MDCs and among LDCs.

In the last half of the 1970s, most of the countries of the Community (particularly Jamaica and Guyana) were adversely affected by severe economic disturbances, which in some cases led to the introduction of stabilization programmes and the tightening of import restrictions. Moreover, the LDCs showed a growing dissatisfaction and claimed a greater and more equitable share of the benefits of integration. In order to co-ordinate financial and technical assistance, the Caribbean Group for Co-operation in Economic Development was formed in late 1977 by Caribbean countries, donor countries and international development institutions, under the chairmanship of the *International Bank for Reconstruction and Development (IBRD).

The Community has made intensive efforts to formulate long-term solutions to the severe energy problems faced by most member countries. In order to ease serious balance-of-payments difficulties, the Multilateral Clearing Facility (MCF), envisaged by the Common Market Annex to the Chaguaramas Treaty, was put into effect in June 1977, while other funds were made available for emergency payments.

In 1980, the seven lesser developed members participating in the ECCM renamed this body the *Organization of Eastern Caribbean States (OECS). Severe difficulties hindered the development of Caribbean trade and integration during the first half of the 1980s. A Group of Experts, set up in 1980, drew up a strategy for the decade with respect to production, export, productivity, marketing, energy policy and air transport. Other meetings of experts were held to review the key components of Caribbean economy.

In July 1984, the Conference of Heads of Government, meeting in Nassau, Bahamas, called for structural adjustment in the economies of the member countries with a view to expanding production and reducing imports and set new target dates for the implementation of the common external tariff. An unsuccessful attempt was also made at relaunching the activities of the MCF which had collapsed in 1983 after having exceeded its credit limit. In July 1986 the Conference agreed to replace the MCF with a Caribbean Export Bank but the plan was ultimately shelved because of the lack of adequate financing. The Conference held in 1989 adopted a series of measures intended to remove by the early 1990s the remaining barriers to the establishment of a single Caribbean market and set new detailed deadlines. It was also decided to set up a 15-member West Indian Commission to explore new avenues to regional political and economic integration. A target date (1994) for the creation of a common market has been agreed. Serious economic problems as well as political instability represent major obstacles preventing the full achievement of the Community's objectives.

Secretary-General: Edwin W. Carrington
Headquarters: Bank of Guyana Building, P.O. Box 10827, Georgetown, Guyana (telephone: 69280; telex 2263 CARISEC GY; fax: 56194)
References: H.J. Geiser, P. Alleyne and C. Gajraj: *Legal Problems of Caribbean Integration* (Leyden, 1976); A.R. Carnegie: 'Commonwealth Caribbean Regionalism: Legal Aspects', *Year Book of World Affairs*, 33 (1979), 180–200; A.W. Axline: *Caribbean Integration. The Politics of Regionalism* (London, 1979); A.J. Payne: *The Politics of the Caribbean Community 1961–79* (Manchester, 1980)

Caribbean Development Bank (CDB; Caribank). The Bank aims to contribute to the harmonious economic growth and development of member countries in the Caribbean and to foster co-operation and integration by financing investment projects and programmes with due regard to the special needs of its less developed members.

The agreement establishing the Bank was signed in October 1969 and entered into effect in January 1970 when the Bank started operations in Barbados. The creation of an autonomous financial body was part of the efforts towards Commonwealth Caribbean co-operation evidenced by the establishment of the Caribbean Free Trade Association (CARIFTA) in 1968. In the early 1970s CARIFTA was succeeded by the *Caribbean Community (CARICOM). The Bank's membership includes the 13 countries now participating in CARICOM and other Commonwealth Caribbean countries (Anguilla, British Virgin Islands, Cayman Islands, Turks and Caicos Islands) plus Canada, Colombia, France, Germany, Italy, Mexico, the UK and Venezuela.

The Bank helps finance capital infrastructure and investment projects, both large and small, public and private, in the productive sectors of the economy, particularly in the less developed countries

(LDCs), as well as regional integration projects in agriculture and air and sea transportation. The main areas covered by Bank lending are: agriculture and rural development (credits to private farmers and loans to governments for infrastructural projects); manufacturing industries (loans to industrialists, development corporations and other agencies); tourism promotion (loans to hotel operators and governments); and education (loans to governments for the development of higher education, teachers' training and technical and vocational training).

The Bank operates with its ordinary capital resources. In addition, a Special Development Fund and other Special Funds have been set up for specific purposes such as development of small farming, livestock production, technical assistance and housing. The initially authorized capital stock amounted to $192 million of which over $155 million had been subscribed. In June 1990, the authorized capital had reached $693.6 million. Financial support has been secured from various governments and institutions, both regional and extraregional. Credits have been granted to the Bank by the *International Bank for Reconstruction and Development (IBRD), the *International Development Association (IDA), the *Inter-American Development Bank (IDB) and the *European Economic Community (EEC). Lending from the Bank's ordinary capital resources is subject to stringent criteria which are unlikely to be fully met by applicants from LDCs. In such cases, the Bank may grant loans on non-commercial terms through a soft window provided by its Special Funds resources earmarked for the benefit of less developed members. In 1990 the decision was adopted to create a Special Development Fund of $124 million.

The Bank's structure consists of the Board of Governors, appointed by governments and meeting annually, the Directors, selected by the Board of Governors for a two-year period, and the President, elected by the Board of Governors for a term not exceeding five years. The Vice-President is appointed by the Directors on the President's recommendation.

The Bank has played a significant role in the process of Commonwealth Caribbean integration and in several cases has effectively operated as a corrective mechanism in favour of the less industrialized and less competitive member countries. The Bank's operations have been considerably smoothed by its close working relations with CARICOM and several financial institutions within and outside the Caribbean.

President: Neville Vernon Nicholls
Headquarters: P.O. Box 408, Wildey, St Michael, Barbados (telephone: 431 1600; telex: WB2287; fax: 426 7269)
Publications: *Annual Report*; *CDB News* (quarterly).

CARICOM. *See* **Caribbean Community.**

Cartagena Agreement. *See* **Andean Group.**

CDB. *See* **Caribbean Development Bank.**

CEAO. Communauté économique de l'Afrique de l'Ouest; *see* **West African Economic Community.**

Central American Bank for Economic Integration (CABEI) [Banco Centroamericano de Integración Económica (BCIE)]. The Bank aims to stimulate and support efforts towards Central American economic integration by financing public and private investment projects particularly related to industrialization, infrastructure and the promotion of reciprocal trade.

The agreement establishing the Bank was signed in December 1960 in Managua, Nicaragua, by El Salvador, Guatemala, Honduras and Nicaragua. These countries were also contracting parties to the General Treaty of Central American Economic Integration which laid the foundations for the *Central American Common Market (CACM). Although created as a separate and autonomous body, the Bank is intended to act within the framework of CACM. The founding agreement entered into effect in May 1961 and the Bank started operations in Tegucigalpa, Honduras. Costa Rica decided to join the Bank in 1962. Argentina, Mexico, Venezuela and Taiwan are extraregional members.

The Bank is intended to finance: infrastructural projects for the completion of existing regional systems and the reduction of disparities in basic sectors, excluding undertakings of merely local or national scope; long-term investment projects in industries of a regional character; coordinated projects related to specialization in agriculture and livestock; enterprises wishing to improve their efficiency and adjust to growing competition; other productive projects concerning economic complementation and the development of Central American trade. Special provisions were subsequently introduced to grant preferential treatment to Honduras.

The Bank operates with its ordinary capital resources; funds for special operations have been set up. The capital stock initially amounting to $20 million was gradually increased to $600 million. Financial support has been secured from several public and private sources and international and national financial institutions operating within and outside Latin America.

The Bank's structure consists of the Board of Governors (composed of the Ministers of Economy and the Presidents of the Central Banks of member countries meeting annually) and five Executive Directors (including the President).

By June 1990, the Bank had authorized loans for over $2 billion, mainly destined to infrastructural projects and housing. A Central American Common Market Fund was set up by the Bank's Board of Governors in May 1981. The Bank's future role will largely remain dependent on concrete results achieved by continuing effort towards Central American integration.

President: Rolando Ramirez Paniagua
Headquarters: P.O. Box 772, Tegucigalpa, Honduras (telephone: 372230; telex: 1103; fax: 370793)

Publications: *Annual Report*; *Revista de la integración*

Central American Common Market

(CACM) [Mercado Común Centroamericano]. The Common Market originally aimed to establish a customs union and to achieve full liberalization of trade between the five participating countries (Costa Rica, El Salvador, Guatemala, Honduras and Nicaragua).

From a legal standpoint, the main formal instrument of CACM remains the General Treaty of Central American Economic Integration, signed in Managua in 1960 for a 20-year period which expired in June 1981. However, in July 1980 the contracting parties declared that the Treaty would continue in operation until agreement was reached on a new integration scheme. This might eventually involve the creation of a Central American Economic and Social Community.

Since the early 1950s, attempts to establish a Central American common market as a means of transcending national frontiers, stimulating foreign trade and reducing heavy economic and financial dependence on outside powers, have been encouraged and supported by the *UN Economic Commission for Latin America and the Caribbean (ECLAC).

The move towards closer economic cooperation received additional impetus from the failure by the *Organization of Central American States (ODECA) to make headway on the political plane. A Multilateral Treaty on Free Trade and Central American Economic Integration was signed in Tegucigalpa, Honduras, in June 1958 by all ODECA members, with the exception of Costa Rica which joined in 1962. A Convention on Integration Industries was also adopted at the same meeting. In 1959 another Central American Convention on Equalization of Import Duties and Charges laid the foundation for the setting up of a common external tariff. Additional agreements concerning specific sectors were reached during the ensuing years. Further negotiations led to the signing of a Treaty of Economic Association in February 1960 by El

Salvador, Guatemala and Honduras. These countries plus Nicaragua concluded the General Treaty of Central American Economic Integration, establishing the Central American Common Market, in Managua, Nicaragua, in December 1960. Costa Rica acceded in July 1962. During their meeting of December 1960, the contracting parties to the General Treaty also set up, under a separate agreement, the *Central American Bank for Economic Integration (CABEI) as an autonomous body.

According to the General Treaty, the abolition of barriers to free trade among contracting parties was to be completed within five years. Provision was also made for the erection of a uniform external tariff. Industrial integration and the gradual alignment of foreign economic policies in selected areas were envisaged (within the framework of the Common Market) in several other Central American conventions and protocols. The basic objectives of the General Treaty with regard to trade liberalization and the creation of a common external tariff were largely achieved by 1969 but the integration process virtually came to a halt, mainly because of the Honduran disengagement.

The already limited functions and powers of the Common Market's institutions were further weakened by disputes between member countries. The General Treaty provided for the establishment of three main organs: the Central American Economic Council (composed of the five Ministers of Economy and charged with the direction and co-ordination of the integration process), the Executive Council (consisting of one representative and one alternate from each member country), and the Permanent Secretariat (SIECA) based in Guatemala City. No provision was adopted concerning the formal relationship between these bodies and the corresponding organs of ODECA. Following the disruption caused in Central American relations by the outbreak of hostilities between El Salvador and Honduras in July 1969, the Economic Council and the Executive Council were no longer convened. Both Councils were replaced by a Ministerial Commission composed of

Ministers and Deputy Ministers of Central American Integration; meetings of other Ministers as well as of Presidents of central banks also play a significant role.

Efforts to carry out the liberalization and co-operation programme on an emergency basis led to the creation of *ad hoc* bodies, while SIECA was charged with studying a new integration scheme and preparing the relevant proposals. A Normalization Commission was set up in 1971 but it made little or no headway and was dissolved in 1972. SIECA drew up a set of proposals for submission to the High Level Committee (CAN) established in December 1972. This body, consisting of officials appointed by the governments of member countries, was originally created to examine SIECA's plans. In February 1975 it was entrusted with the responsibility for preparing a draft Treaty for a Central American Economic and Social Community. CAN was dissolved in March 1976 on completion of a draft establishing new organs, regional institutions, and common economic, financial and social policies. Howwever, recurrent political crises due to social and economic factors, long-standing rivalries and conflicts of interests made it impossible to convert the draft into a formally binding instrument.

Since the resumption of diplomatic relations between Costa Rica and Nicaragua and the conclusion of the General Peace Treaty between El Salvador and Honduras in October 1980, there seemed to be brighter prospects for alleviating tensions and unrest with a view to fully reactivating Central American co-operation and integration in both the economic and the political sphere. Several top level meetings involving Ministers of Foreign Affairs and Ministers and Deputy Ministers responsible for Central American Integration took place in an effort to translate the widespread consensus over the urgent need to restructure the Common Market into an operational strategy, based on the implementation of specific projects, rather than on the adoption of a comprehensive plan for market integration.

However, political and social conflicts aggravated by the severe economic recession and the sharp decrease in intraregional trade in the first half of the 1980s dramatically reduced the possibilities of reviving the Central American integration process. In an effort to find a solution to the crisis, the Ministers responsible for Central American Integration meeting in Guatemala in July 1984 expressed the intention to re-establish the Economic Council and the Executive Council of the Common Market and to adapt the legal and institutional mechanism of the integration process to 'the new economic realities existing in Central America and the exigencies of economic development of the sub-region'. Within this framework, the Central American Tariff and Customs Agreement was signed in December 1984 by Costa Rica, El Salvador, Guatemala and Nicaragua, in the presence of Honduran observers; the instrument came into effect in January 1986 but Honduras insisted on bilateral agreements.

The conclusion of an agreement with the *European Economic Community (EEC) in November 1985 provided CACM with badly-needed support to pursue regional integration plans. Although regional meetings at the ministerial level took place regularly, any significant progress continued to be hindered by heavy external and intra-regional debts, protectionist measures by major trade partners and a number of other economic and non-economic factors.

In June 1990, CACM members stressed their renewed willingness to implement a fre trade agreement by 1992, and the following December started the drafting of a framework agreement to set up a regional common market. In July 1991, with the participation of Panama, member countries formally agreed on a timetable for trade liberalization for most agricultural products by the end of 1991 and for substantial tariff cuts on most nonagricultural products by the end of 1992.

Secretary-General: Marco Antonio Villamar Contreras
Headquarters: SIECA, 4a Avenida 10–25, Zona 14, P.O. Box 1237, Guatemala City, Guatemala (telephone: 682151; telex: 5676; fax: 681071).
Publications: *Carta informativa* (monthly); *Cuadernos de la SIECA* (twice a year);

several economic and statistical surveys.
References: S. Dell: *A Latin American Common Market?* (London, 1966); J. Cochrane: *The Politics of Regional Integration: The Central American Case* (New Orleans, 1969); F. Parkinson: 'International Economic Integration in Latin America and the Caribbean: A Survey', *Year Book of World Affairs*, 31 (1977) 236–56

CEPGL. Communauté économique des pays des Grands Lacs; *see* **Economic Community of the Great Lakes Countries.**

CERN. *See* **European Organization for Nuclear Research.**

CND. *See* **Commission on Narcotic Drugs.**

CoCom. *See* **Co-ordinating Committee for Multilateral Export Controls.**

Colombo Plan, The. The Plan links advanced and developing economies in Asia and the Pacific and a number of non-regional members. It is intended primarily to improve the living standards of the peoples of the region by reviewing aid projects, co-ordinating development assistance and providing training and research facilities.

The Plan was founded at a meeting of *Commonwealth Foreign Ministers in Colombo, in January 1950. It was formally established in 1951 for promoting co-operative economic development in South and South-East Asia. Following a proposal by Australia for the adoption of a programme of economic assistance to South and South East Asia, a Consultative Committee was set up to draft a Commonwealth Technical Assistance Scheme, administered by a Council for Technical Co-operation, meeting at regular intervals, and assisted by a small permanent bureau located in Colombo. The founder members were Australia, Canada, Ceylon [renamed Sri Lanka in 1972],

India, New Zealand, the UK, and the Union of South Africa (which subsequently withdrew). They were joined over the years by many other countries within and outside the Commonwealth. The geographical scope of the Plan is described by its full official title: the Colombo Plan for Co-operative Economic and Social Development in Asia and the Pacific. Its present membership includes 20 developing countries (all within the region) and 6 developed countries (the original developed members plus Japan and the USA).

The objectives and principles of the Plan are broadly formulated and its functions and powers are essentially confined to consultation and voluntary co-ordination of efforts. Within the multilateral framework provided by the Plan, aid to developing member countries is negotiated and supplied on a bilateral basis. The elementary organizational structure of the Plan comprises: the Consultative Committee, consisting of Ministers of member countries, which meets every two years to review progress within the region and to consider the general principles of economic and social co-operation; the Council, composed of the heads of member countries' diplomatic missions in Colombo, which meets regularly to identify issues of interest for consideration by the Consultative Committee and to give overall guidance; the Colombo Plan Bureau (whose operating costs are met by equal contributions from member countries) which performs various administrative tasks, represents the Plan, and disseminates information on its activities. The Director of the Bureau is appointed by the Council. Subsidiary bodies, consisting of officials of member countries, hold periodic meetings to review issues for submission to Ministers.

The Plan has a regular liaison with the relevant UN bodies as well as other international and regional agencies concerned with development assistance.

Although basically providing a forum for consultation and co-ordination with no authority to produce a centralized plan for channelling capital aid and technical assistance, the Plan has succeeded to a remarkable extent in harmonizing development assistance policies and assuring a substantial flow of resources to developing countries in Asia and the Pacific. Capital aid to developing member countries (in the form of grants and loans for national economic and social development projects) mainly concerns agriculture, industry, communications, energy and education. Technical co-operation programmes provide experts and volunteers, training fellowships and equipment for training and research. Special emphasis is being placed on promoting economic and technical co-operation among the developing members themselves.

The Drug Advisory Programme was launched in 1973 to supplement national campaigns concerning drug abuse prevention and to provide assistance to member countries in establishing control offices, improving legislation, and training narcotics officials.

The Colombo Plan Staff College for Technician Education, transferred from Singapore to the Philippines in 1987, was established in 1975 as a specialized institution involving all member countries for the development of training facilities; it is separately financed by most member countries and functions under the guidance of its own Governing Board.

Bureau Director: Gilbert Sheinbaum

Headquarters: 12 Melbourne Avenue, P.O. Box 596, Colombo 4, Sri Lanka (telephone: 581813; telex: 21537; fax: 580721)

Publications: *The Colombo Plan Newsletter* (quarterly); *Annual Report of the Colombo Plan Council*; *Proceedings and Conclusions of the Consultative Committee* (every two years)

References: A. Basch: 'The Colombo Plan: A Case of Regional Economic Cooperation', *International Organization*, 9 (1955), 1-18; C. Burns: 'The Colombo Plan', *Year Book of World Affairs*, 14 (1960), 176-206; M. Haas: 'Asian Intergovernmental Organizations and the United Nations', *Regionalism and the United Nations*, ed. B. Andemicael (Dobbs Ferry, New York, 1979)

Commission on Narcotic Drugs (CND). The Commission, set up by the UN

Economic and Social Council in 1946 as one of its functional commissions, is responsible for the review of matters pertaining to the aims of the relevant international drug treaties and the implementation of their provisions; it is empowered to make recommendations to the Economic and Social Council on the control of narcotic drugs and psychotropic substances. The Commission has primary responsibility for amending the schedules annexed to international treaties in order to bring substances under international control, delete them from control, or change the regime of control to which they are subject.

Membership of the Commission, originally 15, has been repeatedly increased eventually reaching the number of 50. Members are elected for a four-year term: (a) from among the members of the UN and members of the specialized agencies and the parties to the Single Convention on Narcotic Drugs, 1961; (b) with due regard to the adequate representation of countries which are important producers of opium or coca leaves, of countries which are important in the field of manufacture of narcotic drugs and of countries in which drug addiction or the illicit traffic in narcotic drugs constitutes an important problem; and (c) taking into account the principle of equitable geographic distribution.

In 1973 the Economic and Social Council established a Sub-Commission on Illicit Drug Traffic and Related Matters in the Near and Middle East whose membership has been gradually enlarged and currently includes 17 countries.

Since the mid-1970s a number of additional regional subsidiary bodies of the Commission have been set up under the name of Heads of National Drug Law Enforcement Agencies (HONLEAs). They currently include: HONLEA, Asia and the Pacific; HONLEA, Africa; HONLEA, Latin America and the Caribbean; and HONLEA, Europe. Regional HONLEAs meet annually, except for years in which an interregional HONLEA meeting is held.

The Division of Narcotic Drugs of the UN Secretariat acted as secretariat to the Commission and also carried out various functions entrusted to the Secretary-General under the international drug control treaties. Following the General Assembly resolution of December 1990 establishing a single body responsible for concerted international actions for drug abuse control, the structures and functions of the Division of Narcotic Drugs have been integrated in the newly-created *UN International Drug Control Programme (UNDCP).

During the session held in early 1991, the Commission focused on ways and means of improving its functioning as a policy-making body pursuant to the direction given by the General Assembly resolution. The need was stressed for the Commission to hold regular annual sessions, instead of meeting biennially as had previously been the case, in order to fulfil more effectively its responsibilities in keeping with the new functions and mandates of the UN in the field of international control of narcotic drugs and psychotropic substances. At the following (early 1992) session, the Commission, in view of the *UN Conference on Environment and Development (UNCED) taking place the following June, adopted a resolution stressing the link that exists between illicit drug cultivation and manufacture and environmental damage.

Location: Vienna International Centre, P.O. Box 500, 1400 Vienna, Austria (telephone: 21131–0; telex: 135612; fax: 232156)

Commonwealth, The. The Commonwealth is a voluntary association of 50 sovereign countries – comprising about one-quarter of the world's population – that meet and consult on a regular basis to foster common links, to co-ordinate mutual assistance for economic and social development, and to contribute to the restructuring of international economic relations and the achievement of a more equitable world community. All member countries, be they monarchies or republics, recognize Queen Elizabeth II as the symbolic Head of the association.

The Commonwealth originated from the effort undertaken after World War I to reorganize the British Empire on the basis of the union of Britain and the Dominions as autonomous countries enjoying equal rights. The significant contribution of the Dominions to the conduct of the conflict, their participation at the peace conference with separate delegations and signatures, and their individual membership in the League of Nations were among the events that paved the way to the establishment of a free association of independent countries linked with Britain on an equal footing. After the Imperial Conferences of 1921 and 1923, devoted respectively to the discussion of major foreign policy issues, and the definition of the rights of the Dominions to conclude international treaties independently, the Imperial Conference of 1926 adopted the Balfour Formula on the status of the Dominions, including at the time six countries – Australia, Canada, Eire [Ireland], Newfoundland, New Zealand, and the Union of South Africa. Britain and the Dominions were defined as 'autonomous communities within the British Empire, equal in status, in no way subordinate one to another in any aspect of their domestic or foreign affairs, though united by a common allegiance to the Crown, and freely associated as members of the British Commonwealth of Nations'.

The Imperial Conference of 1930 confirmed the Balfour Formula and recognized the full legislative autonomy of the Dominions. The basic principles governing relations within the Commonwealth were embodied in the Statute of Westminster of 1931. The Ottawa Imperial Conference, held in 1932, established a preferential system, based on the concession, on a bilateral basis, of preferential tariffs in the trade between Britain and the other members of the British Commonwealth of Nations.

A new Commonwealth, reflecting the changed needs and roles of its member countries, gradually emerged from World War II with the spread of decolonization and the consequent attainment of independence by territories formerly under British jurisdiction or mandate. The requirement of common allegiance to the Crown was dropped while egalitarianism became a more prominent feature of the association, whose membership began to expand. The

countries of the Indian sub-continent were the first to achieve full independence and join the Commonwealth: India and Pakistan became members in 1947 while Ceylon [now Sri Lanka] did so in 1948. A substantial change was brought about in the association in 1949 when India announced her intention to become a republic while retaining full membership. At the London Conference of Commonwealth Prime Ministers in April 1949, unanimous agreement was reached allowing India to continue 'her full membership of the Commonwealth of Nations and her acceptance of the King as the symbol of the free association of its independent member nations and, as such, the Head of the Commonwealth'. Ghana and the Federation of Malaya [now Malaysia] joined in 1957, followed by Nigeria in 1960.

During the 1960s a steady expansion in membership took place with the entry of Cyprus, Sierra Leone and Tanganyika [now Tanzania] in 1961; Jamaica, Trinidad and Tobago, and Uganda in 1962; Kenya in 1963; Malawi, Malta and Zambia in 1964; The Gambia and Singapore, which had seceded from Malaysia, in 1965; Guyana, Botswana, Lesotho and Barbados in 1966; Mauritius and Swaziland in 1968; Tonga, Western Samoa and Fiji in 1970. For obvious reasons membership has grown at a slower pace during the 1970s and 1980s with the entry of Bangladesh, which had seceded from Pakistan, in 1972; Bahamas in 1973; Grenada in 1974; Papua New Guinea in 1975; Seychelles in 1976; Solomon Islands and Dominica in 1978; Saint Lucia and Kiribati in 1979; Zimbabwe and Vanuatu in 1980; Belize, Antigua and Barbuda in 1981; Saint Christopher and Nevis (1983); and Brunei (1984). Since Brunei's admission no other country joined the Commonwealth until the entry of Namibia in March 1990. More than half of the present members of the Commonwealth are republics. Nauru (since 1968) and Tuvalu (since 1978) enjoy the status of 'special' members which entitles them to participate in all functional activities but not to attend meetings of Heads of Government. Saint Vincent and the Grenadines (since 1979) and the Maldives (since 1982) were also special members but their status was subsequently upgraded to full membership. The Commonwealth also encompasses about 25 self-governing countries and dependencies of the UK, Australia and New Zealand.

Governments of member countries are represented in other Commonwealth countries by High Commissioners whose rank is equivalent to that of Ambassadors.

Upon attainment of independence, a number of territories did not join the Commonwealth for various reasons. Among these territories were Egypt, Iraq, Transjordan, Burma [recently renamed Myanmar], Palestine, Sudan, British Somaliland, Southern Cameroons, and Southern Yemen. The Maldives and Western Samoa joined some years after independence. Of the seven original members of the Commonwealth, three no longer belong to the association: Eire withdrew in 1949; Newfoundland abandoned Dominion status, became a crown colony, and eventually became the tenth province of Canada in 1949; the Republic of South Africa withdrew in 1961 but is expected to rejoin in the near future. Pakistan, which had left in 1972 when its former Eastern province was recognized by the UK and other Commonwealth member countries as an independent state under the name of Bangladesh, rejoined the Commonwealth in October 1989. The membership of Fiji was declared lapsed in October 1987 after the constitutional changes which had followed the coups d'etat.

The objectives of the contemporary Commonwealth are not defined in a written document such as a charter or a founding treaty but are to be found in consultation, co-ordination and co-operation procedures in the political, economic, financial, technical and social fields, with special regard to the needs of the less developed members. The peculiar nature of the association, characterized by full equality and consensus of members and freedom from rigid patterns, has remarkably improved its ability to survive through swift and effective adjustment to changed circumstances.

Commonwealth Heads of Government have agreed a number of statements or declarations to which Commonwealth member countries are committed: the Declaration of Commonwealth Principles (1971); the Gleneagles Agreement on apartheid in sport (1977); the Lusaka Declaration on Racism and Racial Prejudice (1979); the Melbourne Declaration on relations between developed and developing countries (1981); the Goa Declaration on International Security (1983); the New Delhi Statement on Economic Action (1983); the Nassau Declaration on World Order (1985); the Commonwealth Accord on Southern Africa (1985); the Vancouver Declaration on World Trade (1987); the Okanagan Statement and Programme of Action on Southern Africa (1987); the Kuala Lumpur Statement on Southern Africa (1989); and the Langkawi Declaration on the Environment (1989).

Membership of the Commonwealth is based on the voluntary acceptance of the Queen's status as symbolic Head by independent countries which have previously been a part of the British Empire; final decision on admission requires the unanimous consent of member countries. There is no incompatibility between membership in the Commonwealth and participation in other international organizations of a political and/or economic nature.

In fact, the Declaration of Commonwealth Principles commits member countries to international co-operation, to 'support the UN and seek to strengthen its influence for peace in the world, and its efforts to remove the causes of tension between nations'. The Commonwealth is also an active supporter of regional co-operation and has helped strengthen regional groupings in Africa, the Caribbean, Asia and the Pacific.

The basic guidelines of Commonwealth activities are laid down at the meetings of the Heads of Government which take place regularly at biennial intervals. In alternate years senior government officials hold meetings to review policies and consider important matters of common concern. Finance Ministers meet annually in the week prior to the annual meeting of the *World Bank and the *International Monetary Fund (IMF). Regular meetings are also held by Ministers of Education,

Labour, Health, and others as appropriate. Several other meetings take place at different levels, on a regular or ad hoc basis, to ensure close co-ordination on specific issues. Meetings are open to all member countries and are held in different cities and regions within the Commonwealth in conformity with the multilateral character of the association; votes are not taken.

The central organization for joint consultation and co-operation is provided by the Commonwealth Secretariat which was established in 1965 upon decision of the Heads of Government. The Secretariat – headed by a Secretary-General elected by the Heads of Government and located in London – organizes and services meetings and conferences, co-ordinates a broad range of activities and disseminates information on questions of common concern. It is organized in divisions and sections which reflect the main areas of operation: political affairs, economic affairs, export market development, food production and rural development, information, management development, training, education, science and technology, legal affairs, health, women and development, youth programmes.

Multilateral technical assistance for economic and social development is provided through the Commonwealth Fund for Technical Co-operation (CFTC), established in 1971 and subsequently integrated into the Secretariat for administration. The CFTC, which is supported by the voluntary contributions of member countries, particularly the most developed, provides specialist advice in a wide variety of fields, offers training facilities and sends out experts. Government and private funds are channelled to the less privileged member countries through the Commonwealth Development Corporation. Several special programmes and other minor undertakings are also carried out with a view to improving socio-economic conditions of the poorest members and/or strengthening the extensive network of co-operation links existing between members at both the inter-governmental and non-governmental level.

The Commonwealth maintains close links with many international institutions both within and outside the UN system; observer status was granted to the Commonwealth by the UN General Assembly in October 1976. Special co-operative relations have developed with the international agencies concerned with development work, such as the World Bank, the IMF, the *Food and Agriculture Organization (FAO), the *UN Conference on Trade and Development (UNCTAD), the *General Agreement on Tariffs and Trade (GATT), and the *Organization for Economic Co-operation and Development (OECD). Important relationships are developing with regional economic bodies in Europe, especially the *European Economic Community (EEC), Africa, Latin America, the Caribbean and the South Pacific.

The expenses of the Secretariat are apportioned among member countries according to a scale which is related to UN contributions. Canada, Australia, India, and the UK are among the largest contributors; smaller amounts are contributed by the overwhelming majority of the other members.

The contemporary Commonwealth generally provides an effective and flexible framework for consultation and co-operation between countries characterized by wide disparities in political and economic power, interests and ideological views. Major adaptations and adjustments have been necessary in order to help the association maintain and enhance its unique character and role on the world scene.

Severe political strains have been suffered by the association on a number of occasions, such as armed conflicts between members (India and Pakistan) or within the boundaries of a member (Nigeria). The situation in the countries of Southern Africa and the concrete steps to be taken have been, for a considerable period of time, one of the Commonwealth's most important concerns. The Commonwealth played an active role in achieving majority rule in Zimbabwe, provided humanitarian technical assistance and support in international forums to Namibia and opposed apartheid in South Africa. It took a lead in the international efforts to isolate South

Africa in sport through its 1977 Gleneagles Agreement and supported the efforts of majority-ruled countries in the region to reduce their economic dependence on South Africa through the *Southern African Development Co-ordination Conference (SADCC). Attempts have consistently been made by representatives of Commonwealth countries to establish a common position on sensitive matters discussed by major international organizations, especially the UN. The Commonwealth plays a growing role in the fields of economic and financial co-operation and technical assistance, especially since the creation of the CFTC. Assistance is also being granted to enable developing members of the Commonwealth to participate effectively in the Uruguay Round of multilateral trade negotiations.

The development of human resources and the promotion of human rights throughout the Commonwealth are other areas on which increasing emphasis is being placed at different levels within the framework of the association.

The Commonwealth has contributed to international thought on North-South economic disparities through a number of expert group reports, such as those proposing measures to reduce protectionism, reform the Bretton Woods institutions, relieve the debt problems of developing countries and increase the security of small countries. The participation of the UK as a full member of the EEC has been moulded in such a way as to safeguard to a remarkable extent its economic links with other Commonwealth members.

Secretary-General: Chief Emeka Anyaoku
Headquarters: Marlborough House, Pall Mall, London SW1Y 5HX, England (telephone: 839 3411; telex: 27678; fax: 930 0827)
Publications: *The Commonwealth Today*; *The Commonwealth Factbook*; *Report of the Commonwealth Secretary-General* (every two years); *Commonwealth Currents* (every two months)
References: K. Bradley, ed.: *The Living Commonwealth* (London, 1961); H.D. Hall: *Commonwealth: A History of the British Commonwealth* (London and New York, 1971); A. Walker: *The Modern Commonwealth* (London, 1976); D. Judd and P. Slinn: *The Evolution of the Modern Commonwealth 1902–80* (London, 1982); A. Smith and C. Sanger: *Stitches in Time. The Commonwealth in World Politics* (New York, 1983); A.J.R. Groom and P. Taylor (eds): *The Commonwealth in the 1980s. Challenges and Opportunities* (London, 1984); R.J. Moore: *Making the New Commonwealth* (Oxford, 1987); D. Adamson: *The Last Empire. Britain and the Commonwealth* (London, 1989)

Communauté économique de l'Afrique de l'Ouest (CEAO). *See* **West African Economic Community.**

Communauté économique des pays des Grands Lacs (CEPGL). *See* **Economic Community of the Great Lakes Countries.**

Conference on Security and Co-operation in Europe (CSCE). The Conference is a grouping of over 50 countries (all European states, including republics of the former USSR and Yugoslavia, plus Canada and the USA) originally devoted to the promotion of co-operation in three main areas (military security, economic and trade relations, and observance of human rights) and later extended to cover practically all aspects of pan-European relations.

The origins of the Conference date back to the proposals put forward in the 1960s by the USSR with a view to sanctioning the political/territorial status quo in Europe and the inviolability of the frontiers resulting from World War II. After considerable diplomatic efforts, the invitation of the Finnish government was accepted by over 30 European countries, Canada and the USA and the multilateral preparatory talks started in Helsinki in November 1972. The talks developed over three stages, the first and last taking place in Helsinki and the second in Geneva. At the end of the first stage, in July 1973, the foreign ministers of the 35 participating countries approved the Final Recommendations which were to constitute the scheme for the Final Act of the Conference. Negotiations continued intermittently in Geneva from September 1973 to 21 July 1975. From 30 July to 1 August 1975 the Conference was held in Helsinki with the participation of leaders from 35 countries and the European Community (EC).

The Final Act was signed in Helsinki on 1 August 1975 and represented a major achievement in the process of detente which characterized those eventful years. The Final Act consisted of three main 'baskets': methods to prevent accidental confrontations between the opposing military blocs; proposals for economic, scientific and technological co-operation respecting the two different economic and social systems; an understanding on closer contacts between peoples of the two different systems, together with a reaffirmation of respect for human rights. The problems of the Mediterranean were also dealt with.

It is important to stress that the Final Act envisaged a follow-up to the Conference and meetings were held in 1977–78 in Belgrade, in 1980–83 in Madrid, and in 1986–89 in Vienna. In July 1990 the heads of government of the member countries of the *North Atlantic Treaty Organization (NATO) proposed to strengthen the role of the Conference so as 'to provide a forum for wider political dialogue in a more united Europe'.

A summit meeting of CSCE heads of government took place in November 1990 in Paris ending with the signature of a far-reaching agreement on the reduction of conventional forces in Europe and of the 'Charter for a New Europe' pledging steadfast commitment to democracy based on human rights and fundamental freedoms, prosperity through economic liberty and equal security for all countries. The inclusion of a section on 'New Structures and Institutions of the CSCE Process' was a major step toward the institutionalization of the Conference, a development strongly resisted by many Western European governments for several years. Besides the intensification of consultations at all levels, the heads of government meeting in Paris decided the establishment of a Conflict Prevention Centre in Vienna and of an Office for Free Elections in Warsaw. Even more important was the decision to establish a permanent CSCE Secretariat based in Prague. The creation of a CSCE parliamentary assembly 'involving members of parliaments from all participating states' was also called for as a recognition of the 'parliamentary dimension' still missing from the Helsinki process.

The events resulting from the disintegration of the USSR and Yugoslavia, with long-standing ethnic rivalries degenerating into open conflicts, have tested the ability of the Conference to settle disputes by peaceful means and to foster effective co-operation. In this context, the full and continuing participation of both European and North American countries is deemed to be 'essential to the future of the CSCE process'.

References: L.V. Ferraris (ed): *Report on a Negotiation: Helsinki–Geneva–Helsinki 1972–1975* (Leiden, 1979)

Conseil de l'Entente. *See* **Entente Council.**

Co-operation Council for the Arab States of the Gulf. The Council – generally known as the Gulf Co-operation Council (GCC) – aims to strengthen political and economic co-operation and to promote greater solidarity between the Arab oil countries on the western side of the Gulf, in view of the recurring threats to the region's stability.

The need to co-ordinate efforts for the solution of common problems through the establishment of a regional organization of comprehensive aims was emphasized by the Ministers of Foreign Affairs of Saudi Arabia, Bahrain, Kuwait, Oman, Qatar and the United Arab Emirates, at a meeting held in Riyadh, Saudi Arabia, in February 1981. The decision to create the Council was announced by the Foreign Ministers of the six countries meeting at Muscat, Oman, the following March; finally, at Abu Dhabi, in May, the Heads of State of the countries concerned solemnly approved the establishment of the new body.

According to the founding document,

the member countries of the Council intend to establish between them a community whose scope of activity embraces the economic and financial spheres, as well as education and culture, social affairs, health, transportation and communications, trade, customs and legislation. In a Declaration adopted by the Heads of State at Abu Dhabi, emphasis was also placed on the commitment of the member countries to join in efforts to preserve their sovereignty, territorial integrity and independence and to ensure the stability of the Gulf region which should remain 'outside the sphere of international conflicts'.

The institutional structure of the Council is growing steadily and reflects the progressive development of co-operation among member-countries.

The Supreme Council consists of the heads of member states meeting in ordinary session once a year to decide the general policy and action of the Organization. A special body, the Commission for Settlement of Disputes, is to be attached to the Supreme Council. The Ministerial Council consists of the Foreign Ministers meeting in ordinary session at quarterly intervals and in emergency session at the request of at least two members. It is the responsibility of the Ministerial Council to prepare for the sessions of the Supreme Council and to draw up policies, recommendations and projects for the improvement of co-operation and co-ordination between member countries. Periodic meetings are also held by Ministers of Agriculture, Industry, Energy, Transport, Defence, Finance and Economy, assisted by specialized committees. The Secretariat General assists member countries in the implementation of the recommendations adopted by the Supreme and Ministerial Councils. The Secretary-General, appointed by the Supreme Council upon the recommendation of the Ministerial Council for a renewable three-year term, performs administrative and technical functions, in collaboration with two Assistant Secretaries-General, for Political Affairs and for Economic Affairs, respectively. The seat of the Secretariat is in Riyadh.

During its initial period, the Council has laid out the strategy for co-operation activities in several fields – in particular the liberalization of the movement of goods, capital, and people between member countries. In June 1981 the Finance Ministers prepared an economic co-operation agreement dealing with petroleum, the abolition of customs duties, and financial and monetary co-ordination. The Ministers of Petroleum met in Riyadh at the beginning of 1982 with a view to drawing up a joint comprehensive strategy on oil matters to be carried out *vis-à-vis* third countries and international organizations, including the *Organization of the Petroleum Exporting Countries (OPEC) and the *Organization of Arab Petroleum Exporting Countries (OAPEC). A unified policy on the acquisition of technology was also adopted. In December 1987, a plan was approved by the Supreme Council in order to allow a member whose production had been disrupted to 'borrow' petroleum from other members and fulfil its export obligations.

As regards the movement of goods, certain customs duties on domestic products of the member countries were abolished in early 1983, while a common minimum tariff on foreign imports was established in 1986. The imposition of higher tariffs on imports representing a threat to manufacturing industries of the Council's member countries has been under consideration for a number of years.

In February 1987 the governors of the central banks reached an agreement for the co-ordination of exchange rates which was subsequently approved by the Supreme Council. To finance specific projects, mainly in the energy and transport sectors, the Gulf Investment Corporation, having an initial capital of $2100 million and based in Kuwait, was established in 1983. At the beginning of 1990, paid-up capital amounted to $540 million and a dozen investment projects had been approved.

In the late 1980s a number of measures were adopted within the framework of a common industrial strategy for the protection of industrial products of the Council's member countries, the co-ordination of industrial projects and the unification of legislation on foreign investment. Progress has also been made for the adoption of a unified agricultural policy. The establishment of a joint telecommunications network has been decided since the mid-1980s.

Co-operation on military and security issues, not expressly mentioned in the founding agreement, was formally included among the Council's activities by a decision of the Supreme Council at the end of 1981. At their meeting in February 1982, the Foreign Ministers stressed that an attack against any member-country will be considered an attack against all member-countries. In May 1982 the Ministers of Foreign Affairs held an emergency meeting to discuss the issues arising from the conflict between Iraq (supported by the Council's member countries acting individually) and Iran; a peace plan was proposed in May 1983. To foster mutual defence co-ordination, joint military exercises were held in 1983 and 1984. In November 1984 it was decided to set up the 'Peninsula Shield Force' for rapid deployment, under a central command, against external aggression. Repeated offers by the Council to mediate between Iraq and Iran failed to materialize and no joint policy could be adopted *vis-à-vis* Iran following the cease-fire between that country and Iraq in August 1988.

Immediately after Iraq's invasion of Kuwait in August 1990, the Ministerial Council formally demanded the withdrawal of Iraqi troops; the Defence Ministers for their part decided to put on alert the Peninsula Shield Force to prevent an invasion of Saudi Arabia by Iraq. The Supreme Council, meeting in December 1990 in Qatar, demanded Iraq's total and unconditional withdrawal from Kuwait and recognized that military action might be necessary to expel Iraq from Kuwait. The Peninsula Shield Force subsequently took part in the US-led anti-Iraqi alliance which also saw the development of close links between the Council's member countries on the one hand and Egypt and Syria on the other. The six members of the Council plus Egypt and Syria issued in March 1991 the 'Declaration of Damascus' announcing plans to establish a regional peace-keeping force which, however, failed to materialize because of persisting disagreements concerning its composition. In the face of the urgent need to provide conditions for greater political and economic stability in the region, the Council announced in April 1991 the creation of a multi-million dollar development fund mainly to assist friendly countries, notably Egypt and Syria, that had played a major role in the Gulf War.

Secretary-General: Abdullah   Yacoub Bishara

Headquarters: P.O. Box 7153, Riyadh 11462, Saudi Arabia (telephone: 482 7777; telex: 403635; fax: 482 9089)

Reference: M. Rumaihi: *Beyond Oil: Unity and Development in the Gulf* (London, 1986)

Co-ordinating Committee for Multilateral Export Controls (CoCom). The Committee is an informal body – not based on a treaty, executive agreement or other constitutive document – established by Western nations to control exports of goods and technology of military and strategic relevance to potential adversaries. It was intended primarily to deny the USSR and its allies any item that would strengthen their military potential, thereby threatening the security of the West. The radical changes in Central and Eastern Europe have obviously led the Committee – currently including all members of the *North Atlantic Treaty Organization (NATO), except Iceland, plus Australia and Japan – to liberalize substantially its control measures over the past three years.

The Committee was set up in 1949 at the instigation of the USA in order to secure measures by Western Europe and Canada parallel to American controls over exports to the USSR and other 'Communist-dominated nations'. American efforts were originally directed at weakening the socialist regimes economically, militarily and politically. The Export Control Act, adopted by the US Congress in February 1949, called for the use of restrictive measures in order to safeguard the national security and economic interests of the USA. Under the Act, export controls had to be applied to the maximum extent possible in co-operation with all the countries with which the USA had defence treaty commitments and within the framework of a unified Western commercial and trading policy.

After an unsuccessful attempt by the USA to press the case for multilateral controls on exports to the USSR and Eastern European countries in the context of the newly-created Organization for European Economic Co-operation (OECC), closed-door negotiations between American and West European delegates took place in 1949 and eventually resulted in the creation of a mechanism for the implementation and review of export control measures.

The CoCom system started operating in January 1950, with the participation of seven countries: Belgium, France, Italy, Luxembourg, the Netherlands, the UK and the USA. Five more countries – Canada, Denmark, the Federal Republic of Germany, Norway and Portugal – joined in 1950, followed by Japan in 1952, and by Greece and Turkey in 1953. Australia and Spain joined the Committee in the 1980s bringing to 17 the total number of members.

On the institutional plane, a structure was set up consisting of two distinct bodies: (a) a high-level Consultative Group (CG) performing policy-making functions; and (b) a Co-ordinating Committee (CoCom), of a largely executive and technical nature, responsible for carrying out the directions issued by the CG. The meetings of the CG were discontinued in the late 1950s and its competences were *de facto* transferred to the Committee which thus became the sole body in charge of multilateral export controls with the assistance of a small permanent secretariat based in Paris.

A significant development from an institutional standpoint took place during the Korean war when the control of Western exports to China and other Communist countries in Asia had become crucial. In September 1952, a China Committee (ChinCom) was appointed, consisting of the same delegates as CoCom but under a different chairmanship and applying more

stringent rules. In September 1957, however, ChinCom ceased to exist as a separate body and its competence was transferred to CoCom.

The delegates of the member countries meet regularly to discuss both the guidelines of export controls and specific exception requests. Critical to any effort is the necessity to reconcile the legitimate rights of the exporters and their importance to the economy with the exigencies of national security. At present, the militarily relevant products and technologies to be controlled are grouped into three lists: the International (Industrial) List; the International Munitions List; and the International Atomic Energy List. Unanimity is required to include an item in the lists as well as to take it off.

The Committee reviews the requests of individual member countries to permit shipment of specific embargoed items to 'proscribed destinations' when the risk of diversion to military use is sufficiently small. The list of proscribed destinations included the then USSR, its Warsaw Pact allies (collectively referred to as Eastern Europe), Albania, China, Mongolia, North Korea, Cambodia and Viet Nam. The revolutionary events which have been taking place in the Eastern half of Europe since 1989 have induced the Committee to reduce or eliminate many restrictive measures without abandoning, however, its basic approach of strict control of trade in strategically relevant items. This seems to a very large degree justified by the marked instability in Central and Eastern European countries and by the growing danger represented by a proliferation of highly sophisticated weapons in other parts of the world.

It is important to stress that no official relationship ever existed between the Committee and NATO. In principle, CoCom's organizational mechanism and activities were surrounded by secrecy and very few details were available about its structure, tasks, policy guidelines and decisions on specific issues. Conflicts, mostly between the USA and West European countries, have arisen from time to time over the inclusion or deletion of specific items in the international lists administered by the Committee as well as over the proper enforcement of restrictive measures.

Although the future prospects of the Committee, after the sea change in East-West relations, are hard to predict, it may well be that emphasis will gradually shift towards the control of technology transfer to developing countries, with special regard to the industrial techniques for the production of advanced weapons and strategic equipment. Such course of action would also require the establishment of a closer and more stable relationship with a number of non-member countries, in Europe and elsewhere, which are actively involved in the exportation of Western strategic goods and technology.

Chairman: Menno Goedhart

Headquarters: 58bis rue La Boetie, 75008 Paris, France

References: G. Adler-Karlsson: *Western Economic Warfare 1947–1967. A Case Study in Foreign Economic Policy* (Stockholm, 1968); G.K. Bertsch: *East-West Strategic Trade, COCOM and the Atlantic Alliance*, The Atlantic Papers no. 49 (Paris, 1983)

Council of Europe, The. The Council is a regional organization which aims to achieve a greater unity between its member countries in order to safeguard and realize the ideals and principles which represent their common heritage and to facilitate their economic and social progress.

The Council was created in 1949, following protracted negotiations between the representatives of several Western European nations. After 1945, the idea of the political unification of Europe had gained considerable impetus and led to the creation of numerous movements, at both the international and national levels, sponsoring the project of a European Union. In May 1948, the International Committee of the Movements for European Unity organized the Congress of Europe in The Hague, the Netherlands, bringing together in a private capacity nearly 1000 influential Europeans, including many prominent statesmen. One of the resolutions adopted by the Congress called for the establishment of a European Assembly and a European Court of Human Rights. The proposal concerning the Assembly was considered with the Consultative Council of the Brussels Treaty Organization, an institution set up in March 1948 by Belgium, France, Luxembourg, the Netherlands, and the UK. In January 1949, the Ministers of Foreign Affairs of these countries agreed in principle to establish a Council of Europe, consisting of a ministerial committee and a consultative assembly. Proposals concerning the basic features of the new organization were subsequently submitted to a conference of ambassadors including, besides the five Brussels Treaty countries, representatives of Denmark, Ireland, Italy, Norway and Sweden who had been invited to participate.

The Statute of the Council was signed by the representatives of the 10 countries in May 1949, in London, and formally went into effect two months later; subsequently it has been amended on a number of occasions. The founder members were joined by Greece and Turkey later in 1949; Iceland in 1950; the Federal Republic of Germany in 1951 (having been an associate member since 1950); Austria in 1956; Cyprus in 1961; Switzerland in 1963; Malta in 1965; Portugal in 1976; Spain in 1977; Liechtenstein in 1978; San Marino in 1988; Finland in 1989; Hungary in 1990; Czechoslovakia and Poland in 1991; Bulgaria in 1992. Greece withdrew from the Council in December 1969 and rejoined in November 1974. Israel has permanent observer status.

The desire for a united Europe expressed by the representatives of the various movements who met at The Hague Congress of 1948 was fulfilled only to a certain extent by the creation of the Council, which is based upon the principle of voluntary co-operation of the member countries which retain their full sovereign powers. According to the Statute, the basic aims of the Council are to be pursued by discussion of questions of common concern and by agreements and common action in economic, social, cultural, scientific, legal and administrative matters and in the maintenance and further realization of human rights and fundamental freedoms. It is worth noting that matters relating to national defence are specifically excluded from the competence of the Council. Although the scope of the Council embraces a very wide range of subjects, defence being the only notable exception, the powers entrusted to the principal organs are rather limited and substantially confined to the promotion of voluntary co-ordination of efforts, the adoption of recommendations and the drawing up of conventions and agreements.

Every member country is bound to accept 'the principles of the rule of law and of the enjoyment by all persons within its jurisdiction of human rights and fundamental freedoms' and must collaborate 'sincerely and effectively' in the realization of the Council's objectives. Any European country which is deemed to be able and willing to fulfil these obligations may be invited to become a member of the Council; associate membership may be envisaged under special circumstances. Invitations to join the Council are issued by the Committee of Ministers after consulting with the Parliamentary Assembly. While a full member is entitled to participation in both the principal organs of the Council, an associate member is entitled to representation in the Parliamentary Assembly only. The right of withdrawal may be exercised upon giving formal notice and generally takes effect at the end of the financial year in which it is notified. Any country which seriously violates the fundamental obligations arising from membership in the Council may be suspended from its rights of representation and formally requested to withdraw; if such country does not comply with the request, the other member countries may decide its expulsion from the Council.

According to the Statute, the organs of the Council are the Committee of Ministers and the Parliamentary Assembly (more precisely referred to as the Consultative Assembly), both of which are serviced by the Secretariat. The Committee of Ministers consists of the Ministers of Foreign Affairs of all member countries, each country being entitled to one representative and one vote. When a Minister of Foreign Affairs is unable to attend, an alternate may be appointed, possibly from among members of the government. Members of the Committee take the chair in rotation. The Committee is responsible for taking decisions with binding effect on all matters of internal organization, making recommendations to governments and drawing up conventions and agreements; it also discusses matters of political concern. The Committee usually meets in private twice yearly, in April/May and November, at the seat of the Council in Strasbourg, France. From 1952 onwards, Ministers' Deputies were appointed to deal with most of the routine work at monthly meetings; they are entitled to take decisions having the same force and effect as those adopted by the Ministers themselves, provided that important policy matters are not involved. Deputies are usually senior diplomats accredited to the Council as permanent representatives of member countries. Decisions of the Committee normally require the unanimity of the representatives casting a vote and must include a majority of all members sitting on the Committee. Questions arising under the rules of procedure or under financial and administrative regulations may be decided by simple majority. A number of matters, concerning *inter alia* admission of members, adoption of the budget, rules of procedure, financial and administrative regulations, and amendment of the Statute, require a two-thirds majority of the votes cast and a majority of the representatives entitled to sit on the Committee.

The Parliamentary Assembly is empowered to discuss any matter within the aim and scope of the Council, and to present conclusions, in the form of recommendations, to the Committee of Ministers. It consists of 184 parliamentarians elected or appointed by national parliaments; political parties are represented in each national delegation according to the proportion of their strength in the respective parliament. Each member country is represented by a number of parliamentarians corresponding to its population size. France, Germany, Italy and the UK are entitled to 18 representatives each; Spain and Turkey to 12 each; Belgium, Greece, Hungary, the Netherlands and Portugal to 7 each; Austria, Sweden and Switzerland to 6 each; Denmark, Finland and Norway to 5 each; Ireland to 4; Cyprus, Iceland, Luxembourg and Malta to 3 each; Liechtenstein and San Marino to 2. For domestic reasons, Cyprus is not at present represented in the Assembly. Representatives sit in the Assembly in alphabetical order, not in national delegations, and vote in their individual capacity. Five major groups have been formed according to common political views: Socialist Group; Group of the European People's Party (Christian Democrats); European Democratic (Conservative) Group; Liberal Democratic and Reformers' Group; United European Left Group. The Assembly meets in ordinary session once a year for not more than a month in public at the seat of the Council. It elects its own President who controls its proceedings; the session is usually divided into three parts (held in January-February; April-May; and September-October), each part lasting approximately one week. Annual joint meetings with the European Parliament of the European Communities are generally held for one day only. The Assembly may address recommendations to the Committee of Ministers by a two-thirds majority of the representatives casting a vote; resolutions on matters relating to internal procedure and opinions generally require simple majority.

Committees have been set up by the Assembly to consider and report on various matters, to examine and prepare questions on the agenda, and to advise on procedural matters. The Standing Committee represents the Assembly when it is not in session and consists of the President, Vice-Presidents, Chairmen of the Ordinary Committees, and a number of ordinary members; it meets at least three times a year. Ordinary Committees include the following: political; economic and development; social; health and family affairs; legal; culture and education; science and technology; environment; regional planning and local authorities; migration; refugees and demography; rules of procedure; agriculture; relations with European non-member countries;

parliamentary and public relations; budget and inter-governmental work programme.

An additional channel of contact between the Committee of Ministers and the Parliamentary Assembly was provided in 1950 by the creation of a Joint Committee including representatives of both the principal organs of the Council and acting essentially as a co-ordinating and liaison body.

The establishment of a parliamentary assembly of the *Conference on Security and Co-operation in Europe (CSCE) in April 1991 in Madrid originated the problem of a 'division of labour' among the new body and existing parliamentary institutions such as the North Atlantic Assembly and the Parliamentary Assembly of the Council of Europe. A formula is being devised whereby the Assembly of the Council of Europe will contribute to the work of the CSCE assembly in human rights matters, putting its expertise at the service of the newly-created pan-European body.

The Secretariat is headed by a Secretary-General responsible to the Committee of Ministers. The Secretary-General and Deputy Secretary-General are appointed by the Assembly on the recommendation of the Committee of Ministers.

The Council has concluded agreements with the UN and several of its specialized agencies in order to exchange observers and documents and to co-ordinate mutual relations. Relationships are particularly close with the *Organization for Economic Co-operation and Development (OECD) and with other European organizations, notably the *European Community (EC) and the *European Free Trade Association (EFTA), in order to arrange reciprocal communication on matters of important European interest, provide for consultation and co-ordinate initiatives with a view to avoiding duplication and waste of efforts. It is worth mentioning that the Assembly of the *Western European Union (WEU) is composed of representatives of the Union's member countries to the Parliamentary Assembly of the Council. Observers from non-governmental organizations take part in many activities of the Council.

The budget of the Council is submitted annually by the Secretary-General for adoption by the Committee of Ministers. The expenses of the Secretariat as well as all other common expenses are shared between members according to proportions determined by the Committee of Ministers. France, Germany, Italy and the UK together account for about two-thirds of the Council's ordinary budget.

Despite the fluctuating relationship between its principal organs and its fairly limited powers, the Council has succeeded in furthering regional co-operation in several key areas, lowering barriers between European countries, harmonizing legislation or introducing common European laws, eliminating discrimination on grounds of nationality, and undertaking a number of ventures on a joint European basis.

Of paramount importance is the building up by the Council of a common law of Europe through multilateral conventions and agreements. The European Convention for the Protection of Human Rights and Fundamental Freedoms represents a major achievement; its object is to guarantee internationally fundamental rights and freedoms and special machinery is provided for the observance and enforcement of the basic standards. The Convention, prepared under the auspices of the Council, was signed in Rome in November 1950 and went into effect in September 1953; several additional protocols have been drawn up subsequently and have gradually entered into force. Unlike the UN Universal Declaration of Human Rights of 1948, whose value essentially lies in the moral sphere, the European Convention is a binding treaty, though important reservations and denunciation are expressly permitted.

A European Commission of Human Rights, composed of a number of members equal to the number of contracting parties and elected by the Committee of Ministers of the Council, investigates alleged violations of the Convention submitted to it either by signatory countries or, in certain cases, by individuals. It must be stressed that the right of individual petition (that is petition from any person, non-governmental organization or group of individuals claiming to be the victims of a violation of the rights set out in the Convention) may be exercised only if a particular defendant country, signatory to the Convention, has specifically accepted it. The function of the Commission is basically one of conciliation. If no friendly settlement is reached within the prescribed period, the Commission sends a report to the Committee of Ministers in which it states an opinion as to whether there has been a violation of the Convention. It is then the responsibility of the Committee of Ministers or the European Court of Human Rights (if the case is referred to it) to decide whether or not a violation has taken place. The Court was established in 1959 and consists of a number of judges equal to that of the member countries of the Council. Acceptance of its jurisdiction is optional for the signatory countries. The compulsory jurisdiction of the Court has so far been recognized by about 20 countries. The judges are elected by a majority vote of the Parliamentary Assembly from a list of nominees submitted by the member countries. In the event of a dispute as to whether the Court has jurisdiction, the matter is settled by decision of the Court itself. The judgment of the Court is final. Under certain circumstances, the Court gives advisory opinions at the request of the Committee of Ministers.

The Council's Steering Committee for Human Rights is in charge of promoting inter-governmental co-operation in human rights and fundamental freedoms; it prepared, *inter alia*, the European Ministerial Conference on Human Rights which took place in 1985 and the European Convention for the Prevention of Torture which entered into force in February 1989.

In an effort to harmonize national laws, to put the citizens of member countries on an equal footing and to pool certain resources and facilities, about 140 conventions and agreements have been concluded within the framework of the Council to cover a variety of aspects: social security; extradition; patents; medical treatment; training of nurses; equivalence of degrees and diplomas; hotel-keepers' liability; compulsory motor insurance; protection of television broadcasts; adoption of children; transportation of animals; movement of persons; archaeological heritage. A European Social Charter came into force in 1965, setting out the social and economic rights which the signatory countries agree to guarantee to their citizens and complementing to a certain extent the European Convention on Human Rights; in May 1988 the Charter was completed by an Additional Protocol. Two important conventions adopted in 1977 concern the suppression of terrorism, and the legal status of migrant workers. Additional protocols have been adopted to amend and supplement the provisions contained in certain conventions.

In the economic and social field, particular attention is given to the protection of the socio-economic rights of the individual. The work of the Council ranges from consumer education and participation to specific aspects of social policy, welfare and labour law. The European Convention on the Legal Status of Migrant Workers is in force since 1983. With regard to health, the Council aims to increase the exchange between member countries of medical techniques and equipment, to encourage study projects, to draw up common standards on the proper use of pharmaceuticals and on the medical and functional treatment of disabled persons. About 20 member countries co-operate within the framework of the 'Pompidou Group' to combat drug abuse and illicit drug trafficking.

A Committee for Population Studies, set up in 1973, observes population trends and their implications. In 1956, the Council's Social Development Fund was set up, under the name of Resettlement Fund for National Refugees and Over-Population, with a view to giving financial aid, particularly in the spheres of housing, vocational training, regional planning and development. By 1989, total loans granted by the Fund amounted to about $7500 million.

In 1970, the Council set up a European Youth Centre, equipped with audio-visual workshops, reading and conference rooms; about 1500 people can be accommodated annually. In order to provide financial assistance to European activities of non-governmental youth organizations, the Council created the European Youth Foundation which began operations in 1973.

On the legal plane, the European Committee on Legal Co-operation supervises the Council's work programme for international, administrative, civil and commercial law and has prepared numerous conventions. The European Committee on Crime Problems has also prepared conventions on matters falling within its competence such as mutual assistance in procedural matters, international validity of criminal judgments and transfer of proceedings. The Council for Cultural Co-operation (CCC) carries out the educational and cultural activities of the Council, based on the concepts of permanent education and cultural development. The CCC, which includes the members of the Council plus other signatories of the Cultural Convention, administers the Cultural Fund for the promotion and financing of educational and cultural activities. Several committees and expert groups assist the CCC. The Committee for the Development of Sport has the same membership as the CCC and administers the Sports Fund. Its activities concentrate on the implementation of the European Sport for All Charter of 1975 and related issues.

The Steering Committee on the Mass Media covers all aspects of mass communication with special reference to broadcasting; it prepared a European Convention on transfrontier television which was adopted in 1989.

The Steering Committee for the Conservation and Management of the Environment and Natural Habitats, established in 1962, draws up policy recommendations and promotes co-operation in all environmental questions. It introduced a European Water Charter in 1968, a Soil Charter in 1974 and a Charter on Invertebrates in 1986. The Conference of Local and Regional Authorities of Europe, created in 1957, is chiefly concerned with local government matters, regional planning, regional policy of the European Communities, protection of the environment, town planning, and social and cultural affairs; the Steering Committee on

Local and Regional Authorities was established in 1988 to provide a forum for senior officials from ministries of local government. The Cultural Heritage Committee promotes contacts between authorities in charge of historic buildings and encourages public interest. A Convention for the Conservation of the Architectural Heritage of Europe entered into force in 1987.

Secretary-General: Catherine Lalumière

Headquarters: Palais de l'Europe, 67006 Strasbourg, France (telephone: 88 41 20 00; telex: 870943; fax: 88 41 27 81)

Publications: *Forum* (quarterly); *European Yearbook*; *Yearbook on the European Convention on Human Rights*

References: A.H. Robertson: *The Council of Europe. Its Structure, Functions and Achievements* (London, rev. 2/1961); A.H. Robertson: *European Institutions* (London, rev. 3/1973)

CSCE. *See* **Conference on Security and Co-operation in Europe.**

Customs and Economic Union of Central Africa [Union douanière et économique de l'Afrique centrale] (UDEAC). The Union aims to promote the gradual establishment of a Central African common market and improve the living standards of the peoples of member countries.

The Union was established by the Brazzaville Treaty of December 1964 (revised in 1974) and came into operation in January 1966. Signatories were Cameroon, Central African Republic, Chad, Congo and Gabon. With the addition of Cameroon, it replaced the Equatorial Customs Union [Union douanière équatoriale] (UDE) formed in June 1959 by the Central African Republic, Chad, Congo and Gabon, the four autonomous republics participating in the French Community after having been territories of French Equatorial Africa. The Central African Republic and Chad withdrew from the Union in April 1968 in an attempt to set up another common market, the Union des états de l'Afrique centrale (UEAC),

together with the Democratic Republic of the Congo [now Zaire]. In December 1968 the Central African Republic decided to rejoin UDEAC. Chad was given observer status in December 1975. Equatorial Guinea was admitted to full membership in December 1983.

According to the founding document, the Union has no supranational features and is based on the full equality of member countries which take all decisions by unanimous consent. The Union, which is considered a step towards the establishment of an African common market, envisages the elimination of customs duties and other obstacles to trade between member countries, the adoption of a common external tariff, the harmonization of national investment codes, the setting up of a Solidarity Fund to counterbalance regional disparities of wealth and economic development, and the holding of regular consultations on economic matters. The Brazzaville Treaty was extensively revised and supplemented in December 1974 with a view to fostering economic, financial and industrial integration, as well as promoting the formation of multinational companies within the Union.

In spite of the relatively loose character of co-operation between its member countries, the Union is endowed in principle with significant functions and powers. Acts and decisions formally adopted by the main organs have binding force and are directly applicable in member countries. Any independent and sovereign African country wishing to join the Union may be admitted upon unanimous decision of all member countries.

The organizational structure of the Union comprises three principal organs: the Council of Heads of State; the Management Committee; and the General Secretariat. The Council is the supreme organ vested with full powers and meets at least once a year to set down the basic guidelines to be implemented by the other organs. Its decisions are taken unanimously and are legally enforceable in each member country. The presidency of the Council is by annual rotation in alphabetical order of member countries.

The Management Committee consists of

two representatives from each country: the Finance Minister and the minister in charge of matters related to economic development. The Committee meets as often as required but at least twice a year and is responsible for the Union's general operation under the powers which have been delegated by the Council. Decisions adopted by unanimous consent are directly enforceable. Both the Council and the Committee may establish subsidiary bodies whenever the need arises. Several specialized working groups and commissions have been created.

Administrative functions are carried out by the General Secretariat whose seat is in Bangui, Central African Republic. It is headed by a Secretary-General appointed by the Council of Heads of State.

Relations have been established by the Union with UN agencies and programmes concerned with various aspects of economic as well as technical and scientific co-operation; close links are being developed on a regional plane, especially with the *UN Economic Commission for Africa (ECA), with a view to accelerating the process of economic integration in Central Africa.

Although unable to resolve some highly controversial issues, the Union has achieved a number of significant results in the sphere of customs and economic co-operation and integration. Trade within the Union has been liberalized and a basic common tariff is applied to imports from third countries. According to a convention signed in 1972, the right of establishment within the Union has been granted to nationals of member countries. Foreign investments are regulated by a common code and a single taxation system is in force, although rates are fixed by each member country. As regards monetary co-operation, a *Bank of Central African States [Banque des états de l'Afrique centrale] (BEAC) was founded in 1973 in

Yaoundé, Cameroon, as the central bank of issue. The activity of the Solidarity Fund is being supplemented by the *Development Bank of Central African States [Banque de développement des états de l'Afrique centrale] (BDEAC) which has been operating since 1976 in Brazzaville, Congo. The co-ordination of national industrial policies and the promotion of regional multinational companies represent another major area for co-operation. Several industrial projects of a regional scope are under consideration.

In order to take full advantage of economies of scale and to strengthen and rationalize co-operation throughout the region, the member countries of the Union agreed in principle, in December 1981, to establish a wider economic grouping – the *Economic Community of Central African States [Communauté économique des états de l'Afrique centrale] (CEEAC) – also including, as full members, Angola, Burundi, Chad, Rwanda, São Tome and Príncipe, and Zaire; the new organization began operations in Libreville, Gabon, in January 1985.

Secretary-General: Ambroise Foalem

Headquarters: P.O. Box 969, Bangui, Central African Republic (telephone: 610922; telex: 5254)

Publications: *Annuaire du commerce extérieur de l'UDEAC*; *Bulletin des statistiques générales* (quarterly)

References: P. Robson: 'Economic Integration in Equatorial Africa', *African Integration and Disintegration: Case Studies in Economic and Political Union*, ed. A. Hazelwood (London, 1967); L.K. Mytelka: 'Competition, Conflict and Decline in the Union Douanière et Economique de l'Afrique Centrale (UDEAC)', *African Regional Organizations*, ed. D. Mazzeo (Cambridge, 1984)

D

Danube Commission. The purpose of the Commission is to regulate navigation on the Danube in its various aspects, ensuring the application of uniform rules and providing the related services.

The Commission was constituted in 1949 according to the Convention regarding the control of navigation on the Danube which was signed in Belgrade, Yugoslavia, in August 1948. The need to provide uniform navigation rules on international rivers in Europe led to the establishment of international river commissions under the Peace Treaties of Paris (1814) and Vienna (1815). A European Danube Commission was established on a temporary basis under the Peace Treaty of Paris in 1856 and reconstituted as a permanent institution in 1865. The problems concerning navigation on the Danube were again dealt with in the Peace Treaties with Austria, Bulgaria, Germany and Hungary between 1919 and 1921 and a Convention regarding the 'definitive statute' of the Danube was signed in July 1921. A European Commission of the Danube was set up with jurisdiction over the maritime portion of the river while an International Commission exercised jurisdiction over the international waterway. After World War II, the navigation rules of the Danube were reconsidered in the Peace Treaties with Bulgaria, Hungary and Romania of February 1947, and subsequently became the specific object of the Belgrade Convention providing for the establishment of the present Commission.

The Commission holds annual sessions and is composed of one representative from each of its member countries – Austria, Bulgaria, Czechoslovakia, Hungary, Romania, Russia, Ukraine and Yugoslavia. Since 1957, representatives of the Ministry of Transport of the Federal Republic of Germany have attended the meetings of the Commission as guests of the Secretariat.

The Belgrade Convention solemnly declares that navigation on the Danube from Ulm, in the Federal Republic of Germany, to the Black Sea (with access to the sea through the Sulina arm and the Sulina Canal) is equally free and open to the nationals, merchant shipping and merchandise of all countries as to harbour and navigation fees as well as conditions of merchant navigation. The Commission, which enjoys legal status and has its own seal and flag, is empowered to: supervise the implementation of the provisions of the Belgrade Convention; establish the basic regulations for navigation on the river; ensure facilities for shipping; approve projects for maintenance of navigability and supervise technical services; establish a uniform buoying system on all navigable waterways; co-ordinate the regulations for customs, sanitation control, and the hydrometeorological service; collect relevant statistical data. Administrative and technical functions are performed by the Secretariat, comprising a technical section, an administrative section and an accounts department. Members of the Commission and elected officers are granted diplomatic immunity.

Headquarters: Benczur utca 25, 1068

Budapest, Hungary (telephone: 228083)

Publications: *Basic Regulations for Navigation on the Danube*; *Hydrological Yearbook*; *Statistical Yearbook*

References: R.W. Johnson: 'The Danube since 1948', *Year Book of World Affairs*, 17 (1963); S. Gorove: *Law and Politics of the Danube* (1964)

E

EBRD. *See* **European Bank for Reconstruction and Development.**

ECA. *See* **Economic Commission for Africa.**

ECE. *See* **Economic Commission for Europe.**

ECLAC. *See* **Economic Commission for Latin America and the Caribbean.**

Economic and Social Commission for Asia and the Pacific (ESCAP). The Commission provides the only intergovernmental forum for the whole of Asia and the Pacific and fulfils a wide range of functions. It is intended to assist in the formulation and implementation of co-ordinated policies for promoting economic and technological development in the region and to foster the expansion of trade and economic links among member countries and with other countries of the world. It is a regional economic commission operating within the UN system under the authority of the Economic and Social Council, like the *Economic Commission for Africa (ECA), the *Economic Commission for Europe (ECE), the *Economic Commission for Latin America and the Caribbean (ECLAC) and the *Economic and Social Commission for Western Asia (ESCWA).

The Commission was founded in March 1947 upon adoption of a resolution by the Economic and Social Council. Its members include the countries of Asia (except the Arab countries of South Western Asia pertaining to ESCWA, and Israel pertaining to ECE), the Pacific, the USA, France, the Netherlands and the UK. A few Asian and Pacific territories that have not attained full independence enjoy associate membership. Previously known as the Economic Commission for Asia and the Far East (ECAFE), the Commission was reorganized and renamed by the Economic and Social Council in 1974.

Besides furthering regional co-operation on economic issues and extending assistance to individual governments to formulate and implement balanced development programmes, the Commission gives increasing attention to the social aspects of economic development and the relationship between economic and social factors with special emphasis on alleviating poverty in the least-developed areas of the region. Initially involved in the urgent economic problems following World War II, the Commission subsequently took into consideration a wider range of objectives in an increasing effort to cover new areas as well as to intensify practical action for the benefit of the least-developed, land-locked and island countries of the region. Under the terms of reference laid down by the Economic and Social Council, the Commission is also responsible for undertaking or sponsoring investigations and studies of economic and technological problems and developments within the region, and for evaluating and disseminating economic, technological and statistical information originating from this work.

The Commission enjoys considerable autonomy with regard to the fulfilment of its functions since the corresponding terms of reference are rather broadly formulated. These functions are related to the basic task of initiating and participating in measures with a view to facilitating concerted action for economic and social progress in Asia and the Pacific. The Commission is entitled to make recommendations to both the Economic and Social Council and the governments of member countries. Other powers conferred on the Commission include the adoption of the relevant rules of procedure, the appointment of the Chairman, and the establishment of any necessary subsidiary bodies. The Commission must submit an annual report on its activities and plans to the Economic and Social Council; the budget is sent for approval to the UN General Assembly.

The Commission ordinarily holds sessions at ministerial level once a year, with participation by the representatives of all member countries, to consider basic policies, set priorities and review projects and programmes which are being carried out. Decisions and resolutions are customarily adopted by consensus, without casting votes. Under no condition is the Commission allowed to take action against any member country without the latter's consent.

Committees, *ad hoc* conferences, working groups, and other minor subsidiary bodies have been created by the Commission to provide adequate technical support for its activities. At present there are 11 Divisions which are respectively in charge of: administration; agriculture and rural development; development planning; industry, human settlements and environment; international trade and tourism; natural resources; population; social development; statistics; transport and communications; and technical co-operation.

The Secretariat, located in Bangkok, provides the technical and administrative services for the meetings of the Commission and its subsidiary bodies and is responsible for a wide range of general and specialized publications. The Executive Secretary is designated by the UN Secretary General and acts on his behalf. A Pacific Operations Centre was set up in Vanuatu, in 1984, by merging the ESCAP Pacific Liaison Office (Nauru) and the UN Development Advisory Team (Fiji).

Close relations exist between the Commission and the relevant UN specialized agencies and bodies in operation in Asia and the Pacific, as well as with the other regional economic commissions. Co-operative links with the economic, technical and financial institutions in the region have been growing steadily with a view to co-ordinating and implementing programmes and projects of both regional and subregional scope.

Since its inception, the Commission has gradually adapted its work programmes and priorities to the changing political, economic and social conditions in the region, as well as extending co-operation to new fields. The vastness of the area concerned and the huge disparities in levels of development and available resources of member countries as well as the persistence of sharp ideological cleavages have made it difficult to establish region-wide multilateral organizations of a political and economic nature. The Commission has therefore acted, within the UN framework, as a truly Asian-Pacific centre for furthering subregional, regional and interregional co-operation.

Within recent years the Commission has made considerable efforts to implement projects of regional or subregional scope; it acts as executing agency for several programmes and projects. In the past decade, it has concentrated its efforts in the following main areas: food and agriculture; energy; raw materials and commodities; transfer of technology; international trade, transnational corporations and external financial resources transfers; integrated rural development; environmental policies, management and laws; preferential treatment in favour of the least-developed, land-locked and island countries in Asia and the Pacific. A number of specialized bodies have been set up under the aegis of the Commission or with its assistance; they are located in different Asian cities and their membership varies according to their field of action.

As regards development planning, the Commission has been active investigating issues relating to external debt, trade in primary commodities and foreign investment. An important function has been carried out by the Commission in the creation and subsequent improvement of the Generalized System of Preferences (GSP). Assistance from the Commission was also extended for the creation in 1976 of the Asian Free Trade Zone, and for the establishment of groupings dealing with commodities such as the *Asian and Pacific Coconut Community (APCC), the *International Pepper Community (IPC), the *International Jute Organization (IJO) and the *International Natural Rubber Organization (INRO). In the sphere of clearing arrangements and insurance, a significant role is played by the Asian Clearing Union (ACU) and the Asian Re-insurance Corporation; the *Asian Development Bank (AsDB) was set up under the Commission's auspices and has been in operation since the end of 1966. Several agencies have been created to assist member countries in the discovery and use of natural resources such as the Regional Mineral Resources Development Centre, the South East Asia Tin Research and Development Centre, the Committee for Co-ordination of Joint Prospecting for Mineral Resources in Asian Offshore Areas and the Committee for Co-ordination of Joint Prospecting for Mineral Resources in South Pacific Offshore Areas. In this connection the Commission is increasingly stressing the relevance of the environmental impact of the exploitation of natural resources. A new regional training and research institution, the Asian and Pacific Development Centre was established in 1980 to provide assistance and facilities to member countries. Other bodies have been set up in the fields of technology transfer, transport and communications, and typhoon, cyclone and flood warning systems. The period 1985-94 has been designated by the Commission as the Transport Decade for Asia and the Pacific, in the light of the crucial role played by transport improvements in the development process. The Programme on Marine Affairs has been set up in 1986 to advise member countries with regard to the 'exclusive economic zones' established under the 1982 UN Convention on the Law of the Sea.

In agriculture the Commission helps to formulate regional and national policies that lead to increased agricultural production; a close co-operation has been developed with the *Food and Agriculture Organization (FAO) and the *International Labour Organization (ILO). Investigation is being carried out concerning new and renewable energy sources in the region, with special reference to solar, wind and biomass energy. The high rate of population growth in the region has prompted studies on demography and the efficiency of national family-planning programmes, mostly funded by the *UN Population Fund (UNFPA). The Commission is also involved in health programmes covering basic community services and in health planning as part of overall development schemes.

Executive Secretary: Shah A.M.S. Kibria

Headquarters: United Nations Building, Rajadamnern Avenue, Bangkok 10200, Thailand (telephone: 282 9161; telex: 82392; fax: 282 9602)

Publications: Economic and Social Survey of Asia and the Pacific (annually); Economic Bulletin (twice a year); Statistical Yearbook for Asia and the Pacific; Quarterly Bulletin of Statistics for Asia and the Pacific

References: B.G. Ramcharan: 'Equality and Discrimination in International Economic Law (VIII): The United Nations Regional Economic Commissions', Year Book of World Affairs, 32 (1978), 268–85; P.W. Newman, Jr.: 'Regionalism in Developing Areas: UN Regional Economic Commissions and their Relations with Regional Organizations', Regionalism and the United Nations, ed. B. Andemicael (Dobbs Ferry, New York, 1979)

Economic and Social Commission for Western Asia (ESCWA). The Commission acts within the UN framework under the authority of the Economic and Social Council; its purposes are primarily the formulation, co-ordination and implementation of policies for the promotion of economic and social development at regional level and the improvement, through individual and collective actions, of commercial and economic relations among member countries and with the rest of the world. The Commission is one of the five regional economic commissions of the UN – the *Economic Commission for Africa (ECA), the *Economic Commission for Europe (ECE), the *Economic Commission for Latin America and the Caribbean (ECLAC), and the *Economic and Social Commission for Asia and the Pacific (ESCAP).

Initially, attempts to set up an economic commission specifically responsible for the Middle East met with considerable difficulties of a political rather than economic nature. For a while the countries of the region had to be served by an *ad hoc* body, the UN Economic and Social Office in Beirut (UNESOB). In 1974 it finally proved feasible to establish a Commission in charge of the region and a resolution was adopted by the Economic and Social Council. The region included Egypt and the Arab countries of South West Asia and excluded the remaining countries of the Middle East, that is Iran, Israel, and Turkey. Actually Israel and Turkey belong to ECE while Iran belongs to ESCAP. In response to the Egypt-Israel peace treaty concluded in Washington in March 1979, the Commission had unsuccessfully recommended to the Economic and Social Council the suspension of Egypt's membership.

As a body that is specifically in charge of a developing region, the Commission – under the terms of reference laid down by the Economic and Social Council – must deal as appropriate with the social aspects of economic development and the relationship between economic and social factors. It has a broad mandate to consider any action that may be necessary for the attainment of its basic objectives. Besides its primary task of furthering through practical action the development of member countries, the Commission is responsible for promoting investigations and studies of economic and technological problems and developments within Western Asia as well as for collecting, evaluating and disseminating the resultant economic, technological and statistical information.

The Commission is entitled to address recommendations on any matter falling within its competence not only to the Economic and Social Council but also directly to governments of member countries. Among the other powers conferred on the Commission are the following: drawing up its own rules of procedure; appointment of the Chairman of its session; establishment of subsidiary bodies appropriate for the fulfilment of its functions. An annual report on its activities and plans is submitted to the Economic and Social Council; the budget is subject to formal approval by the UN General Assembly.

The Commission holds ordinary sessions every two years with the participation of representatives of all member countries. Beirut was chosen as seat of the Commission until 1979 at a special session which took place in September 1974; the sixth session, held in 1979, decided to move the Commission to Baghdad where permanent headquarters were established in 1982. Temporary headquarters were established in 1991 in Amman. Decisions and resolutions are customarily adopted by consensus, without formal voting. The Commission may act only with the agreement of the governments of the countries concerned. Subsidiary bodies consisting of government officials and experts have been set up by the Commission to consider specific issues of interest to countries of the region. The Secretariat is headed by an Executive Secretary, nominated by the UN Secretary General and acting on the latter's behalf.

The Commission participates in the work of UN specialized agencies and other bodies operating in Western Asia and keeps close contacts with the other four regional economic commissions. Co-operation links have been established with Arab economic and financial institutions in the region.

Since its creation the Commission has made efforts with a view to fostering intersectoral co-ordination and co-operation at the regional level, despite the serious and long-standing problems represented by marked imbalances in economic structures and large income disparities existing between and within its member countries. Because of limits on recruitment imposed during the last half of the 1980s, the Commission's programme of activities had to be substantially reduced.

Executive Secretary: Tayseer Abdel Jaber

Headquarters: P.O. Box 27, Baghdad, Iraq (telephone: 556 9400; telex: 213303)

Temporary address: P.O. Box 927115, Amman, Jordan (telephone: 694 351/8; fax: 694 981/2)

Publications: *Survey of Economic and Social Developments in the ESCWA Region* (annually); *Agriculture and Development* (annually); *Statistical Abstract* (annually)

References: B.G. Ramcharan: 'Equality and Discrimination in International Economic Law (VIII): The United Nations Regional Economic Commissions', *Year Book of World Affairs*, 32 (1978), 268–85

Economic Commission for Africa (ECA). The Commission is called upon, under the authority of the UN Economic and Social Council, to initiate and participate in measures for facilitating concerted action for economic development, to maintain and strengthen the economic relations of member countries among themselves and with other countries of the world, and to produce and disseminate economic, technological and statistical information. It is one of the five regional economic commissions operating within the UN system: the *Economic Commission for Europe (ECE), the *Economic Commission for Latin America and the Caribbean (ECLAC), the *Economic and Social Commission for Western Asia (ESCWA) and the *Economic and Social Commission for Asia and the Pacific (ESCAP).

The Commission was created in 1958 by resolution of the Economic and Social Council as a subsidiary organ of the UN. Its membership has varied considerably over the years. At the very beginning six European nations (Belgium, France, Italy, Portugal, Spain and the UK) with special interests in the region participated as full members alongside ten independent African countries; nine African countries which were not yet independent were associate members. Subsequently, Italy and Belgium withdrew, France, Spain and the UK became associate members and Portugal was excluded. As they gained independence, all other African countries joined the Commission as full members; the participation of the Republic of South Africa was suspended in 1965. The Commission's present membership includes all African states and is the same as that of the *Organization of African Unity (OAU) plus Morocco which no longer belongs to OAU.

Established at the end of the 1950s, when the other UN economic bodies responsible for Europe, Asia and Latin America had already been in operation for a decade, the Commission was involved from the start in the problems of Africa's economic and social development. Its sister commissions primarily had been faced with the urgent issues of the period following World War II in their respective regions. As a body specifically intended to serve a developing region and according to the terms of reference laid down by the Economic and Social Council, the Commission was also endowed with rather wide functions concerning technical co-operation and other forms of operational activity. In addition, appropriate consideration should be given to the social aspects of economic development and the relationship between economic and social factors. The basic goals of promoting self-sustaining processes of development at both regional and subregional level, alleviating unemployment and mass poverty, protecting the environment, and establishing equitable and mutually beneficial relations between the continent and the rest of the world, are to be achieved, *inter alia*, through: development of self-sufficiency in food; foundation and strengthening of a sound industrial base; improvement of the physical infrastructure, especially transport and communications; development of natural resources, technology and services; co-ordinated planning of economic growth; and the advancement of economic co-operation and integration within subregional groupings.

The functions of the Commission are of an operational rather than deliberative nature and are closely connected with the fundamental task of promoting sound economic and social progress in the African continent. In accordance with its terms of reference, the Commission may directly address recommendations on any matter falling within its competence to its member countries as well as to the Economic and Social Council. It is empowered to draw up its own rules of procedure, to elect the Chairman of its sessions and to create the necessary subsidiary bodies. The Commission must submit a full annual report on its activities and plans to the Economic and Social Council; the UN General Assembly is responsible for the formal approval of the Commission's budget.

Until 1965 the Commission customarily held annual sessions, with participation by representatives of all member countries. Biennial sessions were subsequently held until a resolution was adopted in 1969 that these ordinary biennial sessions should be held at ministerial level; they became known as meetings of the Conference of Ministers. At the fourteenth session of the Commission and fifth meeting of the Conference of Ministers in March 1979, it was decided that the Conference of Ministers, as the Commission's highest decision-making organ, should meet annually. It is the responsibility of the Conference, customarily attended by Ministers of economic or financial affairs, to consider the Commission's basic policies, to set priorities, and to review the course of programmes and projects being implemented together with international economic issues of interest to Africa. Decisions and resolutions are normally adopted by consensus without any formal vote being cast. Under no circumstances is it possible to take action against any country without the latter's consent. A number of technical committees and other ad hoc subsidiary bodies composed of specialists and government officials have been created over the years by the Commission according to its needs.

The Secretariat has its headquarters in Addis Ababa, Ethiopia. It services the meetings of the Conference of Ministers and the various subsidiary bodies and performs a wide range of technical and administrative functions. It is organized into Divisions responsible for: food and agriculture, jointly with the *Food and Agriculture Organization (FAO); industry and human settlements; natural resources; trade and development finance; transport, communications and tourism; socio-economic research and planning; public administration, human resources and social development; statistics; population; administration and conference services. The Commission's Executive Secretary is designated by the UN Secretary General.

A number of Multinational Programming and Operational Centres (MULPOCs), located in different African cities and serving different subregions, act as field agents for the implementation of development programmes, thus replacing the former UN Multidisciplinary Development Advisory Teams (UNDATs).

The Commission works in close collaboration with the relevant UN specialized agencies operating in Africa and with the other four regional economic commissions. Effective co-operation links exist in particular with African international organizations, notably OAU, subregional integration bodies such as the *Economic Community of West African States (ECOWAS) and financial institutions such as the *African Development Bank (AfDB) and the Association of African Central Banks (AACB). Technical support has been provided by the Commission in the establishment of several of these bodies. Ties between the Commission and Arab countries outside Africa have been growing since the late 1970s within the framework of the Declaration of Afro-Arab Economic and Financial Co-operation adopted at the first Afro-Arab Summit Conference held in March 1977. Regarding development assistance financing in particular, projects are being submitted for consideration to the *Arab Bank for Economic Development in Africa (BADEA). On the whole, the Commission has been playing a role in fostering intraregional co-ordination and co-operation, as well as establishing mutually beneficial and equitable relations between African countries and the rest of the world.

The work programmes of the Commission include a wide range of objectives covering several fields. A strong emphasis is being laid on agricultural problems in order to expand activities in the field of food development and to co-ordinate guidelines for drawing up additional programmes and projects concerning food, livestock, fishery and forestry products. Industrial policies and strategies are especially aimed at improving co-operation between African countries for the mutual supply of raw materials, exchange of technical expertise and implementation of joint projects. Training of personnel for research and development programmes, improvement of indigenous technologies, and import of adequate foreign technologies represent other major fields of action. Assistance is provided by the Commission to enable member countries to inventory mineral, land and water resources and further to develop both conventional and non-conventional sources of energy, including solar, geothermal and biogas energy. The African Regional Centre for Solar Energy started operations in 1989 in Bujumbura, Burundi. Substantial efforts are being made to expand road, rail, sea and air links between member countries and to improve the Pan-African Telecommunication network (PANAFTEL). The promotion of intraregional trade and financial relations is carried forward, *inter alia*, through the negotiation of several protocols after the completion of background technical studies on imports and exports and related production capacities. An international conference was organized by the Commission in 1987 to address the major issues which hamper African economic recovery, notably the heavy external debt and the unfavourable trading conditions for African commodities. A meeting of African ministers of trade was organized by the Commission in December 1990 to devise means for the revitalization and recovery of regional trade.

Executive Secretary: Layachi Yaker
Headquarters: Africa Hall, P.O. Box 3001, Addis Ababa, Ethiopia (telephone: 517200; telex: 21029)

Publications: *Annual Report*; *Survey of Economic and Social Conditions in Africa* (annually); *African Socio-Economic Indicators* (annually); *African Statistical Yearbook*; *African Trade Bulletin* (twice a year)

References: UN: *ECA today: its Terms of Reference, Past Activities and Potential Role in the Socio-Economic Development of Africa* (Addis Ababa, 1979); I. V. Gruhn: *Regionalism Reconsidered: the Economic Commission for Africa* (Boulder, Co., 1979); OAU: *ECA and Africa's Development: 1983–2008. A Preliminary Prospective Study* (Addis Ababa, 1983); T. M. Shaw: 'The UN Economic Commission for Africa: Continental Development and Self-reliance', *The United Nations in the World Political Economy*, ed. D. P. Forsythe (London, 1989)

Economic Commission for Europe (ECE). The Commission is charged with the promotion of concerted action for raising the levels of economic activity, expanding trade and economic relations among member countries as well as with other countries and carrying out investigations of economic and technological developments within the region. The Commission is also responsible for undertaking the collection and evaluation and, if appropriate, the publication of economic and statistical information.

The Commission operates within the UN framework, under the authority of the Economic and Social Council, like the other four regional economic commissions, that is the *Economic Commission for Africa (ECA), the *Economic Commission for Latin America and the Caribbean (ECLAC), the *Economic and Social Commission for Western Asia (ESCWA) and the *Economic and Social Commission for Asia and the Pacific (ESCAP).

The Commission was established in March 1947 by a resolution of the Economic and Social Council as an operational body to deal with the urgent economic problems arising from World War II. Its full members included several European countries plus the USA; a number of non-UN members in Europe, such as Switzerland, were for a while granted consultative status. Subsequently membership increased considerably, despite various obstacles of a mainly political nature that delayed the effective participation of some countries; Switzerland gained full admission in 1972. Another country outside the region, Canada, joined the Commission in 1973 as full member followed at the beginning of the 1990s by Israel which had never before participated in a regional economic commission. The disintegration of the USSR and the subsequent entry into the UN of former Soviet republics has increased the Commission's membership which now also includes the Baltic countries and Moldova.

Originally devoted to the primary task of post-war reconstruction in Europe, in its early years the Commission had to face the tensions originating from the Cold War and could only gradually take on the role of fostering economic co-operation between countries with different economic and social systems, as well as between subregional economic groupings. In the late 1980s and early 1990s, following the collapse of communism in Europe, the Commission has been striving to forge a new partnership between the two halves of the continent in a truly pan-European context.

The Commission's functions and powers, according to the rather broad terms of reference laid down by the Economic and Social Council, are essentially related to the initiation of and participation in measures for facilitating concerted action for economic progress in Europe. The Commission is empowered to address recommendations on any matter within its competence directly to its member countries as well as to the Economic and Social Council. It is also entitled to draw up its rules of procedure and to establish such subsidiary bodies as are deemed appropriate for the implementation of its functions. A detailed annual report on its activities and plans has to be submitted to the Economic and Social Council; the budget is incorporated into the overall UN budget and is subject to formal approval by the General Assembly.

The Commission normally holds an annual session in Geneva, with the participation of the representatives of all member countries, while meetings of subsidiary bodies are convened throughout the year. Decisions and resolutions (both classes of actions having identical legal effects) are customarily adopted by consensus without any formal vote being cast; abstentions are not recorded. Under no circumstances is the Commission allowed to take action against any country without the latter's consent.

Over the years a number of Principal Subsidiary Bodies have been established by the Commission with the approval of the Economic and Social Council and after discussion with the specialized agencies operating in the same fields. At present there are several bodies performing tasks of a mainly technical nature in specific sectors or charged with the study of intersectoral problems. These bodies include the Committees on: Agricultural Problems; Timber; Coal; Electric Power; Gas; Housing, Building and Planning; Inland Transport; Steel; Chemical Industry; and Development of Trade; the Conference of European Statisticians; the Senior Economic Advisers to ECE Governments; the Senior Advisers to ECE Governments on Science and Technology; the Senior Advisers to ECE Governments on Environmental and Water Problems; and the Senior Advisers to ECE Governments on Energy. The work of these organs is supplemented by several minor specialized bodies and *ad hoc* groups.

The Secretariat is located in Geneva and provides the services necessary for the meetings of the Commission and its subsidiary bodies. It is responsible, *inter alia*, for the publication of general and specialized periodic surveys and reviews, including statistical bulletins. The Commission's Executive Secretary is nominated by the UN Secretary General and acts on his behalf but enjoys considerable autonomy in practice. A well-known Swedish economist, Gunnar Myrdal, served as Executive Secretary from the beginning until 1957 and left a remarkable imprint on the Commission's activities and diplomatic initiatives.

The Commission co-operates with the relevant UN specialized agencies and other international organizations as well as with the other four regional economic commissions. Effective co-operation has existed since the mid-1960s between the Commission and the *UN Conference on Trade and Development (UNCTAD); there are also close ties with the *UN Environment Programme (UNEP) and the *UN Development Programme (UNDP). The Commission serves as executing agency for the latter. The *European Economic Community (EEC) and the *Danube Commission were granted consultative status within the Commission in 1975. The Commission is also linked with the *Conference on Security and Co-operation in Europe (CSCE) whose Final Act was signed in Helsinki in August 1975. It formally records the wish of the signatory countries to take advantage of the possibilities offered by the Commission with respect to the multilateral implementation of the pertinent provisions of the Act.

Since its foundation the Commission has been deeply involved in a wide variety of activities, ranging from its early reconstruction problems following World War II through to East-West economic co-operation issues. Although inevitably affected by the overall political climate prevailing in East-West relations, the Commission has made substantive efforts effectively to use the available opportunities and to adopt a realistic and essentially pragmatic approach to the most controversial issues, ultimately acting as a bridge between the two halves of the continent. In this connection the Commission has attempted to develop intra-European co-operation to the fullest extent practicable within its competence and resources.

The Commission's continuing search for solutions to problems of common concern to member countries has concentrated on the areas covered by its Principal Subsidiary Bodies. A strong emphasis has been placed for several decades on the expansion of trade between centrally-planned and market-economy countries on mutually favourable terms and the correlative elimination of restrictive and discriminatory practices. Facilities have been provided with regard to arbitration, insurance, standardization of general conditions of sale of goods, payment arrangements, and compensation procedures and consultations. The Commission has rendered valuable technical assistance in the field of industrial co-operation; long-term agreements rose from 100 to 1000 within a decade, thereby contributing to the growth of specialization between East and West. Major studies have been completed by the Commission in the fields of industrial co-operation, compensation trade and inventory of obstacles to trade. Continuing attention has been given to various branches of industrial activity, particularly steel, chemicals, engineering and automation. The Commission's work has also proved fruitful with regard to problems arising from mechanization and rationalization in agriculture, and market conditions of agricultural products.

Selected problems of economic policy are considered at regular intervals by high-level governmental experts and medium- and long-term projections, joint research projects and other studies are carried out with a view to facilitating the harmonization of economic policies of member countries. Scientific and technological developments and their related problems are kept under close review and proposals have been put forward towards further international co-operation.

With regard to energy problems, including energy resources and national policies, special attention has been devoted by the Commission to the economic and technical aspects of energy supplies in the face of growing demand and complex conservation and substitution problems. Rising demand for water has led the Commission to undertake a review of major trends and policies concerning use and development of water resources. With regard to environmental questions, the Commission surveys and assesses the state of the environment in the region and considers national policies, institutions and laws, as well as the international implications of environmental policies.

A number of international agreements covering aspects of road, rail, and inland water transport are in force following their adoption through the Commission; increased attention is devoted to transport policy and infrastructure while operational projects are being carried out in conjunction with UNDP. Improvement of national statistics in various fields, exchange of technical information and publication of general and specialized reports have also helped strengthen links between the countries of the region.

Most industrial countries of the world are members of the Commission which has therefore been actively engaged in working out concessions from developed to developing countries. Besides facing the new tasks of integrating the emerging market economies of Eastern Europe into a wider European framework, steps have been taken by the Commission to develop activities of special interest to its less privileged member countries, particularly in the fields of trade statistics, electric power, transport, agriculture and co-operation in the Mediterranean basin.

Executive Secretary: Gerald Hinteregger

Headquarters: Palais des Nations, 1211 Geneva 10, Switzerland (telephone: 731 0211; telex: 412962; fax: 733 9879 – 734 9825)

Publications: *Economic Survey of Europe* (annually); *Economic Bulletin for Europe*; *Annual Report*; separate annual and quarterly bulletins of statistics covering agriculture, timber, coal, general energy, electric energy, gas, chemicals, steel, housing and building, transport and engineering products

References: J. Siotis: 'The United Nations Economic Commission for Europe and the Emerging European System', *International Conciliation*, 561 (1967), 5–72; UN: *ECE: Three Decades of the UN ECE* (New York 1978); F. Parkinson: 'The Role of the UN Economic Commission for Europe', *East-West Relations. Prospects for the 1980s*, ed. G. Schiavone (London, 1982), 111–32

Economic Commission for Latin America and the Caribbean (ECLAC). The Commission is responsible for facilitating and stimulating concerted action by member countries with regard to regional and national development problems, the expansion of mutual trade, and economic integration. It is one of the five regional economic commissions of the UN operating under the authority of the Economic and Social Council – the *Economic Commission for Africa (ECA), the *Economic Commission for Europe (ECE), the *Economic and Social Commission for Western Asia (ESCWA) and the *Economic and Social Commission for Asia and the Pacific (ESCAP).

It came into being in February 1948 by resolution of the Economic and Social Council as a subsidiary organ of the UN under the name of Economic Commission for Latin America. The reference to the Caribbean was added to the title in 1984. Besides the countries of the region, the Commission includes as full members: Canada, France, the Netherlands, Portugal, Spain, the UK and the USA. There are five associate members: Aruba, the British Virgin Islands, Montserrat, the Netherlands Antilles, and the US Virgin Islands.

Established under the pressure of several Latin American countries concerned about the urgency and magnitude of their economic difficulties and dissatisfied with the policies of the USA towards its southern neighbours, the Commission initially considered measures for dealing with the basic problems of the period following World War II and for raising the levels of economic activity in the region. Subsequently, considerable emphasis has been given to a wide range of objectives including: systematic preparation of indicators of economic and social development at national, subregional and regional levels; improvement of planning machinery and techniques and the training of officials and experts; management of the environment and water resources; promotion and strengthening of economic integration within subregional and regional groupings and between these groupings and other organizations of the inter-American and world systems.

The Commission's functions and powers, according to the terms of reference laid down by the Economic and Social Council, are essentially related to the primary task of promoting economic development through concerted measures including technical co-operation and other forms of operational activities. The Commission is also responsible for dealing with the social aspects of economic development and the relationship between economic and social factors. The annual report of the Commission is submitted to the Economic and Social Council; the budget is subject to the approval of the UN General Assembly.

The Commission normally holds biennial sessions, with participation of the representatives of all member countries, in one of the Latin American capitals. Permanent subsidiary bodies have been created by the Commission such as the Central American Economic Co-operation Committee, the Caribbean Development and Co-operation Committee, the Committee of High-Level Government Experts, and many specialized subcommittees. The Secretariat is located in Santiago, Chile, with a subregional office in Mexico City, a subregional headquarters for the Caribbean in Port of Spain, and offices in Bogotá, Brasilia, Buenos Aires, Montevideo and Washington. The Secretariat operates in the following areas: development issues and policies; energy; environment, jointly with the *UN Environment Programme (UNEP); food and agriculture, jointly with the *Food and Agriculture Organization (FAO); human settlements, jointly with the *UN Centre for Human Settlements (UNCHS); industrial development; international trade and development financing; natural resources; population; science and technology; social development and humanitarian affairs; statistics; transnational corporations; and transport.

A significant role was played in the early years of the Commission by the Argentine economist Raúl Prebisch who served as its first Executive Secretary.

The Latin American and Caribbean Institute for Economic and Social Planning (ILPES) was set up in June 1962 under the aegis of the Commission with financial support from the UN, the *Inter-American Development Bank (IDB), and several Latin American governments, and with the co-operation of the *Organization of American States (OAS), the *International Labour Organization (ILO), the *UN Children's Fund (UNICEF) and other international agencies. The Institute, whose headquarters are located in Santiago, Chile, provides training services with international and national courses and advisory assistance mainly concerning long-term strategies and medium-term plans and fosters co-operation among national planning bodies.

The Latin American Demographic Centre (CELADE), set up in 1957 and located in Santiago, Chile, became an integral part of the Commission in 1975. The Centre, with financial assistance from the *UN Development Programme (UNDP) and the *UN Population Fund (UNFPA), investigates the determining factors and consequences of population dynamics, prepares population estimates and projections, carries out advisory activities through numerous technical assistance missions to different countries of the region and conducts post-graduate courses and seminars.

The Latin American Centre for Economic and Social Documentation (CLADES) undertakes the collection, evaluation and publication of socio-economic documentation and information.

The Commission works in close collaboration with UN Headquarters and with specialized agencies and other organizations. Several programmes of activities are carried out by the Commission with UNDP, UNEP, UNFPA, UNICEF, UNIDO, FAO, ILO, the *UN Conference on Trade and Development (UNCTAD), the *International Maritime Organization (IMO) and the *International Bank for Reconstruction and Development (IBRD). Intense working relations are also maintained with regional organizations such as OAS, IDB and the *Latin American Economic System (SELA).

Since its establishment, the Commission has played a very active role in fostering intraregional co-operation and integration, assisting in the creation of the Latin American Free Trade Association

(LAFTA), the *Central American Common Market (CACM) and SELA, and co-operating with the *Andean Group and the *Caribbean Community (CARICOM). Intraregional co-operation has been improved and extended to cover a growing number of areas. Substantive steps have been taken to define different degrees of preferential treatment among Latin American countries according to their respective level of economic development. In 1980 this concept was embodied in the treaty establishing the *Latin American Integration Association (LAIA) as an area of economic preferences.

While retaining the specific economic and social needs of Latin America as its basic priority, in recent years the Commission has approached regional issues within the broader framework of North-South relations with the aim of gradually reducing inequality between developed and developing countries. A major contribution has been made by the Commission in order to establish and improve the Generalized System of Preferences (GSP). Other fields of action are represented by the transfer of resources, international monetary reform, science and technology, industrialization, food and agriculture.

In collaboration with SELA, the Commission organized the Latin American Economic Conference held in Quito, Ecuador, in January 1984, to discuss, in particular, the problems of renegotiation and service of the foreign debt. A special conference to examine national and international strategies for the region's economic recovery was held in January 1987; a regional conference on poverty took place in August 1988. The deterioration of the economic and social situation in the region throughout the 1980s prompted the Commission in May 1990 to advance proposals for overcoming the most serious obstacles to growth such as the heavy external debt, high interest rates, barriers against Latin American exports and low commodity prices. The strategies of Latin America and the Caribbean for the 1990s are being considered by the Commission in the prospect of the eventual transformation of the productive structures of the region within a context of increased democracy, progressively greater social equity and overall improvement in the quality of life.

Executive Secretary: Gert Rosenthal
Headquarters: United Nations Building, Avenida Dag Hammarskjold, P.O. Box 179 D, Santiago, Chile (telephone: 485051; telex: 340295 Transradio)
Publications: *Economic Survey of Latin America* (annually); *Statistical Yearbook for Latin America*; *CEPAL Review* (three times a year)
References: B.G. Ramcharan: 'Equality and Discrimination in International Economic Law (VIII): The United Nations Regional Economic Commissions', *Year Book of World Affairs*, 32 (1978), 268–85; F.H. Cardoso: *The Originality of the Copy: ECLA and the Idea of Development* (Cambridge, 1977)

Economic Community of the Great Lakes Countries [Communauté économique des pays des Grands Lacs] (CEPGL). The general purpose of the Community is to foster economic and political co-operation between Burundi, Rwanda and Zaire. From the mid-1960s onwards several meetings were held and attended by Heads of State and Foreign Ministers; the Community was formally established in September 1976. Its aims are to protect the security of member countries and their peoples by maintaining order and tranquillity at the respective borders, to promote and expand the free movement of persons and goods, and to undertake concerted efforts with respect to economic and political matters.

The Community's supreme organ is the Conference of the Heads of State which ordinarily meets once a year and issues directives to be implemented by its executive organ, the Council of Ministers of Foreign Affairs. The Permanent Executive Secretariat, based in Rwanda, provides administrative services. There are also a Consultative Commission and three Specialized Technical Commissions.

Four specialized agencies have been set up: the Development Bank of the Great Lakes Countries (BDEGL), based in Goma, Zaire; the Organization of CEPGL for

Energy, based in Bujumbura, Burundi; the Institute of Agronomic and Zoological Research, based in Gitega, Burundi; and a regional electricity company (SINELAC), based in Bukavu, Zaire. A number of projects in selected fields of the economy, including agriculture and industry as well as energy production from both renewable and non-renewable sources, are being developed. There are links with several international and national institutions.

Executive Secretary: Salvador Matata
Headquarters: P.O. Box 58, Gisenyi, Rwanda (telephone: 40228; telex: 602; fax: 40785)
Publication: *Grands Lacs* (quarterly)

Economic Community of West African States (ECOWAS). The Community involves 16 English-, French-, Portuguese- and Arab-speaking West African countries in a wide-ranging economic integration scheme originally aimed at establishing a customs union and the free movement of people, services and capital, as well as developing common economic policies and promoting physical integration – especially regarding energy, transportation and communications.

The basic legal instrument of the Community is the Treaty signed in Lagos, Nigeria, in May 1975 by the Heads of State and Government of Benin, Côte d'Ivoire, Gambia, Ghana, Guinea, Guinea-Bissau, Liberia, Mali, Mauritania, Niger, Nigeria, Senegal, Sierra Leone, Togo, and Upper Volta [now Burkina Faso]. Cape Verde joined the Community in 1977.

The implementation of several basic provisions of the Treaty required the subsequent adoption of five different Protocols concerning: (a) the definition of the contents of products originating from member countries; (b) the re-export within the Community of goods imported from third countries; (c) the assessment of loss of revenue incurred by member countries as a result of their participation in the Community; (d) the functioning of the Fund for Co-operation, Compensation and Development; and (e) the determination of contributions of member countries to the

budget of the Community. All of these Protocols were ratified in November 1976.

The conclusion of the Treaty of Lagos represented a significant step towards the implementation of a flexible economic co-operation and integration scheme embracing the entire West African subregion. The first attempts to institutionalize co-operation between the English and French-speaking groups of countries in West Africa were undertaken in the early 1960s under the auspices of the *UN Economic Commission for Africa (ECA). As a result, a document entitled 'Articles of Association for the Establishment of an Economic Community of West Africa' was signed by the representatives of 14 countries in May 1967 in Accra, Ghana. It provided for the creation of an interim body in charge of the preparation of a draft treaty for the proposed Community. In practice, however, the initiative proved overly ambitious and met with stubborn resistance from many prospective participants. As a result, plans to set up an organization overcoming linguistic and cultural barriers and comprising the whole of West Africa had to be shelved for a number of years. A new and more realistic approach to subregional co-operation was proposed by Nigeria and Togo in early 1972 and later materialized in a detailed draft which was extensively discussed and revised at several meetings of experts and summit conferences. The formal document establishing the Community was eventually approved by the 14 original countries plus Guinea-Bissau at the Lagos Conference.

The Community is based on the full recognition of the 'realities' prevailing in the different member countries and of the existence of other inter-governmental organizations and economic groupings within the subregion. Relations between member countries are governed by the principles contained in the Declaration on African Co-operation, Development and Economic Independence adopted at Addis Ababa in 1973 by the Assembly of the Heads of State and Government of the *Organization of African Unity (OAU).

The aim of the Community is to promote co-operation and development in all fields of economic activity, especially industry, transport, telecommunications, energy, agriculture, natural resources, commerce, monetary and financial questions, as well as social and cultural matters, with a view to raising the standard of living of the peoples of the subregion, increasing and maintaining economic stability, improving relations among member countries and contributing to the progress and development of the African continent. Member countries are supposed to plan and direct their respective policies with a view to creating favourable conditions for the achievement of the aims of the Community and to take all steps to ensure the enactment of such legislation as may be necessary to implement the provisions of the Treaty.

The Community's objectives are to be pursued by stages through a pragmatic and flexible approach since no rigorous scale of priorities has been set. More precisely, the Community is responsible for gradually ensuring: (a) the elimination of customs duties and quantitative and administrative restrictions on trade between member countries; (b) the establishment of a common tariff and common commercial policy *vis-à-vis* third countries; (c) the removal of all types of barriers to the free movement of persons, services and capital between member countries; (d) the harmonization of agricultural policies and furtherance of joint projects concerning research, marketing and agro-industrial activities; (e) the co-ordination of policies in the fields of transport, communication, energy and infrastructural projects; (f) the harmonization of economic and industrial policies in the most important sectors with a view to eliminating disparities in the levels of economic development; (g) the harmonization of monetary and financial policies; and (h) the setting up of a Fund for Co-operation, Compensation and Development.

The functions and powers of the Community, in conformity with its objectives, are illustrated by the sections of the Treaty of Lagos which define the main guidelines, indicate the basic ways and means to be adopted and set the deadlines for carrying out certain tasks. The full establishment of the customs union was planned over a 15-year transitional period. During the first two years import duties on intra-

Community trade had to be frozen, that is maintained at their existing levels, and then progressively eliminated over the next eight years; due account had to be taken of the effects of such elimination on the revenue of the member countries concerned. Quotas, restrictions, prohibitions and other administrative obstacles to trade of equivalent effect, as well as internal charges and revenue duties imposed for the protection of domestic goods, were to be abolished in the first ten years. In the remaining five years of the transitional period, existing differences in external customs tariffs of member countries had to be gradually eliminated, common customs and statistical nomenclatures had to be adopted and finally a common customs tariff had to be introduced in respect of all goods imported into the Community from third countries.

As regards the movement of persons, agreements had to be concluded in order to ensure for all citizens of the Community the rights of entry, residence and establishment, allowing them to work and undertake industrial and commercial activities in any member country. Efforts had to be directed by member countries towards the harmonization of their internal and external agricultural policies and the joint development (including research, production, processing and marketing) of their natural resources, especially in agriculture, forestry, animal husbandry and fisheries. Common transport and communication policies – involving *inter alia* the drafting of plans for a comprehensive system of all-weather road links, possible merger of national air carriers, establishment of multinational shipping companies for both maritime and river navigation, and restructuring of national telecommunications network – were considered a necessary condition for the free circulation of goods, services and persons. Consultations were envisaged among member countries for the co-ordination of the various national policies in the fields of energy and mineral resources. On monetary and financial issues the harmonization of the policies of the member countries had to be attained through various means and at different levels. With respect to payments, it was envisaged to set up, in the short term, bilateral systems for the settlement of accounts between member countries and, in the long term, a multilateral system covering the whole Community.

Membership in the Community is open to any West African country on terms and conditions to be established by the Community itself. A member may withdraw from the Community by giving one month's written notice; however, for one full year thereafter the seceding country will still be bound by the provisions of the Treaty and remain liable for the discharge of its obligations. Members of the Community may participate in other regional or subregional institutions to the extent that such participation is not incompatible with the Treaty of Lagos.

The principal organs through which the Community accomplishes its purposes are the Conference of Heads of State and Government, the Council of Ministers, and the Executive Secretariat, assisted by Technical and Specialized Commissions and Committees. Provision was also made for the establishment of a judicial organ, the Tribunal of the Community, responsible for the interpretation of the provisions of the Treaty and for the settlement of disputes referred to it; the organization and powers of the Tribunal have not, as yet, been set out in detail.

Under the present organizational structure, the Conference of Heads of State and Government is the supreme body whose decisions are binding on all other organs. It meets once a year in the capital of a member country under a chairman drawn from members in annual rotation.

The Council of Ministers consists of two representatives from each country and meets not less than twice a year. It is empowered to keep under review the general operation of the Community, to address recommendations to the Conference, and to give directions to all subordinate institutions. The Council's decisions and directions are binding on these institutions unless otherwise provided by the Conference. Each country in turn has the chairmanship of the Council for one year.

The Executive Secretariat – headed by an Executive Secretary appointed by the Conference for a four-year term renewable once only – is in charge of the administrative and technical functions servicing and assisting the institutions of the Community. The Executive Secretary is assisted by two Deputy Executive Secretaries and a Financial Controller.

There are five Specialized Commissions which are responsible for: (a) trade, customs, immigration, monetary and payments matters; (b) industry, agriculture and natural resources; (c) transport, telecommunications and energy; (d) social and cultural affairs; and (e) administration and finance. Additional commissions may be set up by the Conference whenever the need arises. Each commission consists of one representative from each member country and meets as often as necessary to consider the specific problems within its competence. Reports and recommendations are submitted periodically through the Executive Secretary to the Council of Ministers. Two Committees have been created to further co-operation in monetary and financial matters with a view to liberalizing capital movements and facilitating investments within the territory of the Community.

The Fund for Co-operation, Compensation and Development is intended: to finance subregional programmes; to provide compensation to member countries which have suffered losses by reducing duties or granting concessions in consequence of the establishment of the Community; to mobilize internal and external financial resources towards investment; and to support development projects in the least-developed member countries.

The Community has established links with other international economic organizations operating within and outside the African continent. Delicate problems have arisen with regard to relations with other economic and political groupings in West Africa, such as the *West African Economic Community (CEAO) and the *Entente Council. A promising area of co-operation is represented by the Community's growing ties with non-African economic institutions, especially the *European Economic Community (EEC).

The Community's budget, including all

ordinary expenditures other than those in respect of the Fund for Co-operation, Compensation and Development, is prepared by the Executive Secretariat and submitted to the Council of Ministers for approval. Each member country is supposed to pay its annual contributions regularly, unless prevented by exceptional circumstances that adversely affect its economy. Unjustified failure to pay might result in suspension from participation in the Community's institutions. However, substantial arrears have accumulated over the years and have seriously hindered the Community's prospects of development.

The Community started operations in 1977 after the ratification of the Protocols bringing some key provisions of the Treaty of Lagos into effect, the appointment of the Executive Secretary, and the decision to establish the headquarters of the Community in Lagos. The Fund for Co-operation, Compensation and Development initiated its activities at Lomé, Togo in 1982. The authorized capital was raised from $90 million to $360 million in 1986. The decision was taken in 1988 to open the Fund to the participation of non-regional countries.

The implementation of the basic goals of the Community has met with several obstacles, the major one probably being the lack of commitment on the part of the governments of the member countries which has materialized, *inter alia*, in the failure to pay contributions on a regular basis and in the unwillingness to translate into effective national policies the Community's decisions. Customs duties on intra-Community trade were frozen for a two-year period from May 1979 to May 1981; the elimination of duties had to be completed by 1989. However, a number of difficulties have made it necessary to set new deadlines, providing for a different treatment according to the stage of development of the member countries concerned. The countries which are relatively more developed (Côte d'Ivoire, Ghana, Nigeria and Senegal) will abolish certain import duties faster than the 'intermediate' members, while even longer periods have been fixed for the 'least developed' countries (Burkina Faso, Cape Verde, The

Gambia, Guinea-Bissau, Mali, Mauritania and Niger). Common customs and statistical nomenclatures and a code of standards and definitions have been agreed upon. A free trade area has been established since May 1981 for handicrafts and unprocessed agricultural products. Agreement was reached during 1982 on an Agricultural Development Strategy aimed at achieving regional self-sufficiency by the year 2000.

In 1983 the decision was taken to initiate studies on the formation of a single monetary zone; in June 1990 the Conference of the Heads of State and Government adopted measures with a view to setting up the zone by 1994. Studies undertaken in 1984 concerning the establishment of a regional investment bank led to the creation of Ecobank Transnational which started operations in Lomé in March 1988. New road and rail links between member countries are being developed; a programme for the improvement of air traffic safety is under way. As regards the free circulation of citizens of the Community, the provision concerning the right of entry without visa came into force in July 1980. A programme for the improvement and integration of the telecommunications network is under way, the first two phases having already been completed in October 1988. Specific projects concerning co-operation in the field of energy are under consideration. The creation of an Energy Resources Development Fund was approved in 1982.

The problems of political co-operation and security are not envisaged by the Treaty of Lagos but are being considered increasingly by member countries. A protocol on non-aggression was signed in April 1978 by the Heads of State and Government and was followed in May 1981 by a pact on mutual defence agreed upon by 13 members. An attempt at mediating in the civil war in Liberia was made in 1990 and an ECOWAS Monitoring Group (ECOMOG) was sent to that country in order to prevent further conflict and establish an interim government until elections could be held. Despite the subsequent increase in the number of troops participating in ECOMOG, further fighting took place among rival groups but ultimately an agreement was reached by the various factions for restoring peace in the country. A special committee was created in 1991 to review the Treaty of Lagos in order to accelerate the enforcement of decisions.

Executive Secretary: Dr Abass Bundu

Headquarters: 6 King George V Road, PMB 12745, Lagos, Nigeria (telephone: 636841; telex: 22633)

References: T.O. Elias: 'The Economic Community of West Africa', *Year Book of World Affairs*, 32 (1978), 93–116; O.J.B. Ojo: 'Nigeria and the Formation of ECOWAS', *International Organization*, 34 (1980), 571–604

ECOWAS. *See* **Economic Community of West African States.**

EFTA. *See* **European Free Trade Association.**

Entente Council [Conseil de l'Entente]. The Council is an association pledged to promote harmonization of mutual relations among member countries in political and economic matters. It was founded in May 1959 in Abidjan, Côte d'Ivoire, by the representatives of Côte d'Ivoire, Dahomey [renamed Benin in 1975], Niger, and Upper Volta [renamed Burkina Faso in 1984], which were at that time autonomous republics within the French Community after having been territories of French West Africa from 1904; the four countries attained full independence in August 1960. Togo, independent from April 1960, joined the Council in June 1966.

According to the founding document, the Council has no supranational features and its co-ordination activities are based on the principles of friendship, fraternity and solidarity among members. The Council's functions and powers are broadly defined in conformity with the loose character of the association; all decisions are to be taken by unanimous consent.

The main organ of the Council – originally conceived as the deliberating and executive body of the Union of Sahel-Benin – is the Conference of the Heads of State of member countries, assisted by those ministers who are responsible for the matters on the agenda of each particular meeting. Ordinary sessions are held annually, the place rotating each year between members, and are chaired by the Head of State of the host country; extraordinary sessions may be convened at the request of at least two members. The Conference of the Heads of State held in March 1960 decided to set up a Secretariat charged with limited administrative functions and headed by an Administrative Secretary appointed annually by the Chairman of the Conference. However, secretaries were nominated only for the first three years. In 1963 Dahomey experienced a major political crisis and abstained from participating in the Council's activities until January 1965. In May 1970 the Conference of the Heads of State decided to establish a Council of Ministers in order to improve the activities of the Council and to increase efficiency.

To foster economic and financial co-operation, the Council's founding document provided for the creation of a Solidarity Fund whose resources, mainly contributed by the Côte d'Ivoire, had to be redistributed for the benefit of the least-developed members. The comparative ineffectiveness of the Solidarity Fund led to its transformation in June 1966 into a stronger body, the Mutual Aid and Loan Guarantee Fund (Fonds d'entraide et de garantie des emprunts). The new financial institution aimed to promote economic growth in the region, to assist in the preparation of specific projects and to mobilize funds from other sources, acting as a guarantee fund for loans granted to member countries for profitable agricultural, industrial and infrastructural projects and encouraging trade and investment between member countries. In December 1973 another agreement was signed in order to empower the Fund to finance the reduction of interest rates and the extension of maturity periods of foreign loans to member countries. The resources of the Fund consist of annual contributions from member countries, subsidies and grants, as well as investment returns and commissions from guarantee operations.

At the end of 1989 the Fund's capital amounted to 15,797 million francs CFA. The Fund has supported projects for the improvement of crops, breeding of livestock, assistance to small and medium-sized enterprises, standardization, vocational training, production of geological maps, and improvement of transport and telecommunications network. Financial aid for the projects was also provided by external donors, mainly France and the USA.

The Executive Board of the Fund holds annual sessions and is vested with all governing powers which have been to a large extent delegated to the Management Committee, comprising three representatives from each member country and meeting twice a year. The Executive Board is composed of the Heads of State of member countries and therefore has the same membership as the Entente Council. The Secretariat of the Fund is headed by an Administrative Secretary. It also provides technical and administrative services to the Council which in practice has been gradually absorbed by the Fund. Economic and financial co-ordination among member countries has in fact gained priority over issues related to political co-operation.

Administrative Secretary: Paul Kaya

Headquarters: Mutual Aid and Loan Guarantee Fund, 01 BP 3734, Abidjan, Côte d'Ivoire (telephone: 332835; telex: 23558; fax: 331149)

Publications: *Rapport d'activité* (annually); *Entente Africaine* (quarterly)

ESA. *See* **European Space Agency.**

ESCAP. *See* **Economic and Social Commission for Asia and the Pacific.**

ESCWA. *See* **Economic and Social Commission for Western Asia.**

European Bank for Reconstruction and Development (EBRD). The Bank is intended to provide multilateral financing of projects and investment programmes in the countries of Central and Eastern Europe.

The Bank was established in May 1990 by countries of Western and Eastern Europe along with major industrial countries outside Europe to contribute to the progress and economic reconstruction of the former socialist countries willing to respect and put into practice the principles of multi-party democracy and a market economy. Membership of the Bank totals about 55 countries together with the *European Economic Community (EEC) and the *European Investment Bank (EIB). The Bank started operations at its headquarters in London in April 1991.

The Bank's objectives are to provide advice, loans and equity investment and debt guarantees to qualified applicants with a view to fostering the transition towards democracy and open market-oriented economies and to promoting private and entrepreneurial initiative. The Bank lends and invests exclusively in 'countries of operations', that is the nations of Central and Eastern Europe, including the republics of the former USSR and Yugoslavia. The Bank's mandate gives it a special concern for the promotion of democratic institutions and human rights as well as of environmentally sound and sustainable development in its countries of operations.

The Bank's resources include the subscribed capital stock and the funds borrowed in capital markets to supplement the equity capital. The initially subscribed capital of the Bank amounts to ECU10 billion (about $12 billion), of which ECU3 billion will be paid in. The EEC members together with the European Commission and EIB hold 51 per cent, Central and Eastern European countries 13.5 per cent, the USA 10 per cent, Japan 8.5 per cent.

The Bank is a unique combination of merchant bank and development bank. Not less than 60 per cent of the Bank's funding will be directed to private sector enterprises or state-owned enterprises implementing a programme to achieve private ownership and control; not more than 40 per cent will be directed to public infrastructure or other projects.

Funds are granted in accordance with sound banking and investment principles and within commercial decision-making time frames. More precisely, funding is offered on a market rather than on a subsidized or concessionary basis, including: loans with a maximum final maturity of 10 years for commercial enterprises and of 15 years for infrastructure projects; equity; guarantees and underwriting. Loans are usually denominated in convertible currencies or currency units; as a matter of policy, the Bank does not accept currency risk on repayment. The Bank does not issue guarantees for export credits nor undertake insurance activities. It is important to stress that loans to commercial enterprises, including those made to state-owned enterprises implementing a programme to achieve private ownership and control, are granted without government guarantees and require a full commercial return. The Bank limits its financing normally to 35 per cent of the total cost of a borrower's total capital on a *pro forma*, market-value basis. The Bank does not take controlling interests nor assume direct responsibility for the management of enterprises. In a number of cases, the Bank may offer financial advice and training and technical assistance on the basis of funds specifically provided by certain of its member governments.

The organization of the Bank, which is largely similar to that of other international financial institutions, comprises the Board of Governors, vested with full management powers, the Board of Directors, responsible for current operations, and the President.

The Bank co-operates with other international financial organizations and with a range of public and private financial institutions through co-financing arrangements.

In 1991 the Bank approved 14 projects for a total amount of ECU472 million. Proposals were made at the Bank's first annual meeting in April 1992 in Budapest for extending the institution's mandate to include low-interest loans and the acquisition of equity stakes in high-risk projects; this would have favoured, *inter alia*, the conversion of military industries in the former Eastern bloc to civilian production.

However, the decision was eventually taken not to enlarge the Bank's scope of operations.

President: Jacques Attali
Headquarters: 122 Leadenhall Street, London EC3V 4EB, England (telephone: 338 6000; fax: 338 6100)

European Communities. The basic purpose of the three Communities is to bring about a merging of the essential economic interests of the member countries through the gradual establishment and maintenance of common markets involving the elimination of all barriers to the free movement of goods, persons, services and capital and the adoption of common policies; beyond the attainment of economic and social objectives, political integration is regarded as the ultimate aim of the Communities.

In order to establish co-operation between the old war-enemies, France and Germany, in May 1950 the French Minister of Foreign Affairs, M. Robert Schuman, proposed a plan to place the entire coal and steel production of France and Germany under the control of an independent High Authority, within the framework of an organization open to the participation of other European countries. Belgium, Italy, Luxembourg, the Netherlands and the Federal Republic of Germany (gradually becoming integrated into the Western alliance system as the occupation statute was phased out) accepted the French invitation to take part in a conference to consider the Schuman Plan. Negotiations between the six countries culminated with the signing in Paris, in April 1951, of the Treaty setting up the European Coal and Steel Community (ECSC). The Treaty of Paris, effective from July 1952, provided for the pooling of coal and steel production of the member countries and was regarded as a first step towards a united Europe. However, attempts to establish a political union met with overwhelming difficulties between 1952 and 1953, while plans for the establishment of a European Defence Community (EDC) eventually collapsed after rejection by the French National Assembly in August 1954.

The success of the sectoral integration scheme put into effect by the ECSC encouraged efforts to expand the common market to other major areas. At the Conference of Foreign Ministers of the ECSC member countries held in Messina, Italy, in June 1955, plans were laid down for the creation of two more communities aimed at gradually integrating the economies of the Six as well as paving the way towards closer political co-ordination. The UK was invited to the Messina Conference but refused to attend. After extensive negotiations, the European Economic Community (EEC) and the European Atomic Energy Community (Euratom) were set up under separate treaties signed in Rome in March 1957 and entered into effect in January 1958. The Treaties of Rome contained provisions for the establishment by stages, over a transitional period, of a common market, including as its core a customs union, and the approximation of economic policies, as well as for the promotion of growth in nuclear industries for peaceful purposes. Although the three Communities were established as distinct organizations, based upon separate constituent treaties, their institutional structure was similar. Each Community was endowed with its own executive organ (called Commission in both the EEC and Euratom and High Authority in the ECSC and composed of individuals acting only in the Community's interest) and an organ representing the governments of member countries and responsible for policy-making (called Council in both the EEC and Euratom and Special Council of Ministers in the ECSC).

Simultaneously with the signing of the Treaties of Rome, a 'Convention relating to certain institutions common to the European Communities' was concluded, providing a single Court of Justice to replace the ECSC Court, and one Assembly, to be called the European Parliamentary Assembly, for all three Communities. Subsequently, a Treaty was signed in Brussels in April 1965 and entered into effect in July 1967. It established a single Council and a single Commission, thereby transferring to these institutions the various powers (unchanged) of the corresponding bodies of the ECSC, the EEC and Euratom. The merger of the institutions was envisaged as a first step towards the merger of the Communities; at present each of the three Communities retains its distinct legal personality. The Court of Auditors of the European Communities, created in pursuance of a provision of the second Budget Treaty in force since June 1977, is responsible for the external audit of the Community budget and the ECSC operational budget; the Court, however, does not have the full status of a Community institution. In response to the need for frequent consultation at the highest level on major Community and foreign policy topics, it was decided at a summit held in Paris in December 1974 that the Heads of State or Government of the member countries should meet periodically as the European Council.

The first negotiations over British entry into the Communities took place between 1961 and 1963 and eventually failed because of French opposition. In June 1970 membership negotiations began between the Six and Denmark, Ireland, Norway and the UK; these four countries signed the Treaty of Accession to the EEC and Euratom in January 1972 in Brussels. The accession of the new members to the ECSC was enacted, in accordance with the Treaty of Paris, by a decision of the Council of the European Communities. Ireland, Denmark, and the UK became full members of the Communities in January 1973 when the instruments concerning the accession entered into effect. Norway held a popular referendum in September 1972 which rejected entry into the Communities and eventually decided not to accede. The Treaty concerning the accession of Greece was signed in May 1979 and came into force in January 1981. At the end of a process which had begun in May 1979 with the introduction of home rule and the gradual transfer of certain powers from Denmark to the local government, Greenland left the Community in February 1985 and became an overseas territory associated with the Community. In the consultative referendum, held in February

1982, a 52 per cent majority of Greenlanders had voted for their country's withdrawal from the Community.

Negotiations for the entry of Portugal and Spain had been largely completed by early 1985. The instruments of accession were signed in Lisbon and Madrid in June 1985 and became effective in January 1986. The enlargement of the Community was accompanied by renewed efforts to promote European integration and by a wide-ranging debate about the Community's political and institutional future which culminated in the signing, in February 1986, of the Single European Act. The Single Act, which represents so far the most radical revision of the Treaty of Rome, entered into force in July 1987. Not only did the Single Act constitute an expression of the willingness of the member countries to implement basic objectives – completion of the unified internal market by the end of 1992 and strengthening of economic and social cohesion – but also modified the institutional system by rehabilitating majority voting in the Council of Ministers, providing for greater involvement of the European Parliament in the decision-making process, and strengthening political co-operation.

Meeting in December 1989, the European Council decided to convene an intergovernmental conference on economic and monetary union (EMU); in June 1990 the decision was taken to hold a second intergovernmental conference on political union. Following these decisions, two parallel intergovernmental conferences (IGCs) opened in December 1990 in Rome and continued to work in parallel throughout 1991.

The IGCs ended, at the Maastricht European Council of December 1991, with an agreement on the draft Treaty on European union; after legal editing and harmonization of the texts, the Treaty was actually signed in February 1992 and had to be ratified by the parliaments of all EC member countries. There is now a commitment to progressive economic and monetary union (EMU) based on the introduction of a single currency and the establishment of a European central bank before 1999. The ever closer union agreed upon at Maastricht also incorporates the concept of European citizenship, the creation of a cohesion fund, an increase in Community powers in several fields and the strengthening of democratic legitimacy. Another major step forward is the inclusion of provisions covering all areas of foreign and security policy and establishing systematic co-operation among member countries in the pursuit of their policies in the form of joint action. The decisive stimulus thus given to the integration process should ensure for the Community a real political role in the new world order that emerges in the post-Cold War era. The deepening of the Community will be all the more crucial in the face of the coming enlargement. Besides other Western and Southern European countries applying for membership, the newly democratic countries of Central and Eastern Europe are seeking closer relations with the Community as a means of anchoring themselves firmly in a free and pluralistic Europe. Following the unification of Germany in October 1990, the former German Democratic Republic immediately became part of the Communities, although a transitional period was envisaged before fully applying certain Community legislation.

Future enlargements are likely to affect the structure of the Community and the balance between its institutions to a very great extent. It seems beyond doubt that the present structures, developed over four decades to arrange for six and then 12 countries, cannot be stretched to accommodate 25 or even 30 members. It is expected, however, that future changes will not radically alter the basic functions of the institutions as they are described below.

The Commission – consisting of 17 members chosen on the grounds of their general competence and appointed by mutual agreement between the governments of the member countries for a renewable four-year term – acts independently in the general interest of the Community. Its basic task is the implementation of the Treaties, and in this it has the right of both initiative and execution. The President and Vice-Presidents of the Commission are appointed for renewable two-year terms. The Commission works on the principle of collegiate responsibility but each member is responsible for a particular sector. It may not include more than two members having the nationality of the same country. At present, the Commission includes two members for the following countries: France, Germany, Italy, Spain and the UK; the other countries have one member each. The number of members of the Commission may be altered by the Council of Ministers voting unanimously. In carrying out their tasks, the members of the Commission may not seek or accept instructions from any government or other body; any member who no longer fulfils the conditions required for the performance of his duties, or commits a serious offence, may be declared removed from office by the Court of Justice. Furthermore, the Court is empowered provisionally to suspend a member of the Commission from his duties, at the request of the Council of Ministers or of the Commission itself.

The Commission acts by majority vote and is charged with the following functions: (a) to ensure application of the provisions of the Treaties and the provisions enacted by the institutions of the Communities in pursuance thereof; (b) to formulate recommendations or opinions in matters which are the subject of the Treaties, where the latter expressly so provide or where the Commission itself considers it necessary; (c) to dispose, under the conditions laid down in the Treaties, of a power of decision of its own and to participate in the preparation of acts of the Council of Ministers and of the European Parliament; and (d) to exercise the competence conferred on it by the Council of Ministers for the implementation of the rules laid down by the latter. The Commission operates through 23 Directorates-General.

The Council of Ministers – composed of representatives of the member countries, each government delegating to it one of its members – represents the national as opposed to the Community interest. It is responsible for co-ordinating the general economic policies of the member countries and adopting the decisions necessary for the implementation of the Treaties. In practice, more than one minister from each member country may participate in the Council's meetings. The office of President is exercised for a six-month term by each member of the Council in rotation in the following order: Belgium, Denmark, Germany, Greece, Spain, France, Ireland, Italy, Luxembourg, Netherlands, Portugal, UK. Meetings of the Council are convened by the President acting on his own initiative or at the request of a member or of the Commission.

The voting procedure of the Council depends upon the Treaty under which it acts and on the specific procedure that is required for the particular action to be taken. There are three types of voting: simple majority; qualified majority; and unanimity. Where conclusions require a qualified majority, the total votes (76) of the Council's members are distributed as follows: France, Germany, Italy, and the UK, 10 votes each; Spain 8; Belgium, Greece, the Netherlands and Portugal, 5 each; Denmark and Ireland, 3 each; Luxembourg 2. A minimum of 54 votes is required for decisions by qualified majority. Abstentions do not prevent the taking by the Council of conclusions requiring unanimity. In 1965, the impending changes in the voting procedure (that is, the shift towards majority voting as part of the transition from the second to the third stage under the EEC Treaty) gave rise to disputes between France and the other five member countries. The French boycott of all Council meetings for six months (the 'empty chair' policy) was resolved in January 1966 by a deal called the Luxembourg Compromise. Under the Compromise, all decisions had to be taken unanimously whenever 'very important interests of one or more partners' were involved; in practice, the 'veto' power was gradually extended from major issues to minor ones and the Council seldom took decisions by majority voting except on budgetary and agricultural management affairs.

The Single Act has restricted the right of veto; in particular, proposals concerning the dismantling of barriers to the free movement of goods, persons, services and capital may be approved by majority vote. Unanimity is still required for certain areas, notably harmonization of indirect taxes, legislation on health and safety, veterinary controls, and environmental protection. A new 'co-operation procedure' has also been introduced whereby a proposal adopted by a qualified majority in the Council must be submitted for approval to the European Parliament; if the Parliament rejects the proposal, unanimity will be required for the Council to act on a second reading, and if the Parliament suggests amendments, the Commission must re-examine the proposal and forward it to the Council again.

The Council may request the Commission to undertake any studies which it considers desirable for the achievement of the common objectives and to submit to it any appropriate proposals. The ministers of foreign affairs, economics and finance and agriculture normally meet once a month. The Council holds about 60 sessions a year.

Preparation and co-ordination of the Council's work are entrusted to a Committee of Permanent Representatives, meeting in Brussels and commonly known as COREPER (Comité des Représentants Permanents), which consists of the ambassadors of the member countries to the Communities assisted by working groups.

The meetings of the Heads of State or Government of the member countries, held at least twice a year and generally taking place in the member country which exercises the presidency of the Council of Ministers, have been institutionalized since the mid-1970s and bear the name of European Council. Summit meetings consider matters relating to the Community and matters handled by the 'political co-operation' system.

Under the provisions of the EEC and Euratom Treaties, the Commission and the Council, in order to carry out their tasks, are empowered to make 'regulations', issue 'directives', take 'decisions', make 'recommendations' or give 'opinions'. Regulations have a general application and are binding in every respect and directly applicable in each member country. Directives bind, as to the result to be achieved, any member country to which they are addressed, while leaving to national authorities the choice of form and methods. Decisions are binding in their entirety upon those to whom they are directed. Recommendations and opinions have no binding force. Under the ECSC Treaty, a different system is used: 'decisions' are binding in every respect; 'recommendations' are binding only with respect to the objectives, while leaving to the addressee the choice of the appropriate methods; 'opinions' are deprived of binding force.

The European Parliament consists of 518 members apportioned as follows: France, Germany, Italy, and the UK, 81 each; Spain 60; the Netherlands 25; Belgium, Greece and Portugal, 24 each; Denmark 16; Ireland 15; and Luxembourg 6. Members sit in the Parliament in political, not national groups. The last elections were held in June 1989 for a five-year mandate. Party representation in the Parliament is as follows: Socialists 180; European People's Party (Christian Democratic) 162; Liberal, Democratic and Reform Group 45; European United Left 29; Greens 27; European Democratic Alliance 21; 'Rainbow' group (mixed tendencies) 15; European Right 14; Left Unity 13; Independents 12. Prior to the 1979 elections by direct universal suffrage, the Parliament consisted of 198 members delegated by the national parliaments of the member countries. The Parliament holds an annual session, divided into about 12 one-week part-sessions, taking place either in Strasbourg or Luxembourg; the session opens with the March meeting. The Parliament is run by a Bureau including the President and 14 Vice-Presidents elected by secret ballot. Specialized committees deliberate on proposals for legislation put forward by the Commission before the final opinion of the Parliament is delivered by a resolution in plenary session.

The Parliament is consulted over the annual budget of the Communities, advises on legislation and exercises a democratic control over the Commission and the Council. It is empowered to dismiss the Commission on a motion of censure approved by a two-thirds majority but has never exercised its right. As part of the decision adopted in 1970 with a view to providing the Community with its own independent financial resources, the Parliament has been given more control over the administrative budget consisting of non-mandatory expenditure, that is expenditure not arising directly from the Treaty or from regulations made under it. The budgetary powers of the Parliament (which, with the Council, forms the Budgetary Authority of the Communities) were reviewed in 1973 and enlarged in 1975; the Parliament is empowered to reject the draft budget, acting by a majority of its members and two-thirds of the votes cast. The Parliament has twice exercised its right to reject a draft budget – for 1980 and 1985. Since the Single Act, the Parliament has an increased role in legislation through the 'concertation' procedure under which it can reject certain Council drafts in a second reading procedure. Community agreements with third countries are now subject to the approval of the Parliament. It has adopted resolutions on its own initiative not only on Community matters but on a variety of international issues of major concern to European public opinion. It also conducts an active diplomacy through exchange visits with the parliaments of many countries.

The Court of Justice, composed of 13 judges assisted by 6 advocates-general, bears prime responsibility for ensuring the observance of law and justice in the interpretation and application of the Treaties. The judges and advocates-general are appointed for renewable six-year terms by common accord between the governments of the member countries; they are chosen from persons whose independence can be fully relied upon and who fulfil the conditions required for the exercise of the highest judicial functions in their respective countries or are legal experts of universally recognized ability. A partial renewal of the Court takes place every three years, affecting six and seven judges alternately as well as three advocates-general. The President of the Court is appointed by the judges from among themselves for a renewable three-year term. The Court sits in plenary session but may set up within itself Chambers for the purpose of taking certain measures of procedure or to judge particular classes of cases.

A Court of First Instance was created in 1989, following a decision of the Council of Ministers of October 1988, with jurisdiction to hear and determine certain categories of cases which had hitherto been dealt with by the Court of Justice. These categories include cases arising under the competition rules of the EEC Treaty, cases brought under the ECSC Treaty, and cases brought by Community officials.

The Court of Justice has jurisdiction to settle disputes within the Communities and to award penalties. It may review the legal validity of measures (other than recommendations or opinions) taken by the Commission or the Council and is competent to give judgment on actions by a member country, the Commission or the Council on grounds of incompetence, errors of substantial form, infringement of the Treaties or of any legal provision relating to their application, or abuse of power. Any natural or legal person may, under the same conditions, appeal against a decision directed to him or it or against a decision which, although in the form of a regulation or decision addressed to another person, is of direct and specific concern to him or it. After the creation of the Court of First Instance, the Court is also empowered (appeal) to hear cases concerning compensation for damage, disputes between the Communities and their employees, fulfilment by member countries of the obligations arising from the Statute of the European Investment Bank (EIB), arbitration clauses contained in any contract concluded, under public or private law, by or on behalf of the Communities and disputes between member countries in connection with the objects of the Treaties, where such disputes are submitted to the Court under a special agreement. Preliminary rulings are given by the Court, at the request of national courts, on the interpretation of the Treaties, the validity and interpretation of measures taken by Community institutions, and the interpretation of the statutes of bodies set up by a formal measure of the Council, where those statutes so provide.

The Court of Auditors is composed of 12 members appointed for a six-year term by the Council of Ministers acting unanimously, after consultation with the European Parliament. It examines the accounts of all revenue and expenditure of the Community and of any body created by the Community and also has jurisdiction to audit the operations of the European Development Fund (EDF). The Court cooperates closely with the national audit bodies which supervise the national authorities responsible for enforcing Community law.

There are two major consultative bodies. The Economic and Social Committee – composed of 189 members representing economic and social fields (employers, workers and consumers) appointed for a renewable four-year term by the unanimous vote of the Council of Ministers – performs advisory functions and is consulted by the Council or the Commission, particularly with regard to agriculture, free movement of workers, harmonization of laws and transport. The Single Act has extended the advisory functions of the Committee. The ECSC Consultative Committee – consisting of 84 members representing producers, workers and consumers and dealers in the coal and steel industries, appointed by the Council for a two-year term – is attached to the Commission and performs an advisory role with regard to the coal and steel sectors. Members of both Committees are appointed in their personal capacity and are not bound by any mandatory instructions. Besides the consultative bodies already mentioned, there are several hundred specialized groups, representing a wide variety of interests within the Community, which hold unofficial talks with the Commission.

The European Investment Bank was created in 1958 under the EEC Treaty to which its statute is annexed. Its governing body is the Board of Governors consisting, generally, of the Finance Ministers of the member countries. The Board of Directors and the Management Committee complete the Bank's institutional structure. The Bank, working on a non-profit-making basis, makes or guarantees loans for financing investments, principally in industry, energy and infrastructure, which further: projects for the development of less developed regions; projects for the modernization or conversion of undertakings or the development of fresh activities called for by the progressive establishment of the common market, where such projects by their size or nature cannot be entirely financed by the means available in individual member countries; projects of common interest to several member countries or the Community as a whole. From January 1991 the subscribed capital of the Bank was doubled to ECU57.6 billion.

The 'structural funds' of the Community comprise the Guidance Section of the European Agricultural Guidance and Guarantee Fund (EAGGF), the European Regional Development Fund (ERDF), and the European Social Fund. Following the adoption of the Single Act, the Council of Ministers approved reforms of the structural funds, with effect from January 1989, with a view to selecting priority targets and concentrating action in the least-favoured regions. The European Agricultural Guidance and Guarantee Fund was established in 1962 under the administration of the Commission. The Guidance Section contributes credits for structural reforms in the agricultural sector. The European Regional Development Fund (ERDF), in operation since the mid-1970s, is responsible for encouraging investment and improving infrastructure in depressed regions as a means of compensating the unequal rate of development in different areas of the Community. The European Social Fund was originally set up in 1960 under the EEC Treaty with a view to improving opportunities for employment within the Community by assisting training and workers' mobility. The scope of the Fund was subsequently modified several times. According to new rules adopted in 1983, a special emphasis was placed on the Community's poorest regions; areas of high unemployment and industrial decline were also given priority. Stricter criteria have been applied since 1986 for selection of suitable schemes.

The European Monetary Co-operation Fund (EMCF), originally set up in 1973 to administer the Community's special narrow margin currency system (commonly known as the snake), currently performs its functions under the European Monetary System (EMS), in force since March 1979. The EMCF administers, *inter alia*, the pooling of the Community's gold and dollar reserves and should eventually be replaced by a European Monetary Fund. The EDF is responsible for the Community's financial aid under the terms of the Lomé Conventions.

The general budget of the Communities covers all EEC and Euratom expenditure and the administrative expenditure of the ECSC. Following the decision of the Council of Ministers of June 1988, all revenue (except that expressly designated for supplementary research and technological development programmes) is used without distinction to finance all expenditure; all budget expenditure must be fully covered by the revenue entered in the budget. Expenditure under the general budget is financed by automatic payments made over by the member countries from the revenue they collect in agricultural levies and customs duties, from a percentage of the revenue from value-added tax (VAT) on goods and services, and on the basis of a levy on the GNP of each country. The provision of the Community's 'own resources' has been gradually implemented since 1975 when the six original member countries began to pay a growing proportion of their contributions through the new system of automatic payments; the assessment of the transitional contributions of the three new member countries delayed the full application of 'own resources' financing until 1980. The amount of the contributions of member countries, therefore, is no longer based on the relative shares system but is directly dependent on the economic activity in each member country. From 1992 the maximum amount of 'own resources' that may be called up in any one year must be equivalent to 1.2 per cent of member countries' total GNP. Agriculture is by far the most important item on the Community budget, accounting for about two-thirds of total expenditure, mainly in agricultural guarantees.

The European Unit of Account (EUA) was adopted throughout the Community finances from January 1978, in replacement of the EUR, a budgetary unit representing the value of the American dollar before 1971. Following the introduction of the EMS in 1979, the European Currency Unit (ECU) was created on the basis of a 'basket' of national currencies identical to that used to calculate the EUA. The composition of the ECU currently includes the national currencies of all member countries 'weighted' as follows (in percentage): Belgian franc 7.6; Danish krone 2.45; French franc 19.0; Deutsche mark 30.1; Greek drachma 0.8; Irish pound 1.1; Italian lira 10.15; Luxembourg franc 0.3; Netherlands guilder 9.4; Portuguese escudo 0.8; Spanish peseta 5.3; UK pound sterling 13.0. The EMS aims to create close monetary co-operation, leading to a zone of monetary stability in Europe, chiefly by means of an exchange rate mechanism (ERM) which is supervised by the ministries of finance and the central banks of member countries. Under the ERM, a central rate is fixed for each currency in ECUs, with established fluctuation margins. In the final stage of European monetary union, the ECU should be established as a single Community currency.

European Economic Community (EEC). A complete customs union between the six original member countries was achieved in July 1968. It covers the exchange of all goods, the removal of customs duties, charges having equivalent effect and quantitative restrictions on imports and exports between member countries, and the adoption of a common external tariff in relations with third countries. Denmark, Ireland and the UK had gradually eliminated customs tariffs between each other and between themselves and the original six member countries by July 1977. Greece phased out its customs tariffs with the other nine member countries by the end of 1985. Special transitional periods were adopted for Portugal and Spain. However, the movement of goods between member countries remained restricted by a number of national non-tariff barriers, such as health and safety regulations and technical standards. Under the Single Act, all barriers to free movement of goods, persons, services and capital must be removed by December 1992.

The free movement of workers, except those employed in the public service, between member countries became effective in July 1968. Nationals of member countries are granted equal treatment in every important field relating to employment, including matters relating to taxation, social insurance and dependants. Under the Treaty, individuals, companies and firms from one member country may establish themselves in another member country for the purposes of pursuing an economic activity under the same conditions applied to nationals of that country. Many aspects of company law still require harmonization, although several measures have already been adopted. A number of Community directives have been adopted on equal rights for women in pay, access to employment and social security. A Charter of Fundamental Social Rights of Workers – covering freedom of movement, fair remuneration, improvement of working conditions, right to social security, freedom of association and collective wage agreements, and development of participation by workers in management – was approved in December 1989 by all Community members, except the UK.

A single system of VAT applies throughout the Community; VAT rates, however, are not uniform. In view of the completion of the internal market, national rates of VAT and excise duties should be aligned and VAT should be levied in the country of origin before export.

As regards competition, the provisions embodied in the Treaty for action against practices which restrict or distort competition in the common market have been implemented to a significant degree. The Community has made extensive use of its powers to control cross-frontier amalgamations, takeovers, and other arrangements between firms likely to create abuse of market power. Conflicts between national and Community authorities have arisen in this area. In September 1990 new regulations entered into force concerning mergers of large companies that might create unfair competition. Programmes have been adopted in the last half of the 1980s to help small and medium-sized enterprises prepare for the completion of the single market.

With respect to agriculture, which is the most highly organized area of co-operation in the Community, a common policy has been developed step by step from the early 1960s according to the objectives set out in the Treaty: (a) to increase agricultural productivity through technical progress and the rational development of agricultural production, and the optimum utilization of the factors of production, particularly labour; (b) to ensure a fair standard of living for the agricultural population; (c) to stabilize markets; (d) to assure regular supplies as well as reasonable consumer prices.

The Common Agricultural Policy (CAP) is based on the following main elements: a single market, which calls for common prices, stable currency parities and the harmonization of administrative, health and veterinary legislation; Community preference, for the protection of the Community market from imports and world market fluctuations; and common financing of the European Agricultural Guidance and Guarantee Fund which supports, through its Guarantee Section, all public expenditure intervention, storage costs, marketing subsidies and export rebates. Monetary compensation accounts (MCAs) have been paid for agricultural exchanges between member countries to take account of the difference between the reference rate of exchange (the 'green' currencies) and the real rate; however, this system has not proved beneficial for some net food exporters and its complete dismantling is to take place by the end of 1992. In a number of cases, the CAP has encouraged excess production and the consequent formation of costly surpluses.

Several efforts have been undertaken over the past few years with a view to reforming the CAP and reducing its burden on the Community budget. There seems to be no doubt about the necessity to make the agricultural sector more responsive to the level of supply and demand and to reduce agricultural subsidies, particularly in the context of the GATT-sponsored 'Uruguay Round' of multilateral trade negotiations. The operation of the CAP has been characterized by serious fraud, mainly in the form of false claims for subsidies and intervention payments.

Although the need for a common policy for fisheries is acknowledged by all member countries, agreement on the main elements of such a policy has not proved easy to achieve. In principle, the common fisheries policy (CFP), effective since January 1983, gives all EEC fishermen equal access to the waters of member countries. From 1977 the Community has reserved a zone extending up to 200 nautical miles (370 km) from the shore around all its coastlines, within which all member countries have access to fishing and other economic uses of the sea. According to the CFP, the total allowable catch for each species in each region will be set and then shared out between member countries according to pre-established quotas; special rules will apply in order to conserve fish stocks and financial support will be granted to help fleets adjust capacity and equipment to new circumstances. As with agricultural produce, export subsidies are paid to enable the export of fish and import levies are imposed. Agreements have been signed with several countries allowing reciprocal fishing rights and other advantages.

In the industrial sector, textiles, shipbuilding and petro-chemicals are being given increasing attention as areas with special difficulties. Within the framework of the *Multifibre Arrangement (MFA) bilateral agreements have been concluded between the Community and the principal suppliers in the developing world with a view to limiting Community imports through quotas and ceilings. In the face of the shipbuilding crisis, the Community has tried to control the heavy government subsidies, allowing only those subsidies which are intended to promote reductions in capacity and modernization.

The Single Act deals with research and technology, defining the extent of Community co-operation and introducing new decision-making structures. A revised programme on research and technological development for the period 1990–94 has been adopted by the Council of Ministers, with special focus on information and communication technologies and industrial and materials technologies.

Under the Treaty, the common transport policy should ease the movement of goods and persons by improving the European infrastructure network, financing the implementation of the relevant projects and gradually standardizing the varying national regulations which make difficult and delay traffic within the Community; progress has been made, *inter alia*, towards the establishment of a common air transport policy and a common maritime transport policy. Many difficulties must be overcome in order to establish an effective energy policy at Community level. The reduction of petroleum consumption, the development of new and renewable energy sources, energy conservation and the establishment of a sound energy pricing policy are among the basic objectives of a Community-wide energy policy. Measures have been adopted in 1990 for the completion of the 'internal energy market'.

The promotion of close co-operation between member countries in the social field is among the Community's basic aims, particularly in matters relating to employment, labour legislation and working conditions, occupational and continuation training, social security, protection against occupational accidents and diseases. The Single Act has emphasized the need for 'economic and social cohesion' in the Community and the reduction of disparities between the various regions, principally through the existing 'structural funds'.

Other important areas of interest for the Community are represented by scientific and technical information, education (the postgraduate European University Institute was set up in Florence in 1972), and consumer protection. Increasing emphasis is being laid on the protection of the environment which should become an integral part of economic and social policies. Limits have been imposed on the production of chlorofluorocarbons, the emission of harmful exhaust fumes by cars, and the emissions of carbon dioxide. A network of installations is being established in order to make the Community self-sufficient with regard to waste disposal.

Attempts to create an Economic and Monetary Union between 1969 and 1972, on the basis of the Werner Report, failed for a number of reasons, notably the lack of determination of the member countries in the field of economic policy co-ordination. Plans for the Union, which envisaged a common central bank system, invariable exchange rate parities and Community decisions on important economic questions, were shelved after the crisis of the Bretton Woods international monetary system and the first oil shock of 1973. A major attempt to promote a greater convergence of economic policies of member countries has been made with the establishment of the EMS which formally began operations in March 1979. Unlike its predecessor, the 'snake', which was merely a common exchange rate system, the EMS is intended to keep the cross rates of exchange of the currencies of the participating countries within specific fluctuation margins, to co-ordinate intervention on the foreign exchange markets and to grant credit facilities. The Maastricht Treaty expressly envisages a monetary union to be attained in a number of stages.

International relations are maintained by the Communities – each having a distinct international personality of its own – with non-member countries and other international organizations. Nearly all countries of the world have accredited permanent missions to the Communities in Brussels. External relations are mainly dealt with as a joint Community matter when they concern trade and aid. Under the Single Act, member countries must inform and consult each other on foreign policy matters; a Secretariat has been established to prepare the activities of European political co-operation. Co-ordination of foreign and security policy is envisaged by the Maastricht Treaty.

Through bilateral Free Trade Agreements (FTAs) between each member country of the *European Free Trade Association (EFTA) on the one hand and the Community on the other, a full customs union was achieved in July 1977, mainly with regard to the industrial sector; reciprocal arrangements were concluded for certain agricultural goods. In October 1991 an agreement was signed in Luxembourg providing for close integration between the 'Seven' and the 'Twelve' from January 1993 through the creation of a European Economic Area (EEA). After the negative opinion of the Court of Justice of the Communities, the agreement was renegotiated and is likely to enter into force at the same time as the single unified market of the EEC.

The dramatic changes in political and economic systems in Central and Eastern European countries have led to new forms of partnership between these countries and the Community; 'Europe Agreements' have been signed with Poland, Czechoslovakia and Hungary. Technical assistance programmes, credit guarantees and food aid programmes are among the main aspects of the Community's sustained efforts to help restructure and rehabilitate the economies of the former socialist countries, including the republics of the erstwhile USSR.

Association agreements leading to customs union have been made with Cyprus, Malta and Turkey; all three countries have applied for full membership. A co-operation agreement was signed in 1980 with Yugoslavia; a new financial protocol was concluded in 1987. In the face of the progressive disintegration of Yugoslavia, the Community has recognized the independence of several republics and is extending financial support.

A policy for the Mediterranean area, based on a global approach which envisages similar arrangements on trade preferences, financial aid and technical co-operation, is being developed by the Community. Co-operation agreements along these lines are currently in force with Israel, the Maghreb countries (Algeria, Morocco and Tunisia) and the Mashreq countries (Egypt, Jordan, Lebanon and Syria). The trade provisions of the co-operation or association agreements linking the Community with the countries of the southern Mediterranean were adapted to ensure that the traditional export trade of the countries concerned would be maintained after the accession of Portugal and Spain.

As regards the Indian sub-continent, non-preferential agreements for trade co-operation have been in force with India since 1974, with Sri Lanka since 1975, and with Pakistan and Bangladesh since 1976. A non-preferential trade agreement was signed with the People's Republic of China in 1978. In 1980 China was included in the list of beneficiaries of the Community's preferences scheme. In May 1985, a new Community-China Trade and Economic Co-operation Agreement replaced the 1978 instrument and provided a more adequate framework for the development of economic and technical relations between the two parties.

With respect to Latin America, non-preferential trade agreements came into force with Argentina (1972), Brazil and Uruguay (1974) and Mexico (1975). During the late 1970s, other Latin American countries concluded agreements with the Community, to regulate trade in textiles and handicrafts. A framework agreement for commercial and economic co-operation between the Community and Brazil was signed in 1980.

In 1976 the Community signed its first economic co-operation agreement with an advanced industrial country, Canada, covering not only trade promotion but also wide-ranging collaboration in the economic sphere. Despite efforts made on the part of all the parties concerned, it has not been possible so far to reach agreement on trade and economic co-operation matters between the Community and its major economic and commercial partners, that is the USA and Japan (with the exception of fisheries, environmental matters and the peaceful uses of nuclear energy as regards the USA). The economic relationship between the Community and the USA is currently the most important in the world (bilateral trade flows run at about $190 billion a year) and a system of consultation between the two sides has come into existence since the adoption, in November 1990, of the EC-US transatlantic declaration. In July 1991 a first summit meeting was held between the Community and Japan and a joint declaration was adopted calling for greater co-operation and dialogue between the two parties.

To assist the trade of developing countries, the Community introduced, in July 1971, a Generalized System of Preferences (GSP) to over 90 developing nations, later extended to include additional countries. A revised scheme was adopted in 1980 with a view to granting varying preferential advantages according to the degree of competitiveness of the beneficiary countries. Since 1977 the Community has progressively liberalized GSP access for the least-developed countries by according duty-free entry on all products as well as exemption from virtually all preferential limits. In 1989 the GSP was extended to Hungary and Poland.

At present about 70 African, Caribbean and Pacific (ACP) countries, mainly former colonies of the Community's members, participate in the Lomé Convention, first signed in 1975 and renewed in October 1979, December 1984 and December 1989. The First Lomé Convention (Lomé I) replaced the Yaoundé Conventions and the Arusha Agreement and provided an effective framework for co-operation. Under Lomé I, provision was made for the bulk of ACP agricultural goods to enter the market of the Community duty free; the Stabex (Stabilization of Export Earnings) scheme was introduced to help developing countries withstand fluctuations in the price of their agricultural products by paying compensation for reduced export earnings. The Second Convention (Lomé II) extended certain provisions of Lomé I and introduced additional areas of co-operation, notably the Sysmin scheme concerning certain minerals. The Third Convention (Lomé III) placed stronger emphasis on the autonomous, self-reliant process of development in the ACP countries and on the search for greater aid effectiveness. Special provisions regarding the encouragement of private investment were introduced.

The Fourth Convention (Lomé IV), which has a duration of ten years, includes innovations such as the provision of assistance for structural adjustment programmes, increased support for the private sector, environmental protection and measures to avoid a further increase in the recipient countries' indebtedness. The budget for financial and technical co-operation for the first five years amounts to ECU12 billion, of which ECU10.8 billion from the European Development Fund and the remainder from the European Investment Bank. The ACP-EEC institutions comprise: the Council of Ministers, consisting of one minister from each signatory country and meeting annually under one co-chairman from the EEC and one from the ACP group; the Committee of Ambassadors, composed of one ambassador from each signatory country and meeting at least every six months under a chairmanship which alternates between the EEC and the ACP group; the Joint Assembly, attended by delegates of the ACP countries and members of the European Parliament and meeting twice a year.

The Community maintains relations with several UN organs and specialized agencies; it has observer status at the *UN and was made a full member of the *Food and Agriculture Organization (FAO) in November 1991. Thus the EC became the first regional economic integration organization to join a UN specialized agency. Close links, expressly envisaged by the Rome Treaties, have been established between the Community and the *Council of Europe and the *Organization for Economic Co-operation and Development (OECD) respectively. As regards relations with other regional international organizations specifically concerned with economic co-operation and integration, an economic and commercial co-operation agreement was signed with the member countries of the *Association of South East Asian Nations (ASEAN) in March 1980 and entered into effect the following October. A trade and economic co-operation agreement was signed in 1983 with the *Andean Group. A five-year co-operation agreement with the member countries of the *Central American Common Market (CACM) and with Panama was signed in 1985 and entered into force in 1987. An agreement has been concluded with the countries of the *Gulf Co-operation

Council (GCC) in June 1988 and a further expansion of trade and economic links is being contemplated. Contacts are also developing with the *Southern African Development Co-ordination Conference (SADCC).

European Coal and Steel Community (ECSC). A common market for coal, iron ore and scrap was established in February 1953, for steel in May 1953 and for special steels in August 1954; by the end of 1954 nearly all barriers to trade in products covered by the ECSC Treaty had been removed. Rules for ensuring fair competition have been established, currency restrictions, dual-pricing systems as well as discriminatory transport rates have been abolished within the Community.

To overcome the structural problems of the coal and steel industries, and especially to ensure that the contraction of the coal industry occurs without social or economic dislocation, the Community provides financial aid to resettle and retrain workers whose jobs are put at risk and assists investment and redevelopment programmes. A major crisis occurred among the steel firms of the member countries during the recession of the mid-1970s and special measures had to be adopted in 1977 and renewed in 1979, especially with regard to minimum guide prices, production cuts and reference prices for imports; quotas were negotiated with suppliers of 85 per cent of the Community's steel imports. In October 1980 a state of 'manifest crisis' was declared in the steel industry and production quotas were set in order to maintain price levels; about 75 per cent of steel output was brought under compulsory controls while the remaining 25 per cent, covering mainly special steels, became subject to voluntary quotas. In 1985 further decisions were adopted concerning production quotas and government subsidies; stricter controls on state aid to the coal industry were also introduced. In June 1988 the quota system for steel production was abolished.

European Atomic Energy Community (Euratom). A common market for all nuclear materials and equipment came into force in January 1959, eliminating internal duties and setting a common tariff for imports from third countries. Assistance is given to the free movement of specialized labour and there is a common insurance scheme against nuclear risks. The Agency for the supply of nuclear fuels, with rights to purchase materials within the Community and a monopoly of contracts with third countries, is the exclusive owner of special fissile materials. The Community promotes research:

(a) through the Joint Research Centre (JRC) which has been reorganized in 1989 and comprises nine institutes based at Ispra, Italy; Geel, Belgium; Karlsruhe, Germany; and Petten, Netherlands;

(b) by contracting specific tasks to national centres or firms and by 'association contracts' through the contribution of finance and personnel;

(c) by joining international projects.

Basic standards for health protection throughout the Community as well as an insurance convention for large-scale atomic risks have been elaborated.

To improve mutual co-operation on nuclear energy research and safety problems, an agreement was concluded between the EEC and Euratom on the one hand and the *International Atomic Energy Agency (IAEA) on the other. Co-operation agreements are in force with other European and non-European countries. Changing circumstances in the sector of atomic energy have contributed to the steady decline of the Community since the last half of the 1960s, though several attempts have been made to rationalize research operations and to co-ordinate them with national efforts.

Addresses: *Commission*: 200 rue de la Loi, 1049 Brussels, Belgium (telephone 235 1111; telex: 21877; fax: 235 0122); *Council of Ministers*: 170 rue de la Loi, 1048 Brussels (telephone: 234 6111; telex: 21711); *European Parliament*: Centre Européen, Kirchberg, 2929 Luxembourg (telephone: 43001; telex: 2894; fax: 437009); *Court of Justice of the European Communities*: Palais de la Cour de Justice, 2925 Luxembourg (telephone 4303–1; telex: 2510; fax:

433766); *Court of Auditors of the European Communities*: 12 rue Alcide de Gasperi, 1615 Luxembourg (telephone: 4398–1; telex: 3512; fax: 439342); *European Investment Bank*: 100 blvd Konrad Adenauer, 2950 Luxembourg (telephone: 4379–1; telex: 3530; fax: 437704); *Economic and Social Committee*: 2 rue Ravenstein, 1000 Brussels (telephone: 519 9011; telex: 25983; fax: 513 4893); *ACP Secretariat*: ACP House, 451 avenue Georges Henri, Brussels (telephone: 733 9600)

Members of the Commission with their responsibilities: *President*: Jacques Delors (France), Secretariat-General, Legal Service, Spokesman's Service, Joint Interpreting and Conference Service, Security Office, Monetary Affairs.

Vice-Presidents: Frans Andriessen (Netherlands), External Relations, Trade Policy, Co-operation with other European Countries; Henning Christophersen (Denmark), Economic and Financial Affairs, Structural Funds, Statistical Office; Manuel Marín (Spain), Co-operation and Development, Fisheries; Filippo Maria Pandolfi (Italy), Research and Science, Telecommunications, Information Technology and Innovation, Joint Research Centre; Martin Bangemann (Germany), Internal Market, Industrial Affairs, Relations with the European Parliament; Sir Leon Brittan (UK), Competition Policy, Financial Institutions.

Other Members: . . . (Italy), Environment, Nuclear Safety, Civil Protection; Antonio Cardoso e Cunha (Portugal), Energy, Tourism, Small and Medium-sized Businesses, Personnel and Administration; Abel Matutes (Spain), Mediterranean Policy, Relations with Latin America, North-South Relations; Peter Schmidhuber (Germany), Budget, Financial Control; Christiane Scrivener (France), Taxation and Customs Union; Bruce Millan (UK), Regional Policy; Jean Dondelinger (Luxembourg), Cultural Affairs, Audiovisual Affairs, Information, Citizens' Europe, Publications; Ray McSharry (Ireland), Agriculture and Rural Development; Karel van Miert

(Belgium), Transport, Credit and Investment, Consumer Affairs; Vasso Papandreou (Greece), Employment, Industrial Relations, Social Affairs, Education and Training, Economic and Social Committee.

Composition of the Court of Justice (in order of precedence): Judge O. Due, President; Judge R. Joliet, President of the First and Fifth Chambers; Judge F.A. Schockweiler, President of the Second and Sixth Chambers; Judge F. Grevisse, President of the Third Chamber; First Advocate General G. Tesauro; Judge P.J.G. Kapteyn, President of the Fourth Chamber; Judge G.F. Mancini; Judge C.N. Kakouris; Advocate General C.O. Lenz; Advocate General M. Darmon; Judge J.C. Moitinho de Almeida; Judge G.C. Rodriguez Iglesias; Judge M. Diez de Velasco; Judge M. Zuleeg; Advocate General W. van Gerven; Advocate General F.G. Jacobs; Advocate General C. Gulmann; Judge J.L. Murray; Judge D.A.O. Edward.

J.-G. Giraud, Registrar.

Composition of the Court of First Instance (in order of precedence): Judge J.L. da Cruz Vilaca, President; Judge H. Kirschner, President of the First Chamber; Judge B. Vesterdorf, President of the Third Chamber; Judge R. García-Valdecasas y Fernandez, President of the Fourth Chamber; Judge K. Lenaerts, President of the Fifth Chamber; Judge D.P.M. Barrington; Judge A. Saggio; Judge C. Yeraris; Judge R. Schintgen; Judge C.P. Briet; Judge J. Biancarelli; Judge C. Bellamy.

H. Jung, Registrar.

Publications: *Bulletin of the European Communities* (11 issues a year plus supplements); *General Report on the Activities of the European Communities* (annually); *European Economy* (quarterly); *The Courier EEC-ACP* (every two months); *Official Journal of the European Communities* (daily, in three series: Legislation and Information and notices and Supplements); *Reports of Cases before the Court of Justice and the Court of First Instance of the European Communities*; *Energy Statistics* (monthly); *Eurostatistics: Data for Short-term Economic Analysis* (11 issues a year); *Monthly External Trade Bulletin*

References: J. Calmann, ed.: *The Rome Treaty: The Common Market Explained* (London 1967); R. Pryce: *The Politics of the European Community* (London, 1973); W. Hallstein: *Europe in the Making* (London, 1973); G. Mally: *The European Community in Perspective* (Lexington, Mass., 1973); P. Coffey: *The External Economic Relations of the EEC* (London, 1976); J. Paxton: *The Developing Common Market* (London, 1976); J. Paxton: *A Dictionary of the European Communities* (London, 1977, rev. 2/1982); D. Swann: *The Economies of the Common Market* (Harmondsworth, rev. 4/1978); C. Cook and M. Francis: *The First European Elections* (London, 1979); R. Fennell: *The Common Agricultural Policy of the European Community* (London, 1979); D.M. Palmer: *Sources of Information on the European Communities* (London, 1979); P. Coffey, ed.: *Economic Policies of the Common Market* (London, 1979); J.B. Collester: *The European Communities: a Guide to Information Sources* (Detroit, 1979); J. Cooney: *The EEC in Crisis* (Dublin, 1979); J. Lodge: *The European Community: Bibliographical Excursions* (London, 1983); D.A.C. Freestone and J.S. Davidson: *The Institutional Framework of the European Communities* (London and New York, 1988); J. Lodge (ed): *The 1989 Election of the European Parliament* (London, 1990); P.S. Mathijsen: *A Guide to European Community Law* (London, rev. 5/1990); A.G. Toth: *The Oxford Encyclopedia of European Community Law, vol. I, Institutional Law* (Oxford, 1990); J. Pinder: *European Community: The Building of a Union* (Oxford and New York, 1991)

European Free Trade Association (EFTA). The Association aims to ensure free trade betwen member countries in industrial goods, through the elimination of internal customs tariffs and quotas which was actually achieved at the end of

1966, and to expand trade in agricultural goods through the negotiation of bilateral agreements.

EFTA was set up in 1960 by those countries of Western and Northern Europe which wished to create a larger market for their manufactured goods through the liberalization of mutual trade but were not prepared to accept the far-reaching political and economic obligations inherent in membership of the *European Economic Community (EEC). After the failure of the free trade area negotiations within the framework of the Organization for European Economic Co-operation (OEEC) at the end of 1958, the suggestion was put forward to establish a free trade zone between the countries that remained outside the EEC. Government officials of Austria, Denmark, Norway, Portugal, Sweden, Switzerland, and the UK met at Saltsjobaden, Stockholm, in June 1959 to draft a plan with a view to establishing a European Free Trade Association. Negotiations among the representatives of the seven countries were completed during the last half of 1959; the Convention setting up the Association was signed in Stockholm in January 1960 and went into effect the following May. In March 1961 an Agreement creating an association between the 'Seven' and Finland was signed in Helsinki; the Agreement lapsed in January 1986 when Finland became a full member. Iceland became a full member in March 1970 and was immediately granted duty-free entry for exports of industrial goods while being allowed a ten-year period in order to eliminate her own import duties. Two founder members, the UK and Denmark, left the Association in 1972 to join the European Communities; they were followed by Portugal in 1985. Liechtenstein, formerly associated through its customs union with Switzerland, applied for full membership in March 1991 and subsequently was admitted as the seventh member of the Association.

According to the Convention, the basic objectives of the Association are: (a) to promote within the area of the Association and in each member country a sustained expansion of economic activity, full employment, increased productivity and the rational use of resources, financial stability and continuous improvement in living standards; (b) to secure that trade between member countries takes place in conditions of fair competition; (c) to avoid significant disparity between member countries in the conditions of supply of raw materials produced within the area of the Association; and (d) to contribute to the harmonious development and liberalization of world trade.

The Association is essentially based on a free trade zone progressively achieved through the reduction and ultimately the elimination of customs duties, charges with equivalent effect and quantitative restrictions imposed on industrial goods wholly or partly produced within the territory of the Association. Unlike customs unions, the establishment of a free trade area does not require the erection by the participating countries of a common external tariff on goods entering from third countries. Thus, each member of the Association remains free to impose its own duties and to adopt its own trade policy vis-à-vis non-member countries. Agricultural goods are generally excluded from the free trade area provisions but may be the object of specific agreements between any two or more member countries in order gradually to increase trade and to provide reasonable reciprocity to those members whose economies depend to a great extent on exports of such goods. As regards fish and other marine products, which are also excluded from the free trade area, the objective of the Association is to promote an increase in trade in order to compensate the member countries exporting those products for the loss of tariffs on imported industrial goods.

Accession to EFTA is open to any sovereign country subject to unanimous approval by the Council; withdrawal is allowed provided that 12 months' written notice is given. Any country, union of states or international organization may apply for association; although association agreements are negotiated by the Council, they must be submitted to the member countries for acceptance and do not enter into force unless ratified by each member.

The institutional structure of the Association is extremely simple and reflects the peculiar origin and nature of the organization. The Council is the supreme organ responsible for the supervision and application of the Convention and consists of one representative with one vote for each member country. It operates at two levels, meeting either at ministerial level, normally twice a year, or at the level of Heads of National Delegations, usually every week. The chair is held for six months by each country in turn. The Council has a broad mandate to consider any action that may be necessary in order to promote the attainment of the objectives of the Association and to facilitate the establishment of closer links with third countries, unions of states or international organizations. The Council is empowered to take decisions which are binding on all members and to address recommendations. In principle, decisions and recommendations to members are to be made unanimously, but abstentions are permitted and not considered as negative votes. A majority vote, however, is sufficient on certain issues, such as decisions and recommendations adopted under the general consultations and complaints procedure or under the special procedures envisaged to attenuate or compensate for the effect of restrictions introduced by a member because of balance of payments difficulties.

In the exercise of its powers to set up any subsidiary organs it considers necessary, the Council has created a number of Standing Committees: a Committee of Trade Experts; a Committee of Origin and Customs Experts; a Committee on Technical Barriers to Trade; a Group of Legal Experts; an Economic Committee; a Consultative Committee; a Committee of Members of Parliament of the EFTA Countries; a Budget Committee; an Economic Development Committee; and a Committee on Agriculture and Fisheries. The Consultative Committee was created in 1961 as a forum for an exchange of views and information between the organs of the Association and representatives of the main sectors of economic life in the member countries, including Finland. The Consultative Committee is composed of up to five government-nominated members for each country, including employers'

representatives, trade union leaders and individuals, all of them serving in a personal capacity. Meetings are usually held shortly before each session of the Council at ministerial level. The Chairman of the Committee reports to the Council after each meeting. The Committee of Members of Parliament of the EFTA Countries held its first meeting in November 1977; it is convened at least once a year, acting as a consultative and liaison body between the Association and the parliaments of the member countries.

Administrative functions are carried out by a small permanent Secretariat in Geneva headed by a Secretary-General assisted by a Deputy. The Association also has a Brussels office.

According to the Convention and with a view to facilitating the attainment of the objectives of the Association, the Council was expected to establish relationships with other international organizations, in particular the OEEC. Close relations exist, in fact, with the *Organization for Economic Co-operation and Development (OECD), successor to the OEEC, and with several European bodies. Reports are regularly submitted by EFTA to the Parliamentary Assembly of the *Council of Europe where they are debated together with the reports of the European Communities. Formal relations also exist between the Association and the *Nordic Council.

The Council has full responsibility for establishing the financial arrangements and the budget of the Association as well as for apportioning the expenses between the member countries. The basis for national contributions is determined by reference to the Gross National Product (GNP) at factor cost. At present, Switzerland and Sweden are the largest contributors, accounting together for over 50 per cent of the budget, followed by Austria, Finland and Norway.

The Association has substantially achieved its basic goals and, at the same time, has effectively managed to overcome the major difficulties arising from the changing policies of some member countries – notably the UK and Denmark – towards the integration process in Western Europe. Import duties on industrial goods within the territory of the founder members of the Association were removed in eight stages up to the end of 1966, three years ahead of schedule; Finland removed her remaining tariffs a year later, in December 1967. Iceland had completely eliminated import duties by December 1979. All import quotas were abolished by the end of 1966 while export quotas had been eliminated by the end of 1961. Tariffs or import duties have now been removed on all products except farm products, although a number of goods manufactured from agricultural products are duty free. Free trade in fish and other marine products came into effect in July 1990.

The UK and Denmark withdrew from the Association in December 1972 to become full members of the European Communities from January 1973. Five other members of the Association (Austria, Iceland, Portugal, Sweden and Switzerland) signed Free Trade Agreements (FTAs) with the enlarged EEC in July 1972; the FTAs went into effect in January 1973. Similar agreements with the EEC were concluded by Norway, after the negative result of the popular referendum on her proposed participation in the EEC, in May 1973, and by Finland in October of the same year. Through these agreements between each member country of the Association on the one hand and the EEC on the other, free trade in most industrial goods was achieved in 16 Western European countries in July 1977; the last remaining restrictions were abolished in January 1984. The FTAs also apply to Greece since her entry into the EEC in January 1981. A free trade agreement between the member countries of the Association and Spain has been in force since May 1980. Portugal withdrew from the Association to become a member of the European Communities from January 1986. The free trade between Portugal and the countries remaining in the Association has been preserved; the Industrial Development Fund for Portugal, created in April 1976 for a period of 25 years to help develop small and medium-sized industries, was also maintained. In December 1985 the Statute of the Fund was amended in order to take account of

Portugal's withdrawal from the Association and Finland's assumption of full membership. A similar fund had been set up for Yugoslavia at the end of 1989 to complement the work of the Joint EFTA-Yugoslavia Committee created in 1978.

At a meeting held in Vienna in May 1977, the Heads of Government of member countries adopted a Declaration setting out the guidelines for the future activities of the Association. After the completion of the free trade system covering all members of the Association and the EEC, increasing attention is being given to non-tariff barriers such as differences in compulsory technical requirements for electrical and other products and rules for obtaining patent protection for new products. No longer a counterpart to the EEC, the Association is likely to remain strictly a trading organization, without making any effort to promote political co-operation among its member countries.

For the members of the Association, much more important than the trade among themselves is the trade with the EEC which is the source of more than half of their imports and the destination for more than half of their exports. The broadening and deepening of co-operation in several areas with the European Community led to the EFTA-EC Luxembourg Declaration of April 1984 which stressed the common goal of creating an open economic space comprising the whole of Western Europe. In March 1989 the Heads of Government restressed their commitment to establish a homogeneous and dynamic European Economic Area (EEA) embracing all the members of EFTA and the EEC. Formal negotiations between the two organizations for the conclusion of an EEA treaty opened in June 1990 and lasted until October 1991 when an agreement was signed in Luxembourg providing for close integration between the 'Seven' and the 'Twelve' from January 1993. After the negative opinion of the Court of Justice of the European Communities, the agreement has been renegotiated and eventually approved by the Court and is likely to enter into force at the same time as the single unified market of the EEC. However, the agreement may just represent a preliminary step to full EEC membership for those EFTA countries such as Austria and Sweden that have already applied to join the Community.

The Association also maintains relations with countries of Central and Eastern Europe, notably Czechoslovakia, Hungary and Poland, as well as with countries outside Europe, including Israel and the *Gulf Co-operation Council (GCC).

Secretary-General: Georg Reisch

Headquarters: 9–11 rue de Varembé, 1211 Geneva 20, Switzerland (telephone: 749 1111; telex: 414102 EFTA CH; fax: 733 9291)

Publications: *Annual Report*; *EFTA Bulletin* (quarterly)

Reference: J.S. Lambrinidis: *The Structure, Function and Law of a Free Trade Area* (London, 1965)

European Organization for Nuclear Research [Organisation européenne pour la recherche nucléaire] (CERN). The Organization provides for collaboration among European countries in nuclear research of a pure scientific and fundamental character.

The Convention for the establishment of the Organization was signed in July 1953 under the sponsorship of the *UN Educational, Scientific and Cultural Organization (UNESCO). The present membership includes 18 European countries (among them are France, Germany, Italy and the UK); other countries (Israel, Russia, Turkey, and Yugoslavia) have been granted observer status.

According to the Convention, the work of CERN is for peaceful purposes only and concerns subnuclear, high-energy and elementary particle physics; it is not concerned with the development of nuclear reactors or fusion devices. Moreover, the results of experimental and theoretical work must be published or otherwise made generally available.

The Council is the highest policy-making body composed of two representatives of each member country and headed by a President assisted by two Vice-Presidents. The structure of the Organization also comprises a Committee of the Council, and Committees on Scientific Policy and Finance. The staff is headed by a Director-General. The Organization co-operates with non-member countries such as China, Japan and the USA.

Among the experimental facilities operated by the Organization are the following: the Synchro-Cyclotron (SC) of 600 MeV, in operation since 1957; the Proton Synchrotron (PS) of 28 GeV, in operation since 1959; the Super Proton Synchrotron (SPS) of 450 GeV. The Intersecting Storage Rings (ISR), which began operating in 1971, closed down in 1984. A Large Electron-Positron Collider (LEP) of 27 km circumference (of 50 GeV per beam) was commissioned in July 1989.

Director-General: Prof. Carlo Rubbia

Headquarters: 1211 Geneva 23, Switzerland (telephone: 767 6111; telex: 419000; fax: 767 7555)

Publications: *CERN Courier* (monthly); *Annual Report*

European Space Agency (ESA). The Agency promotes co-operation among European countries in space research and technology and their application for peaceful purposes.

The Agency was established in May 1975 in Paris. It replaced the European Space Research Organization (ESRO) and the European Organization for the Development and Construction of Space Vehicle Launchers (ELDO). The present membership includes 13 countries of Western Europe (among them are France, Germany, Italy and the UK). Finland enjoys the status of associate member. Canada signed a co-operation agreement.

The Agency was formally entrusted with all the functions previously assigned to its forerunners as well as with new tasks, particularly in the space applications field. More precisely, the Agency: elaborates a long-term space policy and recommends space objectives to member countries; implements activities and programmes in the space field; co-ordinates the European space programme and national programmes, integrating the latter, as completely as possible, into the European space programme.

The Council, composed of the representatives of all member countries and headed by a Chairman, is the highest policy-making organ of the Agency. The Director, appointed by the Council, performs executive functions. The Agency runs three centres: European Space Research and Technology Centre (ESTEC); European Space Operations Centre (ESOC); and Space Documentation Centre (ESRIN).

The Agency has entered into co-operation agreements with a number of international and national bodies in order to co-ordinate research and carry on joint efforts. A joint project has been undertaken with the *European Communities. Close co-operative ties have been established with the National Aeronautics and Space Administration (NASA) of the USA, and with Japan.

The activities of the Agency have been rather intense and cover several major areas, especially with regard to scientific and applications satellites. Meteorological satellites have been put into orbit and are providing valuable data for meteorological research and weather forecasts. The European satellites for maritime communications provide links between ships and shore stations. To give Europe a launching capability for its own applications and scientific satellites the Ariane launcher has been developed. Mention has to be made of the Spacelab, a manned and reusable space laboratory, and of the European Retrievable Carrier, a reusable payload carrier. A programme was approved in 1987 concerning a new type of Ariane launcher, a manned space-shuttle (Hermes), and collaboration with the USA on a manned space-station.

Director: Jean-Marie Luton

Headquarters: 8–10 rue Mario Nikis, 75738 Paris Cedex 15, France (telephone: 4273 7654; telex: 202746; fax: 4273 7560)

Publications: *Annual Report*; *ESA Bulletin*; *ESA Journal*

F

FAO. *See* **Food and Agriculture Organization of the UN.**

Food and Agriculture Organization of the UN (FAO). The Organization aims to raise levels of nutrition and standards of living of the peoples of member countries; secure improvement of production and distribution of all food and agricultural products; better the conditions of rural populations; contribute to an expanding world economy, ensuring humanity's freedom from hunger; and act as a co-ordinating agency for development programmes in the whole range of food and agriculture, including forestry and fisheries.

The creation of the FAO was recommended by the UN Conference on Food and Agriculture held at Hot Springs, Virginia, USA, between May and June 1943; an Interim Commission was set up to plan the new international agency and draw up its Constitution. In October 1945, delegates of 42 countries met in Quebec, Canada, and formally adopted the Constitution establishing the Organization. The Constitution has subsequently been amended on a number of occasions. Headquarters of the Organization were first in Washington, D.C. and moved to Rome, Italy in 1951. Under a Protocol signed in March 1946, the International Institute of Agriculture, founded in Rome in 1905, was dissolved and its functions and assets were transferred to the new Organization. A relationship agreement was concluded with the UN and entered into force in December 1946. The present membership of the Organization includes over 160 countries and the *European Economic Community (EEC), which was granted full membership in November 1991. Puerto Rico is an associate member.

According to the Constitution, the term 'agriculture' and its derivatives include fisheries, marine products, forestry and primary forestry products. The Organization is empowered to promote and, where appropriate, recommend national and international action with respect to: (a) scientific, technological, social and economic research relating to nutrition, food and agriculture; (b) the improvement of education and administration, and the spread of public knowledge of nutritional and agricultural science and practice; (c) the conservation of natural resources and the adoption of improved methods of agricultural production; (d) the improvement of the processing, marketing and distribution of food and agricultural products; (e) the adoption of policies for the provision of adequate agricultural credit, national and international; and (f) the adoption of international policies with respect to agricultural commodity arrangements.

Other functions of the Organization include the extension of such technical assistance that governments may request as well as the organization, in co-operation with the governments concerned, of expert missions. The Organization is also entrusted with the task of collecting, interpreting and disseminating information relating to nutrition, food and agriculture.

Any nation submitting an application for membership as well as a formal declaration that it will accept the obligations of the Constitution may be admitted to the

Organization by a two-thirds majority vote of the Conference. The Twenty-Sixth Conference approved amendments to the Basic Texts allowing regional economic organizations to become members of the Organization. Thus the EC was made a member and became the first regional economic integration organization to join a UN specialized agency. Territories or groups of territories not responsible for the conduct of their international relations may be granted associate membership, again by a two-thirds majority vote, upon application made on their behalf by the full member having responsibility for their international relations which must also submit a formal declaration of acceptance of the relevant obligations. The right to withdraw is allowed upon submission of notice to the Director-General; withdrawal takes effect one year thereafter.

The work of the Organization is carried out by three principal organs: the Conference, the Council, and the Secretariat. The Conference, composed of one representative from each member, normally meets biennially to formulate overall policies, determine the programme of work and approve the budget. It also elects the Director-General of the Secretariat and the Independent Chairman of the Council. In alternate years, the Organization also holds conferences in each of its five regions (the Near East, Asia and the Pacific, Africa, Latin America and the Caribbean, and Europe). The Conference may, by a two-thirds majority of the votes cast, make recommendations to members, either full or associate, concerning questions relating to food and agriculture, for consideration by them with a view to implementation by national action. The Conference is also empowered to review any decision taken by the Council or by any commission or committee of the Conference or Council or by any other subsidiary body.

The Council, consisting of representatives of 49 member countries elected by the Conference for staggered three-year terms, meets at least once a year under an Independent Chairman and serves as the interim governing body of the Organization between sessions of the Conference.

The most important standing Committees of the Council are the Programme and Finance Committees and the Committees on Commodity Problems, Fisheries, Agriculture and Forestry and the Committee on World Food Security. The Director-General enjoys full power and authority to direct the work of the Organization under the general supervision of the Conference and the Council. Regional offices, headed by regional representatives, have been established for Africa (in Accra, Ghana), for the Near East (Cairo, Egypt), Asia and the Pacific (Bangkok, Thailand) and Latin America and the Caribbean (Santiago, Chile). The regional office for Europe is based at the Organization's headquarters in Rome. Liaison offices have been set up for North America (Washington, D.C.) and at the UN Headquarters (New York).

The Organization has entered into formal agreements with the specialized agencies of the UN and with other international institutions, both intergovernmental and non-governmental. Close relations exist with the relevant UN bodies; in particular, the Organization acts as an executing agency of the *UN Development Programme (UNDP).

The basic Regular Programme budget of the Organization is voted by the Conference and paid by all member countries in shares relating to their gross national product. Additional funds come from a variety of sources, the most important being the UNDP. Other funds are received from several agencies to cover the cost of specialist services provided by the Organization.

The action of FAO over nearly five decades has covered several areas of paramount importance and has in many ways helped to increase the productivity of agriculture, fisheries and forestry and improved the conditions of that very large part of the world population whose livelihoods come from these basic activities. However, long-standing problems and difficulties continue to beset food production and agriculture, particularly in the developing countries where production increases have been offset by growing population, thereby aggravating dependence on world markets. Moreover, abnormal food shortages, mainly caused by drought and bad weather in some major grain producing and exporting countries, have adversely affected the perspectives of world food and agriculture since the beginning of the 1980s. On the other hand, the remarkable increase in the value of world exports of agricultural, forestry and fishery products has been predominantly price-based rather than due to an increased volume of products.

In its action to improve the quality of life and the economic returns of rural populations, FAO has attacked the problem of widespread hunger not as a mere result of inadequate food production but as the most critical element of an overall situation of poverty. In carrying out its aims, the Organization encourages the development of basic soil and water resources, improved production and protection of crops and livestock, the transfer of technology to agriculture, fisheries and forestry in the developing countries, as well as the promotion of agricultural research. It also promotes the preservation of plant genetic resources and the rational use of fertilizers and pesticides; combats epidemics of animal diseases; promotes effective utilization of resources of the seas and inland waters; provides technical assistance in such fields as nutrition, food management and processing, soil erosion control and irrigation engineering; encourages co-operation among developed and developing countries to achieve stable commodity markets and improve the export earnings of the poorest nations.

The Organization responds to the urgent need for capital for agricultural development by helping developing countries to identify and prepare investment projects that will attract external financing. To this end, it works closely with a number of international and national financing institutions, such as the *International Bank for Reconstruction and Development (IBRD), regional development banks, Arab funds and national development banks. The FAO Investment Centre was established in 1964 and by the end of 1989 it had channelled $34 billion of foreign and domestic capital for 750 projects in developing countries. Joint activities with regional development banks increased during the 1980s. In conformity with the strategy currently followed by many investment financing institutions, increasing emphasis is being placed on projects directly affecting the lives of the poorer farmers in developing nations. A special watch is kept on the food situation of the countries experiencing food shortages through an Early Warning System on areas where famine situations are likely to develop; the Office for Special Relief Operations (OSRO), set up in 1973, channels emergency assistance from governments and other agencies and assists in long-term planning for rehabilitation of agriculture in the affected areas.

In the early 1970s, the Organization put forward proposals to maintain minimum world food security by building up national food reserves to be used in the event of crop failure or high prices under an internationally co-ordinated plan. The World Food Conference, held in Rome in November 1974, endorsed the proposals and requested the Organization to act accordingly. The Food Security Assistance Scheme, set up in 1976, is intended to help developing countries strengthen their food security by creating food reserves as well as by developing national and regional early warning systems. The Organization is also actively engaged in an action programme for the Prevention of Food Losses, launched in 1977. It also attempts to ensure that national nutrition strategies are incorporated by developing countries into their national development plans.

Following upon the World Conference on Agrarian Reform and Rural Development, held in Rome in July 1979, an action programme has been adopted and a special Commission established to support the long-term programme for the control of African trypanosomiasis, a disease which severely limits the survival of livestock.

A special programme was initiated by the Organization in 1979 with a view to helping developing countries to adjust to the imposition of exclusive economic zones (EEZs) which extend the jurisdiction of coastal states over the waters up to 200 nautical miles offshore. A Fishery Law Advisory Programme is also run by the Organization. In 1984 the FAO held the first World Conference on Fisheries Management and Development which ended with the approval of five action programmes on planning and management, small-scale fisheries, aquaculture, trade in fish and fish products, and promotion of the role of fisheries in alleviating undernutrition. Micro-computer technology is being developed by the Organization in order to assist developing countries in the assessment of fish stocks and the improvement of fisheries management.

The first global International Conference on Nutrition (ICN), jointly organized by FAO and the *World Health Organization (WHO) in December 1992 in Rome, is intended: (a) to focus world attention on nutritional and diet-related problems, especially among the poor and other vulnerable groups; (b) to mobilize governments, organizations of the UN system, non-governmental organizations (NGOs), local communities, the private sector and individuals in the fight against hunger and malnutrition; and (c) to look into ways to prevent the increasing incidence of diet-related diseases in both developed and developing countries.

Following a comprehensive study of the world's tropical forest resources, undertaken with the *UN Environment Programme (UNEP), the Organization set up in 1983 the Forest Resources Information System. In 1985 the Organization launched a Tropical Forestry Action Plan, listing major areas for priority action; the Plan was subsequently restructured to meet increasing criticism on the part of environmental groups.

The FAO is a sponsor, together with the UN, of the *World Food Programme (WFP) which became operational in January 1963 and uses food commodities, cash and services (particularly shipping) contributed on a voluntary basis by member countries to back programmes of economic and social development as well as for emergency relief for victims of natural and man-made disasters.

World Food Day (WFD) was established by the Organization in November 1979 with the goal that 'food for all' should become a human right for present and future generations; the date chosen – 16 October – is the anniversary of FAO. It has since been observed every year in more than 150 countries, providing a reminder of the Organization's constant search for a long-term solution to the problems of hunger and poverty in the world.

Under the Technical Co-operation Programme (TCP), founded in 1976, immediate help is provided to countries with unforeseen needs or facing emergency situations. Several projects are carried out in the fields of fisheries and forestry. The Organization collects the latest information on food, agriculture, forestry and fisheries from all over the world and makes it available to all member countries; statistical yearbooks, surveys and scientific monographs cover a very wide range of agricultural questions. Every ten years the Organization co-ordinates and publishes the results of a census of world agricultural resources.

Director-General: Edouard Saouma
Headquarters: Viale delle Terme di Caracalla, 00100 Rome, Italy (telephone: 57971; telex: 610181; fax: 5797 3152)
Publications: *The State of Food and Agriculture* (annually); *Production Yearbook*; *Trade Yearbook*; *Yearbook of Fishery Statistics*; *Yearbook of Forest Products*; *Commodity Review and Outlook*; *Ceres* (every two months); *Food Outlook* (monthly); *Unasylva* (quarterly)
Reference: S. Marchisio and A. Di Blase: *The Food and Agriculture Organization* (Dordrecht, Boston and London, 1991)

G

GATT. *See* **General Agreement on Tariffs and Trade.**

GCC. *See* **Co-operation Council for the Arab States of the Gulf.**

General Agreement on Tariffs and Trade (GATT). The General Agreement is the principal international institution devoted to the achievement of a substantial reduction of trade barriers (tariffs, quantitative restrictions and administrative and technical regulations) and to the improvement of the framework for the conduct of world trading relationships.

The General Agreement was signed in October 1947 in Geneva by the representatives of 23 countries to record the concessions granted in a tariff conference, pending the formal acceptance of a comprehensive code governing trade policies and the establishment of the International Trade Organization (ITO) which would have been a specialized agency of the UN. However, the final version of the ITO Charter, drawn up in March 1948 and generally known as the Havana Charter, was never ratified mainly because of the opposition of the US Congress. The General Agreement entered into force in January 1948 and gradually assumed the commercial policy role originally assigned to the ITO and became the major international agency to deal with trade problems.

Although basically unequipped to fulfil the function of an international organization in the proper sense, the General Agreement has been able to overcome the institutional handicap by pragmatically adapting its rules and procedures to ever evolving circumstances.

The General Agreement, which is open to any country in the world, is applied by over 100 contracting parties, both developed and developing, which together account for over 90 per cent of world trade, while a further 30 countries participate under special arrangements. Several membership applications have been received over the past three years as a number of industrial and developing countries – new and old – decided to participate in the General Agreement. The General Agreement is applied provisionally by all contracting parties which are bound to give effect to most of its rules only to the fullest extent not inconsistent with their existing domestic legislation. The original contracting parties, and also some former territories of Belgium, France, the Netherlands and the UK, apply the General Agreement under the Protocol of Provisional Application of October 1947. The contracting parties which have acceded since 1948 apply the General Agreement under their respective protocols of accession.

The original text of the General Agreement has been amended and supplemented several times since 1947. A new Part IV, dealing with trade and development, was added to the text in February 1965 on a *de facto* basis and became effective, for those countries which had accepted it, in June 1966.

The General Agreement is divided into four parts. Part I consists of only the first two articles devoted respectively to the general most-favoured-nation treatment and the schedules of concession. The most-favoured-nation clause, a most venerable rule of commercial policy, is the cornerstone of the General Agreement immediately and unconditionally ensuring non-discrimination and equality of treatment with respect to customs duties, charges of any kind and all rules and formalities in connection with importation and exportation of goods. The following article, providing for the safeguarding of schedules (that is the consolidated list of all concessions granted by contracting parties), implies that the consent of all contracting parties is needed in order to increase bound rates on scheduled items, thus making the cancellation of bilateral concessions practically impossible. Concessions are normally the result of tariff conferences based on the principle of reciprocity.

Part II, unlike the other parts of the General Agreement which are applicable in full, needs only to be enforced to the extent that its provisions are compatible with the domestic legislation of the participating parties at the time of their accession. Existing legislation inconsistent with the obligations incorporated in Part II was meant to apply during a transitional period and was to be eliminated upon definitive acceptance of the General Agreement. However, in spite of significant efforts, the anomaly of provisional application of the General Agreement persists.

Part II constitutes the bulk of the General Agreement and includes 21 articles embodying the basic commercial-policy rules of the Havana Charter with regard to internal taxes, antidumping and countervailing duties, quantitative restrictions, subsidies, state trading and administrative and technical regulations restricting international trade. The four complex articles dealing with quantitative restrictions set out the general principle that such limitations, generally made effective through quotas or licences, must be abolished, granting at the same time a number of significant exceptions, notably in case of balance-of-payments difficulties.

Part III includes most of the organizational and procedural arrangements and some fundamental provisions such as those concerning regional integration. The General Agreement recognizes the desirability of increasing trade through the establishment of customs unions and free trade areas and sets out the specific conditions under which regional economic groupings are to be permitted.

Part IV, consisting of three dense articles, was added to the General Agreement in the mid-1960s following recognition of the need to secure for developing contracting parties a fairer share in the growth in international trade and to face the growing institutional competition stemming from the *UN Conference on Trade and Development (UNCTAD). A key provision states that the developed contracting parties are not to expect reciprocity for commitments made by them in negotiations to reduce or remove tariffs and other obstacles to the trade of less-developed contracting parties. Specific commitments are included with respect to the elimination of tariff and non-tariff barriers and fiscal protective measures on exports of particular interest to developing countries.

Since the General Agreement is essentially a multilateral trade arrangement rather than the founding document of an international organization, the institutional machinery required to carry out its widening functions has developed gradually over the years. The General Agreement originally provided for joint action and decision by the Contracting Parties, as the signatory countries are officially designated when acting collectively and not merely in their individual capacity. In 1955 a major effort was made to strengthen the structure of the General Agreement through the creation of an Organization for Trade Co-operation (OTC) but it was doomed to failure because of the continuing hostility of the US Congress.

The main functions of the Contracting Parties include consultations on any matter affecting the operation of the General Agreement, various kinds of negotiations, both bilateral and multilateral, for the reduction of tariff and non-tariff barriers to trade, and the granting of 'waivers' on obligations imposed upon a contracting party. In special circumstances, the Contracting Parties may authorize a contracting party to suspend the application to any other contracting party of concessions or other obligations as they determine to be appropriate.

Basing themselves on the 'joint action' provisions mentioned before, the countries participating in the General Agreement have built a framework to remedy the institutional weaknesses occasioned by the unusual legal status of the organization. The main organs of the General Agreement include the Session, the Council of Representatives, and the Secretariat.

The Session of the Contracting Parties normally meets in Geneva once a year for a period lasting from three to four weeks; on occasion biannual sessions have been held. As the highest decision-making body, the Session is entitled to deal with all matters falling within the terms of reference of the General Agreement and to adopt recommendations and decisions. Each contracting party has one vote and simple majority is needed for most decisions. However, decisions are usually arrived at by consensus, not by formal vote. A two-thirds majority of the votes cast, with the majority comprising more than half of the contracting parties, is explicitly requested for the granting of waivers on obligations imposed upon a contracting party. In the interval between regular meetings, votes may be taken by postal or telegraphic ballot.

The Council of Representatives, which superseded a far less authoritative intersessional committee in 1960, is open in principle to all contracting parties wishing to be represented but actually consists of a more limited number of members. The Council is the key executive organ of the General Agreement performing several important functions of the Contracting Parties which thus confine themselves in their sessions to broad policy issues. The Council, which meets usually about ten times a year, establishes the agenda for the meetings of the Contracting Parties, supervises the work of the subsidiary bodies and deals with any urgent matters arising between sessions.

Besides its basic administrative and intelligence tasks, the Secretariat (headed by an Executive Secretary who was renamed Director-General in 1965), performs a very significant though often unknown role in bringing about pragmatic solutions to conflicts between contracting parties and generally contributing to the adoption of more liberal commercial policies. The Secretariat also provides extensive support during the highly complex multilateral trade negotiations periodically held within the framework of the General Agreement. A very active part was played by Eric Wyndham White (UK) who served as Executive Secretary (and then Director-General) from the beginning of the General Agreement until 1968. Olivier Long (Switzerland) succeeded him, followed in October 1980 by another Swiss, Arthur Dunkel. The Director-General is assisted by two Deputy Directors-General.

The subsidiary bodies of the General Agreement include a number of standing committees, working parties and groups of experts which, besides dealing with their specific tasks, practically ensure permanent consultation and negotiation among contracting parties. Three committees were established by the Contracting Parties under the Programme for the Expansion of International Trade adopted after the publication of the so-called Haberler Report in 1958; further committees were appointed in the following years. Besides the important Trade and Development Committee, there are other Committees on trade negotiations, balance-of-payments restrictions, import restrictions, textiles, antidumping practices, and budget, financial and administrative questions. A Consultative Group of Eighteen, composed of high-level officials responsible for their countries' trade policies, was set up on a provisional basis in 1975 and established as a permanent body in November 1979. Working Parties and Groups of Experts, generally smaller in size than Committees, are created to investigate and make recommendations on particular problems. Panels of Conciliation are used for the settlement of trade disputes.

An International Trade Centre was set up in 1964 under the auspices of the General Agreement to promote the exports of developing countries. Since 1968 UNCTAD has joined the General Agreement as a co-sponsor of the Centre, thereby giving it the full official title of

International Trade Centre UNCTAD/ GATT. The Centre, whose headquarters are located in Geneva (54-56 rue de Montbrillant, 1202 Geneva, telephone: 734 6021; telex: 289052), has no governing body of its own, because of its status as a joint subsidiary organ of the General Agreement and the UN, the latter acting through UNCTAD. In 1984 it became an executing agency of the *UN Development Programme (UNDP), directly responsible for carrying out UNDP-financed projects related to trade promotion.

The General Agreement works closely with other institutions, particularly those concerned with the problems of international trade, industrial and agricultural development and technical assistance. The regular budget of the General Agreement is contributed on the basis of each member's share of the total trade among contracting parties.

Although the General Agreement is predominantly known for its sponsorship of several rounds of multilateral tariff negotiations, its record with regard to the removal of other than tariff barriers should not be neglected. One of the basic assumptions of the General Agreement is that the exchange of tariff concessions can be of little use unless import controls and restrictions are eliminated; quantitative restrictions are therefore permitted only under specific conditions. Initially, most countries retained restrictions on nearly all the sensitive areas of their trade. Gradually and with caution the major trading nations removed restrictions on a wide range of raw materials, manufactured products, industrial and consumer goods. Efforts to abolish residual restrictions have met with stubborn resistance and new restrictive measures have been adopted over the past few years thereby making even more difficult the fulfilment of the General Agreement's task of promoting an open and orderly trading system. The growth of countertrade, in which goods are bartered for goods in bilateral arrangements, and the expansion of trade between the subsidiaries of multinational corporations have contributed to a significant extent to reduce the share of international trade which conforms to GATT rules.

Agriculture has been virtually excluded from trade liberalization for three decades, though the provisions of the General Agreement apply in principle to agricultural and industrial products alike. Agricultural problems assumed a prominent place in the 1973-79 round of Multilateral Trade Negotiations (MTN) and were even more relevant in the following round started in 1986. On the whole, major industrial countries have maintained and even increased their restrictions on imports and their subsidies to the production and exports of agricultural products.

The relations between developed and developing countries have been receiving increasing attention from the Contracting Parties. The growing concern regarding certain trends in international trade, such as the failure of the exports of developing countries to expand as rapidly as those of the industrial countries, excessive short-term fluctuations in prices of primary products and widespread resort to agricultural protection, brought about very important changes in the General Agreement intended both as an institution and a legal document. The amendments to the existing rules including the addition of Part IV, the establishment of the Trade and Development Committee, the relaxation of the most-favoured-nation clause to accommodate the Generalized System of Preferences (GSP) and to allow an exchange of preferential tariff reductions among developing countries, as well as other positive steps have improved the trading conditions for developing countries and strengthened the role of the General Agreement.

A major challenge to the General Agreement is represented by regional economic arrangements. The wide variety of integration treaties submitted for approval and the underlying political implications have made it extremely difficult for the Contracting Parties to ensure full conformity with the complex provisions of the General Agreement on customs unions and free-trade areas. In practice, a tacit waiver has been granted in all cases, including the crucial test of the 1957 Rome Treaty establishing the *European Economic Community (EEC). Nevertheless the rules of the General Agreement exercised an effective influence on the drafting of several regional arrangements.

Several rules of the General Agreement can be used as a basis for tariff negotiations besides the article specifically concerning multilateral negotiations which was inserted in 1957. Among the negotiations taking place outside the framework of multilateral conferences, mention should be made of accession negotiations. Countries wishing to accede to the General Agreement are normally required to grant concessions to the interested contracting parties in return for the benefits resulting from membership.

Since 1947, seven major multilateral negotiations have been completed under the auspices of the General Agreement; tariffs have been reduced from an industrial-country average of 40 per cent in 1947 to less than 5 per cent today. The first conference took place in 1947 in Geneva and its results were embodied in the General Agreement. The two subsequent rounds, in 1949 (Annecy, France) and 1951 (Torquay, England), dealt almost entirely with the accession of new members, though at Torquay largely ineffective negotiations also took place among existing contracting parties. A further round, held in 1955–56 in Geneva, brought about very modest results because of the limitations imposed by the US Congress on American negotiating power and the shortcomings of the procedures and methods adopted.

In spite of growing awareness of the substantial inadequacy of the time-honoured product-by-product approach, the Dillon Round, held in 1960–61 in Geneva, was still based on the classical negotiation procedures and led to limited and often disappointing results.

Dissatisfaction with the selective product-by-product method eventually resulted in the adoption of the so-called linear or across-the-board procedure in the context of the Kennedy Round in 1964–67. Under the linear method all countries were supposed to reduce tariffs by a prescribed percentage on all industrial items, with a minimum of exceptions covering individual products. In all, 46 contracting parties (accounting for about 75 per cent of

total world trade), made concessions which affected trade valued at just over $40 billion. The tariff concessions granted by the main industrial countries covered 70 per cent of the dutiable imports; two thirds of the reductions were of 50 per cent or more, while another 20 per cent of the reductions was between 20 and 50 per cent. On average, the rate of duty for manufactured industrial goods was reduced by 36 per cent. On the other hand, limited results were achieved with regard to a number of semi-manufactured products and processed raw materials of significant importance to many developing countries. In addition to the schedules of tariff concessions, separate agreements were concluded on grains, chemical products and anti-dumping policies.

The seventh conference has been the Tokyo Round which lasted from September 1973 to April 1979. The negotiations – involving 99 countries of widely differing levels of development and economic systems, both members and non-members of the General Agreement – were intended not only to bring about the reduction of tariff and non-tariff barriers but also to reshape the multilateral trading system. In the tariff field, there were hundreds of bilateral and multilateral negotiations whose benefits were extended to all countries participating in the round in accordance with the most-favoured-nation rule. The level of all industrial duties taken together was reduced by one third if measured on the basis of customs collections, a cut comparable to that achieved in the Kennedy Round; the reductions were scheduled to take place over a period of several years. With regard to those agricultural products on which concessions were changed (and which represent about 50 per cent of trade in agricultural commodities), the average reduction amounted to about 40 per cent. Concessions by the EEC and eight industrial countries (Austria, Canada, Finland, Japan, Norway, Sweden, Switzerland, and the USA) covered imports valued at $141 billion, of which $14 billion in agriculture and $127 billion in industry. In agriculture, tariff action on products of interest to developing countries was taken mostly in the form of improvements of the GSP in the framework of tropical products negotiations.

A prominent place among the results of the negotiations was held by a number of multilateral agreements covering: subsidies and countervailing duties; customs valuation; government procurement; technical barriers to trade; import licensing procedures; dairy products; bovine meat; trade in civil aircraft; and amendments to the anti-dumping code. The negotiations concerning an improved framework for the conduct of international trade brought about, *inter alia*, the establishment, through the 'enabling clause', of differential treatment for developing countries as an integral part of the General Agreement, making the granting of waivers no longer necessary. Such differential treatment, by way of tariff preferences contemplated by the GSP or under arrangements regulating the use of non-tariff measures, can be modified to respond to the changing development, financial and trade needs of these countries. In spite of intensive efforts, the negotiation of an agreement on the rules governing emergency safeguard action against imports proved impossible. This left a lacuna in the results of the Tokyo Round, especially as these were perceived by developing countries.

Most of the world's trade in textiles and clothing is covered by the Arrangement Regarding International Trade in Textiles, or Multifibre Arrangement (MFA), that entered into force in January 1974, under GATT auspices, for a four-year period. The precursor of the MFA, the Short Term Cotton Textile Arrangement, had been negotiated in 1961, under the auspices of GATT, and had been replaced in October 1962 by the Long Term Arrangement Regarding International Trade in Cotton Textiles (LTA) which remained in force until 1974 when it was superseded by the MFA. Since 1974, the MFA has been extended by two successive Protocols, in December 1977 for the period 1978–81, and at the end of 1981 for the period January 1982–July 1986. China (whose participation in GATT lapsed in 1950) became a party to the MFA in January 1984. The 42 parties to MFA III

(the European Community and its member countries counting as one) concluded negotiations on a new five-year agreement in July 1986 with the signature of MFA IV, further expanding the coverage of fibers subject to trade restrictions.

The upsurge of protectionist pressures and other major changes in the trading environment led the Contracting Parties, meeting at the end of 1985, to examine the subject matter and modalities of a new round of multilateral trade negotiations in the light of the Work Programme and priorities for the 1980s as contained in the Ministerial Declaration of 1982. The eighth round, known as the Uruguay Round, formally began in September 1986 following the guidelines set forth in the January 1986 Punta del Este Ministerial Declaration. Participants agreed that during the course of the negotiations, expected to be completed within four years, they would adopt a 'standstill' in measures restricting or distorting trade and a 'rollback' or phasing-out of existing trade practices inconsistent with GATT rules. About 110 countries are taking part in the negotiations. Besides the traditional issues, new areas became the object of negotiations: trade-related investment measures (TRIMs) that may divert trade and encourage inefficient production; trade-related aspects of intellectual property rights (TRIPs) in order to balance protection of these rights with the needs of developing countries; services, currently covering some 20 per cent of world trade, devising appropriate rules to be brought within a multilateral framework. All these issues are further complicated by the numerous links, both tactical and functional, existing between them. Continuing disagreement over a number of major issues, especially the liberalization of agricultural trade, made it impossible to conclude negotiations on schedule, that is before the end of 1990. Negotiations were resumed in February 1991 and continued well into 1992 but a successful conclusion still appeared unlikely.

Director-General: Arthur Dunkel
Headquarters: Centre William Rappard, 154 rue de Lausanne, 1211 Geneva 21,

Switzerland (telephone: 739 5111; telex: 412324; fax: 731 4206)

Publications: *Basic Instruments and Selected Documents*; *International Trade* (annually); *GATT Activities* (annually); *GATT Focus* (ten times a year); *The Tokyo Round of Multilateral Trade Negotiations* (Report by the Director General of GATT, April 1979); *The Tokyo Round of Multilateral Trade Negotiations, vol. II* (Supplementary Report by the Director General of GATT, Jan 1980)

References: K. Kock: *International Trade Policy and the GATT, 1947–1967* (Stockholm, 1969); K.W. Dam: *The GATT: Law and International Economic Organization* (Chicago and London, 1970); R.E. Hudec: *The GATT Legal System and World Trade Diplomacy* (New York, 1975); O. Long: *Law and its Limitations in the GATT Multilateral Trade System* (Dordrecht, 1985); J.H. Jackson: *Restructuring the GATT System* (London, 1990); C. Raghavan: *Recolonization: GATT, the Uruguay Round & the Third World* (London and New Jersey, 1990); A. Oxley: *The Challenge of Free Trade* (New York, 1990); J. Bhagwati: *The World Trading System at Risk* (New York, 1990)

Gulf Co-operation Council. *See* **Co-operation Council for the Arab States of the Gulf.**

H

HABITAT. *See* **United Nations Centre for Human Settlements.**

I

IAEA. *See* **International Atomic Energy Agency.**

IBRD. *See* **International Bank for Reconstruction and Development.**

ICAO. *See* **International Civil Aviation Organization.**

IDA. *See* **International Development Association.**

IDB. *See* **Inter-American Development Bank.**

IEA. *See* **International Energy Agency.**

IFAD. *See* **International Fund for Agricultural Development.**

IFC. *See* **International Finance Corporation.**

ILO. *See* **International Labour Organization.**

IMF. *See* **International Monetary Fund.**

IMO. *See* **International Maritime Organization.**

INCB. *See* **International Narcotics Control Board.**

Inter-American Development Bank (IDB). The Bank is the oldest regional institution in the world in the field of development financing and its volume of operations is second only to the *International Bank for Reconstruction and Development (IBRD). Recurring Latin American proposals to the USA for the creation of an inter-American agency contributing capital resources and technical assistance on flexible terms and conditions were eventually accepted in 1958 within the framework of an overall plan (Operation Pan America) to further economic co-operation in the Western hemisphere. The agreement establishing the Bank was signed in April 1959 in Washington, D.C., by the representatives of the member countries of the *Organization of American States (OAS), that is the USA and 20 Latin American republics; it entered into effect in December 1959. The Bank actually began operations in Washington, D.C., in October 1960. Membership of the Bank was substantially increased in the last half of the 1970s to include nations outside the Western hemisphere and now totals 44 countries. Most countries in North and South America and the Caribbean (except Cuba) belong to the Bank, along with 15 countries in Western Europe, Israel and Japan.

According to the Charter, the Bank's basic goal is to contribute to the acceleration of development of member countries, individually and collectively, through financing economic and social development projects and provision of technical assistance. To achieve its aims, the Bank promotes public and private investment for development purposes, uses its own capital, the funds borrowed in the world capital markets, and other resources to finance the development of its members, extends financial assistance to encourage private investment in cases where private capital is not available at reasonable terms, and provides technical co-operation with regard to resource surveys, feasibility studies and professional training. Loans are usually granted for specific development projects to governments, public agencies, and private enterprises, without requiring a guarantee from the government concerned; since 1990 loans are also granted for the implementation of economic adjustment programmes.

The Bank operates with its ordinary capital resources and a Fund for Special Operations, both contributed by all member countries. In addition to its own resources, the Bank administers other funds entrusted to it by several donor countries (both member and non-member) for financial assistance to Latin America. The ordinary resources of the Bank are made up of the subscribed capital stock and retained earnings, and, to a very large extent, of the funds raised in the capital markets through the issue of securities and the sale of short-term bonds to central banks. The resources are also replenished through the flow of repayments. The capital stock initially authorized by the Charter amounted to $850 million, divided into 85,000 shares having a par value of $10,000 each. The shares originally subscribed by the USA amounted to $350 million. Due to repeated general increases in the shares and the doubling of the Bank's members, the size of the capital stock has grown substantially. At the end of 1989, the subscribed ordinary capital stock, including inter-regional capital, amounted to $34,455 million, of which $2642 million had been paid in. The remainder was subject to call if required to meet the obligations assumed by the Bank in order to increase its lendable ordinary resources.

Replenishments are made every four years. In 1983 agreement was reached on the Sixth Replenishment raising the authorized capital to $35,000 million. Agreement on the Seventh Replenishment was finally reached in April 1989. Lending from the Bank's ordinary capital resources, that is hard loans made on commercial terms, may not exceed the net amount of subscribed capital. Loans are not tied to the purchase of goods and services in any specific country and are repayable in the currencies lent over a period ranging from 15 to 40 years.

In cases where lending of the more traditional type cannot be effective, the Bank makes concessional (non-commercial) loans through the Fund for Special Operations whose resources are made up of the contributions of all members. Concessional loans are granted under terms and conditions which take into account the particular practical constraints arising in specific countries or with respect to specific projects. Lower interest rates are charged and longer repayment terms are allowed than those applied to loans from the ordinary resources. In most cases loans may be repaid in whole or in part in the currency of the borrower.

Besides the ordinary and special operations resources, a number of funds placed under its administration enable the Bank to extend additional financial assistance to developing member countries. A role of outstanding importance has been played by the Social Progress Trust Fund, established by the USA under the ten-year programme of the Alliance for Progress in 1961 in the sum of $394 million; an additional $131 million contribution in 1964 raised the total amount to $525 million. In spite of repeated Latin American requests to the USA, no further replenishments of the Social Progress Trust Fund have been provided. Several Western European countries, Japan, Canada, and Argentina have been providing aid through the agency of special funds entrusted to the Bank. A fund was established by the UK in 1966 and additional contributions were made in 1971 and 1972. The Vatican set up a $1 million fund in 1969 in connection with the encyclical Populorum Progressio. Another fund, equivalent to $500 million, was established in 1975 by the Venezuelan Investment Fund. Loans from these special funds are extended under terms mutually agreed between the Bank and the countries providing the funds.

The Bank's structure includes the Board of Governors, the Executive Directors, and the President. All the powers are vested in the Board of Governors, which consists of one governor and one alternate governor for each member country and meets once a year, usually in a Latin American capital. Each member has 135 votes, plus one vote for each share of capital stock held. The largest shareholder is the USA which possesses 34.6 per cent of the total voting power; Argentina and Brazil follow immediately, each country holding about 12 per cent of the total vote. Most powers are delegated by the Board of Governors to the Executive Directors, permanently residing in Washington, D.C., who conduct the Bank's general operations. There are at present twelve Executive Directors, eight elected by Latin American countries, two by member countries outside the region, one appointed by the USA and one by Canada. The President of the Bank is elected by the Board of Governors and acts as chairman of the Executive Directors; the Executive Vice-President is nominated by the Executive Directors. Felipe Herrera of Chile served as President from the foundation of the Bank until 1970; he was succeeded by Antonio Ortiz Mena of Mexico. The current President is Enrique Iglesias of Uruguay.

The Bank maintains close working relations with the World Bank and other international and regional agencies in order to assure the co-ordination of technical and financial development assistance activities. Since approval of the Seventh Replenishment, the Bank has initiated programmes of sector-adjustment and structural-adjustment lending and several operations have been cofinanced with the World Bank.

At 31 December 1989, total lending authorized by the Bank amounted to $41,599 million of which $30,113 million from the ordinary and inter-regional capital; $10,038 million from the Fund for Special Operations; $1448 million from the other funds. Almost all the developing member countries of the region are recipients of the Bank's loans: Argentina, Brazil, Chile, Colombia and Mexico have obtained the largest number of loans. The sectoral distribution of loans has covered all major areas: agricultural projects, industry, energy and non-fuel minerals, water and sewerage facilities, low-cost housing, transportation and communications, electric power, education and tourism, pre-investment funds and export financing. Technical co-operation has been provided in conjunction with specific development loans or arranged independently.

The Bank's attention is being increasingly focused on integrating the poorest sections of population in the development process through an expansion of productive work opportunities and an effort to manage the continuing rapid shift from rural to urban areas. After the capital increase agreed upon in 1989, the Bank has started lending for sectoral reforms in order to allow developing member countries to introduce policy changes and improve institutions. On the whole the Bank has had a remarkable impact on Latin American economic and social development, despite the inadequacy of its resources in relation to the magnitude of the problems which face the poorer developing countries of Latin America and the Caribbean.

The Institute for Latin American Integration (INTAL) was created in 1964 as an international agency for the Bank with headquarters in Buenos Aires (Esmeralda 130, 1035 Buenos Aires). The Institute provides technical co-operation services concerning the various aspects of the integration process to the Bank units, individual developing member countries, organizations for regional co-operation and other public and private institutions. In March 1986, the Charter of the Inter-American Investment Corporation (IIC), an institution affiliated to the Bank, entered into force with a view to encouraging private investment especially in small- and medium-sized enterprises. The initial capital stock of IIC amounted to $200 million, of which 55 per cent was contributed by developing member countries, 25.5 per cent by the USA, and the remainder by members outside the region.

President: Enrique V. Iglesias

Headquarters: 1300 New York Avenue, N.W., Washington, D.C. 20577, USA (telephone: 623 1397; telex: 64141; fax: 789 2835)

Publications: *Annual Report*; *The Process of Integration in Latin America* (annual survey); *Integración Latinoamericana* (monthly)

International Atomic Energy Agency (IAEA). The Agency seeks to accelerate and enlarge the contribution of atomic energy to peace, health and prosperity throughout the world and to ensure that the assistance provided to that effect is not used for the furtherance of military purposes.

The text of the Statute of the Agency was unanimously adopted in October 1956 by a UN International Conference on the Peaceful Uses of Atomic Energy, held in New York, and entered into force in July 1957. A relationship agreement linking the Agency with the UN came into effect in November 1957. According to the agreement, the Agency has a special status *vis-à-vis* the UN: it is 'under the aegis of the UN' and functions 'as an autonomous international organization' reporting annually to the UN General Assembly and, as appropriate, to the Security Council and the Economic and Social Council. The Agency is not, therefore, a 'specialized agency' according to the UN Charter, though administratively it is part of the UN system. The present membership of the Agency includes over 130 countries. With the admission of China in January 1984, all countries with significant nuclear programmes and activities participate in the Agency.

According to the Statute, the Agency is authorized: (a) to encourage and assist research on, and development and practical application of, atomic energy for peaceful purposes; (b) to make provision for materials, services, equipment and facilities to meet the needs of research and practical application; (c) to foster the exchange of scientific and technical information on peaceful uses of atomic energy; (d) to encourage the exchange and training of scientists and experts; (e) to establish and administer safeguards designed to ensure that special fissionable and other materials, services, equipment, facilities and information made available are not diverted to military use; (f) to establish, in consultation or collaboration with the competent organs of the UN and the specialized agencies concerned, standards of safety for protection of health and minimization of danger to life and property; and (g) to acquire or establish facilities, plant and equipment which are deemed useful for the implementation of its tasks.

The Agency is also authorized to provide for the application of safeguards and standards, at the request of the parties, to operations under any bilateral or multilateral arrangement or, at the request of any country, to any of that country's activities in the field of atomic energy. Activities are to be conducted by the Agency in conformity with UN policies furthering the establishment of 'safeguarded worldwide disarmament'. Moreover, resources must be allocated in such a manner as to secure efficient utilization and the greatest possible general benefit in all areas of the world, bearing in mind the special needs of the developing nations.

Any sovereign country, whether or not a member of the UN or of any of the specialized agencies, may be admitted to participation in the Agency, provided that approval has been secured by the General Conference upon the recommendation of the Board of Governors. Any member may withdraw from the Agency by giving written notice to that effect. Provision is made for the suspension from the exercise of the privileges and rights of membership of any country which has persistently violated the Statute.

Each member should make available such information as it judges to be helpful to the Agency. Any member or group of members wishing to set up research projects for peaceful purposes may request the assistance of the Agency in securing special fissionable and other materials.

With respect to any of its projects or

other arrangement where it is requested by the parties concerned to apply safeguards, the Agency has the right to examine and approve the design of specialized equipment and facilities, including nuclear reactors, to require the observance of health and safety measures as well as the maintenance and production of operating records, to call for and receive progress reports, to approve the means for the chemical processing of irradiated materials and to send into the territory of the recipient country inspectors having access at all times to all places and data and to any relevant person. In the event of non-compliance and failure by the recipient to take corrective steps within a reasonable time, the Agency is authorized to suspend or terminate assistance and withdraw any materials and equipment made available.

The Agency's structure is made up of three principal organs: the General Conference, the Board of Governors, and the Secretariat. The General Conference, consisting of representatives of all member countries, meets in regular annual sessions and in such special sessions as may be necessary. It is empowered to discuss any questions within the scope of the Statute and may make recommendations to the membership of the Agency and/or the Board of Governors. The General Conference establishes the Agency's policies and programmes, approves the budget, considers the annual report of the Board of Governors, decides on applications for membership and suspends member countries from the privileges and rights of membership, elects members of the Board of Governors and approves the appointment of the Director-General. Decisions of the General Conference on financial questions, amendments to the Statute and suspension from membership require a two-thirds majority of the members present and voting; decision on other questions is made by simple majority.

The Board of Governors consists of the representatives of 35 member countries. It meets about four times a year and carries out the executive functions. The General Conference elects 22 of the Board members and 13 are designated by the Board itself. The designation criteria, such as the level of advancement in nuclear technology and equitable geographical distribution, ensure adequate representation and continuity of membership. Under its own authority, the Board approves all safeguards agreements, important projects and safety standards. Decisions of the Board are made by a majority of the members present and voting, with the exception of decisions on the Agency's budget which require a two-thirds majority.

The Secretariat is headed by the Director-General who is appointed by the Board of Governors for a renewable four-year term and is responsible for the administration and implementation of the Agency's programme. The Director-General is assisted by five Deputy Directors-General. Each Deputy is head of a Department: Administration; Research and Isotopes; Safeguards; Technical Co-operation; Nuclear Energy and Safety.

Among the subsidiary bodies, mention must be made of the Scientific Advisory Committee, set up in 1958 to advise the Board of Governors and the Director-General upon scientific and technical matters. It was composed of a limited number of distinguished scientists appointed for three-year terms and representing all fields of nuclear science. As of 1988 the role of the Scientific Advisory Committee has been taken over by periodical reviews of the Agency's activities in the different areas, carried out by panels of specialists appointed by the Director-General. Another important body is the Standing Advisory Group on Safeguards Implementation (SAGSI) which provides advice on technical aspects of safeguards. Mention must also be made of the International Nuclear Safety Advisory Group (INSAG) which comprises scientists appointed on their individual merit to advise the Director-General on nuclear safety issues.

Since the very beginning of its activities, the Agency has entered into co-operation agreements with many specialized UN institutions such as the *UN Educational, Scientific and Cultural Organization (UNESCO), the *International Labour Organization (ILO), the *World Health Organization (WHO), the *World

Meteorological Organization (WMO), the *International Civil Aviation Organization (ICAO) and the *Food and Agriculture Organization (FAO). In 1964 the Agency and the FAO combined forces in a Joint Division of Atomic Energy in Food and Agriculture. An International Consultative Group on Food Irradiation, comprising 15 countries, was established in May 1984. Technical assistance programmes are carried out within the framework of the *UN Development Programme (UNDP) and many large-scale projects are in operation. Several projects are also being implemented jointly with the *UN Environment Programme (UNEP). The work of the Agency is carried out in co-operation with dozens of other bodies, both non-governmental and intergovernmental such as the *Organization for Economic Co-operation and Development (OECD).

Annual budget estimates for the expenses of the Agency are prepared by the Director-General and submitted for approval, through the Board of Governors, to the General Conference. Administrative expenses are apportioned by the Board of Governors among member countries in accordance with a scale fixed by the General Conference. The Board of Governors is responsible for establishing periodically a scale of charges, including storage and handling charges, for materials, services, equipment, and facilities furnished to member countries by the Agency.

The Agency has given a substantial contribution to the development of the peaceful uses of atomic energy on a worldwide scale. It has formulated basic safety standards for radiation protection and issued regulations and codes of practice on specific types of operations, including the safe transport of radioactive materials. A system has been established by the Agency to facilitate emergency assistance to member countries in the event of radiation accidents. Codes of practice and safety guides have been prepared in the areas of governmental organization, siting, design, operation and quality assurance with regard to nuclear power reactors. In 1961, the Agency adopted a safeguards system for small research reactors. Subsequent

amendments have expanded the system to cover all types and sizes of nuclear plants. In 1982, with a view to providing member countries with advice on the safe operation of nuclear power plants, the Agency set up operational safety review teams which visit power plants on request. After the accident to the nuclear power plant at Chernobyl, Ukraine, in April 1986, proposals were put forward in order to reinforce the Agency's role in developing safer plants and preventing nuclear terrorism. Two conventions were drawn up in 1986 under the auspices of the Agency: the first commits parties to provide early notification and information about nuclear accidents with possible trans-boundary effects; the second commits parties to endeavour to provide assistance in the event of a nuclear accident.

Assistance is also provided to member countries on technical, safety, environmental, and economic aspects of nuclear fuel cycle technology, including uranium prospecting and radioactive waste management. In co-operation with OECD, the Agency prepares every two years estimates of world uranium resources, demand and production. The Waste Management Advisory Programme (WAMAP) was created in 1987. A code of practice to prevent the illegal dumping of radioactive waste was drawn up in 1989, and another code on the international trans-boundary movement of waste was drawn up in 1990.

In March 1970 the Treaty on the Non-Proliferation of Nuclear Weapons (NPT) entered into force. It requires the 'non-nuclear-weapon' countries to conclude safeguards agreements with the Agency covering all nuclear materials in all their peaceful nuclear activities. Between 1978 and 1981, three nuclear-weapon countries (the UK, the USA and France) concluded safeguards agreements with the Agency. Another nuclear-weapon country, the USSR, concluded in 1985 an agreement with the Agency on the application of safeguards to certain Soviet peaceful nuclear installations. A safeguards agreement with China was signed in 1988. The Agency also administers full applications of safeguards in relation to the 1967 Treaty for the Prohibition of Nuclear Weapons in Latin

America (Tlatelolco Treaty) on the basis of a co-operation agreement concluded in 1972 with the *Agency for the Prohibition of Nuclear Weapons in Latin America and the Caribbean (OPANAL).

A significant role has been played by Agency's teams in inspecting Iraq's nuclear research facilities according to the terms of the UN cease-fire in the Gulf war of 1991.

The Agency's safeguards system is primarily based on nuclear material accountancy, with containment and surveillance as important complementary measures. In 1970, the Agency established the International Nuclear Information System (INIS) which covers virtually every aspect of the peaceful uses of nuclear science and technology and employs a technique of decentralized input preparation combined with centralized processing of information. The Agency co-operates with FAO in an information system for agriculture (AGRIS). Over the years a large number of international conferences and symposia, as well as smaller panel and group meetings, have been organized by the Agency to enable scientists and experts to discuss new ideas and developments. The Agency operates three laboratories, one at Seibersdorf, near Vienna, one at the Agency's headquarters in Vienna, and one in Monaco, devoted to the study of marine radioactivity and other forms of marine pollution.

A remarkable contribution of the Agency in the field of pure science was the establishment in 1964 of the International Centre for Theoretical Physics in Trieste, Italy – now operated jointly with UNESCO. The Centre offers seminars followed by a research workshop, as well as short topical seminars, training courses, symposia and panels.

The Agency's programme in physical sciences is concentrated on practical problems arising from the use of atomic energy, radiations and isotopes, particularly in developing countries. With regard to life sciences, the Agency co-operates with WHO in the fields of medical applications of radioisotopes and instrumentation, dosimetry for intentional radiation applications and radiation biology.

In its technical assistance programme, the Agency seeks to promote the transfer of skills and knowledge relating to the peaceful uses of atomic energy to enable the recipient developing countries to carry out their atomic energy activities more safely and efficiently. Since 1958, the Agency has provided technical assistance to developing countries in the form of services of advisers, fellowships, training opportunities and equipment. In collaboration with FAO, the Agency conducts programmes of applied research on the use of radiation and isotopes in six main fields: efficiency in the use of water and fertilizers; improvement of food crops; eradication or control of destructive insects; improvement of livestock nutrition and health; efficacy of pesticides and increased utilization of agricultural wastes; and food preservation by irradiation.

Director-General: Hans Blix
Headquarters: Vienna International Centre, Wagramerstrasse 5, P.O. Box 100, 1400 Vienna, Austria (telephone: 2360–0; telex: 112645; fax: 234564)
Publications: *Annual Report*; *Nuclear Safety Review* (annually); *IAEA Newsbriefs* (monthly); *IAEA Bulletin* (quarterly); *Nuclear Fusion* (monthly); *Meetings on Atomic Energy* (quarterly); *INIS Atomindex* (fortnightly)

International Bank for Reconstruction and Development [World Bank] (IBRD). The Bank, a specialized agency of the *UN, is the leading organization in the field of multilateral financing of investment and technical assistance and, due to the recent increase in its membership, has become a truly global institution. Together with the *International Monetary Fund (IMF), the Bank originated from the UN Monetary and Financial Conference held at Bretton Woods, New Hampshire (USA), in July 1944, with the participation of 44 countries. According to the 'division of labour' between the two institutions envisaged at Bretton Woods, the Bank was to be essentially concerned with long-term project and economic development finance. while the Fund's activities were primarily intended to provide temporary balance of payments assistance.

The Bank, whose Articles of Agreement came into force in December 1945, began operations in Washington, D.C. in June 1946. Although initially concerned with the reconstruction of Europe after World War II, the Bank has essentially been providing funds and technical assistance to developing nations and underdeveloped areas of the industrialized world. Only members of the IMF are eligible for membership in the Bank; in turn, the latter is a prerequisite for membership of the *International Development Association (IDA). The Bank and IDA, although legally and financially distinct, are from an operational standpoint a closely integrated unit, sharing the same staff. The 'World Bank', as it is commonly known, comprises the IBRD and IDA; these two institutions, together with the *International Finance Corporation (IFC) and the *Multilateral Investment Guarantee Agency (MIGA), form the World Bank Group whose common objective is to meet the entire range of the financial and technical requirements of development by channelling financial resources from industrial countries to the developing world.

Membership of the Bank totals about 170 countries of the industrial and developing world in widely different stages of economic development and representing a variety of economic systems from centrally planned to market economies. Among non-members mention must be made of Cuba, North Korea, and Taiwan, the latter having been replaced as a member by the People's Republic of China in 1980. Russia and the other former Soviet republics joined in early 1992.

The first operations of the Bank included the lending of $497 million to West European countries to facilitate the importation of essential goods. After the launching of the Marshall Plan and the assumption by OEEC of the task of economic recovery in Western Europe, the Bank has concentrated essentially on assisting the economic development of its member nations.

The Bank, using its own capital and funds raised through borrowing in the world capital markets, lends only for productive purposes and pays due regard to the prospects of repayment. Since July 1982, loans have been made at variable interest rates; before then, they were made at fixed rates. The Bank extends financial assistance in cases where private capital is not available at reasonable terms, promotes private investment loans through guarantees or participations and provides technical assistance in the field of overall development plans and specific investment projects. Project loans may include funds earmarked for resource surveys, feasibility studies and training.

The Bank's resources include the subscribed capital stock and its retained earnings and, primarily, the funds borrowed in capital markets. The resources are replenished through the flow of repayments and the sale of portions of outstanding loans, mostly without the Bank guarantee. The capital stock initially authorized by the Articles of Agreement amounted to $10 billion, divided into 100,000 shares with a par value of $100,000 each and available for subscription only by members. The shares subscribed by the original members amounted to $9100 million, the balance of $900 million having been left available for further subscriptions by the founders and by new member countries. Beginning in 1959, due to repeated general increases in the shares and the admission of new members, the Bank's capital stock has been substantially increased. In April 1988 the Board of Governors approved a further increase of about 80 per cent in the Bank's authorized capital to $171 billion. At 30 June 1991, the subscribed capital amounted to $139,120 million, of which less than 10 per cent ($9393 million) was actually paid in, partly in gold or dollars and partly in national currencies. The remainder is subject to call if required to meet the Bank's obligations.

The Bank makes its loans at terms which are fair but sufficient to earn a profit in the form of interest and commission fees. The principal amounts of loans are repayable in the currencies lent. The Bank has not suffered any losses on loans receivable and does not participate in moratoria or reschedulings. Since 1964, it has been the Bank's policy to transfer to IDA part of the year's income which was not needed for allocation to reserves. No dividends are distributed by the Bank to member countries.

The Bank's largest resource is made up by its borrowing operations, including public issues or private placements throughout the world. At 30 June 1991, the Bank's outstanding obligations, denominated in over 20 different currencies, amounted to $84,797 million. The Bank's securities have been placed with investors in more than 100 countries. This diversity allows the Bank flexibility in selecting the markets that will allow optimum borrowing conditions; the same diversity lessens its dependence on any specific market.

The Bank's lending is limited to member countries; the total amount of loans outstanding may not exceed the net amount of subscribed capital stock plus reserves. Each loan must be guaranteed by the government concerned, thus limiting the eligibility for loans to governments and to public bodies and corporations, and virtually excluding private companies.

The Bank's decision to lend should be based only on economic considerations. The general requirements concern the borrower's ability to meet its obligations and the profitability of the projects to be financed, priority being given to those that appear to be most useful. Loans had to be made in principle only for specific development projects which could not be financed from other sources at reasonable terms. The Bank usually finances part of the investment required for each project, and specifically the expenditure in foreign currencies on purchases from other countries of goods and services required for the project, the borrower being required to cover the expenditures in local currency. Each project is closely followed and audited by the Bank in all stages of its implementation. As Bank loans are not tied, borrowers are not required to purchase goods and services in any particular member country. The Bank makes medium- and long-term loans, usually 10 to 20 years, with repayments generally beginning after a grace period of five years. The Bank may make, participate in, or guarantee loans to the IFC for use in its lending operations.

The organization of the Bank, which is similar to that of the IMF, comprises the Board of Governors, the Executive Directors, and the President.

The Board of Governors is vested with full management powers and consists of one governor and one alternate governor appointed by each member country. The Board of Governors normally holds an annual meeting to consider the Bank's operations and set down the basic guidelines to be implemented by the Executive Directors, to whom the Board delegates many of its powers. The powers that cannot be delegated by the governors concern, *inter alia*, the admission of new members, changes in the capital stock and the distribution of the net income of the Bank. The Board's decisions are adopted by a majority of the votes cast, except as otherwise specifically provided. Each member has 250 votes, plus one additional vote for each share of stock held; voting rights are therefore related to the amount of each country's quota in the Bank's capital stock. The largest shareholder is the USA, which subscribed 17.89 per cent of the capital stock and holds 17.32 per cent of the total voting power. Japan subscribed 8.13 per cent and holds 7.89 per cent of the voting power. The respective percentages are 6.28 and 6.09 for Germany; 6.02 and 5.84 each for France and the UK.

There are at present 22 Executive Directors, who permanently reside in Washington, D.C., meet as often as required and are responsible for the Bank's general operations under the powers delegated to them by the Board of Governors. Each of the five largest shareholders (that is the USA, Japan, Germany, France and the UK) appoints a single Executive Director who casts the votes to which each country is entitled. The remaining Directors are elected for a two-year term by the other member countries, grouped according to geographic and other criteria. Each Director casts all the votes of the countries which contributed to his election. It should be noted, however, that the present practice is that most decisions are taken on the basis of consensus, rather than votes cast formally.

The President of the Bank serves as Chairman of the Executive Directors by whom he is elected, conducts the ordinary business of the Bank and is responsible for the organization, appointment and dismissal of the officers and staff. According to a consolidated tradition, the President of the Bank is a US citizen. Robert S. McNamara served as President from 1969 until June 1981 when he was succeeded by A.W. Clausen. The latter was succeeded by Barber Conable who remained in charge until mid-1991. The present President is Lewis T. Preston.

The breadth of the Bank's functions and the multiplicity of the organizations operating in the field of technical and financial development assistance require close interagency co-ordination to prevent overlapping and waste of resources. Guidelines for collaboration between the Bank and its sister Bretton Woods institution, the IMF, have been in place since 1966 and have been periodically reviewed in order to make procedures and practices more effective and systematic. Both organizations share the basic objective of promoting sustained growth and development of member countries and fulfil differing but complementary roles in the pursuit of that objective. The Bank has primary responsibility for development strategies, structural adjustment programmes and efficient allocation of resources whereas the Fund is mainly concerned with the aggregate aspects of macroeconomic policies. Positive results have so far been achieved in a number of areas, including that of debt strategy and arrears. Long-standing relations are maintained by the Bank with UN agencies and programmes concerned with various aspects of development work. Activities have focused increasingly on strengthening the capacity of developing countries to implement and sustain policy reform. The Bank currently acts as executing agency for a growing number of projects financed by the *UN Development Programme (UNDP).

Increasing interagency co-operation involves environmental issues reflecting the widespread concern with the link between environment and development. The UNDP, the *UN Environment Programme (UNEP) and the Bank jointly manage a Global Environment Facility (GEF) to channel scientific and financial resources to middle-income and lower-income countries to help finance programmes and projects affecting the global environment. The facility is intended to cover four main areas: (a) protection of the ozone layer; (b) limitation of greenhouse-gas emissions; (c) protection of biodiversity; and (d) protection against degradation of international water resources. Co-operation has also been rapidly expanding between the Bank and the *UN Centre for Human Settlements (Habitat) with a view to supporting developing countries in the improvement of urban management and disaster preparedness.

The Bank also maintains close working relations with major regional development institutions, such as the *African Development Bank (AfDB), the *Asian Development Bank (AsDB) and the *Inter-American Development Bank (IDB), and with the *European Economic Community (EEC) to assure co-ordination of development assistance activities. The Bank is closely collaborating with other international agencies, including the *Organization for Economic Co-operation and Development (OECD) and the newly-created *European Bank for Reconstruction and Development (EBRD), to help Central and Eastern European countries meet fundamental challenges such as transformation of the economic system, social protection, and environmental clean-up.

Together with the *Food and Agriculture Organization and UNDP, the Bank sponsors the Consultative Group on International Agricultural Research (CGIAR), an informal association of 40 public and private-sector donors supporting a network of 16 international agricultural-research centres. The Bank continues to promote co-operation with non-governmental organizations (NGOs) to ensure that grassroots insights and expertise are duly taken into account at both the policy and project levels.

To ensure the growth of private foreign investment for economic development, the International Centre for Settlement of Investment Disputes (ICSID) was established as a separate international organization, at the Bank's headquarters, under the Convention on the Settlement of Investment Disputes between States and Nationals of Other States, which was opened for signature in 1965 and entered into effect in October 1966. About 100 countries have completed the process of joining the Centre. Subject to the consent of both parties, a Contracting State and a foreign investor who is a national of another Contracting State may therefore settle any legal dispute that might arise out of such an investment by conciliation and/ or arbitration before an impartial international forum. To further its investment promotion objectives, the Centre also carries out a range of research and publications activities in the field of foreign-investment law. The governing body of the Centre is the Administrative Council, consisting of one representative of each Contracting State, all of whom with equal voting power. The President of the IBRD is *ex officio* the non-voting Chairman of the Administrative Council.

The Bank is engaged in providing training for government officials at the middle and upper levels of responsibility who are involved in development programmes and projects through the Economic Development Institute (EDI), founded in 1955. Courses and seminars are held at headquarters in Washington, D.C., or in developing countries. In keeping with the Bank's increased focus on a growth process promoting both equity and financial and environmental sustainability, the Institute concentrates on the issues concerning poverty reduction, human-resource development, protection of the environment, debt and adjustment, public-sector management and private-sector development. The Institute supports training institutions overseas through teaching, advice, course planning and the supply of material. To expand its activities, the Institute has made successful efforts during the 1980s in arranging for co-financing by national and international aid agencies with significant secondary benefits for the expansion of contacts with these agencies and with training institutes in industrial countries.

Between 1947 and 1991, the Bank has made 3302 loans totalling $203 billion to over 110 member countries. The break-

down of the loans according to purpose and region, up to 30 June 1991, is shown in the table.

The Bank has traditionally financed a large number of projects, especially in the field of capital infrastructure, such as roads and railways, airports, ports and power facilities and telecommunications. In response to the deteriorating prospects for the developing countries, a programme of structural-adjustment lending was inaugurated by the Bank in 1980. The lending supports programmes of specific policy changes and institutional reforms in developing countries designed to achieve a more rational use of resources and thereby: (a) to contribute to a more sustainable balance of payments in the medium and long term and to the maintenance of growth in the face of severe constraints; and (b) to provide the basis for regaining momentum for future growth. In 1987 the Bank renewed its efforts to alleviate poverty and to mitigate the unfavourable social effects of economic adjustment programmes. A 'Special Programme of Assistance' for sub-Saharan Africa has increased concessional lending to heavily-indebted and impoverished African countries.In the late 1980s special emphasis was also placed on assisting heavily-indebted middle-income countries, most of them in Latin America. In the past few years the Bank has also been making a sustained effort to provide advice and capital to the countries of Central and Eastern Europe making the transition from command-driven economies to those that are market-oriented. The Gulf crisis initiated with the invasion of Kuwait has affected a large number of developing countries, both inside and outside the Middle East, and the Bank, along with the IMF, has played a significant role in the mobilization of resources in support of the affected countries.

The present developmental strategy of the Bank places a greater emphasis on the financing of projects likely to bring immediate benefits to the poor people in developing countries. The new strategy is particularly directed at operations which promote productive employment and give the poor greater access to social services – health care, basic education, family planning and nutrition; the full integration of women in the development process is another major objective. The protection of the environment is being accorded growing importance – also in the context of the UN Conference on Environment and Development (UNCED) of June 1992 – and the impact of projects (especially in agriculture and energy) on the environment is assessed and monitored. All relevant sectors and all types of projects with potential for major environmental effects are addressed, although the question of the sustainability of economic growth and of the viability of alternative development strategies is still open to considerable debate. In any case, there seems to be little doubt that major adjustments are urgently needed in technologies, policies and institutions. Continuing support is provided to the programme of debt and debt-service reduction; both the Bank and the IMF are actively involved in the negotiation of packages between debtors and commercial banks. Within the context of efforts to encourage private-sector development, a strategy and work programme are being adopted by the Bank in close co-operation with IFC and MIGA. The Bank has undertaken a programme of expanded cofinancing with a view to supporting borrowers' access to private capital markets within the context of the Bank's country-assistance strategies. A 'core poverty programme' for the direct alleviation of poverty among specific groups has been recently introduced. A comprehensive long-term strategy to address the challenge of poverty, which actually increased in many countries during the 1980s, has gradually emerged

International Bank for Reconstruction and Development (IBRD)
Loans to Borrowers in US $ millions
by Major Purpose and Region, at 30 June 1991

Purpose	Africa	Asia	Europe Middle East, and North Africa	Latin America and the Caribbean	Total
Agriculture and Rural Development	3371.8	10,707.7	10,007.0	13,938.5	38,025.0
Development Finance Companies	1059.0	5377.8	6843.7	7311.1	20,591.6
Education	392.1	3390.2	2592.5	1795.4	8170.2
Energy	2167.3	19,362.5	9230.0	12,621.9	43,381.7
Industry	762.7	5424.8	5022.5	4239.5	15,449.5
Non-project	1943.6	3829.3	6085.9	5215.6	17,074.4
Population, Health and Nutrition	289.4	618.8	335.2	1105.8	2349.2
Public-sector Management	0.0	32.0	130.0	1454.0	1616.0
Small-Scale Enterprises	440.7	1431.5	834.0	1985.6	4691.8
Technical Assistance	138.2	53.0	254.8	286.8	733.4
Telecommunications	510.2	1348.2	1091.8	508.3	3458.5
Transportation	2957.8	10,225.0	7497.7	8720.9	29,401.4
Urban Development	933.7	3159.4	981.3	3853.1	8927.5
Water Supply and Sewerage	1059.8	1685.4	3064.8	3373.7	9183.7
Total	16,026.9	66,645.6	53,971.2	66,410.2	203,053.9

Source: *The World Bank Annual Report 1991*, p. 180.

and is going to characterize all assistance programmes undertaken by the Bank in the current decade.

Most Bank activities involve various forms of technical assistance to meet gaps in project preparation and for institution building. Project loans and credits may include funds specifically earmarked for feasibility studies, resource surveys, management and planning advice, and training. Technical assistance, usually reimbursable, is also extended to countries which do not need financial support, notably for training and transfer of technology and for the preparation of overall and sectoral development strategies.

The record of the development experience in over four decades seems to be both encouraging and sobering. A positive role has certainly been performed by the Bank in helping towards a solution of the problems of underdevelopment in the area of both financial and technical assistance. Yet, despite substantial progress in the growth rates of the developing countries, the living standards of the poor in some of the slower-growing countries have not improved or have even deteriorated.

The effective action of the Bank and of the other two institutions (IDA and IFC) of the World Bank Group was seriously obstructed by the sharp increase in the debt service obligations of developing countries, the recession in the industrial economies and resultant decrease in the financial resources to be allocated to developing areas, and the inadequate co-ordination and overlapping in the complex web of international development assistance. The persistent difficulties to reach agreement on the conclusion of the Uruguay Round of multilateral trade negotiations within the framework of the *General Agreement on Tariffs and Trade (GATT) are having serious repercussions on the interests of developing countries. The reform of a number of agricultural and industrial policies of the developed world might substantially enhance the growth prospects of many poor countries. The declining share of the developing nations in the total supply of capital, and the deteriorating balance between medium-term lending from private

sources and long-term lending from the Bank have made it necessary to increase the Bank's capital. Not only will the capital increase enable Bank lending to continue growing in real terms in the future but will also provide assurance to private lenders about the quality of investment programmes and debt management.

The experience of the past few years highlighted the need for the Bank to be able to respond to altered circumstances by having at its disposal a variety of flexible lending strategies. Extensive discussion is being held within the framework of the Bank on lending policies and consideration is given to a range of possible innovations that could be used in exceptional circumstances. Efforts to strengthen planning and policy reform are being stepped up and, where possible, disbursements are accelerated to support governments of developing countries in the difficult decisions they need to make to ensure the effective use of resource flows.

President: Lewis T. Preston
Headquarters: 1818 H Street, N.W., Washington, D.C. 20433, USA (telephone: 477 1234; telex: RCA 248423 WORLDBK – WUI 64145 WORLDBANK; fax: 477 6391)
European Office: 66 Avenue d'Iéna, 75116 Paris, France (telephone: 4069 3000; telex: 842–640651; fax: 4069 3066)
Tokyo Office: Kokusai Building, 1–1, Marunouchi 3–chome, Chiyoda-ku, Tokyo 100, Japan (telephone: 3214 5001; telex: 781–26838; fax: 3214 3657)
Publications: *Annual Report*; *The World Bank Atlas* (annual); *World Development Report* (annual)
References: A. Cairncross: *The International Bank for Reconstruction and Development* (Princeton, 1959); A.J.M. van de Laar: *The World Bank and the World's Poor* (The Hague, 1976); E.H. Rotberg: *The World Bank: a Financial Appraisal* (Washington, 1976); R.T. Libby: *The Ideology and Power of the World Bank* (Ann Arbor, Michigan, 1977); C. Payer: *The World Bank: A Critical Analysis* (London, 1982)

International Civil Aviation Organization (ICAO). The Organization aims to develop the principles and techniques of international air navigation and to help in the planning and improvement of international air transport.

The Organization was established under the Chicago Convention on International Civil Aviation, adopted in December 1944 at the conclusion of the International Civil Aviation Conference, and entered into force in April 1947. For about two years, pending the formal establishment of the permanent organization, an interim organization was in operation – the Provisional International Civil Aviation Organization (PICAO). A relationship agreement with the UN was concluded by PICAO and subsequently ratified by the permanent organization in 1947.

As between contracting parties, the Chicago Convention superseded the provisions of the Convention relating to the Regulation of Aerial Navigation, signed in Paris in October 1919, which established the International Commission for Air Navigation (ICAN), and the Convention on Commercial Aviation concluded at Havana in February 1928. The Chicago Convention is supplemented by a number of Annexes containing specifications concerning international standards and recommended practices and procedures with which member countries are to comply in order to ensure the safety and regularity of international air navigation. Specifications are kept under constant review and are periodically revised in keeping with technological developments and changing requirements. The present membership of the Organization includes over 160 countries.

According to the Convention, the expression 'international air service' means any scheduled air service, performed by aircraft for the public transport of passengers, mail or cargo, which passes through the air space over the territory of more than one country.

The objectives of the Organization are basically the following: to ensure safe and orderly growth of international civil aviation throughout the world; to encourage skills in aircraft design and operation for peaceful purposes; to improve airways, airports and air navigation facilities; to meet the needs of the peoples of the world for safe, regular, efficient and economical air transport; to prevent the waste of resources caused by unreasonable competition; to safeguard the rights of member countries to operate international airlines; to prevent discriminatory practices; to promote safety of flight in international air navigation; to foster the development of all aspects of international civil aeronautics. The most significant functions of the Organization include: establishing international standards and recommended practices and procedures; promoting simpler formalities at international borders; developing regional plans for ground facilities and services; collecting and publishing air-transport statistics; preparing studies on the economic aspects of aviation; and fostering the development of air law conventions.

Members of the UN may accede to the Organization, according to current provisions. Any sovereign country, not a member of the UN, may be admitted to the Organization by means of a four-fifths vote of the Assembly. Withdrawal is permitted upon submission of notice of denunciation; withdrawal takes effect after one year.

The Organization's structure is made up of an Assembly, a Council with various subordinate bodies and a Secretariat. The Assembly, composed of representatives of all member countries, is the legislative body and meets at least once every three years. It lays down basic policies, examines and takes appropriate action on the reports of the Council and decides on any matter referred to it by the Council, approves the budget, considers proposals for the modification or amendment of the Convention and deals with any matter within the sphere of action of the Organization not specifically assigned to the Council. Decisions of the Assembly are taken by a majority of the votes cast, unless expressly provided otherwise.

The Council is the permanent governing body, composed of the representatives of 33 countries elected by the Assembly for a three-year term, and meets in virtually continuous session. Members of the Council are appointed under three headings: countries of chief importance in air transport; countries making the largest contribution to the provision of facilities for international civil air navigation; countries whose designation will ensure that all major geographical areas are represented. The Council: carries out Assembly directives; administers the Organization's finance; adopts international standards and recommended practices, incorporates them as Annexes to the Convention and notifies all member countries to that effect; takes whatever steps are necessary to maintain safety and regularity of operation of international air transport; provides technical assistance; compiles, examines and publishes information on air navigation; and may act, if requested by the member countries concerned, as a tribunal for the settlement of any dispute relating to international civil aviation. The Council elects its President, appoints the chief executive officer who is called the Secretary-General and makes provision for the appointment of the necessary staff. Decisions by the Council normally require approval by a majority of its members.

The Council is assisted by an important subsidiary body, the Air Navigation Commission, composed of 15 people with suitable qualifications and experience and appointed by the Council from among nominations submitted by member countries. The Commission is responsible for: considering and recommending to the Council the adoption or amendment of the Annexes to the Convention; establishing technical sub-commissions; and advising the Council about the collection and communication to member countries of all information that is considered necessary and useful for the advancement of air navigation. Other subsidiary bodies include standing Committees on: Air Transport; Joint Support of Air Navigation Services; Financial Problems; Legal Problems; and Unlawful Interference.

The Secretariat, under the Secretary-General, comprises five Bureaux dealing with: Air Navigation; Air Transport; Technical Assistance; Legal Problems; and Administration and Services. Besides its headquarters in Canada, the Organization has regional offices for: Western and Central Africa (Dakar); Eastern and Southern Africa (Nairobi); Asia and Pacific (Bangkok); Europe (Neuilly-sur-Seine, France); Middle East (Cairo); North America, Central America and the Caribbean (Mexico City); and South America (Lima). These offices assist, expedite and follow up the implementation of the Air Navigation Plans and maintain them up-to-date.

The Organization works in close co-operation with other agencies of the UN such as the *World Meteorological Organization (WMO), the *International Telecommunication Union (ITU), the *Universal Postal Union (UPU), the *World Health Organization (WHO) and the *International Maritime Organization (IMO). Technical assistance is extended to developing countries under the *UN Development Programme (UNDP) and other specific programmes. Non-governmental institutions which participate in the Organization's work include the International Air Transport Association (IATA), the International Federation of Air Line Pilots Associations, and the International Council of Aircraft Owner and Pilot Associations.

Annual budgets, annual statements of accounts and estimates of all receipts and expenditures are submitted to the Assembly by the Council. The expenses of the Organization are apportioned among member countries on a basis which is determined by the Assembly.

From its inception the Organization has provided an efficient machinery for the achievement of international co-operation in the air, improving safety and regularity and promoting the use of new technical methods and equipment. Among the Organization's activities special mention should be made of standardization, that is the establishment and amendment of international standards and recommended practices and procedures in the technical sphere: licensing of personnel; rules of the air; aeronautical meteorology; aeronautical charts; units of measurement; operation of aircraft; nationality and registration marks; airworthiness; aeronautical telecommunications; air traffic services; search and rescue; aircraft accident inquiry; aerodromes; aeronautical information services and aircraft noise. Extensive work has been undertaken by the Organization in the areas of automatic reporting of data on aircraft accidents, all-weather operations, automation of air traffic services and the application of computers in meteorological services. The Organization has become increasingly concerned with the questions regarding aviation and the protection of the environment. For the past two decades, efforts have also been made towards simplification of government customs, immigration, public health and other regulations relating to international air transport. The Organization has also been responsible for drafting several international air law conventions, involving such varied subjects as the international recognition of property rights in aircraft, damage done by aircraft to parties on the surface, the liability of the air carrier to its passengers, crimes committed on board and unlawful interference with civil aviation. A study is under way concerning the UN Convention on the Law of the Sea and its implications for international air law instruments. Through technical assistance, the Organization has helped developing countries to build up air transport services and to train personnel; most of the work has been directed towards the development of ground services and the creation of large civil aviation training centres at regional level.

Secretary-General: Dr Philippe Rochat

Headquarters: 1000 Sherbrooke St West, Montreal, Quebec, Canada H3A 2R2 (telephone: 285 8219; telex: 05–24513; fax: 288 4772)

Publications: *Annual Report*; *ICAO Journal* (monthly)

International Development Association (IDA). The Association is a lending agency intended to finance development projects in the poorer developing member countries for the same general purposes as the *International Bank for Reconstruction and Development (IBRD) but on terms which are more flexible and bear less heavily on the balance of payments than those of conventional loans – thereby furthering the objectives of the IBRD and supplementing its activities. The Association and the IBRD are commonly referred to as the 'World Bank'.

The Association was established as an affiliate of the IBRD by Articles of Agreement which were opened for signature in February 1960 and came into force in September of the same year. The agreement was drawn up by the Executive Directors of the IBRD, pursuant to a resolution of the Board of Governors of October 1959.

Membership is open to all members of the IBRD, and about 150 of them have joined to date. Although legally and financially distinct from the IBRD, the Association is administered by the same staff. These two institutions, together with the *International Finance Corporation (IFC) and the *Multilateral Investment Guarantee Agency (MIGA), form the 'World Bank Group' whose common objective is to help raise the standards of living in the developing countries by conveying financial resources from the developed world. The Association concentrates its assistance on the very poor countries – those with an annual per capita gross national product of $580 or less (in 1989 dollars). More than 40 developing countries are eligible under this criterion.

The funds used by the Association, called credits to distinguish them from IBRD loans, come mostly in the form of subscriptions, general replenishments from the more industrialized and developed members and special contributions by richer members as well as transfers from the net earnings of the IBRD. Membership is divided into two categories. Part I countries pay all subscriptions and supplementary resources in convertible currencies (Australia, Austria, Belgium, Canada, Denmark, Finland, France, Germany, Iceland, Ireland, Italy, Japan, Kuwait, Luxembourg, the Netherlands, New Zealand, Norway, South Africa, Sweden, the United Arab Emirates, the UK, and the USA). Part II countries (including over 130 developing nations) pay 10 per cent of their initial subscriptions in freely convertible currencies and the remaining 90 per cent of their initial subscriptions and all additional subscriptions and any supplementary resources in their own currencies. The currency of any Part II member may not be used for projects located outside the territories of the member except by agreement between the member and the Association. Operations are conducted in the currencies of all member countries. As at 30 June 1991, total subscriptions and supplementary resources (through the various replenishments) amounted to $68,861 million, of which 96 per cent ($65,944 million) was contributed by Part I members. Resources are replenished periodically by contributions from the more affluent member countries. The ninth replenishment became effective in January 1991.

The Association's lending is limited to member countries, normally only for specific projects, and is based on principles similar to those of the IBRD. Each credit must be guaranteed by the government concerned. The decision to lend must be based only on economic considerations in the light of the needs of the area or areas concerned. Funds are made available to the recipient only to meet expenses in connection with the project as they are actually incurred; the use of credits cannot be restricted to the purchase of goods and services in any particular member country. Each project is closely followed in all stages of its implementation with due attention being paid to considerations of economy, efficiency and competitive international trade. Credits are usually extended for a period of 35 or 40 years with a 10-year initial grace period and no interest charge; an annual service fee is charged on both the disbursed and undisbursed portion of each credit.

The organization of the Association comprises the Board of Governors, the Executive Directors, the President and the necessary operating staff. All the powers of the Association are vested in the Board of Governors – consisting of one governor and one alternate from each member country – which delegates to the Executive Directors (at present 22) authority to exercise many of its powers. Governors and Directors of the IBRD serve *ex officio* in the Association; the President of the IBRD (at present Lewis T. Preston of the USA) is *ex officio* President of the Association and Chairman of the Executive Directors. Officers and staff of the IBRD serve concurrently as officers and staff of the Association.

All matters before the Association are decided by a majority of the votes cast, except as otherwise specifically provided. Voting rights are related, at least in part, to the amount of each country's contribution to the Association's resources. The USA, which contributed 27.42 per cent of the total subscriptions and supplementary resources, holds 16.62 per cent of the total voting power. The second largest contributor is Japan which contributed 21.30 per cent of the total resources and holds 9.77 per cent of the vote.

The Association co-operates with several organizations within and outside the UN system. Although co-operative relationships are in some cases spelled out in formal agreements, more often they evolve as informal consultations on specific problems and from joint missions and parallel undertakings, especially as regards assistance to low-income countries whose development prospects have been severely impaired by external factors.

By 30 June 1991 the Association had granted 2108 credits totalling $64,515.3 million to about 90 member countries (joint loans and credits by the IBRD and the Association are not included but are counted instead as IBRD operations). The breakdown of credits according to purpose and region is shown in the table.

While the Association has traditionally financed all kinds of capital infrastructure, its present developmental strategy is focused on projects that directly affect the well-being of the poorest segments of society in the developing countries by mobilizing domestic resources to achieve faster growth. This strategy is increasingly evident in agriculture and rural development projects as well as in projects concerning education, population, health, and nutrition. Besides poverty alleviation, the Association is increasingly focusing on debt and debt-service reduction, private-sector development, the reform of socialist econo-

International Development Association (IDA)
Credits to Borrowers in US $ millions
by Major Purpose and Region, at 30 June 1991

Purpose	Africa	Asia	Europe, Middle East, and North Africa	Latin America and the Caribbean	Total
Agriculture and Rural Development	5975.7	13,993.2	2258.3	250.5	22,477.7
Development Finance Companies	1281.2	578.6	273.7	144.1	2277.6
Education	2045.2	2393.5	730.5	86.2	5255.4
Energy	1557.6	4042.7	504.6	222.7	6327.6
Industry	496.3	1360.7	161.4	49.5	2067.9
Non-project	3127.5	3070.5	395.0	287.4	6880.4
Population, Health and Nutrition	842.1	1337.3	313.2	99.5	2592.1
Public-sector Management	307.7	0.0	0.0	0.0	307.7
Small-Scale Enterprises	228.7	281.5	88.8	27.5	626.5
Technical Assistance	737.3	155.2	44.6	38.5	975.6
Telecommunications	352.1	869.3	142.7	0.0	1364.1
Transportation	4123.8	3036.0	498.0	228.3	7886.1
Urban Development	868.5	1448.7	251.3	127.0	2695.5
Water Supply and Sewerage	675.5	1453.2	573.6	78.8	2781.1
Total	22,619.2	34,020.4	6235.7	1640.0	64,515.3

Source: *The World Bank Annual Report 1991*, p. 181.

mies, and the role of women in development.

President: Lewis T. Preston
Headquarters: 1818 H Street, N.W., Washington, D.C. 20433, USA (telephone: 477 1234; telex: RCA 248423 WORLDBK – WUI 64145 WORLDBANK; fax: 477 6391)
European Office: 66 Avenue d'Iéna, 75116 Paris, France (telephone: 4069 3000; telex: 842–640651; fax: 4069 3066)
Tokyo Office: Kokusai Building, 1–1, Marunouchi 3–chome, Chiyoda-ku, Tokyo 100, Japan (telephone: 3214 5001; telex: 781–26838; fax: 3214 3657)
Publications: *World Bank Annual Report*; *World Development Report* (annually)

International Energy Agency (IEA). The Agency was set up in 1974 by the Council of the *Organization for Economic Co-operation and Development (OECD). It aims to develop collaboration on energy questions between its members, which include most Western European countries (except France) plus Australia, Canada, Japan, New Zealand, and the USA. The Commission of the European Communities is also represented.

The Agency was established as an operating body within the framework of the OECD when the energy problems of Western countries had become acute due to the dramatic increase in oil prices by the members of the *Organization of the Petroleum Exporting Countries (OPEC). It aims to foster co-operation among major oil importing nations, to promote stability in world energy markets and to ensure the security of energy supplies.

The Agreement on an International Energy Programme was signed in November 1974 in Paris and came into force in January 1976. Under the Programme, countries participating in the Agency agree to share oil in emergencies, to strengthen long-term co-operation with a view to reducing dependence on oil imports, to increase the availability of information on the oil markets and to establish closer ties with the oil-producing and the other oil-consuming countries. The Long-Term Co-operation Programme envisages co-ordinated efforts to conserve energy, to accelerate the development of alternative sources through specific and general measures, to encourage research and development of new technologies, and to remove legislative and administrative obstacles to increased supplies.

The decision-making power in the Agency rests with the Governing Board, composed of ministers or senior officials of member countries. Decisions are taken by unanimous vote only if member countries are to be charged with additional obligations, not already specified in the founding Agreement. On all other questions the rule of weighted majority is in use. Qualified majority is required on a number of important questions, such as aspects of stockpiling, oil-sharing contingency plans and relations with the oil companies. Simple majority suffices with regard to routine matters. The Governing Board is assisted by four Standing Groups which are responsible for: Emergency questions; Long-term co-operation; Oil market; and Relations with producer and other consumer countries. There are also a High-Level Committee on Energy Research and Development and a Coal and Oil Industry Advisory Board; the latter body is composed of industrial executives. Administrative functions are performed by the Secretariat headed by a Chairman assisted by an Executive Director and a Deputy Executive Director.

The Agency has adopted an emergency oil-sharing plan to be put into operation in the event of a reduction in oil supplies to member countries. An extensive system providing information and consultation on the oil market and its prospects is in force. Regular reviews are conducted in order to assess the effectiveness of national programmes of member countries in the fields of energy conservation and use of alternative sources.

Executive Director: Helga Steeg

Headquarters: 2 rue André Pascal, 75775 Paris, France (telephone: 4524 8200; telex: 630190)

International Finance Corporation (IFC). The Corporation's function is to assist less developed countries by promoting growth in the private sector of their economies and helping to mobilize domestic and foreign capital, thus supplementing as an affiliate the activities of the *International Bank for Reconstruction and Development (IBRD).

The Corporation was established by Articles of Agreement which were drawn up within the framework of the IBRD and opened for signature in April 1955. The agreement entered into force in July 1956 and has been subsequently amended.

Membership of the IBRD is a prerequisite for membership in the Corporation, which now totals over 140 countries. Legally and financially, the Corporation and the IBRD are separate entities. The Corporation has its own operating and legal staff, but draws upon the IBRD for administrative and other services. These two institutions, together with the *International Development Association (IDA) and the *Multilateral Investment Guarantee Agency (MIGA), make up the 'World Bank Group' whose common aim is to facilitate economic development in the poorer member countries by providing funds and technical assistance.

The Corporation combines the characteristics of a multilateral development bank and a private financial institution. The basic functions of the Corporation are: (a) to provide – in association with private investors and without government guarantee – risk capital for productive private enterprises of economic priority in developing member countries, in cases where sufficient private capital is not available on reasonable terms; (b) to stimulate and to help create conditions conducive to the flow of domestic and foreign private capital into productive investment; (c) to encourage the development of local capital markets; (d) to provide financial and technical assistance to privately controlled development finance companies; (e) to support joint ventures which provide opportunities to combine domestic sponsorship and knowledge of market and other conditions with the technical and managerial experience available in the industrial countries; and (f) to revolve its portfolio and to undertake new commitments by selling parts of its investments to other investors. The Corporation also provides businesses and governments with advisory services and technical assistance on a wide range of topics. The Corporation does not engage in operations intended primarily for refunding, direct financing of exports or imports, or land development.

The Corporation's resources come from subscriptions by its member countries and from accumulated earnings; however, most of the funds for lending activities are raised through bond issues in the international financial markets. The Corporation also borrows from the World Bank with which it has a Master Loan Agreement. An increase in the authorized capital from $110 million to $650 million was approved in 1977; following the authorization, in 1985, of new shares in the amount of $650 million, the capital rose to $1.3 billion. At 30 June 1991, paid-in capital amounted to $1145 million. In the second half of 1991, after more than a year of discussions among shareholders, it was decided to increase the capital stock to $2.3 billion. The $1 billion increase in the capital has been considered crucial to permit the Corporation to embark on a new period of growth and to expand its operations substantially during the 1990s.

The Corporation provides financing by subscribing to shares, usually in conjunction with a long-term loan; loan capital without equity or an equity feature is provided only in exceptional cases. The proportion of equity to loan capital and the interest rate on loan funds are determined

in relation to a number of factors such as the risk involved and the prospective overall return on the investment. The Corporation invests in shares which are denominated in the currency of the country in which the enterprise is located; loans may be denominated in any major international currency but most of them are usually expressed in terms of US dollars. The normal range of final maturities is from 5 to 15 years, although the Corporation is prepared, under exceptional circumstances, to extend loans with longer final maturities; a grace period of 1 to 5 years is customarily allowed before amortization payments begin. All loans are made at market rates; standard front-end and commitment fees are also charged. Financing is also provided by the Corporation through standby or underwriting arrangements in support of public offerings or private placements of shares, debentures or other corporate securities. Joint transactions with development finance companies may involve direct investments, standby or underwriting arrangements or a combination of these.

As the Corporation seeks to supplement and not to compete with private capital, it looks to other investors to provide a substantial part of the capital required for a project. The Corporation generally mobilizes substantial project financing from other sources either indirectly, in the form of co-financing, or directly, through loan syndications, and underwriting of debt and equity issues in domestic and international markets. It expects its investment partners to provide management and does not seek representation on the board of directors. Annual financial statements, audited by independent public accountants, are required by the Corporation from the company in which it invests.

The Board of Governors, in which all powers of the Corporation are vested, consists of the governors and alternates of the IBRD who represent countries which are also members of the Corporation. Most powers are delegated to the Board of Directors, composed *ex officio* of the Executive Directors of the IBRD who represent countries which are also members of the Corporation; project financing operations are approved by the Board of Directors. The voting power of each member country is related to its contribution to the capital stock. The USA paid 24.59 per cent of the capital stock and has 23.88 per cent of the total voting power. Japan paid 6.97 per cent and has 6.78 of the voting power, closely followed by Germany whose percentages are respectively 6.37 and 6.20.

The President of the IBRD serves *ex officio* as Chairman of the Board of Directors and is President of the Corporation. The President is assisted by an Executive Vice President, responsible for overall management and day-to-day decision-making, and by five Vice Presidents. Besides its headquarters in Washington, D.C., the Corporation has offices in London, Paris and Tokyo as well as Regional and Resident Missions in several developing countries. The Foreign Investment Advisory Service (FIAS), established by the Corporation in 1986 and now jointly operated with MIGA, advises governments on laws, policies, regulations, programmes and institutions that can help attract foreign direct investment. The operations of FIAS are financed by the Corporation, MIGA, the *UN Development Programme (UNDP) and the FIAS Trust Fund.

The Corporation co-operates closely with other international agencies involved in development assistance activities and the promotion of investment opportunities. At 30 June 1991, cumulative gross commitments (composed of disbursed and undisbursed balances) totalled $13,544 billion involving over 900 companies in about 100 member countries.

The Corporation has established itself as the largest source of direct financing for private sector projects in developing countries. According to the strategy presently followed by the World Bank Group in order to adjust to the new economic environment, the Corporation's operations are redirected towards becoming more responsive to the evolving needs of its poorer member countries. Private sector development is widely recognized as a major tool for the stimulation of economic growth and the alleviation of poverty in developing countries. Supported by its last capital increase, the Corporation will be expanding the amount and number of investments and adding to the number of countries in which it is active. The catalytic role of the Corporation through the mobilization of large amounts of capital from private sources retains its paramount importance; new mobilization techniques, such as securitized loan sales, are being developed.

Priority will be given to assisting governments with privatization programmes and direct financial and non-financial assistance to small and medium-sized enterprises will be increased. All projects with a potential impact on the environment will be reviewed during the appraisal process and monitored after implementation to ensure conformity with World Bank and international guidelines and host-country rules. Financial and technical assistance is especially needed in the Central and Eastern European countries making their transition to a market-based economy and building their private sectors. It is to be expected that in the near future the Corporation will play a leading part in developing private sector strategies, while the World Bank will retain its primary role in policy dialogue with governments. More precisely, the Corporation will focus on specific transactions and the World Bank, for its part, will help governments establish and strengthen a macroeconomic environment conducive to prosperity for private enterprise; MIGA, on the other hand, will encourage private investment by providing insurance against political risks.

President: Lewis T. Preston
Headquarters: 1818 H Street, N.W., Washington, D.C. 20433, USA (telephone: 477 1234; fax: 477 6391)
Publication: *Annual Report*

International Fund for Agricultural Development (IFAD). The purpose of the Fund is to mobilize additional financial resources for agricultural and rural development in developing countries through projects and programmes directly benefiting the poorest rural populations.

Following one of the proposals put forward by the 1974 World Food Conference, the agreement establishing the Fund was adopted in June 1976 by the representatives of 91 countries at a UN Conference of Plenipotentiaries. After the attainment of initial pledges of $1 billion, the agreement was opened for signature in December 1976; it entered into force in November 1977 and the Fund began its operations the following month. The present membership includes over 140 countries divided into three main groups: Category I consists of developed countries which are members of the *Organization for Economic Cooperation and Development (OECD); Category II is composed of developing countries which are members of the *Organization of the Petroleum Exporting Countries (OPEC); Category III is made up of over 100 other developing countries. Members of Category I and II (donor countries) contribute to the resources of the Fund while members of Category III (recipient countries) may do so.

The Fund makes loans or grants to developing member countries or to intergovernmental organizations in which such members participate for financing projects which introduce or improve methods of food production and strengthen related national policies and institutions. In line with the Fund's focus on the rural poor, priority is given to projects that meet three interrelated objectives: to increase food production, particularly on small farms; to generate employment and additional income for poor and landless farmers; and to improve nutritional levels and food distribution systems.

Financing by the Fund is provided through loans or grants, the latter being limited by statute to 12.5 per cent of the resources committed in any one financial year. Loans are of three kinds: highly concessional loans, repayable over very long periods (50 years including a 10-year grace period), carrying no interest but only an annual service charge of 1 per cent; intermediate term loans, repayable over 20 years (including a 5-year grace period), bearing an interest rate of 4 per cent; and ordinary term loans, repayable over 15 to 18 years (including a 3-year grace period), carrying an interest rate of 8 per cent. The administration of loans is usually entrusted

by the Fund to competent international financial institutions in order to avoid duplication of work. The Fund has succeeded in attracting other external donors and beneficiary governments for the cofinancing of projects thereby stretching the impact of its own resources.

The Fund's total initial resources amounted to a little over $1 billion. Of the total amount pledged, 55.5 per cent was contributed by members of Category I; 42.5 per cent by Category II; and 2 per cent by Category III. Periodical reviews are conducted to appraise the adequacy of available resources. In January 1980 a resolution was adopted recommending replenishment of the Fund's resources at a level sufficient to provide an increase in real terms in the level of its operations. A final agreement on the level of the first replenishment was reached in early 1982. Negotiations took place between 1983 and 1985 on the second replenishment and a compromise was finally reached in January 1986 on a replenishment of $460 million; this was supplemented by an extra $300 million for a Special Programme for Sub-Saharan African Countries Affected by Drought and Desertification (SPA). The third replenishment was agreed upon in June 1989 for an amount of $523 million.

All the powers of the Fund are vested in the Governing Council in which each member country is represented by a governor and an alternate governor. The Governing Council holds ordinary sessions at yearly intervals and may delegate certain powers to the Executive Board. The 18 members and 17 alternates of the Executive Board are elected for a three-year term by the Governing Council, one third by each category. The Executive Board, meeting three or four times a year, is responsible for the general operation of the Fund and for the approval of loans and grants. The Governing Council elects the President of the Fund by a two-thirds majority for a renewable three-year term. The President also acts as Chairman of the Executive Board. The total votes of both the Governing Council and the Executive Board are distributed equally among the three categories of members, thus ensuring that the developing countries (Categories

II and III) have a major influence on the Fund's investment decisions. In the Governing Council voting rights of members of Categories I and II are partly related to the amount of each country's contribution, and are shared evenly among members of Category III. In the Executive Board, each Director casts the votes of the countries that contributed to his election.

The Fund co-operates closely with other international institutions, notably its sister food agencies in Rome, that is the *Food and Agriculture Organization (FAO), the *World Food Programme (WFP) and the *World Food Council (WFC). Co-operative relations exist with the *World Bank and the *International Monetary Fund (IMF) and many other UN agencies and bodies such as the *UN Development Programme (UNDP) and the *UN Population Fund (UNFPA).

Between 1978 and 1990, loans and grants extended by the Fund under the Regular Programme and the Special Programme for Africa amounted to $3271 million of which $3110 million were represented by loans and $161 million by grants. During this period about two-thirds of loans were in the highly concessional category. The size of the Fund's operations had decreased between 1982 and 1986 because actual payments on the part of some member countries were much slower than expected; the Fund's financing levels have fully recovered since that period.

Besides its regular efforts to identify projects and programmes, the Fund organizes programming missions to selected countries to undertake a comprehensive review of the constraints affecting IFAD-type projects among the rural poor, and to help countries to design strategies for the removal of these constraints. Projects recommended by programming missions generally focus on institutional improvements at national and local level with a view to directing inputs and services to small farmers and the landless rural poor. During the late 1980s increased emphasis has been placed on environmental conservation in order to try to alleviate poverty resulting from the deterioration of natural resources.

President: Idriss Jazairy
Headquarters: Via del Serafico 107, 00142 Rome, Italy (telephone: 54591; telex: 620330; fax: 504 3463)
Publication: *Annual Report*

International Labour Organization (ILO). The principal aim of the Organization is to contribute to the establishment of universal and lasting peace based upon social justice by improving, through international action, labour conditions and living standards.

The Organization was established as an autonomous institution within the system of the League of Nations, its Constitution being embodied in a separate part of the Peace Treaties of 1919 and 1920. The supreme body of the Organization met in 1945 and 1946 and amended the Constitution in order to sever the link with the League of Nations and to anticipate a new relationship with the UN. Other amendments were subsequently introduced on several occasions. The Organization became the first specialized agency associated with the UN through the conclusion of a formal relationship agreement which entered into effect in December 1946. The Organization, which originally comprised 45 countries, now numbers over 150 members. In 1977 the USA exercised its right to withdraw from the Organization on mainly political grounds but resumed full participation in February 1980.

Under the Declaration concerning the Aims and Purposes of the Organization adopted in Philadelphia in May 1944, the fundamental principles which inspire the Organization's work include the following: (a) labour is not a commodity; (b) freedom of expression and freedom of association are essential to sustained progress; (c) poverty anywhere constitutes a danger to prosperity everywhere; and (d) the war against want is to be carried on by continuous and concerted international effort in which the representatives of workers and employers, enjoying equal status with those of governments, join with them in free discussion and democratic decision with a view to promoting common welfare.

The Declaration solemnly affirms the right of all human beings, irrespective of race, creed or sex, to pursue both their material well-being and their spiritual development in conditions of freedom and dignity, economic security and equal opportunity. The attainment of such conditions must constitute the central aim of national and international policies and measures, especially those of an economic and financial character, which should therefore be considered by the Organization in the light of this fundamental objective.

According to the Constitution, the improvement of labour conditions is to be achieved, *inter alia*, by the regulation of the hours of work, including the establishment of a maximum working day and week, the regulation of the labour supply, the prevention of unemployment, the provision of an adequate living wage, the protection of the worker against sickness, disease and injury arising out of his employment, the protection of children, young persons and women, the provision for old age and injury, the protection of the interests of workers when employed in countries other than their own, the recognition of the principle of equal remuneration for work of equal value, the recognition of the principle of freedom of association, and the organization of vocational and technical education. To this end, the Organization brings together government, labour and management to recommend international minimum standards and to draft international labour conventions.

Member countries are required to submit conventions, within a prescribed period of time, to the competent national authorities for the enactment of legislation or other appropriate action. When the competent authorities give their consent, the member is bound to communicate the formal ratification of the convention to the Organization and to take all necessary steps. The member is required to make a periodical report to the Organization on the implementation of the provisions of the convention. The obligation to report periodically the position of national law and practice, in regard to the matters dealt with in a convention, also applies to the non-ratifying member which, moreover, must state the difficulties preventing or delaying ratification. In the case of recommendations, members are again required to bring them before the competent national authorities but are under no further obligation other than that of reporting to the Organization, at appropriate intervals, the position of the law and practice in their countries showing the extent to which effect has been given to the provisions of such recommendations with any modifications that have been found necessary. Besides its legislative functions, the Organization provides extensive technical assistance in co-operation with the governments concerned and carries out research and publication activities on social and labour matters.

As distinct from the automatic membership of the Organization originally provided for all members of the League of Nations, membership is now entirely voluntary. Members of the UN may accede to the Organization in conformity with current provisions. Any sovereign country, not a member of the UN, may be admitted to the Organization by a vote concurred in by two-thirds of the delegates attending the session of the International Labour Conference, including two-thirds of the government delegates present and voting. Unilateral withdrawal is allowed upon submission of written notice to that effect to the Director-General and takes effect two years thereafter. Withdrawal shall not affect the continued validity of obligations arising under any international labour convention ratified by the country which terminates its membership.

The Organization's structure is made up of the International Labour Conference, the Governing Body, and the International Labour Office. The Conference is the supreme deliberative organ and meets annually in Geneva, with a session devoted to maritime questions when necessary. National delegations are composed of two government delegates plus one delegate representing employers and one representing workers. As every delegate is entitled to vote individually, non-government delegates can speak and vote independently of the views of their respective governments. The primary function of the Conference is to adopt international labour conventions and recommendations by a two-thirds majority of the votes cast by the delegates present. The Governing Body (elected by the Conference for a three-year term) is the Organization's executive council. It meets three or four times a year in Geneva to implement policies and programmes and to supervise the work of the International Labour Office and of the various committees and commissions. The Governing Body has the same tripartite structure as the Conference. It is composed of 56 members, 28 representing governments, 14 representing employers and 14 representing workers. Of the 28 persons representing governments, 10 are appointed by the members 'of chief industrial importance' (at present Brazil, China, France, Germany, India, Italy, Japan, Russia, the UK and the USA), and 18 are appointed by the members selected every three years by the government delegates to the Conference, excluding the delegates of the 10 members mentioned above. Employers' and workers' members are elected as individuals, not as national candidates.

The International Labour Office is headed by a Director-General. It serves as secretariat, operational headquarters, research centre and publishing house. In particular, it collects and distributes information, assists governments upon request in drafting legislation on the basis of decisions of the Conference, administers the technical co-operation programmes, undertakes special investigations and provides machinery to assist in the effective application of conventions. Operations are decentralized to regional, area and branch offices in about 40 countries. Regional offices are based in Abidjan (for Africa), Lima (for the Americas), Geneva (for Arab States), and Bangkok (for Asia and the Pacific).

The International Institute for Labour Studies was established by the Organization in March 1960 in Geneva. It is an advanced educational and research institution dealing with social and labour policy and bringing together international experts representing employers, manage-

ment, workers and government interests and other specialists. Its activities are financed by grants and an Endowment Fund to which governments and other bodies contribute. The International Centre for Advanced Technical and Vocational Training was opened by the Organization in October 1965 in Turin, Italy. It provides programmes for directors in charge of technical and vocational institutions, training officers, senior and middle-level managers in private and public enterprises, trade union leaders, and technicians, primarily from the developing nations.

The Organization maintains working relations and co-operates closely with UN bodies, including the *UN Development Programme (UNDP) and the *UN Population Fund (UNFPA), and with the specialized agencies operating within the UN system. Arrangements for co-operation or consultation have been concluded with many international institutions, both intergovernmental and non-governmental, and national bodies.

Arrangements for the approval, allocation and collection of the biennial budget of the Organization are determined by the Conference by a two-thirds majority of the votes cast by the delegates present. Expenses are allocated among member-countries in accordance with a scale which is revised from time to time.

The activities of the Organization have met with many serious difficulties owing to a variety of factors. Some of the difficulties and conflicts of interest originated from the participation of member countries which did not possess independent employers' and workers' organizations, with the result that all their delegates were government-instructed. Since it began operations in 1919 the Organization has adopted a large number of conventions and recommendations, which cover almost every aspect of labour conditions: basic human rights; freedom of association and abolition of forced labour; wages; hours of work; minimum ages for employment; conditions of work for various classes of workers; workmen's compensation; social insurance; vacation with pay; industrial safety; employment services; and labour inspection. Between 1919 and 1990, the International Labour Conference had adopted 171 Conventions and 178 Recommendations, which together form the International Labour Code. By mid-1990, over 5500 ratifications of the Conventions had been registered by member countries.

Special emphasis is given to the World Employment Programme, launched by the Organization in 1969 to assist policy-makers in identifying and putting into effect specific measures for promoting employment. Several employment strategy missions have been carried out under the Programme. The work of the missions is complemented by action-oriented research activities covering major project areas such as technology, income distribution, population, education and training, urbanization, trade expansion and emergency schemes in their relation to employment problems. A World Employment Conference took place in June 1976. Technical co-operation, including expert missions and a fellowship programme, is also a major concern for the Organization. In keeping with the recommendations of the Technical Co-operation Programme, adopted in 1979, the Organization's operational activities are oriented toward a stronger tripartite participation, increasingly involving not only government agencies but also workers' and employers' organizations in project preparation and implementation. A growing number of projects are concerned with the complex problems posed by development, especially to disadvantaged groups such as migrants, refugees, women and uneducated youth.

Assistance is extended in a wide field of social and labour matters such as employment promotion, productivity, human resources development (including vocational and management training), development of social institutions, small-scale industries, rural development, social security, industrial safety and hygiene.

The Organization was awarded the Nobel Peace Prize in 1969.

Director-General: Michel Hansenne
Headquarters: 4 route des Morillons, 1211 Geneva 22, Switzerland (telephone 799 6111; telex: 415647; fax: 798 8685)
Publications: *International Labour Review* (six a year); *Official Bulletin* (three a year); *Legislative Series* (two a year); *Bulletin of Labour Statistics* (quarterly); *Year Book of Labour Statistics*; *ILO Information*
References: J.W. Follows: *Antecedents of the International Labour Organization* (Oxford, 1951); G. Foggon: 'The Origin and Development of the ILO and International Labour Organizations', *International Institutions at Work*, eds P. Taylor and A.J.R. Groom (London, 1988), 96–113

International   Maritime   Organization (IMO). The purpose of the Organization is to facilitate international co-operation on technical matters related to merchant shipping, with a view to achieving safe and efficient navigation and to protecting the marine environment from pollution caused by ships and craft.

A provisional Maritime Consultative Council had been set up, to act only until the establishment of a permanent intergovernmental agency in the maritime field, by an agreement concluded in October 1946 in Washington, D.C., and entered into effect in April 1947.

The Convention establishing the Intergovernmental Maritime Consultative Organization (IMCO) was adopted in March 1948, at the conclusion of the UN Maritime Conference held in Geneva, but did not enter into force until March 1958 because of the delay in securing ratifications by at least 21 countries, including seven with at least one million gross tons of shipping each.

The Convention has been amended and supplemented on a number of occasions; in May 1982, upon the entry into force of the relevant amendments, the Organization had the words 'Inter-governmental' and 'Consultative' dropped from its name and adopted the present denomination. On the basis of a relationship agreement, the Organization has been recognized since 1959 as the specialized agency of the UN in the field of shipping. Membership of the

Organization now includes over 135 countries.

The purposes of the Organization are basically to foster co-operation and exchange of information among member countries regarding government regulations and practices relating to technical matters of all kinds affecting shipping engaged in international trade; to encourage the general adoption of the highest practicable standards with regard to maritime safety, efficiency of navigation and the prevention and control of pollution from ships, and to deal with the relevant legal questions; to promote the abolition of discriminatory action and unnecessary restrictions by governments; to consider unfair restrictive practices by shipping concerns; and to deal with any matters concerning shipping that may be referred to it by any organ or specialized agency of the UN.

In order to achieve its purposes, the Organization is endowed with consultative and advisory powers. It considers and makes recommendations upon matters submitted by member countries, by any organ or specialized agency of the UN or by any other inter-governmental institution. It is also responsible for: convening international conferences on matters within its competence; drafting international maritime conventions, agreements or other suitable instruments and recommending these to governments and intergovernmental organizations. Finally, the Organization provides appropriate machinery for consultation and exchange of information. At the request of one of the countries concerned, the Organization may consider any matter related to unfair restrictive practices by shipping concerns, provided that such matter has proved incapable of settlement through the normal processes of international shipping business and has been the subject of direct negotiations between members.

Members of the UN may accede to the Organization in conformity with current provisions. Any sovereign country not belonging to the UN may be admitted to the Organization provided that, upon the recommendation of the Council, the application has been approved by two-thirds of the full members. Territories that do not enjoy full sovereignty, and to which the Convention has been made applicable either by full members responsible for their international relations or by the UN, may be granted associate membership. Any member may withdraw from the Organization by written notification given to the UN Secretary-General; the withdrawal takes effect twelve months thereafter.

The Organization's structure consists of an Assembly, a Council, a Maritime Safety Committee, a Secretariat, and several subsidiary bodies in charge of specific questions. The Assembly is the policy-making body and is composed of representatives from all member countries meeting for regular sessions every two years. It elects the members to be represented on the Council and the Maritime Safety Committee, considers the reports of the Council and decides upon any question referred to it by the Council, approves the budget, and refers to the Council for consideration or decision any matters within the scope of the Organization. The Assembly also recommends to member countries measures concerning maritime safety as well as the prevention and control of pollution caused by ships and craft operating in the marine environment.

Between sessions of the Assembly, the Council, elected for a two-year term and normally meeting twice a year, performs all the functions of the Organization but is not empowered to make recommendations on maritime safety and pollution control to member countries, a function expressly reserved for the Assembly. The Council receives the recommendations and reports of the Maritime Safety Committee and transmits them to the Assembly, together with its comments and recommendations. With the approval of the Assembly, it appoints the Secretary-General. It makes a report to the Assembly at each regular session.

The Council consists of 32 members, of which 8 represent countries with the largest interest in providing international shipping services, 8 represent countries with the largest interest in international sea-borne trade, and 16 represent other countries which have a special interest in maritime transport or navigation and whose participation ensures representation of all major geographical areas.

The Maritime Safety Committee is open to all members of the Organization and meets at least once a year. It has set up a number of specialized sub-committees to deal with specific problems: bulk chemicals; containers and cargoes; carriage of dangerous goods; fire protection; life-saving, search and rescue; radiocommunications; safety of navigation; standards of training and watchkeeping; ship design and equipment; stability and load lines and fishing vessel safety. The Committee, through the Council, submits proposals to the Assembly on technical matters affecting shipping, including prevention of marine pollution.

Decisions are generally taken by the Assembly, the Council, or the Maritime Safety Committee by a majority of members present and voting; where a two-thirds majority is required, decisions are taken by a two-thirds majority vote of the members who are present.

The Secretariat comprises the Secretary-General, the Secretary of the Maritime Safety Committee and the necessary staff. Divisions and sub-divisions of the Secretariat deal with maritime safety, navigation, technology, marine environment, legal affairs and external relations, administration, conference, and technical co-operation.

The main subsidiary bodies of the Organization are: the Legal Committee, the Facilitation Committee (dealing with measures to facilitate maritime travel and transport), and the Committee on Technical Co-operation (for the evaluation and review of technical assistance programmes and projects), all established by the Council between 1967 and 1972. Another important subsidiary body, the Marine Environment Protection Committee, was set up by the Assembly in 1973 to co-ordinate work on the prevention and control of pollution. These Committees are open to full participation by all members of the Organization.

The Organization works in close co-operation with UN bodies and specialized agencies as well as with other international institutions, both intergovernmental and non-governmental. Technical assistance in the field of shipping is extended to developing countries under the *UN Development Programme (UNDP) and other specific programmes.

Financial statements for each year and budget estimates on a biennial basis, with estimates for each year shown separately, are prepared by the Secretary-General for consideration by the Council, which submits them to the Assembly with its comments and recommendations. The expenses of the Organization are apportioned among member countries according to a scale which is fixed by the Assembly after consideration of the proposals of the Council.

Besides the activities carried out over the years by its various organs in the fields of maritime safety and environmental protection, the Organization has been working in connection with many international instruments, of which it is the depository. These instruments include Conventions concerning: Prevention of Pollution of the Sea by Oil (1954); Facilitation of International Maritime Traffic (1965); Load Lines (1966); Tonnage Measurement of Ships (1969); Intervention on the High Seas in Cases of Oil Pollution Casualties (1969); Civil Liability for Oil Pollution Damage (1969); Establishment of an International Fund for Compensation for Oil Pollution Damage (1971); International Regulations for Preventing Collisions at Sea (1972); Safe Containers (1972); Prevention of Pollution from Ships (1973, modified by Protocol of 1978); Safety of Life at Sea (1974, modified by Protocol of 1978); Carriage of Passengers and their Luggage by Sea (Athens Convention, 1974); International Maritime Satellite Organization (1976); Limitation of Liability for Maritime Claims (1976); Safety of Fishing Vessels (Torremolinos Convention, 1977); Standards of Training, Certification and Watchkeeping for Seafarers (1978); Maritime Search and Rescue (1979); Suppression of Unlawful Acts against the Safety of International Shipping (1988); Salvage (1989). Some conventions have not yet entered into force, pending formal ratification by the prescribed number of countries.

The Organization also works with: the Oslo Commission (OSCOM), established by the Convention for the Prevention of Marine Pollution by Dumping from Ships and Aircraft; and the Paris Commission (PARCOM), established by the Convention for the Prevention of Marine Pollution from Land-based Sources. The World Maritime University (WMU) opened in July 1983 in Malmo, Sweden.

Secretary-General: William A. O'Neil

Headquarters: 4 Albert Embankment, London SE1 7SR, England (telephone: 735 7611; telex: 23588; fax: 587 3210)

Publications: *IMO News* (quarterly); specialized publications, including international conventions of which IMO is depository

International Monetary Fund (IMF). The Fund is a specialized agency of the UN which aims to promote international monetary consultation, co-operation and stabilization of currencies, to facilitate the expansion and balanced growth of world trade, and to help member countries meet temporary difficulties in foreign payments. It is unique among intergovernmental organizations in its combination of consultative, financial, and regulatory functions with a view to ensuring a stable world financial system and sustainable economic growth.

Together with the *International Bank for Reconstruction and Development (IBRD), the Fund originated from the Final Act of the UN Monetary and Financial Conference held at Bretton Woods, New Hampshire (USA), in July 1944, with the participation of representatives of 44 countries. According to the 'division of labour' between the two institutions envisaged at Bretton Woods, the Fund's activities were primarily intended to provide temporary balance of payments assistance while the IBRD was to be essentially concerned with long-term project and economic development finance.

The Articles of Agreement of the Fund came into force in December 1945 when 35 countries, whose quotas amounted to 80 per cent of the Fund's resources, had deposited their ratification of the Bretton Woods Agreement. The Fund began operations in Washington in March 1947. 'Original members' of the Fund include the countries participating in the Bretton Woods Conference which accepted the Articles of Agreement within a prescribed time limit; 39 out of 44 countries became original members, the then USSR being the only important exception. 'Other members' are the countries which have subsequently joined the Fund under the terms and conditions set out in the Fund's resolutions admitting them to membership. A few countries – Czechoslovakia, Indonesia and Poland – withdrew from the Fund and later rejoined.

Membership of the Fund, which is a prerequisite for membership of the IBRD, totals about 160 countries of the industrial and developing world in widely different stages of economic development and representing a variety of economic systems from centrally planned to market economies. Among non-members mention must be made of Cuba, North Korea and Taiwan, the latter having been replaced as a member by the People's Republic of China in 1980. Switzerland is the first member of the Fund that is not a member of the UN. Russia and the other former Soviet republics are expected to join in 1992.

The original purposes of the Fund are: to provide the machinery for consultation and collaboration on international monetary problems; to promote exchange stability, to maintain orderly exchange arrangements among members, and to avoid competitive exchange depreciation; to assist in the establishment of a multilateral system of payments in respect of current transactions between members and in the elimination of foreign exchange restrictions which hamper the growth of international trade; to make resources available to members, under adequate safeguards, so as to enable them to correct maladjustments in the balance-of-payments without resorting to measures destructive of national or international prosperity; to shorten the duration and lessen the degree of disequilibrium in the international balance-of-payments of members. The Fund was not intended to provide facilities for relief or reconstruction or to deal with international indebtedness arising from World War II.

Members commit themselves to mutual collaboration to promote orderly exchange arrangements and a system of stable exchange rates and undertake certain specific obligations relating to domestic and external policies that affect the balance-of-payments and the exchange rate. Members are bound to furnish such information as the Fund deems necessary for its operations and the effective discharge of its duties, including national data on: official holdings as well as holdings by banking and financial agencies, at home and abroad, of gold and foreign exchange; production, exports and imports of gold; total exports and imports of merchandise, according to countries of destination and origin; international balance-of-payments; international investment position; national income; price indices; buying and selling rates for foreign currencies; and exchange controls.

Each member country is assigned a quota related to its national income, monetary reserves, trade balance and other economic indicators. A member's subscription is equal to its quota and is payable in special drawing rights (SDRs), in other members' currencies or in its own currency. The quota approximately determines a member's voting power, the amount of foreign exchange it may purchase from the Fund, and its allocation of SDRs. In 1978, under the Seventh General Review of Quotas, agreement was reached on a 50 per cent increase in members' quotas so as to raise the Fund's resources from SDR39,011.2 million to SDR58,616.3 million. Under the Eighth General Review of Quotas, completed in 1983, a 47 per cent increase was decided, raising the total quota to SDR90,000 million. At the latest such review, the Ninth General Review of Quotas, agreement was reached on a 50 per cent increase in overall quotas, bringing the Fund's general resources to SDR135,214.7 million (that is about $180 billion). According to the Fund's rules, the Tenth General Review of Quotas must be conducted not later than the end of March 1993.

Each member deals with the Fund only through its Treasury, central bank, stabilization fund, or other similar fiscal agency and the Fund deals only through the same agencies. The Fund's resources are made available, on an essentially short-term and revolving basis, to members which need temporary assistance for the solution of their payments problems. More precisely, exchange transactions take the form of members' purchases (drawings) from the Fund of the currencies of other members for the equivalent amounts of their own currency. A member is entitled to buy the currency of another member from the Fund subject to certain conditions, including its likely ability, with the help of resources provided by the Fund, to overcome payments difficulties within a short time. Drawings are limited by provisions governing both the rate of increase and the total amount of the Fund's holdings of a member's currency expressed as a percentage of its quota. Reserve-tranche purchases, that is purchases that do not bring the Fund's holdings of the member's currency to a level above its quota, are allowed more or less automatically and unconditionally. Further purchases on the part of a member are subject to the principle of 'conditionality' which, although not expressly mentioned in the Fund's Articles of Agreement, is the guiding concept of the various policies and facilities based on the requirement that resources be made available to members 'under adequate safeguards'. In line with this principle, a member must commit itself to sound economic management and agree to adjust its fiscal, monetary, exchange and trade policies as stipulated by the Fund. The revised Guidelines on Conditionality, adopted in 1979, obliged the Fund to take a much broader view of a country's economic requirements making express reference to the social and political objectives of member countries and to the causes of their balance-of-payments difficulties. Conditionality, therefore, is not based on a rigid set of operational rules but may vary according to individual programmes and the types of policies or facilities that are used.

A member's purchases of currency from the Fund must be repaid by repurchases or by the purchase of that member's currency by another member. As a general rule members undertake to repay within a period not exceeding three to five years; exceptions are made in the case of extended arrangements. Repurchases are made in SDRs or in usable currencies. Purchases outside the reserve tranche are made in four credit tranches, each equivalent to 25 per cent of the member's quota; repurchases must be made within a specified period of time.

The Fund is expected to depend primarily on its own capital – that is on its quota-based or subscribed resources – but when members have to face extraordinary financing requirements it is authorized to supplement its resources by borrowing. Although it can borrow a member's currency, with the concurrence of the member itself, from any source, the Fund has borrowed thus far only from official sources, primarily member countries and their central banks. Since a member's access to Fund financing is no longer strictly limited to the size of its quota, borrowing has enabled the Fund to expand its lending capability although the exercise has often proven to be costly and time-consuming.

Under the General Arrangements to Borrow (GAB) of 1962, ten industrialized members – the 'Group of Ten' including Belgium, Canada, France, the Federal Republic of Germany, Italy, Japan, the Netherlands, Sweden, the UK, and the USA – undertook to lend the Fund up to $6 billion, in their own currencies, should this be necessary to forestall or cope with an impairment of the international monetary system. Switzerland became associated with the GAB in 1964. Since their inception, the Arrangements have been activated on several occasions and have been periodically reviewed and renewed with some modifications. In January 1983, the Group of Ten reached an agreement on major revisions and a substantial enlargement of the GAB from SDR6.4 billion to SDR17.0 billion. The Swiss National Bank became a full participant in the GAB in April 1984. At the end of June 1990, credit

available to the Fund under borrowing arrangements amounted to SDR1.6 billion, in addition to SDR18.5 billion under the GAB and the associated agreement with Saudi Arabia.

Stand-by Arrangements, introduced in 1954, enable members to negotiate credit in advance of actual needs with a view to forestalling speculative attacks which might aggravate impending difficulties. Under these arrangements, drawings up to specified limits may be made within an agreed period, subject to certain conditions. The usual duration of a stand-by arrangement does not exceed 12 months, with repayment within a period of 3 to 5 years.

To further support members facing temporary balance-of-payments problems, the Fund has adopted a number of devices, including the establishment of: a compensatory financing facility (February 1963, replaced in 1988); a buffer stock financing facility (1969); an oil facility (June 1974); an extended facility for medium-term assistance to members in special circumstances of balance-of-payments difficulty (September 1974); another oil facility (April 1975); a Trust Fund (May 1976) which was terminated in April 1981; a supplementary financing facility for members facing serious payments imbalances (1978). In 1981 the Fund inaugurated the policy of 'enlarged access', allowing for a maximum cumulative use of its resources of up to 450 per cent of quota over a period of three years. This policy enabled the Fund to provide assistance to members whose balance-of-payments deficits are large in relation to their quotas and which need resources in larger amounts and for longer periods than are available under the regular credit tranches.

The Fund established in August 1988 the Compensatory and Contingency Financing Facility (CCFF) which replaced and expanded the former compensatory financing facility of 1963. A Structural Adjustment Facility (SAF) was set up in March 1986 in order to provide balance-of-payments assistance to low-income developing countries on concessional terms; loans are granted to support medium-term macroeconomic and structural adjustment programmes. To provide additional assistance to the adjustment efforts of heavily-indebted countries the Enhanced Structural Adjustment Facility (ESAF) was established in December 1987, setting the access limit to 250 per cent of the member's quota (compared with 70 per cent under the SAF). The same countries (currently numbering over 60) that are eligible to use the SAF are eligible for the ESAF. Guidelines for further assistance to indebted countries were adopted in May 1989, allowing about 25 per cent of resources under a member's extended or stand-by arrangement to be used to support operations involving reduction of debt principal.

The Articles of Agreement of the Fund have been amended substantially on a number of occasions. The First Amendment entered into force in July 1969 with the introduction of SDRs, created by the Fund to meet a long-term global need to supplement existing international reserves; SDRs have become usable and acceptable reserve assets and a substitute for gold in international payments. Members are allocated SDRs in proportion to their quotas in the Fund and may use them bilaterally to buy back from other members equivalent amounts of their own currencies or to obtain convertible currency from members designated by the Fund. Reconstitution provisions setting limits to a member's average holdings of SDRs have been introduced to prevent an excessive reliance on SDRs to finance large or persistent balance-of-payments deficits. From January 1981, the calculation of SDRs was reduced from an original basis of 16 leading currencies to a basket including only the currencies of the USA, the UK, Germany, France and Japan. The suspension of the convertibility of the dollar into gold, announced by the USA in August 1971, the modifications of the par values of currencies and other related events in the financial and monetary fields, gave rise to a major crisis in the international monetary order as emerged from the Bretton Woods Agreement. More than four years of intensive efforts on international monetary reform culminated during 1976, when negotiations were completed with the approval of the Second Amendment which

entered into effect in April 1978.

The Second Amendment is designed to adapt the Fund and its operations to current needs in six main areas: (a) the promotion of orderly exchange arrangements and a stable system of exchange rates in compliance with certain obligations undertaken by members with regard to domestic and external economic and financial policies; (b) the reduction of the role of gold (including the elimination of its function as the unit of value of the SDR, the abolition of the official price of gold, and the disposition of part of the Fund's own holdings of gold) with a view to making the SDR the principal reserve asset in the international monetary system; (c) the provision for wider uses of the SDR by endowing the Fund with increased powers over the categories of holders of SDRs, the relevant transactions and the rules for the reconstitution of members' holdings of SDRs; (d) the simplification and expansion of the types of financial operations and transactions carried out by the Fund; (e) the possible establishment of the Council as a new organ of the Fund; and (f) the improvement of the organizational and administrative mechanism of the Fund.

The par value of the dollar is no longer defined in terms of the SDR and gold and the USA is not obliged to establish and maintain a par value for the dollar.

A proposal for a Third Amendment was approved by the Board of Governors in June 1990. The Third Amendment is aimed at suspending voting and certain related rights of members that fail to fulfil their obligations under the Fund's Articles of Agreement. The quota increases proposed under the Ninth General Review of Quotas cannot take effect before the Third Amendment enters into force.

The organization of the Fund, which is similar to that of the IBRD, comprises the Board of Governors, the Executive Directors, and the Managing Director; advisory Committees also play a significant role.

The Board of Governors is vested with all powers and consists of one governor and one alternate governor appointed by each member country. It holds an ordinary annual meeting, usually in September, to consider the Fund's operations and set down the basic guidelines to be implemented by the Executive Directors, to whom the Board has delegated many of its powers; between annual meetings the governors may take votes by mail or other means. Certain fundamental powers cannot be delegated and remain the sole responsibility of the Board of Governors. They concern, inter alia, the admission or suspension of members, the adjustment of quotas, the distribution of the net income, the liquidation of the Fund, and the election of Executive Directors. In principle, the Board's decisions are to be adopted by a majority of the votes cast, except as otherwise specifically provided. Each member has 250 basic votes, plus one additional vote for each part of its quota equivalent to SDR100,000. Voting rights, therefore, are proportionate to the amount of each member's quota. On the basis of the adjustments proposed under the Ninth General Review of Quotas, the USA would remain the largest shareholder in the Fund, with 19.62 per cent of total quotas. Germany and Japan would be the next largest, each with 6.1 per cent, followed by France and the UK, each with 5.48 per cent (at present, the UK is the second largest shareholder, followed by Germany. France and Japan). Saudi Arabia would have a quota share of 3.79 per cent, Italy a share of 3.4 per cent, and Canada 3.2 per cent.

There are at present 22 Executive Directors, who permanently reside in Washington, D.C., meet as often as required under the chairmanship of the Managing Director, and are responsible for the day-to-day operations under the powers delegated by the Board of Governors. The five members with the largest quotas each appoint their Executive Directors, as can the two members with the largest net creditor positions in the Fund over the past two years. The other 15 Directors are elected by the Governors of the remaining member countries, grouped according to geographical and other criteria; each Director casts all the votes of the countries which contributed to his election. Since a member's voting power depends on the size of its quota, quotas also have a bearing on the formation of the constituen-

cies. However, in practice most decisions are taken on the basis of consensus rather than of formally cast votes.

The Managing Director, elected by the Executive Directors for a five-year term which may be extended, is *ex officio* Chairman of the Executive Directors and is assisted by a Deputy. He conducts the ordinary business of the Fund and is responsible for the organization, appointment and dismissal of the officers and staff. According to an established practice, the post of Managing Director of the Fund is reserved to a European citizen while a U.S. citizen is appointed President of the IBRD.

An Interim Committee of the Board of Governors on the International Monetary System and a Joint Committee of the Boards of Governors of the Fund and the IBRD on the Transfer of Real Resources to Developing Countries (Development Committee) were established with advisory functions and held their initial meetings in January 1975. Since that date both organs have met on a semi-annual basis generally at the same time. The Second Amendment to the Articles of Agreement empowers the Board of Governors to decide, by a large majority of the total voting power, the establishment of a new organ, the Council, which would be similar to the Interim Committee as regards composition and terms of reference but would have decision-making powers.

The Fund is actively engaged in the training of officials of member countries and their financial organizations. Courses offered by the Fund's Institute, established in 1964, deal with financial analysis and policy, balance-of-payments methodology and public finance; assistance is also extended to national and regional training centres. Several departments of the Fund provide training and technical assistance in their areas of special competence.

The Fund may co-operate, within the terms of its Articles of Agreement, with 'any general international organization and with public international organizations having specialized responsibilities in related fields'; a relationship agreement was concluded between the Fund and the UN in November 1947. Close relations, mainly of a non-financial character, are maintained by the Fund with its sister Bretton Woods institution, the IBRD. Co-operation has become closer in the past few years as both organizations are increasingly concerned with structural adjustment issues; guidelines establishing the policy areas on which each institution must concentrate are periodically reviewed. Contacts have also been developing between the Fund and the *General Agreement on Tariffs and Trade (GATT) with regard to trade policy issues and their repercussions in the payments field. As regards the provision of technical asistance for the improvement of economic and financial management, the Fund has become, in 1989, an executing agency for the *UN Development Programme (UNDP).

In the course of nearly five decades, the Fund has performed a significant role despite the fundamental political and economic changes that have occurred in many parts of the world and has maintained an effective presence at the centre of the international monetary and payments system. The amendments to the Articles of Agreement adopted so far represent important stages in the evolution towards a new monetary order whose establishment, however, will ultimately depend on a number of factors largely beyond the powers and scope of the Fund. Disruptions and manipulations of exchange rates have often prevented effective adjustments of the balance-of-payments of member countries. The recent expansion of facilities and other types of operations should benefit in particular developing member countries.

The Fund provides reserves and liquidity through the allocation of SDRs and the generation of reserve positions. At the end of 1984, Fund-related reserve assets totalled SDR58 billion, which comprised SDR16.5 billion of SDRs and SDR41.5 billion of reserve positions. These positions consist of members' subscriptions paid in reserve assets, credit extended by the Fund to its members through the sale of other members' currencies, and the credit extended to the Fund by members under several borrowing arrangements. Fund borrowings from members at the end of 1984 equalled SDR12.8 billion, with the

remainder of members' reserve positions, amounting to SDR28.8 billion, accounted for by reserve asset subscriptions and claims arising from the use of members' currencies in the extension of Fund credit.

The role of the SDR and the possibility of new SDR allocation have been discussed extensively; in fact, no allocations of SDRs have been made since January 1981. More precisely, SDRs were allocated in 1970–72 and 1979–81 for a cumulative total of SDR21.4 billion. The value of the SDR is calculated daily on the basis of the market exchange rates of the relevant currencies.

Four central banks, three intergovernmental monetary institutions and seven development institutions have so far been designated by the Fund 'prescribed holders' of SDRs. These 14 institutions are therefore entitled to acquire and use SDRs in transactions and operations with participants in the SDR Department (all Fund members) and other prescribed holders under the same terms and conditions as Fund members. In addition to its uses as a medium of exchange and for settlements among participants and prescribed holders, the SDR is the unit of account for Fund transactions and operations and for its administered accounts. The SDR is also used as a unit of account by a number of international and regional organizations and in capital markets. Several international conventions use the SDR to express monetary magnitudes, notably those expressing liability limits in the international transport of goods and services.

By mid-1991, the exchange rates of the currencies of six member countries were pegged to the SDR.

With a view to reducing the role of gold, in the mid-1970s the Fund undertook a gold sales programme: one-sixth of the Fund's gold (25 million troy ounces or 775 metric tons) has been sold directly to member countries and a further one-sixth has been sold at public auction for the benefit of developing member countries. On completion of the programme, in the first half of 1980, 24.5 million ounces had been sold directly to 126 members in four annual restitution sales and a further 25 million ounces had been sold at public auction. The profits of the gold auction totalled over $4.6 billion, of which $1.3 billion was transferred directly to 104 developing member countries and the remainder made available for loans by the Trust Fund.

In the 1990s the Fund is likely to face new as well as traditional challenges; in any case its role will remain essentially 'catalytic' that is mobilizing additional market financing rather than replacing it. One major problem will remain that of the heavy indebtedness of many developing countries whose situation has not substantially improved because of inadequate policies and/or insufficient financial support. In the area of debt reduction operations, co-operation with the IBRD and the *International Development Association (IDA) will be crucial since these operations represent a major element in a country's financial and development strategy. The large and persistent external payments imbalances among major industrial countries represent another concern of paramount importance. Last but not least is the daunting task of helping the Central and Eastern European countries as well as the republics of the erstwhile USSR make the massive changes in their institutional and regulatory framework that are necessary to establish open market-based economies in a relatively short time.

Managing Director: Michel Camdessus
Headquarters: 700 19th Street, N.W., Washington, D.C. 20431, USA (telephone: 623 7430; telex: 440040; fax: 623 4661)
Publications: *Annual Report*; *Exchange Arrangements and Exchange Restrictions* (Annual Report); *International Financial Statistics* (monthly, with yearbook); *Balance of Payments Statistics* (monthly, with yearbook); *Direction of Trade Statistics* (monthly, with yearbook); *World Economic Outlook* (annually); *IMF Survey* (two a month)
References: S. Horie: *The International Monetary Fund* (London, 1964); H. Aufricht: *The International Monetary Fund. Legal Bases, Structure, Functions* (London, 1964); B.Tew: *International Monetary Co-operation 1945–70* (London, 1970); M.G. de Vries: *The International*

Monetary Fund 1966–1971 (Washington, 1976); A. Van Dormael: *Bretton Woods: Birth of a Monetary System* (London, 1978); J. Gold: *Legal and Institutional Aspects of the International Monetary System: Selected Essays* (Washington, 1979); R. Solomon: *The International Monetary System 1945–1981* (London, 1982); R.W. Edwards, Jr.: *International Monetary Collaboration* (Dobbs Ferry, New York, 1985); M. Garritsen De Vries: *The IMF in a Changing World 1945–85* (IMF, Washington, D.C., 1986); T. Ferguson: *The Third World and Decision Making in the International Monetary Fund: The Quest for Full and Effective Participation* (London, 1988)

International Narcotics Control Board (INCB) [Organe international de contrôle des stupéfiants] (OICS). The Board aims to ensure the continuous evaluation and overall supervision of governmental implementation of drug control treaties as well as the availability of drugs for medical and scientific purposes.

The formal establishment of the Board was envisaged by the Single Convention on Narcotic Drugs (1961) which consolidated earlier Conventions (February 1925, July 1931) placing natural or synthetic narcotics, cannabis and cocaine under international control. The 1961 Convention entered into force in December 1964; the Board, which took over the functions of the Permanent Central Narcotics Board and the Drug Supervisory Body, began operating in March 1968. The growing abuse of several drugs, such as hallucinogens, amphetamines, barbiturates, non-barbiturate sedatives and tranquillizers, not covered by international treaties prompted the *Commission on Narcotic Drugs (CND) to draw up a legal instrument dealing with these substances. As a result, a Convention on Psychotropic Substances was adopted in 1971 in Vienna by a UN Conference and entered into effect in 1976. The 1961 Convention was amended by a Protocol, signed in 1972 in Geneva and entered into force in 1975, which considerably enlarged the functions and membership of the Board and stressed the need for treatment and rehabilitation of drug addicts. The UN Convention against Illicit Traffic in Narcotic Drugs and Psychotropic Substances, adopted in 1988 and entered into force in 1990, deals with areas not previously dealt with by international treaties.

The basic objective of these international instruments is to limit the supply of and demand for narcotics and psychotropic substances to medical and scientific needs through co-ordinated national and international action.

The functions of the Board are to ensure that the aims of the drug control treaties are not endangered because of the failure of any country or territory to implement the relevant provisions; to review and confirm annual estimates of licit narcotic drug requirements submitted by governments and to monitor the licit movement of psychotropic substances; to prevent the illicit cultivation, production and manufacture of, and illicit trafficking in and use of, drugs; to require governments to adopt remedial measures in case of breaches of the treaties and to bring violations to the attention of the parties, the Economic and Social Council and the CND. In order to assist countries that experience difficulties in carrying out the provisions of the treaties, the UN Fund for Drug Abuse Control (UNFDAC), established in March 1971, contributes to projects to replace illicit opium cultivation, treat and rehabilitate drug addicts, strengthen control measures, or organize information and education programmes.

The Board consists of 13 members elected for a five-year period by the Economic and Social Council in their individual capacities and not as representatives of governments. Members are elected as follows: (a) three members with medical, pharmacological or pharmaceutical experience from a list of at least five nominated by the *World Health Organization (WHO); and (b) ten members from a list of persons nominated by the members of the UN and by parties to the Single Convention on Narcotic Drugs which are not UN members.

Meetings are held at least twice a year, in closed session, in order to review the drug situation throughout the world and to supervise the implementation of the drug control treaties. The Board is assisted by a permanent secretariat which receives and evaluates information from governments and submits it for the Board's attention.

According to the General Assembly resolution of December 1990, the Board's secretariat has been integrated in the newly-created *UN International Drug Control Programme (UNDCP) which has also taken over the functions of the Division of Narcotic Drugs of the UN Secretariat and assumed responsibility for the financial resources of UNFDAC.

A significant role has been played by the Board in the surpervision of national control over production and distribution of narcotic drugs in accordance with the relevant treaties. However, both 'classical' and new drugs are increasingly abused by large numbers of persons in most parts of the world, thus making it more and more difficult for the Board to exercise an effective international control.

Headquarters: Vienna International Centre, P.O. Box 500, 1400 Vienna, Austria (telephone: 21131–0; telex: 135612; fax: 232156)

Publications: *Annual Report*; *Estimated World Requirements of Narcotic Drugs* (annually); *Statistics on Narcotic Drugs and Maximum Levels of Opium Stocks* (annually)

International Organization for Migration (IOM). The Organization is a humanitarian agency with a predominantly operational mandate, including the provision of orderly and planned migration to meet the specific needs of both emigration and immigration countries and the processing and movement of refugees, displaced persons and other individuals in need of international migration services to countries offering them permanent resettlement opportunities.

At the initiative of Belgium and the USA an International Migration Conference was convened in Brussels in 1951 at which the Provisional Intergovernmental Committee for the Movement of Migrants from Europe (PICMME) was founded.

The Organization established its headquarters in Geneva and started operations in February 1952 as the Intergovernmental Committee for European Migration (ICEM). The Constitution of ICEM was adopted in 1953 and entered into force the following year. While the early activities of the Organization were confined to population movements from Europe to North America, Latin America and Oceania, international events gradually led to an extension of operations on a worldwide scale. The global role of the Organization was formally recognized in 1980 by member countries which decided to drop the word European from the agency's name. The role and mandate of the Intergovernmental Committee for Migration (ICM) were again modified in May 1987 when a special Council session adopted amendments to the Constitution and changed the name to International Organization for Migration. Amendments, which entered into force in November 1989, recognized, *inter alia*, that international migration services may be needed throughout the world and in a variety of circumstances, such as temporary migration, voluntary return migration, intra-regional migration, migration of refugees, displaced persons and other individuals. The link between migration and development was emphasized and the need for close co-operation and co-ordination among international organizations was explicitly stated. The Organization's current membership includes about 35 countries plus 22 countries enjoying observer status.

To fulfil its basic goals the Organization carries out the following functions: (a) the handling of orderly and planned migration; (b) the transfer of qualified human resources to foster the economic, social and cultural advancement of the receiving countries; (c) the organized transfer of refugees, displaced persons and other individuals compelled to leave their homeland; and (d) the provision of a forum to states and other partners to discuss experiences, exchange views, devise measures and promote co-operation and co-ordination of efforts on migration issues.

The decision-making power with regard to policy, programmes and financing of the Organization rests with the Council, composed of representatives of all member countries. The Executive Committee, consisting of the member countries elected by the Council, prepares the work of the Council and makes recommendations on the basis of reports from the Sub-Committee on Budget and Finance and the Sub-Committee on the Co-ordination of Transport. The Director General, assisted by a Deputy Director General and the necessary staff, is in charge of administrative functions.

The Organization co-operates closely with other international organizations working in the field of refugee assistance or dealing with social, economic and demographic aspects of international migration. Refugee activities are co-ordinated with the *UN High Commissioner for Refugees (UNHCR) and with governmental and non-governmental organizations.

The budget of the Organization has two components: the administrative part funded by assessed contributions from all member countries, according to an agreed percentage scale; the operational part funded through voluntary contributions from governmental sources and from migrants themselves or their sponsors.

Since 1952 the Organization has assisted well over 4 million persons (3 million refugees and 1 million national migrants), an important proportion of whom were family reunion cases. For refugees the Organization provides documentation, processing and medical services to respond to entry requirements in resettlement countries as well as language and cultural orientation courses; for national migrants the Organization arranges for counselling, recruitment, selection and processing in the country of origin, reception, placement and integration in the receiving country and language courses for migrant workers. Reliable transportation for the movement of migrants is financed by the Organization through its Loan Fund. In order to help developing countries meet their urgent needs for highly skilled persons, the Organization has developed specific 'Migration for Development' initiatives which comprise: the Return of Talent programme for Latin America and Africa; the

Selective Migration programme in Latin America; the Integrated Experts programme in Latin America and Asia; the Horizontal Co-operation in the Field of Qualified Human Resources programme in Latin America. Since 1964, the Organization has transferred over 42,000 highly qualified specialists and technicians to developing countries under the above-mentioned programmes. The Organization provides advisory services and carries out studies to co-operate with member countries in the formulation and implementation of their migration policy, legislation and administration. The Centre for Information on Migration in Latin America (CIMAL) was set up in 1983 by the Organization in Santiago, Chile. The Organization also acts as a multilateral forum where key migration issues may be discussed in the course of international seminars.

Director: James N. Purcell

Headquarters: 17 route des Morillons, P.O. Box 71, 1211 Geneva 19, Switzerland (telephone: 717 9111; telex: 415722; fax: 798 6150)

Publications: *Monthly Dispatch*; *International Migration* (quarterly); *IOM Latin American Migration Journal* (three a year)

International Telecommunication Union (ITU). The Union is the oldest intergovernmental organization in existence. Its aims are to maintain and extend co-operation for the improvement and rational use of telecommunication of all kinds, and to promote technical development and operation with a view to making telecommunication services generally available to the public.

The Union was founded in Paris, in May 1865, as the International Telegraph Union, by the representatives of 20 countries, with the adoption of the first Telegraph Convention and the relevant Regulations. A Bureau of the Union was set up in Berne, Switzerland, in 1868. The first international Radio Conference was held in Berlin in 1906, with the participation of 27 countries, and a Convention and Radio Regulations were drawn up.

The Union's full title was changed to the present one at the Madrid Conferences (1932), when the existing Telegraph and Radiotelegraph Conventions were replaced by the first single International Telecommunication Convention, which entered into effect in January 1934. At the Atlantic City Plenipotentiary and Radio Conferences (1947), the Union was reorganized and entered into a relationship agreement with the UN under which it was recognized as the specialized agency for telecommunication; the agreement came into force in January 1949. The seat of the Union was transferred to Geneva in 1948. The International Telecommunication Convention, which is the constitutional document of the Union, has been radically revised several times. At present the Union is governed by the Convention adopted by the Nairobi Plenipotentiary Conference (November 1982) which entered into effect in January 1984. Membership of the Union now includes about 170 countries. The Nice Plenipotentiary Conference (May/June 1989) adopted a permanent Constitution complemented by a Convention which will enter into force 30 days after the deposit of the instrument of ratification of the 55th member of the Union.

The concept of 'telecommunications' applies to any transmission, emission or reception of signs, signals, writing, images and sounds or intelligence of any nature by wire, radio, optical or other electromagnetic systems – that is telegraph, telephone and radio, and all their applications such as television and telex.

The Union works to fulfil its basic purposes in three main ways: international conferences and meetings; publication of information and organization of world exhibitions; technical co-operation. Basic functions of the Union include: allocating radio frequencies and recording the assignments; eliminating harmful interference between stations; establishing the lowest possible rates, consistent with efficient service and taking into account the necessity to keep on a sound basis the independent financial administration of telecommunication; promoting the adoption of measures for ensuring the safety of life through telecommunications; making studies and recommendations which also cover space telecommunication techniques and regulations; and collecting and publishing information for the benefit of its members. As regards technical co-operation with the developing countries, the Union: promotes the development of regional telecommunication networks; helps strengthen technical and administrative services; and develops the human resources required for telecommunications, especially through the training of personnel. Assistance is provided in the specialized fields of telephony, telegraphy, radiocommunications, frequency management, satellite communications, planning, organization, administration and management.

Members of the UN may accede to the Union, according to current provisions. Any sovereign country, not a member of the UN, may be admitted to the Union if the request has secured approval by at least two-thirds of member countries.

The structure of the Union consists of the Plenipotentiary Conference, the World Administrative Conferences, the Administrative Council and four permanent organs: the General Secretariat, the International Frequency Registration Board (IFRB), the International Radio Consultative Committee (CCIR) and the International Telegraph and Telephone Consultative Committee (CCITT). The 1989 Nice Plenipotentiary Conference approved the creation of a new Telecommunications Development Bureau (BDT) built around the staff of the existing Technical Co-operation Department.

The Plenipotentiary Conference is composed of representatives of all member countries and normally meets at intervals of not less than five years. It is the supreme authority of the Union, laying down general policies, reviewing the Union's work, revising the Convention if necessary, and establishing the basis for the budget. World Administrative Conferences, held at irregular intervals to consider specific telecommunication matters, may discuss only items included in their agenda; all decisions must be in conformity with the International Telecommunication Convention. There may also be Administrative

Conferences held at regional level, when specific questions of a regional nature are involved. The Administrative Council is composed of 43 members, elected by the Plenipotentiary Conference with due regard for equitable geographical representation, and normally meets once a year at the Union's headquarters in Geneva. It supervises administrative functions, co-ordinates the activities of the permanent organs between the meetings of the Plenipotentiary Conference, approves the annual budget and conducts relations with other international organizations. The General Secretariat is directed by a Secretary-General elected by the Plenipotentiary Conference for a renewable term. The Secretary-General is responsible for all the administrative and financial aspects of the Union's activities.

The International Frequency Registration Board consists of five independent radio experts, all from different regions of the world, elected by the Plenipotentiary Conference and working full-time at the Union's headquarters. The Board records assignments of radio frequencies throughout the world after technical examination and advises member countries on technical matters concerning harmful interference between stations. The International Radio Consultative Committee studies technical and operating questions in radiocommunication and makes recommendations. The International Telegraph and Telephone Consultative Committee carries out similar functions relating to telephony, telegraphy, telex, data transmission and other non-speech services. All member countries of the Union can participate in the work of the Committees, together with recognized private companies operating telecommunication services. Each Committee holds a Plenary Assembly, normally every three years, to consider technical questions whose investigation is entrusted to a number of study groups composed of experts from different countries.

The Union, mainly within the framework of the *UN Development Programme (UNDP), administers a programme through which telecommunications experts are sent to various countries throughout the world to advise on the operation of telegraph, telephone and radio systems or to help to train technicians. Surveys for modern international telecommunication networks have been conducted in several developing areas. The Union co-operates actively with the *Universal Postal Union (UPU) with a view to preparing and executing joint technical assistance projects, particularly in the vocational training field. Close co-operative contacts are also maintained with other UN specialized agencies, as well as with several intergovernmental and non-governmental institutions.

Each meeting of the Plenipotentiary Conference fixes the maximum amount of expenditure which the Union may reach until the next meeting. Expenses are borne in common by member countries which are divided for this purpose into various contribution classes.

Since its establishment, the Union has made fundamental contributions to the development and improvement of telecommunication, laying down basic principles and provisions and adapting itself to new pressing needs such as man's growing use of outer space. In the field of technical co-operation mention should be made, *inter alia*, of the Plan Committees (World Committee and Regional Committees for Africa, Latin America, Asia and Oceania, and Europe and the Mediterranean Basin). These Committees – which are joint CCIR/CCITT bodies – are responsible for preparing plans establishing circuit and routing requirements for international telecommunications and for providing estimates of the growth of international traffic. The newly-created Telecommunications Development Bureau is responsible for the implementation of projects: it undertakes research and field studies, provides training and advice, and ensures the strict application of international technical and operational standards.

In 1981 the UN General Assembly proclaimed 1983 as World Communications Year, and designated the Union as the leading agency for co-ordinating activities, with special regard to the development of communications infrastructures.

Secretary-General: Pekka Johannes Tarjanne

Headquarters: Place des Nations, 1211 Geneva 20, Switzerland (telephone: 730 5111; telex: 421000; fax: 733 7256)

Publications: *Telecommunication Journal* (monthly); conventions, statistics, technical documents and manuals.

References: G.A. Codding Jr: *The International Telecommunication Union: An Experiment in International Co-operation* (Leiden, 1952, reprinted 1972); G.A. Codding Jr and A.M. Rutkowski: *The International Telecommunication Union in a Changing World* (Dedham, Mass, 1982); G.A. Codding Jr: 'The International Telecommunication Union', *International Institutions at Work*, eds P. Taylor and A.J.R. Groom (London, 1988), 167–83

IOM. *See* **International Organization for Migration.**

IsDB. *See* **Islamic Development Bank.**

Islamic Development Bank (IsDB). The Bank aims to finance the economic development and social progress of its member countries and of Moslem communities in non-member countries, in accordance with the principles of the Shari'a, that is Islamic Law. It is, at present, the biggest of Arab development funds.

The origins of the Bank date back to the Declaration of Intent issued by a Conference of Finance Ministers of Islamic countries, held in Jeddah, Saudi Arabia, in December 1973. The Agreement establishing the Bank was signed under the auspices of the *Organization of the Islamic Conference (OIC) in August 1974 in Jeddah; the Bank began functioning in that town in October 1975 and financial operations actually started in 1976. Present membership includes over 40 Moslem countries in Africa and Asia, plus Turkey and the Palestine Liberation Organization (PLO).

In its activities, the Bank follows the Koranic principle forbidding usury; it does not extend loans or credits for interest and supports economic and social development by taking up equity participation in public and private enterprises in member countries, financing infrastructural projects, granting funds to Islamic communities in non-member countries and providing technical assistance. It may establish and operate special funds for specific purposes in order to preserve the value of its assets. In particular, the Bank seeks to develop new financial instruments, in accordance with Islamic principles, for additional resource mobilization.

The Bank uses as a unit of account the Islamic Dinar (IsD) which is equivalent to one special drawing right (SDR). The size of the authorized capital stock was set at IsD2000 million, divided into 200,000 shares, each of them having a value of IsD10,000. In July 1990 the subscribed capital amounted to IsD1961 million; paid-up capital was IsD1662 million. The five largest subscribers are Saudi Arabia, Libya, Kuwait, the United Arab Emirates and Turkey.

The structure of the Bank comprises the Board of Governors, the Board of Executive Directors, and the President. The Board of Governors is the supreme body composed of one governor, usually the Minister of Finance, or his alternate, appointed by each member country and meeting at least once a year. Many powers have been delegated by the Board of Governors to the executive organ, that is the Board of Executive Directors, consisting of 11 members and responsible for the Bank's general operations. Five directors are appointed by the five largest subscribers; the governors of the remaining subscribers are entitled to elect the other six directors for a three-year term. The President of the Bank serves for a five-year period and acts as Chairman of the Board of Executive Directors by whom he is elected.

Co-operative links are maintained by the Bank with various international institutions, both Islamic and non-Islamic. It is a member of the Co-ordination Secretariat of Arab National and Regional Development Institutions.

Between 1976 and July 1990, the Bank had approved an amount of IsD2014 million for ordinary operations (long- and medium-term project financing and technical assistance for feasibility studies) and an amount of IsD5597 million for foreign trade financing (particularly for the import of raw materials). With respect to ordinary operations, the industrial and mining sector has been by far the major recipient of the Bank's financing, followed by transport and communication, utilities and agriculture. Under the Bank's Special Assistance Account, emergency aid and other forms of assistance are provided mostly with a view to promoting education in Islamic communities in non-member countries. A sizeable share of the Bank's concessional financing goes to about 20 members which are among the world's least-developed countries according to the United Nations classification. The Bank also undertakes the distribution of meat sacrificed by Muslim pilgrims.

In 1987 the Bank launched the Islamic Banks' Portfolio for Investment and Development to finance trade and leasing activities in the private sector. A Longer-Term Trade Financing Scheme was introduced in 1987/88 with a view to promoting trade among member countries especially in nontraditional commodities. In order to mobilize additional resources from the market the Bank introduced a Unit Investment Fund, specifically targeted to institutional investors, in December 1989.

An Islamic Research and Training Institute was established in 1982 to promote research on economic, financial and banking activities conforming to Islamic law and to provide training for staff involved in development activities in the Bank's member countries.

President: Ahmad Muhammad Ali
Headquarters: P.O. Box 5925, Jeddah 21432, Saudi Arabia (telephone: 636 1400; telex: 601137; fax: 636 6871)
Publication: *Annual Report*

ITU. *See* **International Telecommunication Union.**

L

LAIA. *See* **Latin American Integration Association.**

Latin American Economic System [Sistema Económico Latinoamericano] (SELA). The System is intended to provide all Latin American countries with permanent institutional machinery for joint consultation, co-ordination, co-operation and promotion in economic and social matters at both intraregional and extraregional level. After a relatively brief period of negotiation, with Mexico and Venezuela playing a very active role, the agreement establishing SELA was signed in October 1975 in Panama by the representatives of 25 Latin American and Caribbean countries (including Cuba); Suriname joined in 1979, followed by Belize in 1991.

The basic aims of the System are to advance Latin American trade and co-operation, while respecting and supporting the existing regional arrangements, and to co-ordinate the positions and strategies of individual members regarding external countries and agencies with a view to strengthening the bargaining power of the area. SELA has taken over the functions formerly performed by the Special Latin American Co-ordinating Commission (CECLA), which was created in the first half of the 1960s as a forum for the formulation of common policies on trade and development issues towards international organizations and countries outside Latin America.

To achieve its main objectives, the System: (a) promotes the better utilization of regional resources through the creation of Latin American multinational enterprises; (b) defends the prices of raw materials exported from Latin America and encourages the transformation of these materials within the region; (c) formulates measures and policies which ensure that the operations of transnational companies are in accordance with the development goals of the region and the interests of individual members; (d) improves the collective negotiating capacity for acquiring and utilizing capital goods and technology; and (e) furthers the drafting and implementation of economic and social projects of interest to member countries.

The System's institutional structure includes the Latin American Council, several Action Committees and the Permanent Secretariat. The Latin American Council is the supreme body of the System and consists of one representative from each member country, with one vote. It meets annually at ministerial level; extraordinary meetings may be held whenever necessary. The Council establishes the System's general policies, defines common positions of members concerning third countries, groups of countries and international organizations, approves the budget and elects the Permanent Secretary. Decisions concerning basic policies and joint positions must be approved by consensus. Specific agreements and projects are adopted on a fully voluntary basis and therefore need the approval only of those countries choosing to participate in them. Action Committees may be established by the Council or by two or more interested member countries in order to draft and carry out specific programmes and projects as well as to prepare and adopt joint negotiating positions on issues of interest to member countries in international fora. Each Action Committee, funded by participating member states, establishes its own headquarters and secretariat.

The Permanent Secretariat is charged with the technical and administrative functions of the System. It organizes and carries out preliminary studies on projects of common interest to member countries, implements the decisions of the Latin American Council and co-ordinates the activities of the Action Committees. The Permanent Secretary is appointed by the Latin American Council for a four-year term and may be re-elected once, but not for consecutive periods.

The System has been gradually developing active co-operative relations with international organizations, especially Latin American regional economic and financial bodies, and with third countries. An agreement has been signed with the *UN Development Programme (UNDP), under which technical co-operation and financing would be provided for projects adopted within the framework of the Action Committees. The *European Economic Community (EEC) has shown interest in assisting SELA to carry out specific development projects.

In conformity with its basic purposes and principles and in spite of the relative weakness of its organizational machinery, the System has been making a notable effort to expedite regional co-operation and to build up Latin American solidarity on international economic issues in regard to external countries and organizations. After its first ordinary meeting in October 1975, the Latin American Council held an extraordinary technical session in January 1976 in order to fund an operating budget (contributed according to the economic development level of each member country), to determine areas of co-operative action, and to formulate a common Latin American position in preparation for the fourth session of the *UN Conference on Trade and Development (UNCTAD), scheduled to take place in Nairobi in May of the same year. At subsequent meetings, the Latin American Council defined the rules governing the operations of the Action Committees and laid the foundations for

setting up Latin American multinational enterprises in specific sectors of vital importance to the region.

The Action Committee for the manufacture of fertilizers inspired the establishment in May 1980 of MULTIFERT, a Latin American multinational enterprise for the marketing of fertilizers, located in Panama City. In addition to MULTIFERT, the following agencies have been set up within SELA: Action Committee for the Support of Economic and Social Development in Central America (CADESCA), based in Panama City; Action Committee for Latin American Co-operation and Concertation on Plant Germplasm (CARFIT), based in Mexico City; Latin American and Caribbean Trade Information and Foreign Trade Support Programme (PLACIEX), based in Lima; Latin American Features Agency (ALASEI), based in Mexico City; Latin American Fisheries Development Organization (OLDEPESCA), based in Lima; Latin American Programme for Co-operation on Handicrafts (PLACART), based in Caracas; Latin American Shipping Commission (COLTRAM), based in Caracas; Latin American Commission for Science and Technology (COLCYT), based in Caracas; Latin American Technological Information Network (RITLA), based in Brasilia.

At the extraregional level, efforts to establish and maintain a common policy within an appropriate consultative framework have been a regular feature of meetings of the Latin American Council. Joint positions have been adopted towards the Group of 77 and UNCTAD. With regard to the EEC, which represents an integration group of paramount importance to Latin America as a whole, in 1979 the System adopted a resolution setting out guidelines for substantially improved mutual relations. In this connection, the System's Permanent Secretariat closely co-operates with the Group of Latin American Chiefs of Missions (GRULA) in Brussels with a view to developing the dialogue with the EEC.

To examine the problems and prospects of the region in the light of the economic crisis, with special regard to external debt, the System organized – in collaboration with *ECLAC – a Latin American Economic Conference. At the meeting, which took place in Quito, Ecuador, in January 1984, the Heads of State of Latin America and the Caribbean approved a Declaration and an Action Plan.

On the whole, SELA may play an effective role in the promotion of economic integration through the creation of a number of Latin American joint ventures and the formation of a region-wide economic policy, especially now that most member countries have embarked on a major process of political democratization and economic liberalization.

Permanent Secretary: Salvador Arriola

Headquarters: P.O. Box 17035, El Conde, Caracas 1010, Venezuela (telephone: 905 5151; telex: 23294; fax : 951 6953)

Publication: *Capítulos del SELA* (quarterly)

Reference: R.D. Bond: 'Regionalism in Latin America: Prospects for the Latin American Economic System (SELA)', *International Organization*, 32, 2 (Spring 1978), 401–23; SELA: *Latin American-US Economic Relations, 1982–83* (Boulder, Colorado, 1984)

Latin American Integration Association

(LAIA) [Asociación Latinoamericana de Integración (ALADI)]. The Association was founded in 1980 as the successor to the Latin American Free Trade Association (LAFTA). It pursues the long-term goal of establishing a common market through the creation of an area of economic preferences, based on a regional tariff preference and regional and partial scope agreements. In addition, a support system for less-developed member countries is to be put into effect.

The Treaty creating the Association was signed in Montevideo, Uruguay, in August 1980 by the Ministers of Foreign Affairs of the same 11 countries which had founded LAFTA under the Treaty of Montevideo of February 1960, or had subsequently joined it (Argentina, Bolivia, Brazil, Chile, Colombia, Ecuador, Mexico, Paraguay, Peru, Uruguay and Venezuela). At the same time, several resolutions were approved concerning the renegotiation of LAFTA's 'historical heritage', meaning the various commitments arising from LAFTA's Trade Liberalization Programme.

The adoption of a new and more flexible integration scheme for Latin America represented the outcome of complex efforts originally intended to reorganize and update LAFTA's structure and mechanisms. The Montevideo Treaty of 1960 envisaged the establishment within a 12-year period of a free trade area through the gradual elimination of tariff and non-tariff barriers. Tariff reductions covering 55 per cent of intrazonal trade were achieved during the first rounds of negotiations. However, further progress proved extremely difficult and the transition period was extended to 1980 under the Caracas Protocol of 1969. No substantial progress was being made towards the achievement of a minimum measure of harmonization of the external tariffs of member countries. 'Complementation agreements' in particular sectors largely failed to strengthen policies of economic and industrial integration. Despite the introduction of a system of payments and credits to facilitate intrazonal commercial operations, promote multilateral compensation and ease temporary balance-of-payments problems, financial co-operation made little progress and no agreement was reached on the creation of a regional financial institution. In 1967, LAFTA had expressly authorized the drawing up, within its legal framework, of subregional agreements between its members, to encourage the formation of common markets on a more limited scale, with the ultimate goal of a future merger in a single Latin American market. In accordance with this policy, in May 1969, Bolivia, Colombia, Chile, Ecuador and Peru concluded the Cartagena Agreement establishing the *Andean Group.

In recognition of the slow progress on basic issues and the widespread disappointment over the lack of concrete perspectives, LAFTA's Conference of Contracting Parties urged the Permanent Executive Committee to carry out, during 1979, an analysis of the effectiveness of the trade liberalization and development policies and of the ability of the organizational structure to promote the integration process. In December 1979, a detailed agenda was set up for the negotiation of a new Montevideo Treaty. After two preparatory meetings in the early part of the year, in June 1980 the Conference of Contracting Parties held an extraordinary session in Acapulco, Mexico, to consider the final draft of the Treaty. It was actually signed in Montevideo the following August and entered into force in March 1981.

The Montevideo Treaty of 1980 envisages the gradual and progressive establishment of an economic preferences area and not of a free trade area like its predecessor. In addition, no rigid mechanisms, schedules or time limits (which had already proved impracticable) are set out for the achievement of basic objectives. The exact content and scope of the area of economic preferences depend on the nature of the agreements to be reached, whether regional or partial, and on the depth of the regional preference margin to be applied with reference to tariff levels in force for third countries. All members participate in regional agreements while partial scope agreements are applicable only to interested countries but must aim at progressive multilateralization and provide for extension to other members. Partial agreements may be concluded for periods of at least one year in the spheres of trade, economic and industrial complementation, agriculture and livestock and export promotion. Careful consideration should be given to other areas, such as scientific and technological co-operation, environmental protection and the development of tourism.

The Association's objectives are to be pursued paying due regard to a set of basic principles which involve differential treatments based on the classification of member countries, according to their economic structure, into three main categories: most developed (Argentina, Brazil and Mexico); intermediate (Chile, Colombia, Peru, Uruguay and Venezuela); and least developed (Bolivia, Ecuador and Paraguay). More favourable terms are granted to intermediate countries while additional, special benefits are provided for the least developed and landlocked members. The

functions of the Association, in conformity with the rules and mechanisms of the Treaty, include the promotion of reciprocal trade and economic complementation and the development of economic co-operation activities directed to the enlargement of markets.

Membership of the Association is open to other Latin American countries but may not be subject to reservations. Members may withdraw from the Association provided one year's notice is given. However, special rules apply to the withdrawal of concessions granted under the regional tariff preference scheme and regional and partial scope agreements.

At present there are permanent observers representing 11 countries from Latin America as well as Europe and five international agencies, that is the *UN Economic Commission for Latin America and the Caribbean (ECLAC), the *UN Development Programme (UNDP), the *European Communities (EC), the *Inter-American Development Bank (IDB) and the *Organization of American States (OAS).

The Association is endowed with an institutional structure which is more developed and potentially stronger than that of LAFTA. More precisely, the Association accomplishes it purposes by means of three 'political' organs (the Council of Ministers of Foreign Affairs, the Evaluation and Convergence Conference, and the Committee of Representatives) plus a technical organ (the Secretariat). Subsidiary organs performing advisory and technical functions may be set up in order to facilitate the study of specific problems; one such organ is to consist of officials who, in their respective countries, are responsible for integration policies. Other consultative bodies are to include representatives of the various sectors of economic activity of each member country.

The Council, which is the supreme body, has a broad mandate to consider any action that may be necessary for the attainment of the objectives of economic integration. It is empowered to: lay down the essential rules for the harmonious development of the integration process; appraise the results of the tasks performed by the Association;

adopt corrective measures upon the recommendation of the Conference in order to propitiate convergence; direct the work of the other organs; set basic guidelines concerning relations with other regional organizations and international bodies; revise and adapt the fundamental rules on convergence and co-operation agreements concluded with other developing countries and integration groupings; modify and supplement the Treaty; decide on the admission of new members; and appoint the Secretary-General. The Council is convened by the Committee of Representatives and may not meet and take decisions unless all its members are present.

The Evaluation and Convergence Conference, consisting of plenipotentiaries from member countries, is convened by the Committee of Representatives; the presence of all members is required. The Conference is entrusted with responsibility for appraising the integration process in all its aspects and the convergence of partial scope agreements through their progressive multilateralization, as well as for recommending to the Council the adoption of corrective measures of multilateral scope. The Conference is also responsible for: carrying out periodic revisions of differential treatments; assessing the results of the implementation of the system for supporting the relatively least-developed members; effecting multilateral negotiations with regard to the regional tariff preference; and facilitating the negotiation of regional agreements involving all members.

The Committee is the Association's permanent organ, composed of a permanent and a deputy representative from each country plus representatives from the permanent observers. It may not hold meetings and adopt resolutions unless two-thirds of its members are present. Its principal powers are: to convene governmental meetings for the negotiation of regional agreements, especially with regard to tariff reductions; to take the necessary steps for the implementation of the Treaty; to undertake the work assigned to it by the Council and the Conference; to approve the Association's annual budget and to fix the contributions of each member; to convene the Council and the Conference; to

represent the Association in dealings with third countries; to submit proposals and recommendations to the Council and the Conference; to evaluate multilaterally the partial scope agreements reached by the interested members.

The three political organs of the Association may take decisions when affirmative votes are cast by at least two-thirds of the member countries; non-participation is equivalent to abstention. On highly sensitive issues, which are considered to be vital to the integration process, decisions may be adopted by a two-thirds majority providing that no negative vote is cast.

Eight subsidiary bodies have been created: the Council for Financial and Monetary Affairs, composed of the Presidents of member countries' central banks; the Advisory Commission on Financial and Monetary Affairs; the Meeting of Directors of National Customs Administrations; the Council on Transport for Trade Facilitation; the Advisory Council for Export Financing; the Tourism Council; the Advisory Entrepreneurial Council; and the Advisory Nomenclature Commission.

The Secretariat is headed by a Secretary-General – elected by the Council for a three-year term and re-eligible for another period – who is assisted by two Deputy Secretaries-General. The Secretariat's duties are: to prepare proposals for consideration by the political organs; to carry out studies and other activities included in the annual work programme; to represent the Association in dealings with international economic agencies and bodies; to recommend to the Committee the creation of subsidiary organs; to establish an Economic Promotion Unit responsible for the least-developed members; to submit to the Committee an annual report on the results of the implementation of the Treaty.

As regards the Association's external relations, special emphasis is given to co-ordination and co-operation with other countries and integration groupings in Latin America with a view to establishing a Latin American tariff preference and concluding partial scope agreements. Under special circumstances, partial agreements may also be reached with other developing countries (or the relevant integration areas) outside Latin America.

A series of initiatives have been taken, within the Association's framework, for saving and widening the concessions granted under the auspices of LAFTA and for promoting bilateral and multilateral agreements in the economic and financial fields. Although it inevitably suffers from the uncertainties and contradictions in the economic policies of its leading members as well as from the lack of precise commitments, the Association seems to have, thanks to its flexibility and pragmatism, better opportunities than its predecessor of fostering effective regional co-operation. The multiplicity of ways provided to facilitate agreement on integration actions, together with the effort to propitiate convergence and progressive multilateralization, should lead to the choice of the most feasible means to comply with the ultimate goal of the Montevideo Treaty of 1980. Partial economic complementation agreements with emphasis on the industrial, energy, technological and financial sectors may offer ample possibilities for strengthening co-operation not only among members but with non-members in Central America and the Caribbean.

By the end of 1983 the transition from LAFTA to the Association had been completed with the renegotiation of over 23,000 tariff cuts granted among the partners from 1962 onwards. Some LAFTA institutions have been retained by the Association, such as the Accord on Reciprocal Payments and Credits (revised in 1982) and the Multilateral Credit Agreement to Alleviate Temporary Shortages of Liquidity (revised and extended in 1981).

The agreement on the Regional Tariff Preference (RTP) for goods originating in the 11 member countries was eventually signed in April 1984 and entered into effect the following July. A new system of tariff nomenclature was adopted from January 1986 to facilitate common trade negotiations. A regional round of negotiations was launched by members of the Association in April 1986 in order to promote the establishment of a renewed preferential trade and payments system open to the participation of other Latin American and Caribbean countries. In May 1990 the Council of Ministers established guidelines – to be implemented through a three-year programme of action (1990–92) – with a view to strengthening the role of the Association within the framework of a renewed approach to Latin American integration.

Secretary-General: Jorge Luis Ordonez

Headquarters: Cebollatí 1461, P.O. Box 577, Montevideo, Uruguay (telephone: 401121-28; telex: 26944; fax: 490649)

Publication: *Síntesis ALADI* (monthly, in Spanish)

References: M.S. Wionczek: 'La evaluación del Tratado de Montevideo 1980 y las perpectivas de las acciones de alcance parcial de la ALADI', *Integración Latinoamericana*, 50 (Sept 1980), 4–29; M. Arocena: 'El surgimiento de la Asociación Latinoamericana de Integración', *Integración Latinoamericana*, 59 (July 1981), 11–24

League of Arab States [Arab League]. The purpose of the League is to strengthen the ties between independent Arab countries and to co-ordinate their political activities with a view to realizing close co-operation, to safeguard their sovereignty, and to consider in a general way the affairs and interests of the Arab countries; such co-operation is to take place paying due regard to the structure of each country and the conditions prevailing therein.

The Pact establishing the League was concluded in 1945 by the representatives of seven Arab countries which had achieved independence (Egypt, Iraq, Lebanon, Saudi Arabia, Syria, Transjordan, and Yemen). The original members were joined by Libya (1953); Sudan (1956); Tunisia and Morocco (1958); Kuwait (1961); Algeria (1962); Southern Yemen (1967); Bahrain, Qatar, Oman, and the United Arab Emirates (1971); Mauritania (1973); Somalia (1974); and Djibouti (1977). Palestine is considered independent *de jure* even though, according to the Pact Annex on Palestine, 'the outward signs of this independence have remained veiled as a result of *force majeure*' – and therefore a full member of the League since the beginning. In response to the signing in March 1979 of a peace treaty between Israel and Egypt, the latter's membership of the League was suspended and the League headquarters were transferred from Cairo to Tunis; Egypt's readmission took place in May 1989 and the League moved its headquarters back to Cairo at the end of October 1990.

The foundation of the League as a regional political arrangement for the pursuit of comprehensive goals emerged from an effort to restore the Arab community. However, the existence of many separate states and administrations under mandatory control (as a result of the 1919 peace settlement) and the long-standing tensions and rivalries between conservative and revolutionary groups and movements, as well as between oil-rich and poor countries, led Arab leaders to shelve union or federation plans in favour of a voluntary association of sovereign states. A Pan-Arabic conference was held in autumn 1944. It drew up the Alexandria Protocol outlining the basic features of the new organization, which was formally established by the signing of the Pact of the League of Arab States in March 1945 in Cairo.

As well as the basic aim of promoting co-ordination on the political plane, a close co-operation between member countries is envisaged by the Pact in: economic and financial affairs, including trade, customs, currency, agriculture, and industry; communications, including railways, roads, aviation, navigation, and postal and telegraphic services; cultural affairs; matters related to nationality, passports, visas, execution of judgments and extradition; social welfare; and health.

Each member is bound to respect the form of government existing in other member countries and to refrain from any action tending to change such form. Members are not allowed to use force for the settlement of disputes between them. The League is entitled to mediate in a dispute which may lead to war between two members or between a member and another country in order to conciliate them. In case of aggression or threat of aggression by any country against a member, the League may decide, by unanimous vote, upon the necessary measures to repel the aggression. The collective security aspects of the Pact were further developed and specified in the Joint Defence and Economic Co-operation Treaty, concluded between members of the League in April 1950 and entered into force in August 1952.

Every independent Arab state has the right to adhere to the League, whose Council will decide upon the application presented to this effect. The right of withdrawal is expressly envisaged, provided one year's notice is given; however, a member that does not approve an amendment to the Pact may withdraw before such amendment becomes effective, no minimum period of notice being required. Any member that is not fulfilling its obligations under the Pact may be excluded from the League by a decision taken unanimously.

The basic organizational structure of the League is fairly simple, comprising the Council, assisted by a number of Committees, and the permanent General Secretariat. The Council is the highest policy-making body, composed of the representatives of member-countries and of Palestine, each member having one vote. Ordinary sessions are held twice a year, usually in March and October, either at the seat of the League or at any other designated place, and are presided over by representatives of member countries in turn. Extraordinary sessions may be convened at the request of at least two member countries whenever the need arises. The Council is entrusted with the functions of realizing the purposes of the League, supervising the implementation of agreements concluded between members on specific matters, and setting the guidelines for co-operation with other international organizations in the political, economic and social spheres. In principle, decisions are taken by the Council by unanimity; these decisions are obligatory on all member countries that are bound to act in conformity with their own constitutional rules. Some important questions may, however, be dealt with by majority vote such as decisions relating to arbitration and mediation, personnel, budget, internal organization and termination of sessions. Amendments to the Pact require a two-thirds majority.

At present there are 15 special Committees attached to the Council. It is the responsibility of these Committees to establish the basis and scope of co-operation in the form of draft agreements to be submitted to the Council for consideration. As a rule, decisions are taken by the Committees by simple majority.

The Political Committee, usually composed of the Foreign Ministers of all member countries, reports to the Council sessions on major political questions and may represent the Council itself in dealing with emergencies. The Cultural Committee is charged with the follow-up of the cultural activities of the various organs of the League and of the relevant bodies of member countries. Economic issues have been discussed within the framework of the Economic Council since 1953. Other special Committees deal with communications, social affairs, legal problems, information, health, human rights (with special regard to violations by Israel), administrative and financial matters, and meteorology. Reference should also be made to the Committee of Arab Experts on Co-operation, the Arab Women's Committee, the Organization of Youth Welfare, and the Conference of Liaison Officers for the co-ordination of activities among Arab commercial attaches abroad.

The General Secretariat is composed of the Secretary-General, a number of Assistant Secretaries-General, and the necessary staff. It is the central and permanent organ, carrying out the policies and programmes decided upon by the Council and the Political Committee, and providing administrative services. The General Secretariat includes departments which deal with Arab affairs, economic, international, legal, social and cultural affairs, information, Palestine, administrative and financial affairs. The Secretary-General is elected by the Council by a two-thirds majority for a five-year term. The Assistant Secretaries-General and the principal officials are appointed by the Secretary-General with the approval of the Council.

A significant role within the institutional framework of the League has been played by the periodic meetings of Arab Kings and Presidents, that is the 'Summit Conference', whose first session was held in Cairo in January 1964.

A number of important bodies have been established under the Joint Defence and Economic Co-operation Treaty which was signed in 1950 to supplement the Pact of the League. The Economic Council (which held its first meeting in 1953) consists of the Ministers of Economic Affairs and is responsible for the co-ordination of economic policies of member countries. Membership of the Economic Council does not necessarily imply membership of the military bodies and vice versa. The bodies charged with common defence are: the Joint Defence Council, composed of Foreign and Defence Ministers; and the Permanent Military Commission, composed of representatives of army General Staffs. The Arab Unified Military Command was set up in 1964 to co-ordinate military policies for the liberation of Palestine. Mention must also be made of the Arab Deterrent Force which was created in June 1976 by the Council of the League in order to supervise attempts to cease hostilities in Lebanon and to maintain peace. The mandate of the Force, whose costs were borne mainly by Saudi Arabia and other Gulf states, was repeatedly renewed.

Other institutions have been created by the Council of the League for specific purposes: the Administrative Tribunal of the Arab League; the Special Bureau for Boycotting Israel; the Academy of Arab Music; and the Arab Fund for Technical Assistance to African and Arab Countries.

The member countries of the League participate in the Specialized Agencies which constitute an integral part of the League and are designed to develop specific aspects of co-operation, or to deal with special technical matters of common interest to Arab states. The Specialized Agencies include: the Arab League Educational, Cultural and Scientific Organization; the Arab Organization for

Agricultural Development; the Arab Labour Organization; the Arab Industrial Development Organization; the Arab Civil Aviation Council; the Arab Postal Union; the Arab Telecommunications Union; the Arab States Broadcasting Union; the Arab Organization for Standardization and Metrology; the Arab Organization of Administrative Sciences; the Arab Centre for the Study of Arid Zones and Dry Lands; the Arab Academy of Maritime Transport; the Arab Satellite Communication Organization; the Council of Arab Ministers of the Interior; and the Inter-Arab Investment Guarantee Corporation. The seats of the Specialized Agencies are located in different member countries.

Besides its links with the *UN, the League co-operates closely with several UN specialized bodies, such as the *UN Educational, Scientific and Cultural Organization (UNESCO), the *International Labour Organization (ILO), the *World Health Organization (WHO), and the *International Civil Aviation Organization (ICAO), and other international and national agencies. Arab League Offices and Information Centres have been set up in New York and Geneva and in many capitals throughout the world. All members contribute to the budget of the League according to a scale of quotas determined by the Council.

The activities of the League have developed considerably over the past decades, affecting more or less closely a wide range of aspects of inter-Arab co-operation. Although it lacks the indispensable cohesion to make substantial progress towards a permanent integration of the basic policies of its member countries, the League has achieved a remarkable degree of unity on issues vital to Arab foreign policy. The League maintained a general unity on the Palestinian issue and the non-recognition of Israel until President Sadat's visit to that country in 1977; the Camp David agreements and the consequent peace treaty between Egypt and Israel imposed upon inter-Arab relations a major strain. The League has been dealing with inter-Arab disputes over boundaries and with the recurring crises in Lebanon, obtaining so far only modest results. On the economic plane, a boycott has been carried out against Israel, and public and private establishments throughout the world dealing with Israel. On the cultural and technical plane, rather elaborate structures have been established and various records of achievements are to be found. In any case, the Palestinian issue and the consequent inter-Arab tensions have long exerted a major influence on all aspects and forms of co-operation and on the prospects for the achievement of effective Arab unity within the framework of the League.

Efforts to bring about a negotiated settlement of the Iran-Iraq conflict were undertaken by the League in 1984; unanimous support for Iraq in the defence of its legitimate rights against Iran was expressed in 1987. In May 1990 a Summit Conference held in Baghdad (and boycotted by Syria and Lebanon) criticized the emigration of Soviet Jews to Israel and the efforts of Western governments to prevent Iraq from acquiring advanced weapons technology. In August 1990 an emergency Summit Conference was convened to discuss the invasion and annexation of Kuwait by Iraq; 12 members approved a resolution condemning Iraq and requesting its withdrawal from Kuwait while the remaining members condemned the presence of foreign troops in Saudi Arabia. Growing inter-Arab conflicts over the conduct to be followed in the Gulf crisis (especially Western military presence in Saudi Arabia) and the proposed return of the League's headquarters to Cairo led to the resignation of the Secretary-General in September 1990. The divisions in the Arab world made it impossible to convene another meeting of the League until March 1991 when a session took place at ambassadorial, rather than ministerial, level and any discussion of the war in the Gulf was avoided. In May 1991 the Egyptian Minister of Foreign Affairs was unanimously elected Secretary-General confirming in a certain sense the return of Egypt to its former position of eminence in the Arab world.

Secretary-General: Ahmad Esmat Abd al-Meguid
Headquarters: Tahrir Square, Arab League Bldg, Cairo, Egypt (telephone:

750511; telex: 92111; fax: 775626)
Publications: *Information Bulletin* (daily);
separate reports covering specific problems; bulletins of treaties and agreements concluded between member
countries; monthly and fortnightly bulletins in several languages issued by
Offices and Information Centres
abroad especially to present the
Palestinian case

References: M. Khalil: *The Arab States and
the Arab League* (Beirut, 1962); R.W.
Macdonald: *The League of Arab States*
(Princeton, 1965); H.A. Hassouna: *The
League of Arab States and Regional Disputes*
(Dobbs Ferry, New York, 1975); A.M.
Gomaa: *The Foundation of the League of
Arab States* (London, 1977)

M

Mercado Común Centroamericano. *See* **Central American Common Market.**

MIGA. *See* **Multilateral Investment Guarantee Agency.**

Multilateral Investment Guarantee Agency (MIGA). The Agency, established in 1988 as an affiliate of the *International Bank for Reconstruction and Development (IBRD), aims at encouraging the flow of investment for productive purposes among its member countries, through the mitigation of non-commercial barriers to investment, notably political risk. The Agency thus complements the developmental efforts of the other members of the World Bank Group with which it co-operates closely.

The Convention setting up the Agency entered into effect in April 1988 and has been signed by over 100 countries. Membership of the Agency, currently amounting to about 60 countries, is open to all countries belonging to the IBRD. The Agency is owned by its member countries and is capitalized at SDR1 billion.

The Agency, which is legally and financially separate from the IBRD, is supervised by a Board of Directors. The USA, which is by far the largest subscriber, holds 24.55 per cent of the total voting power; Japan and Germany hold 6.25 and 6.23 respectively, followed by France and the UK with 5.97 per cent each.

The basic objective of the Agency is to guarantee eligible investments against losses resulting from non-commercial risks, under four main categories: (a) transfer risk resulting from host government restrictions on currency conversion and transfer; (b) risk of loss resulting from legislative or administrative actions of the host government; (c) repudiation by the host government of contracts with investors in cases in which the investor has no access to a competent forum; and (d) risk of armed conflict and civil unrest. Eligible investments include contributions in cash or in kind in the form of equity, loans made or guaranteed by equity holders, and certain forms of non-equity direct investment. The Agency's standard policy covers investments for 15 years; in exceptional cases, coverage may be extended to 20 years. In addition to new projects, the Agency can insure the expansion of existing ones, including privatizations and financial restructurings. No minimum investment is required to be eligible for insurance. The Agency co-operates with national investment insurance agencies and private insurers to co-insure or re-insure eligible investments.

The Agency also provides policy and advisory services with a view to encouraging foreign investment in developing countries. In co-operation with the *International Finance Corporation (IFC), the Agency operates the Foreign Investment Advisory Service (FIAS) which provides advice to governments on legislation and policies affecting foreign investment.

In its first years of operations, the Agency has already issued guarantees for several projects in developing countries involving investors from major industrial countries and provided policy and advisory services. European and Japanese investors have shown an increasing interest in the guarantees extended by the Agency. Investment-promotion conferences have also been held under the Agency's sponsorship and as a result several joint ventures have been finalized.

President: Lewis T. Preston

Headquarters: 1818 H Street, N.W., Washington, D.C. 20433, USA (telephone: 477 1234; telex: 248423; fax: 477 6391)

Publications: *Annual Report*; *MIGA News* (quarterly)

N

NATO. *See* **North Atlantic Treaty Organization.**

NEA. *See* **Nuclear Energy Agency.**

Nordic Council. The Council aims to arrange co-operation among Scandinavian countries on economic, social, cultural, legal, labour and environmental matters.

The Council was established in March 1952 and inaugurated in 1953 as an advisory body on economic and social co-operation, consisting of delegates elected from the parliaments of Denmark, Iceland, Norway, and Sweden; Finland joined in 1955. In March 1962 the five Scandinavian countries concluded a Treaty of Co-operation (Treaty of Helsinki) concerning economic, social, cultural, legal and communications questions which has been amended several times (in 1971, 1974, 1983 and 1985). The need to strengthen and institutionalize joint efforts in many areas of mutual concern led the five northern countries to sign a Treaty on cultural co-operation in 1971 (subsequently amended in 1983 and 1985). The new agreements provided for the creation of the Nordic Council of Ministers, to be advised by the already existing Nordic Council of parliamentary delegates.

The basic objectives of the Council cover co-operation in a large number of fields, with the exclusion of defence and foreign affairs. Formal decisions taken by unanimous consent are immediately binding on member countries in all cases where ratification by national parliaments is not required.

The Council of Ministers is the highest decision-making organ, meeting for formal or informal sessions which are attended by Cabinet members responsible for the subjects under discussion. Annual reports on progress and prospects of co-operation are sent by the Council of Ministers to the Nordic Council. This advisory body holds annual ordinary sessions and is made up of 87 delegates elected annually by and from the respective parliaments of member countries. The various parties are proportionately represented on the basis of their representation in the national parliaments. The Faeroe Islands and Aland Islands were granted representation in 1970 within the Danish and Finnish delegations respectively. Greenland has been entitled to separate representation within the Danish delegation since 1984. Recommendations adopted by delegates are submitted to the Council of Ministers for consideration. The delegates are divided into six Standing Committees (Economic; Legal; Communications; Cultural; Social and Environmental; Budget and Control) which are also entitled to discuss the subjects within their competence with the Council of Ministers. Each delegation to the Nordic Council has a secretariat at its national parliament. The work of the Council between sessions is directed by a Presidium composed of 11 parliamentary delegates; the secretariat of the Presidium is based in Stockholm. The Secretariat of the Council of Ministers, located in Copenhagen, performs technical and administrative functions under the direction of the Secretary-General.

The amount of each country's contribution to the ordinary budget of the Council is determined in proportion to the respective national product; many forms of co-operation are financed directly from national budgets.

Nordic co-operation has been developing over the years through the setting up of a large number of specialized institutions and other permanent bodies and the implementation of common programmes and projects. The Nordic Investment Bank was established in 1975 to provide finance and guarantees for investments and exports, with special regard to energy, metal and wood-processing industries and manufacturing; the authorized and subscribed capital amounts to IMF Special Drawing Rights (SDR) 1600 million. Under the Nordic Project Investment Loan Scheme, established in July 1982, loans are also made outside the Nordic region, mainly to developing countries.

Efforts towards closer co-ordination of national policies in economic, financial and trade spheres are being made, despite Denmark's full membership of the *European Economic Community (EEC) and the participation of Finland, Iceland, Norway and Sweden in the *European Free Trade Association (EFTA). Educational, cultural and scientific co-operation has been actively promoted and has contributed to improving national standards. Other successful areas of implementation of joint programmes and projects have been transport and communications, social welfare, health and environment.

Secretariat of the Presidium of the Nordic Council: P.O. Box 19506, Stockholm, Sweden (telephone: 143420; telex: 12867; fax: 117536)
Publications: *Yearbook of Nordic Statistics*; *Nordisk Kontakt* (periodical)
Secretariat of the Nordic Council of Ministers: Store Strandstraede 18, Copenhagen, Denmark (telephone: 33114711; telex: 15544; fax: 33114711)
References: E. Solem: *The Nordic Council and Scandinavian Integration* (New York, 1977); F.W. Wendt: *Nordisk Råd, 1952–1978: Struktur, Arbejde, Resultater* (Stockholm, 1979)

North Atlantic Treaty Organization (NATO). The Organization was basically designed, in 1949, as a military alliance, linking West European countries (then numbering 10) with the USA and Canada, established to prevent or repel aggression from the Soviet Union and its Eastern European allies. It was also intended to provide a framework for continuous co-operation and consultation on political, economic and other non-military issues between member countries. During four decades, the Organization's basic aim was to maintain sufficient forces to preserve the military balance with the USSR and Eastern Europe (allied since May 1955 in the Warsaw Pact) and to provide a credible deterrent against aggression.

The dramatic and revolutionary events which began in the Eastern half of Europe in the autumn of 1989 have brought about a far-reaching process of transformation which involves all those political and military aspects of the Organization which had been built up over the past decades. In an increasingly complex security environment – characterized by the demise of the Warsaw Pact in 1991 and the disintegration of the Soviet Union and Yugoslavia – the new NATO remains first and foremost a means of common defence through collective arrangements. In spite of the fact that the process of transformation is being carried out quickly and in an atmosphere of common purpose among the member countries, many questions still have to be solved with regard to the Organization's future role and tasks. There seems to be a widespread consensus among the participating countries that if the Organization is needed less for short-term protection, it is needed more for long-term stability.

In the light of the challenges and prospects of the new Europe, the role of the European members is being enhanced and the North American commitment is being reduced although it is expected to remain militarily meaningful. Instability and uncertainty in the republics of the former Soviet Union, in Central and Eastern European countries, in the Balkans and in the 'crisis belt' from the Maghreb to the Middle and Near East call for the continued presence of NATO which remains the only functioning collective security organization with binding treaty commitments among its members and common military assets.

The North Atlantic Treaty was signed in Washington, D.C., in April 1949 and entered into force the following August. It represented the outcome of initiatives taken on both sides of the Atlantic. In March 1948 widespread concern over the security of Western Europe in the face of the steadily deteriorating political climate led to the signing of the 50-year Brussels Treaty of economic, social and cultural collaboration and collective self-defence by the Foreign Ministers of Belgium, France, Luxembourg, the Netherlands, and the UK. The following April, the Canadian Secretary of State for External Affairs suggested that the Brussels Treaty Organization be replaced by an Atlantic defence system including the countries of North America. The beginning of the Berlin blockade by the USSR and other grave political events on the European continent prompted the American Senate, in June 1948, to adopt the Vandenberg Resolution calling, *inter alia*, for the 'progressive development of regional and other collective arrangements for individual and collective self-defence' in accordance with the UN Charter and recommending 'the association of the USA with such regional and other collective arrangements'. In October 1948, the Consultative Council of the Brussels Treaty powers announced 'complete agreement on the principle of a defence pact for the North Atlantic and on the next steps to be taken'. The following December, negotiations on the drafting of the North Atlantic Treaty opened in Washington, D.C., between the countries party to the Brussels Treaty, the USA and Canada. Among European countries, Denmark, Iceland, Italy, Norway, and Portugal accepted the invitation to participate in the Atlantic Alliance, while Ireland and Sweden declined. In April 1949, the Foreign Ministers of Belgium, Canada, Denmark, France, Iceland, Italy, Luxembourg, the Netherlands, Norway, Portugal, the UK, and the USA signed the Treaty establishing an Alliance for the defence of

Western Europe and North America. Greece and Turkey acceded to the Treaty in February 1952, followed by the Federal Republic of Germany in May 1955. The accession of Spain was approved by the Organization in December 1981 and formally took place in May 1982.

In March 1966, General de Gaulle announced France's intention to withdraw from the military structure of the Alliance and consequently Allied military forces and military headquarters were removed from France. The military coup d'etat in Cyprus and the subsequent landing of Turkish troops in July 1974 resulted in the withdrawal of Greek forces from the integrated military structure of the Alliance the following August. Greece agreed to rejoin the military structure in October 1980. It is important to stress that, despite the withdrawal by France and Greece of their military personnel from the integrated commands, neither country ever ceased to be a party to the Treaty which, therefore, remained unaffected.

The Preamble to the Treaty emphasizes the determination of the signatory countries to safeguard the freedom, common heritage and civilization of their peoples, founded on the principles of democracy, individual liberty and the rule of law, with a view to promoting conditions of stability and well-being in the North Atlantic area. Under the Treaty, the member countries undertake to settle international disputes in which they may be involved by peaceful means and to refrain in their international relations from the threat or use of force in any manner inconsistent with the purposes of the UN. It is the intention of the member countries to contribute towards the further development of peaceful and friendly international relations, to eliminate conflict in their international economic policies and to encourage economic collaboration between any or all of them. To this end, the member countries, separately and jointly, by means of continuous and effective self-help and mutual aid, agree to maintain and develop their individual and collective capacity to resist armed attack. They are bound to consult together whenever the territorial integrity, political independence or security of any of them is threatened; joint consultation must take place whenever a member country believes that such a threat exists. Of great importance is the provision in which the members agree to consider an armed attack against one or more of them in Europe or North America as an attack against them all and consequently to assist the member or members so attacked. More precisely, each member is under the obligation to take forthwith, individually, and in concert with the other members, 'such action as it deems necessary, including the use of armed force, to restore and maintain the security of the North Atlantic area'. Although members are committed to help each other in the event of an armed attack, it is for each individual member to decide on whatever action it considers appropriate. The area in which the provisions of the Treaty apply is the North Atlantic area north of the Tropic of Cancer.

The Organization was essentially conceived as a defensive Alliance maintaining military preparedness in order to prevent war. Its political task was to provide for consultation on all political problems of relevance to members or to the Alliance as a whole and to give directions to the military side. In peacetime, the Organization was responsible for drawing up joint defence plans, setting up the necessary infrastructure and arranging for joint training and exercises. Apart from the integrated staffs at the Organization's different military headquarters and certain defence units on constant alert, all national forces have always received orders only from national authorities.

The new strategic concept of the Alliance – according to the Declaration of the Heads of State and Government of the member countries meeting in Rome in November 1991 – maintains the 'core functions' of the Organization while making it possible, within the radically changed situation in Europe, to realize in full the members' approach to 'stability and security encompassing political, economic, social and environmental aspects, along with the indispensable defence dimension'. Within a broad concept of security, the Alliance will retain 'its purely defensive purpose, its

collective arrangements based on an integrated military structure as well as co-operation and co-ordination agreements, and for the foreseeable future an appropriate mix of conventional and nuclear forces'. Conventional forces will be substantially reduced; an even greater reduction will affect nuclear forces while multinational formations will play a greater role within the integrated military structure.

According to the Treaty, any other European country in a position to further the principles of the Alliance and to contribute to the security of the North Atlantic area may be invited to join by unanimous consent of the member countries. The enlargement of the Organization with the entry of countries of Central and Eastern Europe is not unlikely, although such an enlargement would require, on the part of the Organization itself, the assumption of full responsibility for organizing and managing security on a truly European scale. The right to withdraw is expressly envisaged after the Treaty has been in force for 20 years, that is from 1969; withdrawal takes effect one year after notice of denunciation has been given.

The Treaty dealt very briefly with the institutional aspects, mentioning only the establishment of a Council empowered to set up subsidiary organs, in particular a defence committee; as a result, the organizational structure has developed in keeping with the growing requirements of co-operation and co-ordination. The highest decision-making body and forum for consultation and negotiation within the Alliance is the North Atlantic Council, composed of representatives of all member countries and 'so organized as to be able to meet promptly at any time'. At ministerial meetings of the Council, which are held at least twice a year, members are represented by Ministers of Foreign Affairs. The Council also meets on occasion 'at the summit', that is at the level of Heads of State and Government. In permanent session, at the level of Permanent Representatives (Ambassadors), the Council meets at least once a week. The Council, which is also empowered to give political guidance to the military authorities, is not bound to follow any voting procedure and, in practice, votes are never cast. Decisions are therefore expressions of the collective will of the members, arrived at by common consent. The Defence Planning Committee (DPC) is composed of the representatives of those member countries which participate in the Organization's integrated military structure and includes, at present, all member countries except France. It deals with matters specifically related to defence and is the highest forum for discussion of military policy. Like the Council, the DPC meets both in permanent session at the level of Permanent Representatives and at ministerial level, twice a year, with the participation of Defence Ministers. The Council and the DPC are chaired by the Organization's Secretary-General, regardless of the level of the meeting. Opening sessions of ministerial meetings of the Council are presided over by the President, an honorary position held annually by the Foreign Minister of a member country, following the English alphabetical order. Nuclear matters are discussed by the Nuclear Planning Group (NPG) in which 14 countries fully participate under the chairmanship of the Secretary-General; France does not attend the meetings while Iceland participates as an observer. The NPG meets regularly at the level of Permanent Representatives and twice a year at the level of Defence Ministers.

A number of Committees have been established by the Council over the years; the Committee on the Challenges of Modern Society (CCMS), founded in 1969, examines the methods of improving cooperation in creating a better environment and undertakes pilot studies of relevance to member countries. There are also Committees for Political Affairs, Economic Affairs, Science, Defence Review, Armaments, Information and Cultural Relations, Civil Emergency Planning, Civil and Military Budgets, Infrastructure, Logistics, and Communications. All Committees perform advisory functions and are supported by an International Staff, made up of personnel drawn from all member countries, responsible to the Secretary-General. The Secretary-General is responsible for promoting and directing the process of consultation within the Alliance. He may propose items for discussion and is empowered to use his good offices at any time in cases of dispute between members and, with their consent, to initiate enquiries or mediation, conciliation or arbitration procedures. The Deputy Secretary-General assists the Secretary-General in his functions. The International Staff comprises the Office of the Secretary-General, five major Divisions (Political Affairs; Defence Planning and Policy; Defence Support; Infrastructure, Logistics and Civil Emergency Planning; and Scientific and Environmental Affairs), the Office of Management, and the Financial Controller.

Besides the civil structure, the Organization has a military structure which also operates under the authority of the Council. The Military Committee (MC), the highest military body in the Alliance, is responsible for addressing recommendations to the Council and the DPC on military matters and for providing guidance on military questions to Allied Commanders and subordinate military authorities. The MC, composed of the Chiefs-of-Staff of all members, except France and Iceland (which has no military forces), meets at Chiefs-of-Staff level normally three times a year but functions in permanent session, with effective powers of decision, at the level of Permanent Military Representatives. Liaison between the MC and the French High Command is effected through the Chief of the French Military Mission. The Presidency of the MC rotates annually in the alphabetical order of countries; the Chairman, elected for a period of two to three years, represents the MC on the Council. The MC is assisted by an integrated International Military Staff (IMS), headed by a Director; the IMS is responsible for the implementation of the policies and decisions of the MC, the preparation of plans, the carrying out of studies and the formulation of recommendations on military matters.

The strategic area covered by the Treaty is divided among three Commands; the Allied Command Europe (ACE) – whose headquarters near Mons, Belgium, are known as Supreme Headquarters Allied

Powers Europe (SHAPE) – covers the area extending from the North Cape to the Mediterranean and from the Atlantic to the eastern border of Turkey, excluding the UK and Portugal; the Allied Command Atlantic (ACLANT), with headquarters in Norfolk, Virginia, USA, covers an area in the Atlantic Ocean extending from the North Pole to the Tropic of Cancer and from the coastal waters of North America to the coasts of Europe and Africa, excluding the Channel and the British Isles; the Allied Command Channel (ACCHAN), with headquarters in Northwood, UK, covers the English Channel and the southern areas of the North Sea. Plans for the defence of the North American area are drawn up by the Canada-United States Regional Planning Group which meets alternately in Washington, D.C., and Ottawa and makes recommendations to the MC. The authority exercised by the Commands varies in accordance with geographical and political factors and with peace or wartime conditions. The Commanders are responsible for the development of defence plans for their respective areas, for the determination of force requirements and for the deployment and exercise of the forces under their Command.

Several civilian and military agencies have been gradually created and charged with specific tasks. These agencies do not necessarily include all the member countries of the Organization and are located in various towns of Western Europe. Generally, civilian agencies are under the authority of the Council while military agencies are responsible to the MC.

Two 'unofficial' bodies, the Eurogroup and the North Atlantic Assembly, also operate within the framework of the Organization. The Eurogroup is an informal association of Defence Ministers of the European members of the Organization, except France and Iceland. It was created in response to a desire for closer European co-operation and co-ordination within the Alliance, with a view to making the European contribution to the common defence as strong and effective as possible. The North Atlantic Assembly – known be-tween 1955 and 1966 as the NATO Parliamentarians' Conference – is basically a forum where members of parliaments from the countries of the Alliance meet regularly with a view to encouraging Atlantic solidarity and co-operation in national parliaments. It provides a link between parliamentarians and authorities of the Organization. The Assembly is composed of 184 members delegated by national parliaments; representation is weighted according to the population of each country. The Assembly meets in plenary session every autumn to discuss reports of the Committees and to address recommendations to the Secretary-General of the Organization; the comments of the Secretary-General on these recommendations are discussed by the Council in permanent session and subsequently transmitted to the Assembly.

The Assembly has developed relations over the past few years with the countries of Central and Eastern Europe as soon as democratically elected parliaments have begun to operate. The status of 'associate delegate' has already been granted to parliamentary delegations from Bulgaria, Czechoslovakia, Estonia, Hungary, Latvia, Lithuania, Poland, Romania and Russia. The establishment of a parliamentary assembly of the *Conference on Security and Co-operation in Europe (CSCE) in April 1991 in Madrid originated the problem of a 'division of labour' among the new body and existing parliamentary institutions such as the North Atlantic Assembly and the Parliamentary Assembly of the Council of Europe. A formula is being devised whereby the North Atlantic Assembly will contribute to the work of the CSCE assembly in security matters, putting its expertise at the service of the newly-created pan-European body.

The relationship between NATO and its former adversaries is being developed within the framework of the North Atlantic Co-operation Council (NACC) set up by the Heads of State and Government at their Rome Summit in November 1991 as a forum of consultation and co-operation on security matters and related issues. The inaugural session of NACC, at the level of Foreign Ministers, took place in Brussels in

December 1991 and adopted a Statement on Dialogue, Partnership and Co-operation.

The Organization has always maintained close relations with several international institutions, in particular those operating in Western Europe. In the new Europe, the Organization plans to work toward a security architecture in which the Organization itself, the CSCE, the *European Communities (EC), the *Western European Union (WEU) and the *Council of Europe complement each other. Appropriate links and consultation procedures are being developed especially between the EC and the WEU on the one hand and the Organization on the other hand to ensure that the countries which are not participating in the forging of a European identity in foreign and security policy and defence may be effectively involved in decisions which are likely to affect their own security.

The Organization has substantially achieved its primary purpose, that is the safeguard of the security of member countries by deterring aggression, through a policy based on the twin principles of defence and détente. The dual approach of maintaining credible collective defence while at the same time pursuing a policy of detente through improved dialogue with the Soviet Union and its Warsaw Pact allies provided the foundation for NATO policy for over two decades until the dramatic events of late 1989 began to change fundamentally the European and global environment. NATO has now embarked on a new era of expanding relations with its former adversaries, replacing confrontation with co-operation and offering assistance to the peoples of the former Soviet Union.

The Organization, in fact, is gradually evolving from a military alliance into a forum for political consultation on vital issues of foreign policy and security on a Euro-atlantic scale. In 1990 and 1991 a series of high-level meetings redefined NATO's role and mission in the new Europe. The meeting of the Heads of State and Government in November 1991 in Rome marked a watershed in the history of NATO as well as in the history of Europe deciding: the establishment of a new relationship with the countries of Central and Eastern Europe; the elaboration of a new military strategy; the pursuit of the arms control process beyond the Conventional Forces in Europe (CFE) Treaty with a view to limiting the offensive potential of armed forces to the point at which surprise attack or major aggression would become impossible.

Secretary-General: Manfred Wörner

Headquarters: 1110 Brussels, Belgium (telephone: 728 4111; telex: 23867; fax: 728 4579)

Publications: *NATO Review* (six a year); *NATO Facts and Figures*; *NATO Handbook*

References: P. Hill-Norton: *No Soft Options: the Politico-Military Realities of NATO* (London, 1978); R.S. Jordan: *Political Leadership in NATO: a Study in Multinational Diplomacy* (Boulder, Colorado, 1979); J. Godson: *Challenges to the Western Alliance* (London, 1986); G. Williams and A. Lee: *The European Defence Initiative* (London, 1986); S.R. Sloan: *NATO's Future: Towards a New Transatlantic Bargain* (London, 1986); D. Cook: *The Forging of an Alliance* (London, 1989); S.R. Sloan: *NATO in the 1990s* (Washington, 1989); J. Smith (ed): *The Origins of NATO* (Exeter Univ. Press, 1990)

Nuclear Energy Agency (NEA). The Agency aims to promote, within the framework of the *Organization for Economic Co-operation and Development (OECD), the development and application of nuclear power for peaceful uses.

The Agency was originally established as a Western European body – under the title of European Nuclear Energy Agency (ENEA) – by a decision adopted, in December 1957, by the Council of the Organization for European Economic Co-operation (OEEC); the decision took effect from February 1958. The Agency represented a response, on a regional scale, to the creation in March 1957 of the *European Atomic Energy Community (Euratom) by the 'Six' (that is Belgium, France, Germany, Italy, Luxembourg, and the Netherlands). The Council of the OECD, which succeeded the OEEC in 1960, formally decided to retain the Agency within the framework of the new Organization. The Agency dropped the term 'European' from its official title and adopted its present name in April 1972. Between May 1972 and October 1976 four of the five OECD members outside Europe (that is Australia, Canada, Japan and the USA) as well as Finland were admitted to full participation. Membership of the Agency now includes all OECD countries, with the exception of New Zealand.

The Agency's basic task is to promote a common effort between member countries in the peaceful use of nuclear energy through international research and development projects, as well as the exchange of scientific and technical experience and information. It is also concerned with the safety and regulatory aspects of nuclear energy, including the adoption of uniform standards governing safety and health protection, and a uniform legislative regime for nuclear liability and insurance. Conferences and symposia on specific subjects are held under the sponsorship of the Agency from time to time.

The controlling body of the Agency is the OECD Steering Committee for Nuclear Energy presided over by a Chairman assisted by Vice-Chairmen. A number of Committees have been set up and are charged with: Technical and Economic Studies on Nuclear Energy Development and the Fuel Cycle; Safety of Nuclear Installations; Nuclear Regulatory Activities; Radiation Protection and Public Health; Radioactive Waste Management; Nuclear Science. There is a Group of Governmental Experts on Third Party Liability in the Field of Nuclear Energy. The Agency's Secretariat performs administrative functions under a Director-General, assisted by a Deputy Director-General, and two Deputy Directors taking charge of Science and Computer Processing, and Safety and Regulation, respectively.

The Agency conducts and publishes studies on world uranium resources, production and demand, long term nuclear fuel cycle requirements, and nuclear legislation in close co-operation with other international institutions, in particular the

*International Atomic Energy Agency (IAEA).

A substantial part of the Agency's work is focused on the safety and regulation of nuclear power, including studies and projects for the prevention of nuclear accidents and the long-term safety of radioactive waste disposal systems.

One of the Agency's most significant undertakings has been the European Company for the Chemical Processing of Irradiated Fuels (Eurochemic), an international company established under a Convention signed in December 1957 to build and operate a plant for re-processing used uranium fuels from nuclear reactors; the plant ceased operations in 1974 and Eurochemic went into liquidation in 1982.

The International Project on Food Irradiation, set up in January 1971 and terminated in December 1981, was aimed at testing irradiated food items and carrying out reviews of the relevant data available from national institutes, under the joint sponsorship of the Agency, the IAEA and the *Food and Agriculture Organization of the UN (FAO).

A project concerning an experimental boiling heavy water reactor, located in Halden, Norway, has been carried out, under successive agreements, since the late 1950s. Research institutions in over ten countries participate in the Halden Project.

Among the international programmes of scientific investigations, launched in the early 1980s, mention should be made of the following: the Incident Reporting System for the exchange of experience in operating nuclear power plants in OECD member countries; the Programme for Inspection of Steel Components; the Information System on Occupational Exposure; the Decommissioning of Nuclear Installations for developing the operational experience needed for future decommissioning of large nuclear power plants.

The Co-operative Programme on Three Mile Island, established in 1986, examines samples from the Three Mile Island nuclear reactor in Pennsylvania, USA (where a serious accident took place in 1979) and elaborates computer codes for analysis of accidents, in particular with regard to the behaviour of fission products. The Alligator Rivers Analogue Project, set up in 1988, aims to gain insight into the long-term processes which influence the transport of radionuclides through rock masses.

A Data Bank was set up in January 1978 in Saclay, France, to allow the 17 participating countries to share larger computer programmes used in reactor calculations and nuclear data applications; it also operates as one of a worldwide network of four nuclear data centres.

The Agency has undertaken a programme of co-operation with Central and Eastern European countries and the republics of the former Soviet Union notably to provide assistance in the field of nuclear safety.

Director-General: Dr Kunihiko Uematsu

Headquarters: Le Seine St Germain, 12 Bld des Iles, 92130 Issy-les-Moulineaux, France (telephone: 4524 1010; telex: AEN/NEA 630668; fax: 4524 1110)

Publications: *Annual Report*; *NEA Newsletter*; *Nuclear Law Bulletin* (periodical)

O

OAPEC. *See* **Organization of Arab Petroleum Exporting Countries.**

OAS. *See* **Organization of American States.**

OAU. *See* **Organization of African Unity.**

ODECA. *See* **Organization of Central American States.**

OECD. *See* **Organization for Economic Co-operation and Development.**

Office of the United Nations Disaster Relief Co-ordinator (UNDRO). The purpose of the Office is to mobilize and co-ordinate international emergency relief to disaster-stricken areas and to co-operate in promoting disaster preparedness and prevention.

In the wake of two major calamities that occurred in 1970 – an earthquake in Peru and a tidal wave in East Pakistan [now Bangladesh] – the UN General Assembly recognized the need to strengthen the capacity of the UN system to render assistance in such calamities and requested, in 1971, the Secretary-General to appoint a Disaster Relief Co-ordinator, whose Office began operations in Geneva in March 1972.

The Office is a separate entity within the UN Secretariat and consists of a Relief Co-ordination Branch and a Disaster Mitigation Branch. It has three main functions: (a) to ensure that, in case of natural or man-made disaster, the emergency relief activities of all donor sources are mobilized and co-ordinated so as to comply with the needs of the disaster-stricken country in a timely and effective manner; (b) to raise the level of pre-disaster planning and preparedness, including disaster assessment and relief management capability, in disaster-prone developing countries; and (c) to promote the study, prevention, control and prediction of natural disasters, including the collection and dissemination of information related to technological developments.

The Office maintains contact during the post-emergency phase with a view to advising governments on the inclusion of disaster-prevention concepts in rehabilitation or reconstruction programmes and on the improvement of disaster preparedness planning generally.

The Co-ordinator is empowered, on behalf of the Secretary-General, to direct all relief activities of the UN system, to receive contributions in kind or cash for disaster relief assistance and to serve as a clearing house for information on assistance provided by all sources of external aid.

The Office is represented in developing countries by the Resident Representatives of the *UN Development Programme (UNDP). A Liaison Office is also maintained at UN Headquarters in New York. A warehouse was established in Pisa, Italy, in 1986 to stock relief supplies ready for shipment anywhere in the world. The Office co-operates closely with donor and recipient governments as well as with various UN bodies and inter-governmental organizations, the League of Red Cross

Societies and other voluntary agencies. Following the decision of the UN General Assembly in 1988 to designate the 1990s as the International Decade for Natural Disaster Reduction, the Office acts as a secretariat for the said Decade.

The Office is basically a co-ordinating body and is not to be regarded as a major source of relief assistance. The Co-ordinator was originally authorized to spend up to $200,000 in a year for emergency assistance, with a ceiling of $20,000 for any single disaster. In 1979, the General Assembly requested that additional funds be provided in the regular budget of the Office for 1980-81 to permit its response to at least 12 requests for emergency assistance in a year, with a ceiling of $30,000 for any one disaster and a global ceiling of $360,000 in one year. In 1982, the General Assembly decided to make UNDRO's Trust Fund permanent and authorized an increase in the budget for direct emergency grants to $600,000 per year with a ceiling of $50,000 for any one disaster. Since it started operations in 1972, the Office has co-ordinated emergency relief in hundreds of disasters, including major catastrophes such as floods in China, the Philippines, Pakistan and Bangladesh and earthquakes in China, Nicaragua, Guatemala, Indonesia, Turkey and the former USSR. It has channelled substantial amounts in contributions to disaster victims and has directly allocated relief assistance from UN funds to meet immediate needs such as medicines, food or the transport of life-saving equipment. The Office may also seek the financing for carrying out specific projects concerning pre-disaster planning and organization. Technical advice on pre-disaster planning has been provided to a large number of disaster-prone developing countries. Another important area of activity is represented by the elimination of the legal and administrative obstacles which hamper the movement of relief goods and personnel from the donor to the recipient countries.

Co-ordinator: M'Hamed Essaafi
Headquarters: Palais des Nations, 1211 Geneva 10, Switzerland (telephone: 734 6011; telex: 28148; fax: 733 5623)

Publications: *Annual Report to the UN General Assembly*; *UNDRO News* (six times a year); *Disaster News in Brief* (annual); technical papers
References: T. Stephens: *The UN Disaster Relief Office* (Washington, D.C., 1978); P. MacAlister Smith: *International Humanitarian Assistance: Disaster Relief Actions in International Law and Organizations* (1985)

OFID. *See* **OPEC Fund for International Development.**

OICS. Organe international de contrôle des stupéfiants; *see* **International Narcotics Control Board.**

OPANAL. Organismo para la Proscripción de las Armas Nucleares en la América Latina y el Caribe; *see* **Agency for the Prohibition of Nuclear Weapons in Latin America and the Caribbean.**

OPEC. *See* **Organization of the Petroleum Exporting Countries.**

OPEC Fund for International Development (OFID). The purpose of the Fund – established by the members of the *Organization of the Petroleum Exporting Countries (OPEC) – is to assist developing countries that do not produce oil through the provision of financial support on appropriate terms.

A special Fund to provide loans to finance balance-of-payments deficits and development projects was created by OPEC countries through an agreement signed in Paris in January 1976. In May 1980, OPEC Finance Ministers decided to convert the special Fund into an autonomous development agency for financial co-operation and assistance enjoying legal personality and renamed it the 'OPEC Fund for International Development'.

The Fund is empowered to: (a) provide concessional loans for balance-of-payments support; (b) provide concessional loans for the implementation of development projects and programmes; (c) contribute and provide loans to eligible international agencies; and (d) finance technical assistance and research through grants. Beneficiaries of the assistance may be the developing countries other than OPEC members and international development agencies; countries with the lowest income are given priority. The loans are not tied to procurement from Fund members or any other countries.

The resources of the Fund, initially set at $800 million, have been replenished repeatedly; the pledged contributions to the Fund by the end of 1990 amounted to $3435 million of which $2725 paid-in. Payments of contributions by member countries are made voluntarily upon demand by the Governing Committee with a view to ensuring the timely disbursement of the loans committed.

The structure of the Fund is similar to that of other international financing institutions and comprises: the Ministerial Council, which is the supreme authority and consists of the Ministers of Finance of the member countries; the Governing Board performing executive functions and consisting of one representative and one alternate for each member country; and the Director-General.

A variety of loans to about 90 developing countries have been granted, on advantageous terms, since the Fund began operations. The geographic distribution of lending operations concentrated mainly on African countries (nearly 50 per cent of the total), followed by Asian countries (over 40 per cent) and Latin American and Caribbean countries (about 10 per cent). By the end of December 1990, an amount of about $2530 million had been committed in the form of about 530 loans; of this total over 70 per cent had been disbursed. Two-thirds of the total amount of loans were granted for project financing and about 28 per cent for balance-of-payments support, leaving less than five per cent for programme financing. Most projects financed by the Fund are co-financed by other development agencies. Direct loans are supplemented by grants for technical assistance, food aid and research. By the

end of 1990, 285 grants had been extended for a total amount of $215 million. An additional amount of nearly $1 billion had been contributed by the Fund to other international institutions by the end of 1990.

The Fund has played a significant role in the co-ordination of the policies of its member countries in various international forums and *vis-a-vis* international organizations, in particular the *International Fund for Agricultural Development (IFAD).

Director-General: Yesufu Seyyid Abdulai

Headquarters: P.O. Box 995, 1011 Vienna, Austria (telephone: 515640; telex: 131734; fax: 513 9238)

Publications: *Annual Report*; *OPEC Fund Newsletter* (three a year); *OPEC Aid and OPEC Aid Institutions* (annually)

References: I. Shihata: *The OPEC Fund for International Development: The Formative Years* (London, 1983); A. Benamara and S. Ifeagwu (eds): *OPEC Aid and the Challenge of Development* (London, 1987)

Organe international de contrôle des stupéfiants (OICS). *See* **International Narcotics Control Board.**

Organisation européenne pour la recherche nucléaire (CERN). *See* **European Organization for Nuclear Research.**

Organismo para la Proscripción de las Armas Nucleares en la América Latina y el Caribe (OPANAL). *See* **Agency for the Prohibition of Nuclear Weapons in Latin America and the Caribbean.**

Organización de Estados Centroamericanos (ODECA). *See* **Organization of Central American States.**

Organization for Economic Co-operation and Development (OECD). The Organization aims to promote economic and social welfare in member countries, by assisting them in the formulation and co-ordination of the appropriate policies, and to stimulate and harmonize its members' efforts in favour of developing nations.

The Convention establishing the Organization was signed in Paris in December 1960 and entered into effect in September 1961. The Organization succeeded – with a new title, an enlarged membership and wider aims and functions – the Organization for European Economic Co-operation (OEEC). The OEEC had been created in April 1948 primarily to administer Marshall Plan aid, in conjunction with the Economic Co-operation Administration (ECA) set up by the USA, with the long-term objective of promoting the achievement of a sound European economy through the co-operative effort of its members. Although participation was formally open to 'any signatory European country', the OEEC became in fact a Western European body, since the USSR and the Eastern European countries refused to join; in particular, Poland and Czechoslovakia recanted, under Soviet pressure, their affirmative replies to the Marshall Plan Conference held in Paris between July and September 1947. In early 1949, the USSR and the countries of Eastern Europe riposted on the institutional plane by establishing the Council for Mutual Economic Assistance (CMEA; Comecon) with the basic goal of organizing a wider commercial and economic co-operation between them. Notwithstanding the lack of any reference to the possibility of associate membership in the OEEC Convention, Canada, Japan, and the USA were granted the status of associate members.

At the end of the 1950s, it was felt that the fundamental aims of the OEEC had been largely fulfilled with the economic recovery of Western Europe and that a new institution, with an emphasis on the promotion of economic growth and development aid to developing nations and a broadened field of operation, should be set up, with the accession of Canada and the USA as full members. A proposal to that effect was put forward in a communique issued in Paris in December 1959 by the

representatives of France, the Federal Republic of Germany, the UK, and the USA. Discussions took place throughout 1960 and a Preparatory Committee was entrusted with the task of drafting the Convention creating the new institution. The reconstitution of the OEEC as the Organization for Economic Co-operation and Development (OECD) was eventually accomplished in December 1960 with the signature of the Convention by the representatives of 18 Western European countries plus Canada and the USA. Another European country, Finland, and three non-European countries, Australia, Japan, and New Zealand, acceded to the Convention in the subsequent years. Yugoslavia was granted a special status. The Commission of the *European Communities takes part in the work of the Organization.

According to the Convention, the Organization is responsible for promoting policies designed: (a) to achieve the highest sustainable economic growth and employment and a rising standard of living in member countries, while maintaining financial stability, and thus to contribute to the development of the world economy; (b) to contribute to sound economic expansion in member as well as non-member countries in the process of economic development; and (c) to contribute to the expansion of world trade on a multilateral, non-discriminatory basis in accordance with international obligations.

To this end, the member countries undertake, both individually and jointly, obligations with regard to: the efficient use of economic resources; the promotion of research and vocational training and the development of resources in the scientific and technological field; the pursuit of policies for the achievement of economic growth and internal and external financial stability, without endangering the economies of other countries; the reduction or abolition of obstacles to the exchange of goods and services and current payments and the maintenance and extension of the liberalization of capital movements; the economic development of both member and non-member countries in the process of economic development by appropriate means, in particular the flow of capital, taking into account the importance of technical assistance and of securing expanding export markets.

With a view to fulfilling these undertakings, the member countries agree: (a) to keep each other informed and provide the Organization with the information necessary for the accomplishment of its tasks; (b) to consult together on a continuing basis, carry out studies and participate in agreed projects; and (c) to co-operate closely and, where appropriate, take co-ordinated action.

The Organization is empowered to adopt decisions which, except as otherwise provided, are binding on all members, to address recommendations to members and to enter into agreements with members, non-members and international institutions. Decisions and recommendations are adopted by mutual consent of all members, each having one vote; in special cases, a majority vote may suffice, if the Organization unanimously agrees to that effect. Abstentions do not impair the vote and abstaining members are not bound by any act adopted without their consent. Moreover, no decision is binding on any member until it has complied with the requirements of its own constitutional procedures. Although the legal personality possessed by the OEEC continues in its successor, it is expressly provided that all decisions, recommendations and resolutions adopted by the OEEC require the approval of the new Organization to remain effective.

Any sovereign country may be invited, by unanimous decision, to join the Organization; the right of withdrawal may be exercised by giving 12 months' notice to that effect. Unlike the OEEC Convention, there is no provision concerning the expulsion of members.

The Council, from which 'all acts of the Organization derive', is the supreme governing body, composed of one representative for each member country. It meets either at the level of permanent representatives (that is the heads of national delegations with rank of ambassador), about once a week, under the chairmanship of the Secretary-General, or at ministerial level, usually once a year, under the chairmanship of a minister elected annually. The Council is responsible for all questions of general policy and is empowered to establish an Executive Committee and such subsidiary bodies as may be required to achieve the aims of the Organization. Each year the Council designates 14 of its members to form the Executive Committee which is called upon to prepare the work of the Council itself and, where appropriate, to carry out specific tasks. The Executive Committee has power of decision only upon express delegation by the Council.

The Secretariat, performing technical and administrative functions, is headed by a Secretary-General appointed by, and responsible to, the Council. The Secretary-General assists the Council in all appropriate ways and has the power of submitting his own proposals to the Council or any other body of the Organization. Three Deputy Secretaries-General as well as special counsellors and advisors assist the Secretary-General.

The Council has made ample use of its authority to set up subsidiary organs for the performance of the Organization's functions. The largest part of the work is prepared and carried out by specialized committees and working parties currently numbering more than 200. Among the main subsidiary bodies are: the Economic Policy Committee, composed of governments' senior officials with a major responsibility for the formulation of general economic policies, which is chiefly concerned with economic growth and the related policy measures; the Economic and Development Review Committee, in charge of the preparation of the annual economic surveys of individual member countries whose results are regularly published; the Development Assistance Committee (DAC) – consisting of the representatives of major OECD capital-exporting nations – which aims to expand the aggregate volume of resources made available to developing countries, to improve their effectiveness and to conduct periodical reviews of the amount and nature of its members' contributions to aid programmes, both bilateral and multilateral; the Trade Committee, dealing with commercial policies and practices and specific trade problems; the Payments Committee, considering questions relating to invisible transactions and multilateral settlements.

Other important Committees are responsible for: Environment; Technical Co-operation; International Investment and Multinational Enterprises; Capital Movements and Invisible Transactions; Financial Markets; Fiscal Affairs; Tourism; Maritime Transport; Consumer Policies; Agriculture; Fisheries; Scientific and Technological Policy; Education; Industry; Steel; Energy Policy; Manpower and Social Affairs. Moreover, there are a High-Level Group on Commodities and a Group on North-South Economic Issues.

The variety of functions assigned to the Organization has involved the establishment of a number of operating agencies, related in varying degrees to the Organization's machinery, which enjoy autonomous or semi-autonomous status. These bodies comprise – besides the *International Energy Agency (IEA) and the *Nuclear Energy Agency (NEA) – the Development Centre, set up in 1962 for the analysis of development and aid problems and policies as well as for the training of specialists, and the Centre for Educational Research and Innovation (CERI), set up in 1968 to facilitate the introduction of reforms in the educational systems of member countries.

The Organization has gradually developed a complex network of co-operative relations with many international agencies, including those belonging to the UN system. Particularly close relations exist with international economic and social institutions, both inter-governmental and non-governmental, operating in Europe, in order to achieve an effective co-ordination of policies and efforts.

Each year the Secretary-General presents to the Council for approval an annual budget, accounts and such subsidiary budgets as may be necessary. The general expenses of the Organization are apportioned among member countries according to a scale fixed by the Council. Other expeditures are financed on such basis as the Council may decide.

The Organization has been actively engaged over the past three decades in a wide range of activities which have represented, to a certain extent, a continuation of the work of the OEEC within an expanded framework and with revised purposes to reflect the changes in the world and European contexts. In spite of the purely voluntary character of co-operation, since the ultimate implementation of the Organization's decisions rests with each member country, co-ordinated action has been carried out in a number of areas of major importance, such as international trade rules, capital movements, export credits and aid to developing countries. The publication of regular surveys, specialized reports and monographs, and statistics on economic and social subjects has largely contributed to a deeper understanding of the state of the economies of both member and non-member countries. Conferences, seminars and other meetings at different levels have often provided an in-depth analysis of many problems affecting the growth prospects of industrial countries and their relations with developing nations. However, periods of low growth in developed countries, inflation, high interest rates, and unemployment have often encouraged protectionist trading and industrial policies and consequently involved reductions in the level of concessional aid. Conflicts of economic interests between the European countries and the USA as well as long-standing tensions between all of them and Japan – as illustrated, *inter alia*, in the Uruguay Round of multilateral trade negotiations – may adversely affect the prospects for better co-operation within the framework of the Organization in the present decade.

Secretary-General: Jean-Claude Paye

Headquarters: 2 rue André Pascal, 75775 Paris, France (telephone: 4524 8200; telex: 620160; fax: 4524 8500)

Publications: *Activities of OECD* (annual report); *News from OECD* (monthly); *The OECD Observer* (every two months); *Main Economic Indicators* (monthly); *Economic Survey* (annually for each member country); *Development Co-operation Report* (annually)

References: H.G. Aubrey: *Atlantic Economic Co-operation: The Case of OECD* (New York, 1967); M.J. Esman and D.S. Cheever: *The Common Aid Effort. The Development Assistance Activities of the OECD* (Columbus, Ohio, 1967)

Organization of African Unity (OAU). The Organization operates to promote unity and solidarity among African countries, through the co-ordination of efforts in the fields of politics and diplomacy, economy, science and technology, education and health, defence and security, and finally to eliminate all forms of colonialism and apartheid in the continent.

The Organization's Charter was signed in May 1963 in Addis Ababa by the heads of state or government of 30 countries of Africa and Madagascar. The present membership of the Organization comprises about 50 African countries, including Madagascar and other islands surrounding Africa. Any 'independent sovereign African state' is eligible for membership; decision on admission requires a simple majority of the member countries.

The Organization's basic principles are the equality of members, non-interference in internal affairs, respect for territorial integrity, peaceful settlement of disputes, unconditional condemnation of political subversion and dedication to the goal of the complete emancipation of dependent African territories; reference had also been made to the principle of international non-alignment.

The Organization's functions and powers are very briefly described by the Charter; this reflects the proper nature of the body, designed to promote a rather loose co-operation, not bound by rigid patterns which, in any case, would be hardly applicable in practice.

The main organs are the Assembly of the Heads of State and Government, the Council of Ministers, the General Secretariat and the Commission of Mediation, Conciliation and Arbitration. The Assembly, which is the supreme organ, meets in ordinary sessions once a year to consider matters of common concern to Africa, to co-ordinate and harmonize the Organization's general policy and, when required, to change the structure, functions and activities of the organs and specialized institutions formed in accordance with the Charter. The Assembly's resolutions are taken by a two-thirds majority, each member having one vote, with the exception of procedural matters, for which a simple majority is sufficient. The Council of Ministers, formed in principle by the Foreign Ministers of the member countries, is the executive body responsible for the implementation, in conformity with the policies laid down by the Assembly, of inter-African co-operation; it meets at least twice a year and decides by simple majority. The General Secretariat, headed by a Secretary-General appointed by the Assembly for a four-year term, performs administrative duties.

The Commission of Mediation, Conciliation and Arbitration was established by a special protocol signed in Cairo in 1964 to promote the peaceful settlement of disputes between member countries. It consists of 21 members elected by the Assembly for a five-year term; no country may have more than one member.

The subsidiary bodies include specialized commissions for economic, social, transport and communications affairs; education, science, culture and health; defence; human rights; and labour. In May 1963 the Co-ordinating Committee for Liberation Movements in Africa was established, with the participation of a certain number of the Organization's member countries. The African Liberation Committee, with headquarters in Dar-es-Salaam, Tanzania, provided financial and military assistance to nationalist liberation movements such as those operating in Angola, Mozambique and Zimbabwe.

Member countries contribute to the budget of the Organization in accordance with their UN assessment; no country may be assessed for an amount exceeding 20 per cent of the regular budget. In this connection it should be emphasized that the existence of substantial budgetary arrears, due to delays in the payment of national contributions, has led the Organization into serious problems that threaten its ability to address the continent's pressing economic and social needs.

The Organization has traditionally been geared towards fighting colonialism and apartheid and has contributed only to a very limited extent to lowering intra-African tensions and fostering regional unity. Strongly diverging views among major member countries on several important issues have considerably weakened the Organization, making the promotion of African solidarity an extremely hard task. Despite the solemn declaration adopted by the Assembly of Heads of State and Government in 1964 on the inviolability of the colonial boundaries existing at the time of gaining independence by the member countries, the Organization has proved unable to mediate effectively in territorial and other disputes and to stop civil wars and secession attempts. Proposals to set up a permanent pan-African military force have been rejected.

Many important issues, such as the Western Sahara, have raised heated contrasts, bringing about a polarization into 'moderate' and 'progressive' countries. The Sahrawi Arab Democratic Republic (SADR), proclaimed by Polisario, was eventually recognized by 26 member countries which called for its admission to the Organization. Admission took place in February 1982 but was disputed by Morocco and other countries which claimed that a two-thirds majority was needed to admit a state whose very existence was in question. Morocco declared its intention to withdraw from the Organization, with effect from November 1985, when a delegation from the SADR took part in the works of the Assembly in November 1984.

Throughout the second half of the 1980s various meetings of the Assembly called for the imposition of comprehensive economic sanctions against South Africa, condemning the links still maintained with that country by some Western and African countries. The African Anti-Apartheid Committee was set up in 1989 in Brazzaville, Congo, to co-ordinate the activities and strategies of anti-apartheid movements within and outside Africa.

Repeated requests by the Assembly to convene an international conference of creditors and borrowers in order to seek a solution to the problem of Africa's heavy external debt proved unsuccessful. The radical political and socio-economic changes taking place in Central and Eastern Europe have led the Assembly to review the implications of such changes for the African continent. A treaty on the creation of the African Economic Community was adopted by the Assembly in June 1991 and will enter into force after ratification by two-thirds of the Organization's member countries. The Community should be established within a period not exceeding 34 years, starting with a five-year stage during which measures would be adopted to strengthen existing economic groupings.

Secretary-General: Salim Ahmed Salim

Headquarters: P.O. Box 3243, Addis Ababa, Ethiopia (telephone: 517700; telex: 21046; fax: 512622)

Publication: *OUA Echo* (twice a year)

References: B. Boutros-Ghali: 'The Addis Ababa Charter', *International Conciliation*, 546 (1964); T.O. Elias: 'The Charter of the Organization of African Unity', *American Journal of International Law*, 59 (1965); M. Wolfers: *Politics in the Organization of African Unity* (London, 1976); A. Sesay, O. Ojo and O. Fasehun: *The OAU after Twenty Years* (Boulder, Colorado, 1985)

Organization of American States (OAS). The Organization is the oldest international regional agency in the world; it is devoted to the strengthening of the security of the Western hemisphere, the settlement of inter-American disputes by pacific means, and the promotion, through co-operative efforts, of its members' economic, social and cultural development. The Organization has a formal relationship with the *UN as a regional arrangement for the maintenance of peace and security.

The Organization's Charter was signed in April 1948 in Bogotá, Colombia, by the representatives of 20 Latin American countries and the USA in order to consolidate the principles, purposes and policies that had been evolving since 1890 within the framework of the inter-American system. The original members were subsequently joined by several Commonwealth Caribbean countries and Suriname. Although Cuba as a national entity is still considered a member, its 'present government' was excluded from participation in the inter-American system in 1962. Several European, African and Asian countries enjoy the status of permanent observers. Canada, a long-time permanent observer, eventually requested to join the Organization in October 1989 and was granted full membership. Member countries of the Organization now total 34.

The first move towards a coalition of the American republics dates back to the signing by Colombia, Central America, Peru and Mexico in 1826 of the Treaty of Perpetual Union, League and Confederation at the Amphictyonic Congress of Panama convoked by Simon Bolivar. The bases for the inter-American system were formally laid at the First International Conference of American States (held in Washington, D.C., from October 1889 to April 1890), with the establishment of the International Union of American Republics served by a central office, the Commercial Bureau located in Washington, for the promotion of trade and the exchange of commercial information among the member states. The 1890 agreement was signed on 14 April, a date which has ever since been celebrated as Pan American Day. The conferences held in 1901 and 1906 extended the scope of inter-American co-operation, approved conventions on international law and arbitration and developed the role of the Commercial Bureau. At the Fourth International Conference of American States in 1910 the name of the organization was changed to Union of American Republics and the Commercial Bureau was renamed the Pan American Union. The four conferences that followed in 1923, 1928, 1933 and 1938 laid the foundation for closer economic, social, cultural and juridical co-operation within the Union, established 'non intervention' as a basic principle of the inter-American system and proclaimed the solidarity of the member countries against all foreign intervention or aggression.

Substantial headway toward the consolidation and strengthening of inter-American peace and security was made through the adoption in 1945 of the Act of Chapultepec on Reciprocal Assistance and American Solidarity. The provisions of the Act were embodied in the Inter-American Treaty of Reciprocal Assistance (Rio Treaty) of 1947 which represented the first comprehensive convention on collective security to which all the American states became parties.

Finally, in 1948, at the Ninth International Conference of American States at Bogotá, a Charter was adopted and the Union of American Republics changed its name to Organization of American States, while the General Secretariat of the Organization continued to be called the Pan American Union until 1970. The Ninth Conference also approved the American Treaty on Pacific Settlement (Pact of Bogotá) which was intended to replace the existing agreements for the prevention and peaceful solution of disputes. The Organization's Charter was substantially revised by the Protocol approved at the Third Special Inter-American Conference held in Buenos Aires in 1967; the amendments, setting new standards for co-operation and establishing the General Assembly as the supreme organ in place of the Inter-American Conference, entered into effect in February 1970. Further amendments to the Charter are contained in the Protocol of Cartagena, approved in 1985 and entered into force in November 1988. These amendments have increased the powers of the Secretary-General and of the Permanent Council.

The basic goals of the Organization are to achieve an order of peace and justice, foster mutual solidarity and co-operation and defend the sovereignty, territorial integrity and independence of the member states. The Charter reaffirms the principle that 'an act of aggression against one American state is an act of aggression against all the other American states' and solemnly proclaims the fundamental rights of the individual regardless of race, nationality, creed or sex and the equal rights and duties of states. The duty to abstain from intervention in the internal or external affairs of any other state is meant to imply proscription not only of armed force but also of 'any other form of interference or attempted threat against the personality of the state or against its political, economic and cultural elements'. Besides the submission of inter-American disputes to peaceful procedures and the safeguard of collective security, the Charter provides a wide range of mechanisms to improve economic, social, educational, scientific and cultural standards and to support regional economic integration.

Any independent American state wishing to join the Organization may be admitted, upon recommendation of the Permanent Council, by decision of the General Assembly; both the recommendation and the decision require a two-thirds majority. However, no entity whose territory was subject before 1964 to dispute between an extra-continental country and one or more member states can be admitted until a peaceful settlement has been reached. The status of permanent observer was officially created in 1971 to enable co-operating non-member countries to participate in the Organization's meetings.

The highly complex structure of the Organization includes the following principal organs: the General Assembly; the Meeting of Consultation of Ministers of Foreign Affairs; the three Councils; the Inter-American Juridical Committee; the Inter-American Commission on Human Rights; the Inter-American Court of Human Rights; and the General Secretariat. Subsidiary organs may be established whenever necessary.

The General Assembly consists of the representatives of all members, each state having one vote, and holds its regular sessions during the second quarter of the year, either in one of the member countries or at headquarters; special sessions may be convoked by the Permanent Council with the approval of two-thirds of the member states. It is the responsibility of the General Assembly to determine the basic policies and functions of the Organization and to consider any matter of common interest to the member states; decisions are taken by absolute majority, except in those cases such as budgetary questions that require a two-thirds vote. The Meeting of Consultation of Ministers of Foreign Affairs may be held to consider urgent problems of common interest to the American states under the Organization's Charter or to serve as Organ of Consultation under the Rio Treaty of 1947 in cases of armed attack or other threats to peace and security.

The three Councils, where all member states are equally represented, are directly responsible to the General Assembly and make proposals and recommendations on matters within their respective competence. The Permanent Council, meeting regularly at the Organization's headquarters in Washington, oversees the maintenance of friendly relations among members assisting them in the peaceful settlement of their disputes and serves as a provisional Organ of Consultation in case of an armed attack. According to the Protocol of Cartagena, the Permanent Council is now allowed to try to resolve a dispute among members regardless of the fact that all the parties concerned (as previously stipulated) agree to take the matter before the Organization. A subsidiary body, the Inter-American Committee on Peaceful Settlement, assists the Permanent Council in its peace-keeping function. The Permanent Council is also responsible for supervising the operation of the General Secretariat, improving the functioning of the Organization and developing co-operation with the UN and other American agencies.

The Inter-American Economic and Social Council (CIES), created in 1945 and incorporated into the Organization's Charter in 1948, has for its principal purpose the furthering of inter-American co-operation for economic and social development through the recommendation of programmes and courses of action and the co-ordination of all economic and social activities. The Council's Permanent Executive Committee periodically reviews the development of the member countries and the status of financial and technical co-operation. The objectives of the Inter-American Council for Education, Science and Culture (CIECC) are to foster not only inter-American cultural relations but also education and cultural advancement in individual countries. The Council is concerned with the preservation of the cultural heritage of the Hemisphere, the co-ordination of educational curricula at all levels and the equivalence of certificates and degrees, and the abolition of illiteracy in Latin America.

The Inter-American Juridical Committee, consisting of 11 jurists from different member states and functioning in Rio de Janeiro, advises the Organization on legal matters, promotes the development and codification of international law and investigates the problems related to the integration of the developing members and the possibility of achieving uniformity in their legislation. The Inter-American Commission on Human Rights (IACHR) – a consultative organ set up in 1960 and composed of seven members chosen from panels presented by governments – seeks to promote the observance and protection of human rights and recommends measures and legislation conforming to the rules of the American Convention on Human Rights (Pact of San José) signed in 1969. The Inter-American Court of Human Rights, based in San José, Costa Rica, was established in 1978 as an autonomous judicial institution, composed of seven members, responsible for the application and interpretation of the American Convention on Human Rights.

The General Secretariat, located in Washington, is the central and permanent organ carrying out the policies and programmes decided upon by the General Assembly, the Meeting of Consultation of Ministers of Foreign Affairs and the Councils and performing several functions assigned to it in other inter-American treaties and agreements. The Protocol of Cartagena has strengthened the role of the Secretary-General who is now empowered to bring to the attention of the Permanent Council matters that 'might threaten the peace and security of the hemisphere or the development of the member states'. Both the Secretary-General and the Assistant Secretary-General are elected by the General Assembly for a five-year term and may not be re-elected more than once or succeeded by a person of the same nationality. The Assistant Secretary-General, who serves as adviser to the Secretary-General and may act as his delegate, is also Secretary of the Permanent Council.

A significant role is played by the Specialized Organizations which are inter-governmental agencies established by multilateral agreements with specific functions concerning technical matters. While preserving their status as integral parts of the Organization and complying with the recommendations of the General Assembly and the Councils, these agencies enjoy full technical autonomy and maintain close relations with international bodies working in the same fields. At present there are six Specialized Organizations dealing respectively with the promotion of health, the protection of children, the extension of women's rights, geographical and historical studies, the welfare of American Indians, and agricultural co-operation. The headquarters of the organizations are located in different member countries on the basis of geographical representation. The Pan American Health Organization (PAHO), whose seat is in Washington, is the oldest international sanitary agency in the world, serving also as a regional organization of the *World Health Organization (WHO).

In addition to the Specialized Organizations, a number of agencies co-operate with various bodies of the Organization for the achievement of specific objectives within fields of common interest to all American states. These agencies, all of which are based in Washington, include the Inter-American Defence Board (IADB) for military co-operation, the Inter-American Statistical Institute (IASI) for the advancement of the science and administration of statistics, the Inter-American Nuclear Energy Commission (IANEC) for the peaceful use of nuclear energy, the Inter-American Emergency Aid Fund (FONDEM) for the supply and co-ordination of assistance in the event of natural disasters, and the Administrative Tribunal competent to pass judgment upon applications alleging non-observance of conditions established in appointments or contracts regarding staff members of the Organization's General Secretariat.

Besides the formal link with the UN as a

regional arrangement, the Organization co-operates more or less closely with UN specialized agencies and with many inter-American economic, technical and financial institutions. All member states are supposed to contribute to the regular budget of the Organization according to a scale of quotas determined by the General Assembly on the basis of several elements; however, substantial arrears in payments of contributions caused a financial crisis by the end of the 1980s. Specific projects are financed by voluntary contributions to special multinational funds.

The Organization's status and role have remarkably changed over the past decades as a result of a number of critical issues emanating from within the inter-American system and not always conducive to the strengthening of an association embracing the USA, Latin American and later also Caribbean countries. In addition, the evolution of the inter-American system itself has been importantly affected by crucial extra-hemispheric events and worldwide problems and pressures. The fundamental questions of peace and security have increasingly been linked to economic and social development, the effective exercise of representative democracy and the respect for human rights. As regards the maintenance of international peace within the hemisphere, the Organization has been dealing with inter-American disputes (mainly occurring in the Caribbean and Central American region) and with threats of subversion and extracontinental intervention. Apart from the crises in Guatemala (1954) and the Dominican Republic (1965) and several boundary disputes, it was the Cuban issue which imposed the major strain upon inter-American relations. Despite the suspension of Cuba in 1962 and the repeated condemnation of Cuban sponsorship of subversive activities and acts of terrorism, the Organization proved unable to adopt a common policy towards the Castro regime. A resolution leaving the parties to the Rio Treaty free to normalize relations with Cuba was eventually approved in 1975. The continued troubles and tensions in Central America pose other major challenges to the Organization's functions in the sphere of peace-keeping.

As regards the long-standing dispute between Argentina and the UK over the Falkland (Malvinas) Islands, the Ministers of Foreign Affairs called on both parties to negotiate a peaceful settlement of the conflict taking into account Argentina's 'rights of sovereignty' as well as the interests of the islanders.

Inter-American co-operation in the economic and social fields has been given growing attention over the past three decades in an effort to reconcile the primary concern of the USA for hemispheric security with Latin American economic interests and rising expectations. The foundation in 1959 of a regional development bank, the *Inter-American Development Bank (IDB), as an autonomous agency designed to finance loans to governments and public and private enterprises, represented a significant step towards more effective financial co-operation. A vast co-operative plan (the Alliance for Progress) to stimulate economic and social development in Latin America during the 1960s was officially launched at a Special Meeting of the Inter-American Economic and Social Council held in Punta del Este, Uruguay, in August 1961. However, despite the strong initial commitment of the USA, only modest results were attained. The Organization has been effectively operating through comprehensive development programmes and specific projects in the field of technical assistance and co-operation, while mostly leaving to the *UN Economic Commission for Latin America and the Caribbean (ECLAC) the task of encouraging and supporting the establishment of regional integration groups and 'common markets' largely patterned after the Western European models. The protectionist practices and trade restrictions that are frequently used as instruments of 'economic aggression' against Latin American countries, and problems connected with unemployment, food shortages, strong inflationary pressures and the energy crisis constitute matters of concern for the Inter-American Economic and Social Council and its Special Committee for Consultation and Negotiation (CECON). Various records of achievement are to be found in other areas of inter-American co-operation – tourism, educational services, statistics, the protection of the historical and archaeological heritage and the improvement of traditional handicrafts.

The Organization – through its highly controversial organ, the Inter-American Commission on Human Rights – has become deeply involved with the alleged violations of human rights by some of its members. Several resolutions on the subject have been adopted by the General Assembly, recommending *inter alia* the creation of the Inter-American Court of Human Rights subsequently installed in Costa Rica. The questions related to the consolidation of democracy and to the observance of human rights and their full legal recognition in the juridical as well as economic, social and cultural spheres exert considerable influence on inter-American relations and on the prospects for the integral development of the Latin American countries.

Secretary-General: João Clemente Baena Soares

Headquarters: Pan American Union Building, 17th Street and Constitution Avenue NW, Washington, D.C. 20006, USA (telephone: 458 3000; telex: 440118)

Publications: *Americas* (six times a year); *OAS Chronicle* (quarterly); *Annual Report of the Secretary General*

References: G. Connell-Smith: *The Inter-American System* (London, 1966); M.M. Ball: *The OAS in Transition* (Durham, North Carolina, 1969); Galo Plaza: *The Organization of American States: Instrument for Hemispheric Development* (Washington, 1969); L.J. LeBlanc: *The OAS and the Promotion and Protection of Human Rights* (The Hague, 1977); B. Wood: 'The Organization of American States', *Year Book of World Affairs*, 33 (1979), 148–66

Organization of Arab Petroleum Exporting Countries (OAPEC). The basic aim of the Organization is to safeguard the interests of member countries and to deter-

mine ways and means to implement mutual co-operation and co-ordination in various forms of economic activity in the petroleum industry. Established in January 1968 by the governments of Saudi Arabia, Kuwait and Libya, the Organization was subsequently joined by other Arab oil-exporting countries in Africa (Algeria, Egypt and Tunisia) and Asia (Bahrain, Iraq, Qatar, Syria and the United Arab Emirates). Tunisia withdrew at the end of 1986. Egypt's membership, suspended in April 1979 after the signing of the bilateral peace treaty with Israel, was restored in May 1989.

Besides the establishment of close co-operative links and the protection of the legitimate interests, invididual as well as collective, of member countries, the Organization is entrusted with the tasks of securing the supply of petroleum to consumer countries at equitable and reasonable prices and creating favourable conditions for capital and technological investments in the oil industry.

The basic institutional structure of the Organization includes the Ministerial Council, the Executive Bureau and the Secretariat. The Council, which is the supreme authority meeting at least twice a year, consists of the representatives of all members, normally the Ministers of Petroleum, each with one vote. The Council formulates the general policy of the Organization, directs its activities and lays down its governing rules; it is chaired for one-year terms by the representative of each country in turn. The Bureau, whose members are senior officials appointed by each country, is the principal executive organ, normally meeting before the sessions of the Council and responsible for the management of the Organization's affairs, the implementation of resolutions and recommendations and the drawing up of the Council's agenda. The Secretariat, headed by the Secretary-General, performs administrative functions. Within the framework of the Secretariat operate four Departments (Finance and Administrative Affairs; Information and Library; Economics; and Technical Affairs). There is also a Tribunal consisting of nine judges whose task is to settle differences in the interpretation and application of the Organization's Charter.

A number of joint undertakings have been set up, particularly over the last few years, to supplement the Organization's activities in several specialized fields and thus to promote and strengthen Arab participation. These undertakings, based in different member countries, include: the Arab Maritime Petroleum Transport Company (AMPTC) and the Arab Shipbuilding and Repair Yard Company (ASRY), both created in the early 1970s to increase Arab participation in the transport of hydrocarbons; the Arab Petroleum Services Company (APSC), providing various services and training specialized personnel; the Arab Petroleum Training Institute; the Arab Petroleum Investments Corporation (APICORP), with an authorized capital of $1200 million (of which $400 million subscribed), granting funds for a wide range of projects related to the oil industry, with priority being given to Arab joint ventures.

The Organization maintains close working relations with the *League of Arab States and its numerous specialized institutions. It also co-operates with several UN organs and agencies, such as the *UN Conference on Trade and Development (UNCTAD), the *UN Industrial Development Organization (UNIDO), and the *International Maritime Organization (IMO), and other international and national bodies.

The Organization has played a significant role in its efforts to improve inter-Arab co-operation on vital petroleum issues and to co-ordinate, as far as possible, Arab policies within the broader framework of the *Organization of the Petroleum Exporting Countries (OPEC). Several conferences and seminars as well as training and research programmes have been carried out under the auspices of the Organization. Special emphasis was placed on the promotion of inter-Arab trade in petroleum products and petrochemicals. However, the invasion of Kuwait by Iraq in August 1990 and the subsequent Gulf war severely affected the Organization's activities and prospects. In December 1990 headquarters were temporarily moved to Cairo; the Ministerial Council also decided to postpone the fifth Arab Energy Conference, originally scheduled to take place in mid-1992, to mid-1994.

Secretary-General: Abd al-Aziz al-Turki
Headquarters: P.O. Box 20501, Safat, 13066 Kuwait (telephone: 244 8200; telex: 22166; fax: 242 6885)
Publications: *Secretary-General's Annual Report*; *OAPEC Monthly Bulletin*

Organization of Central American States [Organización de Estados Centroamericanos] (ODECA). The Organization is devoted to strengthening the political, economic and social bonds among its member countries with a view to restoring Central American unity.

The present Charter of the Organization was signed in December 1962 in Panama City by the Foreign Ministers of five Central American republics (Costa Rica, El Salvador, Guatemala, Honduras, and Nicaragua); Panama has not joined the Organization, although the possibility of its admission to membership is expressly envisaged in the Charter.

The first moves towards a coalition of the five republics date back to the disintegration of the Spanish colonial empire and the subsequent establishment by the newly independent countries of the 'United Provinces of Central America', a federation that lasted from 1823 to 1839. Since then there have been a number of attempts to restore some form of unity among the Central American states, possibly including Panama, which declared its independence from Colombia in 1903. At a conference of Central American states, held in Washington, D.C., in 1907 under the sponsorship of the USA and Mexico, measures were adopted, *inter alia*, for the peaceful settlement of disputes, including the creation of a permanent Court of Justice. It was also agreed not to grant recognition to any new government set up in Central America by revolution until free elections had been held (Tobar Doctrine). Other experiments to build up 'Central American fraternity' looking forward to political union were subsequently undertaken but no progress was made until the signature, in October 1951, by the representatives of Costa Rica, El Salvador, Guatemala, Honduras and Nicaragua of the Charter of San Salvador establishing the Organization of Central American States. In 1962, in order to restructure and give greater effectiveness to the Organization, the same five countries decided to substitute for the original founding document a new Charter of San Salvador, which came into force in March 1965.

The Charter solemnly declares that the contracting parties 'constitute an economic-political community aspiring to the integration of Central America'; such ultimate goal is to be pursued through the joint promotion of economic and social progress and the strengthening of Central American solidarity, the elimination of barriers, the gradual improvement in standards of living, the steady expansion of the industrial sector and the establishment of a consultation mechanism to ensure the peaceful settlement of disputes and collective security. The functions and powers of the Organization are very briefly described in the Charter in harmony with the rather loose and pragmatic character of Central American co-operation.

The main organs are the Meeting of Heads of State, the Conference of Ministers of Foreign Affairs, the Executive Council, the Legislative Council, the Central American Court of Justice, the Central American Economic Council, the Cultural and Educational Council, and the Central American Defence Council. A Secretary, assisted by the necessary staff, is designated by the Executive Council.

The Charter defines the Meeting of Heads of State as the 'supreme' organ, but gives no details about its precise functions. The highest authority is actually the Conference of Ministers of Foreign Affairs, holding regular annual meetings and deciding on substantive matters by unanimous vote. The Executive Council is the permanent body, with headquarters in San Salvador, consisting of the Foreign Ministers or their delegates (usually the ambassadors resident in San Salvador); its primary duties are the direction and co-ordination of the Organization's policies.

The Legislative Council, composed of three representatives from the parliaments of each member country, is formally entrusted with advisory and consultative responsibilities in legislative matters; although, according to the Charter, meetings are to be held annually, commencing on 15 September, no such meeting has taken place thus far. The Central American Court of Justice, composed of the Presidents of the Supreme Courts of member countries, is endowed with fairly limited functions, far less important than those entrusted to its ill-fated predecessor in 1907. The Economic Council consists of the Ministers of Economy and is responsible for planning, co-ordinating and implementing integration; all organs of Central American integration 'belong to this Council'. The Cultural and Educational Council and the Defence Council are to meet periodically at the ministerial level. The Secretary, appointed by the Executive Council, performs the administrative tasks formerly entrusted, under the Charter of 1951, to the Central American Bureau. Several subsidiary bodies, responsible for specific sectors such as agriculture, health, labour and manpower and tourism, have been set up by the Conference of Ministers of Foreign Affairs.

In spite of an imposing institutional machinery, the Organization has proved unable to attain its ambitious political goals while the activities concerning economic co-operation and integration have been entrusted to the *Central American Common Market (CACM). The long-standing dispute between Honduras and El Salvador which culminated in the 'football war' of July 1969 negatively affected the prospects for closer Central American co-operation until the signature of the General Peace Treaty between the two countries in October 1980. The temporary break in diplomatic relations between Costa Rica and Nicaragua further weakened Central American solidarity, while the persistent Guatemalan claims to sovereignty over Belize represented another disturbing factor. During 1980, an improvement in Central American relations made it possible to undertake serious efforts with a view to reactivating the process of political integration. The Meeting of Ministers of Foreign Affairs of the Central American Isthmus, which took place in San José, Costa Rica, in March 1980, decided to restructure Central American integration in all its aspects, including the 're-activation of ODECA'. The development of elastic processes of consultation and co-ordination of efforts within a simple but firm institutional framework might lead to a revitalization of the Organization after the political and social conflicts of the past. Regional meetings at various levels have been taking place over the past few years and the commitment to adapt the institutional framework of Central American integration to the new realities has been solemnly emphasized.

Secretary-General: Ricardo   Juarez Marquez

Headquarters: Oficina Centroamericana, Paseo Escalón, San Salvador, El Salvador (telephone: 235136)

Publications: annual reports and periodic information bulletins on specific sectors (in Spanish)

References: N.J. Padelford: 'Cooperation in the Central American Region: the Organization of Central American States', *International Organization*, 11 (1957), 41–54; J.S. Nye: 'Central American Regional Integration', *International Conciliation*, 562 (1967), 1–66

Organization of the Islamic Conference (OIC). The purpose of the Organization is to promote effective solidarity and to strengthen co-operation among Islamic countries in the most important and vital fields.

The Organization was formally established in May 1971, following a summit meeting of the Heads of State of the Islamic countries held in Rabat, Morocco, in September 1969 and conferences of the Foreign Ministers of those countries held in Jeddah, Saudi Arabia, in March 1970, and Karachi, Pakistan, in December 1970. The present membership includes over 40 Moslem countries in Africa and Asia, plus

Turkey; the Moslem community of the 'Turkish Federated State of Cyprus' has observer status. Mozambique also enjoys observer status. The Palestine Liberation Organization enjoys full membership. Egypt's membership was suspended in May 1979 after it signed a peace treaty with Israel and restored in March 1984. The suspension of Afghanistan took place in January 1980 in consequence of the Soviet invasion; in March 1989 Afghanistan was readmitted as represented by the 'interim government' formed by the Mujaheddin after the withdrawal of Soviet troops.

Besides the general promotion of Islamic solidarity, the Organization's basic aims are: to improve co-operation in the economic, social, cultural and scientific fields; to arrange consultations among members participating in international institutions; to endeavour to eliminate racial segregation and discrimination as well as colonialism in all its forms; to take the necessary measures to support the establishment of international peace and security based on justice; to co-ordinate all efforts for the safeguard of the Moslem Holy Places; to help the Palestinian people regain their rights and liberate their land; to help Moslem peoples preserve their dignity, independence and national rights; to create a suitable atmosphere for the development of co-operation and mutual understanding between members and third countries.

The basic institutional structure of the Organization is fairly simple and comprises the Conference of the Heads of State, the Conference of Foreign Ministers and the Secretariat; several subsidiary bodies have been created over the past two decades. The Heads of State had met at irregular and rather long intervals until the session held in 1981 which decided that summit meetings should be held every three years; issues of paramount importance to Islamic countries are usually discussed on the basis of reports prepared by the Conference of Foreign Ministers. This latter organ holds ordinary sessions once a year in the capital or other important town of a member country and is entrusted with the functions of fulfilling the Organization's tasks and setting the guidelines for relations with third countries. General and administrative services are provided by the General Secretariat, based in Jeddah, which is composed of a Secretary-General (elected by the Conference of Foreign Ministers for a non-renewable four-year term), four Assistant Secretaries-General, and the necessary staff.

The Islamic Committee for economic, cultural and social affairs – established in 1976 – is an important subsidiary organ, meeting at least twice a year, that is empowered to supervise the implementation of the resolutions adopted by the Conference of Foreign Ministers and may address recommendations to the said Conference. The Al-Quds (Jerusalem) Committee was set up in 1975 to carry out the resolutions concerning the status of the Holy City and has met at the level of Foreign Ministers since 1979.

A number of bodies have been established to supplement the Organization's activities in selected fields, such as: the Statistical, Economic and Social Research and Training Centre for the Islamic Countries (located in Ankara); the Islamic Centre for Technical and Vocational Training and Research (Dhaka); the Islamic Foundation for Science, Technology and Development – IFSTAD (Jeddah); the Islamic Chamber of Commerce, Industry and Commodity Exchange (Karachi); the Islamic Educational, Scientific and Cultural Organization – ISESCO (Rabat); the International Islamic News Agency (Jeddah); and the Islamic States Broadcasting Organization (Jeddah). Two specialized bodies are responsible for monetary and financial co-operation: the Islamic Solidarity Fund, founded in 1974 to accord emergency aid and to support Islamic hospitals, schools, cultural centres and universities; and the *Islamic Development Bank which started its financial operations in 1976. A decision was taken in 1982 by the Conference of Foreign Ministers to set up offices for boycotting Israel. In 1983 it was decided to set up the Islamic Reinsurance Corporation with an authorized capital of $200 million, while the Islamic Centre for the Development of Trade began operations in 1983 in Casablanca.

The Organization, which was granted observer status by the *UN General Assembly in 1975, maintains links with several international bodies, such as the *UN Educational, Scientific and Cultural Organization (UNESCO), in order to promote understanding between Islamic and non-Islamic countries, and especially to present the Palestinian issues.

The effective pursuit of the Organization's goals has been adversely affected by recurring tensions and disputes between member countries which hold widely differing views on many fundamental issues. A general unity on the Palestinian question and the status of Jerusalem was maintained until Egypt's recognition of Israel. With regard to Afghanistan, the Conference of Foreign Ministers held an extraordinary session in January 1980 and called for the immediate and unconditional withdrawal of Soviet troops. Resolutions were also adopted opposing foreign pressures exerted on Islamic countries in general, and Iran in particular, and condemning armed aggression against Somalia. The third session of the Conference of the Heads of State of member countries took place in January 1981, in Saudi Arabia, to consider broad political, economic and financial issues; an agreement was reached in principle on the establishment of an Islamic Court of Justice responsible for the settlement of disputes between Moslem countries. The problems in Afghanistan and Iran, and the armed conflict between Iran and Iraq, continued to be major topics of discussion within the framework of the Organization.

The fourth Summit Conference, held in January 1984 in Casablanca, agreed to restore the full membership of Egypt, despite the opposition of seven member countries. The fifth Summit Conference took place in Kuwait in January 1987 and debated issues related to the Iran-Iraq war as well as to conflicts in Chad and Lebanon. In August 1990 a majority of Ministers of Foreign Affairs condemned Iraq's invasion of Kuwait and demanded the withdrawal of the occupation forces.

The sixth Summit Conference was held in Dakar in 1991.

Secretary-General: Hamid Algabid

Headquarters: Kilo 6, Mecca Road, P.O. Box 178, Jeddah 21411, Saudi Arabia (telephone: 680 0880; telex: 401366; fax: 687 3568)

Reference: H. Moinuddin: *The Charter of the Islamic Conference. The Legal and Economic Framework* (Oxford, 1987)

Organization of the Petroleum Exporting Countries (OPEC). The basic aim of the Organization is the co-ordination and unification of the petroleum policies of member countries and the protection of their individual and collective interests. Established in September 1960 at a conference held in Baghdad with the participation of Saudi Arabia, Iran, Iraq, Kuwait, and Venezuela, the Organization was subsequently joined by several other oil-exporting countries: Qatar in 1961; Indonesia and Libya in 1962; Abu Dhabi in 1967 (membership afterwards transferred to the United Arab Emirates); Algeria in 1969; Nigeria in 1971; Ecuador in 1973 (after a few months as an associate member); the United Arab Emirates in 1974; and Gabon in 1975 (an associate member from 1973).

Initially established to consider measures for coping with cuts in the posted price for crude oil introduced by oil companies in the late 1950s, the Organization gained increasing importance as a result of the admission of new countries and of the development of a strategy deliberately using oil supplies as an instrument of political as well as economic pressure. The Organization's members currently produce about one-third of the world's oil (compared with 45 per cent in 1980 and over 55 per cent in 1973) and possess over three-quarters of the total known reserves.

The Organization's Statute, adopted by the conference held in January 1961 in Caracas, has been extensively amended on several occasions.

To achieve its basic aim, the Organization devises methods to ensure the stability of prices in international oil markets with a view to eliminating harmful fluctuations. Under the Statute, this goal is to be attained giving due regard to the necessity of securing a steady income to the producing countries, an efficient, economical and regular supply to the consuming countries, and a fair return on their capital to those investing in the oil industry.

Membership of the Organization is open to any country which is a substantial net exporter of crude and has fundamentally similar interests to those of member countries. Admission requires acceptance by a majority of three-fourths of the full members, including the concurrent vote of the five founders. A country which does not meet all the requirements for full membership may be admitted as an associate member.

The main organs of the Organization are the Conference, the Board of Governors, and the Secretariat. The Conference, which is the supreme authority meeting at least twice a year, consists of the representatives of all members, each with one vote. All decisions, other than those concerning procedural matters, must be adopted unanimously.

The Conference formulates the general policy of the Organization and determines the ways and means for its implementation; confirms the appointments of the members of the Board of Governors, whose activities it directs; considers or decides upon the reports and recommendations submitted by the Board of Governors; and approves the budget. The Conference's resolutions become effective 30 days after the conclusion of the meeting at which they were adopted, unless in the meantime one or more members have given to the Secretariat notification of their opposition.

The Board of Governors, whose members are appointed for a two-year term by each country and confirmed by the Conference which appoints the Chairman, is responsible for the management of the affairs of the Organization and for the implementation of the decisions of the Conference. The Board of Governors, each of whom has one vote, meets no less than twice a year and adopts its decisions by a simple majority of attending members.

The Secretariat, consisting of the Secretary-General, the Deputy Secretary-General and such staff as may be required, performs the executive functions under the direction of the Board of Governors. Within the framework of the Secretariat operate a Legal Office and five Departments responsible for Energy Studies; Economics and Finance; Data Services; Personnel and Administration; OPECNA and Information. The last-mentioned Department was created in 1990 by the merging of the former Public Information Department and the OPEC News Agency (OPECNA) which had been set in 1980 to provide accurate information on the Organization and its activities as well as on member countries' oil and energy issues.

In 1964 the Economic Commission was established as a specialized body, operating within the framework of the Secretariat, in order to assist the Organization in promoting stability of international oil prices at equitable levels; it meets at least twice a year.

Since 1965 the Organization has maintained formal relations with the UN Economic and Social Council, and with a number of bodies such as the *UN Conference on Trade and Development (UNCTAD).

Despite frequent disagreements between the 'moderates', led by Saudi Arabia, and the 'radicals', such as Algeria, Libya and Iraq, over the policies to be followed on pricing, production, export capacity and royalties, the Organization showed during the 1970s a remarkable degree of cohesion *vis-a-vis* the major industrial countries, especially Western Europe and Japan (which are more or less heavily dependent on oil imports). On the other hand, the setting and maintenance of a single level of prices throughout the Organization proved to be an extremely difficult goal.

For a long period, almost from the end of World War II to 1973, oil prices had been decreasing appreciably in both monetary and real terms, thus contributing to the establishment in the industrial countries of a development pattern based on the extensive use of low-cost energy sources. Following the Teheran agreement of 1971 between the producing countries of the Gulf and the major oil companies, the situation began to change radically. The failure of subsequent negotiations with oil companies to revise the Teheran

agreement and to adjust prices induced the Organization's members to increase prices unilaterally. The posted price of crude oil (which at the beginning of the 1970s was less than $2 per barrel) was raised to $11.65 per barrel in December 1973. Subsequent meetings of the Organization decided on further increases, some of them to take place in several stages, but not all members agreed or observed the various stages. In the mid-1970s proposals had been put forward to index prices to world inflation rates and to quote oil in Special Drawing Rights (SDRs) of the *International Monetary Fund (IMF) instead of dollars, but no measures were actually taken to that effect. After the Iranian revolution and the further deterioration of the overall climate in the Middle East, including the armed conflict between Iran and Iraq, agreement on a long-term pricing and production strategy applicable by all member countries became even harder to reach.

In order to defend an OPEC-wide price structure, it was decided in March 1982 (for the first time in the Organization's history) to impose an overall production ceiling of 18 million b/d. No agreement, however, was reached on individual production quotas. Despite continuing efforts over the following years, it proved very difficult to establish and maintain an official marker price and production ceiling effectively applicable to all members of the Organization. Differences over the Organization's strategy, particularly with respect to production quotas, became even more intractable in early 1986 when the collapse in the oil market and the continued decline of the United States dollar brought prices, in real terms, to their lowest level since the middle of 1973. A return to production quotas and to a fixed pricing system, decided in late 1986, succeeded in stabilizing prices, despite the fact that a number of members had exceeded the agreed production limit. Increases in production were allowed in 1989 but again some member countries declared that they did not feel bound to respect the limits, thereby further weakening the Organization's credibility. Effective co-operation with non-OPEC members for common production strategies has also proved unfeasible. After Iraq's invasion of Kuwait in August 1990 and the subsequent international embargo on oil exports from the two countries there was a marked increase in the price of oil which reached a peak of $40 a barrel in early October but subsequently fell to about $25 per barrel. During the last months of 1990 and the beginning of 1991 several members of the Organization produced in excess of their agreed quotas. A reduction in the members' output was subsequently agreed upon while meetings were organized with consumer countries and international organizations to discuss possible forms of cooperation with respect to the international oil market.

Secretary-General: Dr Subroto

Headquarters: Obere Donaustrasse 93, 1020 Vienna, Austria (telephone: 211120; telex: 134474; fax: 264320)

Publications: *Annual Report*; *Annual Statistical Bulletin*; *OPEC Review* (quarterly); *OPEC Bulletin* (monthly)

References: F. Ghadar: *The Evolution of OPEC Strategy* (Lexington, 1977); F. Abolfathi: *The OPEC Market to 1985* (Lexington, 1977); R.S. Pindyck: 'OPEC's Threat to the West', *Foreign Policy*, 30 (1978), 36–52; T.H. Moran: *Oil Prices and the Future of OPEC: the Political Economy of Tension and Stability in the Organization of Petroleum Exporting Countries* (Washington, 1978); I. Seymour: *OPEC, Instrument of Change* (London, 1980); J. Griffin and D. Teece (eds): *OPEC Behaviour and World Oil Prices* (London, 1982); D. Aperjis: *OPEC Oil Policy and Economic Development* (Cambridge, Mass., 1982); J. Perce (ed): *The Third Oil Shock: the Effect of Lower Oil Prices* (London, 1983); S.M. Ghanem: *OPEC: The Rise and Fall of an Exclusive Club* (London, 1986); L. Skeet: *OPEC: 25 Years of Oil and Politics* (Cambridge, 1988)

P

Pacific Economic Co-operation Council
(PECC). The Council is a non-
governmental organization bringing
together academic, business and government leaders to discuss co-operation and
policy co-ordination in areas that would
promote economic growth and development in the Pacific Region. At present
PECC consists of member committees representing 18 nations in the Pacific Basin
(including three Latin American
countries), and the Pacific Island Nations;
the latter are collectively represented by
the *South Pacific Forum (SPF). In addition, two international non-governmental
organizations – the *Pacific Basin
Economic Council (PBEC) and the Pacific
Trade and Development Conference
(PAFTAD) – are 'institutional members'
participating in all activities but without
voting power. Applications for membership have been made by Colombia,
Mongolia, Papua New Guinea and Russia.
   The Council traces its origins to the
Pacific Community Seminar held in
Canberra, Australia, in September 1980 at
the initiative of Australian and Japanese
top government leaders. The Canberra
Seminar – convened to explore ways and
means for a loosely structured but purpo-
seful approach to region-wide co-operation
– was attended by participants from 11
countries, that is the five Pacific industrial
powers (Australia, Canada, Japan, New
Zealand and the USA), the then five members of the *Association of South-East
Asian Nations (ASEAN), and South Korea,
plus a delegation representing collectively
the Pacific Island Nations. Among the
special features of what turned out to be
the first PECC general meeting was the

tripartite structure of the delegations, comprising representatives from business and
industry, mainly members of PBEC, aca-
demics, mainly members of PAFTAD, and
government officials, all of them participating in their private capacities and deciding
on the basis of consensus. Particular emphasis was laid on the need for all members
to be placed on an equal footing, excluding
any form of associate membership for the
developing economies of the region.
Particular elements of Pacific regional co-
operation were identified in the exclusion
of military and security issues – so as 'to
create a sense of community without creating a sense of threat' – and the furtherance
of the 'economic aims and interests' of the
countries belonging to ASEAN and to the
SPF.
   A follow-up meeting – under the official
name of Pacific Economic Co-operation
Conference and now known as PECC II –
was held in Bangkok in June 1982 to concentrate on economic issues 'which are
neither sufficiently nor effectively dealt
with at international and bilateral fora'. On
the institutional plane, it was decided to set
up a Standing Committee, made up of representatives of the national member committees, as the highest decision-making
body of the Conference responsible for the
evolution of the PECC process. It was also
decided to establish a number of task
forces to report on specific issues.
   The results of the work of the task forces
were discussed at PECC III, in November
1983 in Bali, where the 'task force
approach' was confirmed and new topics
were selected for further study. Institutional arrangements were considered
identifying five components: the Confer-

ence (holding periodic general meetings); the Standing Committee; the Task Forces; the Co-ordinating Group (composed of task-force leaders and other experts); and the Member Committees (set up on a national basis). At PECC IV, in the spring of 1985, special attention was devoted to trade policy issues in view of the proposed new round of multilateral negotiations within the framework of the *General Agreement on Tariffs and Trade (GATT).

The launching of the Uruguay Round was welcomed by participants in PECC V (Vancouver, November 1986) which included for the first time delegations from both China and Taiwan (the latter under the name of Chinese Taipei) as full members. A remarkable achievement was the endorsement of the 'Vancouver Statement on Pacific Economic Co-operation' enshrining the basic aims, institutional features and practices of PECC as they had been developing since 1980. A framework thus emerged of 'open regionalism', committed on the one hand to achieving greater region-wide economic co-operation and interaction, while recognizing, on the other, 'both the realities of and the benefits accruing from global interdependence and continuing to encourage increased economic co-operation and interaction with other nations and regions'. The 'Vancouver Statement' now forms the basis for the preamble to the PECC Charter and must be considered a prerequisite for joining the Conference.

At PECC VI (Osaka, May 1988), the Central Fund was formally set up with a view to providing financial support for member committees from developing countries; the establishment of the Fund represented, *inter alia*, the first step towards the creation of a permanent PECC Secretariat. The focal point of PECC VII,

held in Auckland in November 1989, was the relationship of the Conference to the *Asia-Pacific Economic Co-operation (APEC) ministerial meeting held the previous week in Canberra. To consolidate the institutional capability of the Conference, it was decided to set up a permanent PECC Secretariat in Singapore.

The eighth general meeting of the Conference (PECC VIII) took place in Singapore in May 1991 and saw a further expansion of the co-operative links with APEC. For the first time representatives from the member committees of Chile, Hong Kong, Mexico and Peru attended the meeting as full PECC members. A major institutional development was the adoption of the PECC Charter, consisting of eight articles codifying past practice and including the entire text of the 'Vancouver Statement' as an Appendix. In January 1992 it was decided to change the original name of Pacific Economic Co-operation Conference to Pacific Economic Co-operation Council.

The next general meetings of PECC are scheduled to take place in September 1992 in San Francisco and in Malaysia in the spring of 1994. By virtue of its peculiar tripartite structure and its accumulated experience, the Council appears to be in a position to complement and support the APEC process laying the foundations for stronger economic links among Pacific Basin countries.

Director General: Dr Hank Lim

Headquarters: 4 Nassim Road, Singapore 1025 (telephone: 737 9822/23; fax: 737 9824)

PECC. *See* **Pacific Economic Co-operation Council.**

S

SAARC. *See* **South Asian Association for Regional Co-operation.**

SADCC. *See* **Southern African Development Co-ordination Conference.**

SELA. Sistema Económico Latinoamericano; *See* **Latin American Economic System.**

Sistema Económico Latinoamericano (SELA). *See* **Latin American Economic System.**

South Asian Association for Regional Co-operation (SAARC). The Association basically aims at increased economic, social and cultural collaboration among the countries of South Asia with a view to accelerating the pace of economic development and enhancing stability in the region.

The Association originated in December 1985 in Dhaka, Bangladesh, when a solemn document, known as the Dhaka Declaration, and a Charter setting out the objectives and structure of the new organization where signed at a summit meeting attended by the Heads of State and Government of Bangladesh, Bhutan, India, the Maldives, Nepal, Pakistan and Sri Lanka. The summit meeting was held at the recommendation of the Foreign Ministers of the seven countries grouped in the Committee for South Asia Regional Co-operation (SARC).

The need for closer co-operation among the countries of South Asia had been recognized since the early 1980s. Between 1981 and 1983 several multilateral meetings were convened at foreign secretariat level in order to forge operational and institutional links for the pursuit of common goals. A declaration setting up the SARC Committee was eventually approved in August 1983 in New Delhi by a ministerial conference which launched an integrated programme of action (IPA) covering agriculture, rural development, health and population and telecommunications, as well as arts and culture. The tasks of supervising the programme, identifying additional areas of co-operation and mobilizing regional and external resources were entrusted to the Committee while a technical body was created to oversee the actual implementation of the co-ordinated programmes in the various fields. The ministerial meetings held in the Maldives in July 1984 and in Bhutan in May 1985 reviewed the implementation of the action programme and paved the way for the Dhaka summit which agreed upon the formal establishment of the Association.

Regional co-operation is envisaged by the Dhaka Declaration as a 'logical response' to the dramatic challenges posed to the countries of South Asia by 'poverty, underdevelopment, low levels of production, unemployment and pressure of population compounded by exploitation of the past and other adverse legacies'. Effective co-operation is expected to lay the grounds for optimum use of national and regional strengths, human and natural resources and economic complementarities.

According to the Charter, the objectives of the Association are: (a) to promote the

211

welfare and improve the quality of life of South Asian peoples; (b) to accelerate economic growth, social progress and cultural development; (c) to foster collective self-reliance among the member countries; (d) to contribute to mutual trust, understanding and appreciation of one another's problems; (e) to promote active collaboration and mutual assistance in the economic, social, cultural, technical and scientific fields; (f) to strengthen co-operation with other developing countries; (g) to strengthen co-operation among member countries in international fora on matters of common interest; and (h) to co-operate with international and regional organizations having similar aims and purposes.

These widely-phrased objectives appear to leave ample room for further negotiations on specific issues and areas of operational activity. Co-operation within the framework of the Association should not interfere with existing bilateral and multilateral obligations and should be conducted according to the principle of non-interference in internal affairs.

The Association's functions and decision-making powers bear no supranational features and are fairly limited by the unanimity principle which is required for all deliberations; 'bilateral and contentious issues' are expressly excluded from the competence of the Association.

The basic structure of the Association is made up of the Summit Meeting of Heads of State and Government taking place annually, the Council of Foreign Ministers meeting at least twice a year, the technical committees, and the Secretariat. The technical committees are established to study and supervise co-operation programmes in: agriculture and forestry; rural development; health and population; education; telecommunications; postal services; science and technology; transport; meteorology; sports, arts and culture; women and development; prevention of drugs trafficking and drug abuse. Terrorism 'as it affects the stability' of member countries also falls within the competence of technical committees.

Following the decision taken at the Bangalore Summit in November 1986. to establish a Secretariat, a Secretary-General assumed charge in January 1987 and further steps were taken to recruit and establish the Secretariat itself in Kathmandu. It was decided that the Secretary General would be appointed on the basis of rotation among the countries concerned; it is not a policy-making body but co-ordinates the implementation of the Association's activities.

The creation of the seven-member Association represented no small achievement for South Asia, a region with a total population of around a billion (of which three-quarters in India) which had not yet set up an institutional machinery of its own to promote full-scale co-operation. Although the Association does not deal with bilateral matters, it may well be that the very existence of a multilateral framework will help South Asian countries concentrate on common problems and solutions and ultimately lessen tensions arising from crucial issues such as the activities of separatist and terrorist groups.

The Third Summit of the Association was held in Kathmandu in November 1987 and saw the signing of the Regional Convention on the Suppression of Terrorism which entered into force in August 1988. Proposals were made for a SAARC Audio Visual Exchange Programme and a SAARC Documentation Centre. An agreement was also concluded with a view to establishing a SAARC Food Security Reserve which began operations in 1988; it provided, in 1991, nearly 250,000 metric tons of grain to meet emergency food needs in member countries. The SAARC Agricultural Information Centre was set up in 1988 in Dhaka.

At the Fifth Summit of the Association, in 1990, a convention was signed on Narcotic Drugs and Psychotropic Substances; member countries also asked for Iraq's withdrawal from Kuwait. Studies are under way on the causes and consequences of natural disasters and the protection of the environment; the 'greenhouse effect'; and trade, manufacturing and services.

Secretary General: Kant Kishore Bhargava
Headquarters: GPO Box 4222,

Kathmandu, Nepal (telephone: 221785; telex: 2561; fax: 227033)

Southern African Development Co-ordination Conference (SADCC). The general purpose of the Conference is to harmonize national development plans, to foster economic co-operation in all major areas, to reduce the region's economic dependence, especially on the Republic of South Africa, and to co-ordinate and secure support from 'co-operating partners' (foreign donors).

In July 1979, the first Southern African Development Co-ordination Conference took place in Arusha, Tanzania, with the participation of the economic ministers of the Front-Line States (FLS) – Angola, Botswana, Mozambique, Tanzania and Zambia – and of representatives from governments of industrial countries and international agencies that had been promoting closer co-operation among majority-ruled states in the sub-region. After a series of contacts at different levels, the representatives of the five FLS, joined by Lesotho, Malawi, Swaziland and Zimbabwe, meeting in April 1980, signed the Lusaka Declaration on Economic Liberation and formally brought SADCC into existence. A programme of action was approved, allotting specific studies and tasks to member countries, as follows: energy conservation and security to Angola; animal disease control and agricultural research to Botswana; soil conservation and land utilization to Lesotho; fisheries, forestry and wildlife to Malawi; transport and communications to Mozambique; manpower development and training to Swaziland; industrial development co-ordination to Tanzania; mining and studies for a Southern African development fund to Zambia; regional food security to Zimbabwe. Namibia became a member of the Conference in 1990.

All SADCC members are eligible for membership in the *Preferential Trade Area for Eastern and Southern Africa (PTA) and eight of them have actually joined it. Four SADCC members (Botswana, Lesotho, Namibia, and Swaziland) belong with South Africa to the *Southern African Customs Union (SACU).

In contrast to the more traditional philosophy of economic co-operation and integration bodies elsewhere, the primary responsibility for co-ordinating the activities of the Conference rests with individual national governments that enjoy substantial freedom as regards the ways to handle their area assignments, both domestically and regionally.

The formal structure of the Conference is made up of the Summit Meeting of Heads of State and Government which takes place annually, the Council of Ministers meeting at least twice a year, and the Secretariat headed by an Executive Secretary with administrative duties. Special meetings and consultations are held regularly to co-ordinate regional policy in a particular field at ministerial, official, and technical levels. A Southern African Transport and Communications Commission (SATCC) was established in 1980 in Maputo, Mozambique, to carry out transport development projects; the Commission has its own charter, budget, revenue and bureaucratic structure. The Southern African Centre for Co-operation in Agricultural Research (SACCAR) began operations in 1985 in Gaborone, Botswana, to co-ordinate national research systems and to operate a small research grants programme. In March 1989 it was decided to set up a regional investment council with a view to identifying and promoting opportunities for investment in the member countries.

Since its inception the Conference has developed close links with other international organizations – notably the *European Economic Community (EEC) and the *African Development Bank (AfDB), Western aid agencies and donor countries, such as Italy and the USA. Annual conferences with SADCC's 'international co-operating partners' are intended to serve as an effective mechanism for jointly surveying results, evaluating performance and drafting new projects. Operational agreements with donor agencies are negotiated by the parties concerned while the final terms of settlement assume the form of interrelated bilateral agreements. On the whole EEC member countries remain the major contributors, bilaterally and collectively through the Lomé Convention, to SADCC projects.

Transport and communications, energy, trade, industry, agriculture and food security are the most important areas currently being developed through studies and projects. Over the past few years, the Conference has been actively promoting the development of the sub-region without any attempt at creating a common market or an economic community; however, increasing emphasis is being placed on the promotion of intra-regional trade which accounts for only a small fraction of the members' total external trade. Representatives of private-sector businesses are also becoming increasingly involved in the Conference's activities; efforts are being made with a view to improving the investment climate and effectively addressing the problem of human resource development, especially the shortage of well trained manpower. The commitment to consultation and purely voluntary co-ordination, both regional and bilateral, has offered some real benefits to each participating country and might contribute, in the longer term, to a strengthening of a network of functional relations in the sub-region. Despite the fact that its members' dependence on South Africa has not diminished, the Conference has, on the whole, been successful in presenting its programmes and strategies to the international community and attracting interest and financial resources from abroad. The end of apartheid in South Africa and the admission in due course of that country as a full member of the Conference may, however, induce an in-depth re-examination of the functions and structure of SADCC. The research of a new raison d'etre for the Conference should not necessarily involve the demise of its characteristic approach, that is the search for joint solutions to common problems and the co-ordination of development policies without calling into question the sovereignty of member countries.

Executive Secretary: Dr Simbarashe Makoni

Headquarters: Private Bag 0095, Gaborone, Botswana (telephone: 51863; telex: 2555)

Publications: *Annual Progress Report*; *SADCC Energy Bulletin*

References: D.G. Anglin: 'Economic Liberation and Regional Cooperation in Southern Africa: SADCC and PTA', *International Organization*, 37 (1983), 681–711; D.G. Anglin: 'SADCC in the Aftermath of the Nkomati Accord', *Confrontation and Liberation in Southern Africa: Regional Directions after the Nkomati Accord*, ed. I.S.R. Msabaha and T.M. Shaw (London, 1987) 173–97; OECD/SADCC: *Implementing the SADCC Programme of Action* (Paris and Gaborone, 1988)

South Pacific Commission (SPC). The basic purpose of the Commission is to promote the economic and social welfare and the advancement of the peoples of the South Pacific region. It was established by an agreement signed in February 1947 in Canberra, Australia, and effective from July 1948. The founder members were six governments with territories in the region: Australia, France, the Netherlands, New Zealand, the UK, and the USA; the Dutch government withdrew when it ceased to administer the western part of New Guinea. The original agreement has been supplemented by several documents in order to extend the territorial scope of the Commission and to adapt its functions and powers to the changing needs and aspirations of the peoples of the region.

Under the new arrangements adopted in 1983, full membership in the Commission currently includes 27 governments and administrations, that is the developing islands of the Pacific plus Australia, New Zealand, France, the UK and the USA.

The Commission, as a consultative and advisory body to the participating governments in matters affecting the economic and social development of the region, has the power to make recommendations in respect of agriculture, communications, transport, fisheries, forestry, industry, labour, marketing, production, trade and finance, public works, education, health, housing and social welfare – having due regard to the necessity of co-ordinating local projects which are of regional significance. In addition the Commission has the responsibility to facilitate research in scientific, economic and social fields, to ensure the maximum co-operation among research bodies and to provide technical assistance.

The South Pacific Conference is the supreme organ which meets ordinarily every year in October to discuss the Commission's basic policies and to adopt the programme of activities and the budget. Since 1974 the Conference has combined into a single meeting the former Commission Session attended by the delegates of the member governments and the former South Pacific Conference representing the territorial administrations. A representative having one vote is sent by each government and territorial administration.

The Committee of Representatives of Governments and Administrations (CRGA) comprises delegates of the 27 member states and territories, having equal voting rights. It was established in 1983 to replace the former Committee of Representatives of Participating Governments (consisting of only 13 members) and the Planning and Evaluation Committee. The CRGA, which operates as a Committee of the Whole, meets before the annual South Pacific Conference to consider and recommend the administrative budget, evaluate the effectiveness of the preceding year's work programme, examine the draft budget and work programme presented by the Secretary-General and agree on a suitable and relevant theme of economic, social or cultural importance to the region to be discussed by the Conference. The Secretariat, headed by the Secretary-General who is the chief executive officer of the Commission, has a Management Committee with supervisory and advisory functions over all the activities carried out by the Commission.

The Commission maintains working relations with other international agencies such as the *UN Economic and Social Commission for Asia and the Pacific (ESCAP) and with many national institutions directly concerned with the region. The member governments and administrations contribute to the regular budget of the Commission on the basis of a formula related to per capita income; special voluntary contributions from governments, international organizations and other sources account for a substantial proportion of the Commission's total budget.

The Commission arranges conferences and training courses and provides assistance to applied research, information services and data analysis. Special attention is given to the needs of the smaller countries not endowed with mineral resources such as phosphates and nickel and largely based on subsistence farming and fishing. The Commission's main areas of interest currently include agriculture, plant protection and forestry, price stabilization programmes, conservation and environmental management, socio-economic statistics and cultural exchanges in arts, sports and education. In particular, the development and control of marine resources (fish and, less immediately, the mineral riches of the sea bed) is likely to prove a very important test for the Commission's ability to organize and foster effective co-operation on a broad regional basis.

The Commission served as the implementing agency for the South Pacific Regional Environment Programme (SPREP) until 1990 when it was decided to establish SPREP as an independent agency, though retaining associate status with the Commission. In November 1986 the Commission hosted a Conference which adopted the Convention for the Protection of the Natural Resources and Environment of the South Pacific Region aimed to 'prevent, reduce and control pollution'. The Commission also assists governments and aministrations in the region to develop the range of socio-economic statistics and to improve their quality. The Commission was instrumental in establishing the Festival of Pacific Arts and acts as the Secretariat of the Council of Pacific Arts; the activities carried out within the framework of the Festival are supported by a Revolving Fund especially set up to promote the culture and traditions of Pacific island member countries.

Secretary General: Atanraoi Baiteke
Headquarters: P.O. Box D 5, Nouméa, New Caledonia (telephone: 26 20 00;

telex: SOPACOM 3139 NM; fax: 26 38 18)

Publications: *Annual Report*; *Report of the South Pacific Conference* (annually); *Pacific Impact* (quarterly)

South Pacific Forum (SPF). The Forum is the gathering of Heads of Government of the independent and self-governing countries of the South Pacific. The Forum's first meeting was held in Wellington, New Zealand, in August 1971 by the Heads of Government of Australia, Cook Islands, Fiji, Nauru, New Zealand, Tonga, and Western Samoa; SPF was subsequently joined by Papua New Guinea and several Pacific islands as they gained independent or self-governing status and at present has 15 members. There exists no written constitution or other international instrument governing the Forum's activities, its functions and powers. A meeting is held every year by the Heads of Government to discuss political and economic issues of common concern. Decisions are arrived at by consensus and no formal vote is taken. Each meeting has been followed since 1989 by 'dialogues' with representatives of major countries interested in the region such as Japan, China, the USA, Canada, France, the UK and the *European Economic Community (EEC).

The Forum Secretariat was established in 1973 – under the name of South Pacific Bureau for Economic Co-operation (SPEC) – by an agreement signed at the third meeting of the Forum held in Apia, Western Samoa.

The Secretariat's executive board is the Committee consisting of representatives and senior officials from all member countries. The Committee meets twice a year, immediately before the meetings of the SPF and at the end of the year to examine the Secretariat's work programme and annual budget. Australia and New Zealand each contribute one-third of the annual budget, the remaining third being equally shared among the other members.

The Secretariat – formerly headed by a Director whose status was upgraded to that of Secretary-General when, in 1988, SPEC was renamed the Forum Secretariat – performs administrative functions; it has been responsible for the day-to-day operations of the SPF since 1975 when the then SPEC became the Forum's official secretariat. Since 1981 SPEC had acted also as the secretariat to the Pacific Group Council of African, Caribbean and Pacific (ACP) countries receiving assistance from the European Community under the Lomé Conventions. A SPEC Energy Unit was established in 1982 to co-ordinate regional energy policies and carry out research on alternative energy sources. An important role was also played by the Forum Secretariat in the South Pacific Regional Environment Programme (SPREP) along with the South Pacific Commission.

The Forum has undertaken practical measures for the expansion of regional commercial relations through the removal of tariff and non-tariff barriers and the promotion of trade in products of particular interest to the smaller countries. The then SPEC assisted these countries in negotiating, with Australia and New Zealand, the South Pacific Regional Trade and Economic Co-operation Agreement (SPARTECA), in force since January 1981. Under the SPARTECA, Australia and New Zealand allow duty-free and unrestricted access to specified products originating from the developing island members; further liberalization measures have been applied by Australia since 1987.

The August 1984 meeting, held in Tuvalu, besides discussing the grave situation in New Caledonia, charged a group of experts to draft a treaty for establishing a South Pacific Nuclear-Free Zone. The treaty was eventually signed in August 1985 in Rarotonga, Cook Islands, and entered into force in December 1986. Major nuclear powers had been invited to sign protocols in support of the treaty but the offer was accepted only by the then USSR and China.

Other activities include the preparation of programmes for the revitalization of specific traditional industries, the development of tourism, the co-ordination of efforts related to the improvement of intraregional transport and communications and the provision of advisory services. The most recent meetings of the

Forum discussed topics of paramount importance to South Pacific islands such as the threats posed by the predicted rise in sea-level (caused by heating of the atmosphere in consequence of the 'greenhouse effect') and by the extensive and indiscriminate use of drift-net fishing.

Secretary-General: Ieremia T. Tabai
Headquarters: P.O. Box 856, Suva, Fiji (telephone: 312600; telex: 2229)

Publications: *Annual Report*; *Forum Secretariat Directory of Aid Agencies*; *Forum Secretariat Series for Trade and Investment in the South Pacific*

SPC. *See* **South Pacific Commission.**

SPF. *See* **South Pacific Forum.**

U

UDEAC. Union douanière et économique de l'Afrique centrale; *see* **Customs and Economic Union of Central Africa.**

UN. *See* **United Nations.**

UNCED. *See* **United Nations Conference on Environment and Development.**

UNCHS. *See* **United Nations Centre for Human Settlements.**

UNCTAD. *See* **United Nations Conference on Trade and Development.**

UNDP. *See* **United Nations Development Programme.**

UNDRO. *See* **Office of the United Nations Disaster Relief Co-ordinator.**

UNEP. *See* **United Nations Environment Programme.**

UNESCO. *See* **United Nations Educational, Scientific and Cultural Organization.**

UNFPA. *See* **United Nations Population Fund.**

UNHCR. *See* **United Nations High Commissioner for Refugees.**

UNICEF. *See* **United Nations Children's Fund.**

UNIDO. *See* **United Nations Industrial Development Organization.**

Union douanière et économique de l'Afrique centrale (UDEAC). *See* **Customs and Economic Union of Central Africa.**

UNITAR. *See* **United Nations Institute for Training and Research.**

United Nations (UN). The UN is a voluntary association of sovereign countries which have committed themselves, through signing the Charter, to ensure international peace and security and to further international co-operation in solving economic, social, cultural and humanitarian problems and in promoting respect for human rights and fundamental freedoms. The UN is not a world government and is not authorized to intervene in the internal affairs of any country.

The name 'United Nations' was devised by President Franklin D. Roosevelt and was first used in the Washington Declaration by United Nations in January 1942, when representatives of 26 countries pledged their governments to continue fighting together against the Axis Powers. In October 1943, the Moscow Conference of Foreign

Ministers of China, the UK, the USA and the USSR recognized the necessity of establishing 'a general international organization, based on the principle of the sovereign equality of all peace-loving states, and open to membership by all such states, large and small, for the maintenance of international peace and security'. The following year, the basic principles of the proposed organization were worked out during the discussions, held at Dumbarton Oaks (near Washington, D.C.), between the UK, the USA, and the USSR from August to September and between China, the UK, and the USA from September to October. At the Yalta Conference of February 1945, an agreement was reached by Churchill, Roosevelt and Stalin on the voting procedure to be adopted in the Security Council of the UN and the granting of the 'veto power' to the permanent members.

The Charter of the new institution was drawn up by the representatives of 50 countries at the UN Conference on International Organization, held in San Francisco between April and June 1945, and was eventually signed on 26 June. Poland, not represented at the Conference, signed the Charter later and became the fifty-first original member of the Organization. The UN formally came into existence on 24 October 1945, when the Charter became effective following ratification by China, France, the UK, the USA, and the USSR, and by a majority of other signatories; 24 October is now universally celebrated as United Nations Day. In April 1946, the League of Nations – predecessor of the UN – was officially dissolved following a decision of its Assembly.

The number of member countries of the UN has risen from the original 51 to about 180, including practically all independent nations in the world; the only notable exceptions are Switzerland, Taiwan (which occupied the Chinese seat from 1945 till 1971, when replaced by the People's Republic of China), and the Vatican City State (Holy See). All the republics of the former USSR have been granted UN membership. The Russian Federation has succeeded the USSR in all organs of the UN, thereby occupying a permanent seat in the Security Council. The Byelorussian SSR [now Belarus] and the Ukrainian SSR [now Ukraine], although being at the time integral parts of the USSR and therefore not independent countries, have been enjoying separate UN membership as 'original members' since 1945.

The primary purpose of the UN, as it was with the League of Nations, is to maintain peace and security throughout the world and to develop friendly relations among nations. In the Charter, the peoples of the UN express their determination to save succeeding generations from the scourge of war. To this end, they pledge themselves to live in peace as good neighbours, to unite their strength in order to maintain peace and security, and to ensure that armed force shall not be used except in the common interest. The UN is based on the sovereign equality of all its member countries which undertake: to fulfil in good faith their Charter obligations; to settle their international disputes by peaceful means and without endangering peace, security and justice; to refrain in their international relations from the threat or use of force against other countries; to give the UN every assistance in any action it may take in accordance with the Charter, and not to assist countries against which preventive or enforcement action is being taken. The UN is to ensure that non-member countries act in accordance with these principles insofar as it is necessary for the maintenance of international peace and security. However, the UN as such has no competence in matters 'which are essentially within the domestic jurisdiction' of any country and its member countries are not required 'to submit such matters to settlement' under the Charter.

Unlike the Covenant of the League of Nations, the UN Charter reflects the awareness of its draftsmen of the close relationship existing between the maintenance of world peace and the promotion of international economic and social stability, including the safeguard of human rights and fundamental freedoms. The UN must act as 'a centre for harmonizing the actions of nations in attaining these common ends' in both the political and non-political fields through the furtherance of co-operation and co-ordination.

Year	No.	Original Member States
1945	51	Argentina, Australia, Belgium, Bolivia, Brazil, Byelorussian Soviet Socialist Republic, Canada, Chile, China, Colombia, Costa Rica, Cuba, Czechoslovakia, Denmark, Dominican Republic, Ecuador, Egypt, El Salvador, Ethiopia, France, Greece, Guatemala, Haiti, Honduras, India, Iran, Iraq, Lebanon, Liberia, Luxembourg, Mexico, Netherlands, New Zealand, Nicaragua, Norway, Panama, Paraguay, Peru, Philippines, Poland, Saudi Arabia, South Africa, Syria, Turkey, Ukrainian Soviet Socialist Republic, Union of Soviet Socialist Republics, United Kingdom, United States, Uruguay, Venezuela, Yugoslavia

		New Member States
1946	55	Afghanistan, Iceland, Sweden, Thailand
1947	57	Pakistan, Yemen
1948	58	Burma
1949	59	Israel
1950	60	Indonesia
1955	76	Albania, Austria, Bulgaria, Democratic Kampuchea, Finland, Hungary, Ireland, Italy, Jordan, Lao People's Democratic Republic, Libyan Arab Jamahiriya, Nepal, Portugal, Romania, Spain, Sri Lanka
1956	80	Japan, Morocco, Sudan, Tunisia
1957	82	Ghana, Malaysia
1958	83	Guinea
1960	100	Benin, Burkina Faso, Cameroon, Central African Republic, Chad, Congo, Cyprus, Gabon, Ivory Coast, Madagascar, Mali, Niger, Nigeria, Senegal, Somalia, Togo, Zaire
1961	104	Mauritania, Mongolia, Sierra Leone, United Republic of Tanzania
1962	110	Algeria, Burundi, Jamaica, Rwanda, Trinidad and Tobago, Uganda
1963	112	Kenya, Kuwait
1964	115	Malawi, Malta, Zambia
1965	118	Gambia, Maldives, Singapore
1966	122	Barbados, Botswana, Guyana, Lesotho
1967	123	Democratic Yemen
1968	126	Equatorial Guinea, Mauritius, Swaziland
1970	127	Fiji
1971	132	Bahrain, Bhutan, Oman, Qatar, United Arab Emirates
1973	135	Bahamas, Federal Republic of Germany, German Democratic Republic
1974	138	Bangladesh, Grenada, Guinea-Bissau
1975	144	Cape Verde, Comoros, Mozambique, Papua New Guinea, São Tome and Príncipe, Suriname
1976	147	Angola, Samoa, Seychelles
1977	149	Djibouti, Viet Nam
1978	151	Dominica, Solomon Islands
1979	152	Saint Lucia
1980	154	Saint Vincent and the Grenadines, Zimbabwe
1981	157	Antigua and Barbuda, Belize, Vanuatu
1983	158	Saint Kitts and Nevis
1984	159	Brunei
1990	159*	Liechtenstein, Namibia
1991	166	Democratic People's Republic of Korea, Estonia, Federated States of Micronesia, Latvia, Lithuania, Marshall Islands, Republic of Korea
1992	179	Armenia, Azerbaijan, Bosnia and Herzegovina, Croatia, Georgia, Kazakhstan, Kyrgyzstan, Moldova, San Marino, Slovenia, Tajikistan, Turkmenistan, Uzbekistan

* In 1990 the gain of two members was offset by the loss of two members because of the unification of Democratic Yemen and Yemen and of the two German states.

Membership of the United Nations

Member	Date of Admission		Member	Date of Admission	
Afghanistan	19 Nov.	1946	Estonia	17 Sep.	1991
Albania	14 Dec.	1955	Ethiopia	13 Nov.	1945
Algeria	8 Oct.	1962	Federated States of		
Angola	1 Dec.	1976	Micronesia	17 Sep.	1991
Antigua and Barbuda	11 Nov.	1981	Fiji	13 Oct.	1970
Argentina	24 Oct.	1945	Finland	14 Dec.	1955
Armenia	2 Mar.	1992	France	24 Oct.	1945
Australia	1 Nov.	1945	Gabon	20 Sep.	1960
Austria	14 Dec.	1955	Gambia	21 Sep.	1965
Azerbaijan	2 Mar.	1992	Georgia	31 July	1992
Bahamas	18 Sep.	1973	Germany[3]	18 Sep.	1973
Bahrain	21 Sep.	1971	Ghana	8 Mar.	1957
Bangladesh	17 Sep.	1974	Greece	25 Oct.	1945
Barbados	9 Dec.	1966	Grenada	17 Sep.	1974
Belarus[1]	24 Oct.	1945	Guatemala	21 Nov.	1945
Belgium	27 Dec.	1945	Guinea	12 Dec.	1958
Belize	25 Sep.	1981	Guinea-Bissau	17 Sep.	1974
Benin	20 Sep.	1960	Guyana	20 Sep.	1966
Bhutan	21 Sep.	1971	Haiti	24 Oct.	1945
Bolivia	14 Nov.	1945	Honduras	17 Dec.	1945
Bosnia and Herzegovina	22 May	1992	Hungary	14 Dec.	1955
Botswana	17 Oct.	1966	Iceland	19 Nov.	1946
Brazil	24 Oct.	1945	India	30 Oct.	1945
Brunei Darussalam	21 Sep.	1984	Indonesia[4]	28 Sep.	1950
Bulgaria	14 Dec.	1955	Iran	24 Oct.	1945
Burkina Faso	20 Sep.	1960	Iraq	21 Dec.	1945
Burundi	18 Sep.	1962	Ireland	14 Dec.	1955
Cambodia	14 Dec.	1955	Israel	11 May	1949
Cameroon	20 Sep.	1960	Italy	14 Dec.	1955
Canada	9 Nov.	1945	Jamaica	18 Sep.	1962
Cape Verde	16 Sep.	1975	Japan	18 Dec.	1956
Central African Republic	20 Sep.	1960	Jordan	14 Dec.	1955
Chad	20 Sep.	1960	Kazakhstan	2 Mar.	1992
Chile	24 Oct.	1945	Kenya	16 Dec.	1963
China	24 Oct.	1945	Kuwait	14 May	1963
Colombia	5 Nov.	1945	Kyrgyzstan	2 Mar.	1992
Comoros	12 Nov.	1975	Lao People's Democratic		
Congo	20 Sep.	1960	Republic	14 Dec.	1955
Costa Rica	2 Nov.	1945	Latvia	17 Sep.	1991
Côte d'Ivoire	20 Sep.	1960	Lebanon	24 Oct.	1945
Croatia	22 May	1992	Lesotho	17 Oct.	1966
Cuba	24 Oct.	1945	Liberia	2 Nov.	1945
Cyprus	20 Sep.	1960	Libya	14 Dec.	1955
Czechoslovakia	24 Oct.	1945	Liechtenstein	18 Sep.	1990
Democratic People's			Lithuania	17 Sep.	1991
Republic of Korea	17 Sep.	1991	Luxembourg	24 Oct.	1945
Denmark	24 Oct.	1945	Madagascar	20 Sep.	1960
Djibouti	20 Sep.	1977	Malawi	1 Dec.	1964
Dominica	18 Dec.	1978	Malaysia[5]	17 Sep.	1957
Dominican Republic	24 Oct.	1945	Maldives	21 Sep.	1965
Ecuador	21 Dec.	1945	Mali	28 Sep.	1960
Egypt[2]	24 Oct.	1945	Malta	1 Dec.	1964
El Salvador	24 Oct.	1945	Marshall Islands	17 Sep.	1991
Equatorial Guinea	12 Nov.	1968	Mauritania	27 Oct.	1961

Membership of the United Nations—continued

Member	Date of Admission		Member	Date of Admission	
Mauritius	24 Apr.	1968	Seychelles	21 Sep.	1976
Mexico	7 Nov.	1945	Sierra Leone	27 Sep.	1961
Moldova	2 Mar.	1992	Singapore	21 Sep.	1965
Mongolia	27 Oct.	1961	Slovenia	22 May	1992
Morocco	12 Nov.	1956	Solomon Islands	19 Sep.	1978
Mozambique	16 Sep.	1975	Somalia	20 Sep.	1960
Myanmar	19 Apr.	1948	South Africa	7 Nov.	1945
Namibia	23 Apr.	1990	Spain	14 Dec.	1955
Nepal	14 Dec.	1955	Sri Lanka	14 Dec.	1955
Netherlands	10 Dec.	1945	Sudan	12 Nov.	1956
New Zealand	24 Oct.	1945	Suriname	4 Dec.	1975
Nicaragua	24 Oct.	1945	Swaziland	24 Sep.	1968
Niger	20 Sep.	1960	Sweden	19 Nov.	1946
Nigeria	7 Oct.	1960	Syria[7]	24 Oct.	1945
Norway	27 Nov.	1945	Tajikistan	2 Mar.	1992
Oman	7 Oct.	1971	Thailand	16 Dec.	1946
Pakistan	30 Sep.	1947	Togo	20 Sep.	1960
Panama	13 Nov.	1945	Trinidad and Tobago	18 Sep.	1962
Papua New Guinea	10 Oct.	1975	Tunisia	12 Nov.	1956
Paraguay	24 Oct.	1945	Turkey	24 Oct.	1945
Peru	31 Oct.	1945	Turkmenistan	2 Mar.	1992
Philippines	24 Oct.	1945	Uganda	25 Oct.	1962
Poland	24 Oct.	1945	Ukraine	24 Oct.	1945
Portugal	14 Dec.	1955	United Arab Emirates	9 Dec.	1971
Qatar	21 Sep.	1971	United Kingdom	24 Oct.	1945
Republic of Korea	17 Sep.	1991	United Republic of		
Romania	14 Dec.	1955	Tanzania[8]	14 Dec.	1961
Russian Federation[6]	24 Oct.	1945	United States	24 Oct.	1945
Rwanda	18 Sep.	1962	Uruguay	18 Dec.	1945
Saint Kitts and Nevis	23 Sep.	1983	Uzbekistan	2 Mar.	1992
Saint Lucia	18 Sep.	1979	Vanuatu	15 Sep.	1981
Saint Vincent and the			Venezuela	15 Nov.	1945
Grenadines	16 Sep.	1980	Viet Nam	20 Sep.	1977
Samoa	15 Dec.	1976	Yemen[9]	30 Sep.	1947
San Marino	2 Mar.	1992	Yugoslavia	24 Oct.	1945
Sao Tome and Principe	16 Sep.	1975	Zaire	20 Sep.	1960
Saudi Arabia	24 Oct.	1945	Zambia	1 Dec.	1964
Senegal	28 Sep.	1960	Zimbabwe	25 Aug.	1980

Membership of the United Nations—continued

[1]   On 19 September 1991, Byelorussia informed the United Nations that it had changed its name to Belarus.

[2]   Egypt and Syria were original Members of the United Nations from 24 October 1945. Following a plebiscite on 21 February 1958, the United Arab Republic was established by a union of Egypt and Syria and continued as a single Member. On 13 October 1961, Syria, having resumed its status as an independent State, resumed its separate membership in the United Nations. On 2 September 1971, the United Arab Republic changed its name to the Arab Republic of Egypt.

[3]   The Federal Republic of Germany and the German Democratic Republic were admitted to membership of the United Nations on 18 September 1973. Through the accession of the German Democratic Republic to the Federal Republic of Germany, effective from 3 October 1990, the two German States have united to form one sovereign State.

[4]   By letter of 20 January 1965, Indonesia announced its decision to withdraw from the United Nations "at this stage and under the present circumstances". By telegram of 19 September 1966, it announced its decision "to resume full cooperation with the United Nations and to resume participation in its activities". On 28 September 1966, the General Assembly took note of this decision and the President invited representatives of Indonesia to take seats in the Assembly.

[5]   The Federation of Malaya joined the United Nations on 17 September 1957. On 16 September 1963, its name was changed to Malaysia, following the admission to the new federation of Singapore, Sabah (North Borneo) and Sarawak. Singapore became an independent State on 9 August 1965 and a Member of the United Nations on 21 September 1965.

[6]   The Union of Soviet Socialist Republics was an original Member of the United Nations from 24 October 1945. In a letter dated 24 December 1991, Boris Yeltsin, the President of the Russian Federation, informed the Secretary-General that the membership of the Soviet Union in the Security Council and all other United Nations organs was being continued by the Russian Federation with the support of the 11 member countries of the Commonwealth of Independent States.

[7]   Egypt and Syria were original Members of the United Nations from 24 October 1945. Following a plebiscite on 21 February 1958, the United Arab Republic was established by a union of Egypt and Syria and continued as a single Member. On 13 October 1961, Syria, having resumed its status as an independent State, resumed its separate membership in the United Nations.

[8]   Tanganyika was a Member of the United Nations from 14 December 1961 and Zanzibar was a Member from 16 December 1963. Following the ratification on 26 April 1964 of Articles of Union between Tanganyika and Zanzibar, the United Republic of Tanganyika and Zanzibar continued as a single Member, changing its name to the United Republic of Tanzania on 1 November 1964.

[9]   Yemen was admitted to membership of the United Nations on 30 September 1947 and Democratic Yemen on 14 December 1967. On 22 May 1990, the two countries merged and have since been represented as one Member with the name "Yemen".

The United Nations System

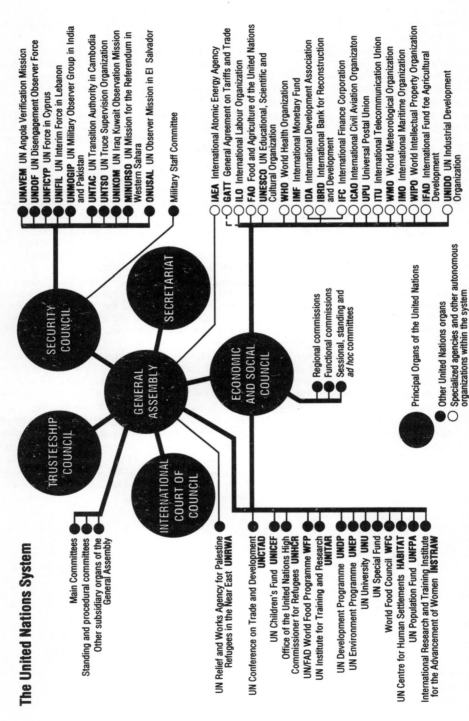

UNAVEM UN Angola Verification Mission
UNDOF UN Disengagement Observer Force
UNFICYP UN Force in Cyprus
UNIFIL UN Interim Force in Lebanon
UNMOGIP UN Military Observer Group in India and Pakistan
UNTAC UN Transition Authority in Cambodia
UNTSO UN Truce Supervision Organization
UNIKOM UN Iraq Kuwait Observation Mission
MINURSO UN Mission for the Referendum in Western Sahara
ONUSAL UN Observer Mission in El Salvador

Military Staff Committee

IAEA International Atomic Energy Agency
GATT General Agreement on Tariffs and Trade
ILO International Labour Organization
FAO Food and Agriculture of the United Nations
UNESCO UN Educational, Scientific and Cultural Organization
WHO World Health Organization
IMF International Monetary Fund
IDA International Development Association
IBRD International Bank for Reconstruction and Development
IFC International Finance Corporation
ICAO International Civil Aviation Organizaton
UPU Universal Postal Union
ITU International Telecommunication Union
WMO World Meteorological Organization
IMO International Maritime Organization
WIPO World Intellectual Property Organization
IFAD International Fund foe Agricultural Development
UNIDO UN Industrial Development Organization

SECURITY COUNCIL

SECRETARIAT

GENERAL ASSEMBLY

ECONOMIC AND SOCIAL COUNCIL

TRUSTEESHIP COUNCIL

INTERNATIONAL COURT OF COUNCIL

Regional commissions
Functional commissions
Sessional, standing and *ad hoc* committees

Main Committees
Standing and procedural committees
Other subsidiary organs of the General Assembly

Principal Organs of the United Nations

Other United Nations organs

Specialized agencies and other autonomous organizations within the system

UN Relief and Works Agency for Palestine Refugees in the Near East **UNRWA**
UN Conference on Trade and Development **UNCTAD**
UN Children's Fund **UNICEF**
Office of the United Nations High Commissioner for Refugees **UNHCR**
UN/FAD World Food Programme **WFP**
UN Institute for Training and Research **UNITAR**
UN Development Programme **UNDP**
UN Environment Programme **UNEP**
UN University **UNU**
UN Special Fund
World Food Council **WFC**
UN Centre for Human Settlements **HABITAT**
UN Population Fund **UNFPA**
International Research and Training Institute for the Advancement of Women **INSTRAW**

224

Amendments to the Charter enter into effect when they have been adopted by a two-thirds vote of the members of the General Assembly and ratified by two-thirds of the members of the UN, including all the permanent members of the Security Council. The amendments introduced so far have related to the expansion of two main organs, the Security Council and the Economic and Social Council.

Membership of the UN is open to all peace-loving nations which accept the obligations of the Charter and, in the judgment of the Organization, are able and willing to carry out these obligations. The original members of the UN are those countries which, having participated in the San Francisco Conference of 1945 or having previously signed the Declaration by the United Nations of 1942, have signed and ratified the Charter. Other countries may be admitted to membership by a two-thirds majority vote by the General Assembly upon the recommendation of the Security Council. The Assembly, therefore, may decide to reject the application of a candidate country having the support of the Security Council but may not admit a country in the absence of a recommendation of the Security Council. Members may be suspended or expelled by the Assembly on the recommendation of the Security Council; they may be suspended if the Security Council is taking enforcement action against them or expelled if they persistently violate the principles of the Charter. The rights of a suspended member may be restored by the Security Council.

There are six principal organs of the UN: the General Assembly, the Security Council, the Economic and Social Council, the Trusteeship Council, the International Court of Justice, and the Secretariat. Actually, both the Economic and Social Council and the Trusteeship Council are auxiliary bodies whose basic task is to assist and advise the General Assembly and the Security Council. The official languages in all these organs, other than the International Court of Justice, are Chinese, English, French, Russian and Spanish. Working languages are English and French, with the addition of Russian, Chinese and Spanish in the General Assembly and the Security Council, and Spanish in the Economic and Social Council. Arabic has been added as an official language of the General Assembly, the Security Council and the Economic and Social Council. English and French are the working languages of the Secretariat in New York. The official languages in the International Court of Justice are English and French.

The General Assembly is the main deliberative organ and consists of all the members of the UN, each country having one vote and being entitled to be represented at meetings by five delegates and five alternates. Regular sessions are held once a year, commencing on the third Tuesday in September and normally lasting until mid-December; there is a resumption for some weeks in the new year, if necessary. Special sessions may be convened by the Secretary-General at the request of the Security Council, of a majority of the members of the UN or of one member if the majority of the members concurs. An emergency special session may be convoked within 24 hours of a request by the Security Council on the vote of any nine members of the Council itself or by a majority of the UN members or by one member concurred with by the majority of the members. The Assembly elects its President and 21 Vice-Presidents for each session.

The General Assembly is empowered to discuss any matter within the scope of the Charter or affecting the powers and functions of any UN organ and, except where a dispute or situation is being discussed by the Security Council, to make recommendations on it. In addition, the following specific competences of the Assembly are envisaged by the Charter: (a) to make recommendations on the principles of co-operation in the maintenance of international peace and security, including the principles governing disarmament and the regulation of armaments; (b) to make recommendations for the peaceful settlement of any situation, regardless of origin, which might impair friendly relations among nations; (c) to initiate studies and make recommendations to promote international political co-operation, the development of international law and its codification, the realization of human rights and fundamental freedoms for all, and international collaboration in economic, social, cultural, educational and health fields; (d) to receive and consider reports from the Security Council, the Secretary-General and other organs; (e) to supervise, through the Trusteeship Council, the execution of the trusteeship agreements for all areas not designated as strategic; (f) to approve the UN budget, to apportion the contributions among members, and to examine the budgets of specialized agencies; (g) to elect the non-permanent members of the Security Council, the members of the Economic and Social Council and those members of the Trusteeship Council which are elected; (h) to take part with the Security Council in the election of judges of the International Court of Justice; and (i) to appoint the Secretary-General upon recommendation of the Security Council.

Under the 'Uniting for Peace' resolution, adopted by the General Assembly in November 1950, the Assembly may take action if the Security Council, because of lack of unanimity of the permanent members, fails to exercise its primary responsibility in any case where there appears to be a threat to the peace, breach of the peace or act of aggression. More precisely, the Assembly is empowered to consider the matter immediately with a view to making recommendations to members for collective measures – including, in the case of a breach of the peace or act of aggression, the use of armed force when necessary to maintain or restore international peace and security. If the Assembly is not in session, an emergency special session may be convened at very short notice.

The General Assembly has a substantive right of decision only with regard to the internal affairs of the UN; as a general rule, recommendations, whatever their political and/or moral force, have no legally binding character and cannot create direct legal obligations for members. All members are entitled to equal voting rights, with decisions on 'important questions' – such as recommendations on peace and security, election of members to organs, admission,

suspension and expulsion of members, trusteeship questions and budgetary matters – being taken by a two-thirds majority of the members present and voting, and decisions on 'other questions' by a simple majority. The term 'decision', in relation to the General Assembly and the other organs of the UN, is used in a wide sense and covers all types of actions, including 'recommendations', 'resolutions' and the like. The vote can be by 'acclamation', show of hands, roll-call, secret ballot or 'consensus', this last practice being followed whenever direct confrontation is to be avoided.

An elaborate structure of committees and subsidiary organs is required to enable the General Assembly to carry out its wide range of functions. There are seven Main Committees on each of which every member has the right to be represented by one delegate. They are: First Committee (disarmament and related international security questions); Special Political Committee; Second Committee (economic and financial); Third Committee (social, humanitarian and cultural); Fourth Committee (decolonization); Fifth Committee (administrative and budgetary); Sixth Committee (legal). In addition, there is a General Committee – composed of the President and 21 Vice-Presidents of the Assembly and the Chairmen of the seven Main Committees – which meets frequently during a session to co-ordinate the proceedings of the Assembly and its Committees and generally to supervise the smooth running of the Assembly's work. The Credentials Committee, consisting of nine members appointed by the President at the beginning of each session of the Assembly, is charged with the task of verifying the credentials of representatives. There are also two standing committees – an Advisory Committee on Administrative and Budgetary Questions (ACABQ), consisting of 16 members, and a Committee on Contributions, composed of 18 members, which recommends the scale of members' payments to the UN. Many subsidiary and ad hoc bodies have been set up by the Assembly in order to deal with specific matters.

As a rule, the Assembly refers all questions on the agenda to one of the Main

Committees, to a joint committee, or to an *ad hoc* committee; these bodies, which decide by a simple majority, submit proposals for approval to a plenary meeting of the Assembly. Although regular sessions last about three months each year, the work of the Assembly goes on continuously: in special committees and commissions, such as those dealing with colonialism, apartheid, peace-keeping operations, disarmament, sea bed and ocean floor, outer space, human rights, international law; in the activities of specialized bodies established by the Assembly itself, such as the *UN Development Programme (UNDP), the *UN Children's Fund (UNICEF), the *UN Environment Programme (UNEP), the *UN Conference on Trade and Development (UNCTAD), and many others; in the work programme of the Secretariat, and at international conferences on specific problems, such as the environment, food, population, status of women, law of the sea, peaceful uses of atomic energy and outer space.

The Security Council has the primary responsibility for maintaining peace and security and consists of 15 members, each of which has one representative and one vote. There are five permanent members, China, France, Russia, the UK and the USA, and ten non-permanent members elected for a two-year term by a two-thirds majority of the General Assembly and ineligible for immediate re-election. Any member of the UN not on the Council may participate, without vote, in the discussion of questions specially affecting its interests. Both members and non-members of the UN, if they are parties to a dispute being considered by the Council, are invited to take part, without vote, in the discussions; the conditions regulating the participation of non-members are laid down by the Council. The Presidency of the Council is held by members in monthly rotation in the English alphabetical order of their names. The Security Council is so organized as to be able to function continuously, and a representative of each of its members must be present at all times at the seat of the UN. The Council may meet elsewhere than at UN Headquarters if it considers

this advisable; in 1972 a session was held in Addis Ababa, Ethiopia, and in the following year another session took place in Panama City, Panama.

Besides its basic function relating to the maintenance of international peace and security in accordance with the purposes and principles of the UN, the Security Council is empowered: (a) to investigate any dispute or situation which might lead to international friction and to recommend methods of adjustment or appropriate terms of settlement; (b) to determine the existence of any threat to the peace, breach of the peace, or act of aggression and to make recommendations or decide what action should be taken; (c) to call on members to apply economic sanctions and other measures not involving the use of force in order to prevent or stop aggression; (d) to take military action against an aggressor; (e) to formulate plans for the establishment of a system to regulate armaments; (f) to exercise trusteeship functions in 'strategic areas'; (g) to recommend the admission of new members and the terms on which states may become parties to the Statute of the International Court of Justice; and (h) to recommend to the General Assembly the appointment of the Secretary-General and, together with the Assembly, to elect the judges of the International Court of Justice.

The Security Council acts on behalf of all UN members which 'agree to accept and carry out' its decisions; members also undertake to make available to the Council 'armed forces, assistance, and facilities' necessary to maintain international peace and security. While other organs of the UN make recommendations to governments, the Council alone has the power to take decisions which members are obligated under the Charter to carry out. Decisions on procedural matters are made by an affirmative vote of at least nine of the 15 members of the Council; decisions on substantive matters also require nine votes, including the concurring votes of all five permanent members. Any of the permanent members may therefore exercise a 'veto right' in relation to all questions, except those of a procedural character, and prevent the taking of a decision having the support of a majority of the Council; the veto, however, may not be exercised if the permanent member concerned is itself a party to a dispute. All five permanent members have exercised the right of veto at one time or another. The practice of abstention of a permanent member is generally accepted and not regarded as a veto; a valid decision may therefore be taken.

The Committee of Experts on Rules of Procedure, the Committee on Council Meetings Away from Headquarters, and the Committee on the Admission of New Members are composed of representatives of all the members of the Council. The Military Staff Committee is composed of the chiefs of staff of the permanent members of the Council or their representatives; this body, although established since 1946 in order to advise and assist the Council for the application of armed force, has performed so far no real function despite proposals made from time to time for its 'revitalization'.

The Economic and Social Council, under the authority of the General Assembly, is the organ responsible for the economic and social work of the UN and the co-ordination of the policies and activities of the specialized agencies and institutions – known as the UN 'family' of organizations. It consists of 54 members, 18 of whom are elected each year by the General Assembly for a three-year term; each member has one representative and one vote. Retiring members are eligible for immediate re-election. The Council generally held two month-long sessions each year, one in New York and the other in Geneva; since 1992 the Council holds only one annual session, lasting about four to five weeks, alternately in New York and Geneva. The President is elected for one year and may be re-elected immediately.

The Economic and Social Council is empowered: (a) to make or initiate studies, reports and recommendations on international economic, social, cultural, educational, health and related matters; (b) to make recommendations for the purpose of promoting respect for, and observance of, human rights and fundamental freedoms; (c) to call international conferences and prepare draft conventions for submission to the General Assembly on matters within its competence; (d) to negotiate agreements with the specialized agencies, defining their relationship with the UN; (e) to address recommendations to the specialized agencies, the General Assembly and members of the UN; (f) to perform services, approved by the Assembly, for members of the UN and, upon request, for the specialized agencies; and (g) to make arrangements for consultation with non-governmental organizations concerned with matters falling within its competence. Decisions of the Council are made by a simple majority of the members present and voting.

A number of standing committees, commissions and other subsidiary bodies have been set up by the Economic and Social Council and meet at UN Headquarters or in other locations. There are standing Committees on: Non-Governmental Organizations; Natural Resources; Development Planning; Crime Prevention and Control; and Negotiations with Intergovernmental Agencies. The Commissions on Human Settlements and on Transnational Corporations are also standing bodies. The functional commissions include the Statistical Commission, Population Commission, Commission for Social Development, Commission on the Status of Women, *Commission on Narcotic Drugs (CND), and Commission on Human Rights. The Commission on Human Rights has a Sub-Commission on Prevention of Discrimination and Protection of Minorities within whose framework operates a five-member Working Group on Contemporary Forms of Slavery.

Also under the Economic and Social Council's authority are the regional economic commissions aimed at assisting the development of the major regions of the world and at strengthening economic relations of the countries in each region, both among themselves and with other countries of the world. These are the *Economic Commission for Africa (ECA), based in Addis Ababa, the *Economic and Social Commission for Asia and the Pacific (ESCAP), based in Bangkok, the *Economic Commission for Europe (ECE), based in Geneva, the *Economic Commission for

Latin America and the Caribbean (ECLAC), based in Santiago, and the *Economic and Social Commission for Western Asia (ESCWA), based in Baghdad. The commissions are responsible for studying the problems of their respective regions and recommending courses of action to member countries and specialized agencies. The Economic and Social Council may consult with non-governmental organizations dealing with matters falling within its competence.

The Trusteeship Council bears prime responsibility for supervising the administration of territories placed under the International Trusteeship System established by the UN. The basic goals of the system – that is the promotion of the advancement of the inhabitants of the trust territories and their progressive development towards self-government or independence – have been fulfilled to such an extent that only one of the original 11 trusteeships remains. The other trust territories, mostly in Africa, attained independence, either as separate states or by joining neighbouring independent countries. The Council acts under the authority of the General Assembly or, in the case of a 'strategic area', under the authority of the Security Council. Membership of the Council is not based on a predetermined number, since the Charter intended to provide for a balance between members administering trust territories and members which did not. At present, the Council, whose size has progressively decreased, consists of the only administering country, the USA which is responsible for the Trust Territory of the Pacific Islands (now comprising only the Republic of Palau, part of the archipelago of the Caroline Islands), plus the four permanent members of the Security Council not administering territories, that is China, France, Russia, and the UK. China, however, did not take part in the work of the Council until May 1989. Being a strategic area, the Trust Territory of the Pacific Islands falls within the responsibility of the Security Council which voted in December 1990 to abolish UN trusteeship over several islands; all but one of the islands which were part of the Trust Territory are now independent. The Trusteeship Council meets regularly once a year; special sessions may be convened whenever necessary. Decisions of the Trusteeship Council are made by a majority of the members present and voting, each member having one vote.

The International Court of Justice is the principal judicial organ of the UN; only states may be parties in cases before it. The Court's governing instrument is the Statute which forms an integral part of the UN Charter and is based on the Statute of the Permanent Court of International Justice of the League of Nations. All members of the UN are ipso facto parties to the Statute. A country which is not a member of the UN may become a party to the Statute on conditions determined in each case by the General Assembly upon the recommendation of the Security Council; under this rule, Switzerland has become a party. All countries which are parties to the Statute of the Court can be parties to cases before it; other countries can refer cases to it under conditions laid down by the Security Council. The Security Council may recommend that a legal dispute be referred to the Court. The General Assembly and the Security Council can ask the Court for an advisory opinion on any legal question; other organs of the UN and the specialized agencies, when authorized by the General Assembly, can ask for advisory opinions on legal questions falling within the scope of their activities.

The Court – which has its seat at The Hague, Netherlands, but may sit elsewhere whenever it considers this desirable – consists of 15 'independent' judges elected with an absolute majority for a renewable nine-year term by the General Assembly and the Security Council voting independently. To safeguard continuity, the terms of office of the judges are so staggered that one-third of the seats becomes vacant every three years. The judges are elected, regardless of their nationality, among persons 'who possess the qualifications required in their respective countries for appointment to the highest judicial offices' or are 'jurisconsults of recognized competence in international law'. Care is taken, however, to see that the principal legal systems of the world are represented in the Court and it is expressly provided that no two judges can be nationals of the same country. Candidates are chosen from a list of persons nominated by the various national groups on the panel of arbitrators of the Permanent Court of Arbitration (established by the Hague Conventions of 1899 and 1907) or by equivalent groups. The Court is permanently in session, except during the judicial vacations. It elects its own President and Vice-Presidents for three years. The full Court of 15 judges normally sits, but a quorum of nine members is sufficient. The Court may form chambers of three or more judges for dealing with particular categories of cases, and forms annually a chamber of five judges to hear and determine, at the request of the parties, cases by summary procedures. Judgments given by any of these chambers are considered as rendered by the Court.

An important feature of the Court is the inclusion of 'national' judges. In fact, judges of the nationality of the parties continue to sit in cases in which their own countries are involved; if these is no judge on the bench of the nationality of the parties to the dispute, each of the parties may designate an *ad hoc* judge. Such a judge, who need not possess the nationality of the party which appoints him, participates on terms of complete equality with the other judges. All questions are decided by a majority of the judges present; in case of a tie, the President of the Court casts the deciding vote. The judgment is final and without appeal, but a revision may be applied for within 10 years from the date of the judgment on the ground of a new decisive factor.

The jurisdiction of the Court is twofold, contentious and advisory, and covers all questions which the parties refer to it, and all matters provided for in the UN Charter or in treaties and conventions in force. Disputes concerning the jurisdiction of the Court are settled by the Court itself. States may bind themselves in advance to accept the jurisdiction of the Court in special cases, either by signing a treaty or convention which provides for reference to the Court or by making a special declaration to this effect. In early 1984, the USA stated

that it would not accept the Court's compulsory jurisdiction in cases involving Central America for the next two years.

According to the Statute, the Court may apply in its decisions: (a) international conventions establishing rules recognized by the contesting countries; (b) international custom as evidence of a general practice accepted as law; (c) the general principles of law recognized by nations; and (d) judicial decisions and the teachings of the most highly qualified publicists of the various nations, as a subsidiary means for determining the rules of law. If the parties concerned so agree, the Court may decide *ex aequo et bono*, that is according to practical fairness rather than strict law. The Court may give an advisory opinion on any legal question to any organ of the UN or its agencies. The Security Council can be called upon by one of the parties in a case to determine measures to be taken to give effect to a judgment of the Court if the other party fails to perform its obligations under that judgment.

The Secretariat services the other organs of the UN and administers the programmes and policies laid down by them. At the head of the Secretariat is the Secretary-General who is the chief administrative officer of the UN appointed by the General Assembly deciding by a simple majority on the recommendation of the Security Council adopted by an affirmative vote of at least nine members, including the concurring votes of the permanent members. The Secretary-General appoints the necessary staff in conformity with the regulations established by the Assembly in order to guarantee the international character, integrity and efficiency of the civil service of the UN. Under the Charter, each member country undertakes to respect the exclusively international character of the responsibilities of the Secretary-General and the staff and not to seek to influence them in the discharge of their duties. Each staff member takes an oath not to seek or receive instructions from any government or outside authority. The Secretary-General performs a number of important political, representative and administrative functions and is required to submit an annual report to the General

Assembly. He is empowered to bring to the attention of the Security Council any matter which, in his opinion, threatens international peace and security and to address the Assembly on any question it has under consideration. In his capacity of chief administrative officer, the Secretary-General acts, in person or through deputies, at all meetings of the Assembly, the Security Council, the Economic and Social Council, and the Trusteeship Council and may be entrusted by these organs with additional functions.

The personal contribution of those who have served successively at the head of the Secretariat has been of paramount importance in many cases. The first Secretary-General was Trygve Lie (of Norway) who was appointed in 1946 and resigned in 1953. Dag Hammarskjöld (of Sweden) succeeded Lie and held office until his death in a plane crash in Africa in 1961 during his Congo mission. After Hammarskjold's death, U Thant (of Burma) was elected acting Secretary-General and a year later elected to office for a full five-year term, retroactive to 1961. Thant served a second five-year term until December 1971 when Kurt Waldheim (of Austria) was appointed. Waldheim served two full terms from January 1972 to December 1981 when the Assembly appointed Javier Pérez de Cuéllar (of Peru) whose second term of office expired in December 1991. Boutros Boutros Ghali (of Egypt) was appointed for a full term starting from January 1992. The Secretary-General is assisted by several Under-Secretaries-General and Assistant Secretaries-General.

The whole structure of the Secretariat has been reorganized and streamlined in 1992 to make it a more flexible and efficient tool in the pursuit of the traditional and new tasks of the UN. There are separate staffs serving subsidiary organs established by the General Assembly or the Economic and Social Council, including: the *UN Children's Fund (UNICEF), the *UN Development Programme (UNDP), the *UN High Commissioner for Refugees (UNHCR), the *UN Relief and Works Agency for Palestine Refugees (UNRWA), the *UN Institute for Training and Research (UNITAR), and the *UN Conference on Trade and Development (UNCTAD).

The external relations of the UN are extremely vast and varied in keeping with its universalist character and comprehensive scope and its attempt at providing a permanent institutional framework for international society. Several intergovernmental bodies are linked to the UN by special agreements which entitle them to work in partnership with the Organization and each other in economic, social, scientific and technical fields. Sixteen organizations are known as 'specialized agencies', according to the definition used in the Charter of the UN. These are: the *International Labour Organization (ILO); the *Food and Agriculture Organization (FAO); the *UN Educational, Scientific and Cultural Organization (UNESCO); the *World Health Organization (WHO); the *International Bank for Reconstruction and Development (IBRD); the *International Development Association (IDA); the *International Finance Corporation (IFC); the *International Monetary Fund (IMF); the International Civil Aviation Organization (ICAO); the *Universal Postal Union (UPU); the *International Telecommunication Union (ITU); the *World Meteorological Organization (WMO); the *International Maritime Organization (IMO); the *World Intellectual Property Organization (WIPO); the *International Fund for Agricultural Development (IFAD); the *UN Industrial Development Organization (UNIDO). They report annually to the Economic and Social Council. The *International Atomic Energy Agency (IAEA), an intergovernmental agency for atomic energy set up 'under the aegis of the UN', reports annually to the General Assembly and, as appropriate, to the Security Council and the Economic and Social Council. The *General Agreement on Tariffs and Trade (GATT), formally a multilateral treaty setting forth the basic rules accepted by countries responsible for most of the world's trade, co-operates with the UN at the secretariat and intergovernmental levels. Important international organizations, such as the European Communities, have been granted observer status by the

General Assembly. The Economic and Social Council has made arrangements for consultation with international non-governmental organizations and, after consultation with the member countries, with national organizations. There are over 600 non-governmental organizations, classified into three categories, having consultative status with the Economic and Social Council; they may send observers to public meetings of the Council and its subsidiary bodies and may submit written statements. They may also consult with the Secretariat of the UN on matters of mutual concern.

The biennial budget of the UN is initially submitted by the Secretary-General and reviewed by the Advisory Committee on Administrative and Budgetary Questions (ACABQ) which is empowered to recommend modifications to the General Assembly. The programmatic aspects are reviewed by the 34-member Committee for Programme and Co-ordination. The regular budget covers the administrative and other expenses of the central Secretariat and the other principal organs of the UN, both at Headquarters and throughout the world. Many activities of the UN are financed mainly by voluntary contributions outside the regular budget; such activities include the UNDP, WFP, UNICEF, UNHCR, UNRWA, and UNFPA. Additional activities are financed by voluntary contributions to trust funds or special accounts established for each purpose.

Contributions of member countries are the main source of funds for the regular budget, in accordance with a scale of assessments specified by the General Assembly on the advice of the Committee on Contributions. The amount of the contribution of a member country is determined primarily by the total national income of that country in relation to that of other member countries. The Assembly has fixed a maximum of 25 per cent of the budget for any one contributor and a minimum of 0.01 per cent. As a result of arrears in payments by some members, a serious financial crisis developed in 1986 and 1987. The USA had withheld its contributions and demanded financial reforms and the introduction of 'weighted voting'

on budgetary matters. A panel of 18 experts was set up in December 1985 to review UN administration and finance; the resulting report was submitted to the Secretary-General in August 1986 and the recommendations were subsequently approved by the General Assembly. The most significant innovation has involved greater control over spending and the adoption of the budget by consensus, giving major contributors a substantial power, although the budget itself remains eventually subject to approval by the General Assembly. Despite the following decision of the USA to initiate payments of both current and overdue contributions, arrears by several other member countries and the increase in expenditure resulting from the extension of peace-keeping activities remain a source of grave preoccupation for the financial future of the UN.

In the scale of assessments for 1992, 1993 and 1994, more than 90 countries, or approximately 60 per cent of the membership of the UN, were each contributing between 0.01 and 0.03 per cent of the budget. The six largest contributors were the USA (25 per cent), Japan (12.45), Russia Germany, France, and the UK.

The UN has undergone major changes in the nearly half a century of its existence, one such change being the enormous increase in membership. The goal of a peaceful world remains first and foremost in UN theory and practice. Activities related to the maintenance of international peace and security, however, account for only part of the current work. Economic and social co-operation has become increasingly important while new fields of interest and activity have emerged. As regards human rights, several international instruments have been adopted over the past decades. The UN has assisted countries under colonial rule to exercise their rights of self-determination and gain independence. At present, the progress towards general and nuclear disarmament, the reduction of economic and social disparities in the world, the achievement of sustainable development and the fight against drug abuse and illicit trafficking are issues of grave concern for UN member countries. The intrinsic limitation of the powers of the UN on matters concerning functional international co-operation and human rights and the climate of continuing confrontation which characterized for more than four decades the relationship between the two superpowers and their respective allies account for the varying record of achievements of the Organization in several important spheres; as in all intergovernmental bodies, the authority and effectiveness of the UN ultimately depend on the political resolve and collective will of the member countries.

In the furtherance of the basic objectives of international peace and security, the UN has taken many actions for the settlement of international disputes and the restoration of peaceful conditions. In its early years, the General Assembly condemned warlike propaganda (1947); called on nations to refrain from the threat or use of force contrary to the Charter and from any threat or act aimed at impairing the independence of any country or at fomenting civil strife (1949); condemned intervention by a country in the internal affairs of another country in order to change its legally established government by the threat or use of force (1950); and called upon all countries to develop friendly and co-operative relations and to settle disputes by peaceful means (1957). Following the 1965 Declaration on the Inadmissibility of Intervention in the Domestic Affairs of States and the Protection of their Independence and Sovereignty, the Assembly adopted in December 1981 another document on the inadmissibility of intervention and interference in the internal affairs of states. Two important declarations were adopted in 1970 on the strengthening of international security and the principles of international law concerning friendly relations and co-operation among states. A difficult task, initiated in 1950, was completed in 1974 with the adoption of a definition of aggression as 'the use of armed force by a state against the sovereignty, territorial integrity or political independence of another state, or in any other manner inconsistent with the Charter of the UN'.

Among the more recent documents, mention should be made of the Declaration on the Prevention of Nuclear Catastrophe, adopted in 1981; the Manila Declaration on the Peaceful Settlement of International Disputes (1982); the Declaration on the Right of Peoples to Peace (1984); the Declaration on the Enhancement of the Effectiveness of the Principle of Refraining from the Threat or Use of Force in International Relations (1987); the Declaration on the Prevention and the Removal of Disputes and Situations Which May Threaten International Peace and Security and on the Role of the United Nations in the Field (1988). In 1980, the General Assembly approved the establishment of the University for Peace, based in Costa Rica, and devoted to research on disarmament, mediation, the resolution of conflicts and the relationship between peace and economic development. The year 1986 was proclaimed the International Year of Peace.

On many occasions the UN, through the Security Council, the General Assembly and the Secretary-General, has been directly involved in efforts to resolve a number of international crises and has developed its capacity as a peace-keeping and peace-making body. In some disputes, the UN has acted through peace-keeping forces, observer or fact-finding missions, plebiscite supervision, good offices missions, conciliation panels, mediators and special representatives; in other cases, the UN has provided the forum for negotiation and a channel for quiet diplomacy. The Security Council has undertaken measures of a military nature (as in the Korean war), an economic embargo (against Southern Rhodesia, now Zimbabwe), an arms embargo (against South Africa), and economic sanctions and use of force (against Iraq in the Gulf crisis). Military observer missions – as in the Middle East or Kashmir – are composed of unarmed officers made available by member countries that are considered impartial by the parties concerned. Peace-keeping forces – as in the Middle East, the Congo [now Zaire] and Cyprus – consist of contingents of lightly-armed troops made available by member countries in order to assist in preventing the recurrence of fighting, restoring and maintaining law and order and promoting a return to normal conditions; the use of force is allowed only for self-defence as a last resort.

The end of the Cold War has contributed to a significant renewal of interest for UN peace-making and has brought about an increasing demand for peace-keeping forces. After almost eight years of negotiations, accords were signed in 1988 in Geneva, in the presence of the Secretary-General, for the withdrawal of foreign troops from Afghanistan paving the way for a comprehensive political settlement in that troubled country. The situation in Cambodia (Kampuchea), a major concern of the UN for more than a decade, has remarkably improved after the withdrawal of Vietnamese forces and international efforts are promoting national reconciliation and the realization of the Cambodian people's right to self-determination. The creation of the UN Transitional Authority in Cambodia (UNTAC) and the consequent UN involvement in the management of the transitional period have represented an important achievement. An important role has also been played in the late 1980s by the UN in the Central American peace process; for the first time the Organization set up an observer mission in order to monitor the electoral process in a sovereign country (Nicaragua). With regard to the Iran-Iraq conflict, after the adoption in July 1987 of a resolution of the Security Council containing a peace plan, the Secretary-General negotiated a cease-fire agreement between the two sides in 1988. A major preoccupation of the UN remains the situation in the Middle East despite the beginning of a peace process involving dialogue between Israelis and Palestinians and the improvement of the situation in Lebanon. In August 1989 the Secretary-General, for the first time, used his authority under the Charter to call for a meeting of the Security Council which appealed for an immediate end of hostilities in Lebanon.

The Security Council condemned Iraq's invasion of Kuwait in August 1990 only a few hours after it had taken place and demanded the immediate and unconditional withdrawal of all Iraqi forces. Subsequent resolutions, taking into account Iraq's failure to comply with the requests of the UN, called for a range of economic sanctions, declared the annexation of Kuwait 'null and void', imposed a deadline for withdrawal and ultimately sanctioned the use of force against Iraq which culminated in the liberation of Kuwait by the end of February 1991.

A new generation of peace-keeping activities began for the UN in 1988 and 1989 when military observer missions were undertaken in Afghanistan and Pakistan, in Iran and Iraq, in Angola and in Central America; a major operation, involving military, police and civilian personnel, was launched in March 1989 in Namibia to oversee the transition of that country to independence under free and fair elections supervised by the UN. A significant role may also be played by the UN in the territories of former Yugoslavia with the establishment of UN Protected Areas (UNPAs).

In 1959, the General Assembly declared the question of general and complete disarmament to be 'the most important one facing the world today' and called on governments to make every effort to achieve a constructive solution: however, it soon became clear that such a goal was not attainable within a specific period of time. Since 1962 a multilateral disarmament negotiating forum – now known as the Conference on Disarmament – has been active in Geneva within the context of a close relationship with the UN. As a result of UN efforts, several important multilateral and bilateral arms regulation and disarmament agreements have been concluded; among these agreements, the 1968 Treaty on the Non-Proliferation of Nuclear Weapons deserves special attention. In the wake of the inadequate results of the First Disarmament Decade – in the 1970s – the General Assembly decided to declare the 1980s as the Second Disarmament Decade and held two special sessions (in 1978 and 1982) devoted entirely to disarmament. A third special session on disarmament was held in 1988 but, despite the remarkable improvement in the relations between the two superpowers, no substantive final document could be adopted. The fundamental changes in Europe and in the major-power relationship have contributed to a considerable extent to efforts for achieving reductions in both nuclear and conventional armaments and the UN is likely to play a more active role either as a negotiating forum or as a catalyst. At present about 50,000 nuclear weapons remain deployed worldwide, enough to destroy the world several times.

The UN Institute for Disarmament Research (UNIDIR) – based in Geneva – has been issuing, since the last half of the 1980s, a number of studies on various aspects of arms control and disarmament. It had been set up by the General Assembly in 1980 on a provisional basis and in 1982 was established as an autonomous institute of the UN to undertake independent research on disarmament and related questions, particularly international security issues; its statute became effective in January 1985. The Institute, besides organizing conferences, publishing papers and conducting research projects, has a fellowship programme for scholars from developing countries.

The question of the peaceful uses of outer space has been on the agenda of the General Assembly since 1958. The UN is concerned not only with the orderly uses of outer space but also seeks to ensure that the benefits yielded by space research and technology are shared by all countries. Several legal instruments have resulted from the activities of the Assembly in this area. Two major conferences on the exploration and peaceful uses of outer space have been held, in 1968 and 1982, under the auspices of the UN. In 1986, the General Assembly adopted Principles relating to remote sensing of the earth from outer space with a view to ensuring that such activities were conducted for the benefit of all countries and to protect mankind from natural disasters.

The establishment of a law governing the use of the sea in all aspects represents another major concern of the UN. So far, three conferences have been organized: the First Conference (1958) adopted five conventions but left many basic issues unresolved; the Second Conference (1960) brought no progress; the Third Conference (1973–82) has adopted an important Convention whose full implementation, however, might be seriously impaired by the opposition of certain industrial countries. A Preparatory Commission has been established to pave the way for the two major institutions to be set up under the Convention – the International Sea-Bed Authority, with headquarters in Jamaica, and the International Tribunal for the Law of the Sea, to be located in Hamburg, Germany.

The questions of apartheid, as enforced in the Republic of South Africa, and racial discrimination have been before the UN since the very beginning of its activities in 1946. The General Assembly has condemned apartheid as a 'crime against humanity' and has kept the situation in South Africa under continuous review, adopting a variety of measures to exert pressure on South African authorities. Taking into account the significant changes occurring in that country, the General Assembly adopted in December 1989, at a special session on apartheid, a Declaration setting out the preconditions for negotiations among all the parties concerned in view of the creation of a united, non-racial and democratic South Africa. In December 1991, the General Assembly unanimously approved a resolution recommending that member countries phase out economic sanctions and drop other sanctions against South Africa.

The UN aim of 'social progress and better standards of life in larger freedom' has received growing attention over the past decades. The UN system currently devotes most of its personnel and financial resources to the economic and social development of the poorer member countries in which two-thirds of the world's people live. A wide-ranging international action was initiated by the UN with the proclamation of the Development Decades, beginning with the 1960s. The need for a world plan or 'strategy' on the necessary measures became evident before the first Decade ended. Intensive work, over several years, led to the agreement on the International Development Strategy for the Second Decade (the 1970s), intended to cover virtually every area of economic and social development; among other goals, the Strategy stressed the need for fairer economic and commercial policies and greater financial resources for developing countries. However, no substantial progress was deemed to be possible without a far-reaching modification of the structures and rules governing international economic and financial relations.

In 1974 the General Assembly held its first special session on economic problems and adopted a Declaration and a Programme of Action on the Establishment of a New International Economic Order so as 'to eliminate the widening gap between the developed and the developing countries and ensure steadily accelerating economic and social development in peace and justice'. In December 1974, a few months after the call for a new international economic order, the Assembly adopted a Charter of Economic Rights and Duties of States with a view to establishing 'generally accepted norms to govern international economic relations systematically and to promote a new international economic order'.

The International Development Strategy for the Third Development Decade was proclaimed by the Assembly in December 1980. Despite modest progress in some areas, the key targets were not met and the overall situation in developing countries actually worsened while the proposed global negotiations between North and South failed to materialize. The especially critical situation in Africa prompted the General Assembly to convene in May 1986 a special session devoted to that region; the session adopted the UN Programme of Action for African Economic Recovery and Development (UNPAAERD), 1986-90, seeking to mobilize political and financial support for economic reforms. Also in 1986, the Assembly sought to promote international co-operation for resolving the external debt problems of developing countries. In subsequent sessions the Assembly broadened the area of agreement on measures to cope with major problems arising from the persistent external indebtedness of developing countries. The situation of the 'least developed' countries has been discussed by two UN Conferences held in Paris in 1981 and 1990 respectively and policies and measures have been formulated. A new international development strategy for the 1990s has been adopted by the General Assembly.

The work of the UN in the social field originally centred on the urgent problems arising from World War II and subsequently began to focus on the needs of the less developed countries. The emphasis on a unified approach to economic and social planning for the promotion of balanced and sound development is reflected in the provisions of the Declaration on Social Progress, adopted by the General Assembly in 1969 as a common basis for national and international policies. An autonomous research institute created in 1963, the United Nations Research Institute for Social Development (UNRISD) based at Geneva, conducts research into problems and policies of social development during different stages of economic growth.

In its efforts to achieve social development involving very large sectors of the population, the UN has stressed the importance of popular participation in the rural areas and has urged agrarian reform. The General Assembly has endorsed the Declaration and Programme of Action approved by the World Conference on Agrarian Reform and Rural Development held in Rome in 1979 under the sponsorship of FAO. The co-operative efforts of the UN and its related agencies in economic and social fields are currently being expanded and streamlined with priority given to problems having a more direct impact on the development process. Direct field activities are carried out by UNDP in co-operation with UN-related agencies and institutions. UNCTAD was established as a permanent organ of the General Assembly in 1964. UNITAR, created in 1965, carries out training and research programmes with a view to improving the effectiveness of the UN.

The UN University (UNU), which opened the doors of its world headquarters in Tokyo in 1975, operates through global networks of associated institutions and research units. A new kind of academic institution, UNU – which is sponsored jointly by the UN and UNESCO and is not a university in the proper sense since it does not have students or award degrees – undertakes multidisciplinary research, provides post-graduate fellowships for scholars from developing countries and conducts several training activities. Research and training centres have been created by UNU in Finland (for development economics), in the Netherlands (for new technologies), in Côte d'Ivoire and Zambia (for natural resources in Africa), in Macau (for software technology) and in Japan (for advanced studies).

On the recommendation of the 1975 World Conference of the International Women's Year, the General Assembly decided to establish the International Research and Training Institute for the Advancement of Women (INSTRAW) whose Statute was endorsed in 1985. The objectives of INSTRAW, with headquarters in Santo Domingo, Dominican Republic, are to stimulate and assist, through research, training and the collection and exchange of information, the efforts of intergovernmental, governmental and non-governmental organizations aimed at the advancement of women and their integration in development both as participants and beneficiaries.

With a view to providing a forum for the presentation and discussion of the relevant policies, the General Assembly authorized in 1950 the convening, at five-year intervals, of a UN Congress on the Prevention of Crime and the Treatment of Offenders; such congresses have been regularly held since 1955. Research and training activities in the field of crime prevention and control are the responsibility of the UN Interregional Crime and Justice Research Institute (UNICRI) – formerly the UN Social Defence Research Institute (UNSDRI), restructured and renamed in 1989 – with headquarters in Rome, Italy, and of regional institutes in Africa, Asia and the Pacific, Latin America, the Arab States and Europe. The UN Trust Fund for Social Defence promotes technical co-operation and the exchange of information in the field of crime prevention and control.

As regards food problems, in 1974 the General Assembly set up the *World Food Council (WFC) and sponsors, jointly with FAO, the *World Food Programme (WFP), in operation since 1963 to stimulate economic and social development through aid in the form of food.

In order to seek solutions to the widespread problems of pollution, the Assembly convened a Conference on the Human Environment in Stockholm in 1972 and subsequently created the *UN Environment Programme (UNEP) to monitor changes in the environment and to encourage and co-ordinate appropriate practices. The urgent need to agree on strategies for sustainable and environmentally sound development in all countries prompted the General Assembly to convene in June 1992 in Rio de Janeiro, Brazil, the *UN Conference on Environment and Development (UNCED). Population problems are dealt with by the *United Nations Population Fund (UNFPA) – set up by the Assembly in 1967 under the name of UN Fund for Population Activities – which has become the largest internationally funded source of assistance to population programmes in developing countries.

The control of narcotic drugs has been representing a widespread concern since the beginning of this century. A series of treaties have been adopted under the auspices of the UN requiring signatory countries to exercise control over the production and distribution of narcotic drugs and psychotropic substances and to combat drug abuse and illicit traffic, duly reporting to international organs.

The *Commission on Narcotic Drugs (CND) was established by the Economic and Social Council in 1946 to advise the Council and prepare draft international agreements on all matters relating to the control of narcotic drugs. The *International Narcotics Control Board (INCB), which started operations in 1968, is composed of members elected by the Economic and Social Council with a view to supervising governmental implementation of drug control treaties. Following resolutions of the Economic and Social Council and of the General Asssembly, the UN Fund for Drug Abuse Control (UNFDAC) was set up in April 1971 to develop programmes and to provide funds for their execution. Despite its limited financial resources,

UNFDAC has served as a catalyst through the mobilization of funds for achieving its basic objectives in key narcotics producing or transit countries. Since the early 1980s financial resources were mostly devoted to comprehensive national and regional plans known as 'Masterplans'.

In 1984 the General Assembly adopted a Declaration on the Control of Drug Trafficking and Drug Abuse calling for renewed efforts and strategies aimed at the eradication of the increasingly complex drug problems. The first International Conference on Drug Abuse and Illicit Trafficking was held in June 1987 in Vienna and adopted, *inter alia*, a Comprehensive Multidisciplinary Outline of Future Activities in Drug Abuse Control. The UN Convention against Illicit Traffic in Narcotic Drugs and Psychotropic Substances (adopted in 1988 and entered into force in November 1990) addresses areas not envisaged in pre-existing international drug treaties.

The UN anti-drug-trafficking activities were reviewed in February 1990 by the General Assembly which concluded a special four-day session with the adoption of a Global Programme of Action. In December 1990, the General Assembly adopted a 40-power resolution giving new impetus to UN efforts in the field of drug abuse control through the establishment of a single programme – the *UN International Drug Control Programme (UNDCP). The newly-created programme integrates and co-ordinates the activities of the existing bodies, including the secretariat of the INCB as well as the UNFDAC; the latter's financial resources have been placed under the direct responsibility of the head of UNDCP.

A number of bodies have been set up by the UN in order to assist groups needing 'special help' in emergency conditions. The General Assembly created UNICEF in 1946 and extended its mandate indefinitely in 1953. UNHCR was established by the Assembly with effect from January 1951; UNRWA began work in 1950 as a subsidiary organ of the General Assembly. The UN has provided assistance for emergency relief and longer-term rehabilitation on several occasions and has

appointed a Disaster Relief Co-ordinator whose Office (UNDRO) started operations in March 1972. The UN Sudano-Sahelian Office (UNSO) was created in 1973 to assist in medium- and long-term rehabilitation and development programmes for that African region affected by prolonged drought, accelerating desertification and other disasters since the 1960s; the mandate and functions of UNSO were subsequently extended.

In furtherance of the UN purpose to achieve international co-operation in promoting and encouraging respect for human rights and fundamental freedoms for all, regardless of race, sex, language or religion, the General Assembly adopted in December 1948 the Universal Declaration of Human Rights, under which, for the first time in history, responsibility for the protection and pursuit of human rights was assumed by the international community and was accepted as a permanent obligation. The Universal Declaration covers not only civil and political rights but also economic, social and cultural rights. Another important accomplishment has been the coming into force in 1976 of legally binding international agreements for the protection and promotion of human rights. These are the International Covenant on Economic, Social and Cultural Rights and the International Covenant on Civil and Political Rights, the latter including an Optional Protocol, all adopted by the General Assembly in 1966. An additional protocol (Second Optional Protocol) to ban capital punishment, under the International Covenant on Civil and Political Rights, was adopted by the General Assembly in 1989.

Besides torture and other cruel, inhuman or degrading treatment or punishment, attention is being given by the UN to other human rights questions such as slavery and slave trade, genocide, statelessness, religious intolerance, and the treatment of migrant workers. The rights of children have been brought by the UN within an all-encompassing document, the Convention on the Rights of the Child, adopted by the General Assembly in 1989. The rights of the disabled, the elderly and the young as well as human rights in armed conflicts have also been considered. Another basic commitment of the UN concerns the achievement of equality of rights for men and women, both in law and in fact.

The UN has played a crucial role in the transition of peoples belonging to more than 80 nations from colonial domination to freedom. Decolonization made early significant gains under the International Trusteeship System; the progress was greatly accelerated by the Declaration on the Granting of Independence to Colonial Countries and Peoples, proclaimed by the General Assembly in 1960, and by the work of the Special Committee established by the Assembly in 1961 to examine on a regular basis the application of the Declaration and to make recommendations to help speed its implementation. When the Special Committee started operations in 1962, the non-self-governing territories placed on its list amounted to 64; these have now been reduced to 18, located mainly in the Pacific Ocean and the Caribbean and with a total population of about 2 million. To observe the 30th anniversary of the Declaration in 1990, the Assembly designated the final decade of this century (1990-2000) as the International Decade for the Eradication of Colonialism. The independence of Namibia and its subsequent entry into the UN in 1990 represented the most recent demonstration of the UN long-standing commitment to the principle of self-determination.

As regards international law, in 1947 the Assembly established the International Law Commission which held its first session in 1949 with a view to promoting the progressive development of international law and its codification. The Commission – composed of 34 members serving in their individual capacity and meeting annually – has prepared drafts on a number of topics. International conferences of plenipotentiaries – convened by the General Assembly on the basis of such drafts – have adopted conventions opened for states to become parties. Two conferences, held in Vienna in 1961 and 1963 respectively, approved the Vienna Convention on Diplomatic Relations and the Vienna Convention on Consular Relations. A conference which met in Vienna in 1968 and again in 1969 approved a Convention on the Law of Treaties. Another conference, which met in Vienna in April 1977 and again in August 1978, completed and adopted the Vienna Convention on Succession of States in Respect of Treaties. Following a 1984 decision of the General Assembly, a UN Conference met in Vienna in March 1986 and adopted the Vienna Convention on the Law of Treaties between States and International Organizations or between International Organizations.

In response to the need for the UN to play a more active role in reducing legal obstacles to the flow of international trade, the Assembly established in 1966 the UN Commission on International Trade Law (UNCITRAL) for the progressive harmonization and unification of the law of international trade; the 36-nation Commission also offers training and assistance in international trade law, taking into account the needs of the developing countries. The Commission's activities have chiefly focused on the preparation of uniform rules concerning the international sale of goods, international payments, international commercial arbitration, and international legislation on shipping.

The major changes in the international situation which have taken place since the autumn of 1989 and the general shift towards a new world order have had a significant impact on the UN, its functioning and its prospects both in the short and in the long term. The dissolution of the USSR and of its network of alliances in Europe and elsewhere has brought to an end the traditional East-West confrontation and opened up new avenues for cooperation unhindered by ideological conflicts. The North-South polarization itself has been substantially affected and to a certain extent softened in consequence of the said events. The almost abrupt return to the realities of a multipolar world has altered deep-rooted balances of power which had inspired UN theory and practice for several decades.

The long-overdue reform of the Organization, both in the sense of a return to the 'original' spirit and in the sense of an adaptation to the challenges of the present times, seems now less far away. The new spirit of co-operation among the 'great powers' and the growing awareness of the interdependence among all countries, large and small, could induce the international community to avail itself of the UN in the most appropriate and effective way. The reorganization and streamlining of the Secretariat, undertaken at the beginning of 1992 by the new Secretary-General, may be viewed as the first and encouraging sign of a wholly new period in the life of the world body. The restructuring of other principal organs, in particular the Security Council, and of many subsidiary bodies to respond more adequately to today's needs will represent a much harder task requiring the co-operation of all member countries.

Headquarters: United Nations Plaza, New York, N.Y. 10017, USA (telephone: 754-1234; telex: 232422)

Geneva Office: Palais des Nations, 1211 Geneva 10, Switzerland (telephone: 31 02 11 – 34 60 11; telex 289696)

Members of the Security Council: *Permanent members*: China, France, Russia, UK, USA; *Elected members*: Austria, Belgium, Ecuador, India and Zimbabwe (until December 1992); Cape Verde, Hungary, Japan, Morocco and Venezuela (until December 1993)

Members of the Economic and Social Council: Algeria, Bahrain, Bulgaria, Burkina Faso, Canada, China, Ecuador, Finland, Iran, Jamaica, Mexico, Pakistan, Romania, Russia, Rwanda, Sweden, UK, Zaire (until December 1992); Argentina, Austria, Botswana, Chile, France, Germany, Guinea, Japan, Malaysia, Morocco, Peru, Somalia, Spain, Syria, Togo, Trinidad and Tobago, Turkey, Yugoslavia (until December 1993); Angola, Australia, Bangladesh, Belarus, Belgium, Benin, Brazil, Colombia, Ethiopia, India, Italy, Kuwait, Madagascar, Philippines, Poland, Suriname, Swaziland, USA (until December 1994)

Members of the Trusteeship Council: *Administering Country*: USA; *Other Countries*: China, France, Russia, UK.

Members of the International Court of Justice, in order of precedence (terms end on 5 February of the year indicated in parentheses): Sir Robert Yewdall Jennings of the UK (2000), President; Shigeru Oda of Japan (1994), Vice President; Manfred Lachs of Poland (1994); Bola Ajibola of Nigeria (1994); Roberto Ago of Italy (1997); Stephen M. Schwebel of the USA (1997); Mohammed Bedjaoui of Algeria (1997); Ni Zhengyu of China (1994); Jens Evensen of Norway (1994); Nikolai K. Tarassov of Russia (1997); Gilbert Guillaume of France (2000); Mohamed Shahabuddeen of Guyana (1997); Andres Aguilar Mawdsley of Venezuela (2000); Christopher G. Weeramantry of Sri Lanka (2000); Raymomd Ranjeva of Madagascar (2000). The terms of office of Judges Sir Robert Yewdall Jennings and Shigeru Oda as President and Vice-President respectively expire in 1994.

Registrar: Eduardo Valencia-Ospina

Secretary General: Boutros Boutros Ghali

Publications: *UN Chronicle* (quarterly); *Yearbook of the UN* (comprehensive account, organized by subject, of UN activities); *Basic Facts About the UN*; *Everyone's United Nations*; *The UN Disarmament Yearbook*; *Monthly Bulletin of Statistics*; *Statistical Yearbook*; *Yearbook of International Statistics*; *World Economic Survey* (annually)

References: T. Lie: *In the Cause of Peace* (London, 1954); H.G. Nicholas: *The United Nations as a Political Institution* (Oxford, 1959); S.D. Bailey: *The General Assembly* (London, 1960); U Thant: *Towards World Peace* (New York, 1964); R. Ogley: *The United Nations and East-West Relations* (University of Sussex, 1972); M. Elmandjra: *The United Nations System: An Analysis* (London, 1973); R. Hiscocks: *The Security Council: A Study in Adolescence* (New York, 1974); T. Meron: *The United Nations Secretariat: The Rules and Practice* (Lexington, Mass., 1977); U Thant: *View from the United Nations* (Newton Abbot, 1977); M. Hill: *The UN System: Co-ordinating its Economic and Social Work* (Cambridge, 1978); E. Luard: *The United Nations: How it Works and What it Does* (London, 1979); J. Kaufmann: *United Nations Decision*

Making (Alphen a/d Rijn, rev. 3/1980); G.R. Berridge and A. Jennings (eds): *Diplomacy at the UN* (London, 1985); M.J. Peterson: *The General Assembly in World Politics* (Winchester, Mass, 1986); T.M. Franck: *Nation Against Nation: What Happened to the U.N. Dream and What the U.S. Can Do about It* (London, 1986); D. Steele: *The Reform of the United Nations* (London, 1987); D. Williams: *The Specialized Agencies and the United Nations. The System in Crisis* (New York, 1987); D.P. Forsythe (ed): *The United Nations in the World Political Economy* (London, 1989); J.W. Muller: *The Reform of the United Nations: A Report* (Dobbs Ferry, 1991)

United Nations Centre for Human Settlements (UNCHS) – HABITAT. The Centre is intended to serve as a focal point for the co-ordination and evaluation of human settlements activities carried out within the UN system.

The establishment of the Centre in 1978 was the result of the UN long-standing concern with the problems of human settlements, particularly the deteriorating quality of living conditions and the need to link urban and regional development programmes with national plans. The first international meeting on the subject was convened by the UN in Vancouver, Canada, in May–June 1976 under the title: Habitat: UN Conference on Human Settlements.

The adoption by the Conference of the Vancouver Declaration on Human Settlements and the Vancouver Plan of Action represented an important commitment on the part of governments and the international community to improve the quality of life for all people through human settlements development. The Plan of Action contained recommendations for national action regarding settlements policies, settlement planning, provision of shelter, infrastructure and services, land use and land tenure, the role of popular participation, and effective institutions and management.

The Vancouver Conference also recommended the strengthening and consoli-dation of UN activities in a single body concerned exclusively with human settlements. Acting on this recommendation, in December 1977 the UN General Assembly transformed the Committee on Housing, Building and Planning into the Commission on Human Settlements, and in October 1978 established the present Centre to service the Commission and to implement its resolutions.

On the basis of the Vancouver Plan of Action, the Centre's major areas of concern include the provision of technical assistance to government programmes, the organization of expert meetings, workshops and training seminars, the publication of technical documents and the dissemination of information through the establishment of a global information network.

Technical co-operation projects cover, *inter alia*, national settlement policies and programmes, urban and regional planning, rural and urban housing and infrastructure development, slum upgrading and sites-and-services schemes, low-cost building technology, technologies for urban and rural water supply and sanitation systems, and the establishment or strengthening of government institutions responsible for human settlements.

The Commission on Human Settlements is the governing body of the Centre. It meets every two years and consists of 58 members (16 from Africa, 13 from Asia, 6 from Eastern Europe, 10 from Latin America, 13 from Western Europe and other countries) serving for four-year periods. There are Divisions responsible for technical co-operation, research and development, information, audio-visual and documentation, and administration. The Habitat and Human Settlements Foundation (HHSF) serves as the financial arm of the Centre. The Executive Director is the highest official overseeing the work of the Centre.

The Centre maintains relations with UN bodies, the specialized agencies and other intergovernmental, as well as non-governmental, organizations. The financial sources of the Centre are represented by allocations from the regular UN budget and voluntary contributions by governments; operational activities are financed by the *UN Development Programme (UNDP) and several multilateral and bilateral donor agencies.

The Work Programme of the Centre is divided into several sub-programmes: settlement policies and strategies (formulation of policy options, trends and guidelines); settlements planning (specific proposals on the use of resources in relation to needs and priority programmes); shelter and community services (housing programmes and co-operatives, credit unions); land (physical development at the national level or below, formulation and implementation of land policies and supporting legislation); development of the indigenous construction sector (use of indigenous methods and reformulation of building acts and regulations); low-cost infrastructure for human settlements (guidelines for legislation on water supply and sanitation and study of energy-efficient housing); human settlements institutions and management (development of national institutions and training courses in human settlements management); mobilization of finance (performance of finance institutions and role of non-conventional finance mechanisms). Audio-visual and documentary materials are produced by the Centre as an integral part of projects and training programmes.

The Centre is responsible for hundreds of technical co-operation projects in all developing regions of the world. It applies advanced technology through its Urban Data Management System and the Housing Finance Software package which is designed to assist in financial management and reporting for small housing and development schemes.

In 1982, the General Assembly proclaimed 1987 the International Year of Shelter for the Homeless (IYSH) and decided that the objectives of the Year would be to improve the shelter situation of the poor and disadvantaged at both individual and community levels, particularly in developing countries, both before and during 1987, and to demonstrate means of continuing those efforts as on-going national programmes beyond 1987. The General Assembly designated the Commission on Human Settlements as the UN inter-governmental body responsible for organizing the Year and the Centre as the secretariat for the Year and as the lead agency for co-ordinating the relevant programmes and activities of other organizations and agencies concerned. In 1988 the Commission on Human Settlements approved a Global Strategy for Shelter to the Year 2000; the Strategy was unanimously adopted by the General Assembly in December 1988.

Executive Director: Dr Arcot Ramachandran

Headquarters: P.O. Box 30030, Nairobi, Kenya (telephone: 333930; telex: 22996; fax: 520724)

Publications: *UNCHS Habitat News* (three times a year); studies and technical reports

United Nations Children's Fund (UNICEF). The Fund was originally intended to carry out relief in Europe after World War II. Today it is mainly concerned with meeting the essential needs of children living in the developing countries and lacking even the most rudimentary medical, nutritional and educational services.

The Fund was created by the UN General Assembly in December 1946, under the name of United Nations International Children's Emergency Fund, in order to extend massive relief to the young victims of World War II in Europe and China. In the early 1950s, the emphasis was gradually shifted to programmes intended to combat the widespread malnutrition, disease and illiteracy afflicting millions of children throughout the developing world. In 1953 the General Assembly decided to extend the Fund's mandate indefinitely and to drop the words 'International' and 'Emergency' from the official name, but the well-known acronym was retained.

In 1976 the Fund adopted the 'basic services' strategy, affirmed by the General Assembly, in order to provide to the under-served areas of developing countries effective assistance in the interrelated fields of primary health care, formal and non-formal education, applied nutrition, clean water and sanitation, responsible parenthood and family planning, child mental health, and improvement in the lives of women and girls. Assistance is extended by the Fund according to mutually agreed priorities for children, in close co-operation with the governments concerned, with special regard to planning, development and extension of low-cost community-based services. Besides its basic long-term involvement in child health, nutrition and welfare programmes, the Fund may also be called upon to provide emergency relief and supplementary aid for mothers and children whenever necessary because of major natural disasters, civil strife or epidemics. Emergency assistance is generally followed by long-range rehabilitation operations.

The basic policy directives of the Fund are laid down by its governing body, the Executive Board, which is composed of representatives of 41 countries elected for a three-year term by the UN Economic and Social Council from among members of the *UN, or its specialized agencies, or the *International Atomic Energy Agency (IAEA). Nine seats each are reserved for Asia and Africa; four for Eastern Europe; six for Latin America; twelve for Western Europe and other countries; and one seat to be rotated among these groupings. The Executive Board meets annually to review the programmes and make commitments for aid.

The Executive Director is nominated by the UN Secretary-General in consultation with the Executive Board and is responsible for current administrative tasks and the appointment and direction of staff. The headquarters of the Fund are located in New York; several regional offices and around 90 field offices complete the organizational structure. Direct links with the public are maintained by the Fund through 33 National Committees, almost all in the developed countries.

In emergency relief the Fund co-operates very closely with the *UN Development Programme (UNDP) and other UN agencies as well as with numerous non-governmental organizations. Over the past few years, a substantial share of emergency assistance went to alleviate drought and famine in Africa.

The activities of the Fund are financed in their entirety through voluntary contributions from governments, private organizations and individuals. Over 70 per cent of the Fund's income derives directly from governments and about 20 per cent from the general public, through various fund-raising campaigns, greetings card sales and individual donations; the remainder comes from the UN system and miscellaneous sources.

The Fund is currently engaged in programmes in about 120 developing countries to help protect children from disease, malnutrition and other perils of the growing years and to prepare them for healthy, productive adult lives. The child population (age 0–15) of the countries assisted is over 1.3 billion.

The Fund's efforts for the 1980s concentrated on the drastic reduction of infant mortality rates through an attack on the principal causes of preventable death and disease, drawing on a wide variety of national and community organizations for support in mobilizing the necessary human and financial resources. The success of these efforts was linked to a very large extent to the community-based services strategy which had been advocated since the mid-1970s. The General Assembly designated the Fund as the 'lead agency' of the UN system responsible for co-ordinating the activities of the International Year of the Child observed in 1979.

The Fund has participated in drafting the Convention on the Rights of the Child which was adopted by the UN General Assembly in November 1989 and entered into force in September of the following year. Also in September 1990 the Fund organized the World Summit for Children with the participation of the heads of state and government of more than 70 countries. By setting the protection and development of children as the focal point of international commitment, the meeting emphasized the importance of education, nutrition, health, family planning, and empowerment of women and girls in building the foundations for the future. A declaration was issued aimed at committing countries to reduce infant mortality and the dangers of childbirth worldwide, and to guarantee that all children will have access to clean water and education by the year 2000.

The Fund was awarded the Nobel Peace Prize in 1965.

Executive Director: James P. Grant

Headquarters: Three United Nations Plaza, New York, N.Y. 10017, USA (telephone: 326 7000; telex: 760 7848; fax: 326 7260)

Publications: *UNICEF Annual Report*; *State of the World's Children* (annually)

Reference: M. Black: *The Children and the Nations. The Story of UNICEF* (New York, 1986)

United Nations Conference on Environment and Development (UNCED). Called in popular usage the 'Earth Summit', the Conference met in Rio de Janeiro, Brazil in June 1992 to address major environment and development priorities for the initial period 1993–2000 and leading into the 21st century.

The UN General Assembly resolved in December 1989 to convene a Conference on Environment and Development and later urged that representation at the Conference be at the level of head of State or Government. In fact, over the two decades since the UN Conference on the Human Environment in 1972 in Stockholm and the subsequent creation of the *UN Environment Programme (UNEP), concern had been growing over the continued deterioration of the environment as well as the lack of adequate development in the developing countries. In calling for UNCED, it was generally agreed that poverty and environmental degradation were closely interrelated and that environmental protection in developing countries had to be considered as an integral part of the development process.

The 1987 report of the World Commission on Environment and Development (Brundtland Commission) had recognized that international environmental protection measures have to take into account current global imbalances in production and consumption and that development has to be environmentally sound and sustainable. The concept of sustainable development has been defined by UNEP as 'development that meets the needs of the present without compromising the ability of future generations to meet their own needs and does not imply in any way encroachment upon national sovereignty'.

The Preparatory Committee (PrepCom) of the Conference, open to all members of the UN and members of the specialized agencies as well as observers, held its first session in Nairobi in 1990, its second and third sessions in Geneva in 1991, and its fourth session in New York in 1992.

At the Rio Conference, the industrial countries acknowledged that they placed the heaviest strains in world resources and bore a special responsibility to repair the damage but made no substantial financial commitments to help the developing countries overcome their environmental problems. Strong support was given, however, to the *Global Environment Facility (GEF) jointly managed by the *World Bank, the *UN Development Programme (UNDP) and UNEP. More than 150 countries signed the UN Framework Convention on Climate Change and the Convention on Biological Diversity; the USA was the only major industrial country not to sign the latter.

A non-binding Statement of Principles on the management, conservation and sustainable development of forests was also signed together with the Rio Declaration on Environment and Development (proclaiming 27 Principles) and the Agenda 21 action plan. Agenda 21 provides a blueprint for action in all areas relating to the sustainable development of the planet from now until the 21st century; although the document is of a non-binding character, it is expected to have a significant influence on government actions. Moreover, a high-level Commission on Sustainable Development, acting as the main subsidiary organ of the General Assembly and the Economic and Social Council, will be established to integrate environment and development issues and to monitor countries' record on environmental protection.

Secretary-General: Maurice Strong
Headquarters: 160 Route de Florissant, P.O. Box 80, 1231 Conches, Switzerland (telephone: 789 1676; fax: 789 3536)

United Nations Conference on Trade and Development (UNCTAD).

The Conference aims to formulate a co-ordinated set of principles and policies, to be adopted by all its member countries, designed to accelerate progress towards self-sustaining growth of the economy in developing nations. The concern of the Conference covers the entire spectrum of policies, in both industrialized and developing areas, which influence the external trade and payments and related development aspects of developing countries.

The establishment of the Conference as a permanent organ of the UN General Assembly dates back to December 1964. The original session of the Conference had been convened earlier that year within the framework of the UN Development Decade of the 1960s, launched by a General Assembly resolution in December 1961. The General Assembly had also approved a resolution on international trade as the primary instrument for promoting economic progress in the less developed countries; the resolution envisaged an international conference on trade problems, which was eventually held in Geneva between March and June 1964. Participation was open to all countries belonging to the UN, its specialized agencies or the *International Atomic Energy Agency (IAEA). Proposals for continuing the work of the Conference through some kind of institutional arrangement led to its establishment as an autonomous body responsible to the General Assembly. Membership of the Conference now totals about 180 countries.

According to the provisions set forth in the General Assembly resolution adopted in December 1964, the principal functions of the Conference are: to promote international trade, especially with a view to accelerating economic development and taking into account the tasks performed by existing international organizations; to formulate principles and policies on international trade and related problems of economic development; to make proposals for putting the said principles and policies into effect and to take other relevant steps, having regard to differences in economic systems and stages of development; to review and facilitate the co-ordination of activities of other institutions within the UN system; to initiate action, where appropriate, in co-operation with the competent organs of the UN for the negotiation and adoption of multilateral legal instruments; to be available as a centre for harmonizing the trade and related development policies of governments and regional economic groupings.

The Conference generally meets every four years in the capital of a member country. After its original meeting in 1964, the Conference held the second session in New Delhi (1968), the third in Santiago, Chile (1972), the fourth in Nairobi (1976), the fifth in Manila (1979), the sixth in Belgrade (1983), the seventh in Geneva (1987), and the eighth in Cartagena de Indias, Colombia (1992). The Cartagena session took far-reaching decisions with a view to revitalizing the Conference and streamlining its institutional structure.

The Trade and Development Board, which all Conference members may join, is a permanent organ which normally meets twice a year and assures continuity of work between sessions of the Conference. The Cartagena session has strengthened the political functions of the Board and specified the issues to be discussed in the two annual sessions, the first session being devoted to macroeconomic policies and interdependence, and the second to trade policies, structural adjustments and economic reforms.

At the Cartagena session the decision was taken to suspend the activities of the various intergovernmental Committees (also open to the participation of all members) which reported to the Board and adopted policy recommendations in specific areas. However, two bodies have been maintained: the Special Committee monitoring the Generalized System of Preferences and the Group of Experts reviewing the impact of restrictive business practices on the exports of developing countries. Four Permanent Committees have been established dealing respectively with commodities, the elimination of poverty (introducing a new aspect in the activities of the Conference), economic co-operation among developing countries, and the promotion of services in the developing countries. Five *ad hoc* working groups have also been set up to focus on: investments and financial flows; trade efficacy; privatization; trade opportunities; and interdependence between investments and transfer of technology. The Conference has a permanent Secretariat headed by a Secretary-General and located in Geneva. A Liaison Office is maintained at UN Headquarters in New York.

Despite rivalries with other international bodies such as the *General Agreement on Tariffs and Trade (GATT) and serious problems of co-ordination, the Conference has made sustained efforts towards the realization of the goals of the UN Development Decades, the redefinition of the international economic agenda and the negotiation of a number of agreements which have represented a significant evolution of governmental policies. The Conference has become more and more involved in the analysis of broad economic issues and financial problems in a growing effort to move beyond the stage of merely enunciating general principles. In particular, it has recommended measures with a view to: expanding and diversifying the exports of goods and services of developing countries; stabilizing and strengthening the international commodity markets on which most developing countries depend for export earnings; enhancing the export capacity of developing countries through mobilization of domestic and external resources, including development assistance and foreign investment; promoting appropriate national trade and transport policies; alleviating the impact of debt on the economies of the developing countries and reducing the debt burden; providing special support to the 'least developed countries', a category currrently comprising about 50 of the world's poorest and most vulnerable countries; fostering the expansion of trade and economic co-operation among developing countries.

One of the major endeavours of the Conference is the Integrated Programme for Commodities (IPC) which basically aims to secure remunerative, equitable and stable prices for the primary commodities on which developing countries depend heavily for export earnings. Negotiations on individual commodity agreements are carried out within this framework. In April 1982 the International Rubber Agreement became the first agreement on a new commodity under the IPC to come into operation, providing for a buffer stock and limitations on price fluctuations. An International Agreement on Jute and Jute Products, aimed at promoting research and development and improving marketing, was adopted in October 1982. An International Tropical Timber Agreement, concentrating on conservation of supplies rather than price stabilization, was concluded in November 1983. New agreements were concluded for natural rubber in 1987, for cocoa in 1986 and for olive oil also in 1986. Progress on agreements concerning other commodities has, on the whole, been fairly limited while the operation of existing agreements has encountered serious difficulties. Also envisaged by IPC are measures intended to increase the demand for natural products facing competition from synthetics and to expand the processing of raw materials in developing countries. A key factor of IPC is a Common Fund, designed primarily to finance buffer stocks of certain commodities in order to reduce or eliminate the wide fluctuations in commodity prices. Articles of agreement for establishing the Common Fund for Commodities were adopted in June 1980, after four years of negotiations, and opened for signature the following October. The agreement came into effect in 1989 after ratification by 90 countries accounting for two-thirds of directly contributed capital. The Common Fund provides a capital of $470 million to support the functioning of international commodity agreements; voluntary contributions amounting to over $250 million have been made available for longer-term purposes such as research, market promotion and conservation of resources.

Another major effort of the Conference

is directed towards the expansion and diversification of the exports of manufactured and semi-manufactured products of developing countries. An important agreement was reached in 1970 on the introduction, for a ten-year period, of a Generalized System of Preferences (GSP) designed to provide developing countries with wider export opportunities beyond the traditional reciprocity and most-favoured-nation rules. The GSP has been subsequently reviewed and extended and currently covers about $50 billion of annual exports from developing countries.

A Set of Multilaterally Agreed Equitable Principles and Rules for the Control of Restrictive Business Practices, including those of transnational corporations, which adversely affect international trade, especially that of developing countries, was adopted in April 1980. The Conference has also adopted an action programme on policies and measures for structural adjustment related to trade that involves both inter-industry and intra-industry specialization so as to enable developing countries to increase their share in world trade of manufactured goods. The relevant bodies of the Conference follow closely the issues that are of particular concern to developing countries in the Uruguay Round of multilateral trade negotiations conducted within the framework of GATT.

With regard to international financial issues, the Conference has sought to improve the terms and conditions of aid, as well as to increase its flow, to reduce the rising burden of debt service and to establish a reformed international monetary system consistent with the pressing needs of development. A resolution was adopted in 1978 for the retroactive adjustment of terms for the official development assistance debt of low-income countries; guidelines for international action in the area of debt rescheduling were drafted in 1980. At its 1987 session the Conference recognized the need for greater flexibility in the rescheduling of debts though it proved impossible to reach a consensus on the increase of debt relief or the reduction of interest rates.

In the field of technology, lengthy negotiations on the establishment of an International Code of Conduct on the Transfer of Technology have been undertaken. Increasing emphasis is placed by the Conference on the promotion of trade expansion, economic co-operation and integration among developing countries, especially with regard to export credits, transportation, insurance and multinational production enterprises.

A substantial work programme has been undertaken in the field of shipping and ports and international shipping legislation and several Conventions have been concluded under the auspices of the Conference. The Convention on a Code of Conduct for Liner Conferences, adopted in 1974 and entered into force in 1983, provides for the national shipping lines of developing countries to participate on an equal footing with the shipping lines of developed countries; the Convention on the Carriage of Goods by Sea (Hamburg Rules) was adopted in 1978; the Convention on International Multimodal Transport of Goods, adopted in 1980, establishes a single liability regime for the carrying of goods entailing more than one mode of transport. The Conference investigates the implications of open-registry fleets for the merchant marines of developing countries; its efforts in this area led to the conclusion in 1986 of the Convention on Conditions for Registration of Ships which deals with the safety and working conditions aboard ships flying 'flags of convenience'.

Recommendations have been put forward by the Conference to meet the special needs of the least-developed, developing island and land-locked countries. The Statute of a Special Fund for Land-locked Developing Countries was approved by the General Assembly in December 1976 but total sums pledged were not deemed sufficient to enable the Fund to start operations. In 1981 the Conference serviced the special UN Conference on the Least Developed Countries which led to the adoption of the Substantial New Programme of Action (SNPA) for the 1980s for the Least Developed Countries. The targets contained in the SNPA were not met and another Conference, held in 1990 in Paris, adopted a new Programme of Action embodying commitments by both the developed and the developing nations. The International Trade Centre in Geneva is operated jointly by the Conference and by GATT. As an executing agency of the *UN Development Programme (UNDP), the Conference is also engaged in several technical assistance projects in developing countries.

The Cartagena session of 1992 has represented a turning point in the life of the Conference with the formulation of the basic concepts of a 'new partnership for development', as illustrated in two basic documents, a political declaration entitled 'The Spirit of Cartagena' and a document containing the decisions of the session entitled 'Commitments of Cartagena'. The restructuring of the Conference machinery, the adoption of more flexible rules and procedures, and the strengthening of the consultation and negotiation process at the intergovernmental level should lead to the elaboration of a system progressively more responsive to the requirements of developing nations.

Secretary-General: Kenneth K. S. Dadzie

Headquarters: Palais des Nations, 1211 Geneva 10, Switzerland (telephone: 734 6011; telex: 289696; fax: 733 6542)

Publications: *UNCTAD Bulletin* (six a year); *Trade and Development Report* (annually); *The Least Developed Countries Report* (annually)

References: A.K. Koul: *The Legal Framework of UNCTAD in the World Trade* (Leyden, 1977); UNCTAD: *The History of UNCTAD 1964–1984* (New York, 1985)

United Nations Development Programme (UNDP). The Programme is the world's largest organization in the field of multilateral technical assistance and is intended to help developing countries increase the wealth-producing capabilities of their natural and human resources.

The establishment of the Programme dates back to November 1965 when the UN General Assembly decided to merge two bodies which were then responsible for providing multilateral technical assistance – the UN Expanded Programme of Technical Assistance created in 1949 and the UN Special Fund set up in 1958. The new Programme entered into force in January 1966 as the central agency of the UN system for funding economic and social development projects around the world.

As a pragmatic field-oriented agency, the Programme is basically responsive only to clearly identified specific needs. Principal project activities include: locating, assessing and activating latent natural resources and other development assets; support for professional and vocational training; expansion of development-related scientific research and applied technologies; and strengthening of national and regional development planning. The scope of technical assistance has been broadened in order to cover all phases of project lifetime from earliest preparatory studies to long-range follow-up. Large scale decentralization of operations has considerably increased the Programme's speed and efficiency. Responsibility for project execution is being assigned increasingly to governments and institutions in the developing countries receiving assistance. The number of UN and non-UN bodies acting as executing agencies or otherwise participating in the work of the Programme is steadily growing. The Programme is responsible to the General Assembly to which it reports through the Economic and Social Council.

Assistance is rendered by the Programme only at the request of governments and in response to their priority needs, integrated into overall national and regional plans. Almost all projects are carried out by UN-related bodies, including all of the specialized agencies and the *International Atomic Energy Agency (IAEA), as well as the *UN Population Fund (UNFPA), the *UN Conference on Trade and Development (UNCTAD), the *UN Children's Fund (UNICEF), the *World Food Programme (WFP), the *UN High Commissioner for Refugees (UNHCR), the *UN Environment Programme (UNEP), the *UN Centre for Human Settlements (HABITAT) and other bodies.

The Programme's policy-making body is

the Governing Council, consisting of the representatives of 48 countries (of which 27 are developing and 21 are economically more advanced), which meets at yearly intervals; one-third of the membership changes each year. The Administrator is responsible for carrying out the activities of the Programme. Assistant administrators are in charge of the Regional Bureaux attached to the Programme's Secretariat in New York and covering Africa; Asia and the Pacific; the Arab States and Europe; and Latin America and the Caribbean; there is also a Division for Global and Interregional Programmes. A Division for Women and Development has been established in 1986 to ensure a fuller participation of women in UNDP-supported activities; in the same year a Division for Non-Governmental Organizations was also created with a view to encouraging a more effective partnership with NGOs in development work. A Management Development Programme started in 1989 in order to strengthen the management capacity of governments on a long-term basis. A Division for the Private Sector was set up in 1990.

Guidance and advice are provided by the Inter-Agency Consultative Board (IACB) composed of the UN Secretary-General and the heads of the agencies participating in the various activities. A Resident Representative of the Programme is stationed in almost every country receiving technical assistance and is responsible for supervising and co-ordinating field operations, advising the local government on the preparation of the country programme and approving most projects costing $400,000 or less (nearly 90 per cent of the total). The field offices of the Programme actually function as the primary presence of the UN in most developing countries.

The Programme, financed by voluntary contributions from UN member countries and participating agencies, has been gradually entrusted with resources for tasks well beyond its original mandate. Despite some serious cash flow crises, it has assumed increasing responsibility for meeting global as well as regional and national priorities in more than 150 developing countries, offering a variety of services not provided by other bodies, and for co-ordinating the UN development system. There are about 7000 projects currently in operation in agriculture, industry, education, power production, transport, communications, health, public administration, housing, trade and related fields.

Countries receiving assistance from the Programme are allocated an indicative planning figure (IPF) for a five-year period. The IPF is based on a formula which takes into consideration the per capita gross national product(GNP), the population size and several other criteria and represents the approximate total funding that a country may expect to receive. In the Fourth Programming Cycle, covering the period 1987–91, 80 per cent of the resources available were devoted to the poorest developing countries, with a per capita GNP of $750 or less; within this group, countries with a GNP of less than $375 were given particular regard. For the Fifth Programming Cycle (1992–96), 87 per cent of the funds will be reserved for countries with per capita GNP of $750 or less, and 55 per cent of these funds for the 41 countries officially designated as least-developed. The Programme also participates in emergency relief operations.

The Programme administers a number of special purpose funds and programmes. The UN Capital Development Fund (UNCDF), established in 1966 and fully operational since 1974, assists the least-developed countries by supplementing existing sources of capital assistance by means of grants and loans on concessionary terms; all projects are designed to minimize external dependence and ensure sustainability. The execution of projects is usually entrusted to local institutions with a view to promoting grassroots self-help activities.

The UN Revolving Fund for Natural Resources Exploration (RFNRE), established in 1974, provides risk capital to help developing countries carry out exploration of potentially high-return natural resources (particularly minerals); contributing governments commit themselves to make replenishment contributions to the Fund when the projects which have been financed lead to commercial production.

The UN Sudano-Sahelian Office (UNSO) was established in 1973 to help eight countries of the Sahel region carry out their programmes for recovery from drought; in 1978 the mandate of the Office was expanded to cover 14 additional African countries and to assist in the implementation of the Plan of Action to Combat Desertification. Projects are financed in part by the UN Trust Fund for Sudano-Sahelian Activities.

The UN Fund for Science and Technology for Development (UNFSTD), created in 1986, has been given responsibilities and resources formerly attributed to the UN Financing System for Science and Technology for Development. The latter had been set up in 1982 to finance a broad range of activities intended to strengthen the endogenous scientific and technological capacities of developing countries.

The UN Development Fund for Women (UNIFEM) has continued since 1985 on a regular basis the activities of the Voluntary Fund for the UN Decade for Women, established by the General Assembly in 1975 on the occasion of the proclamation of the period 1976-85 as the UN Decade for Women; the Fund supports innovative activities benefiting women, such as credit funds, small scale group enterprises and training in work-saving and fuel-conserving technologies.

The UN Volunteers (UNV) programme was established by the General Assembly in 1971 and remains the only volunteer-sending programme in the UN system, supplying at modest cost middle-level skills, particularly in the least-developed countries. The volunteers currently encompass about 150 professions and serve in both UNDP and UN-assisted projects, as well as development programmes carried out directly by host countries. Over 2000 volunteers from both developed and developing countries currently serve in over 110 nations.

Administrator: William H. Draper III

Headquarters: One UN Plaza, New York, N.Y. 10017, USA (telephone: 906 5000; telex: 236286 – 422862)

Publications: *Annual Report*; *Human Development Report* (annually since 1990); *World Development* (every two months); *Co-operation South* (quarterly)

United Nations Educational, Scientific and Cultural Organization (UNESCO). The basic aim of the Organization is to contribute to peace and security by promoting collaboration among nations through education, science, culture and communication in order to further respect for justice, for the rule of law and for the human rights and fundamental freedoms.

The Constitution of the Organization, adopted at a Conference convened by the government of the UK in association with the government of France in November 1945 in London, came into force in November 1946, after 20 signatories had deposited their instruments of acceptance; it has been amended on several occasions. The present membership includes about 160 countries plus a few associate members; in the early 1980s, the USA, the UK and Singapore left the Organization.

In order to realize its purposes the Organization: collaborates in the work of advancing the mutual knowledge and understanding of peoples through all means of mass communication and to that end recommends such international agreements as may be necessary; gives fresh impulse to popular education and to the spread of culture by collaborating with member countries, at their request, in the development of educational activities and by suggesting educational methods; maintains, increases and diffuses knowledge by conserving the world's inheritance of books, works of art and monuments of history and science, by encouraging co-operation among nations in all branches of intellectual activity and by initiating methods calculated to give the people of all countries access to the printed and published materials produced by any of them. All action is to be carried out according to the principle of preserving the independence, integrity and fruitful diversity of the cultures and educational systems of the member countries.

The activities of the Organization fall into three main categories: international intellectual co-operation; operational assistance; and promotion of peace. This implies *inter alia*: expanding and guiding education in order to enable the people of every country to take their own development in hand more effectively; help in establishing the scientific and technological foundations through which every country can make better use of its own resources; encouragement of national cultural values and the preservation of cultural heritage so as to derive maximum advantage from modernization without the loss of cultural identity and diversity; development of communication for the balanced flow of information and of information systems for the universal pooling of knowledge; prevention of discrimination in education and improvement of access for women to education; and promotion of studies and research on conflicts and peace, violence and obstacles to disarmament, and the role of international law and organizations in building peace.

Membership of the UN automatically carries with it the right to membership of the Organization; countries that do not belong to the UN may be admitted to the Organization, upon recommendation of the Executive Board, by a two-thirds majority vote of the General Conference. Territories not responsible for the conduct of international relations are eligible for associate membership, provided an application is made on their behalf by the authority in charge of international relations. Any member, either full or associate, may withdraw from the Organization by notice addressed to that effect to the Director-General; such notice takes effect on 31 December of the year following that during which the notice was given.

The Organization adopts recommendations, by a simple majority, and international conventions by a two-thirds majority, each member country being under the obligation to submit these to its competent authorities within one year. Moreover, each member country is bound to report periodically to the Organization on its laws, regulations and statistics in the educational, scientific and cultural field as well as on the action taken with regard to recommendations and conventions.

The institutional machinery comprises a General Conference, an Executive Board and a Secretariat. It is for the General Conference, as the supreme governing body, to determine the policies and the main lines of work of the Organization and to decide on programmes submitted to it by the Executive Board. Ordinary sessions of the General Conference are held every two years with the participation of representatives from each member country. Intergovernmental conferences on education, the sciences and humanities or the dissemination of knowledge may be convened by the General Conference. The Executive Board consists of 50 members elected by the General Conference and acting under its authority. It meets at least two times a year and is responsible for supervising the execution of the programme of work adopted by the Conference. Although members of the Executive Board represent their respective governments, they exercise the powers delegated to them by the General Conference on behalf of the Conference as a whole. The chief administrative officer and head of the Secretariat is the Director-General who is nominated by the Executive Board and appointed by the General Conference for a renewable six-year term; he is empowered to formulate proposals for appropriate action by the Conference and the Board. Liaison Offices and Regional Offices for Education, Science and Technology, Culture and Communication exist in most areas served by the Organization. National Commissions or National Co-operating Bodies have been set up in most member countries to act as agencies of liaison between the Organization and the principal bodies interested in educational, scientific and cultural matters in each country.

Among the bodies operating within the Organization's framework, mention should be made of the following: the International Institute for Educational Planning (IIEP), set up in 1963 to serve as a world centre for advanced training and research, which is legally and administratively part of UNESCO and is located in Paris (7–9 rue Eugène Delacroix; telephone: 4504 2822; telex: 640032; fax: 4072 8366); the International Bureau of Education (IBE), founded in 1925 and a part of UNESCO since 1969, providing information on developments and innovations in education and based in Geneva (P.O. Box 199; telephone: 798 1455; telex: 415771; fax: 798 1486); the Intergovernmental Committee for Physical Education and Sport (ICPES), established in 1978 to further development and international co-operation in this area and located in Paris (7 place de Fontenoy).

The Organization is a separate, autonomous body related to the UN by a special agreement and enjoys the status of specialized agency bound to report annually to the UN Economic and Social Council. Effective working relationships have been established with other specialized intergovernmental organizations and agencies whose interests and activities are related to the Organization's purposes; any formal arrangements with such organizations or agencies are subject to the approval of the Executive Board. More than 400 non-governmental bodies maintain close relations with the Organization while some of them take part in the execution of projects.

The Organization's activities are funded through a regular budget provided by member countries and also through other sources, particularly the *UN Development Programme (UNDP). The education programme is based on an overall policy regarding education as a lifelong process and seeking to promote the progressive application of the right to education for all and to improve the quality of education. Priority is increasingly being given to the rural areas of developing countries. The Organization was given responsibility for organizing the International Literacy Year (1990), proclaimed by the UN as a means of initiating a plan of action for the spread of literacy (based on regional literacy programmes that had already been established in the 1980s). In March 1990, the Organization sponsored with other UN agencies the World Conference on Education for All.

In the field of natural sciences and technology, the Organization is active in fostering international co-operation and has set up over the years a number of programmes, such as the Man and Biosphere Programme (MAB) for the solution of practical problems related to environmental resource management; the International Hydrological Programme (IHP) dealing with the scientific aspects of water resources assessment and management; the International Geological Correlation Programme (IGCP), run jointly with the International Union of Geological Sciences; the Intergovernmental Informatics Programme for the promotion of co-operation between developed and developing countries in the field of computer sciences; and UNISIST which ensures worldwide co-operation with regard to scientific and technological information for development. The International Oceanographic Commission encourages scientific investigation into the nature and resources of the oceans. At the regional and subregional level, ministerial conferences are periodically organized to consider science and technology policy as well as the application of science and technology to development. Assistance is also provided at the national level in order to enable individual member countries to carry out training and research programmes and projects, such as those concerning the use of small-scale energy sources for rural and dispersed populations. The social and human sciences programme intends to encourage the development of the social sciences throughout the world by strengthening national and regional institutions; other two programmes concern activities dealing with human rights and peace.

The World Heritage Programme, launched in 1978, is aimed at protecting landmarks of outstanding universal value, in accordance with the 1972 Convention Concerning the Protection of the World Cultural and Natural Heritage, by providing financial aid for restoration, technical assistance, training and management planning. The 'World Heritage List' currently includes over 300 sites all over the world. The International Fund for the Promotion of Culture, set up in 1974, has provided assistance for a great number of projects including translations, recordings and exhibitions.

In the field of communication, the Organization aims to promote a free flow and a wider and better balanced exchange of information among individuals, communities and countries, and lays increasing stress upon the role of the mass media in advancing international understanding and peace. Programmes are being implemented at national, subregional and regional level in order to expand and strengthen the information and communication systems of developing countries. At the General Conference in October 1980 a New World Information and Communication Order (NWICO), including plans for an international code of journalist ethics and for the 'licensing' of journalists, was approved, despite strong objections from the USA and the UK. Following the adoption of NWICO, the Intergovernmental Programme for the Development of Communication (IPDC) was set up and funds were granted for the implementation of regional and international projects.

In late 1983, the USA (which provided around 25 per cent of the Organization's budget) announced its intention to withdraw alleging: political bias against the West; endemic hostility toward the institutions of a free society and decreasing attention to individual human rights; widespread mismanagement; and excessive budget growth. The Organization's Executive Board then appointed a 13-member committee to investigate allegations and recommend reforms. The US withdrawal became effective at the end of 1984; in January 1985 the USA established an Observer Mission at UNESCO. The UK and Singapore gave notice in 1984 and withdrew at the end of 1985. In response, reforms have been undertaken with a view to restructuring the Organization and its activities; however, the reforms are still considered not sufficient by the governments of the UK and the USA which do not seem to envisage rejoining the Organization in the near future.

Director-General: Federico   Mayor Zaragoza

Headquarters: 7 Place de Fontenoy, 75700 Paris, France (telephone: 4568 1000; telex: 204461; fax: 4567 1690)

Publications: *UNESCO Courier* (monthly); *Prospects* (quarterly); *International Social Science Journal* (quarterly); *Impact of Science on Society* (quarterly); *World Education Report* (every two years)

References: D.G. Partan: *Documentary Study of the Politicization of UNESCO* (Boston, Mass., 1975); R. Hoggart: *An Idea and its Servants: UNESCO from Within* (New York, 1978); A. Mahtar M'Bow: *From Concertation to Consensus: UNESCO and the Solidarity of Nations* (Paris, 1979); P.J. Hajnal: *Guide to UNESCO* (Dobbs Ferry, New York, 1983); C. Wells: *The UN, UNESCO and the Politics of Knowledge* (London, 1987); V.-Y. Ghebali: *UNESCO Adrift: Crisis and Reform in an International Organization* (London, 1988); W. Preston, Jr., E.S. Herman and H.I. Schiller: *Hope and Folly: The United States and UNESCO, 1945–1985* (Minneapolis, 1989)

United Nations Environment Programme (UNEP). The purpose of the Programme is to provide machinery for international co-operation in matters relating to the human environment; it monitors significant changes in the environment and encourages and co-ordinates sound environmental practices.

The Programme was established in 1972 by the UN General Assembly, following the recommendations adopted at the UN Conference on the Human Environment held in Stockholm in June of that year. The Conference adopted the Declaration on the Human Environment proclaiming the right of human beings to a quality environment and their responsibility to protect and improve the environment for future generations. It also adopted an Action Plan, containing over 100 recommendations for measures to be taken by governments and international organizations to protect life, control contamination from man-made pollutants and improve cities and other human settlements.

According to the Stockholm Conference Action Plan, the Programme is intended to cover the major environmental issues facing both the developed and the developing areas of the world such as the ecology of rural and urban settlements, the relationship between environment and development, natural disasters, and the preservation of terrestrial ecosystems. It is also responsible for promoting environmental law and education and training for the management of the environment. A number of specific tasks have been assigned to the Programme by the relevant UN bodies and by UN-sponsored meetings and conferences. The various plans and projects drawn up within the framework of the Programme are usually put into practice by governments and other UN agencies.

The basic policy guidelines concerning the development and co-ordination of environment activities within the UN system are adopted by the Programme's Governing Council, composed of representatives from 58 countries (16 African; 13 Asian; 10 Latin American; 6 Eastern European; 13 Western European and other countries) elected by the General Assembly for four-year terms. An important role in the actual co-ordination of environmental action is played by the Secretariat whose headquarters are in Nairobi, Kenya, with liaison and regional offices in Bahrain, Bangkok, Geneva, Mexico City, and New York. The Secretariat is also charged with the administration of the Environment Fund, established in 1973 to encourage voluntary additional financing for new initiatives relating to the environment. The Executive Director of the Programme acts as *ex officio* chairman of the Environment Coordination Board, which consists of the heads of all bodies responsible for the implementation of environmental programmes within the UN system.

The Programme has substantially contributed towards focusing world concern on the growing dangers to the human environment. At a special session, in 1982, the Governing Council reviewed the achievements and shortcomings that had occurred in the human environment since the Stockholm Conference and discussed the Programme's guidelines for the 1980s. The Programme played a significant role in the preparation of the *UN Conference on Environment and Development (UNCED) held in Rio de Janeiro in June 1992; the meeting aimed at a restructuring of UN activities in the field of environmental protection and the adoption of long-term integrated environmental strategies leading to sustainable development.

Under the Stockholm Conference Action Plan, the Programme co-ordinates 'Earthwatch', an international surveillance network consisting of three main components. The Global Environmental Monitoring System (GEMS), which began in 1975, is based on a network of stations providing information on the ecological state of the world and on changes in climate, water pollution and tropical forests; to convert the data collected into usable information, a global resources information data-base (GRID) was established in 1985. The INFOTERRA programme is a computerized referral service to sources in about 130 countries for environmental information and expertise; it is responsible for the annual compilation of a Directory of Sources. The International Register of Potentially Toxic Chemicals works through a network of national correspondents to provide scientific and regulatory information on chemicals that may be dangerous to health and the environment.

Research is being carried out on the 'outer limits' of tolerance of the biosphere and its subsystems to the demands made on it by human activities; studies have been undertaken to assess the effect of carbon dioxide emission on climate, the 'greenhouse effect'. In 1985 the Programme completed a study on the effects of chlorofluorocarbon (CFC) production on the layer of ozone in the earth's atmosphere and stressed the need to limit such production. The international Convention for the Protection of the Ozone Layer was adopted at a Conference held in Vienna in 1985 and represented an important stage in the Programme's efforts. A protocol to the Convention – adopted in September 1987 and known as the 'Montreal Protocol' – commits participating countries to reduce production of CFCs by 50 per cent by the year 2000. Further negotiations have been arranged by the Programme with a view to phasing out completely production of CFCs by 2000. In order to prevent the 'dumping' of wastes from industrialized countries in developing countries, the

Programme promoted the adoption in 1989 of the Basel Convention on the Control of Transboundary Movements of Hazardous Wastes and their Disposal.

The Programme has been entrusted by the 1977 UN Conference on Desertification with the responsibility for carrying out the Plan of Action drawn up to combat the spread of deserts, particularly in the Sudano-Sahelian region; assistance has been provided for the formation of regional networks of non-governmental agencies engaged in anti-desertification activities in Africa, Latin America, and Asia and the Pacific. The Programme is also actively co-operating with the UN Centre for Human Settlements (Habitat) to combat deteriorating environmental standards in towns. The World Conservation Strategy was officially launched in March 1980. The Programme actively supports wildlife conservation in collaboration with the International Union for the Conservation of Nature and Natural Resources (IUCN). The Programme administers the Convention on International Trade in Endangered Species of Wild Fauna and Flora (CITES) which has over 100 contracting parties; a ban on international trade in ivory has been adopted by a CITES-sponsored conference in October 1989.

Substantial efforts are being made under the auspices of the Programme in the struggle against marine pollution, particularly in the Mediterranean; a convention and two protocols were signed to that effect in Barcelona in 1976. A number of priority programmes as well as a long-term study of the development plans of the Mediterranean governments are under way. A treaty for the control of pollution of inland origin was concluded in May 1980 in Athens under the sponsorship of the Programme by most of the countries bordering the Mediterranean. Another important treaty for the protection of natural resources and the marine environment was signed in April 1982 in Geneva. Several other countries outside the Mediterranean are developing various forms of close co-operation against marine pollution within the framework of the Programme. Action plans have been adopted for: the seas

around Kuwait; the Caribbean; the West and Central African region; the East African region; the East Asian region; the Red Sea and the Gulf of Aden; the South Pacific; and the South-East Pacific. As regards the oceans, the Programme collects data on pollution and completed in 1984, jointly with the *Food and Agriculture Organization (FAO), a global Plan of Action for the Conservation, Management and Utilization of Marine Mammals.

Executive Director: Dr Mostafa K. Tolba

Headquarters: P.O. Box 30552, Nairobi, Kenya (telephone: 333930; telex: 22068; fax: 520711)

Publications: *Annual Report of the Executive Director*; *State of the Environment Report* (annually); *Our Planet* (quarterly); *Environmental Events Record* (monthly); studies, reports and technical guidelines

United Nations High Commissioner for Refugees (UNHCR).

The main purposes of the Office of the High Commissioner are to provide international legal protection for refugees, to seek permanent solutions to their problems through voluntary repatriation, resettlement in other countries or integration into the country of present residence, as well as to extend material assistance.

The Office was established by the UN General Assembly in 1950, with effect from January 1951, originally for three years. Since 1954 the mandate has been renewed for successive five-year periods.

According to the Statute of the Office, refugees are persons outside their country of nationality because they have a well-founded fear of persecution by reason of race, religion, nationality or political opinion and, because of such fear, are unable or unwilling to avail themselves of the protection of the government of their nationality. Since 1971 the Office has been empowered to carry out a number of special operations for the benefit of displaced persons who are not refugees according to the above definition but find themselves in similar circumstances and are in need of international aid. Under the terms of the resolutions adopted by the

General Assembly and the Economic and Social Council over the past few years, the importance of the 'essential humanitarian task' performed by the Office 'in the context of man-made disasters, in addition to its original functions' has been expressly recognized.

The primary function of the Office lies in the provision of legal protection on the basis of the main international instrument in the field, that is the 1951 UN Convention relating to the Status of Refugees which defines the rights of refugees and lays down a minimum standard of treatment to which they are entitled with regard to employment, education, residence, freedom of movement and security against 'refoulement', that is forcible return to a country where their life or liberty might be in danger. A Protocol extending the scope of the 1951 Convention to new groups of refugees entered into effect in 1967. More than 100 countries have acceded to the 1951 Convention and/or the 1967 Protocol. International conventions have been adopted at the regional level to define specific rights and duties of refugees.

The basic policy guidelines concerning the activities of the Office are given by the General Assembly or the Economic and Social Council to the High Commissioner, elected by the General Assembly on the nomination of the Secretary-General and charged with current operations. The High Commissioner is responsible to the General Assembly to which he reports through the Economic and Social Council. Guidance and advice with respect to material assistance programmes are provided by the Executive Committee of the High Commissioner's Programme, based in Geneva and composed of the representatives of 43 countries, members and non-members of the UN. Sessions are held at yearly intervals and informal consultations between sessions are customarily held by the High Commissioner with representatives of UN member countries. Besides the High Commissioner's Office there are a Division of Refugee Law and Doctrine and five Regional Bureaus: Africa; Asia and Oceania; Europe and North America; Latin America and the Caribbean; South-West Asia, the Middle East and North Africa. The High Commissioner has Representatives and Charges de Mission in the field, covering over 100 countries.

The basic administrative costs of the Office as well as legal protection activities are covered by the regular budget of the UN while material assistance activities and related programme support costs are financed in their entirety by voluntary contributions from both governmental and non-governmental sources; special operations account for a large percentage of these contributions. The overall financial requirements of the Office are steadily growing as a result of the greatly expanded number of persons of concern to the High Commissioner, including returnees and groups of displaced persons in 'refugee-like situations'. Recurrent financial constraints severely curtail the ability of the Office to provide adequate protection and assistance for refugees.

Refugees and displaced persons in the world number more than 10 million, about half of them children, the greatest concentration being in Africa where they live in camps and settlements administered by the Office. The Office is also heavily involved in assistance and protection for refugees of South-East Asia and co-operates with governments and voluntary groups and organizations in housing and maintaining these persons. Specific measures, made possible by increased offers for the placement of refugees as well as by additional pledges in cash and in kind, are being implemented to ease the difficulties facing Indo-Chinese refugees, many of whom are 'boat people'. Major efforts in Latin America are aimed at finding resettlement opportunities for refugees or organizing the reinstallation and rehabilitation of the returnees, especially in Central America. In separate actions under its resolution 'International co-operation to avert new flows of refugees' of December 1980, the General Assembly expressed grave concern over the increasing flow of refugees in many parts of the world and invited all members to convey to the Secretary-General their comments and suggestions. Major problems resulted in the 1980s from the growing numbers of political refugees (particularly from Africa, the Middle East and the Indian sub-continent) seeking asylum in Europe. Canada and the USA remain major countries of resettlement for refugees and the Office extends counselling and legal services for asylum-seekers in these countries. The Office was awarded the Nobel Peace Prize in 1954 and 1981.

High Commissioner: Sadako Ogata

Headquarters: 154 rue de Lausanne, Geneva, Switzerland (telephone: 739 8111; telex: 412972; fax: 739 8449)

Publications: *UNHCR Report* (annually); *Refugees* (monthly)

United Nations Industrial Development Organization (UNIDO). The purpose of the Organization is to promote and accelerate the industrialization of the developing countries through direct assistance and mobilization of national and international resources, with particular emphasis on the manufacturing sector. The Organization is entrusted with the task of co-ordinating all activities undertaken by the UN family of agencies in the field of industrial development. It also provides a forum for consultation and negotiations among developing countries and between developing and industrialized countries.

Established as an organ of the UN General Assembly in November 1966, the Organization became operational in January 1967 as an action-oriented body, replacing the Centre for Industrial Development which had been operating within the UN Secretariat since July 1961. The conflict of views between the developing and the developed countries over the most suitable institutional arrangements for intensifying and concentrating UN efforts for the industrialization of the developing world delayed the establishment of the new Organization for a number of years. A consensus was only reached by the mid-1960s for the creation of an autonomous body within the UN. In 1975, the Second General Conference of the member countries stressed the urgent need to increase and expand the autonomy and functions of the Organization and recommended its conversion to the status of a

UN specialized agency. The recommendation was subsequently endorsed by the UN General Assembly and several sessions were held to draft a Constitution, which was eventually adopted by consensus in April 1979 in Vienna. The Constitution entered into force in June 1985 and in January 1986 the Organization became the 16th specialized agency related to the UN.

According to the Constitution of April 1979, the primary aim of the Organization is to promote industrial development in the developing countries. Activities cover macro-economic and micro-economic aspects of industrial development. At macro-economic level, questions are considered concerning: the formulation of industrial development policies; application of modern methods of production, programming and planning; building and strengthening of institutions and administration in the matter of industrial technology; co-operation with UN regional economic commissions in assisting regional planning of industrial development within the framework of regional and subregional economic groupings; recommendation of special measures to accelerate the growth of the less advanced among the developing countries. At micro-economic level, assistance is provided with regard to problems of technical and economic feasibility, external financing for specific industrial projects, product development and design, management, marketing, quality and research.

The Organization is also responsible for proposing measures for the improvement of the international system of industrial property, with a view to accelerating the transfer of technical knowledge to developing countries and strengthening the role of patents consistent with national interests as an incentive to industrial innovations. Technical assistance usually consists of expert services, but sometimes involves the supply of equipment or fellowships for training, such as in management or production. Studies and research programmes, designed to facilitate and support operational activities, include in particular the compilation, analysis, publication and dissemination of information concerning various aspects of the process of industrialization, such as industrial technology, investment, financing, production, management techniques, programming and planning. Seminars and other specialist meetings are organized on a wide range of subjects related to industrial and technological development.

The work of the Organization is carried out by the following principal organs: the General Conference, the Industrial Development Board (IDB), the Programme and Budget Committee (PBC) and the Secretariat.

The General Conference, composed of one representative from each member country, normally meets once every two years to formulate overall policies, determine the programme of work and approve the budget. The Industrial Development Board, holding one regular session a year, serves as the governing body of the Organization. It is composed of 53 members (of which 33 from developing countries) elected by the General Conference for a three-year term. The Programme and Budget Committee is made up of 27 members elected by the General Conference for a two-year term. The Secretariat performs administrative functions under a Director-General appointed by the General Conference, upon the Board's recommendation, for a period of four years. There are five departments, each headed by a Deputy Director-General: Programme and Project Development; Industrial Operations; Industrial Promotion, Consultations and Technology; External Relations, Public Information, Language and Documentation Services; and Administration.

The Director-General has overall responsibility for administrative and research tasks as well as for all operational activities, including the activities executed by the Organization as a participating agency of the *UN Development Programme (UNDP). The Industrial and Technological Information Bank provides the relevant information on technologies developed or adapted for developing countries.

Co-operative arrangements link the Organization with several specialized agencies, the UN regional economic commissions, and certain intergovernmental and non-governmental bodies outside the UN system. The expansion of its network of field advisers in industrial development has enabled the Organization to improve co-ordination as well as to promote concerted action at the field level, particularly with the offices of the UNDP resident representatives.

The Organization's finance originally derived from the UNDP, the UN regular budget, the UN Regular Programme of Technical Assistance, and trust funds and contributions from various sources. In December 1976 the General Assembly decided to create the UN Industrial Development Fund to enable the Organization to meet more promptly and flexibly the growing needs of the developing countries. The Fund came into operation in January 1978 with pledges totalling $10 million. The Industrial Development Board remarked on the inadequacy of the amount pledged and therefore recommended a desirable annual funding level of $50 million; however, contributions continue to remain well below the target and there are also serious arrears on the part of some members. As from January 1986 the Organization, in keeping with its new status of specialized agency, has assumed full responsibility for its programme and budget based on assessed contributions of its member countries, currently numbering over 150.

Operational activities include the Special Industrial Services (SIS) Programme, intended to supplement other UN industrial development activities by providing short-term and emergency aid to help solve urgent technical problems. The Organization also provides assistance to developing countries to establish and strengthen research and training institutions, offers fellowships, and organizes study tours and in-plant group training programmes. To establish and increase links between potential investors and businessmen in developed countries and enterprises in developing nations, the Organization has set up Investment Promotion Offices in Cologne, Milan, Paris, Seoul, Tokyo, Vienna, Warsaw, Washington and Zurich.

The System of Consultations, introduced in 1977, is intended to help developing countries increase their share of total world production as much as possible. Representatives of government, labour, industry, consumer interests and financial institutions participate in the consultations with a view to establishing targets for the growth of production of a given product in both developed and developing countries. The Organization assisted in the creation of the International Centre for Genetic Engineering and Biotechnology, based in Trieste (Italy) and New Delhi (India), and linked with national centres.

Director-General: Domingo Siazon

Headquarters: Wagramerstrasse 5, P.O. Box 300, 1400 Vienna, Austria (telephone: 211310; telex: 135612; fax: 232156)

Publications: *Annual Report*; *UNIDO Newsletter* (monthly); *Industry and Development* (annual)

Reference: F. Plasil-Wenger: 'The UNIDO', *Journal of World Trade Law*, 1971, 188–207.

United Nations Institute for Training and Research (UNITAR)

The Institute aims to improve, by means of training and research, the effectiveness of the UN, in particular the maintenance of peace and security and the promotion of economic and social development.

Established in 1965 as an autonomous body within the framework of the UN, the Institute carries out training and research programmes. The training programme is intended for members of permanent missions to the UN and other diplomats, staff members of the specialized agencies and national officials of developing countries concerned with subjects related to the UN. Training is conducted at UN Headquarters in New York, in Geneva, and in the field. Activities include familiarization courses on current UN issues, seminars on the structure and organization of the UN and courses on the basic elements of multilateral diplomacy. The research programme is divided between studies concentrating on the short- and medium-term needs of

the UN and studies devoted to longer-term trends.

The Institute works under the overall policy direction of a Board of Trustees and is headed by an Executive Director. The Board consists of up to 30 members who are appointed by the UN Secretary-General for a three-year term. The UN Secretary-General and the Presidents of the General Assembly and the Economic and Social Council plus the Institute's Executive Director are *ex officio* members. Specialized agencies are represented appropriately at Board meetings, which are usually held once a year to set basic guidelines and to review and adopt the annual budget. The Executive Director, nominated by the Secretary-General after consultation with the Board, is responsible for the organization, direction, and administration of the Institute. He is assisted by the Directors of Training and Research, the Special Assistant to the Executive Director, the Secretary of the Board of Trustees and External Relations Coordinator, and the Administrative Officer. The Institute, whose headquarters are in New York with a branch office in Geneva, is supported by voluntary contributions from governments, inter-governmental organizations, foundations and others. Since the late 1980s the Institute has not received any grant from the UN regular budget as had been the case in the past. Co-operative links are maintained by the Institute with a number of institutions and research bodies.

The Institute has published several studies dealing with peace and security, international organization and development, the effectiveness of various parts of the UN system and aspects of regional co-operation. Under the 'Project on the Future', a continuous programme launched by the Institute in 1975, work is mainly devoted to two broad themes: policy choices related to a restructuring of international economic relations; and the meaning of physical limits and supply constraints in energy and natural resources. A major project on technology, domestic distribution and North-South relations is aimed at preparing a new model of economic growth connected with the socio-economic circumstances prevailing in developing countries.

Executive Director: Michel Doo Kingué

Headquarters: 801 United Nations Plaza, New York, N.Y. 10017, USA (telephone: 754 8621; telex: 232422)

Publications: *UNITAR News* (annually); *Important for the Future* (quarterly); *UNITAR Review on World Issues* (quarterly); periodic reports and studies on specific subjects

United Nations International Drug Control Programme (UNDCP). The Programme has been established by the UN General Assembly in December 1990 as the single body responsible for concerted international actions for drug abuse control.

The Programme integrates fully the structures and functions of the Division of Narcotic Drugs of the UN Secretariat, the secretariat of the *International Narcotics Control Board (INCB) and the *United Nations Fund for Drug Abuse Control (UNFDAC), with the aim of enhancing the effectiveness and efficiency of the UN structure for drug abuse control. In the light of the structural changes involved with the creation of the Programme, the functioning of the *UN Commission on Narcotic Drugs (CND) as a policy-making body will be adequately improved.

The Programme is headed by an Executive Director, appointed by the Secretary-General, who assumed office in March 1991. The Executive Director is in charge of the integration and restructuring of the various units involved in the process and enjoys exclusive responsibility for co-ordinating and providing effective leadership for all UN drug control activities with a view to ensuring coherence of actions within the Programme as well as co-ordination, complementarity and non-duplication of such activities across the UN system. He also has direct responsibility for the financial resources of UNFDAC as a fund for financing operational activities of the Programme, especially in developing countries.

The Programme is structured along the following lines: (a) treaty implementation, which integrates, with due regard to treaty arrangements, the functions of the secretariat of the INCB and the treaty implementation functions of the Division of Narcotic Drugs, taking into account the independent role of INCB; (b) policy implementation and research, with responsibility for implementing policy decisions of the relevant legislative bodies and conducting analytical work; and (c) operational activities, with responsibility for coordinating and carrying out the technical co-operation projects currently executed mainly by UNFDAC, the Division of Narcotic Drugs and the secretariat of INCB.

Executive Director: Giorgio Giacomelli

Location: Vienna International Centre, P.O. Box 500, 1400 Vienna, Austria (telephone: 21131–0; Telex: 135612; fax: 230 7002)

United Nations Population Fund (UNFPA). The purpose of the Fund, as a subsidiary organ of the UN General Assembly, is to provide additional resources to the UN system for technical co-operation activities in the population field.

The UN has been concerned with population problems since 1946, when the Population Commission of the Economic and Social Council was established with a view to improving demographic statistics. Subsequently, the efforts of the General Assembly to shift the emphasis to action-oriented programmes led to the creation in 1967 of the Trust Fund for Population Activities. The Trust Fund was charged with the promotion of population programmes and the extension of systematic and sustained assistance to developing countries, according to their requests. Renamed in 1969 the UN Fund for Population Activities (UNFPA), it officially became a Fund of the General Assembly in 1972 and was made a subsidiary organ of the General Assembly in 1979. In 1987 the name was changed to UN Population Fund but the existing acronym was retained.

A World Population Conference was held in Bucharest, Romania, in 1974 (designated as World Population Year) and adopted the World Population Plan of Action by consensus of 136 countries. An International Conference on Population was held in Mexico City in August 1984 to review and appraise the 1974 Plan of Action and to provide new directions for the coming decades on the integration of population with development.

The Fund is empowered to provide financial support, for periods ranging from three to five years, for national, regional and interregional projects concerning basic population data, population dynamics and policy, family planning, and information and education activities. The major areas covered by the financial assistance granted by the Fund include: (a) collection and analysis of data on population trends and structure; (b) study of the interrelationship between population and food demand, and other aspects of economic and social development; (c) formulation of appropriate population policies within the context of national development objectives; (d) direct support to national family planning programmes and establishment of demonstration and pilot projects; (e) training of personnel for research and operational activities and improvement of communication techniques; and (f) application of existing methods of fertility regulation and promotion of research in human reproduction.

Assistance is generally extended through the UN Regional Economic Commissions and member organizations of the UN system, although in some cases the Fund avails itself of the services of non-governmental organizations or acts as its own executing agency.

The basic guidelines concerning the activities of the Fund are adopted by its governing body, the Governing Council of the *UN Development Programme (UNDP), acting under the supervision of the UN Economic and Social Council. An important role is played by the Fund's Executive Director, based in New York, who is in charge of the general operation and maintains close links with recipient governments, relevant UN agencies and bodies, regional and subregional groups and non-governmental organizations to ensure effective co-ordination in population activities. The Executive Director has the rank of Under-Secretary-General of the UN. The Fund Deputy Representatives and Senior Advisers on Population, attached to the offices of UNDP Resident Representatives in the developing countries, provide assistance to governments in the formulation of requests for aid in the population field and are responsible for co-ordinating the work of the executing agencies operating in the geographical area within their competence.

The Fund has made a significant contribution towards focusing international attention on the different aspects of population problems and encouraging co-operative efforts to that effect in developing countries and territories. Comprehensive country agreements have been negotiated in order to implement national population programmes while hundreds of projects are being carried out at the regional level. A large number of projects are aimed at supporting national family planning activities; many other important projects are in the areas of collection of basic population data and communication and education.

The Fund aims to enhance the status of women and ensure that their needs are taken into account when development and population programmes are prepared. It also has special programmes on youth, on ageing, and on AIDS, involving national as well as regional seminars and training programmes. In November 1989, the Fund convened the International Forum on Population in the Twenty-First Century with the participation of representatives of about 80 countries and numerous UN and other agencies. The Forum adopted a declaration specifying a number of objectives to be attained by the year 2000, including an increase in the use of contraceptives, a reduction in early marriage and teenage pregnancy, and a reduction of infant as well as maternal mortality rates.

The Fund brings together potential donors and developing countries in need of support for population activities through a system of 'multi-bilateral' funding by: aiding a government in developing a project and seeking assistance from a donor to implement it; enlisting donor's help in the provision of expertise, supplies or funds; creating a trust fund to manage donors' contributions; or jointly financing a project with a donor. The Fund has selected a number of 'priority countries' whose per capita income and demographic structure indicate that they are most in need of population assistance.

Executive Director: Nafis Sadik

Headquarters: 220 East 42nd Street, New York, N.Y. 10017, USA (telephone: 963 1234; telex: 422031; fax: 370 0201)

Publications: *Annual Report*; *State of World Population Report* (annually); *Population* (monthly); *Inventory of Population Projects Around the World* (annually)

Reference: R.M. Salas: *International Population Assistance: The First Decade: A Look at the Concepts and Policies which have guided the UNFPA in its First Ten Years* (Oxford, 1979)

United Nations Relief and Works Agency for Palestine Refugees in the Near East (UNRWA). The Agency aims to provide direct relief, health, education and welfare services as well as long-term rehabilitation and vocational training for Palestine refugees in Jordan, Lebanon, Syria, the West Bank and the Gaza Strip.

Established as a subsidiary organ by a resolution of the UN General Assembly in December 1949, the Agency began operations in May 1950. Assistance was to be provided to those needy persons, residing in one of the 'host' countries of the Near East, whose normal residence had been in Palestine for a minimum of two years, before the 1948 conflict and who, as a result of the Arab-Israeli hostilities, had lost both their homes and their means of livelihood. The children and grandchildren of registered refugees were also, under certain conditions, eligible for assistance. After the renewal of hostilities in the Middle East in June 1967, the Agency was additionally empowered by the General Assembly to provide humanitarian aid, as far as practicable, on an emergency basis and as a temporary measure, for persons other than Palestine refugees who were newly displaced and in serious need of continued assistance. Assistance is also extended, at the request and on behalf of the government of Jordan, to displaced persons in eastern Jordan who are not registered refugees of 1948. The activities of the Agency in the territories of the West Bank and the Gaza Strip are carried out with the consent of the Israeli Government. The Agency's mandate has been renewed periodically by the General Assembly, most recently until June 1993.

A Commissioner-General is responsible for the Agency's operations (supervision, planning and budgeting), with the assistance of an Advisory Commission consisting of the representatives of 10 countries (Belgium, Egypt, France, Japan, Jordan, Lebanon, Syria, Turkey, the UK, and the USA). The headquarters are located in Vienna; a smaller office in Amman, Jordan, directs the education, health and relief staff. Field Offices exist in Amman, Beirut, Damascus, Gaza and Jerusalem, while Liaison Offices operate in Cairo and New York. Close co-operative links are maintained by the Agency with several UN bodies and specialized institutions such as the *World Health Organization (WHO) and the *UN Educational, Scientific and Cultural Organization (UNESCO).

The Agency depends to a very great extent on voluntary contributions, almost entirely on the part of governments, the remainder being provided by other sources such as voluntary groups and organizations, and business corporations. Since the mid-1970s worldwide inflation and failure of non-contributing UN member countries to respond to intensified solicitations of contributions from the Commissioner-General have adversely affected the various activities, bringing the Agency to the brink of substantially cutting or suspending programmes. Services included in the Agency's regular programmes are provided by a staff of about 18,000, most of whom are themselves Palestine refugees. In mid-1990 the registered refugee population numbered 2,400,000 (about half the estimated total number of Palestinians). Relief services concentrate on providing food and other welfare assistance to destitute refugees; this new programme replaces the general distribution of basic food rations which was discontinued in 1982. More than one-third of the total refugee population is living in 61 refugee camps, while the remaining refugees have settled in towns and villages already existing.

About 67,000 refugees were temporarily displaced and the Agency's services disrupted by continuing disturbances in Lebanon and by the Israeli military action in southern Lebanon in March 1978. An emergency programme was then launched by the Agency with the help of the *European Economic Community (EEC), several governments and voluntary organizations. As a consequence of the Israeli invasion of June 1982, over 150,000 persons were displaced and many schools, clinics and offices of the Agency were destroyed. An emergency operation was undertaken and extended until spring 1984, when food rations were suspended. Other emergency relief operations were undertaken in Lebanon in the second half of the 1980s. Serious problems also arose in the territories of the West Bank and the Gaza Strip where unrest broke out in December 1987 and has been continuing ever since; services in both territories have been often interrupted as curfews and other restrictive measures were imposed on camps. However, the reconstruction programme and other projects to ameliorate the living conditions of the refugees are continuing.

Commissioner-General: Ilter Türkmen

Headquarters: P.O. Box 700, 1400 Vienna, Austria (telephone: 26310; telex: 135310); P.O. Box 484, Amman, Jordan

Publications: *Annual Report of the Commissioner-General*; *Palestine Refugees Today* (quarterly newsletter); *UNRWA Report* (quarterly); *A Survey of United Nations Assistance to Palestine* (every two years)

Universal Postal Union (UPU). The aim of the Union is to secure the organization and improvement of the postal services and to promote the development of technical assistance and international collaboration. To this end, member countries are considered to form a single postal territory for the reciprocal exchange of letter post items; freedom of transit is guaranteed throughout the entire territory of the Union.

The Union is among the oldest intergovernmental organizations still in existence and has played a leading role in the field of international postal co-operation for well over a century. A Treaty concerning the Establishment of a General Postal Union (Berne Treaty) was signed in October 1874 in Berne, Switzerland, by the representatives of 20 European countries, joined by Egypt and the USA; the Treaty came into force in July 1875. The original name of General Postal Union was replaced by Universal Postal Union in 1878. The Union became a specialized agency in relationship with the UN under the terms of an agreement concluded in July 1947 and entered into effect in July 1948; a supplementary agreement was signed in July 1949.

The Postal Congress held in Vienna in 1964 brought about a major structural change by drawing up for the Union a separate and permanent basic Act (Constitution) not subject to revision at each subsequent Congress. The Constitution containing the organic rules of the Union was adopted in July 1964 and came into force in January 1966. It was amended by the Congresses held in 1969 (Tokyo), 1974 (Lausanne), and 1984 (Hamburg). The 1984 Universal Postal Convention of Hamburg entered into force in January 1986. The General Regulations embody the provisions ensuring the application of the Constitution and the working of the Union. For their part, the Universal Postal Convention and its Detailed Regulations establish the rules applicable throughout the international postal service and the provisions concerning the letter post services. All these Acts are binding on all member countries; since about 170 countries participate in the Union, the provisions embodied in the Acts affect almost the entire population of the world. Optional agreements, supplemented by the relevant regulations, govern the operation of postal services as regards the handling of insured values, parcels, postal money orders and cheques, account transfers, cash on delivery items, collection of bills, savings and subscriptions to newspapers and periodicals. The provisions of the Constitution authorize member countries to establish Restricted Unions and to conclude special agreements on the postal service. However, conditions for the public must not be less favourable than those laid down in the Acts of the Union. Relations are currently maintained by the Union with eight Restricted Unions.

The concept of letter post applies to the following categories of items: letters (including aerogrammes), postcards, printed matter, literature in raised relief for the blind, and small packets. Rates, maximum and minimum weight and size limits, as well as conditions of acceptance, are fixed according to the Universal Postal Convention. The Convention prescribes the methods for calculating and collecting transit charges (for letter post items passing through the territories of one or more countries) and terminal dues (that is the compensation payments which an administration that receives more letter post items than it sends has the right to collect from the dispatching administration). Regulations are also established with regard to the registered items service and the air conveyance of mail and of the objects such as infectious and radioactive substances whose transport requires special precautions.

Members of the UN may accede to the Union, in conformity with current provisions; any sovereign country not belonging to the UN may be admitted to the Union if the request is approved by at least two-thirds of the member countries. Each member country may withdraw from the Union by notice of denunciation of the Constitution given through diplomatic channels to the Swiss Government; withdrawal becomes effective one year thereafter.

The Universal Postal Congress, the Executive Council (EC), the Consultative Council for Postal Studies (CCPS) and the International Bureau are the main bodies of the Union. The Congress, composed of representatives of all member countries, is the supreme authority of the Union, usually meeting every five years. It reviews the Universal Postal Convention and its subsidiary agreements on the basis of proposals put forward by member countries, the Executive Council or the Consultative Council. An Extraordinary Congress may be convened at the request or with the consent of at least two-thirds of member countries. The Executive Council, whose creation dates back to the Paris Congress of 1947, consists of 40 members elected by Congress with due regard for equitable geographical representation and meets each year at the Union's headquarters in Berne. It ensures the continuity of the work of the Union between Congresses, maintains close contact with postal administrations, supervises to some extent the activities of the International Bureau, undertakes studies of administrative, legislative and legal problems of interest to the postal service, draws up proposals and makes recommendations to the Congress. It is also responsible for encouraging, supervising and co-ordinating international co-operation in the form of postal technical assistance and vocational training. The Consultative Council for Postal Studies is the successor to the Consultative Committee for Postal Studies which was created at the Ottawa Congress of 1957 and operated until the Tokyo Congress of 1969. The Consultative Council is composed of 35 members elected by the Congress for the period between one Congress and the next, normally five years, and in principle meets annually at the Union's headquarters. It is entrusted with carrying out studies of major problems affecting postal administrations in all member countries in the technical, operational and economic fields and in the sphere of technical co-operation. It also provides information and advice on these matters and examines teaching and training problems arising in the developing countries.

Since the establishment of the Union, a central office known as the International Bureau has functioned in Berne. Besides serving as the permanent secretariat of the Union, it provides liaison, information, consultation and certain financial services for postal administrations and acts as a focal point for the co-ordination and execution of technical co-operation of all types in the postal sphere. The International Bureau is headed by a Director-General and placed under the general supervision of the Swiss government.

The Union co-operates closely with the *UN Development Programme (UNDP) and executes country and inter-country projects covering practically all aspects of the postal services; priority is given to the needs of the administrations of the postally least developed countries. The Union is in close contact with the *International Telecommunication Union (ITU) for the preparation and implementation of joint technical assistance projects, especially in the vocational training field. Co-operative relations are also maintained with other UN specialized agencies such as the *International Civil Aviation Organization (ICAO) for the development of air mail traffic, the *International Atomic Energy Agency (IAEA) for the postal conveyance of radioactive substances, and the *World Health Organization (WHO) for the transport of perishable biological substances. In addition, contact committees have been set up with several other intergovernmental and non-governmental institutions.

Each Congress fixes the maximum amount which the ordinary expenditure of the Union may reach for the five succeeding years; the annual budget of the Union is approved by the Executive Council. Ordinary and extraordinary expenses of the Union are borne in common by member countries which are divided by Congress for this purpose into 8 contribution classes, ranging from .5 units to 50 units. The Union's Special Fund, set up in 1966 and maintained by voluntary contributions from member countries, is mainly intended to finance training and related activities. Since 1981, the Union also funds 'integrated projects' comprising several components: short-term consultants' missions, vocational training fellowships, and items of minor equipment.

The establishment of the Union has made it possible to conduct international postal exchanges under principles and practices which are largely standardized. Over the past decades the Union has managed to adjust to the new requirements of technology and development in the postal field fostering technical co-operation activities in sectors such as planning, organization, management, operations, training and financial services. To this end, the Union has recruited and sent experts, consultants or volunteers, granted vocational training or further training fellowships for individual or group courses and supplied equipment and training and demonstration aids.

Since the last half of the 1970s the Union has concentrated its efforts on activities aimed at: improving mail routeing and delivery, with special regard to the needs of rural areas; increasing the number of postal establishments; promoting the use of aircraft for forwarding all categories of items; strengthening the monetary articles service; establishing, in developing areas, postal training facilities up to senior staff level; and improving postal staff management and utilization.

Director-General: Adwaldo Cardoso Botto de Barros

Headquarters: Weltpoststrasse 4, 3000 Berne 15, Switzerland (telephone: 432211; telex: 912761; fax: 432210)

Publication: *Union Postale* (quarterly)

UNRWA. *See* **United Nations Relief and Works Agency for Palestine Refugees in the Near East.**

UPU. *See* **Universal Postal Union.**

W

West African Economic Community [Communauté économique de l'Afrique de l'Ouest] (CEAO). The Community's basic purpose is to promote, through the establishment of an economic and customs union, the harmonious and balanced growth of the economies of member countries with a view to improving the living standards of West African peoples.

The basic legal instrument of the Community is the Treaty concluded in Abidjan, Côte d'Ivoire, in April 1973 by the representatives of Côte d'Ivoire, Mali, Mauritania, Niger, Senegal, and Upper Volta [now Burkina Faso], which entered into force in January 1974; Benin joined the Community at a later date. Any other West African French-speaking country may join the Community, subject to the approval of all members. Guinea and Togo have been granted observer status.

The Community replaced the Customs Union of West African States – Union douanière des états de l'Afrique de l'Ouest (UDEAO) – originally established by a treaty signed in Paris in March 1966 by seven West African countries, that is the six countries mentioned above plus Dahomey [later renamed Benin]. It entered into effect the following December after the ratification of five members. The UDEAO had been set up to replace another body, the West African Customs Union – Union douanière de l'Afrique de l'Ouest (UDAO) – whose creation dated from June 1959 when the West African autonomous republics participating in the French Community had agreed to form a customs union based on the equitable apportionment of receipts from duties levied by member countries on imported goods. However, the UDAO sys-

tem failed to benefit the poorer landlocked members and the subsequent revision of the terms of the customs union and the creation of UDEAO in 1966 could not bring about any substantial improvements. This eventually induced member countries to establish the present Community as a more realistic and flexible instrument for levelling economic disparities through a redistribution of benefits from integration.

The Community's objectives are to be attained through the gradual liberalization of the movement of industrial and agricultural goods among member countries and the establishment at the subregional level of an active policy of economic cooperation and integration – particularly in the fields of agriculture, animal husbandry, fisheries, industry, transport and communications, and tourism. The growth of intra-Community trade is considered the most important objective. Community development and solidarity funds and subregional economic programmes also play a role.

The functions and powers of the Community bear no supranational features and are based on the principle of full equality of the member countries taking all decisions unanimously, each country having one vote.

The institutional structure of the Community is based on three main organs: the Conference of Heads of State; the Council of Ministers; and the General Secretariat. The Conference is the supreme authority, meeting every two years in one of the member countries. It lays down the basic guidelines under the chairmanship of the Head of State of the host country. The Council consists of the Finance Ministers or other ministers (depending on the matter under discussion) and meets at least twice a year, usually at the Community's headquarters. It implements the decisions of the Conference and deals with other questions entrusted to it. Administrative and technical tasks are performed by the General Secretariat, located at Ouagadougou, Burkina Faso, and headed by a Secretary-General appointed by the Conference of Heads of State for a four-year term.

Two financial institutions had been established within the Community's framework. The Community Development Fund (FCD), financed by member countries on the basis of their respective shares (revised annually) in the trade of industrial products within the Community, was intended to provide compensation for certain types of trade losses and to finance economic development projects; however, failure on the part of member countries to pay their respective subscriptions has hindered the Fund's activities. For its part, the Solidarity and Intervention Fund [Fonds de solidarité et d'intervention pour le développement de la Communauté] (FOSIDEC) was responsible for granting loans and subsidies and extending guarantees for feasibility studies and specific projects. After an initial period of activity, the Fund ran into very severe difficulties and its Director was dismissed in 1984. In order to finance integration projects and service debts, the Conference of Heads of State decided in 1989 to impose a 'Community solidarity levy' on imports from outside the Community. Efforts are currently being made, with the support of international financial institutions, to revive the Fund.

An agreement on non-aggression and mutual co-operation was concluded with Togo by the Community's member countries in June 1977. Relations have been developed by the Community with other international organizations, particularly those operating within the West African subregion. In January 1978 the Community reached an agreement with the *Entente Council with a view to co-ordinating the exchange of economic information and studies and implementing joint development projects. In August 1980, a co-operation agreement was signed with the *Mano River Union (MRU).

The development of the Community's activities has met with several major obstacles, originating from political differences and economic disparities among member countries. Nevertheless, steps have been taken to increase the volume of intra-Community imports and exports through the abolition of internal taxes on non-manufactured goods and traditional handicrafts, and the introduction, in 1976, of a 'regional co-operation tax' to be gradually applied to industrial products. An agreement providing for the free circulation of persons and the right to establish residence was reached in 1978.

Secretary General: Mamadou Haidara
Headquarters: rue Agostino Neto, 01 BP 643, Ouagadougou, Burkina Faso (telephone: 306187; telex: 5212)

Western European Union (WEU). The Union has the broad aim of strengthening peace and security, promoting the unity and encouraging the progressive integration of Europe through the co-ordination of the defence policy and equipment of member countries as well as through consultation and co-operation with regard to political and economic matters. The events which took place in Eastern Europe and the USSR between 1989 and 1991 have dramatically altered the raison d'etre of the Union which is now trying to find a new role within the framework of the *European Community (EC). The Union could eventually become the 'military and foreign policy arm' of the EC, formulating and implementing a common European defence policy and working in co-operation with the *North Atlantic Treaty Organization (NATO).

The Union came into being in 1955 as a successor – with an enlarged membership, modified purposes and a different denomination – to the Brussels Treaty Organization. Growing concern over the security of Western Europe had prompted the governments of Belgium, France, Luxembourg, the Netherlands and the UK to sign a 50-year Treaty 'of economic, social and cultural collaboration and collective self-defence', with a view, *inter alia*, to taking 'such steps as may be held necessary in the event of renewal by Germany of a policy of aggression'. The Treaty was signed in Brussels in March 1948 and entered into force the following August. The realization of the inadequacy of the Brussels Treaty Organization to ensure regional security, and the need to involve the USA in any serious effort to build up an effective machinery for collective self-defence, led to the creation in 1949 of NATO. In December 1950, the Brussels Treaty Organization transferred its defence functions to the NATO command but retained its competence concerning social and cultural activities, in spite of the creation of the *Council of Europe in 1949. After the collapse of plans for a European Defence Community (EDC) because of French rejection, and the decision of the NATO Council to incorporate the Federal Republic of Germany into the Western system of collective security, a conference was held in London between September and October 1954, with the participation of the signatories to the 1948 Brussels Treaty plus Canada, Germany, Italy and the USA. The decisions of the conference were embodied in a series of protocols amending and completing the Brussels Treaty which were drawn up by a ministerial conference held in Paris in October 1954. The Protocols provided, *inter alia*, for the transformation of the Brussels Treaty Organization into the Western European Union, with the inclusion of Germany and Italy as full members; the ending of the occupation regime in the Federal Republic of Germany and the invitation to the latter to join NATO; and the setting up of an Agency for the Control of Armaments. The Protocols entered into force in May 1955, thus bringing the then seven-member Union formally into existence. Portugal and Spain were admitted to membership in November 1988.

According to the revised Brussels Treaty, the member countries will so organize and co-ordinate their economic activities as to produce the best possible results, by the elimination of conflict in their economic policies, the co-ordination of production and the development of commercial exchanges. Such co-operation will not involve any duplication of, or prejudice to, the work of other economic organizations in which members of the Union are represented. A close co-operation with NATO is expressly envisaged. Moreover, the organs of the Union are to rely on the appropriate authorities of NATO for information and advice on military matters. If any member country should be 'the object of an armed attack in Europe', the other countries will afford the member so attacked 'all the military and other aid and assistance in their power'. Provision was also made for close co-operation between member countries on social and cultural matters according to the principles which form the basis of the common civilization of their peoples.

Any sovereign country may be invited to accede to the Union on conditions to be agreed. Greece, Denmark and Ireland have been invited to join the Union; Iceland, Norway and Turkey are to have closer ties as associate members. The revised Brussels Treaty is to remain in force until August 1998; there is no provision for withdrawal before that date.

In order to ensure the achievement of the aims of the Union, and closer co-operation between themselves and with other European organizations, the member countries have established a Council, meeting in London, which considers matters concerning the execution of the Treaty, its Protocols and their Annexes. The Council consists of the Foreign and Defence Ministers of member countries and meets twice a year in the capital of the presiding country; the presidency rotates annually. The Permanent Council which consists of the ambassadors resident in London and an under-secretary from the British Foreign and Commonwealth Office meets regularly at the seat of the Secretariat-General. At the request of any member country, the Council is convened immediately in order to permit consultations with regard to situations which may constitute a threat to peace, in any area whatsoever, or a danger to economic stability. As a rule, decisions are taken unanimously only on questions for which no other voting procedure has been agreed. In the cases provided for in the relevant Protocols, the Council is to follow the prescribed voting procedures which vary from unanimity to two-thirds or simple majority.

The Council is responsible for: formulating basic policies and issuing directives to the Secretary-General and the various agencies and commissions; ensuring the closest co-operation with NATO; making an annual report on its activities, in particular concerning the control of armaments, to the Assembly.

Three agencies dealing with security questions are currently active within the framework of the Union: the Agency for the Study of Arms Control and Disarmament Questions; the Agency for the Study of Security and Defence Questions; and the Agency for the Development of Co-operation in the Field of Armaments. All of these agencies are based in Paris (43, avenue du Président Wilson).

The Assembly is composed of 108 representatives of the Union's member countries to the Parliamentary Assembly of the Council of Europe and meets twice a year, usually in Paris. It carries out the parliamentary functions arising from the application of the revised Brussels Treaty. Usually taking decisions by majority vote, it considers defence policy in Europe, besides other matters concerning member countries in common, and is empowered to address recommendations or transmit opinions to the Council, national parliaments, governments and international organizations. The Assembly, which officially recognized political parties, has set up Permanent Committees on: Defence Questions and Armaments; General Affairs; Scientific Questions; Budgetary Affairs and Administration; Rules of Procedure and Privileges; and Parliamentary and Public Relations. The Assembly has its own Secretariat and a separate budget.

The Secretariat of the Union is based in London and headed by a Secretary-General, assisted by a Deputy Secretary-General.

The Union co-operates closely with other European international organiz-

ations in order to co-ordinate activities and avoid duplication of efforts and overlapping. The UK, France, Germany and Italy, each country contributing the same amount, bear the largest part of the expenses of the budget of the Union.

One of the first important tasks of the newly-created Union concerned the establishment of an international regime for the Saar territory. Under a Franco-German agreement of October 1954, the Saar was to be granted a statute, within the framework of the Union, subject to approval by the population. In October 1955, the statute was rejected by referendum in favour of return to Germany. The full political and economic re-integration of the Saar territory with Germany was achieved between January 1957 and July 1959. Another important sphere of competence of the Union disappeared in June 1960 when its social and cultural activities were handed over to the Council of Europe.

A new, albeit temporary, role for the Union arose in 1963, after the breakdown of the negotiations for the entry of the UK into the EC. The EC countries proposed to the UK that quarterly meetings should be held by the Council of the Union for an exchange of views on the main political and economic problems of common interest in order to improve co-operation between the Six and the UK. The UK welcomed the proposal and regular meetings took place until the reopening of the negotiations in 1970, which eventually led to the signing of the Treaty of Accession to the EC in January 1972. The Council has since then devoted its meetings to consultations on political matters.

At a meeting of the Foreign and Defence Ministers held in Rome in October 1984 the decision was taken to 'reactivate' the Union through a restructuring of the organizational mechanism and the holding of more frequent ministerial meetings. In October 1987, the Council adopted a 'Platform on European Security Interests' with a view to developing a 'more cohesive European defence identity' while recognizing at the same time that 'the substantial presence of US conventional and nuclear forces plays an irreplaceable part in the defence of Europe'. The dramatic changes occurring in Eastern Europe and the USSR in 1989 and in 1990 were extensively discussed within the framework of the Union which also played a role in co-ordinating the military response of Western European countries to Iraq's occupation of Kuwait in August 1990.

An Institute for Security Studies, operating within the framework of the Union, was set up in Paris in July 1990.

Secretary-General: Willem van Eekelen

Headquarters: 9 Grosvenor Place, London SW1X 7HL, England (telephone: 235 5351)

Publications: *Annual Report of the Council*; *Assembly of WEU: Texts Adopted and Brief Account of the Session* (two a year)

WEU. *See* **Western European Union.**

WFC. *See* **World Food Council.**

WFP. *See* **World Food Programme.**

WHO. *See* **World Health Organization.**

WIPO. *See* **World Intellectual Property Organization.**

WMO. *See* **World Meteorological Organization.**

World Bank. *See* **International Bank for Reconstruction and Development;** *see also* **International Development Association (IDA).**

World Food Council (WFC). The Council's basic aim is to provide overall, integrated and continuing attention to achieve the successful co-ordination and follow up of policies concerning food production, nutrition, food security, food trade, food aid and other related matters, by all organizations and bodies of the UN system.

The UN World Food Conference, held in Rome in November 1974, called on the General Assembly to set up a World Food Council to function at ministerial level as the organ of the UN charged with the responsibility for implementing the 20 substantive resolutions adopted by the Conference itself. The Conference recommendations, endorsed by the General Assembly, led to the creation of the Council in December 1974 and of the *International Fund for Agricultural Development (IFAD) in the last half of the 1970s.

The Council reviews major problems and policy issues affecting the world food situation, recommends actions and co-ordinates activities within the UN system, and co-operates with regional bodies to formulate and follow up the approved policies. The Council, which holds regular annual sessions, consists of 36 members, elected by the UN General Assembly; one-third retire each year. Membership is drawn from regional groups in the following proportions: nine from Africa; eight from Asia; seven from Latin America; four from Eastern Europe; and eight from Western Europe and North America. A President and four regional Vice Presidents are elected every two years. The Secretariat, headed by an Executive Director, assists the Council in implementing the world food strategy and keeping food crisis situations under review.

The Council concentrates on promoting the international political consensus necessary: (a) to increase food production in the developing countries, especially in sub-Saharan Africa; (b) to improve national and international food security measures through policies linking food production, agricultural trade and nutritional concerns; (c) to assure the greater effectiveness of food aid; and (d) to liberalize trade in agricultural commodities between developed and developing countries.

At its third session, held in Manila in 1977, the Council adopted a Programme of Action to Eradicate Hunger and Malnutrition, subsequently endorsed by the General Assembly, recommending ways to improve and accelerate international efforts to help achieve a four per cent annual growth rate in the food production of Food Priority Countries (FPCs), that is countries suffering extraordinarily severe food problems. Other important recommendations aimed to ensure world food security, in order to minimize the effects of cyclical production shortfalls on the food supply of the world's people, improving human nutrition, and reducing barriers to food trade between the industrial and the developing world. In 1978, the Council called on all countries to allocate to development, especially to food production, part of the resources freed by disarmament.

Action taken by the Council at its fifth session, held in Ottawa in 1979, included the launch of national 'food strategies' to increase production in the developing countries and for a greater flow of assistance to their food sectors. The Council also urged all countries to achieve without delay the 500,000-ton target for the International Emergency Reserve. In July 1980 a new Food Aid Convention entered into force, increasing the guaranteed minimum level of food aid from grain exporting countries to developing countries in need from 4.2 to 7.6 million tons a year – a goal which was still short of the 10 million minimum recommended by the Council. In December 1981, the General Assembly requested the Council to give further consideration to a series of feasible measures which comprised a world food security net to ensure international market stability and continuity of world food supplies, especially for developing countries, at a reasonable price and on conditions which they could afford.

The long-standing issue of grain reserves was again raised during the early 1980s in an effort to stabilize trade flows and world market prices but met with the opposition of major grain producers. Despite the overall increase in world food production between 1974 and 1984, the risks of food shortages had become greater for many low-income developing countries, especially in sub-Saharan Africa, in terms both of inadequate levels of food production and of the relative proportion of hungry and malnourished people to total population. The volume of assistance had remained short of agreed objectives and the rate of increase of commitments appeared to be falling. At the 1984 Council session, it was decided to give priority to African food problems, to undertake a review of the implementation of national food sector plans and policies in Africa, and to assess the progress made in international institutions for the liberalization of trade in food. In 1985 the Council stressed the need for a clearer distinction between food aid and the disposal of highly subsidized surpluses with disruptive repercussions on markets and production incentives; in particular, the 'dumping' of surplus cereals by industrialized countries was severely criticized. At the sessions held in 1987 and 1988, the Council noted that, although total food production had increased since the 1974 World Food Conference, the number of undernourished people in the world had risen while the overall conditions of the poorest people had continued to deteriorate.

At its fifteenth session, held in Cairo in 1989, the Council adopted a Declaration and Programme of Co-operative Action for the 1990s and decided to undertake a major effort to raise the level of political support for the elimination of hunger and malnutrition. At the 1990 session, Council members discussed the new challenges and opportunities of the decade and agreed to take additional steps and more effective action with a view to achieving the goals of the Cairo Declaration. Special importance was attached by the meeting to the impact of rapid population growth and environmental degradation on the food production efforts needed to fight today's hunger and to feed the estimated eight billion world population by the year 2020. To meet this challenge on a sustainable basis, the Council called for a renewal of the Green Revolution which should make fuller use of existing technology and enhance the development and transfer of new and appropriate technology within and among countries.

At the seventeenth session in Denmark, in June 1991, the Council discussed the extent to which the great political, economic and social changes in many parts of the world are affecting the poor and hungry; also considered were important long-term issues concerning the food security of future generations. On the basis of these discussions, the Council restressed the primacy of food and hunger issues on the global agenda for the 1990s.

Executive Director: Gerald Ion Trant
Headquarters: Viale delle Terme di Caracalla, 00100 Rome, Italy (telephone: 57971; telex: 610181; fax: 574 5091)

World Food Programme (WFP). The Programme, sponsored jointly by the *United Nations (UN) and the *Food and Agriculture Organization (FAO), seeks to stimulate socio-economic development through aid in the form of food and to provide emergency relief. It became operational in January 1963 after parallel resolutions adopted by the UN General Assembly and the FAO Conference in late 1961.

The Programme is the second largest UN assistance source in terms of actual transfer of resources after the World Bank Group and the largest source of grant aid in the UN system. More than one-quarter of the world's food aid is handled by the Programme. Member countries of the UN and the FAO make voluntary contributions to the Programme of commodities, cash, and services (particularly shipping).

The food is used for economic and social development projects in the developing countries and for emergency relief for victims of natural and man-made disasters. Food may also be used in low income countries as a partial substitute for cash wages paid to workers in labour-intensive projects of many kinds (particularly in the rural economy), or may be provided to families resettled for development purposes until first crops are harvested on the new land. The Programme supports institutional feeding schemes where the main emphasis is on enabling the beneficiaries to have an adequate and balanced diet through operations such as school feeding programmes and supplementary feeding of vulnerable groups, including young mothers and children. Help is also extended to meet emergency food needs created by earthquakes, typhoons, floods and other natural disasters.

The Committee of Food Aid Policies and Programmes (CFA), which meets twice a year, is the governing body of the Programme. The Committee is composed of 42 members (21 elected by the UN Economic and Social Council and 21 by the FAO Council) and is responsible for the overall policy direction of the Programme, including food aid policy, administration, operations, funds, and finances. It also acts as the international body designated to discuss food aid issues and concerns, including bilateral food aid.

In the early 1970s, the Programme made severe cuts in its activities because of soaring prices on the world commodity market. The UN World Food Conference, held in Rome in November 1974, called on developed countries to increase their contributions to the Programme.

At present, the Programme enjoys a wide base of support and substantial amounts of food are being supplied by the world's biggest exporters and cash resources provided by other high-income countries. These donors include, among others, the USA, the *European Community (EC) as well as its member countries, Canada, the Scandinavian countries, Australia and Japan. Although the most frequently donated commodities are grains, the Programme also handles substantial quantities of milk powder and high-protein food blends, and smaller quantities of other products such as cooking oil, salt and sugar. It is thus possible to provide beneficiaries with balanced diets and to cater for differing food habits. Usually, food aid is combined with non-food contributions to the recipient country.

The projects to which the Programme commits food aid fall into two broad categories: human resource development for improving the people's nutritional, physical, and educational well-being; agricultural and rural development projects for creating jobs and increasing food production. Priority is given to low-income, food-deficit countries and to highly vulnerable groups such as pregnant women and children. Some projects are especially intended to alleviate the consequences of structural adjustment programmes undertaken by many developing countries which frequently involve substantial reductions in public expenditure and subsidies for basic foods.

The Programme co-operates closely with other UN bodies, private agencies, and governments making bilateral contributions. Non-governmental organizations (NGOs) play an increasingly larger role in the delivery and monitoring of food aid and the provision of non-food items. In several large-scale relief operations, including those in South-East Asia and Africa, the Programme has taken a leading role in co-ordinating food aid deliveries and/or distribution to recipients.

Since 1963, the Programme has undertaken over 1600 development and quick action projects in about 115 countries at a commitment value of nearly $11 billion, about 1100 emergency operations in over 100 countries at a commitment value of nearly $4 billion, and over 50 protracted refugee and displaced persons operations in 20 countries at a commitment value of over $1.5 billion.

Executive Director: Catherine Bertini
Headquarters: Via Cristoforo Colombo 426, 00145 Rome, Italy (telephone: 57971; telex: 626675; fax: 512 7400)
Publications: *WFP Journal* (quarterly); *World Food Programme Food Aid Review* (annually)

World Health Organization (WHO).

The basic objective of the Organization is the attainment by all peoples of the highest possible level of health.

The International Office of Public Health – Office international de l'hygiène publique (OIHP) – was established in Paris in 1903 and can be regarded as a predecessor of the present Organization. Another specialized health body was subsequently set up within the framework of the League of Nations and based in Geneva. In the Western hemisphere, an International Sanitary Bureau had been established in Washington, D.C., in 1902;

the original name was changed to Pan American Sanitary Bureau in 1923, to Pan American Sanitary Organization in 1947, and eventually to Pan American Health Organization (PAHO) in 1958.

The need for the early establishment of a single international body dealing with health issues had been stressed in a declaration adopted at the UN San Francisco Conference in 1945. An International Health Conference was convened by the UN in 1946 in New York to consider the creation of a global institution co-ordinating and directing health activities; it resulted in the adoption, in July 1946, of the Constitution of the present Organization, which entered into force in April 1948 when the prescribed number of ratifications had been reached. Amendments to the Constitution have been introduced on a number of occasions. The Organization concluded a relationship agreement with the UN in July 1948. Another agreement was concluded with the then Pan American Sanitary Organization, which began to serve as a regional office for the American continent. The present membership of the Organization includes about 170 countries.

The Organization acts as the central authority on international health work and establishes and maintains effective collaboration with international agencies and bodies, national health administrations and professional groups. It assists governments in: strengthening health services; stimulating and advancing work to eradicate epidemic, endemic and other diseases; promoting maternal and child health, mental health, medical research and the prevention of accidental injuries; improving standards of teaching and training in the health, medical and related professions; and promoting the improvement of nutrition, housing, sanitation, recreation, economic or working conditions and other aspects of environmental hygiene. The Organization is also empowered: to propose conventions, agreements and regulations and to make recommendations about international health matters; to revise the international nomenclatures of diseases, causes of death and public health practices; to establish and promote international standards concerning food, biological, pharmaceutical and similar products.

Members of the UN may accede to the Organization, in accordance with the provisions of the Constitution. Any sovereign country, not a member of the UN, may be admitted to the Organization if the relevant request is approved by a simple majority vote of the World Health Assembly. Territories or groups of territories not responsible for the conduct of their international relations may be granted associate membership by the World Health Assembly upon application made on their behalf by the full member having responsibility for their international relations. The World Health Assembly may suspend from the rights and privileges of membership any country if it fails to meet its financial obligations to the Organization or in any other exceptional circumstances.

The work of the Organization is carried out by three principal organs: the World Health Assembly, the Executive Board and the Secretariat. The Assembly is composed of delegates of all member countries, chosen from among persons most qualified by their technical competence and preferably representing national health administrations. It meets in regular annual sessions and in such special sessions as may be necessary. Its main functions are: to determine basic policies and guidelines; to elect the members entitled to designate a person to serve on the Executive Board; to appoint the Director-General; to review and approve reports and activities of the Executive Board and the Director-General and to issue instructions to them; to supervise financial policies and to approve the budget; to promote and conduct research in the field of health. The Assembly may adopt, with respect to any matter within the competence of the Organization and by a two-thirds majority, conventions or agreements which shall come into force for each member accepting them in accordance with its constitutional processes. Members which do not accept a convention or an agreement within the established time limit must state the reasons for non-acceptance. The Assembly has authority to adopt regulations concerning: sanitary and quarantine requirements and other pro-

cedures designed to prevent the international spread of disease; nomenclatures of diseases, causes of death and public health practices; standards covering diagnostic procedures for international use; standards with respect to the safety, purity and potency of biological, pharmaceutical and similar products moving in international commerce; and advertising and labelling of these same products. Decisions of the Assembly on important questions such as the adoption of conventions or agreements, the approval of co-operation agreements with other inter-governmental organizations and amendments to the Constitution are made by a two-thirds majority of the members present and voting; simple majority suffices with respect to other questions.

The Executive Board meets at least twice a year and is composed of 31 health experts designated for a three-year period by, but not representing, as many member countries elected by the World Health Assembly. The Executive Board is empowered to give effect to the decisions and policies of the Assembly and to submit to it advice or proposals and a general programme of work for a specific period. It is also empowered to take emergency measures in case of epidemics or disasters.

The Secretariat consists of technical and administrative staff, headed by a Director-General assisted by a Deputy Director-General and several Assistant Directors-General. Health activities are carried out through six regional organizations which have been established for: Africa (Brazzaville, Congo); the Americas (Washington, D.C.); Eastern Mediterranean (Alexandria, Egypt); Europe (Copenhagen); South-East Asia (New Delhi); Western Pacific (Manila). Each regional organization consists of a regional committee composed of the full and associate members in the area concerned, and a regional office staffed by experts in various fields of health.

The Organization has established effective relations and co-operates closely with UN bodies – among them are the *UN Development Programme (UNDP) and the *UN Population Fund (UNFPA) – and with other specialized agencies such as the *International Labour Organization (ILO), the *Food and Agriculture Organization (FAO), the *UN Educational, Scientific and Cultural Organization (UNESCO), and the *International Atomic Energy Agency (IAEA). Suitable arrangements for consultation and co-operation have also been made with non-governmental international institutions and, subject to the consent of the governments concerned, with national bodies, governmental and non-governmental.

The Director-General is responsible for preparing and submitting to the Executive Board the annual budget estimates of the Organization. The Executive Board considers and submits these estimates to the Assembly, together with its recommendations. Expenses are apportioned among members in accordance with a scale fixed by the Assembly. An additional fund for specific projects is provided by voluntary contributions from members and other sources. Other funds are received from UN bodies for particular projects and programmes.

During more than four decades, the Organization's work has been directed towards a variety of fields such as disease control, environmental health, family health, mental health, training of health workers, strengthening of national health systems, formulation of health regulations for international travel, establishment of drug policies, promotion of biomedical research, and collection and dissemination of statistical data and analyses. All activities have been reoriented to accord with the Global Strategy adopted by the World Health Assembly in May 1981 – 'Health for all by the year 2000' – that is the attainment by all citizens of the world of a level of health that will enable them to lead a socially and economically productive life. Water supply and sanitation needs of around 100 countries have been assessed in connection with the International Drinking Water Supply and Sanitation Decade (1981-90) which was launched by the UN. A Priority Programme for the Control of Diarrhoeal Diseases has been under way since 1979. The Global Programme on AIDS (Acquired Immunodeficiency Syndrome) was started in 1987; the aims of the Global Programme are to prevent

transmission of the human immunodeficiency virus (HIV), to care for HIV-infected people, and to unify national and international efforts against AIDS. The Global Commission on AIDS, made up of biomedical and social scientitists and other experts, began its activities in 1989. The Tobacco or Health Programme aims to reduce the use of tobacco, educating tobacco-users and preventing young people from adopting the habit.

The Expanded Programme on Immunization (EPI), launched in 1974, has provided over 100 countries with assistance against six childhood diseases – diphtheria, measles, pertussis, poliomyelitis, tetanus, tuberculosis. These diseases constitute a major cause of death and disability in the developing countries. To complement the EPI a new vaccine development programme was launched in 1984. Six widespread diseases of the tropics – filariasis, leishmaniasis, leprosy, malaria, schistosomiasis, and trypanosomiasis – are targets of a Special Programme on research and training.

One of the Organization's major achievements has been the eradication of smallpox following a massive international campaign of vaccination and surveillance. In May 1980 the World Health Assembly recommended that vaccination against smallpox be discontinued in every country. In 1988 the Assembly declared its commitment to eradicate poliomyelitis by the year 2000; similar commitments were adopted in 1990 with regard to iodine deficiency disorders and in 1991 with regard to leprosy. Intensive efforts are being undertaken against the recrudescence of malaria in many parts of the world.

With regard to non-communicable diseases, intensified research is being carried out with regard to cardiovascular diseases and cancer. In 1990, the 'Inter-Health' programme was initiated in order to combat non-communicable diseases (such as those arising from an unhealthy diet) and their growing incidence in developing countries. Work on cancer is organized and conducted under the responsibility of the International Agency for Research on Cancer (150 Cours Albert Thomas, 69372 Lyon Cedex 08, France), established in

1965 as a self-governing body within the framework of the Organization; it has its own laboratories and runs a research programme on the environmental factors causing cancer. In addition to the five original participating members (France, Germany, Italy, the UK, and the USA), a dozen other developed countries have subsequently joined the Agency.

Under an Action Programme on Essential Drugs and Vaccines, developing countries receive technical assistance in selection, quality control, and production of effective and safe drugs and vaccines essential to their needs. The Organization maintains and regularly revises a Model List of Essential Drugs numbering about 250 substances that will treat over 80 per cent of the health problems of a given population. In order to survey and combat the global increase in drug abuse through the reduction of the demand for drugs and the control of the supply of psychoactive substances, the Organization has launched a Programme on Substance Abuse in 1990.

Director-General: Dr Hiroshi Nakajima
Headquarters: 20 Avenue Appia, 1211 Geneva 27, Switzerland (telephone: 791 2111; telex: 415416; fax: 791 0746)
Publications: *World Health* (six a year); *Bulletin of WHO* (six a year); *World Health Statistics Quarterly*; *World Health Statistics Annual*; *WHO AIDS Series*; *WHO Drug Information* (quarterly)
Reference: F.W. Hoole: *Politics and Budgeting in the WHO* (Bloomington, Indiana, 1976)

World Intellectual Property Organization (WIPO). The Organization seeks to promote the protection of intellectual property throughout the world through co-operation among member countries and, where appropriate, in collaboration with any other international institution, and to centralize the administration of the various Unions established by multilateral treaties and dealing with legal and technical aspects of intellectual property.

The Organization was established by a Convention signed in Stockholm in 1967 and entered into force in April 1970. It was intended to succeed the United International Bureau for the Protection of Intellectual Property (Bureau international réuni pour la protection de la propriété intellectuelle (BIRPI), which had been set up in 1893 and represented the combined secretariats of the Paris Union (for the protection of industrial property) and the Berne Union (for the protection of literary and artistic works). Because some countries participating in BIRPI have yet to accede formally to the new Organization, BIRPI is still a legal entity. A relationship agreement was concluded by the Organization with the UN and it became a specialized agency in December 1974. The Organization's present membership includes around 130 countries. About 100 countries currently participate in the Paris Union and about 85 in the Berne Union.

The expression 'intellectual property' means the legal rights resulting from intellectual activity in the industrial, scientific, literary or artistic fields. Intellectual property comprises two main branches: industrial property (inventions in all fields of human endeavour, scientific discoveries, industrial designs, trademarks, service marks and commercial names and designations); and copyright and neighbouring rights (literary, musical and artistic works, performances of artists, films, records and broadcasts).

The overall objective of the Organization is to maintain and increase respect for intellectual property throughout the world, in order to favour industrial and cultural development by stimulating creative activity and facilitating the dissemination of literary and artistic works and the transfer of technology, especially to and among developing countries. To promote the protection of intellectual property, the Organization encourages the conclusion of new international treaties and the harmonization of national legislations. It gives legal and technical assistance to developing countries to promote their industrialization through the modernization of their industrial property and copyright systems, prepares model laws, provides traineeships, organizes seminars, finances assistance and encourages the flow of scientific and technical documentation. It also performs the administrative tasks of several international treaties dealing with various subjects of intellectual property, assembles and disseminates information concerning the protection of intellectual property, conducts and promotes studies and publishes their results, and maintains services for international registration or other administrative co-operation among member countries.

Accession to the Organization is open to any sovereign country which is a member of at least one of the Unions, and to other countries which participate in the organizations of the UN system, are party to the Statute of the International Court of Justice, or are invited to join by the Organization itself through its General Assembly. Membership of the Unions is open to any sovereign country.

Nine of the Unions administered by the Organization have their own intergovernmental organs which adopt their own programmes of activities and budgets. The Organization has a Conference, a General Assembly, a Co-ordination Committee and a secretariat which is called the International Bureau. The Conference, composed of all member countries, establishes the basic policies and the biennial programme of legal-technical assistance and approves the biennial budget of the Organization. The General Assembly, composed of those member countries which are also members of the Paris or Berne Unions, appoints and gives instructions to the Director-General, reviews and approves his reports, and adopts the biennial budget of expenses common to the Unions. Separate Assemblies and Conferences of Representatives continue to be held by the Paris and Berne Unions pending the formal accession to membership in the Organization of all the countries belonging to BIRPI. The Paris and Berne Unions elect Executive Committees from among their members and the joint membership of these Committees constitutes the Co-ordination Committee of the Organization.

The International Bureau is headed by a Director-General assisted by three Deputy Directors-General. It prepares the meetings of the various bodies of the Organization and the Unions, mainly through the provision of reports and working documents, carries out projects for the promotion of international co-operation in the field of intellectual property and acts as the depository of most of the treaties administered by the Organization.

The Organization's activities are basically of two sorts: substantive or programme activities, and administrative activities concerned with the international registration of industrial property rights.

Among the substantive activities, mention should be made of the two Permanent Programmes for Development Co-operation which are respectively related to Industrial Property and to Copyright and Neighbouring Rights. Under the first Programme, undertaken in 1973 and directed by a Permanent Committee of representatives of over 100 countries (both developing and industrial), the Organization seeks to improve access to inventions, technology and trademarks for the developing countries. The objectives of the second Programme, which dates back to 1976 and is directed by a Permanent Committee of about 90 countries (both developing and industrial), are to encourage in developing countries intellectual creation in the literary, scientific and artistic domains, to facilitate the dissemination, under fair and reasonable conditions, of intellectual creations, and to assist in the strengthening of national institutions in the fields of copyright and neighbouring rights. Membership of the two Committees is voluntary and involves no financial obligation. In both industrial property and copyright, the role of the Organization consists mainly in providing advice and training as well as documents and equipment.

The Permanent Committee on Patent Information fosters co-operation between national and regional industrial property offices in all matters concerning patent information. Administrative or registration activities are those required for the receiving and processing of international applications under the Patent Co-operation Treaty (PCT) of June 1970 or for the international registration of trademarks, appellations of origin or deposit of industrial designs. The Organization performs the administrative functions conferred by the Paris Convention for the Protection of Industrial Property, signed in 1883, by various special agreements concluded within the framework of the Paris Convention, by the Berne Convention for the Protection of Literary and Artistic Works, signed in 1886, and by other conventions concerning the protection of literary and artistic property. Conventions and agreements are kept under review and submitted to revision with a view, *inter alia*, to meeting the needs of developing countries.

Director-General: Dr Arpad Bogsch

Headquarters: 34 Chemin des Colombettes, 1211 Geneva 20, Switzerland (telephone: 730 9111; telex: 22376; fax: 733 5428)

Publications: *Industrial Property* (monthly); *Copyright* (monthly); *Intellectual Property in Asia and the Pacific* (quarterly)

World Meteorological Organization

(WMO). The Organization aims to coordinate, standardize and improve world meteorological activities and to encourage an efficient and rapid exchange of weather information between members.

An International Meteorological Organization was set up in 1873 at the International Meteorological Meeting held in Utrecht, the Netherlands, and the relevant statutes were subsequently revised several times. The 12th Conference of Directors of the International Meteorological Organization convened at Washington, D.C., in September 1947, drew up a Convention creating the World Meteorological Organization to which activities, resources and obligations of the original Organization had to be transferred. The Convention, opened for signature in October 1947, entered into effect in March 1950. The new Organization was formally established in March 1951 when the first session of its Congress was convened in Paris. A number of amendments to the text of the Convention have been introduced over the years. A relationship agreement with the UN was concluded by the Organization and came into force in

December 1951. The present membership of the Organization includes over 160 countries.

The purposes of the Organization are: (a) to facilitate worldwide co-operation in establishing networks of stations to provide meteorological, hydrological or other geophysical observations related to meteorology, and to promote the establishment and maintenance of centres charged with the provision of meteorological and related services; (b) to promote the establishment and maintenance of systems for the rapid exchange of weather information; (c) to promote standardization of meteorological observations and to ensure the uniform publication of observations and statistics; (d) to further the application of meteorology to aviation, shipping, water problems, agriculture and other activities; (e) to promote activities in operational hydrology and to foster co-operation between meteorological and hydrological services; and (f) to encourage research and training in meteorology and to assist in co-ordinating the international aspects of such activities.

The Organization arranges for the international exchange of weather reports, and assists in establishing meteorological services and improving or increasing the application of meteorology and hydrology to economic development projects.

Any member of the UN with a meteorological service may accede to the Organization, in conformity with current provisions. Sovereign countries with a meteorological service and not belonging to the UN may be admitted to the Organization if their request for membership is approved by two-thirds of the member countries. Any territory or group of territories maintaining its own meteorological service but not responsible for the conduct of its international relations may also be admitted to the Organization, provided that the relevant request is presented by the member responsible for international relations and secures approval by two-thirds of the member countries. Any member may withdraw from the Organization on 12 months' written notice given to the Secretary-General. Provision is made for the suspension from the exercise of the rights and privileges of membership of any country failing to meet its financial obligations or otherwise violating the Convention.

The structure of the Organization comprises the World Meteorological Congress, the Executive Council, Regional Meteorological Associations, Technical Commissions and the Secretariat. The World Meteorological Congress, in which all members are represented by delegations headed by the directors of national meteorological services, is the supreme organ and meets for ordinary sessions at least once every four years. The Congress determines the general policies, makes recommendations to members on any matter within the purposes of the Organization, considers the reports and activities of the Executive Council, establishes Regional Associations and Technical Commissions and co-ordinates their activities, and elects members of the Executive Council. Each member of the Congress has one vote. However, only members which are sovereign countries are entitled to vote or to take a decision on a number of sensitive subjects such as amendments to the Convention, requests for membership, relations with the UN and other intergovernmental institutions and elections of individuals to serve in the Organization. Decisions are taken by a two-thirds majority of the votes cast, with the exception of elections of individuals where simple majority suffices. The 36-member Executive Council consists of 26 directors of national meteorological or hydrological services acting in an individual capacity plus the president and the three vice-presidents of the Organization and the six presidents of the Regional Associations. It meets at least once a year to supervise the implementation of Congress resolutions and regulations, to initiate studies and make recommendations on matters requiring international action, and to provide members with technical information, advice and assistance. Decisions of the Executive Council are taken by two-thirds majority of the votes cast.

Regional Meteorological Associations – which are responsible for Africa, North and Central America, South America, Asia, Europe, and the South West Pacific – meet at least once every four years to promote the execution of the resolutions of Congress and the Executive Council within the region of their competence, to co-ordinate meteorological and associated activities and to consider matters referred to them by the Executive Council.

Technical Commissions are composed of experts meeting at least once every four years to study the applications of meteorology and problems and developments in specialized fields. At present there are eight Commissions responsible for: Basic Systems; Climatology; Instruments and Methods of Observation; Atmospheric Sciences; Aeronautical Meteorology; Agricultural Meteorology; Hydrology; and Marine Meteorology. The Secretariat is headed by the Secretary-General appointed by the Congress and performs administrative functions, organizes meetings of the various bodies, acts as a link between the meteorological and hydrometeorological services of the world, and provides information for the general public.

Working arrangements have been concluded by the Organization with the *International Atomic Energy Agency (IAEA) and with many UN specialized agencies such as the *World Health Organization (WHO), the *Food and Agriculture Organization (FAO), the *International Fund for Agricultural Development (IFAD), the *International Civil Aviation Organization (ICAO), the *International Maritime Organization (IMO) and the *UN Educational, Scientific and Cultural Organization (UNESCO). Technical assistance is extended to developing countries under the *UN Development Programme (UNDP) and other specific programmes; environmental prediction research is conducted in collaboration with the *UN Environment Programme (UNEP). The Intergovernmental Panel on Climate Change (IPCC) has been jointly established in 1988 by the Organization and UNEP to evaluate scientific information on changes in climate and formulate a realistic response. Several non-governmental institutions also participate more or less closely in the Organization's work.

The maximum expenditure which may be incurred by the Organization is determined by the Congress on the basis of estimates submitted by the Secretary-General, after prior examination by, and with the recommendations of, the Executive Council. Annual expenditures, within the limitations fixed by the Congress, are approved by the Executive Council upon the delegation of the Congress. Expenditures are apportioned among members on the basis of a scale of assessment determined by the Congress.

Among the most important activities carried out by the Organization, the 'World Weather Watch' Programme deserves special consideration. Based on a number of polar-orbiting and geostationary meteorological satellites and a system of 3 world meteorological centres (WMCs), 29 regional/special meteorological centres (RSMCs) and 148 national meteorological centres, its primary purpose is to provide all members with adequate information to enable them to operate efficient meteorological services and to make local and specialized forecasts. The Organization's Research and Development Programme includes important components such as the Programme on Short- and Medium-Range Weather Prediction Research and the Programme on Long-Range Forecasting Research with a view to improving the accuracy of weather forecasting, and the Programme on Research in Tropical Meteorology relating to cyclones, monsoons, droughts and disturbances bringing rain. The Global Atmosphere Watch (GAW) is the principal worldwide system responsible for the integration of most monitoring and research activities which involve the measurement of atmospheric composition; it is intended to serve as an early warning system to detect changes in the atmospheric concentrations of 'greenhouse' gases, changes in the ozone layer and in long-range transport of pollutants, including acidity and toxicity of rain, as well as the atmospheric burden of aerosols. Through GAW, the Organization co-operates with the *UN Economic Commission for Europe (ECE) and is in charge of the meteorological part of the Monitoring and Evaluation of the Long-range Transmission of Air Pollutants in Europe. Daily analysis of the transport of pollution over Europe is provided by two meteorological synthesizing centres which have been established in Norway and Russia.

The Organization has engaged in several international projects or in joint action with other international institutions in order to increase the contribution made by meteorology to economic and social progress, the protection of life and property and environmental conservation. Under the Hydrology and Water Resources Programme, the Organization fosters international co-operation in evaluating water resources and assists in their development through systematic formation of hydrological services. Another major programme that has been undertaken by the Organization is the World Climate Programme (WCP), for the improvement of the knowledge of climate and its effects on socio-economic and environmental systems, and the application of such knowledge so as to take optimum advantage of climatic resources and changes. Considerable progress is being achieved in education and training activities which are carried out in the sphere of meteorological and related instruction. Technical assistance is provided in the form of expert missions, fellowships and equipment; a number of projects are implemented under Trust Fund arrangements financed by individual governments for activities either in their own country or in a beneficiary country. The Voluntary Co-operation Programme (VCP) – consisting of expert equipment, services, long-term fellowships, and training – assists members in implementing the World Weather Watch Programme to develop an integrated observing and forecasting system.

Secretary-General: Professor G.O.P. Obasi

Headquarters: 41 Avenue Giuseppe Motta, 1211 Geneva 20, Switzerland (telephone: 730 8111; telex: 23260; fax: 734 2326)

Publications: *Annual Report*; *WMO Bulletin* (quarterly); technical manuals, guides and reports

World Tourism Organization (WTO). The Organization promotes travel and tourism and deals with all aspects of tourism on a worldwide basis.

The Organization was established in 1975 to facilitate and improve travel between and within member countries and with a view to contributing to economic development, international understanding, peace, prosperity and universal respect for, and observance of, human rights and fundamental freedoms.

The objectives of the Organization, according to the indications of the UN General Assembly, are the following: (a) to emphasize the social and cultural function of tourism in society, its role in international trade and its contribution to bringing peoples closer together and safeguarding world peace; (b) to encourage the adoption of measures to facilitate travel as well as for the protection of tourists; (c) to provide for a technical co-operation machinery to assist all countries, especially the developing ones, in the formulation of tourism policies, plans and programmes; (d) to develop the human resources in the sector through the preparation of teaching and training programmes; and (e) to promote research and exchange of information on all aspects of international and domestic tourism, including statistical data, legislation and regulations.

The Organization includes over 110 countries as full members, a number of territories not fully responsible for their external relations as associate members, and about 160 intergovernmental and non-governmental bodies and commercial and non-commercial associations involved in tourism as affiliate members.

The General Assembly, meeting every two years, is the supreme organ of the Organization; it has established six Regional Commissions (Africa; Americas; Europe; Middle East; East Asia and the Pacific; South Asia). The Executive Council, meeting at least twice a year, has one member elected on the basis of equitable geographic distribution for every five full members of the Organization. One associate member, selected by the associate members themselves, and a representative of the Committee of affiliate members participate in the work of the Council without voting rights. A number of subsidiary organs have been established by the Council. The Committee of affiliate members carries out its own programmes of activity within the framework of the Organization. The Secretariat performs technical and administrative functions under the responsibility of a Secretary-General.

The Organization has developed close working relations with several agencies of the UN, notably the *UN Development Programme (UNDP).

Secretary-General: Antonio Enriquez Savignac

Headquarters: Calle Capitán Haya 42, 28020 Madrid, Spain (telephone: 571 0628; telex: 42188; fax: 571 3733)

Directory of International Organizations

(1) Agriculture, Food, Forestry and Fisheries

African Timber Organization [Organisation africaine du bois]. *Formed*: 1975. *Purpose*: To study and co-ordinate ways of influencing prices of wood and wood products, to harmonize commercial policies and to conduct industrial and technical research. *Members*: Angola, Cameroon, Central African Republic, Congo, Côte d'Ivoire, Equatorial Guinea, Gabon, Ghana, Liberia, São Tomé and Principe, Tanzania, Zaire. *Secretary-General*: Mohammed Lawal Garba. *Headquarters*: P.O. Box 1077, Libreville, Gabon (telephone: 732928; telex: 5620). *Publications*: *Annual Report*; *ATO-Information* (every two months).

Cairns Group. *Formed*: 1986. *Purpose*: To bring about reforms in international agricultural trade, including reductions in export subsidies and other support measures, and to represent members' interests in GATT negotiations. *Members*: Argentina, Australia, Brazil, Canada, Chile, Colombia, Fiji, Hungary, Indonesia, Malaysia, New Zealand, Philippines, Thailand, Uruguay. *Chairman*: Dr Neal Blewett. *Headquarters*: c/o Department of Foreign Affairs and Trade, Bag 8, Queen Victoria Terrace, Canberra, ACT 2600, Australia.

Desert Locust Control Organization for Eastern Africa (DLCO-EA). *Formed*: 1962. *Purpose*: To promote the effective control of the desert locust in East Africa and to conduct operational research and training programmes. *Members*: Djibouti, Ethiopia, Kenya, Somalia, Sudan, Tanzania, Uganda. *Director-General*: Hosea Y. Kayumbo. *Headquarters*: P.O. Box 4255, Addis Ababa, Ethiopia (telephone: 611465; telex: 21510). *Publications*: *Annual Report*; *Desert Locust Situation Report* (monthly).

General Fisheries Council for the Mediterranean (GFCM). *Formed*: 1952. *Purpose*: To promote in the Mediterranean and in the Black Sea the development, conservation, rational management and best utilization of living marine resources. *Members*: 19 countries. *Headquarters*: FAO, Via delle Terme di Caracalla, Rome, Italy (telephone: 57971; telex: 610181 FAO I). *Publications*: *GFCM Session Reports*; studies and reviews.

Indo-Pacific Fisheries Commission (IPFC). *Formed*: 1948. *Purpose*: To promote the proper utilization of living aquatic resources by the development and management of fishing and culture operations and by the development of related processing and marketing activities. *Members*: 19 countries, including France, the UK and the USA. *Secretary*: V.L.C. Pietersz. *Headquarters*: FAO Regional Office, Maliwan Mansion, Phra Atit Road, Bangkok, Thailand (telephone: 281 78 44; telex: 82815 FOODAG TH). *Publications*: Proceedings and occasional papers.

Inter-American Tropical Tuna Commission (IATTC). *Formed*: 1950. *Purpose*: To study the biology, ecology and population dynamics of the tropical tuna and related species of the eastern Pacific Ocean with a view to determining the effects of fishing and natural factors on stocks and to recommend appropriate conservation measures. *Members*: Costa Rica, France, Japan, Nicaragua, Panama, USA. *Director*: James Joseph. *Headquarters*: c/o Scripps Institution of Oceanography, La Jolla, California 92093, USA (telephone: 546 7100; telex: 697115; fax: 546 7133). *Publications*: *Annual Report*; *Bulletin* (irregular).

International Commission for the Conservation of the Atlantic Tunas (ICCAT). *Formed*: 1969. *Purpose*: To maintain the populations of tuna and tuna-like fish in the Atlantic Ocean at levels which will permit maximum sustainable catch. *Members*: over 20 countries. *Executive Secretary*: O. Rodriguez Martin. *Headquarters*: Calle Principe de Vergara 17, 28001 Madrid, Spain (telephone: 4310329; telex: 46330). *Publications*: *Statistical Bulletin*; scientific papers; data records.

International Commission for the Southeast Atlantic Fisheries (ICSEAF). *Formed*: 1971. *Purpose*: To promote the rational exploitation of the maritime sector of the Southeast Atlantic region. *Members*: 17 countries. *Executive Secretary*: R.A. Lagarde. *Headquarters*: Paseo de la Habana 65, 28036 Madrid, Spain (telephone: 458 8766; telex: 45533). *Publications*: statistical and scientific reports.

International North Pacific Fisheries Commission (INPFC). *Formed*: 1953. *Purpose*: To provide for scientific studies and the collection and exchange of data, to encourage conservation of fishery resources and to ensure the maximum sustained productivity of such resources. *Members*: Canada, Japan, USA. *Headquarters*: 6640 NW Marine Drive, Vancouver, British Columbia V6T 1X2, Canada (telephone: 228 1128; fax: 228 1135). *Publications*: *Annual Report*; *Bulletin*; *Statistical Yearbook*.

International Red Locust Control Organization for Central and Southern Africa (IRLCO-CSA). *Formed*: 1971 as successor to International Red Locust Control Service (IRLCS) established in 1949. *Purpose*: To promote and undertake the most effective control of the significant populations and swarms of red locust in recognized outbreak areas. *Members*: Botswana, Kenya, Lesotho, Malawi, Mozambique, Swaziland, Tanzania, Uganda, Zambia, Zimbabwe. *Director*: E.K. Byaruhanga. *Headquarters*: P.O. Box 240252, Ndola, Zambia (telephone: 612433; telex: 30072). *Publications*: *Annual Report*; *Monthly Report*.

Northwest Atlantic Fisheries Organization (NAFO). *Formed*: 1979 as successor to International Commission for the Northwest Atlantic Fisheries (ICNAF) established in 1950. *Purpose*: To investigate, protect and conserve fishery resources of the Northwest Atlantic Ocean. *Members*: 13 contracting parties (including the EEC) totalling 23 countries. *Executive Secretary*: J.C.E. Cardoso. *Headquarters*: P.O. Box 638, Dartmouth, Nova Scotia B2Y 3Y9, Canada (telephone: 469 9105; telex: 019-31475; fax: 469 5729). *Publications*: *Annual Report*; *Statistical Bulletin* (annually); *List of Fishing Vessels*.

Western Central Atlantic Fishery Commission (WECAFC). *Formed*: 1973. *Purpose*: To assist international co-operation for the conservation, development and utilization of living resources. *Members*: 28 countries in Africa, America, Asia and Europe. *Headquarters*: FAO, Via delle Terme di Caracalla, Rome, Italy (telephone: 5797 66 16; telex: 611127).

(2) Aid, Development and Economic Co-operation

Agency for Cultural and Technical Co-operation [Agence de coopération culturelle et technique] (ACCT). *Formed*: 1970. *Purpose*: To promote and develop multilateral co-operation among French-speaking countries in the fields of education, culture, and science and to provide technical and financial assistance. *Members*: 30 countries, in all continents but particularly in Africa, of which French is the official or habitual language, plus 9 associated or participating countries. *Secretary-General*: Jean-

Louis Roy. *Headqv~rters*: 13 quai André Citroën, 75015 Parıs, France (telephone: 4575 6241; telex: 2011916). *Publication*: *Agecoop Liaison* (monthly).

Andean Development Corporation. [Corporación Andina de Fomento] (CAF). *Formed*: 1968. *Purpose*: To act as the financing institution of the *Andean Group playing simultaneously the role of development bank, investment bank, and commercial bank. *Members*: Bolivia, Colombia, Ecuador, Peru, Venezuela. *Headquarters*: Avenida Luis Roche-Altamira, Edif. Torre Central, Apartado Postal: Carmelitas 5086, Altamira 69011–69012, Caracas, Venezuela (telephone: 285 5555; telex: 27418; fax: 284 2553/284 2880).

Arab Co-operation Council. *Formed*: 1989. *Purpose*: To promote economic co-operation among member countries, including free movement of workers, joint projects in agriculture, transport and communications, and eventual integration of trade and monetary policies. *Members*: Egypt, Iraq, Jordan, Yemen. *Secretary-General*: Helmi Namar. *Headquarters*: Amman, Jordan.

Economic Community of Central African States [Communauté économique des états d'Afrique centrale] (CEEAC). *Formed*: 1983. *Purpose*: To promote economic co-operation, particularly with regard to free movement of citizens, removal of non-tariff barriers, standardization of trade documents, and establishment of a development fund. *Members*: Burundi, Cameroon, Central African Republic, Chad, Congo, Equatorial Guinea, Gabon, Rwanda, São Tomé and Principe, Zaire; Angola has observer status. *Headquarters*: P.O. Box 2112, Libreville, Gabon.

Economic Co-operation Organization (ECO). *Formed*: 1985 to replace Regional Co-operation for Development (RCD) established in 1964. *Purpose*: To encourage and strengthen economic, technical and cultural co-operation and to promote the economic advancement and welfare of the peoples of the region. Joint postal organization (the South and West Asia Postal

Union) established in 1988; joint Chamber of Commerce and Industry established in 1990. *Members*: Iran, Pakistan, Turkey. *Secretary-General*: Ali Reza Salari. *Headquarters*: 5 Hejab Avenue, Blvd Keshavarz, P.O. Box 14155-6176, Teheran, Iran (telephone: 658045; telex: 213774). *Publication*: *Annual Report*.

Gambia River Basin Development Organization [Organisation de mise en valeur du fleuve Gambie] (OMVG). *Formed*: 1978. *Purpose*: To co-ordinate the development of the Gambia basin and to recommend plans for common projects with special regard to irrigation and hydroelectricity. *Members*: Gambia, Guinea, Guinea-Bissau, Senegal. *Executive Secretary*: Nassirou Diallo. *Headquarters*: P.O. Box 2353, 13 rue Le Blanc, Dakar, Senegal (telephone: 223159).

Indian Ocean Commission (IOC). *Formed*: 1982. *Purpose*: To promote regional co-operation, with special regard to new and renewable energy systems, industrial development, fisheries, trade, air and maritime transport, environment, education and culture. *Members*: Comoros, France (representing Réunion), Madagascar, Mauritius, Seychelles. *Secretary-General*: H. Rasolondraibe. *Headquarters*: Q4, avenue Sir Guy Forget, P.O. Box 7, Quatre Bornes, Mauritius (telephone: 425 9564; telex: 5273; fax: 425 1209). *Publication*: *Guide Import/Export*.

Intergovernmental Authority on Drought and Development (IGADD). *Formed*: 1986. *Purpose*: To co-ordinate measures with a view to combating the effects of drought and desertification and to implement the relevant projects. *Members*: Djibouti, Ethiopia, Kenya, Somalia, Sudan, Uganda. *Executive Secretary*: Makonnen Kebret. *Headquarters*: P.O. Box 2653, Djibouti (telephone: 354200; telex: 5978).

Intergovernmental Co-ordinating Committee of the River Plate Basin Countries [Comité Intergubernamental Coordinador de los Países de la Cuenca del Plata] (CIC). *Formed*: 1967. *Purpose*: To promote the harmonious development and physical integration of the River Plate Basin. *Members*: Argentina, Bolivia, Brazil, Paraguay, Uruguay. *Headquarters*: Paraguay 755, 1057 Buenos Aires, Argentina (telephone: 312 2272).

Lake Chad Basin Commission (LCBC). *Formed*: 1964. *Purpose*: To co-ordinate the development of the Chad basin, to recommend plans for common projects and joint research programmes and to ensure the most efficient use of the subterranean and surface water resources in relation to agriculture, animal husbandry and fisheries. *Members*: Cameroon, Chad, Niger, Nigeria. *Executive Secretary*: Abubakar B. Jauro. *Headquarters*: P.O. Box 727, N'Djamena, Chad (telephone: 514137; telex: 5251).

Latin American Energy Organization [Organización Latinoamericana de Energía] (OLADE). *Formed*: 1973. *Purpose*: To facilitate and promote co-operation and co-ordination among the countries of Latin America with regard to policies concerning the protection, conservation, proper utilization and marketing of the energy resources of the region. *Members*: 26 Latin American and Caribbean countries. *Executive Secretary*: Gabriel Sanchez Sierra. *Headquarters*: Avenida Occidental, OLADE Building, Sector San Carlos, P.O. Box 6413 CCI, Quito, Ecuador (telephone: 538122). *Publication*: Revista Energetica.

Mano River Union (MRU). *Formed*: 1973. *Purpose*: To develop a common policy and co-operation regarding harmonization of tariffs and regulations concerning customs, telecommunications and postal services, forestry, and maritime activities and to promote joint development projects. *Members*: Guinea, Liberia, Sierra Leone. *Secretary-General*: Dr Abdoulaye Diallo. *Headquarters*: Private Mail Bag 133, Freetown, Sierra Leone (telephone: 22 811).

MERCOSUR (Common Market of the Southern Cone). *Formed*: 1991. *Purpose*: To form a common market through the establishment of a common external tariff, the co-ordination of fiscal, foreign exchange and customs policies, and the realization of the free movement of goods, services, capital and labour. *Members*: Argentina, Brazil, Paraguay, Uruguay. *Headquarters*: Cuareim 1384, Montevideo, Uruguay (telephone: 920319/907195; fax: 921 726).

Niger Basin Authority [Autorité du bassin du Niger]. *Formed*: 1964 as River Niger Commission [Commission du fleuve Niger] (CFN), present title adopted in 1980. *Purpose*: To promote the most effective use and development of the resources of the Niger basin in all fields. *Members*: Benin, Burkina Faso, Cameroon, Chad, Côte d'Ivoire, Guinea, Mali, Niger, Nigeria. *Executive Secretary*: Aliyu Magagi. *Headquarters*: P.O. Box 729, Niamey, Niger. *Publication*: Bulletin.

Organization for the Development of the Senegal River [Organisation pour la mise en valeur du fleuve Sénégal] (OMVS). *Formed*: 1972. *Purpose*: To develop, by means of a close co-operation among member countries, the resources of the Senegal basin (agricultural, industrial and mining projects, hydroelectric dams, ports). *Members*: Mali, Mauritania, Senegal; admission of Guinea approved in principle. *Secretary-General*: Founeke Keita. *Headquarters*: 46 rue Carnot, P.O. Box 3152, Dakar, Senegal (telephone: 223679; telex: 670). *Publication*: Fleuve Sénégal (periodical).

Organization for the Management and Development of the Kagera River Basin (Organisation pour l'aménagement et le développement du bassin de la rivière Kagera). *Formed*: 1978. *Purpose*: To achieve the integrated development of the water and land resources of the Kagera River Basin. *Members*: Burundi, Rwanda, Tanzania, Uganda. *Executive Secretary*: Jean-Bosco Balinda. *Headquarters*: P.O. Box 297, Kigali, Rwanda (telephone 84665; telex: 0909 22567; fax: 82172).

Organization of Eastern Caribbean States (OECS). *Formed*: 1981. *Purpose*: To promote co-operation and economic integration among member countries, to defend their sovereignty, territorial integrity and independence, and to establish, as far as possible, common positions on international issues. *Members*: Antigua and Barbuda, Dominica, Grenada, Montserrat, Saint Christopher and Nevis, Saint Lucia, Saint Vincent and the Grenadines; associate member: British Virgin Islands. *Director-General*: Dr Vaughan A. Lewis. *Headquarters*: P.O. Box 179, The Morne, Castries, Saint Lucia (telephone: 22537; telex: 6248; fax: 31628).

Pacific Basin Economic Council (PBEC). *Formed*: 1967. *Purpose*: To provide a forum for business leaders with a view to increasing trade and investment flows through open markets in the Pacific and to co-operate with governments and international organizations on key issues affecting the development of the Pacific region. *Members*: Committees in Australia, Canada, Chile, Fiji, Hong Kong, Japan, Korea, Mexico, Malaysia, New Zealand, Peru, Philippines, Taipei and the USA. *International Director General*: Robert G. Lees. *Headquarters*: Pauahi Tower, 1001 Bishop Street, Suite 1150, Honolulu, Hawaii 96813 (telephone: 521 9044; fax: 599 8690)..

Permanent Inter-State Committee for Drought Control in the Sahel [Comité permanent interétats de lutte contre la sécheresse dans le Sahel] (CILSS). *Formed*: 1973. *Purpose*: To organize joint efforts to control drought and its effects in the Sudano-Sahelian region in co-operation with UN Sudano-Sahelian Office (UNSO). *Members*: Burkina Faso, Cape Verde, Chad, Gambia, Guinea-Bissau, Mali, Mauritania, Niger, Senegal. *Executive Secretary*: Ali Diard Djalbord. *Headquarters*: P.O. Box 7049, Ouagadougou, Burkina Faso (telephone: 33078; telex: 5263).

Preferential Trade Area for Eastern and Southern Africa (PTA). *Formed*: 1981. *Purpose*: To improve commercial and economic co-operation within the region and to facilitate financial transactions between member countries with a view to establishing a Common Market and eventually an Economic Community. *Members*: Angola, Burundi, Comoros, Djibouti, Ethiopia, Kenya, Lesotho, Malawi, Mauritius,

Mozambique, Namibia, Rwanda, Somalia, Sudan, Swaziland, Tanzania, Uganda, Zaire, Zambia, Zimbabwe. *Secretary-General*: Bingu Wa Mutharika. *Headquarters*: P.O. Box 30051, Lusaka, Zambia (telephone: 229725; telex: 40127).

Rio Group. *Formed*: 1986. *Purpose*: To provide a permanent mechanism for political consultation and co-ordination in order to liberalize regional trade and expedite the process of Latin American integration. *Members*: Argentina, Bolivia, Brazil, Chile, Colombia, Ecuador, Mexico, Paraguay, Peru, Uruguay, Venezuela. The Group has no legal status and no permanent headquarters.

Southern African Customs Union (SACU). *Formed*: 1969. *Purpose*: To provide for the free movement of goods and services among member countries and to maintain a common external tariff. *Members*: Botswana, Lesotho, Namibia, South Africa, Swaziland.

Union of the Arab Maghreb [Union du Maghreb Arabe] (UMA). *Formed*: 1989. *Purpose*: To create a customs union and later a 'North African Common Market' and to encourage joint ventures and projects. *Members*: Algeria, Libya, Mauritania, Morocco, Tunisia. *Headquarters*: Office du Président, Tunis, Tunisia.

(3) Banking, Industry and Trade

Asian Productivity Organization (APO). *Formed*: 1961. *Purpose*: To strengthen the productivity movement in the Asian region and to disseminate modern productivity knowledge, techniques and experience in agriculture, industry and service sectors. *Members*: countries in the Asia-Pacific region. *Secretary-General*: Nagao Yoshida. *Headquarters*: 4-14 Akasaka, 8-chome, Minato-ku, Tokyo 107, Japan (telephone:3408 7221; telex: 26477; fax: 3408 7220). *Publications*: *Annual Report*; *APO News* (monthly)

Bank of Central African States [Banque

des états de l'Afrique centrale] (BEAC). *Formed*: 1955; present title adopted in 1973. *Purpose*: To act as exclusive issuing house for notes and coins for circulation in the member countries. *Members*: Cameroon, Central African Republic, Chad, Congo, Equatorial Guinea, Gabon. France is not a member but participates in management. *Governor*: Jean-Felix Mamalepot. *Headquarters*: P.O. Box 1917, Yaounde, Cameroon (telephone 222505; telex: 8343; fax: 233329). *Publications*: *Rapport annuel*; *Etudes et statistiques* (monthly).

Central Bank of West African States [Banque centrale des états de l'Afrique de l'Ouest] (BCEAO). *Formed*: 1955; present title adopted in 1962. *Purpose*: To act as issuing house for the member countries of the West African Monetary Union [Union monétaire ouest-africaine] (UMOA): Benin, Burkina Faso, Côte d'Ivoire, Mali, Niger, Senegal, Togo. *Secretary-General*: Jacques Diouf. *Headquarters*: Avenue Abdoulaye Fadiga, P.O. Box 3108, Dakar, Senegal (telephone: 231615; telex: 21815; fax: 239335). *Publications*: *Annual Report*; *Notes d'information et statistiques* (monthly).

Customs Co-operation Council (CCC). *Formed*: 1950. *Purpose*: To study questions relating to co-operation in customs matters with a view to attaining harmony and uniformity, to prepare draft conventions and recommendations, to ensure uniform interpretation and application of customs conventions and to circulate information on customs regulations and procedures. *Members*: 107 countries or territories. *Secretary-General*: T.P. Hayes. *Headquarters*: 26-38 rue de l'Industrie, 1040 Brussels, Belgium (telephone: 513 9900; telex: 61597; fax: 514 3372). *Publications*: *Bulletin* (annually); *CCC News* (periodical); technical handbooks and brochures.

Eastern Caribbean Central Bank (ECCB). *Formed*: 1983. *Purpose*: To maintain a common currency (Eastern Caribbean Dollar) between members of the *Organization of Eastern Caribbean States (OECS), to establish a central body with powers to issue and manage the common currency, and to pro-

mote monetary stability and a sound financial structure. *Members*: Antigua and Barbuda, Dominica, Grenada, Montserrat, Saint Christopher and Nevis, Saint Lucia, Saint Vincent and the Grenadines. *Governor*: Dwight Venner. *Headquarters*: P.O. Box 89, Basseterre, Saint Christopher and Nevis (telephone: 2537; telex: 6828). *Publication*: *Annual Report*.

International Whaling Commission (IWC). *Formed*: 1946. *Purpose*: To provide for conservation of whale stocks, to encourage research relating to whales and whaling, to collect and analyze statistical information concerning conditions and trend of whale stocks and to appraise and disseminate information about methods of maintaining and increasing whale stocks. *Members*: 36 countries in all continents. *Secretary*: Dr R. Gambell. *Headquarters*: The Red House, Station Road, Histon, Cambridge CB4 4NP, England (telephone: 233971; fax: 232876). *Publication*: *Annual Report*.

West African Development Bank [Banque ouest-africaine de développement] (BOAD). *Formed*: 1973. *Purpose*: To promote the balanced development of member countries and the economic integration of West Africa, to mobilize external capital in the form of both loans and grants, to prepare and finance development projects. *Members*: Benin, Burkina Faso, Côte d'Ivoire, Mali, Niger, Senegal, Togo. *President*: Abou Bakar Baba-Moussa. *Headquarters*: P.O. Box 1172, Lomé, Togo (telephone: 214244; telex: 5289). *Publication*: *Rapport annuel*.

(4) Commodities

African Groundnut Council [Conseil africain de l'arachide]. *Formed*: 1964. *Purpose*: To ensure remunerative prices for groundnut and its by-products, to promote consumption, and to organize exchange of information concerning the production, marketing and possible uses of groundnuts. *Members*: Gambia, Mali, Niger, Nigeria, Senegal, Sudan. *Executive Secretary*: Mour Mamadou Samb.

Headquarters: Trade Fair Complex, Badagry Expressway Km 15, P.O. Box 3025, Lagos, Nigeria (telephone: 880982; telex: 21366) *Publications*: *Groundnut Review*; *Newsletter*.

African Petroleum Producers' Association. *Formed*: 1986. *Purpose*: To reinforce co-operation among African petroleum-producing countries and to stabilize prices. *Members*: Algeria, Angola, Benin, Cameroon, Congo, Côte d'Ivoire, Egypt, Gabon, Libya, Nigeria, Zaire. *Executive Secretary*: Mohammed Souidi. *Headquarters*: Brazzaville, Congo.

Asian and Pacific Coconut Community (APCC). *Formed*: 1969. *Purpose*: To promote, co-ordinate and harmonize all activities of the coconut industry towards better production, processing, marketing and research. *Members*: Fiji, India, Indonesia, Malaysia, Federated States of Micronesia, Papua New Guinea, Philippines, Solomon Islands, Sri Lanka, Thailand, Vanuatu, Viet Nam, Western Samoa; associate member: Palau. *Executive Director*: P.G. Punchihewa. *Headquarters*: P.O. Box 1343, Jakarta, Indonesia (telephone: 510073; telex: 62863; fax: 510073). *Publications*: *Annual Report*; *The Cocomunity* (bimonthly newsletter); *Statistical Yearbook*.

Association of Iron Ore Exporting Countries [Association des pays exportateurs de minerai de fer] (APEF). *Formed*: 1975. *Purpose*: To co-ordinate policies of the exporting countries so as to secure fair and remunerative returns from the exploitation, processing and marketing of iron ore. *Members*: Algeria, Australia, India, Liberia, Mauritania, Peru, Sierra Leone, Sweden, Venezuela. *Secretary-General*: L. Roigart. *Headquarters*: Le Château, 14 chemin Auguste Vilbert, 1218 Grand Saconnex, Geneva, Switzerland (telephone: 982955; telex: 289443).

Association of Natural Rubber Producing Countries (ANRPC). *Formed*: 1970. *Purpose*: To co-ordinate the production and marketing of natural rubber, to ensure fair and stable prices, and to promote technical co-operation among member countries. *Members*: India, Indonesia, Malaysia, Papua New Guinea, Singapore, Sri Lanka, Thailand. *Secretary-General*: Dr Abdul Madjid. *Headquarters*: Natural Rubber Building, 148 Jalan Ampang, 50450 Kuala Lumpur, Malaysia (telephone: 261 1900; fax: 261 3014). *Publications*: *ANRPC News*; *Quarterly Statistical Bulletin*.

Association of Tin Producing Countries (ATPC). *Formed*: 1983 to administer the International Tin Agreement. *Purpose*: To promote co-operation in marketing of tin, to gather data and support research. *Members*: Australia, Bolivia, Indonesia, Malaysia, Nigeria, Thailand, Zaire; observer: Brazil. *Secretary-General*: Redzwan Sumun. *Headquarters*: Menara Dayabumi, 4th Floor, Jalan Sultan Hishamuddin, 50050 Kuala Lumpur, Malaysia (telephone: 274 7620; Telex: 32721; fax: 274 0669).

Cocoa Producers' Alliance (COPAL). *Formed*: 1962. *Purpose*: To examine problems of mutual concern to producers, to ensure adequate supplies at remunerative prices, to promote consumption and to exchange technical and scientific information. *Members*: Brazil, Cameroon, Côte d'Ivoire, Dominican Republic, Ecuador, Gabon, Ghana, Malaysia, Mexico, Nigeria, São Tomé and Principe, Togo, Trinidad and Tobago. *Secretary-General*: Djeumo Silas Kamga. *Headquarters*: Western House, 8-10 Broad Street, P.O. Box 1718, Lagos, Nigeria (telephone 635506).

Group of Latin American and Caribbean Sugar Exporting Countries (GEPLACEA). *Formed*: 1974. *Purpose*: To serve as a forum of consultation on the production and sale of sugar and to co-ordinate policies in order to achieve fair and remunerative prices. *Members*: 22 countries in Latin America and the Caribbean, and the Philippines. *Executive Secretary*: José Antonio Cerro. *Headquarters*: Ejercito Nacional 373, 11520 Mexico DF, Mexico (telephone: 250 7566; telex: 01771042; fax: 250 7591).

Inter-African Coffee Organization

(IACO). *Formed*: 1960. *Purpose*: To further the study of common problems concerning African coffee, including production, processing and marketing, in order to ensure the smooth disposal of production and the optimum level of selling prices. *Members*: 25 coffee-producing countries in Africa. *Secretary-General*: Arega Worku. *Headquarters*: BP V210, Abidjan, Côte d'Ivoire (telephone: 216131; telex: 22406). *Publications*: *African Coffee* (quarterly); *Directory of African Exporters* (every two years).

Intergovernmental Council of Copper Exporting Countries [Conseil intergouvernemental des pays exportateurs de cuivre] (CIPEC). *Formed*: 1967. *Purpose*: To coordinate measures designed to foster growth of real earnings from copper exports and to increase resources for the economic and social development of copper-producing countries, with due regard to the interests of the consumers. *Members*: Chile, Peru, Zaire, Zambia; observer: Yugoslavia. *Secretary-General*: Jorge Fernandez Maldonado Solari. *Headquarters*: 39 rue de la Bienfaisance, 75008 Paris, France (telephone: 4225 0024; telex: 649077; fax: 4289 8911). *Publication*: *CIPEC Quarterly Review*.

International Bauxite Association (IBA). *Formed*: 1974. *Purpose*: To co-ordinate policies of the producing countries in order to secure fair and reasonable profits in the processing and marketing of bauxite, bearing in mind the interests of consumer countries. *Members*: Australia, Ghana, Guinea, Guyana, India, Indonesia, Jamaica, Sierra Leone, Suriname, Yugoslavia. *Secretary-General*: Ibrahima Bah. *Headquarters*: 36 Trafalgar Road, P.O. Box 551, Kingston 5, Jamaica (telephone: 92 64535; telex: 2428; fax: 92 67157). *Publication*: *Quarterly Review*.

International Cocoa Organization (ICCO). *Formed*: 1973 under the first International Cocoa Agreement, 1972, renegotiated several times thereafter. *Purpose*: To supervise the implementation of the agreement and to provide member countries with conference facilities and up-to-date information on the world cocoa economy and the operation of the agreement. *Members*: 18 exporting countries in Africa, Latin America and the Caribbean, and the Pacific which account for over 90 per cent of world cocoa exports, and 22 importing countries (with the important exception of the USA) which represent over two-thirds of world cocoa imports. Executive Director: Edouard Kouame. *Headquarters*: 22 Berners Street, London W1P 3DB, England (telephone: 637 3211; telex: 28173; fax: 631 0114). *Publications*: *Annual Report*; *Quarterly Bulletin of Cocoa Statistics*.

International Coffee Organization (ICO). *Formed*: 1963 under the International Coffee Agreement, 1962, renegotiated several times thereafter. *Purpose*: To achieve a reasonable balance between supply and demand on a basis which assures adequate supplies at fair prices to consumers and expanding markets at remunerative prices to producers. *Members*: 50 exporting countries which account for over 99 per cent of world coffee exports, Brazil being by far the largest supplier, and 22 importing countries which represent nearly 90 per cent of world imports. *Executive Director*: Alexandre Beltrão. *Headquarters*: 22 Berners Street, London W1P 4DD, England (telephone: 580 8591; telex: 267659). *Publication*: *Quarterly Statistical Bulletin*.

International Cotton Advisory Committee (ICAC). *Formed*: 1939. *Purpose*: To review developments affecting the world cotton situation, to collect and disseminate statistics, and to recommend any measures for the furtherance of international collaboration with a view to maintaining and developing a sound world cotton economy. *Members*: 45 countries in all continents. *Executive Director*: L.H. Shaw. *Headquarters*: 1901 Pennsylvania Avenue NW, Suite 201, Washington, D.C. 20006, USA (telephone: 463 6660; telex: 701517; fax: 463 6950). *Publications*: *Cotton – Review of the World Situation*; *Cotton – World Statistics*.

International Institute for Cotton (IIC).

Formed: 1966, under the auspices of the *International Cotton Advisory Committee (ICAC). *Purpose*: To increase the consumption of raw cotton and the products manufactured therefrom and to prepare and carry out cotton market development programmes. *Members*: Brazil, India, Côte d'Ivoire, Mexico, Nigeria, Tanzania, Uganda, USA, Zimbabwe. *Secretary*: Harpal Luther. *Headquarters*: Suite 627, 1511 K Street, NW, Washington, D.C. 20005, USA (telephone: 347 4220).

International Jute Organization (IJO). *Formed*: 1984. *Purpose*: To improve structural conditions in the jute market, to enhance the competitiveness of jute and jute products, and to promote and implement projects for research and development. *Members*: 5 exporting and 27 importing countries. *Executive Director*: Shamsul Haque Chishty. *Headquarters*: 95A Rd No 4, Banani, P.O. Box 6073, Gulshan, Dhaka, Bangladesh (telephone: 883256; telex: 642792; fax: 883641).

International Lead and Zinc Study Group (ILZSG). *Formed*: 1959. *Purpose*: To provide opportunities for regular consultations on international trade in lead and zinc, to conduct studies and to consider possible solutions to any special problems or difficulties. *Members*: 32 countries in all continents. *Secretary-General*: Dr Rolf W. Boehnke. *Headquarters*: Metro House, 58 St James's Street, London SW1A 1LD, England (telephone: 499 9373; telex: 299819; fax: 493 3725). *Publication*: *Lead and Zinc Statistics* (monthly).

International Natural Rubber Organization (INRO). *Formed*: 1980, under the International Natural Rubber Agreement, 1979, subsequently extended and renegotiated. *Purpose*: To achieve a balanced growth between the supply of and demand for natural rubber, thereby helping to alleviate difficulties arising from surpluses or shortages. *Members*: 3 exporting countries (Indonesia, Malaysia, Thailand) and 22 importing countries (including the EEC). *Executive Director*: Pong Sono. *Headquarters*: P.O. Box 10374, 50712 Kuala Lumpur, Malaysia (tele-

phone: 248 6466; telex: 31570; fax: 248 6485).

International Olive Oil Council (IOOC). *Formed*: 1959. *Purpose*: To co-ordinate policies of member countries in order to ensure fair competition in the olive oil trade, to put into operation, or to facilitate the application of, measures designed to expand the production and consumption of olive oil, to reduce the disadvantages arising from the fluctuations of supplies on the market and generally to foster international co-operation concerning world olive oil problems. *Members*: Five mainly producing countries, one mainly importing country, and the European Economic Community (EEC) as parties to the International Olive Oil Agreement (Fourth Agreement) signed in 1986. *Director*: Fausto Luchetti. *Headquarters*: Juan Bravo 10, Madrid 28006, Spain (telephone: 577 4735; telex: 48197; fax: 431 6127). *Publications*: *Information Sheet* (fortnightly); *National Policies for Olive Products* (annually).

International Pepper Community (IPC). *Formed*: 1972. *Purpose*: To promote increased consumption and enlargement of markets and to co-ordinate research on the technical and economic aspects of pepper production. *Members*: Brazil, India, Indonesia, Malaysia. *Executive Director*: Mohamed Ismail. *Headquarters*: 3rd Floor, Wisma Bakrie, Jalan H.R. Rasuna Said, Kav. B1, Kuningan, Jakarta 12920, Indonesia (telephone: 520 0401; telex: 62218; fax: 520 0401). *Publication*: Pepper News (monthly).

International Rubber Study Group (IRSG). *Formed*: 1944. *Purpose*: To provide a forum for the discussion of problems affecting natural and synthetic rubber and to provide statistical and other general information on rubber. *Members*: 27 countries substantially interested in rubber production, consumption or trade. *Secretary-General*: B.C. Sekhar. *Headquarters*: 8th Floor, York House, Empire Way, Wembley, HA9 0PA, England (telephone 903 7727; telex: 895 1293; fax: 903 2848). *Publications*: *Rubber Statistical*

Bulletin (monthly); *International Rubber Digest* (monthly); *World Rubber Statistics Handbook*.

International Sugar Organization (ISO). *Formed*: 1987. *Purpose*: To administer the International Sugar Agreement, 1987, to be succeeded by the International Sugar Agreement, 1992, in force since January 1993. *Members*: 36 exporting countries and 9 importing countries. *Executive Director*: Alfredo A. Ricart. *Headquarters*: 1 Canada Square, Canary Wharf, London E14 5AE, England (telephone: 513 1144; telex: 24143; fax: 513 1146). *Publications*: *Annual Report*; *Sugar Year Book*; *Monthly Statistical Bulletin*.

International Tea Committee. *Formed*: 1933. *Purpose*: To administer the International Tea Agreement and subsequently transformed into statistical and information centre. *Members*: Producer countries (Bangladesh, India, Indonesia, Kenya, Malawi, Sri Lanka, Zimbabwe) and consumer countries. *Chief Executive Secretary*: Peter Abel. *Headquarters*: Sir John Lyon House, 5 High Timber Street, London EC4V 3NH, England (telephone: 248 4672; telex: 887911; fax: 248 3011).

International Tropical Timber Organization (ITTO). *Formed*: 1985 under the International Tropical Timber Agreement, 1983. *Purpose*: To assist timber-producing countries in sustainable forest management, processing and trade, to collect information and to promote research. *Members*: 47 producing and consuming countries. *Executive Director*: Freezailah bin Che Yeom. *Headquarters*: 8F Sangyo Boeki Centre Bldg, 2 Yamashita-cho, Naka-ku, Yokohama 231, Japan (telephone: 671 7045; telex: 382 2480; fax: 671 7007).

International Vine and Wine Office [Office international de la vigne et du vin] (OIV). *Formed*: 1924. *Purpose*: To study the scientific, technical, economic and human problems concerning the vine and its products (wine, grapes, raisins, grape juice) and to spread the relevant knowledge by means of publications, to formulate a rational world policy with respect to viticulture and to address recommendations. *Members*: 33 countries, mostly in Europe. *Director*: Robert Tinlot. *Headquarters*: 11 rue Roquepine, 75008 Paris, France (telephone: 4265 0416; telex: 281196; fax: 4266 9063). *Publications*: *Bulletin de l'OIV* (every two months); *Codex oenologique international*.

International Wheat Council (IWC). *Formed*: 1949. *Purpose*: To administer the Wheat Trade Convention (WTC) of the International Wheat Agreement, 1986, and to further international co-operation in all aspects of trade in wheat and other grains. *Members*: 47 countries and the European Economic Community (EEC). *Executive Director*: J.H. Parotte. *Headquarters*: 28 Haymarket, London SW1Y 4SS, England (telephone: 930 4128; telex: 916128; fax: 839 6907). *Publications*: *Grain Market Report* (monthly); *World Wheat Statistics* (annually).

International Wool Study Group (IWSG). *Formed*: 1946. *Purpose*: To collect and collate statistics relating to the world supply of and demand for wool, to review developments in the world wool situation and to consider possible solutions to problems and difficulties unlikely to be resolved in the ordinary course of world trade in wool. *Members*: 14 countries in all continents. *Secretary-General*: L.J. Lamont. *Headquarters*: Ashdown House, 123 Victoria Street, London SW1E 6RB, England (telephone: (215 6215; telex: 881 3148).

Union of Banana Exporting Countries [Union de Países Exportadores de Banano] (UPEB). *Formed*: 1974. *Purpose*: To determine a co-ordinated policy in order to protect the interests of member countries, to promote the technical and economic development of the banana industry and to further international co-operation in connection with world banana problems. *Members*: Colombia, Costa Rica, Dominican Republic, Guatemala, Nicaragua, Panama, Venezuela. *Executive Director*: Haroldo Rodas. *Headquarters*: P.O. Box 4273, Panama City 5, Panama (telephone:

636266; telex: 2568; fax: 648355). *Publications*: *Informe Mensual*; *Boletin Mensual de Estadisticas*.

West Africa Rice Development Association (WARDA). *Formed*: 1970. *Purpose*: To increase the quantity and quality of rice produced in West Africa with a view to making the area self-sufficient. *Members*: 16 countries. *Director-General*: Dr Eugene Robert Terry. *Headquarters*: 01 BP 2551, Bouaké 01, Côte d'Ivoire (telephone: 634514; telex: 69138; fax: 634714). *Publication*: *Annual Report*.

(5) Education, Culture, Science and Technology

International Centre for the Study of the Preservation and the Restoration of Cultural Property (ICCROM). *Formed*: 1959. *Purpose*: To collect, study and disseminate documentation on the scientific and technical problems of the conservation and restoration of cultural property, to co-ordinate and stimulate research, to undertake training of specialists and to organize regular courses. *Members*: 79 countries in all continents. *Director*: Prof Andrzej Tomaszewski. *Headquarters*: Via di San Michele 13, 00153 Rome, Italy (telephone: 587901; telex: 613114; fax: 588 4265). *Publications*: *Newsletter* (annually); specialized monographs.

International Commission for the Scientific Exploration of the Mediterranean Sea [Commission internationale pour l'exploration scientifique de la mer Méditerranée] (CIESM). *Formed*: 1919. *Purpose*: To serve as a liaison body for research workers and to promote joint international activities on behalf of Mediterranean countries. *Members*: 17 countries bordering the Mediterranean (11 European, 4 African, 2 Asian). *Secretary-General*: J.Y. Cousteau. *Headquarters*: 16 boulevard de Suisse, Monte Carlo, Monaco (telephone: 303879). *Publications*: *Rapports et Procés-Verbaux des réunions de la CIESM*; scientific reports.

International Council for the Exploration of the Sea (ICES). *Formed*: 1902 as Permanent International Council for Exploration of the Sea; present title adopted in 1964. *Purpose*: To promote and encourage research and investigations, particularly those related to the living resources, for the study of the Atlantic Ocean and its adjacent seas. *Members*: 16 European countries plus Canada and the USA. *General Secretary*: Dr E.D. Anderson. *Headquarters*: Palaegade 2-4, 1261 Copenhagen K, Denmark (telephone: 3315 4225; telex: 22498; fax: 3393 4215). *Publications*: *Journal du Conseil*; *Bulletin statistique*.

International Institute for the Unification of Private Law (UNIDROIT). *Formed*: 1926. *Purpose*: To study methods for harmonizing and co-ordinating private law, to prepare drafts of laws and conventions with the object of establishing uniform internal law and to prepare drafts of agreements for the improvement of international relations in the field of private law. *Members*: 53 countries in all continents. *Secretary General*: Malcolm Evans. *Headquarters*: Via Panisperna 28, 00184 Rome, Italy (telephone: 684 1372; telex: 623166; fax: 684 1394). *Publications*: *Information Bulletin* (quarterly); *Uniform Law Review* (twice a year).

Organization of Ibero-American States for Education, Science and Culture [Organización de Estados Americanos para la Educación, la Ciencia y la Cultura]. *Formed*: 1949 as Ibero-American Bureau of Education. *Purpose*: To provide information and documentation on education, science and culture, to encourage cultural and educational exchanges and to organize training courses. *Members*: 20 countries in Latin America, and Spain. *Secretary-General*: Simon Romero Lozano. *Headquarters*: Ciudad Universitaria, 28040 Madrid, Spain (telephone: 449 6954; telex: 48422; fax: 449 3678).

Southeast Asian Ministers of Education Organization (SEAMEO). *Formed*: 1965. *Purpose*: To foster co-operation among the Southeast Asian countries through education, science and culture, to advance the mutual knowledge and understanding of the peoples of Southeast Asia and the rest of the world, and to promote collaboration in joint projects concerning education, science and culture. *Members*: Brunei, Cambodia, Indonesia, Laos, Malaysia, Philippines, Singapore, Thailand; *associate members*: Australia, Canada, France, Germany, New Zealand. *Director*: Prof Jakub Isman. *Headquarters*: Darakarn Building, 920 Sukhumvit Road, Bangkok 10110, Thailand (telephone: 391 0144; telex: 22683; fax: 381 2587). *Publication*: *SEAMEO Quarterly*.

(6) Posts and Telecommunications

African Posts and Telecommunications Union [Union africaine des postes et télécommunications] (UAPT). *Formed*: 1961. *Purpose*: To improve and organize rationally postal and telecommunication services between member countries. *Members*: 12 French-speaking countries. *Secretary-General*: Mahmoudou Samoura. *Headquarters*: Avenue P. Lumumba, P.O. Box 44, Brazzaville, Congo (telephone: 832778; telex: 5212).

Asian Pacific Postal Union (APPU). *Formed*: 1962. *Purpose*: To extend, facilitate and improve postal relations between member countries and to foster co-operation in the field of postal services. *Members*: 23 countries, including China, India, Japan, Australia. *Director*: Tagumpay R. Jardiniano. *Headquarters*: Post Office Building, 1000 Manila, Philippines (telephone: 470760). *Publications*: *Annual Report*; *Newsletter*.

Commonwealth Telecommunications Organization. *Formed*: 1967. *Purpose*: To promote consultation and co-operation among Commonwealth member countries on matters relating to external communications and the Commonwealth common user network. *Members*: 25 countries of the Commonwealth. *Secretary-General*: Graham H. Cunnold. *Headquarters*: 26-27 Oxendon Street, London SW1Y 4EL, England (telephone: 930 5511; telex: 27328; fax: 930 4248).

European Conference of Postal and Telecommunications Administrations [Conférence européenne des administrations des postes et des télécommunications] (CEPT). *Formed*: 1959. *Purpose*: To strengthen relations between members and to harmonize and improve administrative and technical services. *Members*: Postal and telecommunications administrations of 26 countries in Western Europe. *Managing Administration*: rotating among members; Liaison Office providing permanent administrative and secretariat service to the Managing Administration. *Liaison Office*: Aarbergergasse 5, Bern, Switzerland.

European Organization for the Exploitation of Meteorological Satellites (EUMETSAT). *Formed*: 1986. *Purpose*: To establish, maintain and exploit European systems of operational meteorological satellites. *Members*: 16 Western European countries. *Director*: John Morgan. *Headquarters*: Am Elfengrund 45, 6100 Darmstadt-Eberstadt, Germany (telephone: 5392-0; telex: 4 197 335; fax: 539225).

European Telecommunications Satellite Organization (EUTELSAT). *Formed*: 1977. *Purpose*: To design, construct, establish, operate and maintain space segments of telecommunications satellite systems with a view to providing international public telecommunications. *Members*: 26 national telecommunications administrations in Western Europe. *Headquarters*: Tour Maine Montparnasse, 33 avenue du Maine, 75755 Paris, France (telephone: 4538 4747; telex: 203823; fax: 4538 3700).

International Maritime Satellite Organization (INMARSAT). *Formed*: 1979. *Purpose*: To improve maritime communications for distress and safety of life at sea, efficiency and management of ships, maritime public correspondence services and radio determination capabilities and to serve the worldwide maritime community exclusively for peaceful purposes; original agreement subsequently amended to include aeronautical and global land-mobile communications. *Members*: 59 countries. *Director-General*: Olof Lundberg. *Headquarters*: 40 Melton Street, London NW1 2EQ, England (telephone: 387 9089; telex: 297201; fax: 387 2115). *Publications*: *Ocean Voice* (quarterly); *Aeronautical Satellite News* (quarterly).

International Telecommunications Satellite Organization (INTELSAT). *Formed*: 1964. *Purpose*: To establish, operate and maintain a global commercial satellite communications system. *Members*: 117 countries. *Director-General*: Dean Burch. *Headquarters*: 3400 International Drive, NW, Washington, D.C. 20008-3098, USA (telephone: 944 6800; telex: 892707).

Postal Union of the Americas and Spain [Unión Postal de las Américas y España] (UPAE). *Formed*: 1911. *Purpose*: To extend, facilitate, study and perfect the postal relationships of member countries. *Members*: Spain, Canada, USA and 21 countries in Latin America. *Secretary-General*: Pedro Miguel Cabero. *Headquarters*: Calle Cebollatí 1468/70, P.O. Box 20042, Montevideo, Uruguay (telephone: 400070; telex: 22073).

(7) Transport

African Civil Aviation Commission (AFCAC). *Formed*: 1969. *Purpose*: To provide a framework for co-operation in all civil aviation activities, to promote co-ordination and better utilization and development of African air transport systems and to encourage the application of ICAO standards and recommendations. *Members*: about 40 countries. *Secretary*: Edouard Lombolou. *Headquarters*: 15 boulevard de la République, P.O. Box 2356, Dakar, Senegal (telephone: 223030; telex: 3182).

Central Commission for the Navigation of the Rhine. *Formed*: 1815. *Purpose*: To ensure freedom and security of navigation and equality of treatment to ships of all nations, to draw up navigational rules, to standardize customs regulations, to arbitrate in disputes involving river traffic and to approve plans for river maintenance work. *Members*: Belgium, France, Germany, Luxembourg, Netherlands, Switzerland. *Secretary-General*: R. Doerflinger. *Headquarters*: Palais du Rhin, Place de la Republique, Strasbourg, France (telephone: 8832 3584). *Publication*: *Annual Report*.

Central Office for International Carriage by Rail. *Formed*: 1893. *Purpose*: To facilitate and ensure application of the international conventions regulating the carriage of goods, passengers and luggage by rail. *Members*: 35 countries mainly in Western and Eastern Europe. *Director-General*: C. Mossu. *Headquarters*: Thunplatz, Gryphenhubeliweg 30, 3006 Berne, Switzerland (telephone: 431762; telex: 912063; fax: 431164). *Publication*: *Bulletin des transports internationaux ferroviaires* (quarterly).

European Civil Aviation Conference [Commission européenne de l'aviation civile] (CEAC). *Formed*: 1955. *Purpose*: To promote the co-ordination, the better utilization and the orderly development of European air transport and to consider any special problem that may arise in this field. *Members*: 25 countries in Western Europe. *Secretary*: Edward Hudson. *Headquarters*: 3 bis Villa Emile-Bergerat, 92522 Neuilly-sur-Seine, France (telephone: 4637 9545; telex: 610075; fax: 4624 1818).

European Conference of Ministers of Transport (ECMT) [Conférence européenne des ministres des transports] (CEMT). *Formed*: 1953. *Purpose*: To achieve, at general or regional level, the maximum use and most rational development of European inland transport of international importance. *Members*: 19 countries of Western Europe; associate members: Australia, Canada, Japan, USA. *Secretary-General*: J.C. Terlouw. *Headquarters*: 19 rue de Franqueville, 75775 Paris, France (telephone: 4524 8200; telex: 611040; fax: 4524 9742). *Publication*: *Annual Report*.

European Organization for the Safety of

Air Navigation (EUROCONTROL). *Formed*: 1963. *Purpose*: To strengthen co-operation in matters of air navigation and in particular to provide for the common organization of air traffic services in the upper airspace. *Members*: 14 countries. *Director-General*: Keith Mack. *Headquarters*: 72 rue de la Loi, 1040 Brussels, Belgium (telephone: 233 0211; telex: 21173; fax: 233 0353).

International Organizations
Membership Tables

Members of the United Nations, the specialized and IAEA, and contracting parties to GATT

Country	UN	ILO	FAO	UNESCO	ICAO	WHO	World Bank	IFC	IDA	IMF	UPU	ITU	WMO	IMO	WIPO	IFAD	IAEA	GATT	UNIDO
Afghanistan	X	X	X	X	X	X	X	X	X	X	X	X	X			X	X		X
Albania	X	X	X	X	X	X	X	X	X	X	X	X	X		X	X	X		X
Algeria	X	X	X	X	X	X	X	X	X	X	X	X	X	X	X	X	X		X
Angola	X	X	X	X	X	X	X	X	X	X		X	X	X	X	X			X
Antigua and Barbuda	X	X	X	X	X	X	X	X	X	X	X	X	X	X		X		X	
Argentina	X	X	X	X	X	X	X	X	X	X	X	X	X	X	X	X	X	X	X
Armenia	X	X		X		X	X			X		X							
Australia	X	X	X	X	X	X	X	X	X	X	X	X	X	X	X	X	X	X	X
Austria	X	X	X	X	X	X	X	X	X	X	X	X	X	X	X	X	X	X	X
Azerbaijan	X	X		X						X		X							
Bahamas	X	X	X	X	X	X	X	X		X	X	X	X	X	X				X
Bahrain	X	X	X	X	X	X	X	X		X	X	X	X	X					X
Bangladesh	X	X	X	X	X	X	X	X	X	X	X	X	X	X	X	X	X	X	X
Barbados	X	X	X	X	X	X	X	X		X	X	X	X	X	X	X		X	X
Belarus	X	X		X		X	X				X	X	X	X	X		X		X
Belgium	X	X	X	X	X	X	X	X	X	X	X	X	X	X	X	X	X	X	X
Belize	X	X	X	X	X	X	X	X	X	X	X	X	X	X	X	X		X	X
Benin	X	X	X	X	X	X	X	X	X	X	X	X	X	X	X	X		X	X
Bhutan	X		X	X	X	X	X		X	X	X	X	X			X			X
Bolivia	X	X	X	X	X	X	X	X	X	X	X	X	X	X		X	X	X	X
Bosnia-Herzegovina	X																		
Botswana	X	X	X	X	X	X	X	X	X	X	X	X	X	X	X	X		X	X
Brazil	X	X	X	X	X	X	X	X	X	X	X	X	X	X	X	X	X	X	X
Brunei	X		X	X	X	X					X	X	X	X					X
Bulgaria	X	X	X	X	X	X	X	X		X	X	X	X	X	X		X		X
Burkina Faso	X	X	X	X	X	X	X	X	X	X	X	X	X		X	X		X	X
Burundi	X	X	X	X	X	X	X	X	X	X	X	X	X	X	X	X		X	X

Members of the United Nations, the specialized and IAEA, and contracting parties to GATT—continued

Country	UN	ILO	FAO	UNESCO	ICAO	WHO	World Bank	IFC	IDA	IMF	UPU	ITU	WMO	IMO	WIPO	IFAD	IAEA	GATT	UNIDO
Cambodia	X	X	X	X	X	X	X		X	X	X	X	X	X		X	X		
Cameroon	X	X	X	X	X	X	X	X	X	X	X	X	X	X	X	X	X	X	X
Canada	X	X	X	X	X	X	X	X	X	X	X	X	X	X	X	X	X	X	X
Cape Verde	X	X	X	X	X	X	X	X	X	X	X	X	X	X	X	X			X
Central African Republic	X	X	X	X	X	X	X	X	X	X	X	X	X		X	X		X	X
Chad	X	X	X	X	X	X	X		X	X	X	X	X		X	X		X	X
Chile	X	X	X	X	X	X	X	X	X	X	X	X	X	X	X	X	X	X	X
China	X	X	X	X	X	X	X	X	X	X	X	X	X	X	X	X	X		X
Colombia	X	X	X	X	X	X	X	X	X	X	X	X	X	X	X	X	X	X	X
Comoros	X	X	X	X	X	X	X	X	X	X	X	X	X	X		X			X
Congo	X	X	X	X	X	X	X	X	X	X	X	X	X	X	X			X	X
Costa Rica	X	X	X	X	X	X	X	X	X	X	X	X	X	X	X	X		X	X
Côte d'Ivoire	X	X	X	X	X	X	X	X	X	X	X	X	X	X	X	X	X	X	X
Cuba	X	X	X	X	X	X					X	X	X	X	X	X	X	X	X
Croatia	X			X	X														
Cyprus	X	X	X	X	X	X	X	X	X	X	X	X	X	X	X	X	X	X	X
Czechoslovakia	X	X	X	X	X	X	X	X	X	X	X	X	X	X	X		X	X	X
Democratic People's Republic of Korea	X		X	X	X	X					X	X	X	X	X		X		X
Denmark	X	X	X	X	X	X	X	X	X	X	X	X	X	X	X	X	X	X	X
Djibouti	X	X	X	X	X	X	X	X	X	X	X	X	X	X	X	X			X
Dominica	X	X	X	X	X	X	X	X	X	X	X	X		X		X			X
Dominican Republic	X	X	X	X	X	X	X	X	X	X	X	X	X	X		X	X	X	X
Ecuador	X	X	X	X	X	X	X	X	X	X	X	X	X	X	X	X	X	X	X
Egypt	X	X	X	X	X	X	X	X	X	X	X	X	X	X	X	X	X	X	X
El Salvador	X	X	X	X	X	X	X	X	X	X	X	X	X	X	X	X	X	X	X
Equatorial Guinea	X	X	X	X	X	X	X	X	X	X	X	X		X		X			X
Estonia	X	X	X	X	X	X	X	X		X	X	X		X			X		

299

Members of the United Nations, the specialized and IAEA, and contracting parties to GATT—continued

Country	UN	ILO	FAO	UNESCO	ICAO	WHO	World Bank	IFC	IDA	IMF	UPU	ITU	WMO	IMO	WIPO	IFAD	IAEA	GATT	UNIDO
Ethiopia	X	X	X	X	X	X	X	X	X	X	X	X	X	X		X	X		X
Fiji	X	X	X	X	X	X	X	X	X	X	X	X	X	X	X	X			X
Finland	X	X	X	X	X	X	X	X	X	X	X	X	X	X	X	X	X	X	X
France	X	X	X	X	X	X	X	X	X	X	X	X	X	X	X	X	X	X	X
Gabon	X	X	X	X	X	X	X	X	X	X	X	X	X	X	X	X	X	X	X
Gambia	X	X		X		X	X	X	X	X	X	X	X	X	X	X		X	X
Georgia	X									X									
Germany	X	X	X	X	X	X	X	X	X	X	X	X	X	X	X	X	X	X	X
Ghana	X	X	X	X	X	X	X	X	X	X	X	X	X	X	X	X	X	X	X
Greece	X	X	X	X	X	X	X	X	X	X	X	X	X	X	X	X	X	X	X
Grenada	X	X	X	X	X	X	X	X	X	X	X	X		X		X			X
Guatemala	X	X	X	X	X	X	X	X	X	X	X	X	X	X	X	X	X	X	X
Guinea	X	X	X	X	X	X	X	X	X	X	X	X	X	X	X	X			X
Guinea-Bissau	X	X	X	X	X	X	X	X	X	X	X	X	X	X		X			X
Guyana	X	X	X	X	X	X	X	X	X	X	X	X	X	X	X	X		X	X
Haiti	X	X	X	X	X	X	X	X	X	X	X	X	X	X	X	X	X	X	X
Holy See											X	X			X		X		
Honduras	X	X	X	X	X	X	X	X	X	X	X	X	X	X	X	X	X		X
Hungary	X	X	X	X	X	X	X	X	X	X	X	X	X	X	X		X	X	X
Iceland	X	X	X	X	X	X	X	X	X	X	X	X	X	X	X		X	X	X
India	X	X	X	X	X	X	X	X	X	X	X	X	X	X	X	X	X	X	X
Indonesia	X	X	X	X	X	X	X	X	X	X	X	X	X	X	X	X	X	X	X
Iran	X	X	X	X	X	X	X	X	X	X	X	X	X	X	X	X	X		X
Iraq	X	X	X	X	X	X	X	X	X	X	X	X	X	X	X	X	X		X
Ireland	X	X	X	X	X	X	X	X	X	X	X	X	X	X	X	X	X	X	X
Israel	X	X	X	X	X	X	X	X	X	X	X	X	X	X	X	X	X	X	X
Italy	X	X	X	X	X	X	X	X	X	X	X	X	X	X	X	X	X	X	X

Members of the United Nations, the specialized and IAEA, and contracting parties to GATT—continued

Country	UN	ILO	FAO	UNESCO	ICAO	WHO	World Bank	IFC	IDA	IMF	UPU	ITU	WMO	IMO	WIPO	IFAD	IAEA	GATT	UNIDO
Jamaica	X	X	X	X	X	X	X	X	X	X	X	X	X	X	X	X	X	X	X
Japan	X	X	X	X	X	X	X	X	X	X	X	X	X	X	X	X	X	X	X
Jordan	X	X	X	X	X	X	X	X	X	X	X	X	X	X	X	X	X		X
Kazakhstan	X			X															
Kenya	X	X	X	X	X	X	X	X	X	X	X	X	X	X	X	X	X	X	X
Kiribati	X	X		X	X	X	X	X	X	X	X	X							
Kuwait	X	X	X	X	X	X	X	X	X	X	X	X	X	X	X	X	X	X	X
Kyrgyzstan	X	X		X		X	X	X	X	X									
Lao People's Democratic Republic	X	X	X	X	X	X	X	X	X	X	X	X	X			X			X
Latvia	X	X	X	X	X	X				X	X	X	X			X			X
Lebanon	X	X	X	X	X	X	X	X	X	X	X	X	X	X	X	X	X		X
Lesotho	X	X	X	X	X	X	X	X	X	X	X	X	X	X	X	X		X	X
Liberia	X	X	X	X	X	X	X	X	X	X	X	X	X	X	X	X	X	X	X
Libyan Arab Jamahiriya	X	X	X	X	X	X	X	X	X	X	X	X	X	X	X	X	X		X
Liechtenstein	X										X	X			X		X		
Lithuania	X	X	X	X	X	X	X	X		X	X	X	X		X				X
Luxembourg	X	X	X	X	X	X	X	X	X	X	X	X	X	X	X	X	X	X	X
Madagascar	X	X	X	X	X	X	X	X	X	X	X	X	X	X	X	X	X	X	X
Malawi	X	X	X	X	X	X	X	X	X	X	X	X	X		X	X		X	X
Malaysia	X	X	X	X	X	X	X	X	X	X	X	X	X	X	X	X	X	X	X
Maldives	X		X	X	X	X	X	X	X	X	X	X	X	X	X	X		X	X
Mali	X	X	X	X	X	X	X	X	X	X	X	X	X	X	X	X	X	X	X
Malta	X	X	X	X	X	X	X	X		X	X	X	X	X	X	X	X	X	X
Marshall Islands	X				X	X	X	X		X									
Mauritania	X	X	X	X	X	X	X	X	X	X	X	X	X	X	X	X	X	X	X
Mauritius	X	X	X	X	X	X	X	X	X	X	X	X	X	X	X	X	X	X	X
Mexico	X	X	X	X	X	X	X	X	X	X	X	X	X	X	X	X	X	X	X

Members of the United Nations, the specialized and IAEA, and contracting parties to GATT—continued

Country	UN	ILO	FAO	UNESCO	ICAO	WHO	World Bank	IFC	IDA	IMF	UPU	ITU	WMO	IMO	WIPO	IFAD	IAEA	GATT	UNIDO
Micronesia	X					X													
Moldova	X	X		X		X				X	X	X	X		X				
Monaco				X	X	X					X	X	X	X	X		X		
Mongolia	X	X	X	X	X	X	X	X	X	X	X	X	X	X	X	X	X		X
Morocco	X	X	X	X	X	X	X	X	X	X	X	X	X	X	X	X	X	X	X
Mozambique	X	X	X	X	X	X	X	X	X	X	X	X	X	X	X	X		X	X
Myanmar	X	X	X	X	X	X	X	X	X	X	X	X	X	X		X	X	X	X
Namibia	X	X	X	X	X	X	X	X	X	X	X	X	X		X	X	X	X	X
Nauru					X						X	X							
Nepal	X	X	X	X	X	X	X	X	X	X	X	X	X	X	X	X	X		X
Netherlands	X	X	X	X	X	X	X	X	X	X	X	X	X	X	X	X	X	X	X
New Zealand	X	X	X	X	X	X	X	X	X	X	X	X	X	X	X	X	X	X	X
Nicaragua	X	X	X	X	X	X	X	X	X	X	X	X	X	X	X	X	X	X	X
Niger	X	X	X	X	X	X	X	X	X	X	X	X	X	X	X	X	X	X	X
Nigeria	X	X	X	X	X	X	X	X	X	X	X	X	X	X	X	X	X	X	X
Norway	X	X	X	X	X	X	X	X	X	X	X	X	X	X	X	X	X	X	X
Oman	X		X	X	X	X	X	X	X	X	X	X	X	X	X	X	X		X
Pakistan	X	X	X	X	X	X	X	X	X	X	X	X	X	X	X	X	X	X	X
Panama	X	X	X	X	X	X	X	X	X	X	X	X	X	X	X	X	X		X
Papua New Guinea	X	X	X	X	X	X	X	X	X	X	X	X	X	X	X	X			X
Paraguay	X	X	X	X	X	X	X	X	X	X	X	X	X		X	X	X	X	X
Peru	X	X	X	X	X	X	X	X	X	X	X	X	X	X	X	X	X	X	X
Philippines	X	X	X	X	X	X	X	X	X	X	X	X	X	X	X	X	X	X	X
Poland	X	X	X	X	X	X	X	X	X	X	X	X	X	X	X	X	X	X	X
Portugal	X	X	X	X	X	X	X	X	X	X	X	X	X	X	X	X	X	X	X
Qatar	X	X	X	X	X	X	X			X	X	X	X	X	X	X	X		X
Republic of Korea	X	X	X	X	X	X	X	X	X	X	X	X	X	X	X	X	X	X	X
Romania	X	X	X	X	X	X	X	X	X	X	X	X	X	X	X	X	X	X	X

Members of the United Nations, the specialized and IAEA, and contracting parties to GATT—continued

Country	UN	ILO	FAO	UNESCO	ICAO	WHO	World Bank	IFC	IDA	IMF	UPU	ITU	WMO	IMO	WIPO	IFAD	IAEA	GATT	UNIDO
Russian Federation	X	X		X	X	X	X	X	X	X	X	X	X	X			X		X
Rwanda	X	X	X	X	X	X	X	X	X	X	X	X	X		X	X		X	X
Saint Kitts and Nevis	X		X	X	X	X	X	X	X	X	X			X		X			X
Saint Lucia	X	X	X	X	X	X	X	X	X	X	X	X	X	X	X	X		X	X
Saint Vincent and the Grenadines	X		X	X	X	X	X	X	X	X	X	X	X	X	X	X			X
Samoa	X	X	X	X		X	X	X	X	X	X	X		X		X			
San Marino	X	X		X	X	X			X		X	X			X				
Sao Tome and Principe	X	X	X	X	X	X	X		X	X	X	X	X	X	X	X			X
Saudi Arabia	X	X	X	X	X	X	X	X	X	X	X	X	X	X	X	X	X		X
Senegal	X	X	X	X	X	X	X	X	X	X	X	X	X	X	X	X	X	X	X
Seychelles	X	X	X	X	X	X	X	X	X	X	X	X	X	X	X	X			X
Sierra Leone	X	X	X	X	X	X	X	X	X	X	X	X	X	X	X	X	X	X	X
Singapore	X	X			X	X	X	X	X	X	X	X	X	X	X	X	X	X	X
Slovenia	X	X		X	X	X		X	X	X	X	X	X	X	X				
Solomon Islands	X	X	X		X	X	X	X	X	X	X	X	X	X		X			X
Somalia	X	X	X	X		X	X	X	X	X	X	X	X	X	X	X			X
South Africa	X		X		X	X	X	X	X	X	X	X	X	X	X		X	X	
Spain	X	X	X	X	X	X	X	X	X	X	X	X	X	X	X	X	X	X	X
Sri Lanka	X	X	X	X	X	X	X	X	X	X	X	X	X	X	X	X	X	X	X
Sudan	X	X	X	X	X	X	X	X	X	X	X	X	X	X	X	X	X	X	X
Suriname	X	X	X	X	X	X	X	X		X	X	X	X	X	X	X		X	X
Swaziland	X	X	X	X	X	X	X	X	X	X	X	X	X	X	X	X		X	X
Sweden	X	X	X	X	X	X	X	X	X	X	X	X	X	X	X	X	X	X	X
Switzerland		X	X	X	X	X	X	X	X	X	X	X	X	X	X	X	X	X	X
Syrian Arab Republic	X	X	X	X	X	X	X	X	X	X	X	X	X	X	X	X	X	X	X
Tajikistan	X					X													
Thailand	X	X	X	X	X	X	X	X	X	X	X	X	X	X	X	X	X	X	X

Members of the United Nations, the specialized and IAEA, and contracting parties to GATT—continued

Country	UN	ILO	FAO	UNESCO	ICAO	WHO	World Bank	IFC	IDA	IMF	UPU	ITU	WMO	IMO	WIPO	IFAD	IAEA	GATT	UNIDO
Togo	X	X	X	X	X	X	X	X	X	X	X	X	X	X	X	X		X	X
Tonga	X		X	X	X	X	X	X	X	X	X	X	X	X		X			X
Trinidad and Tobago	X	X	X	X	X	X	X	X	X	X	X	X	X	X	X	X		X	X
Tunisia	X	X	X	X	X	X	X	X	X	X	X	X	X	X	X	X	X	X	X
Turkey	X	X	X	X	X	X	X	X	X	X	X	X	X	X	X	X	X	X	X
Turkmenistan	X																		
Tuvalu				X							X					X		X	X
Uganda	X	X	X	X	X	X	X	X	X	X	X	X	X	X		X	X	X	X
Ukraine	X	X		X		X	X	X		X	X	X	X	X	X		X		X
United Arab Emirates	X	X	X	X	X	X	X	X	X	X	X	X	X	X	X	X	X	X	X
United Kingdom of Great Britain and Northern Ireland	X	X	X		X	X	X	X	X	X	X	X	X	X	X	X	X	X	X
United Republic of Tanzania	X	X	X	X	X	X	X	X	X	X	X	X	X	X	X	X	X	X	X
United States of America	X	X	X		X	X	X	X	X	X	X	X	X	X	X	X	X	X	X
Uruguay	X	X	X	X	X	X	X	X	X	X	X	X	X	X	X	X	X	X	X
Uzbekistan	X																		
Vanuatu	X		X	X	X	X	X	X		X	X	X	X	X	X	X			X
Venezuela	X	X	X	X	X	X	X	X	X	X	X	X	X	X	X	X	X	X	X
Viet Nam	X	X	X	X	X	X	X	X	X	X	X	X	X	X	X	X	X		X
Yemen	X	X	X	X	X	X	X	X	X	X	X	X	X	X	X	X	X		X
Zaire	X	X	X	X	X	X	X	X	X	X	X	X	X	X	X	X	X	X	X
Zambia	X	X	X	X	X	X	X	X	X	X	X	X	X	X	X	X	X	X	X
Zimbabwe	X	X	X	X	X	X	X	X	X	X	X	X	X	X	X	X	X	X	X

Membership of Major Regional Organizations: Africa

	AfDB (1)	CEAO	CEEAC	CEPGL	ECA	ECOWAS	Entente Council	IOC (2)	MRU	OAU (3)	PTA	SACU	SADCC	UDEAC
Algeria	X				X					X				
Angola	X		0		X					X	X		X	
Benin	X	X			X	X	X			X				
Botswana	X				X					X		X	X	
Burkina Faso	X	X			X	X	X			X				
Burundi	X			X	X					X	X			
Cameroon	X		X		X					X				X
Cape Verde	X				X	X				X				
Central African Rep.	X		X		X					X				X
Chad	X		X		X					X				0
Comoros	X				X			X		X				
Congo	X		X		X					X	X			X
Côte d'Ivoire	X	X			X	X	X			X				
Djibouti	X				X					X	X			
Egypt	X				X					X				
Equatorial Guinea	X		X		X					X				X
Ethiopia	X				X					X	X			
Gabon	X		X		X					X				X
Gambia	X				X	X				X				
Ghana	X				X	X				X				
Guinea	X	0			X	X			X	X				
Guinea Bissau	X				X	X				X				
Kenya	X				X					X	X			
Lesotho	X				X					X	X	X		
Liberia	X				X	X			X	X			X	
Libya	X				X					X				
Madagascar	X				X			X		X				
Malawi	X				X					X	X		X	

305

Membership of Major Regional Organizations: Africa—continued

	AfDB (1)	CEAO	CEEAC	CEPGL	ECA	ECOWAS	Entente Council	IOC (2)	MRU	OAU (3)	PTA	SACU	SADCC	UDEAC
Mali	X	X			X	X				X				
Mauritania	X	X			X	X				X				
Mauritius	X				X			X		X	X			
Morocco	X				X									
Mozambique	X				X					X	X		X	
Namibia					X					X	X		X	
Niger	X	X			X	X	X			X				
Nigeria	X				X	X				X	X			
Rwanda	X		X	X	X					X				
SãoTomé and P.	X		X		X					X				
Senegal	X	X			X	X				X				
Seychelles	X				X			X		X				
Sierra Leone	X				X	X			X	X				
Somalia	X				X					X	X			
South Africa					X							X		
Sudan	X				X					X	X			
Swaziland	X				X					X	X	X	X	
Tanzania	X				X					X	X		X	
Togo	X	0			X	X	X			X				
Tunisia	X				X					X				
Uganda	X				X					X	X			
Zaire	X		X	X	X					X	X			
Zambia	X				X					X	X		X	
Zimbabwe	X				X					X	X		X	

0 = Observer.
NOTES: 1. Also about 25 non-regional countries.
2. Also France representing Réunion.
3. Sahrawi Arab Democratic Republic admitted in 1982 but membership disputed by Morocco and other countries. Subsequently Morocco withdrew.

Membership of Major Regional Organizations: Asia and The Pacific

	APEC (1)	AsDB (2)	ASEAN	Colombo Plan (3)	ESCAP (4)	PECC (5)	SAARC	SPC (6)	SPF (7)
Afghanistan		X		X	X				
Australia	X	X		X	X	X		X	X
Bangladesh		X		X	X		X		
Bhutan		X		X	X		X		
Brunei	X		X		X	X			
Cambodia		X		X	X				
China	X	X			X	X			
Fiji		X		X	X	X		X	X
Hong Kong	X	X			A	X			
India		X		X	X	X	X		
Indonesia	X	X	X	X	X	X			
Japan	X	X		X	X	X			
Kiribati		X			X			X	X
Korea, Rep. of	X	X		X	X	X			
Laos		X	O	X	X				
Malaysia	X	X	X	X	X	X			
Maldives		X		X	X		X		
Mongolia		X			X				
Myanmar		X		X	X				
Nauru					X			X	X
Nepal		X		X	X		X		
New Zealand	X	X		X	X	X		X	X

Membership of Major Regional Organizations: Asia and The Pacific—continued

	APEC (1)	AsDB (2)	ASEAN	Colombo Plan (3)	ESCAP (4)	PECC (5)	SAARC	SPC (6)	SPF (7)
Pakistan		X		X	X		X		
Papua New Guinea		X	O	X	X			X	X
Philippines	X	X	X	X	X	X			
Samoa		X			X			X	X
Singapore	X	X	X	X	X	X			
Solomon Islands		X			X			X	X
Sri Lanka		X		X	X		X		
Taiwan	X	X				X			
Thailand	X	X	X	X	X	X			
Tonga		X			X			X	X
Vanuatu		X			X			X	X
Viet Nam		X	O		X				

O = Observer.
A = Associate Member.
NOTES: 1. Also Canada, USA.
    2. Also Cook Islands, Marshall Islands, Micronesia and 15 non-regional countries.
    3. Also Iran, Canada, UK, USA.
    4. Also Iran, Tuvalu, France, Netherlands, Russia, UK, USA.
    5. Also Canada, USA, Chile, Mexico, Peru.
    6. Also other regional countries and territories, France, UK, USA.
    7. Also other regional countries.

Membership of Major Regional Organizations: Europe

	Benelux	CERN	Council of Europe	CSCE (1)	EBRD (2)	EFTA	ESA	European Communities	NACC (3)	NATO (4)	Nordic Council	WEU
Albania				X	X				X			
Austria		X	X	X	X	X	X					
Belarus				X	X				X			
Belgium	X	X	X	X	X		X	X	X	X		X
Bosnia-Herzegovina				X	X							
Bulgaria			X	X	X				X			
Croatia				X	X							
Cyprus			X	X								
Czechoslovakia		X	X	X	X				X			
Denmark		X	X	X	X		X	X	X	X	X	
Estonia				X	X				X			
Finland		X	X	X	X	X	A		0		X	
France		X	X	X	X		X	X	X	X		X
Germany		X	X	X	X		X	X	X	X		X
Greece		X	X	X	X			X	X	X		
Hungary		X	X	X	X				X			
Iceland			X	X		X			X	X	X	
Ireland			X	X	X		X	X				
Italy		X	X	X	X		X	X	X	X		X
Latvia				X	X				X			
Liechtenstein			X	X		X						
Lithuania				X	X				X			

Membership of Major Regional Organizations: Europe—continued

	Benelux	CERN	Council of Europe	CSCE (1)	EBRD (2)	EFTA	ESA	European Communities	NACC (3)	NATO (4)	Nordic Council	WEU
Luxembourg	X		X	X	X			X	X	X		X
Malta			X	X								
Moldova				X	X				X			
Netherlands	X	X	X	X	X		X	X	X	X		X
Norway		X	X	X	X	X	X		X	X	X	
Poland		X	X	X	X				X			
Portugal		X	X	X	X			X	X	X		X
Romania				X	X				X			
Russia		0		X	X				X			
San Marino				X								
Slovenia				X	X							
Spain		X	X	X	X		X	X	X	X		X
Sweden		X	X	X	X	X	X				X	
Switzerland		X	X	X	X	X	X					
Turkey		0	X	X					X	X		
Ukraine				X	X				X			
United Kingdom	X	X	X	X	X		X	X	X	X		X

0 = Observer.
A = Associate Member.
NOTES: 1. Also Canada, USA, Armenia, Azerbaijan, Georgia, Kazakhstan, Kyrgyzstan, Tajikistan, Turkmenistan, Uzbekistan.
2. Also the EEC, the EIB, Canada, USA, Japan, Taiwan, Armenia, Azerbaijan, Georgia, Kazakhstan, Kyrgyzstan, Tajikistan, Turkmenistan, Uzbekistan.
3. Also Canada, USA, Armenia, Azerbaijan, Georgia, Kazakhstan, Kyrgyzstan, Tajikistan, Turkmenistan, Uzbekistan.
4. Also Canada, USA.

Membership of Major Regional Organizations: Latin America and The Caribbean

	Andean Group	CABEI (1)	CACM	CARICOM (2)	CDB (3)	CIC	ECLAC (4)	IDB (5)	LAIA	MERCOSUR	OAS (6)	OECS (2)	Rio Group	SELA
Antigua and Barbuda				X	X		X				X	X		
Argentina		X				X	X	X	X	X	X		X	X
Bahamas					X		X	X			X			
Barbados				X	X		X	X			X			X
Belize				X	X		X				X			X
Bolivia	X					X	X	X	X		X		X	X
Brazil						X	X	X	X	X	X		X	X
Chile							X	X	X		X		X	X
Colombia	X				X		X	X	X		X		X	X
Costa Rica		X	X				X	X	O		X			X
Cuba							X		O		X			X
Dominica				X	X		X				X	X		
Dominican Rep.							X	X	O		X			X
Ecuador	X						X	X	X		X		X	X
El Salvador		X	X				X	X	O		X			X
Grenada				X	X		X				X	X		X
Guatemala		X	X				X	X	O		X			X
Guyana				X	X		X	X			X			X
Haiti							X	X			X			X
Honduras		X	X				X	X	O		X			X
Jamaica				X	X		X	X			X			X
Mexico		X			X		X	X	X		X		X	X
Nicaragua		X	X				X	X	O		X			X

311

Membership of Major Regional Organizations: Latin America and The Caribbean—continued

	Andean Group	CABEI (1)	CACM	CARICOM (2)	CDB (3)	CIC	ECLAC (4)	IDB (5)	LAIA	MERCOSUR	OAS (6)	OECS (2)	Rio Group	SELA
Panama							X	X	0		X			X
Paraguay						X	X	X	X	X	X		X	X
Peru	X						X	X	X		X		X	X
Saint Kitts-Nevis				X	X		X				X	X		
Saint Lucia				X	X		X				X	X		
Saint Vincent				X	X		X				X	X		
Suriname							X	X			X			X
Trinidad and Tobago				X	X		X	X			X			X
Uruguay						X	X	X	X	X	X		X	X
Venezuela	X	X			X		X	X	X		X		X	X

0 = Observer.
NOTES: 1. Also Taiwan.
2. Also Montserrat.
3. Also other 5 regional countries, Canada, France, Germany, Italy, UK.
4. Also Canada, France, Italy, Netherlands, Portugal, Spain, UK, USA.
5. Also 17 non-regional countries.
6. Also Canada, USA.

Membership of Major Regional Organizations: The Middle East

	AFESD (1)	Arab League (1)	BADEA (1)	ECO (2)	ESCWA	GCC	IsDB (3)	OAPEC (4)	OIC (3)
Bahrain	X	X	X		X	X	X	X	X
Egypt	X	X	X		X		X	X	X
Iran				X			X		X
Iraq	X	X	X		X		X	X	X
Jordan	X	X	X		X		X		X
Kuwait	X	X	X		X	X	X	X	X
Lebanon	X	X	X		X		X		X
Libya	X	X	X				X	X	X
Oman	X	X	X		X	X	X		X
Qatar	X	X	X		X	X	X	X	X
Saudi Arabia	X	X	X		X	X	X	X	X
Syria	X	X	X		X		X	X	X
United Arab Em.	X	X	X		X	X	X	X	X
Yemen	X	X	X		X		X		X

NOTES: 1. Also other Arab countries in Africa.
2. Also Pakistan and Turkey.
3. Also about 30 other Islamic countries in Africa and Asia.
4. Also Algeria.

Classification of Countries and Membership of Major Groups

For analytical purposes, several classification schemes, based on various criteria, are used by international organizations and scholars, to arrange the countries of the world into groups and subgroups. The first and most general distinction is between industrial and developing countries; an additional miscellaneous group may be introduced with regard to the 'least developed countries'.

Industrial countries include North America (that is Canada and the USA), Western and Southern Europe (except Cyprus and Malta), Australia, Japan, New Zealand; Israel and South Africa may also be included. Countries in this group may also be defined as developed market economies. The seven largest economies in this group in terms of GNP are collectively referred to as the major industrial countries: USA, Japan, Germany, France, the UK, Italy, and Canada. The European countries include all industrial countries with the exception of Australia, Canada, Japan, New Zealand and the USA. Among the European countries a major subgroup is represented by the 12 members of the European Community: Belgium, Denmark, France, Germany, Greece, Ireland, Italy, Luxembourg, Netherlands, Portugal, Spain, the UK.

Developing countries include all those countries which do not belong to the category of industrial countries, in practice all the countries of Africa (except South Africa), Asia (except Israel and Japan), Latin America and the Caribbean, Oceania (excluding Australia and New Zealand), plus the former 'socialist' countries of Eastern Europe and all the republics that

were part of the Soviet Union, Cyprus, and Malta.

A subdivision of developing countries may be adopted with reference to main geographic regions:
North Africa: Algeria, Egypt, Libya, Morocco, Tunisia;
Sub-Saharan Africa: all developing countries in Africa, except North Africa;
Latin America and the Caribbean: all developing countries in the Western Hemisphere;
Mediterranean: Cyprus, Malta, Turkey, plus the republics of former Yugoslavia;
South and East Asia: Afghanistan, Bangladesh, Bhutan, Brunei, Cambodia, China, Fiji, Hong Kong, India, Indonesia, Laos, Malaysia, Maldives, Mongolia, Myanmar [formerly Burma], Nepal, Pakistan, Papua New Guinea, Philippines, Republic of Korea, Singapore, Sri Lanka, Taiwan, Thailand, Viet Nam.
Western Asia: Bahrain, Iran, Iraq, Jordan, Kuwait, Lebanon, Oman, Qatar, Saudi Arabia, Syria, United Arab Emirates, Yemen.

A further subdivision may be introduced with regard to southern Asia in order to distinguish between **South Asia** (including Bangladesh, Bhutan, India, Maldives, Nepal, Pakistan, and Sri Lanka) and **South**

315

East Asia (Brunei, Cambodia, Indonesia, Laos, Malaysia, Myanmar, Philippines, Singapore, Thailand, and Viet Nam).

The countries of Western Asia listed above plus Egypt and Libya may be considered part of the **Middle East**.

In addition to their broad regional classification, developing countries are grouped according to specific criteria, the main ones being those based on export orientation and on the financial situation with respect to external debt; other criteria are used to identify 'miscellaneous groups'.

According to the 'predominant export' criterion, a major distinction is made between fuel exporters and non-fuel exporters.

Fuel exporting developing countries, whose average ratio of fuel exports exceeds 50 per cent of total exports, are: Algeria, Angola, Brunei, Cameroon, Congo, Ecuador, Gabon, Indonesia, Iran, Iraq, Kuwait, Libya, Mexico, Nigeria, Oman, Qatar, Saudi Arabia, Trinidad and Tobago, United Arab Emirates, Venezuela.

Non-fuel exporting countries are those whose total exports of goods and services include a substantial share of: (a) manufactures; (b) primary products; or (c) services and private transfers. These countries are disaggregated into subgroups on the basis of the predominant composition of their exports.

Developing countries exporters of manufactures, whose exports of manufactures account for over 50 per cent of total exports, are: Brazil, Bulgaria, China, Czechoslovakia, Hong Kong, Hungary, India, Republic of Korea, Poland, Romania, Singapore, Taiwan, Thailand, Tunisia.

Exporters of primary products (55 countries more than half of which are in Africa) are further divided into agricultural exporters (41 countries) and mineral exporters (14 countries). The exporters of services and recipients of private transfers number over 30 in various continents.

Finally, about a dozen countries have a diversified export base, that is their exports are not dominated by any one of the categories mentioned above.

According to financial criteria, a basic distinction is made between **net creditor** and **net debtor** countries. The net creditors' group is by far the smallest and includes: Iran, Kuwait, Libya, Oman, Qatar, Saudi Arabia, Taiwan, and the United Arab Emirates. The very large group of net debtor countries (over 130 countries) is further disaggregated on the basis of two criteria: (a) the predominant type of source of borrowing (official borrowers, including over 70 countries; market borrowers; and diversified borrowers); and (b) the existence of recent debt-servicing difficulties (about 75 countries have incurred external payments arrears or entered into official or commercial bank debt-rescheduling agreements over the past few years).

Reference may also be made to other subgroups, the most common of which are: (1) **major oil exporters** (Algeria, Indonesia, Iran, Iraq, Kuwait, Libya, Nigeria, Oman, Qatar, Saudi Arabia, United Arab Emirates, and Venezuela); (2) **newly industrializing Asian economies** (Hong Kong, Republic of Korea, Singapore, and Taiwan); (3) **heavily indebted countries** (the countries considered by the 1985 'Baker Plan': Argentina, Bolivia, Brazil, Chile, Colombia, Côte d'Ivoire, Ecuador, Mexico, Morocco, Nigeria, Peru, Philippines, Uruguay, Venezuela).

Least developed countries comprise the developing countries whose per capita gross domestic product (GDP) did not exceed the equivalent of $567 based on the average for the years 1985-87, whose share of manufacturing in total GDP did not exceed 10 per cent, and whose adult literacy rate did not exceed 20 per cent. These countries currently include: Afghanistan, Bangladesh, Benin, Bhutan, Botswana, Burkina Faso, Burundi, Cambodia, Cape Verde, Central African Republic, Chad, Comoros, Djibouti, Equatorial Guinea, Ethiopia, Gambia, Guinea, Guinea-Bissau, Haiti, Kiribati, Laos, Lesotho, Liberia, Madagascar, Malawi, Maldives, Mali, Mauritania, Mozambique, Myanmar,

Nepal, Niger, Rwanda, Samoa, São Tomé and Príncipe, Sierra Leone, Solomon Islands, Somalia, Sudan, Tanzania, Togo, Tuvalu, Uganda, Vanuatu, Yemen, Zaire, Zambia.

Low-income countries comprise the developing countries whose per capita GDP did not exceed the equivalent of $425 in 1986. More precisely, the group includes the least developed countries listed above (except Botswana, Cape Verde, Djibouti, Kiribati, Liberia, Solomon Islands, and Tuvalu) plus China, Ghana, Guyana, India, Kenya, Madagascar, Pakistan, Senegal, Sri Lanka, Viet Nam, and Western Samoa.

North generally refers to the industrial countries located in the Northern Hemisphere and is often used to designate the OECD member countries.

South generally refers to the developing countries located mainly in the Southern Hemisphere and was often used interchangeably with the Third World.

Over the years, developing countries have formed a number of groupings based on a convergence of political, ideological and economic interests. The composition of two of these groupings is given below:

Non-Aligned Movement includes: Afghanistan, Algeria, Angola, Bahamas, Bahrain, Bangladesh, Barbados, Belize, Benin, Bermuda, Bhutan, Bolivia, Botswana, Burkina Faso, Burundi, Cambodia, Cameroon, Cape Verde, Central African Republic, Chad, Colombia, Comoros, Congo, Côte d'Ivoire, Cuba, Cyprus, Djibouti, Ecuador, Egypt, Equatorial Guinea, Ethiopia, Gabon, Gambia, Ghana, Grenada, Guinea, Guinea-Bissau, Guyana, India, Indonesia, Iran, Iraq, Jamaica, Jordan, Kenya, Korea DPR, Kuwait, Laos, Lebanon, Lesotho, Liberia, Libya, Madagascar, Malawi, Malaysia, Maldives, Mali, Malta, Mauritania, Mauritius, Morocco, Mozambique, Myanmar, Nepal, Nicaragua, Niger, Nigeria, Oman, Pakistan, Palestine, Panama, Peru, Qatar, Rwanda, São Tomé-Príncipe, Saudi Arabia, Senegal, Seychelles, Sierra Leone, Singapore, Somalia, Sri Lanka, Sudan, Suriname, Swaziland, Syria, Tanzania, Togo, Trinidad-Tobago, Tunisia, Uganda, United Arab Emirates, Vanuatu, Venezuela, Viet Nam, Yemen, Zaire, Zambia, Zimbabwe.

Group of 77 includes: Afghanistan, Algeria, Angola, Antigua-Barbuda, Argentina, Bahamas, Bahrain, Bangladesh, Barbados, Belize, Benin, Bhutan, Bolivia, Botswana, Brazil, Brunei, Burkina Faso, Burundi, Cambodia, Cameroon, Cape Verde, Central African Republic, Chad, Chile, Colombia, Comoros, Congo, Costa Rica, Côte d'Ivoire, Cuba, Cyprus, Djibouti, Dominica, Dominican Republic, Ecuador, Egypt, El Salvador, Equatorial Guinea, Ethiopia, Fiji, Gabon, Gambia, Ghana, Grenada, Guatemala, Guinea, Guinea-Bissau, Guyana, Haiti, Honduras, India, Indonesia, Iran, Iraq, Jamaica, Jordan, Kenya, Korea DPR, Korea Republic, Kuwait, Laos, Lebanon, Lesotho, Liberia, Libya, Madagascar, Malawi, Malaysia, Maldives, Mali, Malta, Mauritania, Mauritius, Mexico, Morocco, Mozambique, Myanmar, Nepal, Nicaragua, Niger, Nigeria, Oman, Pakistan, Palestine, Panama, Papua New Guinea, Paraguay, Peru, Philippines, Qatar, Romania, Rwanda, Saint Christopher-Nevis, Saint Lucia, Saint Vincent-Grenadines, Samoa, São Tomé-Príncipe, Saudi Arabia, Senegal, Seychelles, Sierra Leone, Singapore, Solomon Islands, Somalia, Sri Lanka, Suriname, Swaziland, Syria, Tanzania, Thailand, Togo, Tonga, Trinidad and Tobago, Tunisia, Uganda, United Arab Emirates, Uruguay, Vanuatu, Venezuela, Viet Nam, Yemen, Zaire, Zambia, Zimbabwe.

Index of Foundation Dates

Commission for the Scientific Exploration of the Mediterranean Sea [Commission internationale pour l'exploration scientifique de la mer Méditerranée] (CIESM); International Labour Organization (ILO); League of Nations

1924 International Vine and Wine Office [Office international de la vigne et du vin] (OIV)

1926 International Institute for the Unification of Private Law (UNIDROIT)

1930 Bank for International Settlements (BIS)

1931 The Commonwealth [Statute of Westminster]

1932 International Telecommunication Union (ITU)

1933 International Tea Committee

1939 International Cotton Advisory Committee (ICAC)

1943 United Nations Relief and Rehabilitation Administration (UNRRA)

1944 International Bank for Reconstruction and Development (IBRD); International Civil Aviation Organization (ICAO); International Monetary Fund (IMF); International Rubber Study Group (IRSG)

1945 Food and Agriculture Organization of the United Nations (FAO); League of Arab States [Arab League]; United Nations (UN); United Nations Educational, Scientific and Cultural Organization (UNESCO)

1946 Commonwealth Science Council (CSC); International Whaling Commission (IWC); International Wool Study Group (IWSG); United Nations Children's Fund (UNICEF); World Health Organization (WHO)

1947 Economic Commission for Asia and the Far East (ECAFE); Economic Commission for Europe (ECE); General Agreement on Tariffs and Trade (GATT); South Pacific Commission (SPC); World Meteorological Organization (WMO)

1948 Brussels Treaty Organization; Economic Commission for Latin America and the Caribbean (ECLAC); Indo-Pacific Fisheries Commission (IPFC); International Maritime Organization (IMO); Organization for European Economic Co-operation (OEEC); Organization of American States (OAS)

1949 Co-ordinating Committee for Multilateral Export Controls (CoCom);

Council for Mutual Economic Assistance (CMEA; Comecon); Council of Europe; Danube Commission; Ibero-American Bureau of Education; International Red Locust Control Service (IRLCS); International Wheat Council (IWC); North Atlantic Treaty Organization (NATO); United Nations Relief and Works Agency for Palestine Refugees in the Near East (UNRWA)

1950   Customs Co-operation Council (CCC); Inter-American Tropical Tuna Commission (IATTC); International Commission for the Northwest Atlantic Fisheries (ICNAF); Office of the United Nations High Commissioner for Refugees (UNHCR)

1951   ANZUS Pact; Colombo Plan; European Coal and Steel Community (ECSC); Organization of Central American States [Organización de Estados Centroamericanos] (ODECA); Provisional Intergovernmental Committee for the Movement of Migrants from Europe (PICMME)

1952   General Fisheries Council for the Mediterranean (GFCM); Intergovern-mental Committee for European Migration (ICEM); Nordic Council

1953   European Conference of Ministers of Transport (ECMT); European Organization for Nuclear Research [Organisation européenne pour la recherche nucléaire] (CERN); International North Pacific Fisheries Commission (INPFC)

1954   South East Asia Treaty Organization (SEATO)

1955   Bank of Central African States [Banque des états de l'Afrique centrale] (BEAC); Central Bank of West African States [Banque centrale des états de l'Afrique de l'Ouest] (BCEAO); Central Treaty Organization (CENTO); European Civil Aviation Conference [Commission euro-péenne de l'aviation civile] (CEAC); International African Migratory Locust Organization [Organisation internationale contre le criquet migrateur africain] (OICMA); International Finance Corporation (IFC); Warsaw Pact; Western European Union (WEU)

1956   International Atomic Energy Agency (IAEA); International Olive Oil Council (IOOC)

1957   European Atomic Energy Community (EURATOM); European Economic Community (EEC); European Nuclear Energy Agency (ENEA)

1958   Benelux Economic Union; Economic Commission for Africa (ECA); North Pacific Fur Seal Commission (NPFSC)

1959   Entente Council; Equatorial Customs Union [Union douanière équatoriale] (UDE); European Conference of Postal and Telecommunications Administrations [Conférence européenne des administrations des postes et des télécommunications] (CEPT); Inter-American Development Bank (IDB); International Centre for the Study of the Preservation and the Restoration of Cultural Property (ICCROM); International Lead and Zinc Study Group (ILZSG); International Olive Oil Council (IOOC); West African Customs Union [Union douanière de l'Afrique de l'Ouest] (UDAO)

1960   Caribbean Organization; Central American Bank for Economic Integration (CABEI); Central American Common Market (CACM); European Free Trade Association (EFTA); Inter-African Coffee Organization (IACO); International Development Association (IDA); Latin American Free Trade Association (LAFTA); Organization for Economic Co-operation and Development (OECD); Organization of the Petroleum Exporting Countries (OPEC)

1961   African and Malagasy Union [Union africaine et malgache] (UAM); African Posts and Telecommunications Union [Union africaine des postes et télécommunications] (UAPT); Asian Productivity Organization (APO); International Computing Centre (ICC)

1962   Asian Pacific Postal Union (APPU); Cocoa Producers' Alliance (COPAL); Desert Locust Control Organization for Eastern Africa (DLCO-EA)

1963   African Development Bank (AfDB); European Organization for the Safety of Air Navigation (EUROCONTROL); International Bank for Economic Co-operation (IBEC); International Coffee Organization (ICO); Organization of African Unity (OAU); United Nations Research Institute for Social Development (UNRISD); World Food Programme (WFP)

1964   African and Malagasy Union for Economic Co-operation [Union africaine et malgache de coopération économique] (UAMCE); African Groundnut Council [Conseil africain de l'arachide]; Customs and Economic Union of Central Africa [Union douanière et économique de l'Afrique centrale] (UDEAC); International Council for the Exploration of the Sea (ICES); International Telecommunications Satellite Organization (INTELSAT); Lake Chad Basin Commission (LCBC); Maghreb Permanent Consultative Committee [Comité permanent consultatif du Maghreb] (CPCM); Regional Co-operation for Development (RCD); River Niger Commission [Commission du fleuve Niger] (CFN); United Nations Conference on Trade and Development (UNCTAD)

1965   African and Mauritian Common Organization [Organisation commune africaine et mauricienne] (OCAM); Asian Development Bank (AsDB); Southeast Asian Ministers of Education Organization (SEAMEO); United Nations Development Programme (UNDP); United Nations Institute for Training and Research (UNITAR)

1966   Customs Union of West African States [Union douanière des états de l'Afrique de l'Ouest] (UDEAO); Economic Community of East Africa; International Institute for Cotton (IIC); United Nations Industrial Development Organization (UNIDO)

1967   Agency for the Prohibition of Nuclear Weapons in Latin America and the Caribbean [Organismo para la Proscripción de las Armas Nucleares en América Latina y el Caribe] (OPANAL); Association of South-East Asian Nations (ASEAN); Commonwealth Telecommunications Organization; Intergovernmental Council of Copper Exporting Countries [Conseil intergouvernemental des pays exportateurs de cuivre] (CIPEC); Pacific Basin Economic Council (PBEC); United Nations Fund for Population Activities (UNFPA); World Intellectual Property Organization (WIPO)

1968   Arab Fund for Economic and Social Development (AFESD); Caribbean Free Trade Association (CARIFTA); International Narcotics Control Board (INCB); International Trade Centre UNCTAD/GATT; Organization of Arab Petroleum Exporting Countries (OAPEC)

1969   African Civil Aviation Commission (AFCAC); Andean Group [Cartagena Agreement]; Asian and Pacific Coconut Community (APCC); Caribbean Development Bank (CDB; Caribank); International Commission for the Conservation of the Atlantic Tunas (ICCAT)

1970   Agency for Cultural and Technical Co-operation [Agence de coopération culturelle et technique] (ACCT); Association of Natural Rubber Producing Countries (ANRPC); International Investment Bank (IIB); West Africa Rice Development Association (WARDA)

1971   International Commission for the Southeast Atlantic Fisheries (ICSEAF); International Red Locust Control Organization for Central and Southern Africa (IRLCO-CSA); Organization of the Islamic Conference (OIC); South Pacific Forum (SPF); United Nations Fund for Drug Abuse Control (UNFDAC)

1972   International Pepper Community (IPC); Office of the United Nations Disaster Relief Co-ordinator (UNDRO); Organization for the Development of the Senegal River [Organisation pour la mise en valeur du fleuve Sénégal] (OMVS); United Nations Environment Programme (UNEP); West African Health Community (WAHC)

1973   Caribbean Community (CARICOM); International Cocoa Organization (ICCO); Latin American Energy Organization [Organización Latino-americana de Energía] (OLADE); Mano River Union (MRU); Permanent Inter-State Committee for Drought Control in the Sahel [Comité permanent interétats de lutte contre la sécheresse dans le Sahel] (CILSS); South Pacific Bureau for Economic Co-operation (SPEC); West African Development Bank [Banque ouest-africaine de développement] (BOAD); West African Economic Community [Communauté économique de l'Afrique de l'Ouest] (CEAO); Western Central Atlantic Fishery Commission (WECAFC)

1974   Arab Bank for Economic Development in Africa [Banque arabe pour le développement économique en Afrique] (BADEA); Economic and Social Commission for Asia and the Pacific (ESCAP); Economic and Social Commission for Western Asia (ESCWA); Group of Latin American and Caribbean Sugar Exporting Countries (GEPLACEA); International Bauxite Association (IBA); International Energy Agency (IEA); Islamic Development Bank; Union of Banana Exporting Countries [Unión de Países Exportadores de Banano] (UPEB); World Food Council (WFC)

1975   African Timber Organization [Organisation africaine du bois]; Association of Iron Ore Exporting Countries [Association des pays exportateurs de minerai de fer] (APEF); Conference on Security and Co-operation in Europe (CSCE); Economic Community of West African States (ECOWAS); European Space Agency (ESA); Latin American Economic System [Sistema Económico Latinoamericano] (SELA); Nordic Investment Bank; World Tourism Organization (WTO)

1976   Arab Monetary Fund (AMF); Economic Community of the Great Lakes Countries [Communauté économique des pays des Grands Lacs] (CEPGL); International Fund for Agricultural Development (IFAD); International Research and Training Institute for the Advancement of Women (INSTRAW)

1977   European Telecommunications Satellite Organization (EUTELSAT)

1978   Amazonian Co-operation Treaty [Amazon Pact]; Gambia River Basin Development Organization [Organisation de mise en valeur du fleuve Gambie] (OMVG); Organization for the Management and Development of the Kagera River Basin (Organisation pour l'aménagement et le développement du bassin de la rivière Kagera); United Nations Centre for Human Settlements (UNCHS) – HABITAT

1979 International Maritime Satellite Organization (INMARSAT); Northwest Atlantic Fisheries Organization (NAFO); Southern African Development Co-ordination Conference (SADCC)

1980 Development Bank of the Great Lakes States [Banque de développement des états des Grands Lacs] (BDEGL); Intergovernmental Committee for Migration (ICM); International Natural Rubber Organization (INRO); Latin American Integration Association (LAIA); Niger Basin Authority [Autorite du bassin du Niger]; OPEC Fund for International Development (OFID); Pacific Economic Co-operation Council (PECC); Pan African Postal Union (PAPU)

1981 Gulf Co-operation Council (GCC); Organization of Eastern Caribbean States (OECS); Preferential Trade Area for Eastern and Southern Africa (PTA)

1982 Indian Ocean Commission (IOC)

1983 Association of Tin Producing Countries (ATPC); Eastern Caribbean Central Bank (ECCB); Economic Community of Central African States [Communauté économique des états d'Afrique centrale] (CEEAC)

1984 International Jute Organization (IJO)

1985 Economic Co-operation Organization (ECO); International Tropical Timber Organization (ITTO); South Asian Association for Regional Co-operation (SAARC)

1986 African Petroleum Producers' Association; Cairns Group; European Organization for the Exploitation of Meteorological Satellites (EUMET-SAT); Intergovernmental Authority on Drought and Development (IGADD)

1987 International Organization for Migration (IOM); International Sugar Organization (ISO)

1988 Multilateral Investment Guarantee Agency (MIGA)

1989 Arab Co-operation Council; Asia-Pacific Economic Co-operation (APEC); Union of the Arab Maghreb [Union du Maghreb Arabe] (UMA); United Nations Interregional Crime and Justice Research Institute (UNICRI)

1990 European Bank for Reconstruction and Development (EBRD); United Nations International Drug Control Programme (UNDCP)

1991 MERCOSUR; North Atlantic Co-operation Council (NACC)

Classified Index

The purpose of this classification of international organizations is to simplify presentation and provide a key to systematic reading of the entries included in the book.

I Universal Organizations

General Competence
United Nations

UN Specialized Agencies
Food and Agriculture Organization
General Agreement on Tariffs and Trade
International Atomic Energy Agency
International Bank for Reconstruction and
   Development
International Civil Aviation Organization
International Development Association
International Finance Corporation
International Fund for Agricultural
   Development
International Labour Organization
International Maritime Organization
International Monetary Fund
International Telecommunication Union
UN Educational, Scientific and Cultural
   Organization
UN Industrial Development Organization
Universal Postal Union
World Health Organization
World Intellectual Property Organization
World Meteorological Organization

Other Specialized Agencies
International Maritime Satellite Organization
International Telecommunications Satellite
   Organization
World Tourism Organization

Other UN Bodies
International Research and Training Institute
   for the Advancement of Women
Office of the UN Disaster Relief Co-ordinator

UN Centre for Human Settlements
UN Children's Fund
UN Conference on Trade and Development
UN Development Programme
UN Environment Programme
UN High Commissioner for Refugees
UN Institute for Training and Research
UN International Drug Control Programme
UN Population Fund
UN Relief and Works Agency for Palestine
   Refugees in the Near East
UN Research Institute for Social Development
World Food Council
UN/FAO World Food Programme

II Regional Organizations

AFRICA

General Political Competence
Organization of African Unity

General Economic Competence
UN Economic Commission for Africa

Economic Co-operation and Integration
Customs and Economic Union of Central
   Africa
Economic Community of Central African States
Economic Community of the Great Lakes
   Countries
Economic Community of West African States
Entente Council
Indian Ocean Commission
Mano River Union
Preferential Trade Area for Eastern and
   Southern Africa

Index of Acronyms

Italicized entries indicate organizations which are no longer in existence or have been reorganized and renamed.

Index of Names

Italicized entries indicate organizations which are no longer in existence or have been reorganized and renamed.